JEWISH LAW | HISTORY, SOURCES, PRINCIPLES | *Ha-Mishpat Ha-Ivri*

VOLUME I
PART ONE
The History and Elements of Jewish Law
and
PART TWO
The Legal Sources of Jewish Law
SECTION 1
Exegesis and Interpretation

VOLUME II
PART TWO (*continued*)
The Legal Sources of Jewish Law
SECTION 2
Legislation, Custom, Precedent, and Legal Reasoning

VOLUME III
PART THREE
The Literary Sources of Jewish Law

VOLUME IV
PART FOUR
Jewish Law in the State of Israel
and
Appendixes, Glossary, Bibliography, Indexes

A PHILIP AND MURIEL BERMAN EDITION

M E N A C H E M E L O N

DEPUTY PRESIDENT, SUPREME COURT OF ISRAEL

JEWISH LAW

HISTORY, SOURCES, PRINCIPLES

Ha-Mishpat Ha-Ivri **VOLUME I**

Translated from the Hebrew
by Bernard Auerbach
and Melvin J. Sykes

THE JEWISH PUBLICATION SOCIETY Philadelphia Jerusalem 5754 / 1994

Originally published in Hebrew under the title
Ha-Mishpat Ha-Ivri
by the Magnes Press, The Hebrew University, Jerusalem

First English edition

Manufactured in the United States of America

The author and publisher gratefully acknowledge the support of the Philip and Muriel Berman Book Fund of The Jewish Publication Society, sponsored by Mr. and Mrs. Philip I. Berman, Allentown, Pennsylvania, in the publication of this book.

Library of Congress Cataloging-in-Publication Data

Elon, Menachem.
[Mishpaṭ ha-'Ivri. English]
Jewish law : history, sources, principles / Menachem Elon ; translated from the Hebrew by Bernard Auerbach and Melvin J. Sykes.
p. cm.
Includes bibliographical references and index.
Volume I, ISBN 0–8276–0385-1
Volume II, ISBN 0-8276-0386-X
Volume III, ISBN 0-8276-0387-8
Volume IV, ISBN 0-8276-0388-6
Four-volume set, ISBN 0-8276-0389–4
1. Jewish law—History. 2. Rabbinical literature—History and criticism. 3. Law—Israel—Jewish influences. I. Title.
BM520.5.E4313 1993
296.1′8′09—dc20 93–9278
CIP

Designed by Arlene Putterman

Typeset in Meridien and Perpetua by Graphic Composition, Inc.
Printed by Hamilton Printing Company

PHILIP AND MURIEL BERMAN EDITION

The Author

JUSTICE MENACHEM ELON was first appointed to the Supreme Court of Israel in 1977 and was named Deputy President of the Court in 1988. A legal scholar and teacher, he was awarded the Israel Prize in 1979 for *Ha-Mishpat Ha-Ivri.*

Justice Elon has published many works on the history and nature of Jewish law and the relation between it and the modern State of Israel, including *The Freedom of the Person of the Debtor in Jewish Law* (1964) and *Religious Legislation in the Laws of the State of Israel and Within the Jurisdiction of the Civil and Rabbinical Courts* (1968). From 1968 to 1971 he was editor of the Jewish Law section of the *Encyclopaedia Judaica,* which was subsequently collected in his *Principles of Jewish Law* (1975). By 1984 he had edited 10 volumes of *The Annual of the Institute for Research in Jewish Law of The Hebrew University of Jerusalem* and was also editing a digest of the responsa of the medieval authorities. He has been a member of government committees for the preparation of various bills of the Israeli Civil Law Coordination.

An ordained rabbi, Justice Elon earned his diploma from the Tel Aviv School of Law and Economics in 1948, received a master's degree in humanities, and was awarded a doctor of laws degree *cum laude* from The Hebrew University of Jerusalem. He began his affiliation with The Hebrew University in 1954 as an instructor of law and was subsequently appointed teaching associate, senior lecturer, associate professor, and, in 1972, Professor of Jewish Law.

Translators

BERNARD AUERBACH, Professor of Law, University of Maryland School of Law (retired, 1992). B.A. (Yeshiva University), J.D. (New York University), LL.M. (Yale University), Rabbinic Ordination (Rabbi Isaac Elchanan Theological Seminary, Yeshiva University), Sterling Fellow, (Yale University). *Consultant:* Court of Appeals of Maryland Standing Committee on Rules of Practice and Procedure (1965–1980). *Reporter:* Maryland Judicial Conference (1967–1970). *Recipient:* Bernard Revel Memorial Award for Arts and Sciences, Yeshiva College Alumni Association. *Member:* Jewish Law Association; American Bar Association.

MELVIN J. SYKES, A.B. (Johns Hopkins University), LL.B. (Harvard University), Diplomate, Baltimore Hebrew College. *Fellow:* American College of Trial Lawyers, American College of Trust and Estate Counsel, American Bar Foundation, Maryland Bar Foundation (former president). *Member:* American Law Institute, Court of Appeals of Maryland Standing Committee on Rules of Practice and Procedure; American and Maryland State Bar Associations, Bar Association of Baltimore City. *Sole Practitioner, Baltimore, Maryland:* General practice, trial and appellate litigation, probate and trusts. *Adjunct Faculty Member:* University of Maryland School of Law.

Editorial Consultant

DANIEL D. CHAZIN, *Member:* New Jersey and New York Bars. B.A. (Yeshiva University), J.D. (New York University). *Member:* American Bar Association, New Jersey and New York State Bar Associations. Gruss Fellow, 1989–90, New York University School of Law.

Assistant Editorial Consultant

NORMAN MENACHEM FEDER, A.B., M.A. (Columbia University), J.D. (New York University). Editor-in-Chief, N.Y.U. Journal of International Law & Politics (1986–1987). Luce Scholar (1987–1988). Law Clerk to Judge Roger J. Miner, United States Court of Appeals for the Second Circuit (1988–1989). Law Clerk to Deputy President Menachem Elon, Supreme Court of Israel (1989–1990). Associate, Cleary, Gottlieb, Steen & Hamilton, New York.

SUMMARY OF CONTENTS

	INTRODUCTION	xlvii
	ABOUT THE TRANSLATION	lvii
	BIBLIOGRAPHICAL ABBREVIATIONS OF BOOKS AND ARTICLES FREQUENTLY CITED	lxix
	ABBREVIATIONS USED IN CITING RABBINIC WORKS AND SCHOLARLY LITERATURE	lxxiii
	ABBREVIATIONS USED IN CITING MODERN LEGAL MATERIALS	lxxv
	ACRONYMS AND APPELLATIONS OF HALAKHIC AUTHORITIES	lxxvii
	TRANSLITERATION GUIDE	lxxx

VOLUME I

PART ONE
The History and Elements of Jewish Law

Chapter 1	THE HISTORY OF JEWISH LAW	1
Chapter 2	THE DEVELOPMENT OF JEWISH LAW: SOME IMPORTANT FACTORS	46
Chapter 3	THE SCIENTIFIC STUDY OF JEWISH LAW	75
Chapter 4	*MISHPAT IVRI:* DEFINITION AND NATURE	92
Chapter 5	THE ORAL LAW: DEFINITION AND GENERAL PRINCIPLES	190
Chapter 6	THE BASIC NORM AND THE SOURCES OF JEWISH LAW	228
Chapter 7	THE PREROGATIVES OF THE HALAKHIC AUTHORITIES	240

PART TWO
The Legal Sources of Jewish Law
SECTION 1 *Exegesis and Interpretation*

Chapter 8	EXEGESIS AND INTERPRETATION (MIDRASH AND *PARSHANUT*): INTRODUCTION	275
Chapter 9	EXEGETICAL INTERPRETATION OF THE TORAH	281
Chapter 10	INTERPRETATION OF THE *HALAKHAH*	400

Chapter 11 INTERPRETATION OF DOCUMENTS 422
Chapter 12 INTERPRETATION OF COMMUNAL ENACTMENTS 444

GLOSSARY G•1

VOLUME II

PART TWO *(continued)*
The Legal Sources of Jewish Law
SECTION 2 *Legislation, Custom, Precedent, and Legal Reasoning*

Chapter 13 LEGISLATION: INTRODUCTION 477
Chapter 14 LEGISLATION: NATURE, OBJECTIVES, AND PRINCIPLES OF LEGISLATION BY THE HALAKHIC AUTHORITIES 494
Chapter 15 LEGISLATION: ENACTMENTS THROUGH THE END OF THE TANNAITIC PERIOD 545
Chapter 16 LEGISLATION IN THE AMORAIC PERIOD 622
Chapter 17 LEGISLATION IN THE GEONIC PERIOD 643
Chapter 18 POST-GEONIC LEGISLATION: INTRODUCTION 666
Chapter 19 COMMUNAL ENACTMENTS 678
Chapter 20 SURVEY OF LEGISLATION FROM THE TENTH CENTURY C.E. TO THE PRESENT 780
Chapter 21 CUSTOM *(MINHAG)*: ITS NATURE AND THE SOURCE OF ITS BINDING FORCE 880
Chapter 22 CUSTOM: OPERATION AND CATEGORIES 895
Chapter 23 *MA'ASEH* AND PRECEDENT 945
Chapter 24 LEGAL REASONING *(SEVARAH)* 987

GLOSSARY G•1

VOLUME III

PART THREE
The Literary Sources of Jewish Law

Chapter 25 THE LITERARY SOURCES OF JEWISH LAW: NATURE AND DEFINITION 1017
Chapter 26 THE LITERARY SOURCES FROM THE SINAITIC REVELATION UNTIL THE *TANNAIM* 1020
Chapter 27 THE LITERARY SOURCES FROM THE TANNAITIC PERIOD UNTIL THE REDACTION OF THE TALMUD: INTRODUCTION 1038
Chapter 28 THE LITERARY SOURCES IN THE TANNAITIC PERIOD 1041
Chapter 29 THE LITERARY SOURCES IN THE AMORAIC PERIOD 1083

Chapter 30	THE LITERARY SOURCES AND OTHER HALAKHIC LITERATURE IN THE POST-TALMUDIC PERIOD: INTRODUCTION	1101
Chapter 31	COMMENTARIES AND NOVELLAE	1104
Chapter 32	THE CODIFICATORY LITERATURE: NATURE AND STRUCTURE; THE PROBLEM OF CODIFICATION	1138
Chapter 33	THE CODIFICATORY LITERATURE: FROM THE GEONIC PERIOD UNTIL MAIMONIDES' *MISHNEH TORAH*	1149
Chapter 34	THE CODIFICATORY LITERATURE: MAIMONIDES' *MISHNEH TORAH*	1180
Chapter 35	THE CODIFICATORY LITERATURE: FROM MAIMONIDES UNTIL THE *SHULḤAN ARUKH;* THE *SEFER HA-TURIM*	1236
Chapter 36	THE CODIFICATORY LITERATURE: THE WORKS OF JOSEPH CARO AND MOSES ISSERLES	1309
Chapter 37	THE CODIFICATORY LITERATURE: REACTIONS TO THE *SHULḤAN ARUKH,* AND ITS FINAL ACCEPTANCE	1367
Chapter 38	THE CODIFICATORY LITERATURE: COMMENTARIES ON AND CODIFICATION AFTER THE *SHULḤAN ARUKH*	1423
Chapter 39	THE RESPONSA LITERATURE	1453
Chapter 40	LITERATURE FACILITATING RESEARCH IN JEWISH LAW: COMPILATIONS OF LEGAL DOCUMENTS, REFERENCE WORKS	1529
	GLOSSARY	G•1

VOLUME IV

PART FOUR
Jewish Law in the State of Israel

Chapter 41	INTRODUCTION: JEWISH LAW FROM THE ABROGATION OF JEWISH JURIDICAL AUTONOMY TO THE ESTABLISHMENT OF THE STATE OF ISRAEL	1575
Chapter 42	JEWISH LAW IN THE GENERAL LEGAL SYSTEM OF THE STATE OF ISRAEL	1619
Chapter 43	THE LAW OF PERSONAL STATUS IN THE RABBINICAL AND GENERAL COURTS: ADDITIONAL ASPECTS OF THE PROBLEM OF THE STATUS OF JEWISH LAW IN THE LAW OF THE STATE OF ISRAEL	1752
Chapter 44	THE FOUNDATIONS OF LAW ACT, 1980	1827
Chapter 45	THE RELIGIOUS AND CULTURAL ASPECTS OF THE QUESTION OF THE STATUS OF JEWISH LAW IN THE JEWISH STATE	1898

Appendixes, Glossary, Bibliography, Indexes

Appendix A	CROSS-REFERENCE TABLE—THE *MISHNEH TORAH* AND THE *SHULḤAN ARUKH*	1949

Appendix B ADDITIONAL COMPARISONS OF THE LANGUAGE AND STYLE OF THE *MISHNEH TORAH,* THE *TURIM,* AND THE *SHULḤAN ARUKH* 1979
Appendix C A LISTING OF THE MOST WIDELY KNOWN COMPILATIONS OF RESPONSA 1989

GLOSSARY 2009
BIBLIOGRAPHY 2025
INDEX OF SOURCES 2063
SUBJECT INDEX 2129

CONTENTS

INTRODUCTION xlvii

ABOUT THE TRANSLATION lvii

BIBLIOGRAPHICAL ABBREVIATIONS OF BOOKS AND ARTICLES FREQUENTLY CITED lxix

ABBREVIATIONS USED IN CITING RABBINIC WORKS AND SCHOLARLY LITERATURE lxxiii

ABBREVIATIONS USED IN CITING MODERN LEGAL MATERIALS lxxv

ACRONYMS AND APPELLATIONS OF HALAKHIC AUTHORITIES lxxvii

TRANSLITERATION GUIDE lxxx

VOLUME I

PART ONE
The History and Elements of Jewish Law

Chapter 1 THE HISTORY OF JEWISH LAW 1

I. Introduction, 1
II. Jewish Law—A Living and Functioning System, 3
- A. The Religious and National Character of Jewish Law, 4
- B. The Jewish Legal Order and the Extent of Its Authority, 6
- C. Methods of Enforcement of Judicial Decisions, 10
- D. The Prohibition Against Litigating in Non-Jewish Tribunals (*Arka'ot Shel Goyim*), 13
- E. Arbitration, 19
- F. Lay Tribunals (*Battei Din Shel Hedyotot*), 20
- G. Criticism of Lay Tribunals by the Halakhic Authorities, 30
- H. The Basic Distinction between the Various Forms of Jewish Adjudication on the One Hand and Adjudication by Non-Jewish Tribunals on the Other, 34

I. The Legal-Political Viewpoint of the General Government, and the Economic-Social Relationship between the Jewish Community and the Government, 36
J. Summary, 38
III. The Different Periods of Jewish Law, 39
A. The Two Broad Periods, 39
B. The Division of the Two Periods into Subperiods, 40

Chapter 2 **THE DEVELOPMENT OF JEWISH LAW: SOME IMPORTANT FACTORS** **46**
I. Development in the Various Areas of the Law, 46
II. Creativity in Halakhic Literature as a Reflection of Practical Application, 51
III. Public Leadership as a Creative Factor in the Jewish Legal System, 54
A. The King's Law, 55
B. Jewish Government in the Land of Israel and the Diaspora, 58
C. Local Jewish Self-Government, 60
D. Lay Adjudication, 61
IV. The Relationship Between Jewish Law and Non-Jewish Law, 62
A. Reciprocal Influences Between Jewish Law and Non-Jewish Law, 62
B. *Dina de-Malkhuta Dina* ("The Law of the Land Is Law"), 64

Chapter 3 **THE SCIENTIFIC STUDY OF JEWISH LAW** **75**
I. Classification in Jewish Law, 75
A. Classification and Definition of the Fields of Law, 75
B. Substantive Changes in Various Subject Areas, 76
1. Law of Obligations, 76
2. Public and Administrative Law, 77
3. Conflict of Laws, 78
II. The Concreteness of Jewish Legal Terminology, 79
III. The Need for Research into All Periods of Jewish Law; The Historical-Dogmatic (also called Historical-Analytical) Method, 80

Chapter 4 ***MISHPAT IVRI:* DEFINITION AND NATURE** **92**
I. The Concept of *Halakhah*, 93
II. The Reciprocal Relationship between *Halakhah* and *Aggadah*, 94
III. The Term *Mishpat Ivri*, 105
A. The Terms *Mishpat* and *Din*, 105
B. The Term *Ivri*, 110
IV. Common Features of "Religious" *Halakhah* and "Legal" *Halakhah*, 111
A. Common Thought Patterns and Terminology, 111
B. Common Legal Principles, 112
C. Dependence of "Religious" Precepts on "Legal" Precepts, 113
D. Common Fictions, 115

E. Interaction between Different Parts of the *Halakhah*, 116
1. The Obligation of Child Support, 116
2. "The Payment of a Debt is a Religious Obligation", 117
3. The Creation of an Obligation by Vow, Ban, or Oath, 119
4. The Nature of a Divorce Judgment, 120
V. Distinction between "Religious" and "Legal" *Halakhah*—"*Issur*" and "*Mamon*", 122
A. Freedom of Contract—"Contracting Out of a Law Contained in the Torah", 123
B. Illegal Contracts, 128
C. Legislation (*Takkanot*), 130
D. Custom (*Minhag*), 130
E. Different Rules for Decision Making, and Other Distinctions, 131
F. Distinction between Matters of *Issur* and Matters of *Mamon* with Regard to *Dina de-Malkhuta Dina* ("The Law of the Land Is Law"), 132
G. Logic and Legal Reasoning as the Major Creative Source of Law in the Area of *Mamon*, 137
VI. Law and Morals in the Jewish Legal System, 141
A. Reciprocal Relationship between Law and Morals—Recourse by the Legal System to the Moral Imperative, 142
B. "Exempt by Human Law but Liable by Divine Law", 145
C. The Imprecation "He Who Punished" (*Mi she-Para*), 148
D. "Fulfillment of Duty in the Sight of Heaven" (*Laẓeit Yedei Shamayim*), 148
E. "The Sages are Displeased with Him," and Other Forms of Moral-Religious Sanctions, 149
F. *Lifnim Mi-Shurat Ha-Din*—Acting More Generously than the Law Requires, 155
G. Law, Justice, and Equity, 167
1. "Judge Your Neighbor Fairly", 168
2. Justice as a Supplement to Law, 169
3. Justice as a Primary Norm, 175
4. Law and Equity—Rule and Discretion, 176
H. Good Faith (*Tom Lev*), 183

Chapter 5 **THE ORAL LAW: DEFINITION AND GENERAL PRINCIPLES** **190**

I. The Concept of the Oral Law, 190
II. The Antiquity of the Oral Law, 192
A. Noahide Laws, 194
B. Legal Practices Antedating the Sinaitic Revelation, 195
1. The Purchase of the Cave of Machpelah, 195
2. The Liability of a Paid Bailee, 196
C. Biblical Law Modifies Earlier Legal Practices, 197
1. Levirate Marriage—The Account of Judah and Tamar, 197
2. The Murderer Who Takes Hold of the Corners of the Altar, 199

D. The Oral Law Elucidates and Supplements the Written Law, 200
III. *Divrei Kabbalah* ("Matters of Tradition"), 203
IV. *Halakhah Le-Moshe Mi-Sinai* ("Law Given to Moses at Sinai"), 204
V. Biblical Law (*De-Oraita*) and Rabbinic Law (*De-Rabbanan*), 207
A. Classification into Biblical Law and Rabbinic Law, 208
B. Differences in Legal Consequences of Classification as Biblical or Rabbinic, 212
1. Leniency in Regard to Rabbinic Law, 212
2. "The Sages Gave Their Laws the Same Force as Biblical Law", 214
3. "The Sages Gave Their Laws Greater Force than Biblical Law", 215
4. Legal Enforcement of Rabbinic Laws, 217
VI. Reduction of the Oral Law to Writing, 224
A. The Nature of the Prohibition Against Reduction to Writing and the Reasons Therefor, 224
B. Dating the Reduction of Talmudic Literature to Writing, 227

Chapter 6 **THE BASIC NORM AND THE SOURCES OF JEWISH LAW** **228**
I. The Three Meanings of the Term "Sources of Law", 228
II. The Basic Norm of a Legal System, 230
III. The Basic Norm of Jewish Law, 232
IV. The Sources of Jewish Law, 235
A. The Literary Sources, 235
B. The Historical Sources, 236
C. The Legal Sources, 236

Chapter 7 **THE PREROGATIVES OF THE HALAKHIC AUTHORITIES** **240**
I. "The Torah Is from Heaven" and "The Torah Is Not in Heaven", 240
II. No Suprahuman Authority in Halakhic Determinations, 242
A. "A Prophet Is No Longer Authorized to Innovate", 242
B. The Torah Was Entrusted to the Halakhic Authorities, 243
C. Law and Equity—"Right" That Is "Left" and "Left" That Is "Right", 247
D. The Oven of Akhnai, 261
E. Differences of Opinion with Regard to Suprahuman Influences in the Determination of the *Halakhah:* The Accepted View, 264
III. The Prerogatives of the Halakhic Authorities as Existing in Every Generation, 266
IV. The Principle that "The Law Is in Accordance with the Views of the Later Authorities" (*Hilkheta ke-Vatra'ei*), 267

PART TWO
The Legal Sources of Jewish Law
SECTION 1 *Exegesis and Interpretation*

Chapter 8 **EXEGESIS AND INTERPRETATION (MIDRASH AND *PARSHANUT*): INTRODUCTION** **275**

I. Explanation of the Terms *Midrash* and *Parshanut*, 275
II. Interpretation of the *Halakhah*, of Documents, and of Communal Enactments, 277
III. Scriptural Authority for Biblical Exegesis, 278

Chapter 9 **EXEGETICAL INTERPRETATION OF THE TORAH** **281**

I. Nature and Function of Exegesis of the Torah, 283
A. Creative Interpretation (*Midrash Yozer*) and Integrative Interpretation (*Midrash Mekayyem*), 283
B. Midrash as a Creative Source in Jewish Law, 286
C. Comparison with Other Legal Systems, 290
D. Differences in Legal Rules Resulting from Differences in Methods of Interpretation, 292
E. Integrative Interpretation, 297
II. *Asmakhta* (Supportive Interpretation) in Midrash, 300
III. Different Literary Forms for Creative and Integrative Interpretation, 305
IV. Development of the Use of Midrash, 308
A. Antiquity of Exegetical Activity, 308
B. Exegetical Interpretation from Ezra the Scribe until the *Zugot* ("Pairs"), 309
C. Exegetical Interpretation in the Period of the *Zugot*, 314
D. Exegetical Interpretation in the Academies of R. Akiva and R. Ishmael, 316
V. The Thirteen Canons (*Middot*) of Interpretation, 318
VI. Explicative Exegesis, 319
A. Terms and Expressions—Generally, 320
B. Terms and Expressions—Conjunctive and Disjunctive, Masculine and Feminine, 321
1. The Letter *Vav*—Conjunctive or Also Disjunctive?, 321
2. Masculine and Feminine, 322
C. Generalization and Specification, 323
1. Inference from a Generalization Followed by a Specification (*Kelal u-Ferat*), 324
2. Inference from a Specification Followed by a Generalization (*Perat u-Khelal*), 325
3. Inference from a Generalization Followed by a Specification Followed in Turn by a Generalization (*Kelal u-Ferat u-Khelal*), 326
4. The Relation between the Canons on Generalization and Specification and the Other Canons, 327
5. A Generalization that Requires a Specification or a Specification that Requires a Generalization, 328

a. A Generalization that Requires a Specification, 329
b. A Specification that Requires a Generalization, 330
D. A Matter Included in a Generalization and Also Specifically Mentioned (*Davar she-Hayah bi-Khelal ve-Yaẓa Min ha-Kelal*), 330
E. An Ambiguous Word or Passage Is Explained from Its Context or from a Subsequent Expression (*Davar ha-Lamed me-Inyano, ve-Davar ha-Lamed mi-Sofo*), 333
1. Explanation on the Basis of a Subsequent Expression, 334
2. Explanation on the Basis of Context, 334
F. Two Contradictory Passages, 335
1. Contradiction between Two Passages in Two Sections, 336
2. Contradiction between Two Passages in the Same Section, 337
3. Contradiction between Two Parts of the Same Verse, 338
VII. Logical Interpretation, 339
A. Violation of a Betrothed Girl, 339
B. The Law of Pledges, 340
C. Damage Due to a Pit, 341
D. The Law of Agency, 342
VIII. Analogical Exegesis, 343
A. Scriptural Analogy (*Hekkesh ha-Katuv*), 344
1. Explicit Analogy, 344
2. Analogy by Implication, 346
B. Inference *A Fortiori* (*Kal va-Ḥomer*), 347
1. Inference from the More Lenient to the More Stringent, 348
2. Inference from the More Stringent to the More Lenient, 349
3. "It Is Enough for the Conclusion That It Be like the Premise", 349
C. Inference from the Similarity of Words or Phrases (*Gezerah Shavah*), 351
D. Application of a General Principle (*Binyan Av*), 355
1. Application of a General Principle Derived from a Single Verse, 356
2. Application of a General Principle Derived from Two Verses, 356
3. Application of a General Principle Derived from Three Verses, 357
4. Application of a General Principle Derived from Four Verses, 358
E. Order of Priority in the Use of the Analogical Canons, 360
IX. Restrictive Interpretation, 360
A. Acceptance of Proselytes from National Groups with Whom Marriage Was Forbidden, 361
B. The Rebellious Son, 365
1. Halakhic Interpretation with Regard to the Son, 365

2. Halakhic Interpretation with Regard to the Parents, 366
C. The Idolatrous Town, 367
1. How an Idolatrous Town Comes into Being, 367
2. Towns That Cannot Become Idolatrous Towns, 367
D. Opposition to Drastically Restrictive Interpretation, 369
X. The Methods of Interpretation of R. Ishmael and R. Akiva, 371
A. The Principal Differences in the Methods of Interpretation by the Academies of R. Ishmael and R. Akiva, 371
B. The Dispute Related Mainly to the Methods of Integrating the Law with Scripture, Not to the Substance of the Law, 374
C. Criticism by the Sages of Symbolic Methods of Interpretation, 380
XI. Exegetical Interpretation of the Torah in the Amoraic Period, 383
A. Decline in the Use of Exegetical Interpretation of the Torah, 383
B. Dispensing with the Need for Integrative Interpretation, 384
C. General Guidelines for Use of Interpretive Methods, 387
XII. Biblical Exegesis in the Post-Talmudic Period, 391
A. Consecration of Something Not Yet in Existence, 392
B. "Moving a Landmark" (*Hassagat Gevul*), 394
C. "Scheming Witnesses" (*Edim Zomemim*), 397

Chapter 10 **INTERPRETATION OF THE *HALAKHAH*** **400**

I. The Nature of Halakhic Interpretation, 400
II. Halakhic Interpretation in Ancient and Tannaitic Times, 402
A. Legislation Concerning *Agunot*—The Enactment Speaks of the Usual Situation, 402
B. Maintenance and Support of Daughters—Analogy from a Parallel Rule, 403
C. Indirect Evidence of Halakhic Interpretation, 404
1. Agency for the Purpose of Divorce, 404
2. Bailments, 405
III. Halakhic Interpretation in the Amoraic Period, 407
A. Legal Capacity of Minors in the Law of Finders—Plain Meaning versus Nonliteral Interpretation, 409
B. Liability in Tort—Restricting the Rule to Limited Facts, 411
IV. Halakhic Interpretation in the Post-Talmudic Period, 414
A. Guidelines for Judicial Decision Making—How Far Do Authoritative Materials Bind the Judge?, 416
B. Fraudulent Conveyances—Resourcefulness of the Halakhic Authorities in Combating Fraud, 416
C. Use of Traditional Canons in Interpreting Post-Talmudic Responsa, 418

Chapter 11 **INTERPRETATION OF DOCUMENTS** **422**

I. *Doreshin Leshon Hedyot*, 422
A. *Doreshin Leshon Hedyot* as Meaning "Interpreting Ordinary Language", 422
1. Interpretation of a *Ketubbah* by Hillel the Elder, 424
2. The Right to Collect the Amount of the *Ketubbah* on the Strength of the Testimony of the Wife Alone, 426
3. A Daughter's Legal Right to Support, 427
4. Interpretation of a Sharecropping Lease, 428
B. *Doreshin Leshon Hedyot* as Meaning "Ascertaining Lay Usage", 429
II. Principles of Documentary Interpretation, 432
A. Two Principles: (1) The Later Part of the Document Controls; and (2) Ambiguities Are Resolved Against the Holder of the Document (lit. "The Holder of the Document Has the Lower Hand"), 433
B. Interpretation According to the "Colloquial Usage of the People" (*Leshon Benei Adam*), 437

Chapter 12 **INTERPRETATION OF COMMUNAL ENACTMENTS** **444**

I. Authority to Interpret Communal Enactments, 445
II. Interpretation in Accordance with the Language of the Enactment, Not the Subjective Intent of Those Who Enacted It, 449
A. Tax Law, 450
B. Family Law, 452
C. The Law of Landlord and Tenant, 453
D. Scope of Authority to Interpret as Limited by the Text of the Enactment, 457
E. "Scribal Errors" in the Text of the Enactment, 458
III. Circumstances that Permit the Background and Objectives of the Enactment to Be Taken into Account, 459
A. Universally Agreed Intent, 459
B. Condemnation of Overnice Technicality in Interpreting Enactments, 461
C. Giving Weight to the Preamble and to the Promotion of Good Public Order, 462
D. Explanatory Remarks of the Enactors—Use and Limitations, 462
IV. Inconsistency or Ambiguity in the Text, 464
V. Methods of Interpreting Enactments, 468

GLOSSARY **G•1**

VOLUME II

PART TWO *(continued)*
The Legal Sources of Jewish Law
SECTION 2 *Legislation, Custom, Precedent, and Legal Reasoning*

Chapter 13 **LEGISLATION: INTRODUCTION** **477**

I. The Relationship Between Midrash and Legislation, 477
II. Legislation in Jewish Law and in Other Legal Systems, 478
III. The Source in the Written Law for the Legislative Power of the Halakhic Authorities, 481
IV. Legislative Authority of Other Competent Bodies and the Source of That Authority, 486
V. Explanation of Terms, 490
  A. *Takkanah* and *Gezerah*, 490
  B. *Tenai Bet Din, Minhag*, 492

Chapter 14 **LEGISLATION: NATURE, OBJECTIVES, AND PRINCIPLES OF LEGISLATION BY THE HALAKHIC AUTHORITIES** **494**

I. The Scope of Legislative Activity by the Halakhic Authorities, 495
II. The Nature of Legislative Activity by the Halakhic Authorities; the Meaning of the Prohibitions "You Shall Not Add" and "You Shall Not Take Away", 496
III. The Fundamental Objective of Legislative Activity by the Halakhic Authorities, 503
IV. Principles and Guidelines for Legislative Activity by the Halakhic Authorities, 505
  A. "The Court May Direct that an Affirmative Precept of the Torah Not Be Carried Out" (*Shev ve-Al Ta'aseh*), 505
  B. "The Court Has the Power to Expropriate Property" (*Hefker Bet Din Hefker*), 507
    1. The Initial Stages of the Principle, 507
    2. *Hefker Bet Din Hefker* as a Legislative Principle, 508
    3. Scope of the Principle's Application, 510
    4. Application of the Principle to a Religious Question Turning on the Ownership of Property; Enactment of the *Prosbul*, 511
    5. *Hefker Bet Din Hefker* and Communal Enactments, 514
  C. "The Court May Impose Punishment Not Prescribed in the Torah", 515
  D. Temporary Measures to Restore the People to the Faith, 519
  E. The Court in Special Circumstances and "Where There Is Good Cause" May Direct Performance of an Act the Torah Prohibits (*Kum va-Aseh*) Even in Matters of Religious Law, 521

1. Annulment of Marriages "Improperly Effected", 521
2. Legislation Concerning *Agunot*, 522
3. Extension of This Principle to Legislation in Criminal Law, 531
V. The Terms *Le-Migdar Milta* (To Safeguard the Matter), *Lefi Sha'ah* (Temporarily), *Hora'at Sha'ah* (A Temporary Measure), etc., 533
VI. Legislation in Jewish Law and the Problem of *Ultra Vires*, 536
VII. The Role of the Public in the Legislative Activities of the Halakhic Authorities, 538
VIII. "One Court May Not Overturn the Legislation of Another Unless Greater than the Other in Wisdom and Number", 541

Chapter 15 **LEGISLATION: ENACTMENTS THROUGH THE END OF THE TANNAITIC PERIOD** **545**

I. Introduction, 546
II. Earliest Legislation, 550
A. The Enactments of Joshua Concerning the Relationship between the Individual and the Public in Property Matters, 551
B. Military Legislation by King David, 554
III. Legislation at the Time of Ezra and the Great Assembly, 554
A. The Men of the Great Assembly, 554
B. Sessions of Court, 556
C. Extension of the Proscription of Incestuous Relationships from the First to the Second Degree of Consanguinity, 556
IV. The Sanhedrin, 558
A. The Sanhedrin as a Legislative Body, 558
B. The Enactment of Simeon b. Shataḥ Concerning the *Ketubbah*, 559
C. The Enactments of Hillel, 561
D. The Enactments of Rabban Gamaliel the Elder, 563
1. Writing of Names in a *Get* (Bill of Divorcement), 563
2. Nullification of a *Get* Sent to a Wife Through an Agent, 564
3. Enactment Concerning *Agunot*, 566
E. The Enactments of Usha, 566
1. Obligation of Child Support, 567
2. Sale by a Wife of Her Usufruct (*Melog*) Property, 568
V. Anonymous Enactments in Various Fields of Law, 569
A. Legislation Concerning Family Law and the Law of Succession, 570
1. Spousal Support, 570
2. The Wife's Handiwork; Waiver of Rights Conferred by Legislation, 571
3. Ransom of the Wife; Usufruct of *Melog* Property, 572
4. The Husband's Right of Inheritance and the Widow's Right to Maintenance, 573
5. Support of Daughters out of Their Father's Estate, 574
6. Enactment Concerning Inheritance Rights of the Wife's

Sons; Ensuring Daughters a Share in Their Father's Property, 575
7. Enactment of "One-Tenth of the Estate"; the Daughter's Status as an Heir, 578
B. Legislation Concerning Modes of Acquisition (*Kinyan*), 580
1. Acquisition by "Pulling" (*Kinyan Meshikhah*), 581
2. Acquisition by Barter (*Kinyan Ḥalifin*) and Acquisition by Symbolic Barter (*Kinyan Sudar*), 581
3. Acquisition of Personalty Incidental to Acquisition of Land (*Kinyan Agav Karka*), 583
4. "A Meeting of the Three", 584
5. Legal Capacity, 585
C. Legislation Concerning the Law of Obligations, 587
1. Nature of the Law of Obligations; Personal and Real Character of Obligations in Jewish Law, 587
2. Legislation Concerning Liens on Property, 591
a. Encumbered Property Sold by the Debtor Can Be Seized Only If the Debtor Has No Other Assets, 591
b. Encumbered Property Cannot Be Seized If the Debt Is Unliquidated, 592
c. Encumbered Property Can Be Seized for a Debt Evidenced by a Document but Not for a Debt Created Orally, 593
3. Market Overt, 596
D. Legislation Concerning the Law of Torts, 601
1. Enactment for the Encouragement of Penitents, 601
2. Latent Damage, 602
3. Exemption from Liability for Damage Inadvertently Caused by a Person Acting Pursuant to Public Authority, 604
E. Legislation Concerning Criminal Law, 605
F. Legislation Concerning the Law of Procedure and Evidence, 605
1. Inquiry and Examination of Witnesses, 605
a. The Solution of R. Ḥanina, 606
b. The Solution of Rava, 607
c. The Solution of R. Papa, 607
2. Authentication and Certification of Legal Instruments, 610
G. Legislation Concerning Labor Law; Enactment That the Laborer May Take an Oath and Receive His Wages, 614

Chapter 16 **LEGISLATION IN THE AMORAIC PERIOD** **622**

I. Introduction, 622
II. Principles of Legislation, 623
A. "Do What Is Right and Good", 623
1. The Adjoining Landowner's Preemptive Right, 625
2. The Debtor's Right to Redeem Land Seized to Satisfy a Debt, 627
B. Prevention of Strife and Enmity, 628

III. "All Who Marry Do So Subject to the Conditions Laid Down by the Rabbis, and the Rabbis Annul This Marriage", 631

Chapter 17 **LEGISLATION IN THE GEONIC PERIOD** **643**
I. Introduction, 643
II. Enactments of the *Geonim*, 646
A. Equalizing Real and Personal Property for the Satisfaction of Debts, 646
B. Power of Attorney from the Plaintiff to Litigate against the Defendant; "Four Cubits in the Land of Israel", 649
C. The Oath "I Have Nothing" in Proceedings to Enforce Civil Judgments, 651
D. Abrogation of the *Ketubbah* Clause Concerning Inheritance Rights of a Wife's Sons, 655
E. Legislation on Marriage and Divorce, 656
1. Enactment Concerning the Manner of Effecting Betrothal, 656
2. Enactment Concerning the Grant of a Divorce to a *Moredet* (Wife Who Refuses to Cohabit with Her Husband), 658

Chapter 18 **POST-GEONIC LEGISLATION: INTRODUCTION** **666**
I. The Diffusion of Spiritual Hegemony and the Rise of the *Kehillah* (Local Jewish Community), 666
II. Contraction of the Territorial Scope of Legislative Jurisdiction, 668
III. Contraction of the Substantive Scope of Legislative Authority, 676
IV. Local Legislation and Conflict of Laws, 677

Chapter 19 **COMMUNAL ENACTMENTS** **678**
I. Legislation by the Townspeople and the Community, 679
II. The Source of the Authority and Legal Effectiveness of Communal Enactments, 685
A. Civil Law, 685
B. Criminal Law, 688
C. Equating the Standing of the Community with That of the Court, 699
D. Communal Legislation and Matters of *Issur* ("Religious" Law), 707
E. Binding Force of Communal Enactments, 713
III. Majority and Minority in Communal Enactments, 715
A. The Principle of Majority Rule, 715
B. What Constitutes a Majority, 723
IV. Communal Enactments by Communal Representatives, 727
V. The Applicability of Communal Enactments to Minors, Persons Yet Unborn, and Persons Joining the Community subsequent to the Adoption of the Enactment, 731
VI. The Relation between the Substantive Content of Communal Enactments and the Provisions of the *Halakhah*, 736

A. Competence of Testimony in Communal Matters by Witnesses Halakhically Incompetent to Testify, 737
B. Competence of Judges Related to the Litigants or Having a Personal Interest in the Case to Sit in Communal Matters, 739
C. Signature of the Town Scribe Instead of Signatures of Witnesses, 741
D. Enactment of a Limitation Period for Asserting Claims of Ownership, 744
E. Enactments in Tax Law, 745
VII. The Integration of Communal Enactments into the Halakhic System, 751
A. Approval of Communal Enactments by a "Distinguished Person", 751
B. Consonance of Communal Enactments with the Principles of Justice and Equity Embodied in Jewish Law, 760
1. An Enactment Must "Build Fences and Tend to Improve" and Not "Breach Fences and Spoil What Is Good", 760
2. A Majority of the Public Must Be Able to Conform to the Enactment, 762
3. An Enactment Must Not Arbitrarily Prejudice Minority Rights, 763
4. An Enactment Must Apply Equally to All Members of the Community, 771
5. An Enactment Must Apply Prospectively and Not Retroactively, 772
C. Interpretation of Communal Enactments by the Halakhic Authorities, 777
VIII. Summary, 778

Chapter 20 **SURVEY OF LEGISLATION FROM THE TENTH CENTURY C.E. TO THE PRESENT** **780**
I. Introduction, 782
II. Legislation in the Various Centers: Personages and Legislative Bodies and the Scope of Their Legislative Activity, 783
A. Germany and France, 783
1. Enactments of Rabbenu Gershom Me'or Ha-Golah ("Light of the Exile"): Prohibitions against Polygamy, and against Divorce without the Wife's Consent, 783
2. Enactments of Rashi, 786
3. Enactments of Rabbenu Tam and of the Community of Troyes, 786
a. Enactments Concerning the Relation Between Jews and Non-Jews, 786
b. Enactment Limiting a Husband's Right to Inherit, 787
c. Enactment Prohibiting Challenge to the Validity of a Divorce after Its Delivery, 787

d. Enactment Prohibiting Prolonged Separation by a Husband from His Wife, 787
4. Enactments of David b. Kalonymus, 788
5. Enactments of "Shum" (Speyer, Worms, and Mainz), 788
6. Enactments of Maharam of Rothenburg and Rabbenu Perez of Corbeil, 789
7. Enactment of Ḥayyim Or Zaru'a Against *Ex Parte* Decisions, 791
8. Enactments of Mainz at the End of the Fourteenth Century, 792
9. Enactments in the Fifteenth and Sixteenth Centuries, 793
a. Enactment of the Synod of Nuremberg on the Language to Be Used in Court Proceedings, 793
b. Enactments of Bingen, 793
c. Enactments of Frankfurt, 794
B. Spain and North Africa, 796
1. Legislation by Local Communities: Toledo and Molina, 796
2. Countrywide Legislation, 797
3. Enactments of the Aragonian Communities, 1354, 797
4. Enactments of the Castilian Communities at Valladolid, 1432, 798
a. The Educational System: Organization and Financing, 799
b. Appointment of Judges and Other Public Officials; Judicial Authority; Civil and Criminal Procedure, 799
c. Enactments Concerning Informers and the Relation between the Government and the Jews, 801
d. Enactments Concerning Tax Law, 803
e. Enactments Outlawing Extravagance in Dress and Festive Banquets, 803
5. Enactments of the North African Center, 804
a. Algerian Enactments, 1394, 804
b. Enactments of Fez, 806
C. The Mediterranean Countries and Italy, 809
1. Enactments of Maimonides in Egypt, 809
2. Enactments of Candia (Crete); Enactment for the Protection of Tenants, 811
3. Italy, 813
a. Enactments of Forli, 1418, 813
(1) Enactments Concerning Taxes, 813
(2) Prohibition of Games of Chance, 814
(3) Limits on Luxuries and Extravagant Festive Banquets, 814
(4) Sumptuary Legislation, 815
b. Enactments of Florence, 816
c. Enactments of Ferrara, 816
4. Enactments of Corfu, 817
D. Enactments of the National and Regional Councils of

Poland, Lithuania, and Moravia in the Seventeenth and Eighteenth Centuries, 817
1. Enactments of the Council of the Four Lands (*Va'ad Arba Araẓot*), 818
2. Enactments of the Council of the Principal Communities of Lithuania, 818
3. Enactments of Moravia, 819
E. Enactments of Individual Communities in the Seventeenth and Eighteenth Centuries, 820
1. The Book of Enactments of the Community of Cracow, 821
a. Jails and Imprisonment, 821
b. Imprisonment for Gambling, 821
2. Other Compilations, 823
F. Legislation after the Onset of Emancipation, 824
G. Enactments of the Chief Rabbinate of the Land of Israel, 824
1. Establishment of a Rabbinical Court of Appeals, 824
2. Procedural Enactments for the Rabbinical Courts of the Land of Israel, 1943, 826
a. Procedure for Litigation and the Payment of Court Costs, 826
b. Adoption, 827
c. Equalization of Daughters with Sons, and Wives with Husbands, in Regard to Inheritance, 828
3. Enactments of 1944, 829
a. The Minimum Amount of the *Ketubbah*, 830
b. Support by a *Levir* of His Brother's Widow, 830
c. Support of Children up to the Age of Fifteen, 831
4. Enactments of 1950, 833
5. Termination of Legislative Activity, 834
III. The Special Legislative Trend in Regard to Some Aspects of Family Law and the Law of Succession, 835
A. Exercise of Full Legislative Authority over Financial Aspects of Family Law and the Law of Succession, 835
1. Restriction on the Husband's Right of Inheritance, 835
a. Enactment of Rabbenu Tam; Enactments of "Shum", 836
b. Enactments in Spain; Enactments of Toledo, Molina, Algeria, and Fez, 838
2. Right of a Mother to Inherit, 840
3. Restriction on a Widow's Right to Recover the Amount of Her *Ketubbah*, 841
4. Equal Rights of Inheritance for Sons and Daughters in Certain Circumstances, 842
B. Decline in Legislation Directly Affecting the Validity of Marriage and Divorce, 846
1. Controversy Between the Authorities of Mainz and the Authorities of Worms and Speyer in the Twelfth Century, 848
2. Annulment of Marriage on the Strength of an Explicit

Enactment; the Views of Asheri, Rashba, and Rabbenu Jeroham, 850
3. The Demand for "The Approval of All the Halakhic Authorities of the Region"; the View of Ribash, 856
4. Basic Distinction Between Theory and Practice in Regard to Legislative Authority; the Views of Rashbeẓ (Simeon b. Ẓemaḥ Duran) and Rashbash (Simeon b. Solomon Duran), 859
5. Explanation for Abstention from Exercising Legislative Power to Annul Marriages; the View of Maharam Alashkar, 864
6. The Difference between the Enactment of Fez, 1494, and the Enactment of Fez, 1592, 869
7. The Rulings of Joseph Caro and Rema (Moses Isserles) Concerning Abstention from the Exercise of Legislative Power to Annul Marriages, 870
8. The Sixteenth and Seventeenth Centuries in Italy and the Mediterranean Countries, 872
9. Enactments in the Eastern Countries in the Eighteenth and Nineteenth Centuries Providing for Annulment of Marriages, 874
10. Contemporary Legislative Authority Concerning the Law of Marriage, 878

Chapter 21 **CUSTOM (*MINHAG*): ITS NATURE AND THE SOURCE OF ITS BINDING FORCE** **880**

I. Introduction, 880
II. Custom as a Historical Source of Law, 880
III. Custom as a Legal Source of Law, 881
IV. Extent and Rationale of the Efficacy of Custom as a Legal Source of Law, 883
V. Explanation of Terms; Meanings of *Minhag;* Other Hebrew Terms for "Custom", 885
VI. Distinctions between Laws Derived from Custom and Laws Derived from Other Legal Sources, 888
VII. Scriptural Support for the Binding Force of Custom, 893

Chapter 22 **CUSTOM: OPERATION AND CATEGORIES** **895**

I. Introduction, 895
A. Functions of Custom, 896
B. Categories of Custom, 896
1. Custom and Usage, 896
2. General and Local Custom, 897
II. Custom as Determining the Law, 898
III. Custom as Supplementing the Law, 901
IV. Custom as Changing Existing Law, 903
A. Distinction between Matters of *Mamon* (Civil Law) and Matters of *Issur* ("Religious" Law) in Regard to the Creative Power of Custom, 903
B. The Maxim "Custom Overrides the Law", 905
C. Custom in Matters of *Issur* and in Other Areas of Jewish Law, 909

V. Custom as a Creative Force in Various Areas of the Law, 911
A. Preparation and Certification of Documents; Recovery of Debts; Financial Relations Between Husband and Wife, 912
B. Custom in the Development of the Modes of Acquisition and the Creation of Obligations, 913
C. Custom in Tax Law, 920
D. Custom in Jewish Law in the State of Israel; Severance Pay, 924
E. Local Custom as Overriding the Law, 926
VI. Proof of Custom, 927
VII. Custom and Usage, 930
VIII. General and Local Custom, 932
IX. Custom and the Conflict of Laws, 936
X. Control by the Halakhic Authorities over Custom, 937
A. Custom Based on Error, 937
B. Unreasonable or Illogical Custom, 940
C. "Bad Custom", 941
D. Integration of Custom into Existing Law: Fundamental Principles of Equity and Justice in Jewish Law, 942

Chapter 23 ***MA'ASEH* AND PRECEDENT** **945**
I. *Ma'aseh* as a Legal Source, 945
II. The Caution Shown by the Halakhic Authorities in Their Actions, 949
III. *Ma'aseh* in Judicial Decision Making, 950
A. The Tannaitic Period, 951
1. Preparation and Signing of Legal Instruments, 951
2. Grounds for Release from a Vow, 952
3. Suretyship Undertaken after Creation of the Principal Debt, 953
B. The Amoraic Period, 954
1. Laws Concerning Conversion to Judaism, 954
2. Laws Concerning Return of Lost Property, 956
IV. *Ma'aseh* in the Conduct of Halakhic Authorities, 958
A. The Tannaitic Period, 958
1. Laws Concerning the Sabbath, 958
2. Laws Concerning the *Sukkah*, 959
B. The Amoraic Period: Assets of a Deceased Proselyte, 959
V. Distinguishing a *Ma'aseh*, 960
A. The Process of Distinguishing in Jewish Law, 960
B. Distinguishing as a Technique in Drawing Conclusions from a Judicial Decision; An Example from the Law of Bailments, 964
C. Distinguishing as a Technique in Drawing Conclusions from Incidents Involving Conduct of a Halakhic Authority; An Example from the Law of Interest, 966
VI. *Ma'aseh* in the Post-Talmudic Period, 968
A. Deducing Legal Conclusions from an Incident Recorded in Talmudic Literature, 968
1. Law Concerning the Reciting of the *Shema*, 969

2. One Life May Not Be Sacrificed to Save Another, 969
B. *Ma'aseh* Occurring in the Post-Talmudic Period, 973
C. *Ma'aseh* and the Responsa Literature, 975
VII. Precedent in Jewish Law, 978
A. "Case" and Precedent in Other Legal Systems, 978
B. Similarities and Differences between *Ma'aseh* in Jewish Law and Precedent in the Common Law, 980
C. The Nature of a Judgment in Jewish Law and the Problem of Precedent, 981
D. The Approach to Decision Making in Jewish Law and the Problem of Precedent, 983

Chapter 24 **LEGAL REASONING (*SEVARAH*)** **987**
I. Definition of Legal Reasoning as a Legal Source, 987
II. Legal Reasoning as the Creative Source of Various Legal Rules; The Rule "Be Killed Rather than Transgress" in the Law of Murder, 990
III. Legal Reasoning as the Creative Source of General Legal Principles, 992
A. "The Burden of Proof Is on the Claimant", 992
B. "The Mouth That Has Prohibited Is the Mouth That Has Permitted", 993
C. Legal Presumptions; Reliance on a Majority, 995
IV. Legal Reasoning in the Amoraic Period, 998
A. "A Half-Measure Is Biblically Prohibited", 998
B. Parallel Rationales: Biblical Verse and Legal Reasoning, 1000
1. The Law Pertaining to Witnesses, 1000
2. The Law of *Ḥaliẓah*, 1002
V. Legal Reasoning in the Post-Talmudic Era, 1004
VI. Search by the Halakhic Authorities for the Legal Source of Particular Rules, 1007

GLOSSARY **G•1**

VOLUME III

PART THREE
The Literary Sources of Jewish Law

Chapter 25 **THE LITERARY SOURCES OF JEWISH LAW: NATURE AND DEFINITION** **1017**
I. The Literary Sources of Law, 1017
A. In General, 1017
B. Official Publications, 1017
C. Legal Literature and General Literature, 1018
II. The Literary Sources of Jewish Law, 1019

Chapter 26 **THE LITERARY SOURCES FROM THE SINAITIC REVELATION UNTIL THE *TANNAIM*** **1020**

I. The Written Law, 1020
II. The Prophets and the Hagiographa, 1021
A. The Laws of the Sabbath, 1021
B. Modes of Acquisition, 1022
C. The King's Law, 1024
D. "A Person Shall Be Put to Death Only for His Own Crime", 1025
E. The Law of Suretyship, 1026
III. Legal and General Literature, 1027
A. Introduction, 1027
B. The Papyri, 1028
C. The Septuagint, 1029
D. Philo of Alexandria, 1030
E. Flavius Josephus, 1031
F. The Apocrypha, 1033
IV. Summary, 1037

Chapter 27 **THE LITERARY SOURCES FROM THE TANNAITIC PERIOD TO THE REDACTION OF THE TALMUD: INTRODUCTION** **1038**

I. Form and Substance of Talmudic Halakhic Literature, 1038
II. The Types of Literary Sources, 1039

Chapter 28 **THE LITERARY SOURCES IN THE TANNAITIC PERIOD** **1041**

I. The Term *Tanna*, 1042
II. The Generations of the *Zugot* and the Major *Tannaim*, 1043
III. Aramaic Translations of Scripture, 1045
IV. Compilations of Halakhic *Midrashim*, 1047
A. From the School of R. Ishmael, 1048
B. From the School of R. Akiva, 1048
V. The Mishnah—in General, 1049
A. The Literary Form of the *Halakhah* in the Mishnah as Compared with That in the Halakhic *Midrashim*, 1049
B. The Development and Redaction of the Mishnah, 1050
VI. The Literary Structure of the Mishnah, 1052
A. Etymology of the Term *Mishnah*, 1052
B. The Divisions of the Mishnah and Their Contents, 1053
C. The Arrangement of the Laws in the Mishnah, 1055
VII. The Codificatory Nature of the Mishnah, 1057
A. The Content of the Mishnah, 1057
1. Comparison Between the Law as Set Forth in the Mishnah and the Law in Cognate Sources, 1058
2. Statement of the Law without Attribution to a Source, or by Attribution to "the Sages", 1060
3. The Amoraic View of the Authoritative Character of the Mishnah, 1061
4. Diversity and Uniformity in Jewish Law, 1061
5. Multiplicity of Opinions in the Mishnah, 1070

B. The Legal Style of the Mishnah, 1072
1. The Casuistic Style, 1073
2. The Hybrid Casuistic-Normative Style, 1074
a. Possession of Real Property for Three Years as Proof of Ownership, 1075
b. Division of Property Owned in Common, 1075
3. The Normative Style, 1076
C. The Literary Style of the Mishnah, 1078
VIII. The *Tosefta*, 1078
IX. Summary, 1082

Chapter 29 **THE LITERARY SOURCES IN THE AMORAIC PERIOD** **1083**
I. Introduction, 1083
A. The Two Talmuds, 1083
B. Some Preliminary Definitions, 1083
1. *Amora*, 1083
2. Talmud, 1084
3. *Gemara*, 1084
II. The Leading *Amoraim* Listed by Generations, 1085
III. The Babylonian Talmud, 1087
A. The Babylonian Diaspora, 1087
B. The Teachings of the Babylonian *Amoraim* and the Contents of the Babylonian Talmud, 1088
C. The Redaction and Completion of the Babylonian Talmud, 1091
D. The *Savoraim*, 1093
E. Compilation of the Talmud on Only Part of the Mishnah, 1094
IV. The Jerusalem Talmud, 1095
A. Contents of the Jerusalem Talmud; Differences from the Babylonian Talmud, 1095
B. The Redaction of the Jerusalem Talmud, 1097
V. The Literary-Legal Nature of the Talmud and the Place of the Talmud in the Jewish Legal System, 1098

Chapter 30 **THE LITERARY SOURCES AND OTHER HALAKHIC LITERATURE IN THE POST-TALMUDIC PERIOD: INTRODUCTION** **1101**
I. *Geonim*, *Rishonim*, and *Aḥaronim*, 1101
II. The Three Major Types of Literary Sources of the *Halakhah*; the Various Kinds of Other Halakhic Legal Literature, 1102

Chapter 31 **COMMENTARIES AND NOVELLAE** **1104**
I. The Nature of Commentaries and Novellae, 1105
II. Commentaries and Novellae on the Mishnah, 1106
A. The Geonic Period, 1106
B. Maimonides' Commentary, 1106
C. Obadiah of Bertinoro's Commentary, 1108
D. *Tosafot Yom Tov* by Yom Tov Lipmann Heller, 1108
E. *Melekhet Shelomo* by Solomon Adeni, 1109

F. *Tiferet Yisra'el* by Israel Lipschutz, 1109
G. Ḥanokh Albeck's Commentary, 1110
III. Commentaries and Novellae on Halakhic *Midrashim* and the *Tosefta*, 1110
A. Halakhic *Midrashim*, 1110
1. Rabad's Commentary on the *Sifra*, 1110
2. Rabbenu Hillel's Commentary on the *Sifra* and the *Sifrei*, 1111
B. The *Tosefta*, 1111
1. *Ḥasdei David* by David Pardo, 1112
2. *Tosefta ki-Feshutah* by Saul Lieberman, 1112
IV. Commentaries on the Babylonian Talmud, 1113
A. The Geonic Period, 1113
B. Rabbenu Hananel's Commentary, 1114
C. Rabbenu Gershom Me'or Ha-Golah and His Students, 1115
D. Rashi's Commentary on the Talmud, 1116
V. Novellae on the Babylonian Talmud, 1118
A. The Ashkenazic Novellae; the Tosafists, 1118
1. In General, 1118
2. How the Novellae of the Tosafists Were Created, 1119
3. The Leading Tosafists, 1120
a. Samuel b. Meir (Rashbam), 1120
b. Jacob b. Meir (Rabbenu Tam), 1120
c. Isaac b. Samuel (Ri), 1120
d. Samson b. Abraham (Rash) of Sens, 1121
e. Meir b. Baruch (Maharam) of Rothenburg, 1121
4. Decisions and Responsa in the *Tosafot*, 1122
B. The Sephardic Novellae/Commentaries, 1123
1. Joseph ibn Migash (Ri Migash), 1123
2. Abraham b. David (Rabad) of Posquières, 1123
3. Meir Abulafia (Ramah), 1124
4. Naḥmanides (Ramban), 1124
5. Solomon b. Abraham Adret (Rashba), 1124
6. Yom Tov Ishbili (Ritba), 1125
7. Nissim Gerondi (Ran), 1125
8. Menahem Meiri, 1126
9. Beẓalel Ashkenazi, 1126
C. Novellae in the Period of the *Aḥaronim*, 1127
1. *Ḥiddushei Halakhot* by Samuel Eliezer Edels (Maharsha), 1128
2. *Penei Yehoshu'a* by Jacob Joshua Falk, 1129
VI. Commentaries and Novellae on the Jerusalem Talmud, 1130
A. The Jerusalem Talmud—Its Study and Use as a Basis for Legal Decisions, 1130
B. Solomon Sirillo's Commentary, 1132
C. *Sedeh Yehoshu'a* by Joshua Benveniste, 1134
D. Elijah of Fulda's Commentary and Novellae, 1134
E. David Fraenkel's Commentary and Novellae, 1135
F. Moses Margoliot's Commentary and Novellae, 1135
G. The Gaon of Vilna's Commentary, 1136

Chapter 32 **THE CODIFICATORY LITERATURE: NATURE AND STRUCTURE; THE PROBLEM OF CODIFICATION** **1138**

I. The Relationship of Codificatory Literature to Commentaries, Novellae, and the Responsa Literature, 1138
II. The Two Basic Types of Codes, 1139
III. Codification in Other Legal Systems, 1140
  A. The Term "Codification", 1140
  B. Codification in Continental Europe, 1141
  C. Codification in Common-Law Countries, 1142
IV. The Nature and Problem of Codification in Jewish Law, 1144

Chapter 33 **THE CODIFICATORY LITERATURE FROM THE GEONIC PERIOD UNTIL MAIMONIDES' *MISHNEH TORAH*** **1149**

I. Codificatory Works in the Geonic Period, 1150
  A. *Sefer ha-She'iltot* by Aḥa of Shabḥa, 1150
  B. *Halakhot Pesukot* by Yehudai Gaon, 1153
  C. *Halakhot Gedolot*, 1155
  D. Motivating Factors for and against Codification in the Geonic Period, 1156
  E. Halakhic Monographs, 1158
    1. Saadiah Gaon, 1159
    2. Samuel b. Ḥophni Gaon, 1161
    3. Hai Gaon, 1164
    4. The Objectives of Halakhic Monographs, 1166
II. *Sefer ha-Halakhot* by Isaac Alfasi (Rif), 1167
  A. The Nature and Content of *Sefer ha-Halakhot*, 1167
  B. Commentaries on *Sefer ha-Halakhot*, 1173
    1. Zeraḥiah ha-Levi Gerondi (Rezah), 1173
    2. Abraham b. David (Rabad) of Posquières, 1173
    3. Naḥmanides (Ramban), 1174
    4. Jonathan of Lunel, 1175
    5. Nissim Gerondi (Ran), 1175
    6. Joseph Ḥabiba, 1176
    7. Joshua Boaz b. Simon Baruch, 1176
    8. Other Commentators, 1176
III. Codificatory Works from Alfasi to Maimonides, 1177
  A. Spain, 1177
    1. Isaac ibn Ghayyat (Riẓag), 1177
    2. Judah al-Bargeloni, 1177
  B. France and Germany, 1178
    1. The School of Rashi, 1178
    2. Eliezer b. Nathan (Raban), 1179

Chapter 34 **THE CODIFICATORY LITERATURE: MAIMONIDES' MISHNEH TORAH** **1180**

I. Strengthening of the Tendency toward Codification at the Beginning of the Rabbinic Period, 1181
II. Maimonides and his Codificatory Work, 1184
  A. Goals, 1184
  B. Compiling and Reworking the Halakhic Material, 1186
  C. Topical Arrangement and Classification, 1195
  D. Categorical Statement of Legal Rules with No Reference to Sources or Contrary Opinions, 1203

E. Style and Draftsmanship of the *Mishneh Torah*, 1206
F. Factual-Casuistic Formulation, 1211
G. A Legal Code for the People, 1214
III. Critical Reaction to Maimonides' Codificatory Methodology, 1215
A. Correspondence with *Dayyan* (Judge) Phinehas b. Meshullam of Alexandria, 1216
B. Correspondence with Joseph ibn Aknin; Rendering Decisions on the Basis of the *Mishneh Torah*, 1222
C. Rabad's Critical Glosses, 1223
D. Asheri's Reaction, 1226
E. Interim Summary of the Stages of Codification of Jewish Law, 1229
IV. Commentaries on the *Mishneh Torah*, 1231
A. *Migdal Oz* by Shem Tov ibn Gaon, 1232
B. *Maggid Mishneh* by Vidal of Tolosa, 1232
C. *Kesef Mishneh* by Joseph Caro, 1233
D. *Yekar Tiferet* by David ibn Zimra (Radbaz), 1233
E. *Leḥem Mishneh* by Abraham di Boton, 1233
F. *Mishneh la-Melekh* by Judah Rosanes, 1234
G. *Haggahot Maimuniyyot* by Meir ha-Kohen of Rothenburg, 1234
V. The Ultimate Achievement of the *Mishneh Torah*, 1235

Chapter 35 **THE CODIFICATORY LITERATURE: FROM MAIMONIDES UNTIL THE *SHULḤAN ARUKH;* THE *SEFER HA-TURIM*** **1236**

I. Codificatory Literature Until the *Sefer ha-Turim*, 1237
A. Books Following the Order of the Talmud, and/or Organized in Whole or in Part According to Topic, 1238
1. *Sefer Avi ha-Ezri* and *Sefer Avi'asaf* by Eliezer b. Joel ha-Levi (Raviah), 1238
2. *Sefer ha-Roke'aḥ* by Eleazar b. Judah, 1239
3. *Sefer ha-Terumah* by Baruch b. Isaac, 1239
4. *Sefer ha-Manhig* by Abraham b. Nathan ha-Yarḥi, 1240
5. *Or Zaru'a* by Isaac b. Moses (Riaz), 1241
6. Codificatory Works by Naḥmanides (Ramban), 1242
7. *Sefer ha-Hashlamah* by Meshullam b. Moses of Beziers, 1243
8. *Sefer ha-Terumot* by Samuel Sardi, 1244
9. *Sefer Shibbolei ha-Leket* by Zedekiah b. Abraham ha-Rofe, 1247
10. *Sefer ha-Tanya*, 1248
11. *Sefer ha-Neyar*, 1248
12. *Sha'arei Dura* by Isaac b. Meir of Düren, 1248
13. *Sefer ha-Mordekhai* by Mordecai b. Hillel ha-Kohen, 1249
14. *Piskei ha-Rosh* by Asheri, and Its Commentaries, 1251
a. *Piskei ha-Rosh*, 1251
b. Commentaries on *Piskei ha-Rosh*, 1253
(1) *Haggahot Asheri* by Israel of Krems, 1253
(2) *Peri Megadim et al. by* Yom Tov Lipmann Heller, 1254

(3) *Korban Netanel* by Nethanel Weil, 1255
15. *Sefer ha-Tashbeẓ* by Samson b. Ẓadok and *Sefer ha-Parnas* by Moses Parnas of Rothenburg, 1255
16. *Sefer Eẓ Ḥayyim* by Jacob b. Judah Ḥazzan, 1255
17. *Sefer Orḥot Ḥayyim* by Aaron b. Jacob ha-Kohen, 1257
18. *Sefer Kol Bo*, 1258
B. Books Organized on the Basis of an Enumeration of the Biblical Commandments, 1259
1. *Sefer Yere'im* by Eliezer b. Samuel (Re'em), 1259
2. *Sefer Miẓvot Gadol* (*Semag*) by Moses of Coucy, 1261
3. *Sefer Miẓvot Katan* (*Semak*) by Isaac of Corbeil, 1263
4. *Sefer ha-Ḥinnukh*, 1265
C. Books Organized According to Idiosyncratic Criteria, 1267
1. *Sefer ha-Ittur* by Isaac of Marseilles, 1267
2. *Sefer Meisharim* and *Toledot Adam ve-Ḥavvah* by Rabbenu Jeroham b. Meshullam, 1269
D. The Codificatory Methodology of Solomon b. Abraham Adret (Rashba), 1273
1. *Torat ha-Bayit ha-Arokh, Torah ha-Bayit ha-Kaẓer,* and Other Codificatory Works by Rashba, 1273
2. *Bedek ha-Bayit* and *Mishmeret ha-Bayit*, 1276
II. *Sefer ha-Turim* by Jacob b. Asher, 1277
A. Jacob b. Asher's Codificatory Methodology, 1277
B. The Structure and Organization of *Sefer ha-Turim*, 1287
III. Commentaries on *Sefer ha-Turim*, 1302
A. *Bet Yosef* by Joseph Caro and *Darkhei Moshe* by Moses Isserles (Rema), 1303
B. *Bet Yisra'el* by Joshua Falk, 1303
C. *Bayit Ḥadash* (*Baḥ*) by Joel Sirkes, 1303
D. Compilations of Responsa Arranged According to the Organization of *Sefer ha-Turim*, 1304
IV. Codificatory Literature from *Sefer ha-Turim* to the *Shulḥan Arukh*, 1304

Chapter 36 **THE CODIFICATORY LITERATURE: THE WORKS OF JOSEPH CARO AND MOSES ISSERLES** **1309**

I. Joseph Caro and His Codificatory Achievement, 1309
A. Historical and Halakhic Circumstances, 1309
B. A Two-Part Code: A Book of *Halakhot* and a Book of *Pesakim*, 1312
C. *Bet Yosef*, 1313
1. Compendious Presentation of All the Halakhic Material, 1313
2. Methodology of Determining the Law, 1316
D. The *Shulḥan Arukh*, 1319
1. Codificatory Approach, 1319
2. Structure and Arrangement, 1323
3. Language and Style As Compared to the *Turim* and the *Mishneh Torah*, 1327
E. The Crystallization of the Methodology for Codifying Jewish Law, 1341
II. Moses Isserles (Rema) and His Contribution to the Codificatory Literature, 1345

A. The Polish Jewish Community, 1345
B. Jacob Pollack and Shalom Shakhna, and Their Attitude toward Codification, 1345
C. Moses Isserles (Rema), 1349
D. *Darkhei Moshe:* Its Purpose and Methodology, 1350
E. *Torat Ḥattat* and Its Methodology, 1357
F. Glosses to the *Shulḥan Arukh:* The *Mappah*—Its Objectives and Methodology, 1359
G. The *Shulḥan Arukh* as the Authoritative Code of Jewish Law, 1365

Chapter 37 **THE CODIFICATORY LITERATURE: REACTIONS TO THE *SHULḤAN ARUKH,* AND ITS FINAL ACCEPTANCE** **1367**

I. Introduction, 1368
II. The Eastern Countries, 1368
A. Joseph ibn Lev (Maharibal), 1368
B. The Agreement of Two Hundred Rabbis to Caro's Principle of Decision Making, 1369
C. Critiques of Specific Laws in the *Shulḥan Arukh,* 1370
1. Jacob Castro (Maharikash), 1371
2. Samuel Aboab, 1371
3. Yom Tov Ẓahalon (Maharitaẓ), 1372
D. The Acceptance of the *Shulḥan Arukh,* 1373
III. The Western Countries, 1374
A. Opposition to the *Shulḥan Arukh* without Proposing Any Alternative Type of Code, 1375
1. Ḥayyim b. Beẓalel, 1375
2. Judah Loew b. Beẓalel (Maharal of Prague), 1379
3. Samuel Eliezer Edels (Maharsha) and Meir b. Gedaliah (Maharam of Lublin), 1383
B. Opposition to the *Shulḥan Arukh* as Manifested by the Composition of Alternative Types of Codes, 1385
1. Solomon Luria (Maharshal), 1385
2. Mordecai Jaffe, 1394
3. Yom Tov Lipmann Heller, 1403
C. Opposition to the *Shulḥan Arukh* as the Sole Basis for Legal Decisions; Commentaries on the *Shulḥan Arukh,* 1407
1. Joshua Falk, 1408
2. Joel Sirkes, 1415
IV. The Acceptance of the *Shulḥan Arukh* as the Definitive and Authoritative Code of Jewish Law, 1417
A. The Completion of the Codificatory Structure of the *Shulḥan Arukh* by Its Commentaries, 1417
B. Historical Circumstances as a Factor in the Acceptance of the *Shulḥan Arukh,* 1419

Chapter 38 **THE CODIFICATORY LITERATURE: COMMENTARIES ON AND CODIFICATION AFTER THE *SHULḤAN ARUKH*** **1423**

I. Introduction, 1424
II. Commentaries on *Ḥoshen Mishpat,* 1424
A. *Sefer Me'irat Einayim* (*Sema*) by Joshua Falk, 1424
B. *Turei Zahav* (*Taz*) by David b. Samuel ha-Levi, 1425

C. *Siftei Kohen* (*Shakh*) by Shabbetai b. Meir ha-Kohen, 1425
D. *Be'er ha-Golah* by Moses Rivkes, 1426
E. *Urim ve-Thummim* by Jonathan Eybeschütz, 1426
F. *Be'ur ha-Gra* by Elijah, Gaon of Vilna, 1427
G. *Kezot ha-Hoshen* by Aryeh Leib Heller, 1428
H. *Netivot ha-Mishpat* by Jacob Lorbeerbaum, 1429
III. Commentaries on *Even ha-Ezer*, 1429
A. *Turei Zahav* (*Taz*) by David b. Samuel ha-Levi, 1429
B. *Ḥelkat Meḥokek* by Moses Lima, 1429
C. *Bet Shemu'el* by Samuel Phoebus, 1430
D. *Be'er ha-Golah* by Moses Rivkes, 1430
E. *Be'ur ha-Gra* by Elijah, Gaon of Vilna, 1430
F. *Avnei Millu'im* by Aryeh Leib Heller, 1431
IV. Commentaries on *Oraḥ Ḥayyim* and *Yoreh De'ah*, 1431
V. Responsa Compilations Arranged in the Topical Sequence of the *Shulḥan Arukh*, 1432
A. *Panim Ḥadashot* by Isaac Jesurun, 1433
B. *Keneset ha-Gedolah* by Ḥayyim Benveniste, 1434
C. *Be'er Heitev* by Judah Ashkenazi and Zechariah Mendel b. Aryeh Leib, 1437
D. *Leket ha-Kemaḥ* by Moses Ḥagiz, 1437
E. *Yad Aharon* by Aaron Alfandari, 1438
F. *Birkei Yosef* by Ḥayyim Joseph David Azulai (Ḥida), 1439
G. *Matteh Shim'on* by Simon Mordecai Bekemoharar, 1439
H. *Sha'arei Teshuvah* by Ḥayyim Mordecai Margolioth, 1440
I. *Pitḥei Teshuvah* by Abraham Eisenstadt, 1441
J. *Oraḥ Mishpat* by Raḥamim Elijah Ḥazzan, 1442
K. *Darkhei Teshuvah* by Ẓevi Hirsch Shapira and His Son Ḥayyim Eleazar Shapira, 1442
L. *Ozar ha-Posekim*, 1442
M. *Halakhah Pesukah*, 1443
VI. Codificatory Literature after the *Shulḥan Arukh*, 1443
A. In General, 1443
B. Compilations of Tax Laws, 1444
1. *Massa Melekh* by Joseph ibn Ezra, 1445
2. *Avodat Massa* by Joshua Abraham Judah, 1446
3. *Massa Ḥayyim* by Ḥayyim Palache, 1447
C. Codificatory Literature Devoted Mainly to Religious Law, 1447
D. *Arukh ha-Shulḥan* by Jehiel Michal Epstein, 1448
E. Causes of the Decline of Codificatory Authority and Activity, 1450
F. The Problem of Codification at the Present Time, 1451

Chapter 39 **THE RESPONSA LITERATURE** **1453**
I. Introduction, 1454
II. Responsa in the Talmudic Literature, 1454
III. The Nature and Content of the Responsa Literature, 1456
A. The Distinctiveness of the Responsa Literature as Compared with the Other Types of Post-Talmudic Halakhic Literature, 1456
B. The Special Significance and Weight of the Rulings in the Responsa, 1457

C. The Respondent as a Supreme Judicial Tribunal, 1460
D. Responsa and the Development of Jewish Law, 1461
E. Matters of *Mishpat Ivri* as the Major Subjects of the Responsa, 1461
F. The Magnitude of the Responsa Literature, 1462
G. Responsa as a Source for Knowledge of Enactments, Customs, Legal Documents, and Non-Jewish Law, 1463
H. Responsa on Questions of Textual Interpretation, Philosophy, and Religious Beliefs, 1464
I. Responsa as a Source for the History of Halakhic Literature, 1464
J. Responsa as a Historical Source, 1465
K. Responsa and Parallels in Other Legal Systems, 1466

IV. The Different Periods of the Responsa Literature, 1468
A. The Geonic Period, 1468
B. The Period of the *Rishonim* (Early Authorities), 1473
1. The Nature and Content of the Responsa in the Period of the *Rishonim*, 1473
2. The Twelfth to Fourteenth Centuries, 1477
3. The Fifteenth Century, 1479
4. Summary, 1480
C. The Period of the *Aḥaronim* (Later Authorities) up to the End of the Eighteenth Century, 1482
1. The Nature and Content of the Responsa in the Period of the *Aḥaronim*, 1482
2. The Sixteenth Century, 1486
3. The Seventeenth Century, 1488
4. The Eighteenth Century, 1489
D. The Period of the Emancipation—the Nineteenth Century, 1491
1. Nature and Content of the Responsa of the Nineteenth Century and Thereafter, 1491
2. The Responsa in Different Jewish Centers, 1495
E. The Period of National Awakening, the Holocaust, and the Establishment of the Jewish State—the Twentieth Century, 1496
1. The Responsa Literature until the 1940s, 1496
2. The Responsa Literature in the 1940s and Thereafter, 1497
F. Summary, 1499

V. General Overview of the Methodology, Structure, and Form of the Responsa, 1501
A. The Questioners; Submission of Questions, 1501
B. The Structure, Form, Style, Transmittal, and Copying of the Question and Response, 1507
C. Fictitious Names of Persons and Places in the Responsa, 1512
D. Hypothetical Responsa; *Terumat ha-Deshen*, 1516

VI. Compilations of Responsa—Redaction and Organization, 1517

VII. Research in the Responsa; Digest of the Responsa Literature, 1523

Chapter 40 **LITERATURE FACILITATING RESEARCH IN JEWISH LAW: COMPILATIONS OF LEGAL DOCUMENTS, REFERENCE WORKS** **1529**

I. Introduction, 1530
II. Compilations of Legal Documents, 1531
  A. Enactments, 1531
  B. Legal Instruments (*Shetarot*), 1533
    1. *Sefer ha-Shetarot* [The Book of Legal Instruments] by Saadiah Gaon, 1535
    2. *Sefer ha-Shetarot* by Hai Gaon, 1536
    3. *Sefer ha-Shetarot* of Lucena, Spain, 1536
    4. *Sefer ha-Shetarot* by Judah al-Bargeloni, 1536
    5. Compilation of Legal Instruments in *Maḥzor Vitry*, 1537
    6. Compilations in *Sefer ha-Ittur* and *Yad Ramah*, 1537
    7. Compilations of Legal Instruments Used by English Jews in the Eleventh to Thirteenth Centuries, 1537
    8. Legal Instruments Used in Christian Spain in the Twelfth to Fifteenth Centuries, 1538
    9. *Tikkun Soferim* [The Scribe's Handbook] by Solomon b. Simeon Duran (Rashbash), 1538
    10. *Tikkun Soferim* by Moses Almosnino and Samuel Jaffe, 1538
    11. *Tikkun Shetarot* by Eliezer Milli, 1538
    12. The Compilation in *Naḥalat Shiv'ah* by Samuel ha-Levi, 1539
    13. *Et Sofer* [The Scribe's Quill] by Jacob ibn Ẓur, 1539
    14. *Oẓar ha-Shetarot* [A Treasury of Legal Instruments] by Asher Gulak, 1539
    15. Legal Instruments Used in Spain and North Africa in the Eleventh to Fifteenth Centuries, 1540
III. Reference Works, 1540
  A. Guidebooks, 1541
    1. *Seder Tannaim va-Amoraim* [Chronicles of the *Tannaim* and *Amoraim*], 1541
    2. *Iggeret Rav Sherira Gaon* [The Epistle of Rabbi Sherira Gaon], 1542
    3. *Mevo ha-Talmud* [Introduction to the Talmud] by Samuel ha-Nagid of Egypt, Attributed to Samuel ha-Nagid of Spain, 1543
    4. Maimonides' Introduction to His *Commentary on the Mishnah;* The Introductions of Menahem Meiri to *Bet ha-Beḥirah*, 1543
    5. *Sefer Keritut* by Samson of Chinon, 1544
    6. *Halikhot Olam* by Joshua ha-Levi, 1545
    7. *She'erit Yosef* by Joseph ibn Verga, 1545
    8. *Kelalei ha-Gemara* [Principles of the *Gemara*] by Joseph Caro, 1545
    9. *Kelalei ha-Talmud* [Principles of the Talmud] by Beẓalel Ashkenazi, 1547
    10. *Yavin Shemu'ah* by Solomon Algazi, 1547

11. *Yad Malakhi* by Malachi ha-Kohen, 1547
12. Guidebooks from the Nineteenth Century and Thereafter, 1548
B. Encyclopedias, 1551
1. *Paḥad Yiẓḥak* by Isaac Lampronti, 1551
2. *Sedei Ḥemed* by Ḥayyim Hezekiah Medini, 1552
3. *Die Exegetische Terminologie der Jüdischen Traditionsliteratur* [The Exegetical Terminology of the Literature of the Jewish Tradition] by Wilhelm Bacher, 1553
4. *Mafte'aḥ ha-Talmud* [Key to the Talmud] by Jehiel Michal Guttmann, 1553
5. *Enẓiklopedyah Talmudit* [Talmudic Encyclopedia], 1554
6. Halakhic Works Arranged Alphabetically, 1554
7. *Mishpat Ivri* Alphabetically Arranged by Subject, 1554
C. Biographies of Halakhic Authorities, 1556
1. Biographies According to Historical Periods, 1557
2. Biographies According to Geographical Areas, 1558
3. Biographies of Individual Authorities, 1559
4. Encyclopedias with Biographical Articles, 1560
D. Bibliographies, 1560
1. General Bibliographies, 1561
2. Bibliographies According to Type of Halakhic Literature, 1562
3. Bibliographies of Scholarly Literature on *Mishpat Ivri*, 1562
E. Lexicons, 1564
F. Books Explaining Abbreviations, 1566
G. Textual Variants, 1567
H. Concordances, 1568
I. Source References, Sayings, and Aphorisms, 1568
J. Scholarly Research in *Mishpat Ivri*, 1569
K. Journals and Periodicals on *Mishpat Ivri*, 1570

GLOSSARY **G•1**

VOLUME IV

PART FOUR
Jewish Law in the State of Israel

Chapter 41 **INTRODUCTION: JEWISH LAW FROM THE ABROGATION OF JEWISH JURIDICAL AUTONOMY TO THE ESTABLISHMENT OF THE STATE OF ISRAEL** **1575**

I. The Period of the Emancipation, 1576
A. Internal-Spiritual and External-Political Changes, 1576
B. The Change with Regard to the Hebrew Language, 1577

C. The Change in Attitude to Jewish Law, 1578
D. Warnings by the Halakhic Authorities at the Onset of the Change in Attitude to Jewish Law, 1579
E. The Abrogation of Juridical Autonomy and the Reconciliation of the Halakhic Authorities to the New Situation, 1582
F. The Continuation of Juridical Autonomy among the Jews of the Eastern Countries, 1584
G. Consequences of the Abrogation of Jewish Juridical Autonomy, 1586
II. The Era of National Awakening, 1588
A. Ha-Mishpat Ha-Ivri (Jewish Law) Society, 1588
B. Mishpat Ha-Shalom Ha-Ivri (The Jewish Court of Arbitration), 1592
C. Jewish Law in the Rabbinical Courts in the Land of Israel, 1596
1. Establishment of the Chief Rabbinate and Setting the Course of Its Activity in the Area of Jewish Law, 1596
2. Judicial Procedure and the Law of Personal Status, 1598
3. Civil Law, 1600
D. The Religious Leadership and Jewish Law, 1605
E. Jewish Law and the Hebrew Language, 1607
1. The Restoration of the Hebrew Language as the Language of Daily Life, 1607
2. The Position of Jewish Law, 1608
III. On the Eve of the Establishment of the State of Israel, 1611
A. The Legal System under the British Palestine Mandate Immediately before the Establishment of the State of Israel, 1611
B. The Deliberations Regarding the Place of Jewish Law in the Legal System of the State of Israel, 1612
C. Proposals to Require Recourse to Jewish Law, 1617

Chapter 42 **JEWISH LAW IN THE GENERAL LEGAL SYSTEM OF THE STATE OF ISRAEL** **1619**
I. The Official Position of Jewish Law and the Hebrew Language in the State of Israel, 1620
A. Section 11 of the Law and Administration Ordinance, 1948, 1620
B. The Hebrew Language, 1621
C. Dependence on English Law and Non-Recourse to Jewish Law, 1621
II. The Actual Position of Jewish Law in the State's Legal System, 1623
III. Jewish Law in Legislation, 1624
A. The Two Legislative Periods, 1624
B. Legislative Policy, 1625
C. Legislation Based on Principles of Jewish Law, 1627
1. The First Legislative Period, 1627
a. Civil Law, 1627

(1) The Cooperative Houses Law, 1627
(2) Labor Law, 1629
(3) Imprisonment for Debt, 1635
b. Criminal and Public Law, 1639
(1) The Penal Law Revision (Bribery) Law, 1640
(2) The Defamation Law, 1642
(3) Immunity of Judges, 1645
(4) Laws Incorporating Basic Tenets of the Jewish Tradition, 1646
(5) The Law of Return, 1647
(6) The Basic Law: Israel Lands, 1651
c. Personal Status, Family, and Succession Law, 1652
(1) The Marriage Age Law, 1654
(2) The Woman's Equal Rights Law, 1656
(3) The Family Law Amendment (Maintenance) Law, 1660
(4) The Capacity and Guardianship Law, 1663
(5) The Succession Law, 1671
(a) Provisions Generally Incorporating Jewish Law, 1671
(b) Provisions Not in Accord with Jewish Law, 1683
(6) Who Is a Jew?, 1688
2. The Second Legislative Period, 1690
a. The Bailees Law, 1692
b. The Unjust Enrichment Law, 1696
c. Admonition of Witnesses and Abrogation of the Witness Oath, 1697
d. The Crime Register and Rehabilitation of Offenders Law, 1707
e. Self-Help—The Land Law, 1709
f. Illegal Contracts, 1716
D. Legislation Contrary to Jewish Law, 1721
1. Suretyship—The Guarantee Law, 1721
2. The Gift Law, 1724
3. Limitation of Actions, 1724
E. Self-Sufficiency of the Law of the State of Israel, 1728
IV. Jewish Law in Israeli Judicial Decisions, 1729
V. Jewish Law in the Interpretation of Israeli Legislation, 1731
A. Problems of Statutory Interpretation and Interpretive Approaches to Israeli Legislation, 1732
B. The Proper Method of Interpreting Israeli Legislation, 1735
1. Value-Laden Legal Terms, 1738
2. Other Problems of Statutory Construction, 1737
3. *Bank Kupat Am v. Hendeles*—The First Hearing, 1739

Chapter 43 **THE LAW OF PERSONAL STATUS IN THE RABBINICAL AND GENERAL COURTS: ADDITIONAL ASPECTS OF THE PROBLEM OF THE STATUS OF JEWISH LAW IN THE LAW OF THE STATE OF ISRAEL** **1752**

I. Adjudication in Matters of Personal Status, 1753
A. Continuation of the Basic Allocation of Jurisdiction, 1753

B. The Nature of the Problems Discussed in This Chapter, 1756
II. The Law Applied by the Rabbinical Courts in Matters of Personal Status, 1758
A. Jewish Law, 1758
B. Statutes Mandating Their Application by the Rabbinical Courts, 1760
III. Application of the Jewish Law of Personal Status by the General Courts, 1765
A. Conflict of Laws, 1766
B. Evidence and Procedure, 1767
C. Privately Performed Marriages, 1770
1. Marriage Between a *Kohen* and a Divorcée, 1771
2. Marriages Permitted under the *Halakhah*, 1782
IV. The Weight Given by the General Courts to the Decisions of the Rabbinical Courts Interpreting Jewish Law, 1784
A. The Earnings of a Wife from Her Employment, 1785
B. The Rights and Obligations of Parents in the Education of Their Children, 1794
V. Legislation Contrary to Jewish Law—A Case Study of the Solution to a Problem, 1802
A. The Obligation of a Husband to Support His Wife as Affected by Her Income from Employment and from Her Property, 1802
B. Amendment of the Woman's Equal Rights Law, 1805
VI. Differing Trends in Regard to the Employment of Legislation in the Rabbinical System, 1807
A. Decline in Legislation as an Instrument of Halakhic Creativity, 1807
B. The Rabbinical Court of Appeals—Accomplishments and Limitations, 1809
VII. Civil Law in the Rabbinical Courts, 1818
VIII. The Rabbinical Courts and the General Legal System of the State, 1819
A. The *Wiloszni* Case, 1820
B. The *Nagar* Case, 1824

Chapter 44 **THE FOUNDATIONS OF LAW ACT, 1980** **1827**

I. The Purpose and Meaning of the Foundations of Law Act, 1827
A. Repeal of Article 46 of the Palestine Order in Council, 1828
B. The Principles of the Jewish Heritage as a Part of the Positive Law of the Israeli Legal System, 1831
C. According Full Operative Force to the Fundamental Principles of the Israeli Declaration of Independence, 1832
D. Legislation, Judicial Precedent, Analogy, 1834
E. "A Legal Issue Requiring Decision"; Lacuna, 1835

F. The Principles of Freedom, Justice, Equity, and Peace of the Jewish Heritage, 1839
G. The Principles of the Jewish Heritage in the Decisions of the Courts, 1841
1. The Fundamental Rights of Detainees and Prisoners, 1841
2. Freedom from Detention, 1842
3. Freedom of Thought and Speech, 1846
4. Human Dignity and Equality, 1850
5. Attitude toward National and Religious Minorities, 1854
6. The Right of Privacy, 1856
7. Other Court Decisions Discussing the Principles of the Jewish Heritage, 1860
8. How the Sources of the Jewish Heritage Are to Be Used, 1861
II. The Interpretive Function of Jewish Law in the Israeli Legal System in Light of the Foundations of Law Act, 1863
A. Uncertainty as to the Meaning of a Statute—The *Hendeles* Case, Additional Hearing, 1863
B. The Interpretation of Value-Laden Legal Terms, 1871
C. Terms and Expressions Unique to Jewish Law, 1874
D. An Institution of Jewish Law Incorporated Into Israeli Law—The *Koenig* Case, Additional Hearing, 1875
III. The Foundations of Law Act, 1980, and the Incorporation of the English Statute of Elizabeth, 1571, 1885
IV. Conclusion, 1894

Chapter 45 **THE RELIGIOUS AND CULTURAL ASPECTS OF THE QUESTION OF THE STATUS OF JEWISH LAW IN THE JEWISH STATE** **1898**
I. In General, 1898
II. Jewish Law in the Independent Israeli Legal System from the Perspective of the Traditional Jewish Legal System, 1906
A. The Nature of the State's Incorporation of Jewish Law, 1906
B. The Prohibition Against Litigating in Non-Jewish Courts, 1914
C. The Problems When Jewish Legislation and Adjudication Are Not Based on Jewish Law, 1917
III. Jewish Law in the Independent Israeli Legal System from the Perspective of the Law of the State, 1918
A. The Legislature, 1918
B. The Courts, 1920
IV. Subjective and Objective Factors Affecting Recourse to Jewish Law, 1923
A. Subjective Factors, 1924

B. Objective Factors, 1931
C. Observations Concerning Fears and the Fearful, 1938
V. Concluding Reflections, 1940

Appendixes, Glossary, Bibliography, Indexes

Appendix A	**CROSS REFERENCE TABLE—THE *MISHNEH TORAH* AND THE *SHULḤAN ARUKH***	**1949**
Appendix B	**ADDITIONAL COMPARISONS OF THE LANGUAGE AND STYLE OF THE *MISHNEH TORAH*, THE *TURIM*, AND THE *SHULḤAN ARUKH***	**1979**
Appendix C	**A LISTING OF THE MOST WIDELY KNOWN COMPILATIONS OF RESPONSA**	**1989**
	GLOSSARY	**2009**
	BIBLIOGRAPHY	**2025**
	INDEX OF SOURCES	**2063**
	SUBJECT INDEX	**2129**

INTRODUCTION

I I am gratified by the publication of this English translation of my Hebrew work *Ha-Mishpat Ha-Ivri.* This work is the fruition of long labor in the field of Jewish law: researching and writing, lecturing in the Law School of the Hebrew University of Jerusalem and other universities, and, during the past fifteen years, drawing upon the resources of Jewish law to help decide cases as a justice of the Supreme Court of Israel. The book surveys Jewish law as a legal system, reviewing the system's history, sources, principles, literature, and modes of creativity.

Jewish Law, however, is more than a law book. It is intended for a wider readership than scholars of Jewish law or even jurists generally; it should be of value to anyone interested in religion and religious philosophy, and particularly to anyone who seeks insightful understanding of Judaism itself. Jewish law is a window on Jewish history, religion, and philosophy. Jewish life and Jewish law are two sides of one coin, and the literature of Jewish law is a treasure-trove of information about all aspects of Jewish daily life throughout the ages in every kind of circumstance—tranquillity and persecution, prosperity and calamity, ascent and decline.

The Hebrew original of the present translation has found acceptance in Israel as a resource for instruction in law school courses in Jewish law and in university courses in Talmud, Jewish history, and Jewish thought. It has also found an audience among general readers interested in acquiring or deepening their understanding of the spiritual and cultural wellsprings of Judaism and the Jewish people.

I first sensed the desirability of an English translation of *Ha-Mishpat Ha-Ivri* in the 1984/85 academic year, during which I was privileged to inaugurate the chair in Jewish law at The New York University School of Law; and this impression was intensified as a result of teaching a course in Jewish law that I introduced at Harvard Law School in 1990/91. The burgeoning interest in Talmudic legal studies in the Jewish community in recent years, the course offerings in Judaic studies in hundreds of universities and theological seminaries, and the numerous courses in Jewish law in law schools throughout the English-speaking world all attest to a pressing need for a survey of Jewish law in English. It is my hope that these volumes will help to satisfy this need.

II The objective of these volumes is to provide a comprehensive overview of the entire field of Jewish law. Part One outlines the history and basic principles of Jewish law. Part Two studies the legal sources of Jewish law, namely, exegesis and interpretation, legislation, custom, precedent, and legal reasoning. These are the creative processes and modes of growth that enable the law to take account of changing circumstances and adapt to changing needs. Part Three surveys the literary sources of Jewish law—including pre-Biblical, Biblical, and immediately post-Biblical literature; the Babylonian and Jerusalem Talmuds; post-Talmudic commentaries, novellae, and codes; the responsa literature; and scholarly studies and reference works.

The overview presented by all four volumes combines two different perspectives: one, from within the Jewish legal system, thoroughly reviews the literature of the system itself; and the other, from outside the system, uses the techniques of comparative law and the methodologies of general jurisprudence in order to provide broader insight and a better appreciation of the nature and quality of Jewish law in relation to other legal and social systems. The summary of contents at the beginning of each volume and the detailed analytical table of contents of the entire work at the beginning of Volume I indicate the vastness of the field and the scope of the present study.

From the internal perspective, Jewish law is a seamless web in which elements from the earliest to the most recent are woven into an integrated analytical whole for which history is in a sense irrelevant. The rabbinic authorities entrusted with responsibility for the Jewish legal system felt bound to treat the law as a unitary construct, all of a piece; this is an approach characteristic of all legal systems that take existing law as their starting point for solving new legal problems.

Full understanding of any area of Jewish law, however, requires an appreciation of the law's creative, vitalizing impulse, which can be attained only by careful study of the changes in that area over the course of time, the relationship of those changes to the general nature and circumstances of each historical period, and the particular characteristics of the various centers of Jewish population where Jewish law governed Jewish life. As these volumes demonstrate, the history of Jewish law and of the processes by which the contributions of each historical period were integrated into the total corpus of that law makes clear that the rabbinic authorities themselves, although operating within the system's seamless web, understood, and even stressed, that Jewish law reflects dynamic growth and ongoing development.

Accordingly, I have attempted to survey the important doctrines of Jewish law from their inception through every subsequent stage of their history. Such an approach has been taken only lately in the study of Jewish law; until quite recently, most scholarly activity in the field was confined to the Biblical and Talmudic periods. The reasons for this limitation on the scope of Jewish legal research are explored in some detail in Chapter 3, but one of the most important is worthy of mention here: the failure to appreciate the significance of the juridical autonomy enjoyed in most Jewish population centers from the time of the Talmud until the eighteenth century (and in certain "eastern" Jewish communities even later) and the consequent widespread ignorance of the continuous creativity and development of Jewish civil, administrative, public, and even criminal law throughout that long period. Indeed, thanks to this juridical autonomy and the tight religious and cultural discipline of the organized Jewish community, whose members regarded Jewish courts and the governance of all aspects of everyday life by Jewish law as of paramount importance, post-Talmudic law continued to be a living, practical, dynamic, and adaptive system, sensitive and responsive to ever-changing needs.

For jurists and those interested in political science, Jewish law up to the eighteenth century is an instructive example of the successful resolution of one of the prime challenges to a legal system: how to achieve a balance between tradition and innovation, continuity and growth, stability and change—in Dean Pound's terminology, how to keep the law stable yet not standing still. The rabbinical authorities and Jewish communal leaders, to whom responsibility for the operation of the Jewish legal system was entrusted, successfully discharged an awesome twofold responsibility: on the one hand, unremitting nurture of the continuing growth and creativity of Jewish law, and on the other hand, maintenance of the spirit, continuity, and essential character of Jewish law, as well as preservation of the core value of each Jewish legal concept and institution through all its permutations over time.

The history of Jewish law demonstrates the successful achievement of this delicate balance, not only while Jews had a sovereign state of their own but also during the far longer periods when they were without sovereignty but enjoyed juridical autonomy, as was the case during the Talmudic period in Babylonia and the Land of Israel, and then throughout the post-Talmudic period in all the lands of their dispersion—North Africa, Spain, Germany, France, the Land of Israel, Poland, Turkey, Italy, and other centers of Jewish life. Indispensable to this success was the interaction between Jewish law and Jewish life; law governed life, but life influenced law. Indeed, the decline of creativity in those fields of Jewish law with counterparts in other legal systems is a direct consequence of the attenuation, and ultimately the ending, of Jewish juridical autonomy.

III Volume IV, which constitutes Part Four of the work, focuses on the problems of Jewish law after the Emancipation in the eighteenth century, from the beginnings of the movement for Jewish national revival to the current relationship between Jewish law and the legal system of the State of Israel. Part Four begins with Chapter 41, which describes the great change in Jewish law effected by the abrogation of juridical autonomy in continental Europe in the eighteenth century and in the "eastern" countries of Turkey and North Africa substantially later, as well as by the spiritual, cultural, and national divisions within the Jewish people. These developments have brought about diminished observance of Jewish law in everyday affairs and are at the root of the problems encountered by Jewish law during the period of Jewish national revival and, later, in the legal system of the State of Israel.

Chapter 42 treats the place of Jewish law in the legal system of the Jewish state. In theory, except for a portion of family law and the law of personal status, Jewish law is not part of the positive law recognized and enforced by the State of Israel. In fact, however, both Israeli legislation and judicial decisions have been influenced by Jewish law in no small measure. Chapter 42 explores this influence in some detail, and also examines the broader question of the relationship between the Jewish religion and the State of Israel, as well as the fundamental institutional differences between historic Jewish law and modern Israeli legislation.

Chapter 43 deals with the problems resulting from the adoption of Jewish family law and the Jewish law of personal status as the law of the State of Israel. Both the rabbinical courts and the general courts of the State of Israel must apply Jewish law in these areas; consequently, difficult and complex questions have arisen as to the relationship between the rabbinical courts and the general legal system of the State.

Chapter 44 analyzes the provisions of the Foundations of Law Act enacted by the Knesset (Israeli Parliament) in 1980 and reviews the Israeli Supreme Court's construction and application of that statute. The objective of the Foundations of Law Act was to sever the legal system of Israel from the English legal system, with which it had been historically linked, and to found the legal system of Israel instead upon the principles of "freedom, justice, equity, and peace of the Jewish heritage." Chapter 44 also reviews the divergent approaches of judges, jurists, and legal philosophers in regard to the application of the Act.

Chapter 45, which concludes Volume IV and the entire work, treats the subjective and objective considerations, the different religious orientations, and the social and cultural factors that affect the various viewpoints on the question of the place of Jewish law in the Israeli legal system. It also takes due account of the widespread and worrisome lack nowadays of even the most rudimentary knowledge of the "Jewish heritage" and particularly of Jewish law.

Volume IV, as is evident, has an essentially different focus from the volumes that precede it. The first three volumes review the ongoing creative continuity of a legal system that governed all aspects of everyday life, whereas Volume IV deals with a period when the study of Jewish civil, criminal, and public law has been theoretical and academic ("Torah for its own sake") rather than for the purpose of solving problems of practical life. It focuses on the question of the extent to which Jewish law can and should operate today, particularly in Israel, where the Knesset, a secular legislature, is the supreme legal authority.

Yet in a certain sense, Volume IV carries on a theme of the first three volumes, which depict the continuity that results from a natural and uninterrupted flow of creativity, such as characterized Jewish law prior to the Emancipation. Volume IV likewise deals with the problem of continuity—albeit the continuity generated by a sense of crisis that took hold when the natural creative flow of Jewish law was cut off. Even this different kind of continuity, however, is vital to the future well-being of the legal system of the Jewish state. Application of Jewish law in practical life is, of course, important for the continuous growth and enrichment of Jewish law; yet it is even more important to the legal system of the Jewish state, as the final chapter more fully explains, that that system occupy an honored place in the historic tradition of Jewish law.

It is therefore encouraging that the motive force for the application of Jewish law in the world of practical affairs in the Land of Israel and the Jewish state has come not only from the religious but from every element of the community. This broad sentiment for the incorporation and expression of Jewish law has been reflected in Israeli legislation and judicial opinions both of trial court judges and justices of the Supreme Court of Israel, who have made use, in greater or lesser measure, of the resources of Jewish law.

While these volumes were already in process of publication, the Knesset enacted one of the most important pieces of "constitutional" legislation in the legal system of the State of Israel, entitled "Basic Law: Human Dignity and Freedom." This statute has extremely important implications for the subject of the present work that require mention here: It gives greater legal protection than an ordinary statute to a significant number of fundamental human rights—the right to life, to bodily integrity, to the dignity of each person as a human being, and to the safeguarding of these rights by the State; the right to property; the right to protection against unlawful deprivation or limitation of freedom, whether by imprisonment, restriction of movement, extradition, or any other means; the right of free egress from the State of Israel and the right of free reentry by every Israeli citizen; the right to privacy, including freedom from unlawful intrusion into one's home, from unreasonable searches of person or property, from eavesdropping on private conversations, and from unauthorized reading of correspondence or other private writings.

The very first of the twelve sections of the Act provides:

> This Basic Law is designed to protect human dignity and freedom by giving the force of a Basic Law to the values of the State of Israel as a Jewish and democratic state.

This mission—to give effect to the values of the State of Israel as a state both Jewish and democratic—mandates recourse by the Israeli courts to two sources for shaping the contours of the rights enumerated in the Basic Law. First, to implement the values of Israel as a Jewish state the courts must ascertain how the rights enumerated in the Basic Law have been understood in the Jewish heritage, which has dealt with these rights extensively in the Bible, the Talmud, the post-Talmudic legal literature, and the works of countless generations of Jewish thinkers. Second, to give effect to the values of the State of Israel as a democratic state, the courts must look to the scope and meaning of the enumerated rights in the democracies where freedom is prized. The two strands—the Jewish heritage and the democratic tradition—are parts of a single value system of a state both Jewish and democratic. Each strand reinforces and complements the other, and it is the task of the courts to interweave them into the synthesis mandated by the Basic Law.

IV Some further comments about the general approach and format of this work may be in order. First, in attempting to survey the history and basic principles of Jewish law, the creative processes by means of which, as Lord Coke put it, "out of ould fields [will] spring and grow the new Corne," and the nature of the vast literature of Jewish law throughout its history, I have tried to go beyond mere description and to include critical analysis of problem areas and conflicting opinions.

Second, I have become convinced that for almost any kind of effective study it is not enough that the subject simply be expounded, its history set forth, and the conflicting opinions and their attendant problems explained. A descriptive exposition, no matter how well done, is no substitute for direct contact with the primary sources—the raw material of the law.

I have therefore not merely summarized and expounded but have attempted to convey a feeling for the subject matter that comes only with direct exposure to the primary sources. To this end, I have quoted liberally from the sources themselves and have attempted to weave the quotations into the exposition so that the story of Jewish law not be told merely as a series of points made by the author but flow as a natural consequence of the primary sources from which it derives. This mode of presentation seems particularly desirable today, when, for a number of reasons, many readers find it very difficult to deal with the sources of Jewish law in studying any aspect of Judaism; indeed, to many, those sources are a completely "closed book."

Third, it has been my purpose to provide a global overview of the Jewish legal system, not a legal encyclopedia containing a systematic and detailed treatment of every subject in the *corpus juris* of Jewish law. Such an encyclopedic treatment can be found in the *Encyclopaedia Judaica,* published by Keter Publishing House Ltd., Jerusalem, in 1971, in which almost 150 articles, under my general editorship, cover in detail not only the legal sources and general legal institutions of Jewish law but also evidence and procedure, family law, criminal law, public and administrative law, conflict of laws, and the law of acquisitions, obligations, torts, inheritance, and other subjects. The full scope of these articles is detailed on pages 1554–1556 in Volume III. All of these articles, collected and rearranged, were published under my editorship in 1975 under the title *The Principles of Jewish Law* (Keter Publishing House Jerusalem Ltd.). This collection, in English, has been reprinted several times and complements the present work, providing additional insights and a different perspective.

Fourth, the present volumes are essentially a translation of the third and most recent edition of the Hebrew original, supplemented, so far as feasible, to take into account developments that have taken place since that edition was published in 1988.

I am fully aware that in the present volumes my reach has exceeded my grasp, but I hope that this work will succeed in at least opening a window on the vast and magnificent vistas of Jewish law, will stimulate interest in Jewish law, and will encourage and assist teaching and study of the subject in law schools, *yeshivot* (Talmudical academies), rabbinical schools, theological schools, and university courses in Judaic studies in the English-speaking world. One whose life has been devoted to the study of the intellectual and spiritual achievements of Judaism, of which Jewish law is a signal example, can ask no greater reward, except that others will follow in the field and improve and perfect his work.

V It remains for me to perform the pleasant duty of acknowledging my debt and expressing my thanks to all who have helped to bring about the publication of these volumes. First and foremost, I am grateful to the translators, Melvin J. Sykes, Esquire, and Professor Bernard Auerbach. The labor they have devoted to this task over a period of many years, their keen and careful scholarship, and their lucid English style have produced a gratifying example of the art of translation. My thanks also to Daniel D. Chazin, Esquire, editorial consultant, for his meticulous review of the manuscript and proofs, his many valuable suggestions as to both style and substance, and his assistance in the translation of the appendixes and in the preparation of the indexes; and to N. Menachem Feder, Esquire, assistant editorial consultant, for his valuable general assistance, particularly in reviewing the manuscript and proofs, verifying the citations to Israeli case law, and translating the titles of Israeli legislation.

I acknowledge with appreciation the dedicated assistance of The Jewish Publication Society and those associated with it in publishing this work: Professor Nahum Sarna, Editorial Consultant, who reviewed the manuscript for accuracy and style; Dr. Chaim Potok, Chairman of the Publications Committee; Dr. Ellen Frankel, Editor-in-Chief; Rabbi Michael Monson, Executive Vice President; Jean Sue Libkind, Director of Publishing Operations; Joanna Hill, Production Manager; and especially Diane W. Zuckerman, Managing Editor, who has had primary responsibility for this publication and, with steadfast dedication, unflagging energy, infinite patience, and consummate tact, has coordinated and encouraged the efforts of all concerned. My thanks also to Arlene Putterman, who designed these handsome volumes, and to Diana Witt, the chief indexer, for her performance of a difficult, challenging, and most important task.

I would like to express my gratitude also to Norman W. Redlich, formerly Dean and now Professor of Law, and John Sexton, currently Dean, of The New York University School of Law. The chair in Jewish law at The N.Y.U. School of Law was established during Professor Redlich's tenure as dean, and I was glad to fulfil the request of Dean Sexton to head the school's program in Jewish Law. I am also pleased to acknowledge the cooperation of Dean Robert Clark in the establishment of the Harvard Law School chair in Jewish law in 1990. Both of these chairs were made possible by the benefaction of Mr. Joseph S. Gruss and his late wife, Caroline; and it was Mr. Gruss who also made possible the establishment of the excellent library of Jewish law at The N.Y.U. School of Law, which includes a good working library on Israeli law. Finally, my heartfelt thanks to Shirley Gray, of The

N.Y.U. School of Law, whose efficient and dedicated secretarial service and administrative assistance have been invaluable, and to Joan Stein, Mr. Sykes's secretary, of whom it can be truly said that without her these volumes would never have come to pass.

Menachem Elon
Jerusalem, Israel
12 Tamuz, 5753
July 1, 1993

ABOUT THE TRANSLATION

WHY WE TRANSLATED THIS WORK

When we first read *Ha-Mishpat Ha-Ivri,* we realized that never in the annals of Jewish legal scholarship has there been anything even approaching this work in comprehensiveness, analysis, and perspective. It surveys the political theory, jurisprudence, and entire legal literature of Judaism, and provides insight into the skill and creativity of the Jewish legal masters and the sources and spirit of Jewish law, the subject which for some two millennia was the prime intellectual occupation of the Jewish people. It treats Jewish law from a jurisprudential perspective—viewing the legal system as a whole, and laying bare its basic values, concepts, and modes of thought—while providing examples of the system's operation in a broad range of legal areas, including agency, administrative law, conflict of laws, creditors' rights, criminal law, evidence, family law, guardianship, judicial administration, labor relations, legislation, partnership, procedure, property, and torts. It illuminates Jewish law's solution to perennial legal problems still very much on the contemporary agenda in English-speaking societies—such as rule versus discretion, principles of legislation (including the limits of legislative power), textual interpretation (*e.g.,* when, if ever, may words in a normative text be treated as surplusage), stability versus creativity, law and morals, the problem of codification, the place of dissent in the legal system, spirit versus letter of the law, law versus equity, form versus substance, judicial activism versus "strict construction," and the force of precedent. It compares the Jewish approach to such problems with that of other legal systems. It highlights the distinctive features of Jewish law: the indigenous moral underpinnings stemming from the Jewish religious tradition, the persistence of core Jewish values through permutations of legal doctrine over the course of time, and the maintenance of a viable legal system encompassing a significant body of doctrine not enforced or enforceable by governmental sanction but addressed to individual conscience, with obligations rather than "rights" as the focus of legal precepts.

It was clear that an English translation of this work would be a vital resource for a variety of purposes in the English-speaking world: for the many law-school courses in Jewish law; for Jewish lawyers who would welcome the opportunity to reconnect with their roots through a channel that is familiar to them; for Jewish laypersons who would like to become more knowledgeable about their heritage; for students with a traditional Talmudic education who would profit from a more systematic overview, greater historical sense, and more jurisprudential depth in their study of Jewish law; for Christians seeking their own religious roots, who would like to know more about "the Law" so frequently referred to in Christian writings; and for historians, jurists, philosophers, academicians in the humanities, and anyone else who would like to acquire an understanding of one of the moral and intellectual foundations of western civilization.

Only an author uniquely endowed could have produced such a work. Menachem Elon is an ordained rabbi who has also been a practicing lawyer, legal scholar and author, university professor, Deputy Attorney General of Israel, Adviser on Jewish Law to the Israeli Minister of Justice, and, since 1977, a Justice of the Supreme Court of Israel, of which he is now Deputy President. *Ha-Mishpat Ha-Ivri* exhibits a mastery not only of the vast Jewish legal literature (Biblical literature, the Babylonian and Jerusalem Talmuds, commentaries, novellae, and the thousands of volumes of responsa), but also of Roman, Continental, and common law, jurisprudence, legal philosophy, a number of languages, and a broad expanse of social and political history.

Justice Elon effectively communicates a feeling for Jewish law as a working system that is a cultural expression of Judaism and the Jewish people. His style is remarkably lucid. He presumes no prior knowledge and builds, step-by-step, an imposing edifice; yet his style neither compromises his scholarly rigor nor descends perceptibly beneath the level of those already knowledgeable in Jewish law. He offers to the neophyte a valuable introduction and to the scholar rich new insights.

The reception of *Ha-Mishpat Ha-Ivri* in the Hebrew-speaking world bears out our estimate of its worth. Its appearance was hailed by Israeli critics as "monumental," "an event of national significance," and a "work of genius." It helped win for its author the Israel Prize, Israel's highest civilian award. It is a required text in university courses in Israel. It has gone through three editions and four reprintings. According to the Magnes Press of the Hebrew University of Jerusalem, *Ha-Mishpat Ha-Ivri* has sold approximately four times as many copies as the next most successful work of academic scholarship published in Hebrew on a Jewish subject. In the words of the Israeli author Moshe Shamir, *Ha-Mishpat Ha-Ivri* reveals "the people of Israel in all its glory and grandeur."

We felt that this work had to be made available to the much larger audience awaiting it in the English-speaking world; and when Justice Elon agreed to work closely with us, we undertook the translation.

THE GUIDING PRINCIPLES OF THIS TRANSLATION

The basic problem of all translators is that translation always falls short because it is not merely into a different language but into a different culture as well. Literal equivalents often do not communicate congruent concepts when the cultural frameworks are different. Thus, for example, a correct literal equivalent of a *kenas* is a "fine," but a *kenas* in Jewish law is not the same as a fine in other contemporary legal systems (see *infra* pp. 108–109).

This difficulty, however, does not preclude a reasonable degree of success in conveying to an English-speaking audience the essential meaning of Justice Elon's text, which, after all, is written by a twentieth-century scholar steeped in general scholarship as well as Jewish lore. The style of both the Hebrew original and the translation is conversational and idiomatic, and gaps between the cultures of Hebrew and English are filled by various editorial devices, such as explanatory footnotes, extended paraphrase, parenthetical connections and clarifications, and inclusion of a parenthetical literal translation along with the idiomatic English rendering, where doing so serves a purpose such as to indicate a picturesque mode of thought with no English equivalent, or an echo of some sacred or authoritative text not likely to be familiar to the typical reader of English.

Moreover, a translator has a fair degree of latitude in dealing with a text like Justice Elon's. The essential aim is to convey clearly his meaning in English. By and large, his Hebrew style has permitted us to keep close enough to his text to enable a reader to locate easily in the original any matter in the translation. Thus, we have followed the Hebrew in first quoting rabbinic texts, and then generally paraphrasing and analyzing the quotation; this practice helps the reader to understand the quotations and makes clear the direction of Justice Elon's argument.

There are, however, some additions and changes, all made after consultation with Justice Elon, designed to enhance clarity for the English reader. Thus, some footnotes have been added, legal citations in extensive quotations from judicial opinions have been moved from text to footnotes, a few passages have been restructured, the sequence of footnotes has occasionally been changed, sources of allusive language have been supplied, and new material has been added to reflect developments since the most recent Hebrew edition in 1988. Paragraphing and punctuation are, of course, ours; sentences and paragraphs in English are typically—and should be—shorter than in modern scholarly Hebrew.

The less tractable problem is the translation of rabbinic texts, which are liberally quoted pursuant to Justice Elon's pedagogical technique. The earlier rabbinic texts are written in a cryptic shorthand style, in thought-patterns unfamiliar to an English reader, with staccato bursts and capacious ellipses that the reader was expected to be able to fill. Consequently, one cannot understand Talmudic literature without more help than is provided by the text and a dictionary. Literal translations of early rabbinic texts tend to read like gibberish; it has justly been said of one essentially literal English translation of the Babylonian Talmud that the only way to understand it is to consult the original Hebrew and Aramaic.

A translation must convey the necessary background and a sense of the logic and rhythm of the argument that is beyond the literal text, and it must preserve and explain ambiguities that are the focus of argument or at the root of the problem. Yet only a literal rendering can give an idea of the style and the idiosyncratic aspects of the culture of the original; it is important to preserve the integrity—the tension, liveliness, rich overtones, and sense of thrust and parry of the rabbinic texts.

We have therefore attempted to make these texts intelligible to the modern reader, and at the same time convey a sense of the style and cultural world of the original language by designating deletions and omissions, by inserting in brackets the necessary background and connectors, and by interweaving the bracketed matter with a more or less literal translation of the text. We have placed the bracketed matter in the text rather than in the footnotes because this placement makes the passages easier to read and also because we wanted to conform as closely as possible to the sequence of footnotes in the Hebrew original.

We hope that when the passages are read through, they will convey the sense of the argument. If they are read skipping the bracketed material, they should convey a sense of the flavor and the taut style of the original. Our method may not yield as smooth and elegant a translation as one written completely afresh in present-day English, but it seems to us to be the optimum combination of two inherently conflicting objectives. Recognizing that translation always loses something, we have tried to keep the loss in the translation of early rabbinic texts to a minimum.

Later rabbinic texts are not so cryptic, but they too have their problems for the translator. In many such texts, the Hebrew style is difficult and obscure. The terminology is often archaic; and the Hebrew language has undergone substantial development in the twentieth century, so that the words of the text may no longer mean today precisely what they meant when they were written.

We have also been mindful that there is a wide variation in the knowledge and background of different readers. The rabbinic passages record debates between experts, and it is necessary to make certain that the audience is on a level sufficiently high to understand the debate fully. We have tried to do this for the least knowledgeable reader without "writing down" to an extent that would impair the work's usefulness to the more knowledgeable.

We have called attention to the technical Hebrew term or expression for virtually every legal concept, principle, rule, or standard discussed; and each volume contains a glossary, for the imperfections of which we alone are responsible. For one not familiar with Jewish law, the Hebrew terms or expressions will afford an opportunity to learn some of the technical vocabulary of Jewish law, and for one who already has some familiarity with Jewish law, they will stimulate recognition and strengthen the impact of the text. Even if an English translation of such a term or expression is clear and fair, the English will not have the impact—the resonance and associations—that the Hebrew term has on one who is familiar with it. Thus, *de-oraita* and *de-rabbanan* mean more than "Biblical" and "rabbinic," which are fair English equivalents; seventeen pages of printed text and footnotes (pp. 207–223) are required to explain, to the extent that English can, the full meaning of these terms in the Jewish legal system.

PARTICULAR PROBLEMS OF FORM AND STYLE

Translation of Biblical Texts

In general, our translation of the Hebrew Bible follows The Jewish Publication Society's TANAKH (1985), which has become standard in the field of Jewish studies. However, translation problems sometimes arise because the TANAKH and the rabbinical exegetes view the Hebrew Bible from different perspectives. The aim of the TANAKH is to approximate as closely as possible the meaning the translators believed was intended for the audience to whom the text was addressed at the time it was written. The Rabbis, by contrast, were concerned with interpreting the text in order to derive legal propositions for their own time. Because Biblical texts are rich in ambiguities and nuance, the rendering in the TANAKH sometimes gives no hint of the basis for the rabbinical reading. In these instances and in cases where the rabbinical interpretation involves textual linguistics or style peculiar to Hebrew, we translate so as to make the rabbinical interpretation intelligible, and we often also note the TANAKH's translation in brackets or in a footnote. These references to the TANAKH, which are not in the Hebrew edition of *Ha-Mishpat Ha-Ivri,* should help readers who have not mastered Hebrew to follow the legal argument and also to appreciate the complexities of trying to deal with the Hebrew Biblical texts through translations.

An additional source of possible difficulty is the practice in rabbinical texts of referring to the Bible by quotation of tag lines that identify the verse or passage supporting the rabbinical argument but do not include the Biblical language directly relevant to the argument. In such cases, we have filled out the quotation, supplying the crucial language in brackets.

Citations

In view of the wide range of types of sources cited, it may be helpful to explain the policies we have followed in regard to source citations.

Citation of scholarly works. Citations of books in the Bibliography (Vol. IV) generally include the first (and sometimes a second) initial and the last name of the author, the title, the edition (if there is more than one), and the place and date of publication. Sometimes, a citation in the footnotes will omit some of this material, but footnote references are always sufficient to identify the source cited, and additional details may be obtained from the Bibliography. Books frequently referred to are cited fully the first time they appear and thereafter only by the last name of the author and an abbreviated title. A list of such works, with full bibliographical references and the abbreviated forms of citation, begins on page lxix. When a book not on the list of short titles is cited more than once in any chapter, all citations after the first include the last name of the author and a reference to the footnote where the book is first cited in that chapter, *e.g.*, "Katz, *supra* n. 22 at 105." If the prior footnote cites more than one book by the author referred to, the later footnote will also include the particular title to which reference is made.

Titles in a foreign language are cited in that language, except that Hebrew titles are not in the Hebrew alphabet but are transliterated. Titles that give some indication of the nature of the book are also translated in brackets after the original or transliterated title. Often, however, titles of rabbinical works in Hebrew make fanciful plays on the name of the author, or allusions to Scripture, and tell nothing about the nature of the work. In such instances, we have generally not attempted to translate the title, although we do point out pertinent wordplays that can be made intelligible to an English reader.

When the Hebrew version of these volumes cites to a Hebrew work, and the work has been translated into English, we usually cite the English version, except where the English version does not include the pertinent material. For example, Neubauer's *Sefer ha-Kabbalah* contains matter that Gerson Cohen's translation entitled *Sefer ha-Qabbalah* does not, and the English version of Yitzhak Baer's *History of the Jews in Christian Spain* does not have all the material of the original Hebrew. Where the English version translates a Hebrew source that is quoted in the present work, we have cited the relevant pages of the English version but have made our own translation from the Hebrew whenever we felt that doing so more faithfully conveyed the substance or spirit of the original. Where a book in Hebrew has a title page in English in addition to the Hebrew title page, the English title in the book itself is set forth in brackets after the Hebrew title even if the English title departs significantly from the Hebrew. Thus, the title of A. Neubauer's major work, *Seder ha-Ḥakhamim ve-Korot ha-Yamim,* is translated as "Medievel Jewish Chronicles" even though the literal translation of the Hebrew is "Chronicle of the Sages and Events."

Dates of works in Hebrew present a small problem in that the Hebrew year generally runs September to September, not January through December. Thus, for example, the Hebrew year 5753 has some three months in 1992 and nine months in 1993. The title page of older Hebrew books generally state the Hebrew year, but not the month, of publication. We have converted the Hebrew year of publication to the secular calendar year in which most of the Hebrew year in question falls, although there is a 25 percent chance that actual publication was during the previous calendar year.

Citation of rabbinic materials. The Babylonian Talmud (*Talmud Bavli*) is cited "TB," followed by the tractate title, page, and folio. The Jerusalem Talmud (*Talmud Jerushalmi*) is cited "TJ," followed by the tractate title, chapter number, rule number, page, and folio of the edition currently in general use, with parallel citations in parentheses to the chapter, rule, page, and folio of the less accessible Venice edition. A table of abbreviations used in citing rabbinic works and scholarly literature begins on page lxxiii. Among the more frequently cited rabbinic works are Maimonides' *Mishneh Torah* (*MT*), Jacob b. Asher's *Sefer ha-Turim* (*Tur*), and the *Shulḥan Arukh* (Sh. Ar.).

Citation of legal materials. Cases are cited by the names of the parties and the volume and page of the law reports in which the case may be found. Citations include cases decided by English, American, and Israeli courts. A list of the abbreviations for the various series of law reports begins on page lxxv. We have not followed any hidebound style of citation such as Harvard's *Blue Book* or the University of Chicago's *Maroon Book,* but in general, our citations to contemporary legal materials follow forms familiar in lawyers' briefs and judicial opinions. Names of cases referred to in the text, or in footnotes where the name is not immediately followed by the citation, are italicized. Names of cases merely cited in the notes appear in roman type. There is wide variation in the form of citation of Israeli legal materials in English. We have used the *Israel Law Review* (which is itself not always consistent) as a general (but not invariable) guide.

Spelling of Names

There is no uniform standard for spelling the English equivalent of Hebrew names. In general, we have followed the *Encyclopaedia Judaica,* except that where a Hebrew work has been translated into English or has an English title page in addition to the Hebrew, we have adopted the spelling as it appears in the English translation or on the English title page.

The names of parties to Israeli cases are particularly problematic. It is often difficult to determine the correct pronunciation from the unvocalized Hebrew, particularly where the name is not of Hebrew origin. In such instances even the same Israeli source, let alone different sources, may be inconsistent in the English spelling of names.

In the present translation, the name of the same person may be spelled differently, depending on whether it is being "translated" or transliterated. Thus, the Hebrew name transliterated as *Shelomo* is translated as "Solomon"—except when a particular individual spells the English version of the name differently, *e.g.,* former Chief Rabbi Shlomo Goren, whose name neither follows the technical rules of transliteration we have adopted nor the usual translation of the Hebrew. Similarly, Justice Moshe Silberg's name transliterates as "Zilberg," the Hebrew for the name Joel is Yo'el and for Ezekiel is Yeḥezkel, and the Hebrew name for the Israeli parliament is transliterated as "Keneset" but the English spelling in general use is "Knesset."

There are also inconsistencies in the scholarly literature with regard to names having the guttural "ch" sound (as in the German "ach"), generally transliterated in the present work as "ḥ", and sometimes, as in the name "Menachem Elon," by "ch." The familiar English equivalent of a number of names containing the guttural "h" do not have the underdot used in transliteration—*e.g.,* Hasmoneans, Jehiel, Johanan, Menahem, Nahum, Nehemiah, etc. The index of the *Encyclopaedia Judaica* has "HANUKKAH" without the underdot and "ḤANUKKAH LAMP" with it.

We have generally followed the JPS TANAKH in rendering the names of Biblical persons and places. Post-biblical place names are transliterated or rendered by the accepted English spelling if one exists. Contemporary names and some words with an accepted English form are usually not transliterated. We have made *ad hoc* judgments as best we could.

Translation of Legal Materials

There is no official translation of Israeli legal materials. Selected judgments of the Supreme Court of Israel have been published in English by the "Israel Bar Publishing House on behalf of the Supreme Court," and the Israeli

Ministry of Justice publishes a compilation of Israeli legislation entitled *Laws of Israel;* but these translations have no official status. We have used them, but have felt free to deviate whenever we thought they could be improved.

Quotations

Except when very short (usually within a sentence), quotations are block-indented and printed in slightly smaller size than the author's text, so that primary source material can be instantly identified and distinguished from the author's exposition. For convenience, the quotation of primary sources is repeated rather than simply cited by reference to a previous appearance.

Footnotes and Cross-References

One of the striking features of the Hebrew editions of this work is how copiously the work is footnoted and cross-referenced. The notes are not merely documentation but lively subsidiary exposition that illuminates, elaborates, clarifies, or qualifies the text. They are truly footnotes—printed on the same pages as the text they annotate, so as to spare readers the burden of flipping pages from the text to notes.

Stylistic Conventions

The rabbinical scholars, teachers, judges, and role models who are recognized as authoritative in the Jewish legal system are called in Hebrew *hakhamim* ("wise men" or "sages"). Such authorities in the Talmudic period we refer to as "Sages" (with a capital "S") and preface their names with "R.," for "Rabbi," "Rav," or "Rabban." The generic term we use for those entrusted with responsibility for the system of Jewish law (*Halakhah*) is "halakhic authorities." (As to the concept of *Halakhah,* see pp. 93ff.) All the halakhic authorities in the Jewish legal system were and are rabbis, but, in conformity with conventional practice in scholarly works in English on Jewish law, halakhic authorities of the post-Talmudic period are referred to as "R." or "Rabbi" in the present work only when that designation is material to the discussion, or as "Rabbenu" where that term has become part of the rabbi's name.

In scholarly works written in Hebrew on Jewish law, and in Talmudical academies (*yeshivot*), halakhic authorities active at any time within most of the post-Talmudic period are identified by an acronym that begins with "R." for "Rabbi" (lit. "my master") or "Rabbenu" (lit. "our rabbi," *i.e.,* "our master"). Thus, *Ra*bbi *Sh*elomo *Yi*ẓḥaki is "Rashi" (Hebrew has only one letter for both "y" and "i"), *Ra*bbi *M*oses *b. M*aimon (Maimonides) is "Rambam," *Ra*bbi *M*oses *b. N*aḥman (Naḥmanides) is "Ramban," and *R*abbi *M*oses *I*sserles is "Rema" (Isserles in Hebrew begins with an *aleph,* silent in "Isserles" but sounded as "a"—as in "father" or alternatively, as in "law"—when it is the last letter of the acronym). We use the acronyms more or less interchangeably with the full names of the authorities. In *yeshivah* circles it is customary to precede the acronym with "the"—"the Rambam," etc.—but we have not used this form of reference because it does not conform to customary English usage. We hope that learned readers will not find the omission of the definite article too disconcerting. A list of these acronyms and appellations begins on page lxxvii.

Transliteration

There are wide differences in the various systems (and non-systems) of transliteration from Hebrew to English; the choice of one or another is largely arbitrary. The general adoption of the modern Sephardic pronunciation in the State of Israel and most of the Jewish communities in the diaspora, together with the advantages of simplicity, have weighed against the "scientific" systems that make fine distinctions no longer relevant to spoken Hebrew. We have therefore adopted, with slight modifications, the popularly accepted, simplified version found in the *Encyclopaedia Judaica.* A Transliteration Guide begins on page lxxxi.

SUGGESTIONS FOR STUDY

Knowledgeable readers will be able to go through these volumes without difficulty. For readers without previous exposure to rabbinic literature, it may be wise to start with Volume III, which deals with the literature of Jewish law, and then go on to Volumes I, II, and IV. Volume III is easier reading than the other volumes because it leads chronologically, step-by-step, through the classic texts; it locates the position of each text in the literary spectrum and provides a sense of the historical development of Jewish law without going too deeply into technical legal doctrine. Studying Volume III first will make it easier to follow the historical review of the Jewish legal system and the discussion of Jewish law's concepts, forms, doctrines, procedures, and modes of growth in Volumes I and II; and the bibliographical references in the notes in all the other volumes will be more meaningful.

Those who wish to supplement the insight gained from these volumes with an encyclopedic treatment of the portion of Jewish law that roughly parallels the civil law of other contemporary legal systems can do so with the help of Justice Elon's *Principles of Jewish Law* (Keter Press, Jerusalem, 1975), discussed in his Introduction. For formal instruction in a law school setting, Justice Elon has designed a casebook for use along with the present work. He has been using it in his classes and working to revise it in light of suggestions from colleagues and experience with it in the classroom. He looks forward to publication of the casebook in the near future as the final step in his plan to provide a comprehensive set of English materials for academic instruction in Jewish law at the graduate-school level.

A FINAL WORD

One of the greatest benefits we have derived from our work on these volumes has been the many hours we have spent with Justice Elon. More than just a translation, our work has been a collaboration with him; he has graciously reviewed our results and discussed them with us in all their phases. The quality of the translation has been much enhanced by his suggestions and advice; for the imperfections that remain, we accept responsibility.

We also deeply appreciate the invaluable assistance of Joan Stein, Mr. Sykes's secretary for forty years, who typed many drafts of the entire manuscript, while ably fulfilling the heavy demands upon her as secretary and office manager of a busy trial and appellate legal practice.

Finally, our heartfelt thanks to our wives, Vivien Auerbach and Judy Sykes, for their interest, understanding, encouragement, assistance and forbearance over a long and arduous period.

BERNARD AUERBACH
Jerusalem, Israel

MELVIN J. SYKES
Baltimore, Maryland
16 Tamuz, 5753
July 5, 1993

BIBLIOGRAPHICAL ABBREVIATIONS OF BOOKS AND ARTICLES FREQUENTLY CITED

H. Albeck, *Mavo la-Mishnah* [Introduction to the Mishnah], Jerusalem, 1959 = Albeck, *Mavo.*

G. Alon (or Allon), *Meḥkarim be-Toledot Yisra'el bi-Mei Bayit Sheni u-vi-Tekufat ha-Mishnah ve-ha-Talmud* [Studies in Jewish History in the Days of the Second Temple and in the Mishnaic and Talmudic Period], 2 vols., Tel-Aviv, 1957–1958 = Alon, *Meḥkarim.* (For an English version, *see Jews, Judaism and the Classical World: Studies in Jewish History in the Times of the Second Temple and Talmud,* I. Abrahams and A. Oshery trans., Jerusalem, 1977.)

——— *Toledot ha-Yehudim be-Ereẓ Yisra'el bi-Tekufat ha-Mishnah ve-ha-Talmud* [History of the Jews in the Land of Israel in the Mishnaic and Talmudic Period], 3rd ed., Tel-Aviv, 1959 = Alon, *Toledot.* (For an English version, *see The Jews in Their Land in the Talmudic Age,* G. Levi trans. and ed., Jerusalem, 1 vol., Magnes Press, 1980–1984; reprinted, Harvard University Press, 1989.)

S. Assaf, *Battei ha-Din ve-Sidreihem Aḥarei Ḥatimat ha-Talmud* [Jewish Courts and Their Procedures after the Completion of the Talmud], Jerusalem, 1924 = Assaf, *Battei Din.*

——— *Ha-Onshin Aḥarei Ḥatimat ha-Talmud* [Penal Law After the Completion of the Talmud], Jerusalem, 1922 = Assaf, *Onshin.*

——— *Tekufat ha-Geonim ve-Sifrutah* [The Geonic Period and Its Literature], Jerusalem, 1956 = Assaf, *Geonim.*

Y. Baer, *Toledot Ha-Yehudim bi-Sefarad ha-Noẓrit* [A History of the Jews of Christian Spain], 2nd ed., Tel Aviv, 1965. An English translation, *A History of the Jews in Christian Spain,* JPS, 2 vols., 1961–1966 = Baer, *Spain.*

S.W. Baron, *A Social and Religious History of the Jews,* JPS-Columbia, 18 vols. 1952–1983 = Baron, *History.*

M.A. Bloch, *Sha'arei Torat ha-Takkanot* [On Legislative Enactments], Vienna *et al.,* 7 vols., 1879–1906 = Bloch, *Sha'arei.*

P. Dykan (Dikstein), *Toledot Mishpat ha-Shalom ha-Ivri* [History of the Jewish Court of Arbitration], Tel Aviv, 1964 = Dykan, *Toledot.*

M. Elon, *Ḥakikah Datit be-Ḥukkei Medinat Yisra'el u-va-Shefitah Shel Battei ha-Mishpat u-Vattei ha-Din ha-Rabbaniyyim* [Religious Legislation in the Statutes of the State of Israel and in the Decisions of the General and Rabbinical Courts], Tel Aviv, 1968 = Elon, *Ḥakikah.*

——— "Ha-Ma'asar ba-Mishpat ha-Ivri" [Imprisonment in Jewish Law], *Jubilee Volume for Pinḥas Rosen,* Jerusalem, 1962, pp. 171–201 = Elon, *Ma'asar.*

——— *Ḥerut ha-Perat be-Darkhei Geviyyat Ḥov ba-Mishpat ha-Ivri* [Individual Freedom and the Methods of Enforcing Payment of Debts in Jewish Law], Jerusalem, 1964 = Elon, *Ḥerut.*

——— (ed.) *Principles of Jewish Law,* Jerusalem, 1975 = *Principles.*

——— "Samkhut ve-Oẓmah ba-Kehillah ha-Yehudit, Perek be-Mishpat ha-Ẓibbur ha-Ivri" [Authority and Power in the Jewish Community, A Chapter in Jewish Public Law], in *Shenaton ha-Mishpat ha-Ivri* [Annual of the Institute for Research in Jewish Law], Hebrew University of Jerusalem, III–IV (1976–1977), pp. 7ff. = Elon, *Samkhut ve-Oẓmah.* (For an English translation, *see* "Power and Authority—Halachic Stance of the Traditional Community and Its Contemporary Implications," in *Kinship and Consent, The Jewish Political Tradition and Its Contemporary Uses,* D. Elazar ed., Turtledove Publishing, 1981, pp. 183–213).

——— "Yiḥudah Shel Halakhah ve-Ḥevrah be-Yahadut Ẓefon Afrikah mi-le-aḥar Gerush Sefarad ve-ad Yameinu" [The Exceptional Character of *Halakhah* and Society in North African Jewry from the Spanish Expulsion to the Present], in *Halakhah u-Fetiḥut, Ḥakhmei Morokko ke-Fosekim le-Doreinu* [Halakhah and Open-Mindedness: The Halakhic Authorities of Morocco as Authorities for Our Own Time], 1945, pp. 15ff. = Elon, *Yiḥudah Shel Halakhah.*

J.N. Epstein, *Mavo le-Nusaḥ ha-Mishnah* [Introduction to the Text of the Mishnah], 2nd ed., Jerusalem, 1964 = Epstein, *Mavo.*

——— *Mevo'ot le-Sifrut ha-Tannaim,* [Introduction to Tannaitic Literature], Jerusalem, 1957 = Epstein, *Tannaim.*

——— *Mevo'ot le-Sifrut ha-Amoraim,* [Introduction to Amoraic Literature], Jerusalem, 1963 = Epstein, *Amoraim.*

L. Finkelstein, *Jewish Self-Government in the Middle Ages,* New York 1924 (second printing, New York, 1964) = Finkelstein, *Self-Government.*

Z. Frankel, *Darkhei ha-Mishnah* [The Methodology of the Mishnah], Leipzig, 1859 (facsimile ed., Tel Aviv, 1969) = Frankel, *Mishnah.*

——— *Mevo ha-Yerushalmi* [Introduction to the Jerusalem Talmud], Breslau, 1870 (facsimile ed., Jerusalem, 1967) = Frankel, *Mevo.*

A.H. Freimann, *Seder Kiddushin ve-Nissu'in Aḥarei Ḥatimat ha-Talmud, Meḥkar Histori-Dogmati be-Dinei Yisra'el* [Law of Betrothal and Marriage after the Completion of the Talmud: A Historical-Dogmatic Study in Jewish Law], Mosad ha-Rav Kook, Jerusalem, 1945 = Freimann, *Kiddushin ve-Nissu'in.*

L. Ginzberg, *Perushim ve-Ḥiddushim ba-Yerushalmi* [A Commentary on the Palestine Talmud] (English title by Prof. Ginzberg), New York, 1941 (facsimile ed., New York, 1971) = Ginzberg, *Perushim.*

A. Gulak, *Yesodei ha-Mishpat ha-Ivri* [The Foundations of Jewish Law], Jerusalem, 1923 (facsimile ed., Tel Aviv, 1967) = Gulak, *Yesodei.*

I. Halevy, *Dorot ha-Rishonim* [The Early Generations—A History of the Oral Law to the *Geonim*], Frankfort, 1897–1906 (facsimile ed., Jerusalem, 1957) = Halevy, *Dorot.*

I. Herzog, *The Main Institutions of Jewish Law,* 2nd ed., London, 2 vols., 1965–1967 = Herzog, *Institutions.*

D.Z. Hoffmann, *Das Buch Deuteronomium Übersetzt und Erklärt* [The Book of Deuteronomy: Translation and Commentary] = Hoffmann, *Commentary on Deuteronomy.*

Koveẓ Teshuvot ha-Rambam ve-Iggerotav [Compilation of Responsa and Epistles of Maimonides], Leipzig, 1859 = *Koveẓ ha-Rambam.*

J. Levy, *Wörterbuch über die Talmudim und Midraschim* [Talmudic and Midrashic Dictionary], 2nd ed., Berlin, 1924 = Levy, *Wörterbuch.*

S. Lieberman, *Greek in Jewish Palestine* = Lieberman, *Greek.*

——— *Hellenism in Jewish Palestine* = Lieberman, *Hellenism.*

A. Neubauer, *Seder ha-Ḥakhamim ve-Korot ha-Yamim* [Medieval Jewish Chronicles], Oxford, 1895 (facsimile ed., Jerusalem, 1967) = Neubauer, *Seder ha-Ḥakhamim.*

J.W. Salmond, *On Jurisprudence,* 12th ed., London, 1966 = Salmond.

Shenaton ha-Mishpat ha-Ivri [Annual of the Institute for Research in Jewish Law, Hebrew University of Jerusalem] = *Shenaton.*

M. Silberg, *Ha-Ma'amad ha-Ishi be-Yisra'el* [Personal Status in Israel], 4th ed., Jerusalem, 1965 = Silberg, *Ha-Ma'amad.*

H. Tykocinski, *Takkanot ha-Geonim* [Geonic Enactments], Jerusalem, 1960 = Tykocinski, *Takkanot.*

E.E. Urbach, *Ḥazal, Pirkei Emunot ve-De'ot* [The Sages: Doctrines and Beliefs], rev. ed., Jerusalem, 1971 = Urbach, *The Sages.* (For an English version *see The Sages, Their Concepts and Beliefs,* I. Abrahams trans., Magnes Press, 2 vols., Jerusalem, 1975.)

——— *Ba'alei ha-Tosafot, Toledoteihem, Ḥibbureihem ve-Shittatam* [The Tosafists, Their History, Writings and Methodology], 2nd ed, Jerusalem, 1968 = Urbach, *Tosafot.*

Z. Warhaftig, (ed.); *Osef Piskei ha-Din Shel ha-Rabbanut ha-Rashit le-Ereẓ Yis-*

ra'el [A Compilation of the Rulings of the Chief Rabbinate of the Land of Israel], 1950, = *Osef Piskei ha-Din.*

I.H. Weiss, *Dor Dor ve-Doreshav* [The Generations and Their Interpreters—A History of the Oral Law], 6th ed., Vilna, 1915 = Weiss, *Dor Dor ve-Doreshav.*

ABBREVIATIONS USED IN CITING RABBINIC WORKS AND SCHOLARLY LITERATURE

ad loc.	*ad locum,* "at the place," used after a citation to designate commentary on the passage cited
A.M.	*anno mundi,* "in the year [from the creation] of the world"
b.	ben, bar, "son of"—as in Simeon b. Gamaliel
Baḥ	*Bayit Ḥadash,* a commentary on *Tur* by Joel Sirkes.
B.C.E.	before the common era, equivalent of B.C.
ca.	*circa,* "approximately"
C.E.	common era, equivalent of A.D.
cf.	*confer,* "compare"
EH	*Even ha-Ezer,* part of the *Shulḥan Arukh*
EJ	Encyclopaedia Judaica
ET	*Enẓiklopedyah Talmudit* [Talmudic Encyclopedia]
ḤM	*Ḥoshen Mishpat,* part of the *Shulḥan Arukh*
HUCA	*Hebrew Union College Annual*
ibn	"son of," equivalent of "b." (which *see*)
id.	*idem,* "the same," used instead of repeating the immediately preceding citation
JJGL	*Jahrbuch für jüdische Geschichte und Literatur* [Jewish History and Literature Annual]
JJLG	*Jahrbuch der jüdisch-literarischen* Gesellschaft [Jewish Literary Society Annual]
JPS	The Jewish Publication Society
JQR	*Jewish Quarterly Review*
lit.	literally
loc. cit.	*loco citato,* "in the place [previously] cited"
M	Mishnah, used to designate a Mishnaic tractate
MGWJ	*Monatsschrift für Geschichte und Wissenschaft des Judenthums* [Monthly for the History and Science of Judaism]
ms., mss.	manuscript(s)
MT	*Mishneh Torah* (Maimonides' code)

n.	note
nn.	notes
OḤ	*Oraḥ Ḥayyim,* part of the *Shulḥan Arukh*
op. cit.	*opere citato,* "in the work [previously] cited"
R.	Rabbi, Rav, or Rabban, used in the present work for the Talmudic Sages
Resp.	Responsa
Sema	*Sefer Me'irat Einayim* by Joshua Falk
Semag	*Sefer Miẓvot Gadol* by Moses of Coucy
Semak	*Sefer Miẓvot Katan* by Isaac of Corbeil
Shakh	*Siftei Kohen* by Shabbetai b. Meir ha-Kohen
Sh. Ar.	*Shulḥan Arukh*
"Shum"	Hebrew acrostic for the communities of Speyer, Worms, and Mainz
s.v.	*sub verbo, sub voce,* "under the word," designating the word or expression to which commentary is appended. Equivalent of Hebrew "d.h." (*dibbur ha-matḥil*)
Taz	*Turei Zahav* by David b. Samuel ha-Levi
TB	Talmud Bavli [Babylonian Talmud]
TJ	Talmud Yerushalmi [Jerusalem Talmud, sometimes called Palestine Talmud]
Tur	*Sefer ha-Turim* by Jacob b. Asher
v.l.	*varia lectio,* pl. *variae lectiones,* "variant reading(s)"
YD	*Yoreh De'ah,* part of the *Shulḥan Arukh*

ABBREVIATIONS USED IN CITING MODERN LEGAL MATERIALS

A.2d	Atlantic Reports, Second Series (U.S.)
A.B.A.J.	*American Bar Association Journal*
A.C.	Law Reports Appeal Cases (Eng.)
All E.R.	All England Law Reports, formerly All England Law Reports Annotated
Atk.	Atkyns English Chancery Reports (1736–1755)
Ch.	Chancery (Eng.)
C.L.R.	Current Law Reports (cases decided during the British Mandate)
Colum. L. Rev.	*Columbia Law Review*
D.C. App.	District of Columbia Court of Appeals
DK	*Divrei ha-Keneset* [The Knesset Record]
E.R., Eng. Rep.	English Reports, Full Reprint (1220–1865)
Ex.	Court of Exchequer (Eng.)
Harv. L. Rev.	*Harvard Law Review*
H.L.C.	Clark's House of Lords Cases (Eng.)
I.C.L.Q.	*International and Comparative Law Quarterly*
I.S.C.J.	Israel Supreme Court Judgments
Jur.	Jurist Reports (Eng., 18 vols.)
K.B.	King's Bench (Eng.)
L.J.	Law Journal
L.J.Q.B.	Law Journal Reports, New Series, Queen's Bench (Eng.)
L.Q.	Law Quarterly
L. Rev.	Law Review
Md. L. Rev.	*Maryland Law Review*
Minn. L. Rev.	*Minnesota Law Review*
Mod.	Modern Reports, 1669–1732 (Eng.)
N.E.2d	Northeastern Reporter, Second Series (U.S.)
Ohio App.	Ohio (Intermediate) Appellate Court reports

Osef Piskei ha-Din	a collection of rabbinical court decisions compiled by Zeraḥ Warhaftig
P.D.	*Piskei Din,* Israel Supreme Court Reports
P.D.R.	*Piskei Din Rabbaniyyim,* Israel Rabbinical Court Reports
P.L.R.	Palestine Law Reports (Court Decisions during the British Mandate)
P.M.	*Pesakim Meḥoziyyim,* Israel District Court Reports
Q.B.	Queen's Bench (Eng.)
SCJ	Supreme Court Judgments Annotated (Reports of cases in the Supreme Court of the Land of Israel during the British Mandate)
Vand. L. Rev.	*Vanderbilt Law Review*
Wis. L. Rev.	*Wisconsin Law Review*
W.L.R.	Weekly Law Reports (Eng.)

ACRONYMS AND APPELLATIONS OF HALAKHIC AUTHORITIES

Alfasi	Isaac b. Jacob ha-Kohen of Fez, Rif
Asheri	Asher b. Jehiel, Rosh
Ba'al ha-Roke'aḥ	Eliezer b. Judah
Ba'al ha-Turim	Jacob b. Asher
Baḥ	Joel Sirkes
Ḥafeẓ Ḥayyim	Israel Meir ha-Kohen
Ha-Gra	Elijah b. Solomon Zalman (Gaon of Vilna)
Ha-Kala'i	Alfasi
Ḥakham Zevi	Zevi Hirsch b. Jacob Ashkenazi
Ḥatam Sofer	Moses Sofer
Ḥayyim Or Zaru'a	Hayyim b. Isaac
Ḥazon Ish	Abraham Isaiah Karelitz
Ḥida	Ḥayyim Joseph David Azulai
Mabit	Moses b. Joseph Trani
Maharaḥ	Ḥayyim b. Isaac, also known as Ḥayyim Or Zaru'a
Maharai	Israel Isserlein
Maharal of Prague	Judah Loew b. Beẓalel
Maharalbaḥ	Levi b. Ḥabib
Maharam Alashkar	Moses b. Isaac Alashkar
Maharam Alshekh	Moses b. Ḥayyim Alshekh
Maharam of Lublin	Meir b. Gedaliah of Lublin
Maharam Mintz	Moses b. Isaac Mintz
Maharam of Padua	Meir Katzenellenbogen
Maharam of Rothenburg	Meir b. Baruch of Rothenburg
Maharash Kastilaẓ	Simeon Kastilaẓ
Maharashdam	Samuel b. Moses Medina
Maharaẓ Chajes	Ẓevi Hirsch Chajes
Mahardakh	David ha-Kohen of Corfu
Maharḥash	Ḥayyim Shabbetai of Salonika

Mahari Bruna	Israel b. Ḥayyim Bruna
Mahari Caro	Joseph Caro, also known as Maran
Mahari Minẓ	Judah Minẓ
Mahari Weil	Jacob b. Judah Weil, also known as Maharyu
Maharibal	Joseph ibn Lev
Maharif	Jacob Faraji
Maharik	Joseph b. Solomon Colon
Maharikash	Jacob b. Abraham Castro
Maharil	Jacob b. Moses Moellin
Maharit	Joseph b. Moses Trani
Maharit Algazi	Yom Tov b. Israel Jacob Algazi
Maharitaẓ	Yom Tov b. Akiva Ẓahalon
Mahariẓ	Yeḥaiah (Yaḥya, Yiḥye) b. Joseph Ẓalaḥ (Saliḥ)
Maharsha	Samuel Eliezer b. Judah ha-Levi Edels
Maharshak	Samson b. Isaac of Chinon
Maharshakh	Solomon b. Abraham
Maharshal	Solomon b. Jehiel Luria
Maharsham	Shalom Mordecai b. Moses Schwadron
Maharyu	Jacob b. Judah Weil, also known as Mahari Weil
Malbim	Meir Leib b. Jehiel Michael
Maran	Joseph Caro, also known as Mahari Caro
Neẓiv (Naẓiv)	Naphtali Ẓevi Judah Berlin
Noda bi-Yehudah	Ezekiel b. Judah ha-Levi Landau
Rabad (Rabad I)	Abraham b. David (ibn Daud) of Posquières
Rabad (Rabad II)	Abraham b. David (ibn Daud) ha-Levi
Raban	Eliezer b. Nathan of Mainz
Rabi	Abraham b. Isaac of Narbonne
Radbaz	David ibn Zimra
Ralbag	Levi b. Gershom, Gersonides
Ralbaḥ	Levi ibn Ḥabib
Ramah	Meir Abulafia
Rambam	Moses b. Maimon, Maimonides
Ramban	Moses b. Naḥman, Naḥmanides
Ran	Nissim of Gerona (Gerondi)
Ranaḥ	Elijah b. Ḥayyim
Rash	Samson b. Abraham of Sens

Rashba	Solomon b. Abraham Adret
Rashbam	Samuel b. Meir
Rashbash	Solomon b. Simeon Duran
Rashbeẓ (Rashbaẓ)	Simeon b. Ẓemaḥ Duran
Rashi	Solomon b. Isaac of Troyes
Rav Za'ir	Chaim Tchernowitz
Raviah	Eliezer b. Joel ha-Levi
Redak (Radak)	David Kimḥi
Re'em	Elijah b. Abraham Mizraḥi; Eliezer b. Samuel of Metz
Re'iyah	Abraham Isaac ha-Kohen Kook
Rema	Moses Isserles
Remakh	Moses ha-Kohen of Lunel
Reshakh	Solomon b. Abraham, Maharshakh
Rezah	Zeraḥia ha-Levi Gerondi
Ri	Isaac b. Samuel, also known as Isaac the Elder
Ri Migash	Joseph ibn Migash
Riaz	Isaac b. Moses of Vienna; Isaiah b. Elijah of Trani
Ribash	Isaac b. Sheshet Perfet
Rid	Isaiah b. Mali di Trani the Elder
Rif	Isaac b. Jacob ha-Kohen, Alfasi
Ritba	Yom Tov b. Abraham Ishbili
Riẓag	Isaac ibn Ghayyat
Rogachover	Joseph Rozin (Rosen)
Rosh	Asher b. Jehiel, Asheri
Shadal (Shedal)	Samuel David Luzzatto
Tashbaẓ (Tashbeẓ)	Samson b. Ẓadok
Tukh	Eliezer of Touques
Yaveẓ	Jacob Emden
Yaveẓ of North Africa	Jacob ibn Ẓur of Morocco

TRANSLITERATION GUIDE

LETTERS

NAME OF LETTER	SYMBOL	TRANSLITERATION	SOUND	REMARKS
aleph	א	not transliterated		
bet	בּ	b	as in *b*oy	
vet	ב	v	as in *v*alue	
gimmel	ג, גּ	g	as in *g*ate	no distinction between gimmel with *dagesh lene* and *gimmel* without *dagesh*
dalet	ד, דּ	d	as in *d*ance	no distinction between *dalet* with *dagesh lene* and *dalet* without a *dagesh*
he	ה	h	as in *h*ome	
vav	ו	v	as in *v*alve	when used as a vowel, transliter-ated as "o" or "u"
zayin	ז	z	as in Zion	
ḥet	ח	ḥ	ch as in German *Achtung*	no English equivalent
tet	ט	t	t as in *t*ag	
yod	י	y or i	y as in *y*es or when i, like ee in sh*ee*n	y except when vowel, and then "i"
kaf	כּ	k	k as in *k*ing or c as in *c*ome	English has no equivalent for the difference between *ḥet* and *khaf* in Hebrew
khaf	כ,ך	kh	like ch as in *Achtung*	

LETTERS (*continued*)

NAME OF LETTER	SYMBOL	TRANSLITERATION	SOUND	REMARKS
lamed	ל	l	l as in *l*ean	
mem	מ,ם	m	m as in *m*other	
nun	נ,ן	n	n as in *n*o	
samekh	ס	s	s as in *s*ing	
ayin	ע	not transliterated		indicated by apostrophe
pe	פּ	p	p as in *p*ost	
fe	פ,ף	f	f as in *f*ine	
ẓade / sade / tsade	צ,ץ	z	like ts in fi*ts*	
kof	ק	k	like ck as in lo*ck*	
resh	ר	r	r as in *r*ain	may be rolled
shin	שׁ	sh	sh as in *sh*ine	
sin	שׂ	s	s as in *s*ong	
tav	תּ	t	t as in *t*ame	no distinction between *tav* with *dagesh lene* and *tav* without a *dagesh*
taw	ת			

VOWELS

NAME OF VOWEL	SYMBOL (PLACED BELOW LETTER)	TRANSLITERATION	SOUND	REMARKS
kamatz / kameẓ / kamaẓ	◌ָ	a	like a in f*a*ther	if "long" kamaẓ
		o	like aw in l*aw*	if "short" kamaẓ
pataḥ	◌ַ	a	like a in f*a*ther	
ḥataf-pataḥ	◌ֲ	a	like a in *a*lignment	but no precise English equivalent

VOWELS (*continued*)

NAME OF VOWEL	SYMBOL (PLACED BELOW LETTER)	TRANSLITERATION	SOUND	REMARKS
ẓere tsere	..	e or ei	like *ai* as in pl*ai*n, ei as in "v*ei*n"	except *bet* not *beit*
segol	∵	e	like e in l*e*d	
ḥataf-segol	∵:	e	like second e in heg*e*mony	
sheva	:	e	like e in sh*e*nanigan	*sheva na* is transliterated, *sheva naḥ* is not
ḥirek ḥireq	.	i	between ee in sh*ee*n and i in p*i*n	
holam	וֹ, ˙	o	o as in h*o*me	dot placed above letter
kubbuẓ kibbuẓ	וּ, ⋱	u	u as in bl*ue*	

Notes

1. *Dagesh forte* is represented by doubling the letter, except that the letter *shin* is not doubled.

2. The definite article "ha" is followed by a hyphen, but although the following letter always has a *dagesh forte* in the Hebrew, it is not doubled in the transliteration. The transliteration of the definite article starts with a small "h" except in the name of Rabbi Judah Ha-Nasi, Rosh Ha-Shanah (the holiday) and the beginning of a sentence or title.

3. An apostrophe between vowels indicates that the vowels do not constitute a diphthong, but each is to have its separate pronunciation.

PART ONE

The History and Elements of Jewish Law

Chapter 1

THE HISTORY OF JEWISH LAW

I. Introduction
II. Jewish Law—A Living and Functioning System
  A. The Religious and National Character of Jewish Law
  B. The Jewish Legal Order and the Extent of Its Authority
  C. Methods of Enforcement of Judicial Decisions
  D. The Prohibition Against Litigating in Non-Jewish Tribunals (*Arka'ot Shel Goyim*)
  E. Arbitration
  F. Lay Tribunals (*Battei Din Shel Hedyotot*)
  G. Criticism of Lay Tribunals by the Halakhic Authorities
  H. The Basic Distinction Between the Various Forms of Jewish Adjudication on the One Hand and Adjudication by Non-Jewish Tribunals on the Other
  I. The Legal-Political Viewpoint of the General Government, and the Economic-Social Relationship between the Jewish Community and the Government
  J. Summary
III. The Different Periods of Jewish Law
  A. The Two Broad Periods
  B. The Division of the Two Periods into Subperiods

I. INTRODUCTION

Jewish law has a history of more than three thousand years. For by far the greater part of that period, the Jewish people did not enjoy political independence; and for much of that time, the Jews were scattered about in various places of exile with no clear geographical center.

Normally, when a legal system is deprived of its home base and the source of its vitality—its own sovereign state—it loses its link with a specific people, decays, and ultimately dies. This was the fate of the legal systems of many ancient peoples, of which we retain only the few traces that archeologists have been fortunate enough to unearth. This was what became of even the firmly based and highly developed system of Roman law that greatly influenced other legal systems which, to this day, absorb from its roots and study its principles. Roman law, as a creative, living, and developing system, virtually ended with the fall of the Western Roman Empire in the fifth century C.E. and of the Eastern or Byzantine Roman Empire some thousand years later.[1]

Such was not the case with Jewish law. One of the most significant phenomena in the history of Jewish law is that the loss of political independence (an independence that existed only for a relatively short time) and the rupture of the physical connection with the national homeland, the Land of Israel (*Ereẓ Yisra'el*), did not result in the abrogation of juridical autonomy. During its long and wide dispersion throughout the world, the Jewish people carried with it its own law and its own courts, diligently preserving their prerogatives by charters obtained from the governmental authorities and by the imposition of strict internal discipline.

Not only did the Jewish legal system not shrivel and die in the absence of a homeland, but its most vigorous development occurred during the period when the people were widely scattered throughout the diaspora. The portion of Jewish law that came into being prior to the destruction of the Second Temple in the first century C.E. provided merely the institutional and conceptual foundation for the monumental and multidimensional structure that later developed, initially, in the days of the *tannaim* (first century to 220 C.E.) and *amoraim* (220 C.E. to the end of the fifth century C.E.) and, thereafter, during the geonic era (end of the sixth or middle of the seventh century to the middle of the eleventh century C.E.) and the rabbinic era (eleventh century C.E. to date).

Moreover, although some *tannaim* and *amoraim* still lived and worked in the Land of Israel, it was the Babylonian Talmud, created and edited in the diaspora of Babylonia, that was the major development of Jewish law after the Mishnah; and if the Babylonian Talmud and most of the works of the *geonim* thereafter were composed when there was still a single domi-

1. *See* H.J. Wolff, *Roman Law,* 1951, pp. 177–178:

> In the Byzantine Empire—where central imperial government persisted and Justinian's codification and subsequent legislation remained in force, and where legal instruction and scientific treatment of the law maintained a comparatively high level—Roman law in the form laid down by Justinian survived in the main. In the West, Roman institutions . . . continued in use among the Roman elements of the population, and Roman forms of legal thinking largely dominated legislative and judicial activities of ecclesiastical authorities. But lacking the support of uniform direction by a central imperial government and of a scientifically trained class of legal experts . . . here Roman law nearly ceased to be a living force. The great resurrection which it experienced centuries later . . . and which made possible the tremendous impact it had on Western civilization was a purely scholarly achievement that had, at least at first, little to do with the actual law of the time.

See also the rest of the discussion in Wolff, *supra;* Rudolph Sohm, *Institutionen, Geschichte und System des Römischen Privatrechts* [Institutions, History, and System of Roman Private Law], 17th ed., 1949, pp. 137–146, 151; P. Vinogradoff, *Roman Law in Medieval Europe,* 2nd ed., Oxford, 1929.

nant center of the diaspora, the massive later rabbinic literature, extending over a period of some one thousand years, was produced in widely scattered places—North Africa, Spain, Germany, France, the Land of Israel, Poland, Turkey, Italy, and elsewhere. In all of these periods, Jewish law lived, grew, and developed.

A crucial change in the history of Jewish law was brought about by the decisive transformation of Jewish society—and concurrently, of Jewish law and its juridical authority—with the advent of the Emancipation and the loss of internal autonomy at the end of the eighteenth century. The results of this change were destined to be felt particularly at the beginning of the twentieth century during the Jewish national reawakening that saw the return of the Jewish people to its own land and the restoration there of political sovereignty, of which one important component is full juridical power.

This and the following chapter study in detail the history of Jewish law to the end of the eighteenth century. The later history of Jewish law is discussed in Volume IV of this work.

II. JEWISH LAW—A LIVING AND FUNCTIONING SYSTEM

In order to understand the direction taken by Jewish law, one must appreciate two of its fundamental and essential characteristics. First, in all eras of Jewish legal history, even after the exile of the people from its land, the growth of Jewish law was not the product of abstract speculation—of study for its own sake—but rather the outcome of a living, functioning, and practical system. Although, after the destruction of the Temple, the study of certain subjects such as the laws of ritual purity and impurity and the laws relating to the Temple and to sacrificial offerings became purely theoretical, all other aspects of Jewish law—whether dealing with the relation of people to God, to one another, or to their community—continued to be followed and applied to the actual problems of everyday life. The second fundamental characteristic, which follows from the first, is the continuous and unceasing development of Jewish law.

What is the explanation for the first characteristic, namely, the practical application of Jewish law in actual life situations, notwithstanding exile from its home state?[2] Two factors account for this unique phenomenon. One is internal, based on the nature and quality of Jewish law and on the place of that law in the spiritual and cultural life of the Jewish people. The

2. For the explanation of the second characteristic—continuous and unceasing development—*see infra* pp. 46ff.

second factor is external—the general legal and political consensus that prevailed during the course of political history until the eighteenth century with respect to the concepts of governmental and judicial power.

A. The Religious and National Character of Jewish Law

Let us look first at the internal factor, which is the major key to understanding this phenomenon. As indicated, the internal factor is based on the character of Jewish law as being religious and national. It is religious in that, according to principles of the Jewish faith, the root source of all Jewish law is divine revelation. Just as the purely "religious" aspects of life—the commandments governing the relation of people to God (such as the laws of prayer, the sabbath and holidays, and the dietary laws [*kashrut*])—maintained their vitality when the people were in exile, so too the purely "legal" aspects—the commandments regulating the relations between people in matters such as business, labor, torts, and crimes, or those establishing the framework of relationships between the individual and the public authority of the autonomous community—continued to develop and grow. In both areas—the "religious" and the "legal"—solutions to problems were found in the same source—in the Torah and the *Halakhah,* the *corpus juris* of the Jewish legal system; the same court or halakhic authority that ruled on questions of ritual practice also decided civil law cases involving contracts, leases, sales, and the like.

This inseparability of the "religious" and the "legal" Jewish law found expression even in the educational routine of the Jewish child. A youngster would study the Talmudic tractate of *Bava Meẓi'a,* which deals with civil matters, in exactly the same way that he studied the laws that clarify what is permitted and forbidden in regard to the sabbath or the *sukkah.*[3] The reason for this is clear and well recognized. Just as a Jew is bound to observe "religious" commandments and to avoid transgression, he is also bound by religious sanction no less stringent to observe "legal" commandments, which likewise may not be transgressed. This underlying commonality of "religious" and "legal" obligations is emphasized and re-emphasized at the highest level in the scale of values of the *Halakhah*—in the Written Law. In the Ten Commandments, those commandments requiring observance of the sabbath and prohibiting false swearing in the name of God are included in the same pronouncement and *in pari materia* along-

3. Booth used on the festival of *Sukkot* (Tabernacles); *see* Leviticus 23:34, 39–43. *See also* Josephus, *Antiquities,* IV, 8:12, ed. Thackery, in *Loeb Classical Library,* Vol. I, 1930, p. 577 ("Let your children also begin by learning the laws, most beautiful of lessons and a source of felicity"); ed. Schalit (Hebrew trans.), p. 100 and n. 122, and XX, 11:2; Josephus, *Contra Apionem,* II:18.

side "You shall not steal" and "You shall not murder."[4] The injunction that "You shall not insult the deaf or place a stumbling block before the blind" and the direction that "You shall rise before the aged and show deference to the old" are both rooted in "You shall fear your God. I am the Lord."[5] In the same way, the commandments "You shall not render an unfair decision . . . You shall not falsify measures of length, weight, or capacity. You shall have an honest balance, honest weights . . ." are based upon "I the Lord am your God who brought you out from the land of Egypt."[6] From the earliest beginning, the commands and proscriptions of the entire body of *Halakhah* in all its aspects and at all times have borne the imprint of religious obligation.

In addition to its religious character, Jewish law was also the national legal system of the Jewish people, inasmuch as its development was the product of that people. In this respect, Jewish law differs from other religious legal systems, such as canon law and Moslem law, which were created or developed not by the members of a single nation but by Catholics or Moslems from different national groups. The Jewish people, throughout its dispersion, regarded Jewish law as its national legal system—as an integral and fundamental part of its cultural heritage as a nation. Because the Jewish people, even in exile and dispersion, continued to exist as a national entity and not merely as a religious sect, it constantly needed to make use of the particular national asset that expressed its essential character, namely, its national legal system, which was developed entirely by its own members, the masters of the *Halakhah* and of legal thought.[7]

4. Exodus 20:1–14.

5. Leviticus 19:14, 32.

6. Leviticus 19:35–36.

7. This concept was recently expressed by the President of the Supreme Court of Israel in Skornik v. Skornik, 8 *P.D.* 141 (1954). In this case, a collateral issue arose as to the validity of a marriage celebrated under Jewish law by a Jewish couple in a country whose laws did not recognize such a marriage. Justice Agranat asserted:

> [For] the limited purpose of according legitimacy to such a marriage, the national law, which was then, and continues to be, their law to this day, namely, Jewish law, should override the foreign national law (*lex patriae*) that applied to the parties at the time of their marriage and recognizes only marriages celebrated pursuant to a prescribed civil form (*id.* at 178).

In explaining why Jewish law should be seen as the national law of the Jew, Justice Agranat said:

> When we acknowledge—as we must—the continued existence of the Jews in all the generations and in all the lands of their dispersion as a separate nation, we must in turn examine the character of Jewish law according to the Jewish nation's historical attitude to it. Then we will perforce conclude that the Jewish nation has, indeed, in all eras and in all the lands of its dispersion, treated Jewish law as its special possession, as part of the imperishable values of its culture. In other words, this law served in the past as the national law of the Jewish people, and to this day it bears this national character for Jews wherever they may be (*id.* at 177).

B. The Jewish Legal Order and the Extent of Its Authority

For a legal system to be practical and functional, there must be a court structure and an operating judicial system; otherwise, no valid judgment can be rendered or enforced. A section of the Torah is devoted to the selection of judges;[8] the establishment of a court system is an affirmative commandment,[9] and Jewish courts existed in all places of exile even after the loss of national independence. The Jewish court, together with the institutional independence of Jewish communal organization, was the main foundation for the internal Jewish autonomy from the destruction of the Temple to the period of the Emancipation.

In the Land of Israel, when the Temple was destroyed, Jewish juridical autonomy became limited for a short period[10] but soon regained its full scope:

> At the time of Rabban Gamaliel [of Yavneh], we observe the existence of a Jewish adjudicatory process in its full extent. Rabban Gamaliel himself and some members of his Sanhedrin actually served as judges: R. Tarfon, R. Ishmael, R. Akiva, and others. This era also constitutes one of the great periods in the conceptual development of Jewish law. This phenomenon of the rebirth of the law and its institutions represents one of the major features of the revival of the nation in its land after the destruction of the Temple; and it is reasonable to assume that this was the result of the successful efforts of the people and its leaders to establish an independent life in spite of the hardships and obstacles that it faced as a subjugated people. It was this struggle that, in the end, brought about the consent of the government to recognize, *de jure*

See also Yosipoff v. Attorney General, 5 *P.D.* 481 (1951); M. Silberg, *Ha-Ma'amad ha-Ishi be-Yisra'el* [Personal Status in Israel] (hereinafter, *Ha-Ma'amad*), 1957, pp. 240–242, and the remarks of N. Feinberg and P. Dykan quoted there. For a detailed discussion of this point in connection with the incorporation of Jewish law into the law—both statutory and decisional—of the State of Israel, *see* Muberman v. Segal, 32(iii) *P.D.* 85, 97 (1977); Roth v. Yeshufeh, 33(i) *P.D.* 617, 632 (1979); Hendeles v. Bank Kupat Am, 35(ii) *P.D.* 785 (1981); Bank Kupat Am v. Hendeles, 34(iii) *P.D.* 57 (1980). *See also infra* pp. 1731–1751, 1854–1856.

8. Exodus 18:21–26.

9. Deuteronomy 16:18. *See further* D.Z. Hoffmann, *Das Buch Deuteronomium Übersetzt und Erklärt* [The Book of Deuteronomy: Translation and Commentary] (hereinafter, *Commentary on Deuteronomy*) 17:8–11 (Hebrew trans. pp. 315–325), as to the judicial system up to the destruction of the Second Temple.

10. Jurisdiction over capital cases was abolished as early as forty years before the destruction of the Temple. Jerusalem Talmud (hereinafter, TJ), Sanhedrin 1:1, 1b (1:1, 18a); 7:2, 31a/b (14:2, 24b); Babylonian Talmud (hereinafter, TB), Shabbat 15a. However, it seems that, in fact, the Jewish courts heard capital cases at least until the destruction. *See* G. Alon, *Toledot ha-Yehudim be-Ereẓ Yisra'el bi-Tekufat ha-Mishnah ve-ha-Talmud* [History of the Jews in the Land of Israel during the Period of the Mishnah and the Talmud] (hereinafter, *Toledot*), I, pp. 129–131; H. Cohn, *The Trial and Death of Jesus*, Ktav, 1977, pp. 31–32, 345–350 nn. 42–44.

and *de facto,* the juridical autonomy of the Jewish community in the Land of Israel.[11]

Toward the middle of the second century C.E., the edicts of Emperor Hadrian produced a severe crisis for Jewish juridical autonomy in the Land of Israel, and the halakhic Sages risked their very lives to defend that autonomy and preserve its continuity.[12] According to one tradition,[13] it was said in reference to this period: "In the days of R. Simeon b. Yoḥai,[14] the right to adjudicate civil cases was taken away from Israel." Yet at the end of the second century C.E., broad judicial autonomy again existed, even as to capital cases.[15]

Juridical autonomy continued to exist even in the diaspora, in its various centers and in its different periods. The Jewish community in Babylonia had broad autonomy from early times, and one of the major institutions of that autonomy was the Jewish court.[16] After the disappearance of the Babylonian center, Jewish courts continued to exist in all other centers, carrying out their function of adjudicating disputes among Jews.[17] The leaders of the Jewish communities did all they could to obtain from the rulers

11. Alon, *Toledot,* I, p. 132, *and see id.* at 132–146 for a description of this judicial autonomy.

12. *See, e.g.,* TB Sanhedrin 13b–14a:

> R. Judah said in Rav's name: "May the memory of that man be praised, namely, R. Judah b. Bava; were it not for him . . . the laws of fines and penalties (*kenas*) would have been abolished in Israel. For the wicked government [of Hadrian] once decreed that whoever conferred or received ordination should be put to death, the city in which the ordination took place demolished, and the region where it was performed uprooted. What did R. Judah b. Bava do? He went and sat between two great mountains at a point situated between two large cities—between the sabbath boundaries [two thousand cubits on all sides beyond the city proper] of the cities of Usha and Shepharam—and there ordained five elders: R. Meir, R. Judah, R. Simeon, R. Yose, and R. Eleazar b. Shammua. R. Avia adds R. Nehemiah to the list. When their enemies discovered them, he [R. Judah b. Bava] said to them, 'My sons, flee!' They said to him, 'What will become of you, Master?' He said to them, 'I lie before them like a stone that no one will bother to overturn.' It was said that they [the enemy] did not leave the spot until they had driven three hundred iron spearheads into his body, making it like a sieve."

13. TJ Sanhedrin 1:1, 1b (1:1, 18a); 7:2.

14. This is the reading in TJ Sanhedrin 7:2, and is also the correct reading for 1:1 and not, as in the printed editions, "and in the days of Simeon b. Shataḥ"; *see Korban ha-Edah,* TJ Sanhedrin 1:1, s.v. Hakhi garsinan bi-mei R. Shim'on b. Yoḥai nitlu dinei mamonot, and *Sheyarei Korban, ad loc.,* s.v. Bi-mei Shim'on b. Shataḥ.

15. *See* A. Gulak, *Yesodei ha-Mishpat ha-Ivri* [The Foundations of Jewish Law] (hereinafter, *Yesodei*), IV, pp. 25–27; Alon, *Toledot,* I, pp. 130–131, II, pp. 43–44, 78–79, 111–114; S.W. Baron, *A Social and Religious History of the Jews* (hereinafter, *History*), II, pp. 265–269.

16. *See* S. Assaf, *Tekufat ha-Geonim ve-Sifrutah* [The Geonic Period and Its Literature] (hereinafter, *Geonim*), pp. 18–20; Gulak, *Yesodei,* IV, pp. 27–29.

17. For their jurisdiction over cases between Jew and non-Jew, *see infra* n. 109.

of the countries, upon whose protection they depended, Charters of Privileges to guarantee the independence of Jewish law and to grant enforcement power to the courts and the internal governmental agencies of the Jewish community. Even in those periods and places where the rights of the Jews were limited, Jews were generally granted authority to adjudicate most civil law matters.

Two examples illustrate this judicial authority, one from Spain and the other from Poland.

In the first half of the fifteenth century, Don Abraham Benvenisti served as the Court Rabbi, Chief Judge, and Tax Assessor of the Jewish communities in Castile, Spain. In 1432, Benvenisti convened the communal leaders and halakhic authorities in Valladolid, the place of the King's Court, to enact legislation (*takkanot*) concerning various matters "in the service of the Creator, blessed be He, in honor of the holy Torah, in the service of the King (may God protect him), and for the success of the communities (may God keep and preserve them), and for their benefit." Contained in these enactments is a wide-ranging codification of the judicial and administrative regulations of the Castilian Jewish communities. An interesting rationale for this extensive juridical autonomy, which even included the power to inflict capital punishment on a defendant convicted for the third time of the offense of being an informer, is found in the introduction to the third section of the compilation of these enactments:

> It is the will and the kindness of our lord, the King (may God protect him and may he reign for many years over his kingdom), that our civil and criminal disputes be governed by Jewish law; and he has commanded in his Charter of Privileges that the honored Don Abraham (may God protect him) shall judge over them, he and the judges that he shall appoint.
>
> Out of this emerge many benefits to the communities (may God keep and protect them): first, the Jews will, in this way, observe their Torah; second, they will save themselves the expense and damage that they would incur if they resorted to the gentile courts; third, the gentile judges, although wise, learned, and just, have not been sufficiently exposed to our laws and jurisprudence to have developed expert knowledge of them; fourth, because of this reason, it is a burden to our lords the judges and the *Alkaldim* [alcaldes].
>
> At all times there were decrees and agreements on this matter in the Castilian communities (may God keep and preserve them); in addition, as our lord, the King, in the above mentioned Charter, has commanded his officials and judges not to become involved in disputes among Jews . . . .

What is described here is an extremely broad juridical authority—Jewish civil and criminal law, and a Jewish chief judge who appoints other judges to serve under him. The first and major benefit of this autonomy was, of course, that the Jews were able in this way to observe their Torah and judge according to Jewish law. One may surmise that the desire to relieve the gentile judges of an extra burden was enumerated as one of the purposes of this autonomy in order to make the enactment more attractive and acceptable in the eyes of the king, but was not the real reason why autonomy was so desired.[18]

The second example is the description of the structure of the Jewish courts in the Polish diaspora in the second half of the sixteenth and the first half of the seventeenth century by the historian Meir Balaban:

> The Jewish court is composed of a number of judges, headed by the rabbi. Panels of judges (usually three panels) are found in the large communities, with each panel consisting of at least three judges. At the head of the third panel (the highest) sits the rabbi. The first panel, the lowest, sits in judgment (in Cracow) every day over monetary disputes involving from one *perutah* up to ten golden coins, and also over claims for unlawful encroachment on economic rights, insults, disputes between merchants, small loans, etc. The second panel, on the intermediate level, sits every day and deals with monetary claims of from ten to one hundred gold coins, and also those matters of insult brought before it. The third panel, the highest, sits twice or three times a week, as its business requires, and hears cases involving amounts of one hundred gold coins or more, in addition to religious and moral offenses (profanation of the name of God, moral depravity), and, in Posen, even cases involving capital punishment for religious crimes.
>
> The Jewish court judged according to Jewish law contained in the Talmud and rabbinic literature. Matters involving unclear questions of law were brought before the leading rabbis of the time, who expressed their opinions. These opinions were collected in books of *she'elot u-teshuvot* (responsa) that became sources of authority for later analogous cases. . . . Judgments were legally enforced to the fullest extent. Offenders were sentenced to fines, imprisonment (for bankruptcies, violations of police regulations), corporal punishment, being placed in the pillory,[19] confiscation of property, etc.[20]

18. *See* Y. Baer, *A History of the Jews in Christian Spain* (hereinafter, *Spain*), II, pp. 259–269; M. Elon, "Ha-Ma'asar ba-Mishpat ha-Ivri" [Imprisonment in Jewish Law], *Jubilee Volume for Pinḥas Rosen* (hereinafter, *Ma'asar*), pp. 180–181. On the enactments of Valladolid, their text and content, *see infra* pp. 798–802.

19. On the nature of punishment by pillory (*kuna*), *see* Elon, *Ma'asar,* pp. 197–198; *id., Encyclopedia Judaica* (hereinafter, EJ), VIII, p. 1303 (reprinted in *The Principles of Jewish Law* [hereinafter, *Principles*], p. 539).

20. *Bet Yisra'el be-Folin* [The Jews in Poland], 1948, I, pp. 57–58. *See also* the terms of the Charter of Privileges that the king of Poland, Sigismund Augustus, granted to the Jews of Greater Poland in 1551, *id.,* II, at 238–239. There was also a supreme court for all the Polish Jewish communities, which sat during the major fairs of Lublin and Jaroslaw and was composed of seven judges sent from the leading communities of Poland. (The court of the Council of the Four Lands developed from the court of the fairs.) The jurisdiction of the judges of the fairs (*dayyanei ha-yeridim*) was provided for in various enactments (*takkanot*); a considerable part of their jurisdiction consisted of cases between different regions and

Jewish law was applied, therefore, not only to all aspects of private civil law—such as property acquisitions, obligations, family matters, and succession—but also to a large segment of public law. In consequence of the internal authority of the Jewish community, Jewish law comprehensively governed the administration of the local government of each community and of federations of communities. The structure of the Jewish community and its institutions was based on halakhic laws; and the halakhic authorities were called on to decide constitutional questions relating to legislation by the agencies of the community,[21] matters involving elections to those agencies, methods of tax assessment and collection, the relation of the citizen to the public authority, and similar matters. Such public law questions are the subject of thousands of responsa in which halakhic authorities developed a complete legal system for Jewish public law.[22] In a large proportion of Jewish centers, juridical autonomy included criminal law. This aspect of autonomy varied from place to place in its scope and in its enforcement mechanisms. In some places, it included even capital cases, and in others, only religious delicts, crimes against property, and violations of police and administrative regulations.[23]

C. Methods of Enforcement of Judicial Decisions

As part of their autonomy, the Jewish courts and governing agencies had authority to impose sanctions. The coercive measures employed varied from place to place and from time to time. The usual methods were attachment of property, monetary fines, and corporal punishment. In some places,

---

communities, or between two parties who were subject to the jurisdictional authority of different communities. These cases often raised issues in the area of conflict of laws. *See* S. Assaf, *Battei ha-Din ve-Sidreihem Aḥar Ḥatimat ha-Talmud* [Courts and Their Procedures After the Completion of the Talmud] (hereinafter, *Battei ha-Din*), pp. 57–64; M. Elon, EJ, V, pp. 882–890, s.v. Conflict of laws (reprinted in *Principles*, pp. 715–723). In general, the enactments demarcated the court's jurisdictional boundaries. At times, the jurisdiction encompassed all towns that buried their dead in a particular cemetery (*see, e.g.*, the enactment (*takkanah*) of Rabbenu Tam cited by L. Finkelstein, *Jewish Self-Government in the Middle Ages* [hereinafter, *Self-Government*], p. 193). The halakhic authorities protected local jurisdiction and did not allow a local court to assume jurisdiction over a party not subject to its jurisdiction. *See* Israel Isserlein, *Terumat ha-Deshen*, Pesakim u-Khetavim, #63, #65; *Resp. Mahari Weil* #36. *See also* Pesakim u-Khetavim #252.

21. As to communal enactments, *see infra* ch. 19.

22. *See* M. Elon, EJ, XV, pp. 837ff., s.v. Taxation; *id.*, XIII, pp. 1351ff., s.v. Public authority; *id.*, VIII, pp. 279ff., s.v. Hekdesh (reprinted in *Principles*, pp. 662ff., 645ff., 701ff.). *See also infra* pp. 77–88, 681ff.

23. *See* S. Assaf, *Ha-Onshin Aḥarei Ḥatimat ha-Talmud* [Penal Law after the Completion of the Talmud] (hereinafter, *Onshin*), pp. 15ff. *See also infra* nn. 24, 25, and pp. 47, 515–519, 688–698.

there were Jewish jails, administered by the Jewish community and staffed by Jewish jailers.[24] In a few areas, Jewish courts were even given authority to administer the death penalty, especially against informers.[25] At times, the autonomous Jewish authorities required the help of the gentile government to enforce the sanctions imposed by the Jewish court, particularly the carrying out of the death penalty.[26]

The traditional and perhaps strongest sanction available to Jewish authorities was the *ḥerem,* or ban. The character and severity of the ban varied from place to place and according to the type of transgression and the extent of the sanction deemed necessary. At times, the severity of the ban extended to complete severance of relationships with the transgressor: no one was permitted to speak to him, to engage in any business dealings with him, or to marry him or any member of his household. The use of this sanction was necessary because the Jewish authorities lacked the typical enforcement powers associated with sovereignty. It was an effective measure and a strong deterrent, in view of the conditions of life and society of the Jewish population. The Jewish community lived as an autonomous body, an island unto itself, with all the members of that body dependent upon one another, and frequently even earning their livelihood from one another. One upon whom a ban was pronounced was excluded from the

24. *See* Elon, *Ma'asar,* pp. 178ff.; M. Elon, *Ḥerut ha-Perat be-Darkhei Geviyyat Ḥov ba-Mishpat ha-Ivri* [Individual Freedom and the Methods of Enforcing Payment of Debts in Jewish Law] (hereinafter, *Ḥerut*), 1964, in subject index, s.vv. Battei sohar yehudiyyim, Soharim yehudiyyim, Ma'asar.

25. *See, e.g.,* for Spain, *Resp. Rashba,* I, #181; V, #290; *Resp. Rashba Attributed to Naḥmanides* #240; *Resp. Asheri* 17:1, 17:8; *Resp. Zikhron Yehudah* #58, #79; *Resp. Ritba* #131; *Resp. Ribash* #251; for Poland, *Resp. Maharam of Lublin* #138. *See also Resp. Maharam of Rothenburg,* ed. Cremona, #232; *Resp. Maharam of Rothenburg,* ed. Prague, # 485; *Resp. Maharam of Rothenburg,* ed. Lemberg, #247, #248; *Resp. Mahari Weil* #114; *Resp. Mahari Bruna* #265; *Resp. Eitan ha-Ezraḥi* #45; *Resp. Ḥavvot Ya'ir* #146; *Resp. Rabi Av Bet Din* (ed. Kafaḥ, Jerusalem, 1962) #149 (S. Assaf, *Sifran Shel Rishonim,* Jerusalem, 1935, *Teshuvot ha-Rabi* #41) concerning one who killed while drunk; *Sefer ha-Mikneh,* of Joseph of Rosheim (ed. Ḥavvah Fraenkel-Goldschmidt, Jerusalem, 1970), pp. 7–9, 24–29, concerning two informers sentenced to death by Samuel b. Aaron Scheldtstaat at Strasbourg in the second half of the fourteenth century. *See also id.,* Introduction at xv–xviii.

26. *See, e.g., Resp. Rashba,* V, #290. It should be pointed out that in certain places (*e.g.,* Corfu, Palermo, Candia [Crete], Morocco, Algeria) the reverse situation existed: the Jews were required by the general government to supply hangmen from their own midst to execute death sentences pronounced by the non-Jewish courts on both Jews and non-Jews. *See* S. Assaf, "Talyanim Yehudim" [Jewish Hangmen], *Mekorot u-Meḥkarim* [Sources and Studies], pp. 252ff. (also printed in *Tarbiẓ,* V, pp. 224–226); A.H. Freimann, *Seder Kiddushin ve-Nissu'in Aḥarei Ḥatimat ha-Talmud, Meḥkar Histori-Dogmati be-Dinei Yisra'el* [Law of Betrothal and Marriage after the Completion of the Talmud: A Historical-Dogmatic Study in Jewish Law] (hereinafter, *Kiddushin ve-Nissu'in*), Mosad ha-Rav Kook, Jerusalem, 1945, p. 123 n. 8; Markus, "Toledot ha-Yehudim be-Khene'a ba-I Kretim" [History of the Jews of Candia on the Island of Crete], *Tarbiẓ,* XXXVIII (1969), p. 165 n. 30.

communal Jewish religious and civic life. The far-reaching effects of this sanction led many halakhic authorities to refrain from using it except for the most serious and extreme cases.[27]

An interesting example of the scope of the application of Jewish law in practice can be found in a careful and systematic study of the more than one thousand responsa of Asheri (Asher b. Jehiel [Rosh]), one of the leaders of German and Spanish Jewry in the second half of the thirteenth century and the beginning of the fourteenth century.[28] Responsa make up the "case law" of the Jewish legal system, and include, for the most part, decisions of the halakhic authorities of the various centers and the different eras on questions that arose in actual life situations between members of the Jewish community or between individual Jews and the communal authorities.[29]

In the collection of the responsa of Asheri, about two hundred responsa, *i.e.*, about twenty percent, deal with matters between people and God (laws that were later codified in the *Shulḥan Arukh* sections *Oraḥ Ḥayyim* and *Yoreh De'ah*, such as the laws of blessings, holy days, forbidden foods, the menstrual period, and the *mikveh* [ritual bath]); and all the rest, *i.e.*, approximately eighty percent, or more than eight hundred responsa, concern matters that generally form the corpus of the law in other legal systems (subjects that, for the most part, were later codified in the *Shulḥan Arukh* sections *Even ha-Ezer* and *Ḥoshen Mishpat*). Of these more than eight hundred responsa, approximately 170 deal with family law (laws of marriage and divorce, property relationships between husband and wife, the legal relationship of parent and child); and all the rest, almost seven hundred responsa, concern the other areas of civil, criminal, and administrative law.

This distribution of the subject matter of the collected responsa of one of the leading halakhic authorities of the thirteenth and fourteenth centuries indicates that by far the major portion of the legal questions requiring clarification in the new ambiance of the Spanish and other diasporas related to the legal component of the *Halakhah*.[30] Jewish social life, commerce, and

27. *See* Assaf, *Onshin,* p. 34. As to the sanctions referred to above, as well as additional methods of coercion, *see id.* at 18–44; Assaf, *Battei ha-Din,* pp. 25–34.

28. This study was made in connection with the preparation of the digest of responsa literature by the Institute for Research in Jewish Law of the Hebrew University. *See Mafte'aḥ ha-She'elot ve-ha-Teshuvot* [Digest of Responsa Literature], *Responsa of Asheri,* ed. M. Elon, published by the Institute for Research in Jewish Law, 1965, and the introduction thereto.

29. *See infra* pp. 1453ff.

30. This phenomenon is typical of the entire responsa literature up to the sixteenth century, as is evident from *Mafte'ah ha-She'elot ve-ha-Teshuvot Shel Ḥakhmei Sefarad U-Ẓefon Afrikah* [Digest of the Responsa Literature of Spain and North Africa], *Legal Digest,* 2 vols., ed. M. Elon, Institute for Research in Jewish Law, Magnes Press, Jerusalem, 1986.

economy, Jewish public organization in the framework of the *kehillah* (organized Jewish community) and its governing institutions and elected officials, and the relation of the Jewish community to the surrounding non-Jewish environment and to the general government—all these gave rise, from time to time, to problems for which sometimes there were no clear solutions in the existing Jewish law, or for which it was necessary to find new and different solutions from those that Jewish law had reached in the past. The special, the difficult, and the novel elements in these problems, in addition to the usual clash of interests between litigants, caused these questions to be brought to the central halakhic authority for final decision and resolution.

D. The Prohibition Against Litigating in Non-Jewish Tribunals (*Arka'ot Shel Goyim*)

A striking expression of the religious and national character of Jewish law is found in the prohibition against resorting to non-Jewish tribunals (*arka'ot*)[31]—a prohibition that the halakhic authorities and the communal leaders regarded as particularly strict. At about the time that the Temple was destroyed, when the Roman authorities restricted Jewish legal autonomy for a short period,[32] we are told:

> R. Tarfon[33] said: "In all places that you find *agoriot* (non-Jewish courts),[34] even though the substance of their law is the same as Jewish law, you are not permitted to resort to them, for it is written: 'And these are the laws that you shall set before them.'[35] Before them [the Jewish people] but not before the gentiles."[36]

31. For the explanation of the term *arka'ot, see* Blau, *Hashva'ot Bein ha-Mishpat ha-Ivri le-Hellenisti-Miẓri* [Comparative Study of Jewish and Hellenistic-Egyptian Law], pp. 17–21; Alon, *Toledot,* I, p. 346.

32. *See supra* p. 6.

33. In *Tanḥuma,* Mishpatim, sec. 6 (p. 100), the text reads: "R. Simeon says," and in the *She'iltot* (several printed editions and mss.), She'iltah #2, Parashat Bereshit (p. 23, *and see* the commentaries there), the text reads: "R. Meir says." This indicates that the statement was made in the fourth generation of the *tannaim,* after the Bar Kokhba rebellion, which was a period of great crisis for Jewish juridical autonomy. *See supra* nn. 13, 14, concerning the statement of TJ Sanhedrin 1:1 and 7:2: "In the days of R. Simeon b. Yoḥai, the right to adjudicate civil cases was taken away from Israel."

34. The word *agoria* is of Greek origin; *see* J. Levy, *Wörterbuch über die Talmudim und Midrashim* [Talmudic and Midrashic Dictionary] (hereinafter, *Wörterbuch*), 2d ed., Berlin, 1924, s.v. Agoria; *Arukh ha-Shalem,* s.vv. Agar, Agori. In ms. Munich the reading is *arka'ot shel goyim* (non-Jewish tribunals). *See also Mekhilta de-R. Simeon b. Yoḥai,* ed. Hoffman, p. 117, and M. Kasher, *Torah Shelemah,* XVII, pp. 9–11.

35. Exodus 21:1.

36. TB Gittin 88b. This conclusion is reached as follows by Naḥmanides, *Commentary on Exodus* 21:1: "One would have expected Scripture to have stated, 'that you shall set forth

This determination by the halakhic authorities—based not only on the difference between non-Jewish law and *Halakhah,*[37] but on the very act of resorting to a non-Jewish court, even though "their law is the same as Jewish law"—was promulgated at a time when the Jewish legal system was about to set out on the long and difficult course of maintaining juridical autonomy without a sovereign state; and this pronouncement established one of the sturdiest bulwarks protecting the continuous existence and development of the Jewish court in all the periods of the exile. Resort to a non-Jewish court was compared to the denial of the existence of God and His Torah and to the transgression of the commandment against profanation of God's name.[38] "Anyone who litigates before non-Jewish judges or in

---

to them,' as in Exodus 15:25 ('there He made for [lit. "set forth to"] them fixed rules'), yet [Scripture] states '*before* them.' This shows that they [the Jewish people] shall be the judges—the language 'before them' having reference to judges." *See* other explanations in Rashi, s.v. Lifneihem, and in *Tosafot,* Gittin 88b, s.v. Lifneihem ve-lo lifnei hedyotot.

37. When a non-Jewish court decides a case according to its own law, then, in addition to violating the prohibition against resorting to non-Jewish courts, whoever obtains anything under the judgment is considered to be a robber. *Resp. Tashbeẓ,* II, #290 states:

> . . . and all this [*i.e.,* the prohibition against resorting to non-Jewish courts] applies even when their laws are the same as ours, in which case litigating before them amounts to no more than exaltation of their religion. When, however, their law differs from ours, then it is obviously prohibited, and one who sues before them is a robber and unfit to be a witness, until he restores what by our law he unjustly took from the other party. . . . This is so obvious that it does not need to be put in writing. If he betroths a woman with money that he took by their law and against our law, the betrothal is invalid. . . .

See the full responsum. *See also Resp. Yakhin u-Vo'az,* I, #6; Samuel Aboab, *Sefer ha-Zikhronot,* Zikkaron 10:3.

38. *Tanḥuma,* Mishpatim, sec. 3 (p. 98), states:

> Whence do we know that when Jewish litigants are engaged in a dispute and know that the gentiles rule on it identically with Jewish law, the case may still not be submitted to them? From the Scriptural verse, "That you shall set before them," *i.e.,* before Jews and not before Cutheans [gentiles]; for whoever forsakes Jewish judges and takes his case before gentiles has, first, denied the Holy One, blessed be He, and thereafter denied the Torah.

And see Midrash Tannaim, Deuteronomy (ed. Hoffmann, p. 96) on 16:19:

> "You shall appoint for yourselves"—this denotes that laws were given [by God] only to Israel, and teaches you that whoever takes his case to [a court of] any other nation is viewed as if he worshipped idols, for thus does [Scripture] state: "You shall appoint judges and officials for yourselves," which is followed by "You shall not judge unfairly" (v. 19), "Justice, justice shall you pursue" (v. 20), and "You shall not erect a pole of wood [for idol worship] (*asherah kol eẓ*)" (v. 21). Furthermore, whoever forsakes Jewish laws and goes to a gentile [court] denies the Holy One, blessed be He, as it is written, "For their rock is not like our Rock even in our enemies' own estimations" [*i.e.,* even our enemies agree that their God is not like ours] (Deuteronomy 32:31). Why? Because their laws are not good.

Rashi, Exodus 21:1, s.v. Lifneihem, following the *Tanḥuma,* says:

their courts, even though their law is the same as Jewish law, is an evildoer, as if he has reviled, blasphemed, and raised his hand against the Torah of Moses, our Teacher. . . ."[39]

As stated, the prohibition against the use of non-Jewish courts was more strict than the typical legal rules relating to civil matters, since the use of such courts had the effect of undermining the essence of Jewish autonomy. Therefore, it was agreed by most halakhic authorities that, contrary to the usual rule that all rules of civil law are in the category of *jus dispositivum,* and therefore even Biblical law in this area may be varied by agreement,[40] the parties may not agree to submit to the jurisdiction of a non-Jewish court, and any such agreement is null and void.[41] On the basis of this same rationale, resort to non-Jewish courts could not be permitted even under the doctrine of *dina de-malkhuta dina* ("The law of the land is law").[42]

In the political and social context of the different areas of the diaspora, however, it was not always possible to apply the prohibition against the use of non-Jewish courts in all its stringency. The major problem that arose was when one of the parties was a violent and dangerous individual who refused to appear before the Jewish court or, after he had litigated before the Jewish court and had lost his case, refused to accept the judgment. This was a problem that arose as a natural consequence of the absence of Jewish sovereignty and the resulting lack of a fully adequate power of enforcement. To solve this problem, it was established as early as the middle of the ninth century C.E. by Paltoi Gaon that "if Reuben has a claim against Simeon, who refuses to appear in court, he [Reuben], in order to obtain what is his, may bring [Simeon] before the non-Jewish courts."[43]

Even if you know that they judge a particular matter in the same way as Jewish law, do not bring it before their courts, for whoever brings cases involving Jews before gentiles profanes the name [of God], glorifies idols and enhances their praise. . . .

39. Maimonides, *Mishneh Torah,* also called *Ha-Yad ha-Ḥazakah* (hereinafter, *MT*), Sanhedrin 26:7. For v.1., *see* ed. Rome 1480. *See also Tur* and Sh. Ar. ḤM 26:1.

40. *See infra* pp. 123–127.

41. Naḥmanides, *Commentary on Exodus* 21:1; *Resp. Rashba,* VI, #254 (quoted in *Bet Yosef* on *Tur* ḤM, end of ch. 26, s.v. Katav ha-Rashba); *Tur* ḤM 26:5; Sh. Ar. ḤM 26:1 and 26:3; *Yam Shel Shelomo,* Bava Kamma 8:65; Samuel Aboab, *supra* n. 37; *Birkei Yosef,* ḤM #26, piska 3.

42. *See* sources in n. 41 *supra. See also Resp. Tashbeẓ,* I, #158, quoted *infra* p. 135.

43. *Oẓar ha-Geonim,* Bava Kamma, Responsa, p. 69. The deduction of this principle by Paltoi Gaon from the statement in TB Bava Kamma 92b, "There is a popular saying: If you draw the attention of your fellow [to warn him] and he does not respond, push down a large wall on him," is mere makeweight reasoning, for it is a popular saying that has no bearing on the subject of non-Jewish courts. Meir Dan Plotzki, *Keli Ḥemdah,* Mishpatim #1, argues that the suggestion of this source for this law "is not at all convincing." *See also infra* p. 1583 n. 18.

This innovation, which carried with it some degree of danger for internal Jewish discipline, was not readily accepted; and more than three hundred years later, when Naḥmanides (Moses b. Naḥman [Ramban]) was asked about this rule established by the *geonim,* he answered:

> I do not know that any such thing is permitted. I do not recognize those *geonim.* It is forbidden to summon before a non-Jewish court even a violent debtor who refuses to appear before a Jewish court; but the Jewish court may issue a writ of execution against his property, and if it then becomes necessary to bring the case to the gentiles and they compel him to obey what the Jewish judges have ordered, this is permissible.[44]

Thus, it was Naḥmanides' opinion that the case must always be tried before a Jewish court, and the only legitimate function of the non-Jewish authorities in a dispute between Jews is to enforce the judgment rendered by the Jewish court. However, the distinction made by Naḥmanides was not accepted, and the rule as finally established was that one must first seek relief before the Jewish court; and if the defendant refuses to appear, the claimant, with permission of the Jewish court, may bring his claim against the defendant in the non-Jewish court in order "to prevent the strong and powerful from evading the law."[45]

44. *Resp. Naḥmanides* #63 (S. Assaf, *Sifran Shel Rishonim,* Jerusalem, 1935, p. 98). Only if the other party in the case "is a violent man and the Jewish court is afraid to issue an order against him, so that he is to be classed as wicked, may one pursue the claim against him in the non-Jewish court . . . . Since he does not obey and there is no means of redress through the Jewish authorities, it is as though one retrieved it from a robber."

45. Maimonides, *MT,* Sanhedrin 26:7, and Radbaz, *ad loc.; see also* commentaries on *MT, ad loc.; Tur* ḤM 26:6–7; Sh. Ar. ḤM 26:2 and 4, and commentators *ad loc.; Yam Shel Shelomo,* Bava Kamma 8:65; *Oẓar ha-Geonim,* Bava Kamma, Responsa, p. 100; *Ginzei Schechter,* II, New York, 1929, pp. 118, 127–128; *Resp. Maharashdam,* ḤM, #360; *Takkanot Medinat Mehrin* [Enactments in Moravia], p. 88, #265.

It is instructive to note the surprise of one of the leading halakhic authorities of the nineteenth century at the dispensation to resort to non-Jewish courts when one of the litigants is a violent man. Meir Dan Plotzki (1868–1928), who headed the Jewish court of Ostrava (Ostrog), Poland, in his book *Keli Ḥemdah* (Mishpatim, #1), says, *inter alia:*

> I will not forbear to state here my great perplexity: The Torah said "before them" but not before the gentiles. Nevertheless, the accepted view is that the prohibition applies only if the [other] party to the suit is willing to litigate in a Jewish court; but if he is not willing to do so, his opponent may obtain permission from the Jewish court and take the case to a non-Jewish court in order to protect his rights. *See* Maimonides at the end of [*MT*] Hilkhot Sanhedrin. But why should this be permitted? Since it is a prohibition implicit in the affirmative commandment "before them," implying "but not before the gentiles," why should one be allowed to transgress this rule to protect against loss? Is not a person enjoined to yield all his fortune in order not to transgress a negative commandment? . . . So why should it be permitted for the sake of money to go to a non-Jewish court?

This objection certainly has a great deal of merit, but the halakhic authorities established this dispensation by way of a strained argument from the passage in TB Bava Kamma 92b;

At times, the use of non-Jewish courts was allowed in certain matters in which the general government had a special interest, such as real estate,[46] the payment of promissory notes,[47] government taxes, currency matters,[48] and assault and battery.[49] Sometimes, when a dispute between two Jews was tried before a non-Jewish court, the court applied Jewish law, and in order to do so, it requested an opinion on the case from a halakhic authority.[50] As stated, even if the litigants agreed to take their disputes to the non-Jewish court, the agreement was not effective; however, there were some who disagreed with this rule. In a *takkanah* promulgated by Rabbenu Tam, Rashbam (Samuel b. Meir), and other halakhic leaders of their generation, it was stated:

> We have decided and enacted under the pain of ban and excommunication applicable to all men and women, near and far, that it is forbidden to bring a fellow Jew before the non-Jewish courts or to coerce him by means of the gentiles, whether by a noble, a commoner, a governor, or an officer, unless agreed to by both parties before competent witnesses.[51]

We learn from this *takkanah* that if both sides agree, it is permitted to litigate before a non-Jewish court; and we find similar opinions in the writings of some of the leading *aḥaronim* (later authorities).[52] Another significant, innovative view is found in the writings of Shabbetai ha-Kohen, author of the *Shakh* (*Siftei Kohen*), who denies the validity of agreements between the parties to litigate before non-Jewish courts only if the agreement provides for appearance before non-Jewish courts generally. If, however, the parties make an agreement in due form to litigate before a particular named non-Jewish judge, the agreement is binding because "this

---

for without the dispensation, violent men would have the advantage, which would utterly subvert the entire social order.

46. *Resp. Rema* #109; *Takkanah* #379 of the community of Fürth, published by S. Assaf, "Le-Sidrei Vattei ha-Din be-Ashkenaz" [On Proceedings before Jewish Courts in Germany], *Ha-Mishpat ha-Ivri*, I, p. 117. *See also infra* p. 809.

47. *Naḥalat Shiv'a* #28; *Takkanah* #379 of the Fürth community, *supra* n. 46. *See also Urim ve-Thummim* to Sh. Ar. ḤM, ch. 26, Thummim, subpar. 2.

48. *Netivot ha-Mishpat*, Novellae, ḤM 26, subpar. 2. *See also Kesef ha-Kodashim, ad loc.*; Finkelstein, *Self-Government*, pp. 361–362.

49. *Resp. Maharaḥ Or Zaru'a* #25, #142.

50. *Resp. Rashba*, I, #1148; *Resp. Ritba* #131; *Resp. Ribash* #490, *et al. See also infra* p. 1502 and n. 137.

51. The *takkanah* is quoted in *Resp. Maharam of Rothenburg*, ed. Cremona, #78; *see also Resp. Ran* #73.

52. *See* Maharash Ḥayyun (son of the daughter of Maharashdam), *Benei Shemu'el*, as quoted in Ḥ.J.D. Azulai (Ḥida), *Birkei Yosef*, ḤM #26, piska 3 and Ḥida's comments; *Sefer Me'irat Einayim* (hereinafter, *Sema*), Sh. Ar. ḤM 26, subpar. 11, and *Turei Zahav* (hereinafter, *Taz*) on Sh. Ar. ḤM 26:3.

gentile is trustworthy in their eyes and they have confidence in him, and it is effective in the same way as if they agreed on one who is a relative or is otherwise disqualified."[53]

In some communities, and at various times, there were those who made light of and disregarded the prohibition against the use of non-Jewish courts.[54] However, on the whole, the halakhic authorities and the communal leaders stood firm against every effort to undermine Jewish juridical autonomy, and defended that autonomy by means of special legislation and other stringent countermeasures.[55]

53. *Siftei Kohen* (hereinafter, *Shakh*), Sh. Ar. ḤM 22, subpar. 15; he differs with the view expressed by Joseph Caro in Sh. Ar. ḤM 22:2; *see also infra* p. 1919 n. 44.

54. It sometimes happened that an organized group in the community, and perhaps even some of its leaders, undermined the prohibition against resort to non-Jewish courts. This happened for instance, in Arta, Greece, in the first half of the sixteenth century. Benjamin Ze'ev b. Mattathias described the following episode (*Resp. Binyamin Ze'ev* #282):

> I decided that in a situation such as this, I should not keep silent about what I have seen and have heard with my own ears concerning a conspiracy of wicked men. Six ringleaders, apart from their followers, assembled and went to the [gentile] judge of the town and obtained an order from him that no Jewish scholar, rabbi, or official be allowed to hold court under the laws of the Torah (whether civil or family law or [involving] bans), except by permission of the [gentile] judge (*id.* at 166a).

Benjamin Ze'ev protested against this bitterly:

> Are there no judges among the Jews? Why do the wicked of our people exalt themselves to follow the willfulness of their evil heart to bring family matters and bans before non-Jewish judges? There is no doubt that the men who have sinned at the cost of their souls and who battle mightily to abolish the laws of the Torah deserve to be banned, as [I will explain] further on . . . . These [men] who have deprived the communities of the laws of the Torah should be branded as having read themselves out of their community. Through such wicked men the generation is collapsing. They deserve to be flogged. . . . Likewise, the communities of the city of Arta who have set at naught the laws of the Torah ought to be flogged. . . . (*id.* at 167a).

Benjamin Ze'ev went on to decry the profanation of God's name in the sight of the gentiles, caused by those who undermined the autonomy of the Jewish judicial system:

> The prophet [Ezekiel 36:20] cried out, "They have profaned My holy name." How have they profaned it? When it was said of them [Ezekiel, *loc. cit.*], "These are the people of the Lord, yet they had to leave His land." In other words, when the nations among whom they are exiled say of them, "Behold these, the people of God, whom He could not save from being exiled." Thus, the name of Heaven is profaned and His glory diminished. Thus, the gentiles say of them, "Behold how the Jews, who say that they are the people of God, themselves, by means of the [gentile] judge, proceed to do away with their own law, and He is not able to deliver them from foreign power, but they are in exile under the subjugation of the nations." So you see how through these wicked men the name of Heaven is profaned. Therefore, whoever stands up against them sanctifies the name of Heaven in public. . . . (*id.* at 171b–172a).

See also Resp. Ba'ei Ḥayyai, ḤM, II, #158.

55. *See* bibliography *infra* n. 108; *Resp. Ranaḥ* #58, #63; *Resp. Ba'ei Ḥayyai,* ḤM, II, #1, #158; *Resp. Ne'eman Shemuel* #84.

E. Arbitration

The goal of preventing resort to non-Jewish courts, in order to preserve Jewish juridical autonomy, led halakhic authorities to maintain and encourage the use of tribunals composed of Jewish judges, even when their decisions had an extremely tenuous basis in *Halakhah* or were not based on *Halakhah* at all. These tribunals were: (a) arbitrators and (b) various forms of lay courts.

The beginning of the institution of arbitration took place in the days of R. Meir and his colleagues[56] (the second half of the second century C.E.—the generation of R. Simeon b. Yoḥai referred to previously) when Jewish authority to decide civil cases was taken away.[57] This was the period after the Bar Kokhba revolt, when many Jewish courts ceased to function and their judges were killed, and when those courts that did remain were deprived of the power to enforce their judgments. The Sages directed the people toward the system of arbitration, in which even ordinary shepherds who did not know *Halakhah* could sit and decide the matters brought before them according to their common sense and personal judgment. It is indeed interesting that, as pointed out by Asher Gulak, the Sages sought to give to the method of choosing the arbitration panel at least a Jewish quality (a method that also assured a fair hearing for the dispute)[58] by establishing that there were to be three arbitrators, *i.e.*, each litigant chose one and both litigants or the two selected arbitrators agreed on a third.[59] The institution thus resembled the Jewish court of law, which was made up of at least three judges.[60] This differed from Roman law, under which arbitration generally was conducted by one arbitrator and only in exceptional cases did the parties agree on two or more arbitrators.[61] Even after the restoration of judicial autonomy, arbitration continued to fulfill an important function, complementing the regular court system; and the Sages established the rules and procedures of arbitration.[62]

56. Mishnah (hereinafter, M) Sanhedrin 3:1–2. According to Alon, *Toledot*, I, p. 138, the beginning of the institution of arbitration dates back some time earlier, to the days of Rabban Gamaliel; *see also* G. Alon, *Meḥkarim be-Toledot Yisra'el bi-Mei Bayit Sheni u-vi-Tekufat ha-Mishnah ve-ha-Talmud* [Studies in Jewish History in the Days of the Second Temple and in the Mishnaic and Talmudic Period] (hereinafter, *Meḥkarim*), II, pp. 30, 44.

57. *See supra* p. 7.

58. TB Sanhedrin 23a: "Since each party selects one arbitrator and both agree on a third, a true judgment will be rendered." *See also* TJ Sanhedrin 3:1, 13b (10:1, 21a).

59. M Sanhedrin 3:1.

60. *Id.* 1:1.

61. Gulak, *Yesodei*, IV, p. 31; *and see id.* at 25–27, 30–32.

62. TB Sanhedrin 23a ff.; Maimonides, *MT*, Sanhedrin ch. 7; *Tur* and Sh. Ar. ḤM ch. 13; Assaf, *Battei ha-Din*, pp. 54–57; Warhaftig, "Dinei Borerut ba-Mishpat ha-Ivri" [Arbitra-

F. Lay Tribunals *(Battei Din Shel Hedyotot)*

The institution of lay tribunals had an interesting pattern of development. The Hebrew term *hedyot* ("lay"), as used in *bet din shel hedyotot* ("lay tribunal"), has two different meanings. According to one meaning, the formal-legal, the reference is to judges who are not duly ordained—*i.e.*, judges outside of the Land of Israel, where ordination (*semikhah*) was not practiced, and also those in the Land of Israel after the practice of ordination ceased—even though these judges may be fully knowledgeable, astute, and expert in the laws of the Torah. This is the meaning of the term, for example, in the following Talmudic passage:[63] "'These are the laws that you shall set before them' [Exodus 21:1]. 'Before *them*' [ordained judges] but not before *hedyotot*." And as Abbaye there stated to R. Joseph: "We too are considered to be *hedyotot*."[64]

The second meaning of the term—the sense in which it is ordinarily used—refers to judges who are not fully knowledgeable or are even totally ignorant of the laws of the Torah.[65] These are "the lay people of the mar-

---

tion in Jewish Law], *Mazkeret, A Torah Collection in Memory of Rabbi Herzog*, Jerusalem, 1962, pp. 507–529; Frank, *Kehillot Ashkenaz u-Vattei Dineihem* [Jewish Communities of Germany and Their Courts], pp. 96–99. Related to the institution of arbitration is the institution of compromise. For all the above matters in detail, *see* M. Elon, EJ, III, pp. 294–300, s.v. Arbitration (reprinted in *Principles*, pp. 565–570); EJ, V, pp. 857–859, s.v. Compromise (reprinted in *Principles*, pp. 570–573); Sobol v. Goldman, 33(i) *P.D.* 789, 799ff. (1979).

63. TB Gittin 88b.

64. Maimonides, *MT*, Sanhedrin 26:7, quotes this passage of the *baraita*, "'Before them' but not before *hedyotot*," together with the rest of R. Tarfon's statement, "'Before them' but not before the gentiles," *see supra* p. 13. It seems that Maimonides quotes this passage regarding *hedyotot* incidentally, influenced by the joinder of the two statements in TB Gittin, though it is not pertinent to Maimonides' text at all. It is clear that what Maimonides says concerning the stringency of the prohibition against resort to non-Jewish judges does not refer to litigating before Jewish judges who are expert and knowledgeable and are familiar with the Torah but have not been ordained! Nor can the stringency of this prohibition, the source of which is in *Tanḥuma*, Mishpatim, *supra* n. 33, refer to litigation before Jewish laymen, for the *Tanḥuma* speaks only of one who litigates before non-Jewish judges and bypasses the Jewish judges. The quotation of this passage in *MT* still needs to be clarified. *See* Moses of Trani, *Kiryat Sefer*, who quotes this paragraph from *MT*, but does not include the phrase, "'Before them' but not before *hedyotot*."

65. For example, in TB Bava Meẓi'a 32a, R. Joseph b. Manyumi said in the name of R. Naḥman that the statement in M Ketubbot 11:2 that "a widow may sell [property of her deceased husband's estate for her *ketubbah* or maintenance] without the presence of a court" means that "a widow does not need a court of expert judges (*mumḥin*), but a court of laymen (*hedyotot*) is sufficient." The term "expert judges" here refers to judges knowledgeable in the law who may adjudicate civil cases though they are not ordained, and are therefore *hedyotot* in the first sense; and the term "laymen" in this context refers to "lay people of the marketplace who have no learning at all" (Ritba, quoted in *Shittah Mekubbeẓet*, Bava Meẓi'a 32a).

ketplace who have no learning at all."[66] Since the terms *hedyotot* and *bet din shel hedyotot* appear in various contexts in the Talmud,[67] it has to be determined which of the two meanings is referred to in each case.[68] "Lay tribunal" (*bet din shel hedyotot*) is used in the present discussion in the second sense, *i.e.*, a court that consists partially or completely of judges who do not know the laws of the Torah.

The original purpose and character of this judicial institution are subjects of scholarly dispute.[69] On the question of its place within the structure

---

Here the Talmud utilizes the Hebrew term for "lay tribunal" in the most extreme sense of complete laymen, none of whom has any learning or is able to reason a matter out—a court that according to Talmudic law is not competent to judge, save in exceptional cases such as the sale of an estate for payment of a *ketubbah* or to provide support.

66. Ritba, *supra* n. 65; *see also Resp. Ritba* #190: "Our masters of blessed memory have explained that the laymen referred to here are knowledgeable in the appraisal of property though [otherwise] not fit to judge at all; this is the correct interpretation." This is the way it is also understood by *Tosafot Shanz* (Sens) quoted in *Shittah Mekubbeẓet*, Bava Meẓi'a 32a; also in *Bet ha-Beḥirah* to Bava Meẓi'a 32a (ed. Sofer, p. 116), and in the *Maggid Mishneh* to *MT*, Ishut 17:13: "Though there is not one among them who is learned and can reason [a matter] out and they are not fit to judge civil cases."

67. The term *bet din shel hedyotot* also appears in TB Bava Kamma 14b and TB Nedarim 78b. *See* Rashi, s.v. Ella, *Tosafot*, s.v. Perat le-vet din hedyotot, and *Bet ha-Beḥirah*, to Bava Kamma 14b, all of whom explain that the term refers to unordained judges, and were therefore constrained to regard the issue as being whether such a court could impose a penalty (*kenas*). If *bet din shel hedyotot* is taken to mean a tribunal not merely "unordained" but also "ignorant of Torah law," as it obviously means in *Bava Meẓi'a*, then one can regard the issue as being whether such a tribunal may hear *any* civil case, as seems to be the plain meaning of the *mishnah*.

There is a difference of opinion among the commentators with regard to the term as used in TB Nedarim. *See Enẓiklopedyah Talmudit* [Talmudic Encyclopedia] (hereinafter, ET), III, pp. 160–161, s.v. Bet din. In many other places the term *hedyotot* appears without the words *bet din* ("tribunal"), and there are many differences of opinion as to its meaning. *See id.* at 159, concerning *ḥaliẓah* before *hedyotot*, and at 158–161, regarding a number of additional matters.

68. On the differences of opinion as to the meaning of this term in connection with various laws, *see* ET, *supra* n. 67.

69. According to Gulak, *Yesodei*, IV, pp. 32–33, lay tribunals began to function in the era after the Bar Kokhba rebellion, as was also true of arbitration. On the other hand, Alon, *Toledot*, I, p. 139, asserts:

> There were lay courts, whose members were not ordained scholars, but who were appointed by the public, *i.e.*, by the local authority, to judge. These were called *gimmel benei ha-keneset* (a three-member panel). These courts were connected with the municipal administration, and served as a continuation of the body that existed before the destruction of the Temple (and in the time of the Second Temple) and was called *mishpat ha-edah* (the communal court). Sometimes these judges were chosen from among the strong-armed and violent men of the towns; and their judicial activities did not have the consent of the Sages, nor were they in the spirit of the Torah.

See further Alon, *Toledot*, II, p. 79; *id.*, *Meḥkarim*, II, pp. 15ff.; M Bekhorot 5:5; H. Albeck, Hashlamot, Kodashim, Bekhorot pp. 390–391.

of the Jewish judicial process at the time of the *tannaim,* Gedaliah Alon has accurately observed:[70]

> It is clear that these courts [the lay courts] too should be regarded as a national resource. Indeed, even the halakhic tradition of the *tannaim* acknowledges them. On the other hand, one should not ascribe to them, even to a small extent, the same national and spiritual significance as courts consisting of halakhic authorities. Because a lay court is only local and *ad hoc,* it cannot provide the basis for a uniform and comprehensive national judicial system. This type of adjudication actually constituted a hindrance to the crystallization of a comprehensive national judicial system. When the Sanhedrin and the *Nasi* (Patriarch, or President of the Sanhedrin) set about establishing a national judicial system, they had to contend with these local courts and were forced to acquiesce in their existence (just as in the case of courts of arbitration), although they apparently attempted to draw the local courts into the sphere of influence of the Sages and of the central authorities.

These observations, in both aspects, are not only pertinent for the period of the *tannaim,* but are also fundamentally correct for all the later periods in the history of Jewish adjudication. Nevertheless, at the explicit initiative of the halakhic authorities themselves, lay tribunals frequently performed the function of protecting and guarding Jewish juridical autonomy.[71]

From the teachings of the *amoraim,* we learn that they approved of a court of three laymen for civil cases, so long as one of the three is *gamir, i.e.,* has learned rules and laws from the scholars and judges,[72] and the other two, though not possessing even this minimum qualification, are able at least to understand what is explained to them.[73] The grant of authority to a court of three laymen was justified as a *takkanah* enacted in order to assure the existence of an ongoing forum—even in the absence of a court of judges expert in Torah law—"in order to prevent doors from being closed to borrowers" (*i.e.,* in order to remove a deterrent to the granting of credit).

70. Alon, *Toledot,* II, pp. 78–79.

71. *See infra* pp. 27ff.

72. TB Sanhedrin 3a and Rashi, *ad loc.,* s.v. De-gamir; the qualification required to be a judge is that he be both *gamir* (learned) and *savir* (astute, or as Rashi, Sanhedrin 5a, s.v. Savirna, puts it, "able to contribute original insights and to weigh critically the considerations involved in reaching a decision"). *See also Sema,* Sh. Ar. ḤM 3, subpar. 2. According to other authorities, all three need to be *gamir,* but none need be *savir—see Tur* ḤM 3:1 in the name of Ramah.

73. TB Bekhorot 37a: "That when the law is explained to them they understand." It is reasonable to assume that this requirement also obtains with regard to the three laymen referred to in TB Sanhedrin 3a; and this is the view stated in *Ḥiddushei ha-Ran, ad loc.,* s.v. I efshar de-leika.

As stated, the jurisdiction granted to the three lay judges included all civil law matters,[74] but excluded criminal law.[75] The lay court was also given the power to compel the appearance of the parties before it.[76] The institution of the three-judge lay court became accepted as an essential part of Jewish law at all subsequent times.[77]

The goal of preventing the resort to non-Jewish courts and of protecting Jewish juridical autonomy motivated the halakhic authorities in the post-Talmudic period to permit the appointment of three laymen to function as a court, even if none of them was *gamir,* in a locality where even the minimal requirement that the court include one *gamir* could not be met.

An interesting responsum of Rashba (Solomon b. Adret), the great halakhic authority and leader of Spanish Jewry in the thirteenth century, sheds light on this important change and on the social context that brought it about.

Rashba was asked the following question by Jacob ibn Kadsheff of Toledo:[78]

> Please respond: In regard to the dictum that whoever appoints a judge who is not worthy is as if he has planted an *asherah* [a tree or grove involved in idol worship],[79] what are we to do in the towns where no one knows even one letter and yet we must give to such people the power to make decisions binding on parties to a dispute, for if we do not do so, the people will go to

74. TB Sanhedrin 3a: "Admissions [of debt] and [ordinary cases of] debt." *See also Piskei ha-Rosh, ad loc.,* #1 ("and this applies also to a wife's *ketubbah,* matters of inheritance and gifts . . . in order to shut the door to an evildoer, to the end that he may not rely on the chance that his adversary will not find expert judges"); ET, III, pp. 155ff., s.v. Bet din.

75. TB Sanhedrin 3a. In the course of time, criminal cases also came under the jurisdiction of lay tribunals. *See* the discussion *infra.*

76. *Piskei ha-Rosh,* Sanhedrin, ch. 1, #2; *Tosafot,* Sanhedrin 5a, s.v. Dan afilu yeḥidi; *Tur* ḤM 3:2; Sh. Ar. ḤM 3:1; *see also* ET, III, p. 156, s.v. Bet din, where other views are cited.

77. *Tur* and Sh. Ar. ḤM 3:1. *See also Ḥiddushei ha-Ran* to Sanhedrin 2b, s.v. U-ve-din hu de-liba'ei mumḥin, where he questioned how TB Gittin 88b, which states that cases can be judged "before them [*i.e.,* ordained judges] but not before laymen," could be reconciled with the conclusion reached in TB Sanhedrin that three laymen are qualified to judge. He resolved the difficulty by saying that the response of R. Joseph in the passage in Tractate Gittin (to the question, "What is the authority of a Jewish court in Babylonia to adjudicate inasmuch as the judges were not ordained and are therefore only *hedyotot?*"), namely, "We carry out their commission" (*i.e.,* the Babylonian court is authorized by the halakhic authorities in the Land of Israel), also explains the enactment by the Sages to permit litigation before three laymen: in each instance, jurisdiction is delegated by the competent authority. It should also be pointed out that a lay tribunal differs from a court of experts in that if the former errs, it must pay compensation for the loss caused as a result of the error. *See* TB Sanhedrin 6a; *Tur* ḤM 25:1; Sh. Ar. ḤM 25:3.

78. *Resp. Rashba,* II, #290.

79. TB Sanhedrin 7b.

> the non-Jewish courts and violations of the law will abound. . . . It is the practice in this city to send the elders of the city to appoint elders in other places to adjudicate civil and criminal cases. Should we consent to this or not?

Rashba responded:

> In strict law it is not possible, except with the consent of the parties, to appoint judges who are not experts. . . . Therefore [if such judges must be appointed], you must appoint them—even though they are not expert—according to the needs of the time, with the consent of the townspeople, and may all your actions be for the sake of Heaven. . . . And in any case, one must search out worthy men who fear God, abhor injustice, and can understand instruction. For criminal cases, such judges must be admonished to obtain the approval of the elders of your city so that they will act only when strictly necessary and then only after the most careful deliberation. . . . In the final analysis, it is all for the sake of Heaven and to eliminate evil from among you, inasmuch as you have seen that it is a matter of necessity. You, as a God-fearing man, will lead the others.

Social conditions in towns near Toledo placed the halakhic authorities of Toledo in a painful dilemma: whether to maintain a Jewish court system in those towns even though it was impossible to organize even a lay court that satisfied the requirement that at least one of the judges be *gamir,* or whether, in this particular situation, it would be better to make use of non-Jewish courts rather than maintain a system that, in any case, would not be based on *Halakhah,* since none of the judges knew the *Halakhah.* In order to preserve Jewish juridical autonomy, Rashba ruled that the choice should be made in favor of adjudication by a Jewish court, whose decisions would be made by upright and honest men according to their deliberation and understanding of the circumstances of each case. This ruling applied to both civil law and criminal law, except that Rashba admonished that in criminal cases, such judges should act with even greater caution and deliberation.[80]

80. The halakhic-legal rationale for the competency of a lay tribunal of judges who know absolutely nothing of Torah law is based on Rashba's characterization of the judicial institution *arka'ot she-be-Suria* ("the courts in Syria"), mentioned in TB Sanhedrin 23a, by which is meant Jewish judges who do not know Torah law and hence cannot judge according to the *Halakhah.*

Regarding such judges, it is stated in the name of the Sages, who differed with R. Meir, that a litigant cannot declare them disqualified "for it does not rest with him to reject a judge whom the public has accepted." Consequently, Rashba said with regard to the concrete case before him, "It is permissible for the townspeople to accept [the laymen] over them, and if they do so, none can reject them, for they are the equivalent of *arka'ot she-be-Suria.*"

This explanation of the term is also implied in Rashi's comment, Sanhedrin 23a, s.v. Be-arka'ot she-be-Suria, that "they were not conversant with Torah law." This is also im-

Echoes of the existence of lay courts, as a consequence of this social reality, can be heard again about 150 years later in the previously men-

---

plied by Ran to Sanhedrin, *ad loc.* (ed. Jerusalem, 1958, p. 43a), who comments: "Courts in Syria, composed of idlers [*yoshevei keranot,* lit. "those who sit on street corners"] who are not fit to judge because they are ignorant, but the townspeople chose them as judges over themselves." Likewise in *Yad Ramah, ad loc.,* s.v. U-mefarkinan ke-de-amar R. Yoḥanan: "In the courts in Syria who[se judges] were not conversant at all." Similarly in TJ Sanhedrin 3:2, 14a (3:2, 21a) where *arka'ot she-be-Suria* are contrasted with courts that adjudicate according to Torah law: "Resh Lakish said: 'This statement was made [only] with regard to *arka'ot she-be-Suria,* but not with regard to courts that adjudicate according to Torah law.' R. Johanan said: '[The statement applies] even to courts that adjudicate according to Torah law.'" *See also Resp. Maharam of Padua* #43:

> It is the courts in Syria (of whom it is certain that all three [judges] are idlers and none of them has learned or heard anything from the Sages) that constitute the subject of the dispute between R. Meir and the Sages. Since they were appointed and they at least had experience in judging, the Sages allowed them to judge; they may perhaps be regarded as persons whom the litigants have accepted over themselves, since they were appointed to sit as judges.

The commentator who went furthest was Meiri in *Bet ha-Beḥirah* to Sanhedrin, *ad loc.* (ed. Sofer, p. 78): "The courts in Syria were not versed in Torah law but judged according to their discretion as well as [general] law and usages," *i.e.,* not only did they not judge by the law of the Torah, but they followed other laws and usages! He went on to say (p. 79), "He [*i.e.,* such a judge] is one of those whom the public accepted when he was selected through the political process, as we have explained with regard to 'the courts in Syria.'"

See also Ḥazon Ish, Sanhedrin 15:4, who held that it appears from the Talmud that a judge of "the courts in Syria" is "a judge who rules according to the laws of the Torah, but is disqualified because of the paucity of his knowledge of the Torah and his propensity to err." The majority of *rishonim,* as we have seen, did not explain the Talmudic discussion in this way. As to the further remarks of *Ḥazon Ish* that "the courts in Syria" were not permitted to adjudicate according to established legal principles, but only according to their personal estimate of the case, it would appear that Meiri's opinion was to the contrary, for he emphasized that they judged not only on the basis of their personal estimate of the case, but also on the basis of settled and accepted rules and usages.

See also Gulak, *Yesodei,* IV, p. 27 and n. 7, who considered "the courts in Syria" to be a judicial institution of the non-Jewish government, comprised of Jewish judges not conversant with Torah law. Gulak's argument from the term *arka'ot,* which implies established courts rather than *ad hoc* arbitrators, is not convincing, as it is possible that these courts were established lay tribunals but nevertheless a Jewish institution. *See also* Alon, *Meḥkarim,* II, p. 30, stating that the term "the courts in Syria" refers to Jewish courts. *See also id.* at 46.

As far as the final halakhic ruling is concerned, Rashba—and apparently also the other *rishonim* whom we have mentioned—saw in the institution a source for the existence of lay tribunals, none of whose members is learned and who rule according to their discretion and perhaps also according to other nonhalakhic laws and usages. The basis for their halakhic legitimacy is the consent of the parties to a case, who may waive disqualification of judges, as in the case where they agree that "my father or your father is acceptable to me" (TB Sanhedrin 23a). Indeed, the acceptance of the lay tribunal carries more weight than consent by the parties, because it is an acceptance by the public, "which an individual cannot retract or annul." *Cf. Resp. Rashba Attributed to Naḥmanides* #65; *see also* Naḥmanides, *Commentary on Exodus* 21:1. *See also infra* p. 1915 and n. 46; pp. 1181–1182, quoting *Resp. Ri Migash* #114, and p. 736 n. 221 for Rashbeẓ's opinion on the subject of appointing and appearing before judges who are not conversant with the law.

tioned enactments that were adopted at the synod of the representatives of the Castilian communities in 1432 at Valladolid.[81]

The second section of those enactments, dealing with the selection of judges and other officials, begins as follows:

> WHEREAS, in the abundance of our sins and the weight of our transgressions, there are fewer scholars and masters of Torah and faith who are worthy of acting as judges according to the Torah, to the point that only rarely will there be communities (may God guard and protect them) in the kingdom in which can be found a court of three who are fit to judge in these times according to the laws of the Talmud; and
> WHEREAS, our forefathers (may they rest in Eden) were therefore compelled to go beyond the law of the Talmud in selecting judges; and
> WHEREAS, if there are no judges in each community empowered to adjudicate claims, quarrels, and complaints and to punish transgressors, each man would swallow his neighbor alive, there would be wholesale transgression and perversion of the law, and the everlasting covenant would be nullified; for the world depends on three things—on justice, on truth, and on peace—and where there is no true Torah, there is no peace, there is no civility, and there is no social tranquility;
> THEREFORE, we have ordained and agreed that each and every community shall select judges to decide these cases, as has been said, and the members of the community shall accept them; but they shall select the most fit and worthy that they can obtain and that can be found in the locality, for the Torah is emphatic in its admonition in this regard. Because judgment is the Lord's, man does not judge for himself but for God, Who is his partner in judging. And it is also stated: "You shall not show partiality in judgment," which is an admonition not to appoint a judge who is not worthy. And the intent of every man or group that selects these judges should be for the sake of Heaven without any falsehood, deceit, or collusion; and whoever appoints judges shall select the most fit and worthy that are found in the community for this appointment.

The basic innovation of Rashba became settled law in the *Shulḥan Arukh*. Joseph Caro there stated:[82]

> It is a violation of a negative commandment to designate a judge who is not worthy, not knowledgeable in the Torah, and not fit to be a judge, even if he has a winning personality as well as other good qualities. . . .

On this point, Moses Isserles (Rema) added to Caro's statement:

81. *See supra* p. 8. *See also* S.W. Baron, *The Jewish Community,* II, pp. 70–73.
82. Sh. Ar. ḤM 8:1, and *see Sema, ad loc.*, subpar. 1.

> It is forbidden to designate an ignorant person as a judge on the supposition that he will always consult a scholar; and in the small towns that have no scholars who are worthy of being judges, or where all of the people are ignorant and there is a need for judges to decide their disputes in order that they will not make use of non-Jewish courts, they appoint those deemed by the inhabitants to be the best and most scholarly among them, even if they are not qualified to be judges. Since the townspeople have accepted them, no one may disqualify them; and every community can accept for itself a court, even though the judges are not qualified according to the Torah.[83]

These halakhic prescriptions with regard to the judicial authority of the various types of courts reflect the historical situation in most of the Jewish centers in the diaspora. It is true that as a general rule a considerable proportion of litigation involving private disputes among Jews, and between individual Jews and the Jewish communal leaders, took place before a court of three judges who were expert in the laws of the Torah and who decided in accordance with those laws. However, alongside these courts, in most Jewish population centers there existed arbitration tribunals and lay courts as established judicial institutions.

Many social and economic factors, as well as the level of knowledge and education, had an influence on the extent to which the lay courts were used. Lay judges are known to us under different names in different population centers.[84] As a general rule, they based their decisions on communal

83. *See also* Rema to Sh. Ar. ḤM 22:1 (end) ("If the public appointed unscholarly judges over themselves as though they were expert, the parties cannot object."); Sh. Ar. and Rema ḤM 3:1 ("Any three men may constitute a court even if they are laymen, for it is impossible that there should not be one among them who knows how to reason about the law; but if none of them has such knowledge, they are disqualified to judge"). *Shakh* (subpar. 3) adds: "However, if the public has accepted them, even three idlers are competent, as stated further on at the beginning of ch. 8 and ch. 22, end of par. 1."

There is a view that since the competence of a court is derived from public acceptance, the members of a lay tribunal accepted by the public are exempt from liability to compensate parties injured by their erroneous decision; and in this respect these judges are in a more advantageous position than a court of three laymen—even if one is a *gamir*—who are not accepted by the public. *See Nimmukei Yosef* to Alfasi at the beginning of TB Sanhedrin: "There is the view that the rule is the same even for idlers if they have been accepted as judges by the community; their judgment stands, and even if they erred they do not have to pay compensation, for it cannot be argued that they were accepted for the purpose of judging according to Torah law, when it was well known that they do not know Torah law." *But see Shakh,* Sh. Ar. ḤM 25, subpar. 15.

84. For example: In Spain—*zekenim* (elders), *tovei ha-ir* (the good citizens of the town), *berurei tevi'ot* (claims arbiters) for civil matters, and *berurei averot* (transgressions arbiters) for criminal matters; in Germany—*tovei ha-ir;* in Poland and Lithuania—*ha-parnasim ha-roshiyyim* (the top leaders), *ha-tovim* (the good citizens), *piskei ba'alei battim* (lay judgments), *et al.;* in Italy—*ha-parnasim ha-memunnim* (the appointed leaders), *anshei ha-ma'amad* (communal leaders).

legislation, mercantile customs, the promptings of their intelligence, their sense of justice and equity,[85] and, at times, even on non-Jewish law in a particular subject area.[86] There were occasions when a lay court, no member of which was a halakhic authority, turned to halakhic authorities for advice and legal opinions.[87] In certain places, specific jurisdictional limits were established, the lay judges being given, in the main, criminal and tax matters. Thus, for example, Asheri observed:[88]

> The custom has spread throughout the Jewish diaspora that a tax delinquent is put in prison and is not brought before a regular court, but the city fathers judge him according to their custom.[89]

In the records of enactments of Lithuania we find the following *takkanah* of 1639:[90]

> The lay communal leaders will have jurisdiction over quarrels and discords, concessions and property rentals, liquor taxes,[91] and fines and punishments; and the communal judges will try monetary disputes. The lay leaders shall not deal with monetary disputes, and the judges shall not involve themselves in matters outside their jurisdiction.

An unusual and far-reaching *takkanah* is found in the record of enactments of the community of Leghorn, Italy, from the year 1670, as follows:[92]

85. *See, e.g., Resp. Rashba,* II, #290, III, #393, IV, #311; *Resp. Rashba Attributed to Naḥmanides* #279; *Resp. Maharshal* #93; *Resp. Rema* #33; S. Toaff, "Maḥaloket R. Ya'akov Sasportas u-Farnasei Livorno al ha-Shipput ha-Otonomi 'ba-Umah ha-Yehudit' be-Livorno bi-Shenat 5441" [Controversy between R. Jacob Sasportas and the Communal Leaders of Leghorn Concerning Juridical Autonomy in the "Jewish Nation" in Leghorn in 1681], *Sefunot,* IX (1965), pp. 170ff. *See also infra* n. 92.

86. *See supra* n. 80 for *Bet ha-Beḥirah* on *arka'ot she-be-Suria. See also* the quotation from the *takkanot* of the Community of Leghorn, *infra* p. 29.

87. *See, e.g., Resp. Asheri* 18:13; *Resp. Zikhron Yehudah* #58; S. Aboab, *Sefer ha-Zikhronot,* Zikkaron 10:3. *See also* Elon, *Ma'asar,* pp. 178–179, 187.

88. *Resp. Asheri* 7:11.

89. *See also* Elon, *Ḥerut,* pp. 131–132.

90. *Pinkas Medinat Lita* [Record Book of the Jewish Communities of Lithuania], ch. 364. For similar provisions in other centers, *see* Assaf, *Battei ha-Din,* pp. 86–88; *see also* J. Katz, *Tradition and Crisis,* pp. 94–95; H. H. Ben-Sasson, *Hagut ve-Hanhagah* [Concept and Conduct], pp. 183ff.

91. The enactment uses the term *orandi* for the rental of properties, concessions relating to taxes, and the like, from the government or from private individuals, and the term *tshapui* for a special tax on trading in wine and in other liquors. *See Pinkas Medinat Lita,* pp. 339–340.

92. On the juridical autonomy of the "Jewish Nation" in Leghorn in 1681, *see* Toaff, *supra* n. 85 at 190–191, par. 3. *See also id.,* Introduction to the *takkanot,* stating that they were enacted "by the authority given by the Torah, by permission of our Sages, and by the privileges granted by our Prince to enact *takkanot. . . .*"

> WHEREAS, many claims and complaints in civil and commercial matters are subject to great delay, causing much loss, due to the fact that the parties often demand to be judged according to the strict rules of [Torah] law without regard to business practices and to the customs of the city and country, whose norms and standards do not always coincide with strict law; and
> WHEREAS, we are concerned that this conflict is bound to lead to unjust decisions because these are transactions that have been structured with reference to general civil and commercial norms;
> THEREFORE, in order to eliminate this impediment as well as other difficulties, we determine, decree, and make known that all commercial transactions that shall be declared to be subject to the legal authority of the communal leaders and their subordinates, even if not specifically mentioned herein, shall be governed by mercantile custom, *i.e.*, the law merchant of this city that we take upon ourselves and affirm as if it were specifically determined to be a law of the Torah, and no further authorization is required; and it is incumbent that this law shall be abided by and carried out, and shall be the basis upon which the officials shall render judgment, even when appeal or arbitration is requested. We likewise declare and order that in all cases, claims, and disputes in the realm of religious or spiritual law that are mentioned below and in all similar matters, it shall be the duty of the officials, the appellate judges, and arbitrators duly vested with judicial authority—even if the parties do not so request—to decide and to judge according to Jewish law and custom. Therefore, they are authorized to refer such cases for decision to those halakhic authorities whom they deem appropriate; and the judgment shall be promulgated by the officials, appellate judges, and arbitrators.[93]

One of the unusual features of this *takkanah* is that it incorporates the entire corpus of a non-Jewish legal system in the area of commercial law and validates it "as if it were specifically determined to be a law of the Torah."[94]

93. The *takkanot* specified what subjects are to be governed by Torah law and what subjects are within the jurisdiction of the communal officials (the meaning of various subject headings is not entirely clear):

> Matters concerning Torah law: *Ketubbot,* as ordered [?], inheritances, divorces; *ḥazakot,* as ordered [?], *kashrut,* security arrangements; interest; spiritual matters pertaining to divine law, wills, gifts. Matters pertaining to the communal officials [*adonei ha-ma'amad*]: Marine and inland trade; purchase and sale of merchandise and jewels; pledges, security arrangements on land and sea; insurance, surrender of *ḥazakah,* damage to ships and cargoes; business records and contracts; commissions and brokerages, sureties, deposits, loans, compromise and settlement; barter [*mir*], confiscation, bankruptcies, business associations, arbitration, preference for judicial resolution of disputes [?].

94. *See infra* n. 104 for the strong opposition by Jacob Sasportas to the provision of this *takkanah* that limits the right of a party to request that his case be judged under Torah law.

G. Criticism of Lay Tribunals by the Halakhic Authorities

We can discern in the text of the Lithuanian *takkanah* differences of opinion between the different courts about their respective jurisdictions. As we saw in Rashba's responsum, the institution of the lay court—which does not contain even one *gamir,* and which does not judge according to the *Halakhah* but rather on the basis of personal evaluation and according to the circumstances—was designed to prevent the resort to non-Jewish courts when no Jewish judges were available who could judge according to the *Halakhah.*[95]

It is probable that, at first, some commercial cases that depended on local customs were submitted to a panel of merchants and professionals; but once this institution was created, it not only struck root even where there were regular courts consisting of judges knowledgeable in the Torah, but it also began to arrogate to itself jurisdiction over various other areas of the law. In many places, as we have seen above, the jurisdiction of these lay tribunals over certain matters was recognized even by the halakhic authorities, especially in new legal situations arising out of the social and economic conditions of the particular place and time.[96]

Not always, however, were the halakhic authorities happy with this parallel system of lay tribunals. Because lay adjudication was not based on halakhic rules, the halakhic authorities, justifiably, saw these courts as a serious threat to the proper development of Jewish adjudication according to the *Halakhah.*[97] In addition, the fact that lay tribunals often reached de-

95. Rashba distinguished between two types of tribunals and called them by different names. In one case, in which Reuben wrote to Simeon that he would sell his shop before a "court (*bet din*) of his choosing," Rashba ruled that the intention was "before a court, one of whose members is *gamir* and *savir* (learned and astute), for otherwise, it would not be called a court but a 'lay tribunal' (*bet din shel hedyotot*)" (*Resp. Rashba,* I, #1010). A "court" (*bet din*) as such, then, is one in which at least one judge knows Torah law; it therefore judges according to the rules of the *Halakhah;* but a tribunal consisting entirely of laymen, which does not judge according to the rules of the *Halakhah,* is called a "lay tribunal" (*bet din shel hedyotot*).

96. *See also Resp. Maharshal* #4, and *Resp. Rema* #33.

97. *See, e.g., Resp. Mahari Weil* #146; the author, Jacob Weil, said to Solomon of Breslau: "If you listen to my advice and abide by it, you will not sit with the public in any case, for you know that the judgments of laymen and of scholars are opposite in character. . . . It is befitting for a scholar not to get involved in the affairs of laymen." *See also Resp. Maharshal* #33, #93.

Mahari Weil's statement was quoted somewhat later in *Resp. Ḥayyim ve-Shalom* (by Ḥayyim Palache of Izmir (Smyrna), middle of the nineteenth century), II, #102 in connection with a decision establishing paternity in the absence of sufficient grounds. *See also* A.H. Freimann, "Mezonot Shel Yeled she-Nolad she-Lo be-Nissu'im al pi Dinei Yisra'el" [Maintenance of a Child Born out of Wedlock, According to Jewish Law], *Ha-Praklit,* II, p. 163 (reprinted in *Ha-Praklit,* XXV (1968), pp. 163ff. at p. 171.)

cisions on a basis other than settled law and doctrine was seen as raising grave risks of favoritism and miscarriage of justice.

A detailed summary of the arguments of these halakhic authorities is found in the writings of the scholar and author, Judah Leib Pohovitzer of Pinsk, in the second half of the seventeenth century:[98]

> The conclusion to be drawn from our words is the greatness of the merit of those who appoint proper judges. They deserve all of the benefits and rewards that are promised for the scholars of the Torah. We refer to the leaders of the communities who for the sake of Heaven accept over themselves rabbis who fear God and who watch over all the activities of the town. . . .
>
> However, our Sages have said that, because of the necessities of the time, a court may impose punishment even when not provided for in the Torah, so long as it is done not to violate the Torah but to safeguard it.[99] On this basis, it became the practice that there be leaders and administrators in every town who give judgments according to the circumstances of the case and in accordance with communal legislation, and these are called lay judgments (*piskei ba'alei battim*). There are also towns without persons who know the Torah, and in order to preclude resort to non-Jewish judges it was permitted to establish a Jewish court even though its members do not know the law.
>
> The practice has persisted over time, throughout many generations, until judging according to the Torah has been forgotten; and even where there are those who know the law, ignorant leaders are chosen as judges in order to pay them honor; and they decide cases according to their own whim and desire, as motivated by feelings of respect, affection, or fear. And one sin brings on another, as this practice causes much controversy among the Jews, since each person wants to lord it over his neighbor and not have his neighbor lord it over him. I have found it written in the name of a halakhic authority, who also was critical of lay judgments, as follows: "In my opinion they are worse than gentile judgments, because the latter have some order or system, but in lay judgments, there is neither order nor system. On the same facts, sometimes they find liability, and sometimes they do not. Sometimes their ruling causes harm intentionally, and sometimes unintentionally." Even those who have mastered the Torah and are well versed in the law, when they sit together with the communal leaders, judge as they wish, contrary to the law of the Torah, and do not hesitate to act as advocates rather than as judges.[100]
>
> I myself have not infrequently seen perverse lay decisions that resulted from bias or prejudice, and the loser cried out: "Isn't this the opposite of Torah

98. *Keneh Ḥokhmah,* Frankfurt-am-Oder, 1681, Sermon on *Dayyanim,* pp. 25–26.
99. TB Sanhedrin 46a.
100. *Cf.* M Avot 1:8.

> law as specifically stated in *Ḥoshen Mishpat?*" When he does so, either no one pays any attention to him, or else he is punished with fines and disgrace because of his protests, and who is there that can tell them what to do? . . .
>
> If we do not repair the breaches that have been opened, they will become even greater than in the past; it is therefore necessary for the outstanding halakhic authorities of our generation to give this matter their attention and promulgate appropriate enactments so that the communal leaders will not depart from Torah law or applicable legislation and will not give judgment without good reason; and only then will God be with them and they will aim to give true judgment. . . .

This description indicates an undesirable development in the existence and conduct of the lay tribunals. The first and major purpose of this institution—the maintenance of Jewish adjudication in a place where there are no judges who know the laws of the *Halakhah*—was thwarted when, in the course of time, this type of court began to compete with courts that judged according to the *Halakhah.* The result was that "judging according to the Torah has been forgotten."

Judah Leib Pohovitzer's chief complaint against the lay courts was that they were not governed by established principles, and there was neither certainty nor predictability in their rulings because they decided "according to their own whim and desire." Their decisions not only reflected bias but also perverted justice and caused much contention. Thus, litigation before Jews deteriorated to a level below that of the non-Jewish courts, which, at least, "have some order or system." Judah Leib Pohovitzer went so far as to condemn those who know the Torah law but who, when sitting with a lay tribunal, "judge as they wish, contrary to the law of the Torah." For this reason, he demanded that cases be considered according to Torah law, or at least according to communal legislation (*tikkunim*), *i.e.,* within the framework of legislative enactments duly adopted and accepted by the community, so that judicial decisions would be based on reasoned and articulated grounds.

These very same arguments were even more pointedly stated about one hundred years later, in the latter half of the eighteenth century, near the end of Jewish juridical autonomy, by one of the great halakhic authorities, Ezekiel Landau, author of *Noda bi-Yehudah:*

> A deterioration of the rule of law has come from two sources, both equally damaging. First, from litigants who bring their claims to laymen and do not wish to subject themselves to the laws of the Torah and refuse to carry out the commandment: "Justice, justice shall you pursue." [Second], from the judges and officials who give lay judgments according to their common sense,

> or out of animosity, or affection, or for similar reasons, or, God forbid, because of bribery . . . . I have not found anyone who has acted courageously as a "man" to give righteous judgment. I have found only that some are men of violence and some are sycophants.
>
> They do not give justice to the orphan, and the complaint of the widow gets no sympathy from them. The few among them who are honest are like a drop in the ocean. And even these are not determined fighters for justice. . . . At times, a court of expert judges sends its messenger to summon a person to court—it has happened that I myself have summoned a party to come to the courtroom—and there is no response, as there is no willingness whatsoever to stand trial.[101]

In another passage he added:

> Do you really think that the verse "Zion shall be redeemed with justice" [Isaiah 1:27] refers to the judgments of laymen, most of which rest on bias or bribery or some other improper interest? It is also said in Scripture [Micah 3:9]: "They abhor justice," *i.e.*, they completely abhor the law of the Torah and say: "The importance of being subject to Torah law has passed." At times even the judgments of non-Jewish courts, which are based on human reason, at least have some measure of justice.[102]

In these reactions to lay adjudication, which to some extent reflect a socially and class-based negative attitude to the powerful leaders and officials who acted as if the community belonged to them, the halakhic authorities attempted to limit the spread of lay adjudication beyond what was acceptable and desirable. They tried to minimize the damage done to the development of a judicial system based on Jewish law, and they feared, apparently not always unrealistically, that an adjudicatory system that is not based on legal principles is subject to deterioration, perversion of justice, and the exploitation of the weaker segments of society. This type of controversy, which is typical wherever parallel judicial systems exist, should not obscure the fact that the grant of specific judicial authority to lay Jewish judges and the existence of this authority in the majority of the Jewish population centers during most historical eras were brought about and perpetuated essentially to provide an important supplementary means of preventing resort to non-Jewish courts and to safeguard Jewish juridical autonomy, in the broad sense of this concept.

101. *Derushei ha-Ẓelaḥ,* Sermon #3, par. 12–14.

102. *Id.*, Sermon #8, par. 10. *See also infra* n. 104 for the vigorous opposition of Jacob Sasportas to limiting the right to adjudication under the laws of the Torah.

H. The Basic Distinction between the Various Forms of Jewish Adjudication on the One Hand and Adjudication by Non-Jewish Tribunals on the Other

Samuel Aboab, one of the leading rabbinical authorities in seventeenth century Italy, accurately and concisely described the essence of Jewish juridical autonomy in its various qualities and aspects, as follows:[103]

> The majority of Jews in all places of their habitation, according to all that we have heard and seen, and according to the clear evidence of their writings, establish judges for themselves after obtaining the consent of the king or government (may their glory be exalted), one or more in every town, according to its size; and to them are brought all disputes in the community, and according to their word is judgment given as between man and his neighbor, and in this way the people live in peace.
>
> There are a few places where the lay leaders appointed to govern the community act as judges, having been accepted as such; and sometimes, depending on the subject, they confer with the rabbi who teaches Torah there and request his opinion on a particular question, this act being commendable and indicating a quality of humility and fear of sin,[104] and there are occasions when the option is given to the respective parties to choose an arbitrator; and sometimes when they appear before the leaders and high-ranking officials, and these judges see that the case may be protracted for more than a day or two, the judges themselves give permission for each party to choose an arbitrator within a specified time to judge between them. All of these methods and similar ones are conducted according to the Torah, although one may be superior to another.

103. Samuel Aboab, *Sefer ha-Zikhronot,* Zikkaron 10:3, on law and the judicial process.

104. This statement of Aboab about localities where chosen lay leaders are judges and at times take counsel from the rabbi who disseminates Torah among them fits well the situation with regard to Jewish adjudication in the Leghorn community in that era. (For details *see* I. Tishbi, "Iggerot R. Ya'akov Sasportas Neged Parnesei Livorno mi-Shenat 5441" [Letters of R. Jacob Sasportas against the Communal Leaders of Leghorn in 1681], *Kovez Al Yad,* XIV, Mekizei Nirdamim, Jerusalem, 1946, pp. 145–159; Toaff, *supra* n. 85 at 169–191. *See also* Assaf, *Battei ha-Din,* p. 90). This community gained wide judicial autonomy in civil matters and, to a certain extent, also in criminal matters (Toaff, p. 170). The judges were the elected heads of the community, and they adjudicated a considerable portion of civil litigation according to general mercantile practices or their ideas of justice. They were required to judge certain other civil, family, and religious matters in accordance with the *Halakhah,* for which they sought the opinion of the rabbis (*id.* at 170ff., 190–191; and *see supra* pp. 28–29). In enactments of that period, various regulations were promulgated that limited the right of a litigant to have his case judged by the laws of the Torah. These regulations provoked bitter opposition from Jacob Sasportas; among those who sought to bring peace between the disputants was Samuel Aboab (Tishbi, *supra* at 145ff.; Toaff, *supra* at 169ff.).

> But surely, those who in some places openly use the non-Jewish courts are acting directly contrary to the Torah, are publicly profaning the name of Heaven, and will be held accountable for this action in the Final Judgment.[105]

Aboab's description of the various types and forms of Jewish autonomous adjudication is extremely instructive. One may postulate (and it is apparent from our short survey up to this point) that in each particular place and time one of the forms of decisionmaking listed by Aboab was accepted and practiced more than any other—depending upon the extent of knowledge of the Torah, the relationship between the lay leaders and the halakhic authorities, and the social conditions of the place and time. And it is undoubtedly true that, from the point of view of the effectiveness of Jewish adjudication and its development, not all the methods were of equal value: "One may be superior to another." However, as expressed by Aboab, the common denominator was that "all of these methods and similar ones are conducted according to the Torah," since they maintain and guard Jewish juridical autonomy; those few places that have made use of non-Jewish courts profane the name of Heaven, act against the Torah, and undermine the existence of Jewish adjudication.

Aboab expressed the religious-national viewpoint of the people's spiritual and lay leaders and of the people at large in all of the long periods of exile and dispersion. They recognized that the uniqueness and independence of Jewish adjudication provided the basis for and guaranteed the preservation of the individuality and indivisibility of the people;[106] and it was this primary goal that caused them pointedly to reject any resort to non-Jewish courts. Indeed, their approach and attitude proved to be justi-

105. This essential distinction between adjudication by lay tribunals—in all their forms—in which Jewish judges sat, and courts in which non-Jewish judges sat in judgment, was also clearly laid down in the *Shulḥan Arukh.* Sh. Ar. ḤM ch. 8 deals, *inter alia,* with Jewish judges who do not judge according to the *Halakhah,* and sets forth all the rules on that subject. In Sh. Ar. ḤM ch. 26, the matter of non-Jewish courts is discussed and the special stringency of the prohibition against litigating before them is emphasized. The criticism of the lay tribunals by the halakhic authorities (and, as we have seen, there was such criticism) was directed against lay judgments that did not accord with the *Halakhah;* such judgments diminished the vitality of the *Halakhah,* served as a means to exploit the weak and the powerless, and had no fixed system of procedure. However, these courts were never equated to non-Jewish courts, resort to which was considered blasphemy, rebellion against the Torah, and an undermining of the distinctiveness and unity of the Jewish people. *See also infra* p. 1915 and n. 46.

106. Moreover, the quality of Jewish adjudication, the expeditiousness of the litigation, the minimal court costs, and the fairness of the judges were cited from time to time as reasons for preferring Jewish adjudication to non-Jewish adjudication. *See* Assaf, *Geonim,* pp. 20–23; *id., Battei ha-Din,* pp. 13–17, 20; for an instructive responsum in this connection, *see Resp. Ḥavvot Ya'ir* #136.

fied when the Emancipation brought in its wake an increasing resort to non-Jewish courts—one of the principal causes of the diminution, to the point of virtual disappearance, of Jewish law as a practical force in the real world. This subject is discussed in greater detail in chapter 41.

I. The Legal-Political Viewpoint of the General Government, and the Economic-Social Relationship between the Jewish Community and the Government

The religious-national character of Jewish law and the deep-seated recognition that strict and vigilant protection of this asset is a guarantee of the continued existence and unity of the Jewish people were, as stated, the major and determinative factors in making Jewish law a practical force in the everyday life of the Jewish people, even during exile and dispersion. But the question must still be faced: How was it possible to maintain an autonomous Jewish court system in a sovereign country of another people? Moreover, what induced the general government to respond positively to the request of the Jewish community within its territory for Jewish juridical autonomy?

The answer is found in the second factor mentioned at the beginning of our discussion, namely, the political and legal concepts of government and adjudication accepted up to the eighteenth century, and the economic and social relationship between the government and the various groups, including foreigners, who lived within the territory subject to the government's control. The legal system was based upon an individual's group affiliation, and the state recognized the varied judicial systems of the different groups that lived within it. The state made no demand for centralization. It was a corporate state comprising various autonomous groups, such as the nobles, the burghers, the guilds, and others, who often competed with one another, and sometimes even competed with the central government. In fact, the Jewish group was often the object of competition between the different groups and classes and the central government. Under these political-legal conditions, a Jewish autonomous body possessing its own independent judicial system was able to survive.

The willingness of the general government to grant this autonomy to the Jewish group rested on various considerations: a certain measure of tolerance toward other religions, and motivations based on philosophical, theological, and, especially, economic considerations. The central government and the various classes and groups among whom the Jews lived and sought protection saw it as their "duty" and prerogative to impose heavy taxes on the Jews in return for the privilege of residence and habitation. Collecting these taxes from each individual, especially as the Jews were reckoned to be a foreign people, involved many difficulties, such as the likelihood of tax evasion and similar problems.

Consequently, the government found it convenient to levy taxes on the Jewish community as a whole. To facilitate this practice, the community was empowered to become an autonomous, corporate entity, whose leaders were responsible for raising from the community as a whole the total sum due, which the appropriate institutions within each community would then collect from their individual members. Furthermore, the existence of an autonomous Jewish public body enabled the government to issue directives to and conduct negotiations with the recognized leaders of this body about other governmental prerogatives and responsibilities.[107] "Jewish self-government existed by the will of the Jews, but also owed much to compatible external conditions and factors that favored its existence."[108]

Thus, the will and devotion of the Jewish people to safeguard its religious-national law was reinforced by external conditions and factors that made possible the fulfillment of that desire. In this way, the Jewish people was enabled to preserve its law as a living and functioning system, and its courts faithfully accompanied the people through all its migrations and dispersions.[109]

107. For specific instances, *see infra* pp. 745–746, citing *Piskei ha-Rosh*, Bava Batra, ch, 1, #29 and *Resp. Rashba*, V, #270.

108. H.H. Ben-Sasson, *Perakim be-Toledot ha-Yehudim bi-Mei ha-Beinayim* [Chapters in the History of the Jews in the Middle Ages], p. 91. For additional details on juridical autonomy, the legal-political conditions, and the fiscal-social causes for the granting of Charters of Privileges and juridical autonomy to Jewish groups in the countries of the diaspora, *see* Ben-Sasson, *supra* at 35–53; *id.* (ed.), *Toledot Am Yisra'el* [History of the Jewish People], II, *Toledot Yisra'el bi-Mei ha-Beinayim* [History of the Jews in the Middle Ages], pp. 110–170; Baer, *Spain, passim;* B.Z. Dinur, *Yisra'el ba-Golah* [Israel in Diaspora], I(1), pp. 61–189, I(2), pp. 152–206, II(1), pp. 225–278, II(2), pp. 313–505; J. Katz, *Tradition and Crisis,* chs. 2 and 10 (pp. 11–17 and 91–102); *id., Exclusiveness and Tolerance,* pp. 48–63; J. Mann, "Sekirah Historit le-Dinei Nefashot ba-Zeman ha-Zeh" [Historical Survey of Contemporary Law on Capital Cases], *Ha-Ẓofeh le-Ḥokhmat Yisra'el,* X (1926), pp. 200–208; Z. Hirshberg, *Toledot ha-Yehudim be-Afrikah ha-Ẓefonit* [History of the Jews in North Africa], I, pp. 161–170; Kisch, *Jewry-Law in Medieval Germany,* 1949, pp. 139ff.; J. Parkes, *The Jews in the Medieval Community,* 1938, pp. 101–207; S.W. Baron, *The Jewish Community,* I, pp. 157–374, II, pp. 208–245; Otto Stobble, *Die Juden in Deutschland während des Mittelalters* [The Jews in Germany during the Middle Ages], 3rd ed., 1923, pp. 140ff.; R. Schroeder, *Lehrbuch der Deutschen Rechtsgeschichte* [Textbook on the History of German Law], 6th ed., 1922, pp. 245, 505ff.; J.E. Scherer, *Die Rechtsverhältnisse der Juden in der Deutsch-Österreichischen Ländern* [Legal Relationships of the Jews in the German-Austrian States], 1901, *passim;* Finkelstein, *Self-Government,* pp. 6ff.

109. At this point, at the conclusion of our account of Jewish juridical autonomy, it is appropriate to direct the reader to another problem which arose as a consequence of that autonomy, namely, the problem of jurisdiction over claims between a Jew and a non-Jew. On this subject, *see* M. Balaban, *Bet Yisra'el be-Folin* [The Jews in Poland], I, pp. 58–59; Dinur, *supra* n. 108; S.W. Baron, *supra* n. 108, I, at 191, 228, 240, 249–251, 272, 277–280, 296–298, 330; II, at 48, 116; J. Parkes, *supra* n. 108 at 249–250; Kisch, *supra* n. 108 at

J. Summary

We conclude our discussion of Jewish juridical autonomy with the words of Yehezkel Kaufmann on the significance of that autonomy in Jewish history:

> The common feature of the autonomy in the diaspora, as in the Land of Israel, was the aspiration to live according to Jewish law. Throughout the generations of the exile, this aspiration was the firm basis for this autonomy. It was born, as we have seen, out of the ideal of a life according to the Torah. Judaism, which knew only of religious law, did not recognize secular pagan law. Integral to the desire to live according to the Torah was the desire to live according to Torah law. For this reason, throughout the generations of exile, the Jewish people aspired to juridical autonomy. It was essentially legal independence that made the Jewish community not merely a religious community but also a separate national political entity.
>
> The acknowledgment given by the non-Jewish government to the right of the Jews to be judged under their own law had an enormous significance. First of all, it resulted in the Torah's being a sort of political constitution even in the lands of exile. The study of Torah had high social value. The scholars of the Torah were looked up to as dignitaries and leaders, and the academies where the Torah was studied were highly regarded by the whole people. Furthermore, the Jewish community became recognized to a large extent as a distinct political group. Juridical autonomy is what made the Jewish nation in the diaspora truly "a state within a state."
>
> This unique privilege that the premodern state (pagan, Christian, and Moslem) granted to the Jews of the diaspora was indeed an exceptional phenomenon, in that the Jews almost always lived in gentile cities and possessed no right of urban self-government. Nevertheless, the type of autonomy granted to Jewish communities was feasible in the premodern state because that state was based on a corporative legal order: there was no single general law applicable to everyone alike. Various social classes had different rights, as did different cities and towns. The state recognized distinct bodies of law, each applicable to a different citizen-group. It was therefore also able to recognize the special law of the Jewish "corporate body." For this reason, the modern nation-state [being based on a different principle] has no room for Jewish juridical autonomy. . . . [110]
>
> This autonomy derived from the yearning of the nation to realize in its life, to the maximum possible extent, the ideal of the Torah. It was, in particular, the consequence of the desire to carry out Jewish law, the law of the

---

185ff.; J.E. Scherer, *supra* n. 108 at 171ff. *See also* J. Katz, *Exclusiveness and Tolerance*, pp. 52–53; M. Elon, EJ, V, pp. 882–890, s.v. Conflict of laws (reprinted in *Principles*, pp. 715–723).

110. Y. Kaufmann, *Golah ve-Nekhar* [Exile and Estrangement], 1962, I, p. 518.

Torah, and to organize internal Jewish life on that basis. Hence, the autonomy that formerly existed was fundamentally a juridical autonomy.[111]

III. THE DIFFERENT PERIODS OF JEWISH LAW

As has been pointed out, the history of Jewish law extends over a period of more than three thousand years. We divide this immense period[112] into two broad periods, each of which, in turn, is subdivided further as appropriate.[113]

A. The Two Broad Periods

The first broad period begins with the written Torah and ends with the completion of the Talmud. The second broad period is the post-Talmudic period, from the completion of the Talmud until our own day.

What is the rationale for making the Talmud the dividing line between these two major periods? First, we must make clear and emphasize that this division between the Talmudic *Halakhah* and the post-Talmudic *Halakhah* has no significance at all so far as continuity and development of the *Halakhah* are concerned. As mentioned earlier, the *Halakhah* not only kept on developing continuously after the Talmud was completed but even became, in most of its subject areas, more prolific, and richer in literary expression. What makes the Talmud distinct as a watershed in the history of Jewish law is its character as the authentic source of Jewish law and the attitude of the entire Jewish people toward the *Halakhah* as expressed in the Talmud and its literature. The enormous body of normative laws formulated and contained in the Talmudic literature was received in the Jewish world as the accepted elaboration of the Oral Law, beyond contest or reconsideration:

> Everything in the Babylonian Talmud is binding on all Israel . . . [as agreed to] by the entire Jewish people.[114]

111. *Id.*, II, at 312.

112. As will be seen *infra*, these general divisions and subdivisions are based on various historical and practical considerations. However, one should not exaggerate the extent of precision in the division into periods, since each period is intertwined with the ones preceding and following it.

113. At this stage in our discussion, we will outline only broadly the division into periods and give a general description of each period. Later, we will return to the subject and discuss various details of these periods. *See* the notes on each individual period in section III of this chapter and the relevant headings in the subject index.

114. Maimonides, *MT*, Introduction. *See also infra* p. 1099.

The Talmud is the cornerstone and foundation, the starting point for all study and deliberation in every area of the *Halakhah* in the post-Talmudic period. Of course, at the highest level of the value scale of the *Halakhah,* in all periods, is the written Torah—the divine revelation at Sinai which contained within it "all the niceties of Biblical exegesis, the interpretations of the *Soferim* (Scribes) and all the new interpretations that the *Soferim* would later derive."[115] Until the literary sources of the *tannaim* were compiled and edited (and to a certain extent even until the entire body of Talmudic literature was completed), the written Torah was the source on which the judges based their decisions and into which the Sages delved. As the Talmudic literature became complete, the written Torah continued to be the "constitution" of Jewish law, but the Talmudic literature—the Mishnah, the halakhic *midrashim,* the *baraitot,* and the Talmuds—became the exclusive sources for deriving the *Halakhah.* Halakhic authorities taught their disciples, and judges decided cases, exclusively on the basis of the Talmudic literature. They no longer directly consulted the written Torah to solve problems as they arose.

The law contained in the Talmudic literature is binding because of the very fact of its inclusion as part of the compilation of the literature of Talmudic *Halakhah,* and the halakhic authorities do not go behind it to earlier sources in order to satisfy themselves as to its authenticity. This special status was preserved for Talmudic law even after the *Halakhah* was augmented, during a period of more than 1500 years, by a substantial literature that in scope, arrangement, and facility of use is superior to the literature of the Talmud itself. The primary and authoritative source for any halakhic rule and its analysis is the Talmud and its literature.

There is yet another reason why the completion of the Talmud is a watershed. During the period of the Talmud, Jewish law developed and established its sources for further growth and its procedures for ongoing creativity, all of which set the pattern for the law's continuing creativity and development in the post-Talmudic period. During the Talmudic period, the *Halakhah* established and developed the characteristic patterns, the methods of reasoning, and the forms of expression of halakhic legal thought.

B. The Division of the Two Periods into Subperiods

The two broad periods that we have discussed should be further divided, both for pertinent historical reasons and for convenience of research and study, into a number of subperiods.

115. TB Megillah 19b; TJ Pe'ah 2:4, 13a (2:6, 17a).

1. The first broad period is traditionally divided in the literature of Talmudic research into the following parts:
   a. *The Biblical period to Ezra and Nehemiah (to approximately the middle of the fifth century B.C.E.).*[116]
   b. *The period from Ezra and Nehemiah until the Zugot ("Pairs") (to approximately 160 B.C.E.).*[117] It has been customary to call a significant part of this period by the name given by Nachman Krochmal, "the period of the *Soferim*."[118] Recently, however, strong objections have been made against the use of the term *Soferim* to designate the authorities of only this period, as there is no support for such a limitation either in the Talmudic sources or elsewhere.[119]
   c. *The period of the Zugot (from 160 B.C.E. until the beginning of the common era).* This period is given this name because of the five *Zugot* who were acknowledged to be the leaders of the nation and the primary halakhic authorities of the period. Their names are recorded in the first chapter of Tractate *Avot* and the second chapter of Tractate *Ḥagigah*. The Sages known to us from the Talmudic literature to have immediately preceded the *Zugot* were Simeon the Just, who was one of the last of the Men of the Great Assembly (*Anshei Keneset ha-Gedolah*) and Antigonus of Sokho,[120] from the city of Sokho in Judea.[121] The last of the *Zugot* were Hillel and Menahem, although Menahem served for only a short time: "Menahem departed and Shammai entered."[122] The first in each pair was as a general rule the *Nasi* (Patriarch, or President of the Sanhedrin) and the second was the *Av Bet Din* (the Vice-President of the Court, lit. "father of the court"). Hillel was the *Nasi*, followed by his son, Simeon, who was followed in turn by his son, Rabban Gamaliel the Elder.
   d. *The period of the Tannaim (from the generation of the destruction of the Temple until 220 C.E.).* In this period, five generations of *tannaim* were active, beginning with Rabban Simeon b. Gamaliel and his generation and ending with R. Judah Ha-Nasi, who arranged and edited

116. *See infra* pp. 190–223, 308–309, 550–554.

117. *See infra* pp. 309–314, 554–558.

118. *See* Nachman Krochmal (1785–1840), *Moreh Nevukhei ha-Zeman* [Guide for the Perplexed of the Time], ed. Rawidowicz, pp. 56, 194.

119. *See* Y. Kaufmann, *Toledot ha-Emunah ha-Yisra'elit* [History of the Jewish Religion], IV, Book 1, pp. 481–485; E.E. Urbach, "Ha-Derashah ki-Yesod ha-Halakhah u-Va'ayat ha-Soferim" [Exegesis as the Foundation of the *Halakhah* and the Problem of the *Soferim*], *Tarbiz*, XXVII (1958), pp. 172ff.

120. M Avot 1:2–3.

121. *See* Joshua 15:35, 48; *and see infra* p. 1043.

122. M Ḥagigah 2:2. *See also infra* pp. 314–316, 558–562, 1043.

the Mishnah. The generation after him, which included R. Ḥiyya Rabba (the elder) and his contemporaries, was the generation of transition from the period of the *tannaim* to the period of the *amoraim*. The end of this period saw not only the compilation of the Mishnah, the codificatory work of R. Judah Ha-Nasi, but also compilations of halakhic *midrashim* and *baraitot*.[123]

e. *The period of the Amoraim (from 220* C.E. *until the end of the fifth century* C.E.*)*. In this period there were five generations of *amoraim* who were active in the Land of Israel (until the end of the fourth century C.E.) and seven generations in Babylonia. This was the period that produced the two Talmuds—the Jerusalem Talmud and the Babylonian Talmud.[124]

f. *The period of the Savoraim (to the end of the sixth or the middle of the seventh century* C.E.*)*. The end of the seventh generation of Babylonian *amoraim* marked the transition to the period of the *savoraim*, which extended to the end of the sixth century, or, according to some scholars, to the middle of the seventh century C.E. The *savoraim* had two main activities: (a) they completed the editing of the Babylonian Talmud and (b) they formulated principles for determining the law when there is a conflict of authority.[125]

2. The second broad period, the post-Talmudic, is traditionally divided into the following subperiods:

   a. *The period of the Geonim (from the end of the savoraic period until approximately 1040* C.E.*)*.[126] This period is so described because the title *gaon* was the official designation of the heads of the academies of Sura and Pumbedita in Babylonia during that time. For most of the period, the academies in Babylonia still constituted the spiritual center for the entire Jewish people; and complete legal authority was accorded by most Jewish communities to the opinions and responsa of the *geonim*. The ambition of the *geonim*, which they succeeded in accomplishing, was to establish the Babylonian Talmud as the authoritative source of the *Halakhah* for the entire Jewish people. Those *geonim* whose names are best known are: Yehudai; Amram; Saadiah; Samuel b. Ḥophni; and Sherira and his son, Hai. In this period, others

123. *See infra* pp. 1041–1082.

124. *See infra* pp. 1083–1100.

125. *See infra* pp. 1093–1094.

126. In the East, the geonic period extended until the end of the thirteenth century, and throughout that century there were still *geonim* at the head of the academies of Sura and of Pumbedita. *See* S.D. Goitein, *Sidrei Ḥinnukh bi-Mei ha-Geonim u-Vet ha-Rambam* [Educational Systems from the Geonic Period to Maimonides], p. 12, n. 2. *See also id.* at 12–21, for a detailed description of this period.

who were not officially titled *gaon* were also active, such as Aḥa of Shabḥa, author of the *She'iltot,* and Simeon Kayyara, author of *Halakhot Gedolot.*[127]

At the end of the geonic period, two of its leading authorities, Sherira Gaon and his son, Hai, were in office. However, the position of Babylonia as the authoritative center for all Jews had begun to wane. Its ties with the centers of Torah that arose in North Africa and Spain had weakened, and these communities no longer made it a practice always to refer questions of *Halakhah,* or matters of Torah generally, to the academies in Babylonia. The causes for this were internal to Babylonia, such as the disputes between the academies of Sura and Pumbedita, as well as external, such as the refusal of the Omayyad caliphs of Cordoba, Spain, to allow the Jewish inhabitants of their land to be associated with the academies in Babylonia, which were within the area of control of the Abbasids. In the middle of the eleventh century C.E., the historical phenomenon of a single spiritual center for the entire Jewish diaspora came to an end; and from that time, each of the various centers turned for guidance to its own leaders and teachers. Although some communication continued between the different centers, and from time to time great leaders arose whose rulings were accepted as binding by more than one of the centers, the unifying hegemony of one single center ceased; and this fact had far-reaching consequences on the manner in which Jewish law developed.[128]

An additional circumstance which characterized the geonic period was that it inaugurated the division of the literary sources of Jewish law into the three categories that still exist today: commentaries and novellae, responsa, and codes.[129]

b. *The Rabbinic Period.*[130] The rabbinic period followed the period of the

127. *See infra* pp. 1099, 1106, 1113–1114, 1130–1132, 1149–1167, 1468–1473.

128. Samuel ha-Nagid, in his elegy upon the death of Hai Gaon, states that with Hai's departure, "the Jews of Babylonia, North Africa, and Spain have become equal." *Diwan Shemu'el ha-Nagid, Ben Tehillim,* ed. Dov Yarden, Jerusalem, 1966, p. 235. *See also infra* pp. 489, 666–675, 1167–1168, 1473.

129. *See infra* p. 1102.

130. For "rabbinic period" as the name of the post-geonic period, *see Sefer ha-Kabbalah* of Abraham ibn Daud, in A. Neubauer, *Seder ha-Ḥakhamim ve-Korot ha-Yamim* [Medieval Jewish Chronicles], Oxford, 1895, facsimile ed., Jerusalem, 1967 (hereinafter, *Seder ha-Ḥakhamim*), I, p. 73: "The generation of these three—R. Hananel, R. Nissim, and R. Samuel ha-Levi ha-Nagid—was the first generation of the rabbinate [*ba-rabbanut*], when the power of the Talmud returned to Spain and there were there five rabbis, all named Isaac. Two of them were natives of Spain, the third [came from] close by, and two came from another country." One of these five was Isaac Alfasi (Rif). *See also id.* at 78: ". . . three generations of the rabbinate [*ba-rabbanut*]."

geonim. From the perspective of Jewish law, the rabbinic period is divided into three parts:

(i) *The period of the Rishonim (Early Authorities—from the eleventh century until the sixteenth century* C.E.*)*. This period ended with Joseph Caro (author of the *Shulḥan Arukh*—the "Set Table"), who was among the exiles from Spain, and Moses Isserles ([Rema], author of the *Mappah* ["Tablecloth"]—glosses on the *Shulḥan Arukh*), one of the leading halakhic authorities of Polish Jewry. In this period of the rabbinic era, the classic works of all three types of literary sources of Jewish law were produced: commentaries and novellae, responsa, and codes.[131] The beginning of this period coincided with the beginning of the great flowering of the Spanish center, and the period ended with the disappearance of the center in Spain and the rise of new centers elsewhere, mainly in the Land of Israel, the Turkish Empire, Poland, and Lithuania.

(ii) *The period of the Aḥaronim (Later Authorities—from the time of Joseph Caro and Rema until the beginning of the Emancipation in the latter part of the eighteenth century)*. This period continued to produce the three types of legal literature of the previous era of the *rishonim,* but the major concentration was on the responsa literature, which, quantitatively, now reached its high point. This period also produced a considerable number of collections of communal legislation. These enactments took root and developed mainly in the prior period of the *rishonim,* but the major literary record of them in the form of compilations dates from the period of the *aḥaronim.*[132] The period ended with the great turning point in the development of Jewish law, namely, the advent of the Emancipation of the Jews and the loss of juridical autonomy.

(iii) *The period from the end of the eighteenth century to the present.* This last period is divided into three subperiods:
  (a) From the end of the eighteenth century until the beginning of the twentieth century, *i.e.,* from the time of the loss of juridical autonomy until the period of the Jewish "national reawakening."
  (b) From the beginning of the twentieth century until the establishment of the State of Israel.
  (c) From the establishment of the State of Israel to the present.

131. *See infra* pp. 1106–1108, 1115–1127, 1167ff., 1473–1482.
132. *See infra* pp. 1482–1491, 1525–1527.

The course of the history of Jewish law underwent a radical change from the time Jewish juridical autonomy began to disappear. As a result of this change, many problems arose that were new and completely different from those that had confronted Jewish law before the end of the eighteenth century. For this reason, it is appropriate to discuss this entire period since the eighteenth century separately, in Volume IV of this work.

Chapter 2

THE DEVELOPMENT OF JEWISH LAW: SOME IMPORTANT FACTORS

I. Development in the Various Areas of the Law
II. Creativity in Halakhic Literature as a Reflection of Practical Application
III. Public Leadership as a Creative Factor in the Jewish Legal System
A. The King's Law
B. Jewish Government in the Land of Israel and the Diaspora
C. Local Jewish Self-Government
D. Lay Adjudication
IV. The Relationship Between Jewish Law and Non-Jewish Law
A. Reciprocal Influences Between Jewish Law and Non-Jewish Law
B. *Dina de-Malkhuta Dina* ("The Law of the Land Is Law")

I. DEVELOPMENT IN THE VARIOUS AREAS OF THE LAW

In Chapter 1, we discussed the first significant characteristic of Jewish law fundamental to an understanding of Jewish legal history, *i.e.*, that Jewish law in all of its periods, even after the exile of the nation from its land, was a living law, operative and practiced in the daily life of a juridically autonomous Jewish society. The second important characteristic, namely, the continuous and ongoing nature of the development of Jewish law, follows from the first and is fundamental to an appreciation of the essential quality of Jewish law. Jewish law, as a living and practical law, necessarily partook of the distinctive character of every living thing, namely, continuous development—which may be apparent and recognized as its different stages occur, or hidden and unrecognized as it proceeds, and clearly discernible only after the fact and from the perspective of history. Since the function of law is to provide solutions to problems of everyday life, in every time and place, law, like any other living creation, constantly changes as it reflects the life to which it relates.

The practical need to use Jewish law and Jewish courts brought about continuous creativity and development in the Jewish legal system. Social conditions and economic life continually changed from period to period; and, under the particular conditions affecting the life of the Jewish people, there were also social and economic differences among the various places of the diaspora. Even when the Jewish people had a political center and, later, a single spiritual center, there were various Jewish settlements throughout the diaspora. Geographical dispersion began to show its effects with particular force at the end of the tenth and the beginning of the eleventh century C.E., when the Babylonian center, which had dominated the entire diaspora, declined, and many other centers arose throughout the breadth of the Jewish dispersion, some concurrently and some successively. The new centers included North Africa, Spain, Germany, France, Italy, Turkey, Egypt, the Balkans, Poland, and Lithuania.

Of course, the halakhic authorities in all centers invoked and interpreted the same Talmudic and rabbinic sources, and in many instances there was both oral and written communication between the various centers. However, the radical transformation wrought by the fragmentation of one single center into many local centers, and the consequent enormous differences in the economic and social conditions of the various Jewish centers, necessarily led to substantial development of the Jewish legal system. Local variations in Jewish social, commercial, and economic life, in patterns of community organization, institutions, and government, and in relations with the non-Jewish environment and the general government all frequently produced legal problems. For some of these problems there was no clear solution in existing Jewish law, and for others it was necessary to find a new and different solution from the one traditionally applied.

This constant creativity existed primarily in all aspects of civil law but also to a substantial degree in the area of criminal law—the precise extent depending on the degree of autonomous criminal jurisdiction possessed by any particular Jewish center.[1] Particularly instructive is the enormous creativity that developed in the area of public law. In contrast to the public law of the previous periods that established the legal relationship between the people and the individual national leader such as the king, the *nasi,* or the exilarch, the new legal situation encompassing the community and its des-

1. *See Teshuvot ha-Rabi Av Bet Din* [Responsa of Abraham b. Isaac of Narbonne], ed. Kafaḥ, Jerusalem, 1962, #149, pp. 128ff., and S. Assaf, *Sifran Shel Rishonim,* pp. 42–44; *Resp. Rashba,* III, #393; Judah son of Asheri in *Resp. Zikhron Yehudah* #58; *Resp. Ritba* #131. In general, *see also* Maimonides, *MT,* Sanhedrin 24:4–10; *Tur* and Sh. Ar. ḤM ch. 2; Assaf, *Onshin, passim;* J. Ginzberg, *Mishpatim le-Yisra'el* [Laws for Israel], *passim;* Elon, *Ma'asar,* pp. 171–201. *See also infra* pp. 515–519, 688–698. For details on the subject of creativity and development in the field of criminal law, both substantive and procedural, *see* Nagar v. State of Israel, 35(i) *P.D.* 113, 163–170 (1980). M. Elon, EJ, XII, pp. 109ff. at p. 134, s.v. Mishpat ivri (reprinted in *Principles,* pp. 5ff. at p. 29), may give the erroneous impression that development and creativity ceased in Jewish criminal law. The discussion there requires revision.

ignated and representative institutions generated an elaborate system of public and administrative law. This body of law covered, for example, the relation between citizens and the public authority; relations between the public authority and its employees; the composition of communal institutions; the method of electing and appointing officials of communal institutions and other public officials; the procedure for communal legislation and the legal administration of communal agencies; the procedure for tax assessment and collection; and many other aspects of the economic and fiscal relationships in the community.[2] Geographical dispersion and the consequent proliferation of many local statutes and customs also led to considerable development in Jewish law in the field of conflict of laws.[3]

The development that took place in the various institutions of Jewish law throughout its long history was generated, as stated, by various economic, social, and political causes.[4] How does Jewish law absorb these changes and developments and make them an integral part of its legal corpus? What are the legal methods that it uses to harmonize the existing law with the newly created law? As in all legal systems, these methods constitute the legal sources of the law—in Jewish law, the sources that the halakhic system itself recognizes as instruments to create and develop the *corpus juris* of the Jewish legal system. The second part of this volume and all of Volume II of this work will be devoted to a detailed examination of these sources.

It is indeed obvious to anyone who studies the *Halakhah* that it is a gigantic seamless web containing old and new elements, sources, and in-

2. For details, *see infra* pp. 681ff., 745ff., 920ff.; M. Elon, EJ, XV, pp. 837–873, s.v. Taxation (reprinted in *Principles,* pp. 662–701); EJ, XIII, pp. 1351–1359, s.v. Public authority (reprinted in *Principles,* pp. 645–654); EJ, VIII, pp. 279–287, s.v. Hekdesh (reprinted in *Principles,* pp. 701–708). For a detailed discussion of creativity and development in Jewish administrative law, *see* Lugasi v. Minister of Communications, 36(ii) *P.D.* 449, 467–470 (1981).

3. *See* M. Elon, EJ, V, pp. 882ff., s.v. Conflict of laws (reprinted in *Principles,* pp. 715–723).

4. It cannot always be said that the development of Jewish law involved forward movement in all its institutions. Even in other legal systems, which had the benefit of healthy and organic development under circumstances including a sovereign state and geographical concentration in a single place, development of the law did not always mean progress; so it is not surprising that in Jewish law, which subsisted without political independence and in many different geographical concentrations, there are to be found at times—in one era or another and in one center or another—legal institutions that did not advance the overall legal system (*see, e.g.,* Elon, *Ḥerut,* pp. 238ff., 264). Jewish law as a living, operative legal system was called upon to react to the social, economic, and moral changes that occurred in every place and time, and being so called upon, it solved the problems as they arose in consequence of these changes. At times it was influenced by the social conditions of the environment in which it operated. In the course of time, principles that were essentially alien to it were discarded. *See id.*

terpretations, all intertwined with each other without any attempt at separation by historical period—as if in fact as well as in theory the web is all of one piece. The halakhic authorities justifiably saw it as their legal and practical duty to unify and blend together the results of various halakhic eras into one single body of settled law and not to isolate one stage from another or one period from another for separate treatment.

This point of view is legitimate and accepted in all legal thought, especially under a legal perspective that sees existing law as the essential starting point for any new law. This, for example, was the way the bulk of English law was created and developed. Nevertheless, well understood as this phenomenon is, it should not preclude the scholar, using a dogmatic-historical (sometimes referred to as analytical-historical) approach for the study of each institution in the Jewish legal system, from distinguishing the various stages of development through which the institution has passed.

Moreover, in following the various stages of development and examining the legal methods through which these developmental changes became incorporated into Jewish law, one can perceive that even the halakhic authorities themselves often discerned, and even stressed, the changes that occurred in the course of development of one or another institution in the Jewish legal system. The halakhic authorities emphasize the origin or the establishment of a new stage in the *Halakhah* not only when they make use of legislation (*takkanah,* which by its very nature changes or adds to existing law) as a legal source but even when a different legal source, such as interpretation (*midrash, parshanut*), is the basis for their conclusion.[5]

In this way, Jewish law continued to develop, connected and intertwined with practical circumstances and problems that it regulated and by which, in turn, it was shaped. Facing the halakhic authorities and the communal leaders was a twofold mission: On the one hand, they had a constant concern for the continued creativity and development of Jewish law; on the other hand, they felt a great responsibility to preserve the spirit, objectives, and continuity of that law.[6] Their success in accomplishing this twofold task of reaching legal solutions grounded in the past yet meeting the many needs of the contemporary generation is apparent to the student of

5. For details, *see* Elon, *Ḥerut,* Preface, p. XII, and pp. 261–264. *See also infra* pp. 80ff.

6. A study of the various stages of development of the legal institutions of Jewish law reveals that through all the various changes in a given legal institution the central concept constituting the basis of that legal institution was always preserved. This central concept is the common denominator of all the various stages and changes through which that legal institution passed in the course of its history. The identification of such central concepts calls for comprehensive and thorough research into each and every legal institution in every era. For further discussion, *see* Elon, *Ḥerut,* Preface, pp. XII-XIII, and pp. 255ff. *See also infra* pp. 80ff.

the history of Jewish law in every era, both when the Jewish people possessed political independence and during the long period when they lacked political sovereignty—but enjoyed juridical autonomy—in the Land of Israel, in Babylonia, and in all the lands of Jewish dispersion.

Obviously, in the long history of Jewish law, there were periods of rise and decline, of increasing and decreasing use of the legal sources for the purpose of carrying on the creation and development of Jewish law. The level of use of the legal sources depended at any given time upon the extent of the learning and scholarly attainments of the halakhic authorities and the communal leaders, and upon the extent to which Jewish law was actually applied in real life situations so as to generate the need and desire to create and develop it in order to satisfy the requirements of particular times and places. Indeed, when these conditions were met—and they were met in the overwhelming majority of the periods and the places of Jewish exile—and when the leaders of the people worked in cooperation with the masters of Torah and *Halakhah,* and Jewish law both in theory and in actuality was a living law applied in practice, these legal sources developed the *corpus juris* of the Jewish legal system in the same manner as legal sources develop the *corpus juris* in every living and operative legal system that develops continuously in the course of experience and application in actual life.

It is indeed instructive that in those places where the attachment to Jewish law weakened and the people's use of Jewish courts decreased, Jewish legal creativity declined. In this connection, Maimonides wrote to Phinehas, the *dayyan* (judge) of Alexandria:[7]

> All the Jews who live in the cities of the Christians, even the great scholars among them, do not have expert knowledge of the laws, because they do not customarily use them, inasmuch as the Christians do not permit them to judge [by Jewish law] as the Ishmaelites do; and when a case comes before them, they take more time than they should. They are unable to master the matter until they have engaged in a long search through the Talmud, as we must do today with regard to a law concerning animal sacrifices, since we do not engage in them, whereas at the time when animal sacrifice was actually practiced, everyone was expert in them, just as those who live among the Ishmaelites, including even students, are knowledgeable with respect to legal decisions that have been a regular part of their experience.

Samuel Aboab voiced similar sentiments as he chastised the Jews of seventeenth-century Italy for litigating in non-Jewish courts:

7. *Koveẓ Teshuvot ha-Rambam ve-Iggerotav* [Compilation of Responsa and Epistles of Maimonides] (hereinafter, *Koveẓ ha-Rambam),* Leipzig, 1859, I, #140 (p. 26).

> There is another disadvantage in it [the use of non-Jewish courts]. It impedes the learning of Torah and raises their [the gentiles'] stature. Wherever cases are adjudged according to the law of the Torah, the daily run of cases will produce the kind of deliberation befitting for legal rules that will be applied in practice . . . . In this way, the law emerges clear and polished; and every day thus brings many new and precise laws, and concerning that kind of dispute between litigants it can be said that it is for the sake of Heaven . . . .
>
> The books of responsa that were published in these places testify to this; and we know truly from reliable witnesses that there are more of them unpublished because of the lack of financial resources and the absence of an available printing press than have been published.[8]

Making use of the Jewish court results both in the creation "every day . . . [of] many new and precise laws" and in the proliferation of books of responsa, *i.e.*, development and creativity in the substance as well as the literature of the law. Indeed, Italian Jewry, among whom the resort to non-Jewish courts was usual, is relatively poor in creativity in Jewish law as compared, for example, to Polish Jewry, which seldom resorted to non-Jewish courts and which developed an extensive and wide-ranging creativity in the corpus of Jewish law and its literature.

II. CREATIVITY IN HALAKHIC LITERATURE AS A REFLECTION OF PRACTICAL APPLICATION

As stated, Aboab emphasized that the use of Jewish courts not only produces continuous creativity and development of the *corpus juris* of the Jewish legal system, but also brings with it the growth and expansion of literary creativity in Jewish law. Indeed, this phenomenon is basic to the creation of halakhic literature in every era.

Volume III of this work is devoted to a careful examination of the authoritative literary sources of the *Halakhah*.[9] For the purpose of our present discussion, it suffices to point out that even a cursory examination of the topics with which the literature of Jewish law has dealt during its various periods will reveal that the segment of the *Halakhah* used in actual practice produced incomparably more halakhic literature than was devoted to the part of the *Halakhah* not applied in practice.

8. S. Aboab, *Sefer ha-Zikhronot*, Zikkaron 10:3. *See* Assaf, *Battei ha-Din*, p. 13, who explains that the reference was to the Jews in Poland, where at that time there were few and inferior publishers as compared to Italy, which had a good number of excellent publishing houses.

9. *See infra* pp. 1017ff.

As is well known, the Mishnah, which was edited in the Land of Israel by R. Judah Ha-Nasi at about 200 C.E., is divided into six "Orders" (*sedarim;* sing. *seder*), each of which deals with one main branch of Jewish law, and all of which together comprise the entire *corpus juris* of the halakhic system. However, as early as the major literary source that directly succeeded the Mishnah, namely, the two Talmuds, we note an instructive phenomenon: In the Babylonian Talmud, which was created and developed in Babylonia, there is no Talmud for the Order of *Zera'im* ("Seeds," dealing largely with matters of agriculture, except for Tractate *Berakhot,* which deals with prayer and blessings), whereas, by way of contrast, the Jerusalem Talmud includes an entire Order on this subject. It cannot be doubted that the Babylonian Sages as well as the Sages of the Land of Israel learned and taught all of the six Orders of the Mishnah, and their discussions are extensively recorded in the tractates of the other Orders. However, the fact that no Babylonian Talmud was composed for the Order of *Zera'im* is explained by the nature of the laws covered in that Order, namely, *mizvot ha-teluyot ba-arez* ("precepts dependent upon, *i.e.,* directly relating to, the Land [of Israel]"), such as the sabbatical year, the "corners" of the field (set aside for gleanings by the poor), and the first fruits, all of which had no practical application in Babylonia and were therefore studied there only as a matter of theory. On the other hand, the Jerusalem Talmud, redacted in the Land of Israel, where these laws were applied in everyday life, did include the Order of *Zera'im.*[10]

In the period after the Talmud, the major part of literary creativity in the *Halakhah* centered on "the laws that apply at this time," *i.e.,* those branches of the *Halakhah* that were actually practiced—not the law dealing

10. *See* I. Halevy, *Dorot ha-Rishonim* [lit. "The Early Generations"—A History of the Oral Law to the *Geonim*] (hereinafter, *Dorot*), II, pp. 524–525:

> But the matter is thus: all that was compiled and edited was handed down to us and was preserved by the whole people in exile. But the tractates that have no practical application in our times were not compiled or edited, hence we possess nothing of them.

To the same effect *see* M. Mielziner, *Mavo la-Talmud* [An Introduction to the Talmud], pp. 60–61, which also gives the reasons why the Order of Kodashim was redacted even though its laws have had no practical application since the destruction of the Temple. *See also* TB Zevaḥim 44b-45a:

> R. Naḥman said in the name of Rabbah b. Avuha who said in Rav's name: "The law (*halakhah*) accords with R. Eleazar's ruling in the name of R. Yose [in a matter relating to Temple sacrifices]." Said Rava: "[Do we need] a *halakhah* [for the days of] the Messiah? . . . Why do we need to settle the law [now]? . . ."

See also Rashi, *ad loc.,* s.v. Hilkheta li-meshiḥa and s.v. Amar leih hakha ka amina. *See also* I.H. Weiss, *Dor Dor ve-Doreshav* [lit. "The Generations and Their Interpreters"—A History of the Oral Law], 6th ed., Vilna, 1915 (hereinafter, *Dor Dor ve-Doreshav*), III, pp. 204–206. As to the other tractates for which there is neither Babylonian nor Jerusalem Talmud, *see* Halevy, Mielziner, and Weiss, *supra;* Z. Frankel, *Mevo ha-Yerushalmi* [Introduction to the Jerusalem Talmud] (hereinafter, *Mevo*), pp. 45ff.

with the Temple or with ritual purity, or the law applicable only in the Land of Israel. The creation and growth of halakhic literature generally goes hand-in-hand with the actual use of the *Halakhah*. At times, even study itself is confined to those Orders that are of practical relevance, namely, *Mo'ed* (Festivals), *Nashim* (Family Law, lit. "Women"), and *Nezikin* (lit. "Torts," which includes civil and criminal law). In addition, the tractates of the other Orders of the Talmud which include "laws that apply at this time" were designated for study together with *Mo'ed, Nashim,* and *Nezikin*. Menaḥem Meiri, in the thirteenth century, provided evidence to this effect in his introduction to his work, *Bet ha-Beḥirah:*

> It has been customary to study only three Orders, namely, *Mo'ed, Nashim,* and *Nezikin,* and the other three—*Kodashim* [Consecrated Things], *Tohorot* [Ritual Purity], and *Zera'im* [Seeds]—have been completely neglected, with the rare exception of "one from a city or two from a tribe" [lit. family], because of the virtual absence of any need in these times to know them and because of the great complexity of their subject matter.
>
> Because of this, it was deemed advisable in the days of the *geonim* to remove from the three Orders not regularly studied those tractates felt to be at least as important to know as the tractates of the three Orders that are habitually studied, if not more so. These [tractates from the Orders not regularly studied] are Tractate *Berakhot* (Blessings) (from the Order of *Zera'im*), which was inserted in the Order of *Mo'ed;* Tractate *Ḥullin* [Non-Holy Things] (from the Order of *Kodashim*), which was also inserted in the Order of *Mo'ed;* and Tractate *Niddah* [Menstruant Woman] (from the Order of *Tohorot*), which was inserted in the Order of *Nashim*. In this way, the arrangement of the tractates in those three orders was changed at the time of the *geonim*.[11]

In the period of the *geonim,* many monographs were written on various halakhic subjects, most on matters of clearly civil law, and some on matters of religious law; but almost all of them cover laws that were used in actual practice. These monographs were written primarily for practical reference in the courts throughout the Babylonian diaspora.[12]

This concentration on laws with practical application also occurred in two of the branches of halakhic literature in the post-Talmudic period, namely, the codificatory literature and the responsa literature, and to a certain extent even in the third branch, the literature of commentaries and novellae. Isaac Alfasi included in his Book of Laws (*Sefer ha-Halakhot*) only "laws that apply at this time" and did not include, for example, laws in the Order of *Kodashim* (except Tractate *Ḥullin,* which deals with laws that are

11. *Bet ha-Beḥirah,* Berakhot, Jerusalem, 1960, Preface, p. xxxii.

12. *See also* S.D. Goitein, *Sidrei Ḥinnukh bi-Mei ha-Geonim u-Vet ha-Rambam* [Educational Systems from the Geonic Period to Maimonides], Jerusalem, 1962, pp. 155–156; *infra* p. 1166.

still applicable, such as laws relating to animal slaughter and the dietary laws). The only one who did not follow this approach is Maimonides in his Code, called *Mishneh Torah* or *Yad ha-Ḥazakah.* Maimonides attempted to restore the situation to its "pristine glory" and included in his code all areas of Jewish law, even matters of faith and theology, which he formulated as laws. However, this effort was never repeated; and every code thereafter, such as the code of Asheri, the *Sefer ha-Turim,* and the *Shulḥan Arukh,* followed the method of Alfasi and included only "the laws that apply at this time" and that were followed in practice.

The post-Talmudic responsa literature also largely dealt with questions that concerned actual practice; and no responsa literature developed on the subjects of ritual purity or sacrificial offerings. It is obvious why this happened. Questions arose and problems were presented only as a result of practical everyday application of laws, and it was these questions that were brought before the halakhic authorities for solution. However, in the branch of halakhic literature consisting of commentary and novellae, the fields of *Halakhah* that had no application in practice were also treated, although even that type of literature dealt preponderantly with the part of the *Halakhah* that had practical application.[13]

It is undoubtedly true that Jewish law was studied, to a considerable extent, in every age, from a theoretical point of view, by way of study for its own sake, "to magnify Torah and to glorify it"; and a not insubstantial body of literature was written with this objective. However, this type of study and its literary product are of subsidiary value as vehicles for knowledge of Jewish law needed for everyday use in actual life.

III. PUBLIC LEADERSHIP AS A CREATIVE FACTOR IN THE JEWISH LEGAL SYSTEM[14]

The halakhic authorities and the Jewish courts played the central role in the development of the Jewish legal system; but another factor—namely,

13. Such, for example, was the background situation when commentaries and novellae on the Jerusalem Talmud were composed. *See infra* pp. 1130–1132. It is interesting that in recent years, with the great increase in the Jewish population in the Land of Israel, the creation of all three branches of halakhic literature—commentaries, codes, and responsa—on the laws of the Order of *Zera'im* has greatly increased, because these laws again apply in practice.

14. The reference here is to the leaders of the public, such as communal representatives and the like, as governmental authorities. In addition, the people at large had substantial influence in the creation of *Halakhah* through custom acting as the legal source (*see infra* pp. 881–885) and also in the invalidation of enactments by the halakhic authorities by virtue of the principle that no legislation should be imposed upon the public unless the majority are able to conform to it. *See infra* pp. 538–541.

the duly constituted leadership of the people—also operated throughout the history of Jewish law to promote creativity and development. This leadership took various forms in the course of Jewish history, ranging from individual leaders, such as the king, the *nasi,* and the exilarch, to the collective authority of the public in the form of organized communities or groups of communities, acting through their appointed or elected representatives.

A. The King's Law

The fundamental laws relating to kingship in Israel are found in the Torah,[15] in the Book of Samuel,[16] and in other passages in the Bible.[17] The section on kings in Deuteronomy discusses mainly the king's responsibilities and the manner of his rule, and concludes with his obligation to write a scroll of the Torah for himself and to read from it all the days of his life. "Thus he will not act haughtily toward his fellows or deviate from the Instruction (*mizvah,* lit. "commandment") either to the right or to the left."[18]

The Book of Samuel delineates the king's prerogatives and the people's duties to him. The halakhic authorities deduced additional details of royal authority from passages concerning leaders of the people other than kings. For example, the law that a rebel is subject to the death penalty is based upon the statement concerning Joshua: "Any man who flouts your commands and does not obey every order you give him shall be put to death. Only be strong and resolute!"[19] The royal prerogative is extensive, encompassing executive, legislative,[20] and judicial powers[21] and extending not

15. Deuteronomy 17:14–20.

16. I Samuel ch. 8.

17. *See, e.g.,* I Kings ch. 21, the incident involving the vineyard of Naboth the Jezreelite. For a more detailed discussion of this incident, *see infra* pp. 1024–1025.

18. Deuteronomy 17:20. *See also* Maimonides, *MT,* Melakhim 3:1.

19. Joshua 1:18; TB Sanhedrin 49a.

20. *See infra* pp. 486–487. Joshua 24:25 ("On that day at Shechem, Joshua made a covenant for the people and he made a fixed rule for them") is also explained as indicating the legislative authority of the national leader. *See* Naḥmanides, *Commentary on Exodus* 15:25. The Sages regarded Joshua's enactments as part of the body of legislation enacted pursuant to halakhic authority, which is why we have included these enactments among the legislation of the halakhic Sages. *See infra* pp. 551–553, quoting Maimonides' attribution of Joshua's enactments to "Joshua and his court." The enactment of David in I Samuel 30:24–25 could be viewed as an example of the king's law, but it too was classified by the Sages as an enactment based on halakhic authority; *see also infra* p. 554.

21. On the king's judicial power, *see* I Kings 3:16ff.; Jeremiah 21:12. The king's judicial power was sometimes exercised by his delegate (II Kings 15:5; II Chronicles 26:21). The king also had a considerable influence on the legal system since he appointed the High Court judges; *see* II Chronicles 19:8. *See also* Hoffman, *Commentary on Deuteronomy* 17:8–11 (Hebrew trans. p. 323).

only to various fiscal and economic matters directly associated with the administration of the country[22] but also to matters of criminal law when necessary "*letakken ha-olam* [lit. "to improve the world," *i.e.*, for the welfare of society] as the times demand."[23] The king had the right, in certain instances of legislation and adjudication, to depart from the laws as previously established by the *Halakhah*.[24]

Scholars and students of the *Halakhah* have discussed at length the relation between justice under law and the king's justice. Nissim Gerondi (Ran), one of the leading halakhic authorities in Spain, explained the relation between these two aspects of the Jewish legal system as follows:[25]

> It is possible that they [the laws of the Torah] were concerned more with achieving goals on a higher level than social welfare, since we establish a king over ourselves for this latter objective.
>
> But the goal of the judges and the Sanhedrin was to judge the people according to inherently true and righteous law from which the Godly will be infused into us, whether or not the well-being of society will result from it.
>
> Consequently, it is possible that sometimes non-Jewish law may promote social welfare more than some laws of the Torah do. But we are not without recourse because of this, as whatever needs to be done to promote social welfare may be fully accomplished by the king. . . . The function of the judges was to judge only according to the laws of the Torah, which are inherently just, as it is written "And they shall govern (*shaftu*) [which may also be rendered "judge"] the people with due justice (*mishpat ẓedek*)" [Deuteronomy 16:18], and the function of the king was to perfect the achievement of social welfare and to do whatever the times required.

In Ran's view, adjudication according to the *Halakhah* is "on a higher level" and "inherently just," but does not always fulfill the interests of society and the needs of the time. Consequently, non-Jewish systems of law may perhaps solve particular social problems in a more satisfactory manner than the *Halakhah*. Harmonizing the law with current needs and with the social welfare was achieved by means of the king's law. As a result, the

22. Such as the imposition of various taxes, the conscription of men, and the requisition of property as required for war, for national needs, and for the king's own use. Matters in this category are summarized by Maimonides, *MT*, Melakhim ch. 4, and Gezelah va-Avedah 5:9ff.

23. Such as imposing the death sentence on a murderer who for technical reasons (such as deficiency in the interrogation of the witnesses, incompetency of the witnesses to testify, or the absence of a warning) is not liable to the death penalty under strict law. *See* Maimonides, *MT*, Melakhim 3:10, Roẓe'aḥ u-Shemirat ha-Nefesh 2:4.

24. *See also* Maimonides, *MT*, Sanhedrin 14:2, 18:6; Melakhim 5:1–3; and the sources listed *supra* nn. 18ff. On the king's law in general, *see* Simon Federbush, *Mishpat ha-Melukhah be-Yisra'el* [Jewish Governmental Law].

25. *Derashot ha-Ran* #11, p. 75.

Jewish legal system as a whole is not defective because "whatever needs to be done to promote social welfare may be fully accomplished by the king."

Ran's instructive description, which naturally brings to mind the two historical currents in English legal history, namely, common law and equity (although they served somewhat different functions), concluded with an observation of fundamental importance that describes the basic character of all the different forms that the king's law developed in the course of Jewish legal history:[26]

> This is the difference between the judge and the king: The judge is more bound by the laws of the Torah than the king, and because of this the king was cautioned and commanded to keep a copy of the Torah at hand, and thus it was said: "When he is seated on his royal throne, he shall have a copy of this Torah written for him . . . . Let it remain with him . . . . Thus he will not act haughtily. . . ." In other words, since the king sees that he is not bound by the laws of the Torah in the same way as the judge, a strong admonition is necessary that he should not depart from the commandments to the right or to the left and that he should not feel superior to his brethren because of the great power that God gives him.
>
> But the judge does not need all of these warnings, because his power is limited by the law of the Torah, which states: "And they shall judge the people with due justice;" and he is warned that that judgment should not be slanted in any way, as it is said: "You shall not judge unfairly"; and he is admonished not to take a bribe even to give a correct judgment, as it is said: "You shall not take bribes. . . ."

The wide flexibility available in the king's law to deviate from settled *Halakhah* requires extreme care to prevent the king's law from departing from the general policy and basic values of the Torah. As we shall see later, this was one of the central problems in the relation between the halakhic regime and the institution of communal legislation, which, in general, was a later extension of the basic concept underlying the king's law.[27]

26. *Id.* at 76.

27. Another comment of Ran (*id.* at 75) touches on the historical process that led to the fusion of the two functions—judgment by strict law and the king's law—in the Jewish legal system. His view is expressed in the following argument:

> Do not raise an objection against me from the tannaitic text in chapter "Nigmar ha-Din" [TB Sanhedrin 46a; *see infra* p. 515]: R. Eliezer [b. Jacob] says, "I have heard that the court may impose flogging and punishment not prescribed in the Torah—not to transgress the law of the Torah but in order to make a fence around the Torah . . . ." From this passage it would appear that a court is appointed to judge in accordance with the needs of the time [*i.e.*, the court itself is also charged with this function that Ran attributes to the king]. But it is not so. When there is both a Sanhedrin and a king in Israel, the Sanhedrin judges the people solely according to law and does not act beyond this to meet current needs unless the king delegates to it his power in this

B. Jewish Government in the Land of Israel and the Diaspora

The king's law was the first instance of a basic creative and evolving force in the Jewish legal system not resulting directly from the work of the halakhic authorities. The halakhic authorities themselves later conferred such creative power on the various successive forms of Jewish governance that developed throughout Jewish history. With regard to the head of the internal Jewish government in the diaspora, the halakhic authorities established that "the exilarchs in Babylonia stand in place of the king";[28] and they also taught that "the king's law applies at all times [and] in every generation to

---

> respect. However, when there is no king in Israel, the judge combines both powers, that of the judge and that of the king.

Thus, according to Ran, when the Sanhedrin acted to improve social conditions and to respond to the needs of the time when those needs could not be met under strict law, it performed that function under authority conferred upon it by the king and his law; and only when the monarchy ceased were the two functions—judgment under strict law and also under the king's law—united in the regular judicial authorities. Apparently, even after the monarchy ceased, this special function of the king's law continued to exist in the guise of the various forms of leadership that arose afterward in Jewish history (*see* pp. 58–61). Ran's theory of the merging of the two functions is particularly interesting in that it is reminiscent of a similar process toward the end of the nineteenth century, in regard to common law and equity, the two currents in English law mentioned above. Ran went on to provide another solution to the difficulty:

> One may also say that any question relating to the commandments of the Torah—whether the answer depends upon a correct interpretation of the text or requires meeting the special needs of the time—is a question for the court, as Scripture states: "And they shall judge the people with due justice"; but any reform beyond that is entrusted to the king [and] not to the judge. What follows from this is that the judges are appointed to judge the people with due justice. From this flow two benefits: one which is totally perfect, *i.e.*, that the divine blessing will alight [upon the people] and adhere to them, and second, that the [social] fabric is maintained in good order; and if there is a lapse in peace and good order because of a temporary need, it is for the king to make good. Thus, judgment according to law is essentially and for the most part entrusted to the Sanhedrin, and only to a slight extent entrusted to the king.

However, it is difficult under this theory to determine the line between, on the one hand, "the needs of the time" and "maintaining the [social] fabric in good order," which are entrusted to the court, and, on the other hand, "any reform beyond that," which is entrusted to the king.

28. Maimonides, *MT*, Sanhedrin 4:13, following TB Sanhedrin 5a. *See also* Rashi, *ad loc.*, s.v. Shevet, "that they have authority to expropriate property." *See further* Maimonides' commentary to M Bekhorot 4:4. *See also* Gulak, *Yesodei*, IV, pp. 27–28, and M. Baer, *Rashut ha-Golah be-Vavel bi-Mei ha-Mishnah ve-ha-Talmud* [The Exilarchy in Babylonia in the Period of the Mishnah and the Talmud], esp. pp. 57ff. Baer is of the opinion (pp. 87–91) that the court of the exilarch made no greater use of Persian law than did the courts of the Talmudic Sages. It should be remembered that the exilarch, like the king and the Jewish government in general, was vested by the law itself with the power to deviate from the rules fixed by the *Halakhah*, even in judicial matters; and it is reasonable to assume that the exilarch exercised this power.

the leaders of the time in their respective countries."[29] The following statement of Abraham Isaac Kook, the Chief Rabbi of the Land of Israel in the early part of the twentieth century, concerning the authority of the Jewish government in the Land of Israel in our days, is instructive:[30]

> When there is no king, it would seem that because the king's law concerns the general condition of the nation, the king's law-making prerogatives revert to the nation as a whole. . . . In regard to whatever concerns the governance of the public, whoever leads the nation governs according to the king's law, which encompasses the totality of the needs of the people at any time for the general security.

> The authority of the king was given to the exilarchs in Babylonia.[31]

> *A fortiori,* the duly constituted leaders of the nation, whatever their caliber, when the nation is in its own land and under its own government . . . are certainly not inferior to the exilarchs in Babylonia. . . . He [the leader] certainly stands in the place of the king with regard to the king's law, which concerns the leadership of the public.[32]

29. *Bet ha-Beḥirah,* Sanhedrin 52b (ed. Sofer, p. 212):

> You already know that capital cases may be tried only when the Temple exists and when the Sanhedrin regularly sits there in its appointed place, as it is written [Deuteronomy 17:9], "you shall appear before the priests . . . and the judge . . . ," [from which we derive] that when the priesthood [functions] there, judgment may take place, but when there is no priesthood, there is no judgment. On the other hand, the king's law applies at all times; in every generation the leaders of the time—those preeminent in their respective countries—are authorized to impose sanctions and [even] capital punishment in the ways we have described by legislation as may be exigent.

30. *Mishpat Kohen* #144 (ed. Jerusalem, 1937, p. 337), in a detailed responsum to Zalman Pines.

31. *Id.* at 337–338, which adds:

> Those who have been chosen for the position of general or countrywide leadership of the nation, such as the Hasmonean kings and heads of state, are certainly not inferior to the Babylonian exilarchs; hence no Scriptural verse was needed to include the exilarchs, who actually descended from Judah and the House of David, as is pointed out in *Tosafot,* Sanhedrin 5a, s.v. De-hakha, citing TJ, except to make clear that even in exile they occupy the place of a Jewish king. So when a leader of the people is chosen to be responsible for all its needs after the manner of a king, with the consent of the public and the court, then he assuredly stands in the place of the king as to the laws of the state with regard to matters of general administration.

32. The legal rationale given by various later authorities for the source of the binding force of the king's law was that this binding force flows from an agreement between the people and the king, under which the people yield up to the king their prerogatives in all matters falling within the king's law, while the king obligates himself to preserve and protect the people. This rationale applies to every form of government, and certainly to one chosen by the people, such as the Jewish communal governments in later periods. The notion of a contract between the people and the king as the basis for the authority of the king's law apparently developed under the influence of the accepted medieval theory of popular con-

C. Local Jewish Self-Government

Legislative creativity in Jewish law was also found in the local units of Jewish governance. There is evidence to this effect in halakhic sources as early as the initial part of the era of the second Temple, which discuss certain legislative authority vested in the townspeople. From these modest beginnings, there later developed a rich and extensive corpus of legislation by the autonomous governing bodies of local Jewish communities and the regional organizations of communities and countries. This body of communal legislation, which encompassed every field of civil, criminal, and public law, especially from the tenth century C.E. onward, is reviewed in detail in Volume II of this work.[33] In a manner similar to what we have seen with regard to the king's law, it was possible for communal legislation to be inconsistent with various particulars of the *Halakhah;* and the halakhic authorities established various ways of ensuring that these enactments would

---

sent as the basis of the validity of the king's laws. The same theory has also been cited by various halakhic authorities as the basis for the principle of *dina de-malkhuta dina* ("the law of the land is law"). *See infra* p. 66. This concept is also found in Maimonides, *Sefer ha-Mizvot,* Affirmative Commandment #173: ". . . as the people of Israel declared concerning themselves: 'Any man who flouts your commands . . .' [Joshua 1:18]." *See also Derashot ha-Ran* #11, pp. 75–76. This theory is extensively discussed in Z.H. Chajes, *Torat ha-Nevi'im,* ch. 7, "Din Melekh Yisra'el" [Law of the King of Israel], 46b/47a:

> [A]ll the laws of kingship are only a matter of contract between the king and the people; both sides have agreed to these terms. The people have agreed to yield up their wealth and property for the common good, to the end that there be but one spokesman for the generation, who will lead them and fight their wars. It is also essential that in time of war he should be able to break through fences to gain passage across privately owned fields. When necessary, he is permitted to use the property of another to save his own life, for the king encompasses the entire nation and the welfare of the state depends on him. Even matters that affect merely his prestige are also for the general benefit of the people. He is permitted to conscript their sons and daughters when necessary for administering his state, even with regard to a matter affecting merely his prestige. If his kingdom is graced with all manner of pomp and majesty, this enhances the general welfare and produces vast benefits, for he will be feared far and wide, and his throne will be firm and free from aggression and terror from his neighbors on all sides.

Since the king's authority stems from the mutual covenant between himself and the people, who have yielded up their wealth for the benefit of the state, it follows that "whenever no benefit is seen to flow from the taking of their property, the law of the Torah returns to its place [*i.e.*, becomes again controlling] because the parties did not intend their agreement to apply to such circumstances." That is why, for instance, Ahab was not allowed simply to take the vineyard of Naboth for himself (*see* I Kings ch. 21). *See also* Chajes' further remarks regarding the king's authority to execute rebels, despite the rule that one may not consent to the infliction of bodily injuries on himself. Chajes explains this rule on the basis of the principle of "the pursuer," where it is permitted to save the life of the pursued (namely, the people whose king is being defied) by taking the life of the pursuer (namely, the rebel). *See also* the responsum of Moses Sofer to Chajes, more fully discussed *infra* n. 37.

33. *See infra* pp. 678ff.

remain an integral part of the overall Jewish legal system.[34] One of their principal methods was to be vigilant (as we have seen in regard to the king's law) to assure that communal legislation did not conflict with the basic principles of justice and equity in Jewish law.[35]

D. Lay Adjudication

A contribution to the development of the Jewish legal system was also made by lay communal leaders and men of affairs who sat as members of some Jewish tribunals. We have already noted the existence of the institution of arbitration and lay tribunals in various places in the Jewish diaspora. It is true that at times these tribunals were a hindrance, and even harmful, to the normal development of the Jewish legal system and indeed to basic fairness in adjudication.[36] However, it is reasonable to conclude that when these institutions worked in harmonious cooperation with the halakhic authorities and with courts made up of expert judges, the result of such cooperation between men of affairs and halakhic authorities reflected a significant contribution on the part of the communal leaders to keeping Jewish law closely grounded in practical life and problems of the real world—and, consequently, continuously creative. Because Jewish society until the beginning of the Emancipation was in general a traditional society and acknowledged the supremacy and binding character of the *Halakhah*, such cooperation was generally the norm; and even at the end of this period, when signs of the end of Jewish autonomy began to appear, the halakhic leaders recognized this substantial authority of the people's lay leaders as part of the Jewish legal system.[37]

34. *See infra* pp. 751–779.

35. *See supra* p. 57 for Ran's comments.

36. *See supra* pp. 30–33.

37. *See* the interesting responsum of Moses Sofer to Z.H. Chajes (*Resp. Ḥatam Sofer*, OḤ, #208) discussing various aspects of the latter's book *Torat ha-Nevi'im*. Moses Sofer wrote:

> It seems to me that the source of authority for the leaders to impose the death penalty and other punishments is the verse "[You shall not] bring bloodguilt upon you" [Deuteronomy 19:10] as expounded in TB Mo'ed Katan 5a. No doubt, even if the Torah had not been given, there would have been—and before it was given there were—norms and rules; and every king preserves his country through justice. *See further Resp. Rema* #10. When the Torah was given, it promulgated these norms afresh [*see infra* pp. 195, 233–234], but the Torah's omission of matters such as liability for acts causing latent damages [*see infra* pp. 602–604] surely does not mean that such acts are permitted. Far from it—"Her ways are pleasant ways" [Proverbs 3:17]. It is only that they are not included in the laws of the Torah, and it is for the king and the Sanhedrin to provide [a solution] according to the circumstance and the time; the Torah does not deal with it. The same principle applies with even greater force when it comes to

IV. THE RELATIONSHIP BETWEEN JEWISH LAW AND NON-JEWISH LAW

There are two aspects to the question of the relationship between Jewish law and foreign law. First, To what extent is there a reciprocal relationship and influence between Jewish law and non-Jewish law, such that each legal system is influenced by the other and each absorbs and incorporates legal precepts of the other? Second, To what extent does one legal system recognize laws of the other system without making them part of its own law? Although the two aspects are different, they are related because applying the laws of another system involves recognition, whether conscious or unconscious, that in certain instances the foreign law yields the correct result. Such recognition leads to the possibility that the foreign law may influence the content of the legal system that recognizes it, sometimes even to the point of later complete incorporation.

A. Reciprocal Influences Between Jewish Law and Non-Jewish Law

The first aspect, the extent of reciprocal influence, has been much discussed in scholarly research on Jewish law and has been one of the favorite subjects for such research since the seventeenth century.[38] This area of research, more than any other topic of Jewish law, can be motivated by considerations of apologetics that result in overemphasis on the influence of non-Jewish law on Jewish law or exaggeration of the influence of Jewish law on non-Jewish law. In addition, it is not easy to demonstrate the influence of one legal system upon another, for it is possible for similar forces to be at

---

removing the large numbers of pernicious persons, such as murderers who act when there are no witnesses, and the like. . . .

The responsum discusses at length the king's law, which constitutes a source for governmental authority in all eras. *See also infra* p. 679 n. 1, and p. 714 n. 145.

38. *See* the comprehensive bibliography of S. Eisenstadt, *Ein Mishpat,* pp. 365–386, and *infra* p. 84. *See also* I. Jeiteles, "Fremdes Recht im Talmud" [Foreign Law in the Talmud], *JJLG,* XXI, pp. 109–128; H. Finkelscherer, "Zur Frage fremder Einflüsse auf das rabbinische Recht" [On the Question of Foreign Influences on Rabbinic Law], *MGWJ,* LXXIX (1935), pp. 381–98; D.M. Shoḥet, *The Jewish Court in the Middle Ages,* 1931, pp. 105–119, especially pp. 108–110; the researches of A. Gulak listed in the bibliography of the present work; B. Cohen, *Jewish and Roman Law,* 1966, especially the Introduction, first chapter (pp. 1–30), and bibliography; J.J. Rabinowitz, *Jewish Law, Its Influence on the Development of Legal Institutions,* 1956; Y. Baer, *Yisra'el ba-Ammim* [Israel among the Nations], 1955; *id.,* "Ha-Yesodot ha-Historiyyim shel ha-Halakhah" [The Historical Foundations of the *Halakhah*], *Zion,* XVII, pp. 1–55, 173; XXVII, pp. 117–155 (*see also Zion,* XXVIII, p. 116); Baron, *History,* V, pp. 9–16; Elon, *Ḥerut,* in the subject index, s.v. Hashpa'ah mi-ma'arekhet aḥat al ma'arekhet mishpatit aḥeret.

work in both systems and thereby create similar legal institutions in each system without any direct influence of one system on the other.

However, generally speaking, it can be said that there were reciprocal influences between Jewish law and other legal systems with which Jewish law had contact in the course of its history. The existence of a Jewish community living its social and economic life according to its own law in the midst of various legal systems of the many nations where the various Jewish settlements were located had a distinct effect on those legal systems, and there was a reciprocal effect as well.[39] The halakhic authorities knew the law that was applied in the non-Jewish courts, and at times even recommended the acceptance of a foreign legal practice of which they approved.[40]

39. *See, e.g.,* N. Isaacs, "Influence of Judaism on Western Law," in *Legacy of Israel,* Oxford, 1927, pp. 377–406; *see also* sources cited *supra* n. 38.

40. Halakhic authorities were familiar with non-Jewish law. For examples of this familiarity in the various eras in the history of Jewish law, *see* the sources cited *supra* nn. 38 and 39; and the responsa of the halakhic authorities of the post-Talmudic era often cite non-Jewish law, *see, e.g.,* M. Elon (ed.), *Digest of the Responsa of Asheri,* p. 425; *see also Resp. Rashba,* I, #1129; III, #153, #160; VI, #92; *Resp. Rashba Attributed to Naḥmanides* #16 (neighbors); *Resp. Rashba,* III, #218 (oaths); III, #421; V, #183 (tax exemption); IV, #35, #111 (urban building); V, #167; VI, #149; *Resp. Rashba Attributed to Naḥmanides* #22, #65 (legal documents); *Resp. Rashba,* VI, #254 (succession); *Resp. Rashba Attributed to Naḥmanides* #133 (divorce); #223 (suretyship); *Resp. Ribash* #130 (neighbors); #43 (legal documents); #94 (cursing of prophets); #97 (financial relationship of an engaged couple before marriage); #234 (evidence and criminal procedure—testimony of the accused in a criminal case, the sequence of the testimony, and taking testimony of the defendant in the presence of the complainant); #238 (the informer); #239 (competence of the court); #266 (partnership, solicitation, and accessories in criminal law); #299 (debt recovery and suretyship); #305 (liens on realty as security for a loan); #322 (urban building); #427 (renting and hiring); *Resp. Maimonides* (ed. J. Blau) #5 (renting and hiring); #9 (adjoining landowners, evidence); #32, #93 (partnership); #64 (succession, escheat); #90, #194 (adjoining landowners); #69, #192 (sales); #52, #210 (succession, escheat); #410 (imprisonment for debt); *Resp. Ran* #38 (divorce); *Resp. Ritba* #146 (debt recovery); *Resp. Ri Migash* #106 (the single witness); #118 (*ketubbah* and debt recovery); *Resp. Avraham b. ha-Rambam* #97 (adjoining landowners); *Resp. Tashbeẓ,* II, #176 (confiscation of Jews' property by the government); III, #5 (abandoned realty); *Resp. Alfasi* #156 (suretyship).

In one responsum, Israel Isserlein relied upon his contacts with Christian judges (*Terumat ha-Deshen,* Pesakim u-Khetavim, #83), and he also displayed his knowledge of German law (*id.* #104; *Terumat ha-Deshen* #338 [adjoining landowners]). *See likewise Resp. Maharil* #82. Israel of Bruna recommended the adoption of a rule from non-Jewish law with regard to the appearance of an attorney: "For even the gentiles avoid this; when one party takes an attorney, this attorney may not also plead for the adverse party. How much more should we [avoid this] who are commanded to sanctify ourselves [and avoid] even what is permitted us" (*Resp. Mahari Bruna* #132).

See also S. Eidelberg, "Ḥukkim Germaniyyim be-Aḥat ha-Teshuvot Shel Rabbenu Gershom Me'or ha-Golah" [German Law in a Responsum of Rabbenu Gershom, the Light of the Exile], *Zion,* XVIII, pp. 83–87. For extensive and instructive material on this subject, *see Digest of the Responsa Literature of Spain and North Africa, Historical Digest,* I, Preface, p. 28 and pp. 41, 106, 126, 273 (1981), II, pp. 304–307 (1986); and *id., Legal Digest,* I, Preface, p. 29, II, pp. 561–564 (1986).

At times, the halakhic authorities recognized the particular social utility of non-Jewish law[41] and even did not hesitate to praise the judicial system of the gentiles when it was administered better than the judicial system of the Jews.[42] A certain degree of incorporation of precepts of non-Jewish law into Jewish law came about through custom as a legal source.[43] Non-Jewish law, when incorporated into the Jewish legal system, was so assimilated and internalized that it was rendered consistent with the general principles and ultimate objectives of Jewish law; and when, because of particular social conditions, Jewish law would incorporate a non-Jewish legal precept that was inconsistent with the basic principles of Jewish law, the precept would eventually be discarded.[44]

B. *Dina de-Malkhuta Dina* ("The Law of the Land Is Law")

The question of the recognition by Jewish law of the binding authority of a rule of law contained in a non-Jewish legal system has been extensively

41. *See Derashot ha-Ran* #11 (p. 75): "Consequently, it is possible that sometimes non-Jewish law may promote social welfare more than some laws of the Torah do . . . ," quoted *supra* p. 56.

42. *See, e.g., Sefer Ḥasidim* #1301: "There are localities where the gentiles and not the Jews administer true justice because of the scarcity of Talmudic scholars there, or because they [the Jews of the locality] have come from many places and are made up of many different families; and those of low moral quality who immigrated from another place lead them astray." *See also supra* pp. 31–33 (at times, non-Jewish judicial procedure was superior to that of Jewish lay courts).

43. *See infra* pp. 881–882, 911–927.

44. There are three possible forms of incorporation:

(1) A non-Jewish legal institution may be adopted unaltered when not inconsistent with the general tenor of Jewish law.

(2) Sometimes a non-Jewish institution may be incorporated and adapted to the general tenor of Jewish law—*see, e.g.,* with regard to imprisonment for debt (Elon, *Ḥerut,* pp. 259–260), with regard to imprisonment for criminal offenses (Elon, *Ma'asar,* p. 200), and with regard to administering an oath to witnesses "in accordance with the attitude of the witnesses who were raised according to their custom [*i.e.,* non-Jewish law] and believe it [*i.e.,* taking an oath before testifying] to be [required by the] Torah" (*Resp. Tashbez,* III, #15). Under non-Jewish law, a witness was automatically sworn, whereas in Jewish law, administration of an oath is in the discretion of the court and is applied in special circumstances. *See id.;* Rema to Sh. Ar. ḤM 28:2. *See also* Becker v. Eilat, 32(iii) *P.D.* 370, 378ff. (1978); and *infra* pp. 1697–1707.

(3) Occasionally, because of particular circumstances, Jewish law may absorb a legal principle that is completely alien to its spirit, and for this reason the principle disappears from the system in the course of time. *See, e.g.,* with regard to delaying the burial of one who had not discharged his debt (Elon, *Ḥerut,* pp. 238–254). The incorporation of such foreign law was usual in the field of criminal law in connection with the practice of corporal punishment, which was customary in non-Jewish law. *See* Assaf, *Onshin,* pp. 21–22, 31; Elon, *Ma'asar,* pp. 183, 197. On the subject of the incorporation of non-Jewish law into Jewish law, *see further* Rav Ẓa'ir (Chaim Tchernowitz), *Toledot ha-Halakhah* [History of the *Halakhah*], I, pp. 131ff., III, pp. 300ff.

discussed in the literature of Jewish law because of the fact that Jewish law has a long history as a legal system functioning by the sovereign grace of foreign governments that had their own legal systems. The discussion of this subject centers on the doctrine of *dina de-malkhuta dina,* which means "the law of the land [lit. 'the kingdom'] is law," and is therefore to be followed. Let us examine briefly some of the principal aspects of this doctrine.

Even during the period of the *tannaim,* one may discern the recognition by Jewish law of certain provisions of non-Jewish law, particularly those relating to legal documents, taxes, and punishments. However, it was only with Samuel, one of the first Babylonian *amoraim,* that this was crystallized as a general doctrine.[45] It is noteworthy that the doctrine was established in the diaspora, as a result of the historical situation of a Jewish community that enjoyed Jewish juridical autonomy but nevertheless lived by the sufferance of a sovereign non-Jewish government that had its own legal system.[46] This background in which *dina de-malkhuta dina* arose and took form throughout the long annals of Jewish law was emphasized in the writings of the halakhic authorities[47] and is reflected in the legal rationale for the doctrine. However, knowing this background does not detract from the significance of the doctrine in regard to the general question of the relationship between Jewish and non-Jewish law.

45. TB Nedarim 28a; Gittin 10b; Bava Kamma 113a/b; Bava Batra 54b-55a.

46. This is why, according to most halakhic authorities, the doctrine of *dina de-malkhuta dina* does not apply to a Jewish government. The governmental prerogatives in a Jewish state are governed by the king's law, which applies to all forms of Jewish government as they continue to develop over the course of time (*see supra* pp. 58–61). *See Resp. Ba'alei ha-Tosafot* (ed. Agus) #12, p. 58; Aaron ha-Levi, quoted in *Resp. Ribash ha-Ḥadashot* #9; Novellae of Rashba to Nedarim 28a, s.v. Be-mokhes; Ran, Nedarim 28a, s.v. Be-mokhes ha-omed me-elav; *Nimmukei Yosef* to Alfasi, Nedarim 28a, s.v. Ve-ha-amar Shemuel dina de-malkhuta dina. But there were those who applied this doctrine even to a Jewish government, and this view had many advocates in later periods. *See also* ET, VII, pp. 307–308, s.v. Dina de-malkhuta dina; S. Shilo, EJ, VI, pp. 51–55, s.v. Dina de-malkhuta dina (reprinted in *Principles,* pp. 710–715); and *infra* p. 74.

47. *See Teshuvot Ḥakhmei Provence* (ed. Sofer, p. 427):

> This doctrine [of *dina de-malkhuta dina*] took root only because of necessity, because we are subject to their [the gentiles'] rule, and it is impossible to conduct our commercial affairs unless we follow the customs established by the leader of the country who lays down and enforces its laws, whoever he may be.

See also the rationale cited by the *geonim* for the doctrine of *dina de-malkhuta dina* (*Teshuvot ha-Geonim,* ed. S. Assaf, Jerusalem, 1942, p. 75):

> This was [the meaning of] the dictum of the *amora* Samuel: When the Holy One, blessed be He, granted power to the kingdoms, he also granted them power over the people's property to deal with as they saw fit. This applies even to the Jews, as it is written, "They rule over our bodies and our beasts as they please" (Nehemiah 9:37).

This is a theoretical, philosophical rationale, based on the reality of the existence of the Jewish people in exile. The Jews were subject to non-Jewish law in civil matters, since the government had control over their possessions.

What is the rationale that has been advanced for the doctrine of *dina de-malkhuta dina?*[48] Some authorities explain the doctrine on the basis of the concept of a contract between the citizens and the government—a concept that at that time served as the basis for the executive and legislative authority of the king:[49]

> All taxes, assessments, and practices under the kings' laws that they customarily enact in their kingdoms are law, as all the inhabitants of the kingdom voluntarily consent to be bound by the enactments of the king and his laws, and therefore it is settled law; and one who, by authority of the king's law, retains possession of his neighbor's property is not guilty of thievery.[50]

Somewhat similar is the more "simple" rationale that also had proponents in general political-legal thought:

> Because the land is his and he could say to them: "If you do not obey my laws, I will expel you from my country."[51]

Some authorities grounded the doctrine of *dina de-malkhuta dina* on a combination of halakhic reasoning and considerations based on the conditions under which they lived. Some were of the opinion that just as Jewish law recognizes the legitimacy of legal creativity in the legal system of a Jewish government (as it does in the case of the Jewish king),[52] it also recognizes the legitimacy of the same prerogatives in a non-Jewish government.[53] Other authorities based the doctrine on the legislative principle of

48. *See* I. Herzog, *The Main Institutions of Jewish Law* (hereinafter, *Institutions*), I, pp. 24–32; S. Shilo, "Ha-Bissus ha-Mishpati la-Kelal Dina de-Malkhuta Dina" [The Legal Basis for the Doctrine of *Dina de-Malkhuta Dina*], *Mishpatim*, II, pp. 329–344; ET, VII, pp. 295–297, s.v. Dina de-malkhuta dina; J. Katz, *Exclusiveness and Tolerance*, pp. 48–50; H.H. Ben-Sasson, *Toledot Am Yisra'el* [History of the Jewish People], II, *Toledot Yisra'el bi-Mei ha-Beinayim* [History of the Jews in the Middle Ages], pp. 110–113. In the Talmud itself no reason is given for the doctrine; the first legal rationale was given in the eleventh century C.E. by Rashi. *See supra* n. 47 for the explanation from the geonic era, which is not a legal rationale.

49. *See supra* p. 59 and n. 32.

50. Rashbam, Bava Batra 54b, s.v. Ve-ha-amar Shemuel dina de-malkhuta dina; for a similar explanation, *see* Maimonides, *MT*, Gezelah va-Avedah 5:18. Since there is such an agreement, the applicable rule with regard to civil matters, to which the doctrine of *dina de-malkhuta dina* applies, is that one is free to contract out of the law, for in civil matters one may stipulate to change even a Biblical norm. *See infra* pp. 123–127 and *supra* n. 32.

51. Ran, Nedarim 28a, s.v. Be-mokhes ha-omed me-elav, in the name of the Tosafists. According to this rationale, the doctrine does not apply to Jewish kings because "all Jews are partners in the Land of Israel," and the king may not banish a Jew from the land. *Id. See also supra* n. 46; *Shittah Mekubbeẓet*, Nedarim 28a.

52. *See supra* pp. 55–57.

53. *Bet ha-Beḥirah*, Bava Kamma 113a, s.v. Kevar amarnu (p. 329), 113b, s.v. U-me-aḥar she-be'arnu (p. 331), s.v. Kol mah she-amarnu (pp. 331–332); Ritba's novellae to Bava

hefker bet din hefker (lit. "what the court declares ownerless is ownerless")—the right of the court to expropriate property:

> For the halakhic authorities have expropriated property in the manner of kings, as in the case of enactments for the encouragement of penitents (*takkanat ha-shavim*),[54] the promotion of the public welfare (*tikkun ha-olam*),[55] and the furtherance of the interests of peace and tranquillity (*darkhei shalom*).[56] [They have] also [done this] in the case of a forced marriage and the incident that occurred in Naresh,[57] where they annulled a Biblically valid marriage.[58]

According to this view, the doctrine is a special enactment by halakhic authorities arising out of the conditions in the diaspora. Some added to the foregoing reasons the ancient concept of Jewish law that certain fundamental laws are the heritage of every nation and it is therefore appropriate for Jewish law to recognize them. This idea of the existence of certain legal principles common to all men is embodied in the concept of the Noahide laws (lit. "commandments of the descendants of Noah"), which will be discussed later.[59]

Batra 55a, s.v. Hanei telat millei. Among other arguments, they relied on the fact that Samuel, the *amora* who established the doctrine of *dina de-malkhuta dina* with regard to gentile kings, was also the one who ruled that "whatever is written in the section dealing with kings [I Samuel ch. 8], the king is permitted to do" (TB Sanhedrin 20b), *i.e.*, the chapter states the king's rightful privileges and is not intended merely to instill fear among the people, as his contemporary, Rav, held it is.

54. *See infra* pp. 601–602.

55. *See infra* pp. 504ff.

56. *See id.*

57. *See infra* pp. 636–639.

58. *Resp. Ba'alei ha-Tosafot* (ed. Agus) #12, p. 60. *See further Teshuvot Ḥakhmei Provence* (ed. Sofer), p. 427:

> Just as the Talmudic Sages ruled that the court has authority to expropriate property under certain circumstances, they have likewise ruled that the king has the same power to expropriate as the court; and he may make use of the expropriated property.

We find here a new formulation, *hefker malka hefker* (the king has power to expropriate), analogous to *hefker bet din hefker* (the court has the power to expropriate) and *hefker ẓibbur hefker* (the community has the power to expropriate); *see infra* p. 700 n. 88. For details concerning *hefker bet din hefker, see infra* pp. 507–514.

59. Rashi, Gittin 9b, s.v. Ḥuẓ mi-gittei nashim, to the effect that the doctrine of *dina de-malkhuta dina* is not applied in matters of divorce "since the Jewish laws of divorce and marriage do not pertain to them [the gentiles], but the children of Noah [*i.e.*, gentiles] were commanded to administer justice." According to Rashi, we have here apparently a merging of two reasons: (1) the law of the land is binding under Jewish law for any of the above-cited reasons given by the halakhic authorities; and (2) this doctrine can have force only for civil matters, because they involve universal legal principles, but not for matters of marriage and divorce, which are peculiar to each nation. *See further Tosafot Rid,* Gittin 9b, and I.Z. Meltzer, *Even ha-Ezel,* Hilkhot Nizkei Mamon 8:5.

The Noahide laws include a considerable part of civil and criminal law. *See infra* p.

The full halakhic recognition of the doctrine of *dina de-malkhuta dina* had the potential for becoming a serious danger to the continued development of Jewish law. According to this doctrine, it could be entirely consistent with the *Halakhah* for legal matters to be increasingly conducted in practice according to the law of the country in which a particular Jewish community lived; and needless to say, if that occurred, Jewish law could easily have become a matter of merely theoretical and scholarly interest, its development curtailed and its creative power at an end. The halakhic authorities were alert to this danger and forestalled it by means of special vigilance to assure that Jewish law was applied in practical life.

The principal method that a clear majority of the halakhic authorities used was to limit the scope of application of the doctrine. From a literal reading of some Talmudic passages, one might conclude that this doctrine applied not only to the relation between the individual and the government—such as tax matters[60] and eminent domain for highways and bridges[61]—but even to civil matters between individuals.[62] In the Talmudic era, this did not slow the pace of Jewish civil law, as is well attested by the

---

194. Other halakhic authorities distinguished between the subjects included in the Noahide laws and other subjects, such as legal rules relating to commerce. The doctrine of *dina de-malkhuta dina* applies to these other matters, but not to the law of evidence,

> because the ancient Noahide laws, the seven commandments with which they were charged, included the administration of justice, and all their cases are decided on the evidence of a single witness and by a single judge; but we, the descendants of Abraham, have been placed in a more sanctified category and for all cases we require two witnesses; and since this is one of their ancient rules and practices, it would very much ill become us to invoke *dina de-malkhuta dina* as a basis for practicing as they do; their law of evidence is rather merely *dina di-venei Noah* [law of the descendants of Noah] (*Teshuvot Ḥakhmei Provence,* ed. Sofer, p. 421).

60. TB Nedarim 28a; Bava Kamma 113a/b.

61. This rule was explained by Rava (TB Bava Kamma 113b) by means of the following example: The government expropriates and cuts down palm trees belonging to private individuals, without a *kinyan* (act of acquisition), and builds bridges with the wood. We use these bridges and cross over them, without fear of committing the offense of benefiting from stolen property. The reason we do not have this concern is the doctrine of *dina de-malkhuta dina,* under which the act does not constitute theft. Maimonides (*MT,* Gezelah va-Avedah 5:17) stated the rule as follows: "If a king cuts down trees belonging to individuals and uses them to build a bridge, it is permitted to cross it. Similarly, if he demolishes houses in order to make a roadway or a wall, it is permitted to derive benefit from them. This is the rule in all similar cases, for the law of the king is the law."

62. *E.g.,* TB Bava Batra 54b/55a (law of sale and acquisition of real estate); TB Gittin 10b (giving effect to documents drawn up or authenticated by non-Jewish courts, in spite of their invalidity under Jewish law). According to one view, all kinds of non-Jewish documents are valid except bills of divorcement and manumission of slaves. Others hold that only documents of a declarative nature, *i.e.,* that serve as proof of a legal relationship—*e.g.,* promissory notes—are effective, but not documents of a constitutive nature, *i.e.,* that in themselves create a legal relationship—*e.g.,* deeds of gift.

enormous creativity in that area of the law reflected in the Babylonian Talmud.[63] However, with the dispersion of the people to various centers and the decline, beginning at the end of the tenth century C.E.,[64] of the dominance of a single Jewish center (Babylonia), the tendency among the halakhic authorities to limit the scope of application of the doctrine of *dina de-malkhuta dina* grew stronger. The Talmudic sources that could imply that this doctrine also covered civil matters between individual Jews[65] were explained away by various means, and the principle was accepted among many halahkic authorities that:

> *Dina de-malkhuta dina* applies only to those matters that are the king's interests, such as roads, customs duties, and other taxes, but as to private matters between individuals the Sages did not say that "the law of the land is law." . . . As to the affairs of a Jew with his fellow Jew, we are not to judge between them by the law of the kingdom. . . . So long as we are permitted by the king to be governed by laws of the Talmud, as in our generation when the king says "Judge your cases among yourselves," we are not required to judge ourselves under any law but Jewish law, unless the parties otherwise agree.[66]

Other authorities explicitly emphasized the rationale of the danger of undermining the Jewish legal system:

> All that we have said concerning the law of the land—that it is for us binding law—applies to enactments by the government for its own benefit and its economic requirements, whether the enactment requires each person to pay so much per year, or so much from his business transactions, or so much upon the occurrence of any event that is decreed to be taxable. Such enactments, even though contrary to our laws, are binding; and one is prohibited from stealing from the king by violating what he has decreed. For this is appropriate for him as pertaining to his kingship, as it was said concerning Jewish kings: "Whatever is written in the section dealing with kings, the king is permitted to do."[67] And this is why the doctrine refers [literally] to the "law of the kingdom" (*dina de-malkhuta*) rather than the "law of the king," so as to limit the doctrine to those laws that are appropriate for the kingdom. But anything the king enacts by arbitrary abuse of his position,[68] and any

63. *See* the instructive remarks of Gulak, *Yesodei,* IV, pp. 27–29.

64. *See supra* p. 43.

65. *See, e.g.,* a detailed discussion in connection with this in *Sefer ha-Terumot,* gate 46, ch. 8, par. 5; *see also Teshuvot Ḥakhmei Provence* (ed. Sofer), pp. 420ff.

66. *Sefer ha-Terumot, supra* n. 65. The king's interests also include matters affecting debasement of coinage and changes in the value of currency, "for there is no greater governmental interest than this, for they are the owners of the currency; they mint it, and they issue it in their own country." *See* responsum of Naḥmanides in *Sefer ha-Terumot, supra.*

67. TB Sanhedrin 20b. *See supra* n. 53.

68. *E.g.,* a tax for an undefined sum or a law aimed at a particular person and not applicable to all equally, which has the character of robbery, plunder, and wrong. *See* TB

> laws that the nations retain from their ancient books, or that are based on usage of their wise men of old, and which are contrary to our laws, are not included in this principle, because if they were, all of Jewish law would cease to exist.[69]

Some halakhic authorities, relying on proofs from the Talmud, applied the doctrine of *dina de-malkhuta dina* even to civil matters between fellow Jews;[70] but even they struggled mightily with this problem. An instructive example of such a struggle is provided by Rashba, a leading architect of the Jewish legal system in all aspects of the law in thirteenth-century Spain. While it may be concluded from one of his responsa that "even as to a matter that does not affect the king's interests, we apply *dina de-malkhuta dina*,"[71] in a different responsum he saw in this an "uprooting of the entire law of the Torah," and he ruled that "*dina de-malkhuta dina* is not applicable except where it affects the king's interests."[72] Other authorities are of the opinion that even though the doctrine applies to civil matters between Jews, this is so only for those laws that are not directly inconsistent with the laws of the Torah.[73] The ruling laid down by Moses Isserles (Rema) was the most restrictive:[74]

Bava Kamma 113a; Maimonides, *MT*, Gezelah va-Avedah 5:9–14; Sh. Ar. ḤM 369:4–11. *See also infra* pp. 72–73.

69. Meiri, *Bet ha-Beḥirah*, Bava Kamma 113b, s.v. Kol mah she-amarnu (pp. 331–332); *id.*, Avodah Zarah 16a, s.v. Ha-mishnah ha-shevi'it (p. 41).

70. *See* these views in *Sefer ha-Terumot*, *supra* n. 65; Naḥmanides' novellae to Bava Batra 55a, s.v. Im ken bittalta yerushat beno ha-bekhor; Ran to Alfasi, Gittin 10b, s.v. U-de-amrinan dina de-malkhuta dina; Ran to Alfasi, Bava Batra 55a, s.v. Im ken bittalta yerushat beno ha-bekhor; *Nimmukei Yosef* to Alfasi, Bava Batra 55a, s.v. U-ferush dina de-malkhuta dina; *Maggid Mishneh* to Maimonides, *MT*, Malveh ve-Loveh 27:1. It should be pointed out that the comments of *Bet ha-Beḥirah* on Bava Batra 55a, s.v. Sadeh zeh, also indicate some inclination to this view, but these comments may be reconciled with his comments on Bava Kamma and Avodah Zarah cited *supra* n. 69. *See also Shakh*, Sh. Ar. ḤM 73, subpar. 36 for a detailed discussion.

71. *Resp. Rashba*, I, #895.

72. *Resp. Rashba*, VI, #254, quoted in *Bet Yosef* to *Tur* ḤM 26:7. To the same effect is *Resp. Rashba*, III, #109. *See also* S. Shilo, *Dina de-Malkhuta Dina*, 1974, p. 137, discussing this contradiction and concluding that the responsum limiting the applicability of the principle was composed in Rashba's youth and was later retracted. This theory is not conclusive, and the matter requires further study.

73. *See Shakh*, *supra* n. 70, and the views cited there; ET, VII, pp. 297–301, s.v. Dina de-malkhuta dina; *see also Teshuvot Ḥakhmei Provence* (ed. Sofer), pp. 426–427, where an opinion is cited that the principle of *dina de-malkhuta dina* is not to be applied when the law of the land is contrary to Biblical law, as, *e.g.*, in matters of evidence, but may be applied in derogation of halakhic rules only when it is "contrary to a provision of rabbinic law and so long as it concerns only a civil matter."

74. Rema to Sh. Ar. ḤM 369:11, following *Resp. Maharik* #187. *See further Teshuvot Ḥakhmei Provence* (ed. Sofer), pp. 419–420. On the basic objective that the principle of *dina de-malkhuta dina* must not be allowed to lead to resort to non-Jewish courts and thereby

> We apply *dina de-malkhuta* only to a matter that is for the benefit of the king or is necessary for the general welfare of the state. It does not mean that judgment should generally be given according to the non-Jewish law, for if it did, all Jewish [civil] law would, in effect, be abrogated.

The great and continuous creativity in the various areas of Jewish law in the post-Talmudic period is further proof that the scope of application of the doctrine was confined to the periphery of the Jewish legal system and did not adversely affect the essential functioning of that system. Moreover, the halakhic authorities, by appropriately confining the use of the doctrine, turned it into a positive factor that helped preserve the Jewish legal system: the limited incorporation of some aspects of non-Jewish law enabled the Jewish community to make the necessary adjustments to conditions of the non-Jewish environment.[75]

The lesson of this phenomenon goes beyond the immediate situation; it is also instructive concerning the relationship between Jewish law and other legal systems in general. This relationship was determined, first and foremost, in light of the primary and fundamental objective of protecting the Jewish legal system and, thereby, Jewish juridical autonomy and all that it entailed. Whenever the successful accomplishment of this objective was not endangered, there was no reason not to utilize a rule of non-Jewish law when necessary in a particular situation. This practice, in certain areas of Jewish civil law, was permitted under the various rationales for the doctrine of *dina de-malkhuta dina* discussed above.[76] Abraham b. David (Rabad), a halakhic authority in the twelfth century C.E., laid down as a general proposition that whenever there is a lacuna in the law, it may be filled by resort to non-Jewish law. In a case involving the adoption of non-Jewish law in regard to a mortgage of real estate, he generalized as follows:

> And thus I hold that whenever our law supplies no clear answer and we do not have a definite custom of our own, then we follow their [*i.e.*, the gentiles'] custom by extension of the doctrine of *dina de-malkhuta dina*, since the law of the land is to rule according to custom.[77]

---

undermine Jewish autonomy, *see* the instructive statement in *Resp. Tashbeẓ*, I, #158, quoted *infra* p. 135.

75. *See* Katz, *supra* n. 48 at 54.

76. The doctrine of *dina de-malkhuta dina* does not apply to matters of "religious" law, but to civil matters only. *See infra* pp. 132–137.

77. *Temim De'im* #50; *Teshuvot u-Fesakim Shel ha-Rabad* #131 (ed. Kafaḥ, p. 176). Rabad's responsum is quoted at the end of *Resp. Maharashdam*, ḤM, #328. Samuel de Medina (Maharashdam) adds: "It is even more appropriate to do this on matters that occurred among non-Jews, inasmuch as these Marranos (*anusim*) followed their [the non-Jews']

With regard to the doctrine of *dina de-malkhuta dina* (as in the case of the incorporation into the Jewish legal system of a rule of non-Jewish law,[78] or of any communal enactment or custom that is contrary to a given rule of Jewish law[79]), Jewish law will not recognize the applicability of non-Jewish law if such application would violate the basic principles of justice and equity embodied in Jewish law. The classic example is the rule that the law of the land is not binding unless that law applies equally and in a non-discriminatory manner to all inhabitants of the nation:

> The principle of the matter is this: Any law enacted by the king that applies generally and not only to a single individual is not robbery, but whenever he takes discriminatorily from a particular individual only, and not by law applicable to everyone, he acts lawlessly against that individual, and this is robbery.[80]

Similarly, the levy of a monetary fine against an entire community because of the misdeeds of two or three individuals is "utter robbery," because it is contrary to the principle of Jewish law that forbids collective punishment, or punishment of one person for the transgressions of another:

---

practices." *See also* the responsum of Radah (David ha-Kohen) quoted there by Maharashdam with regard to a *shekhiv me-ra* (one dangerously ill or otherwise facing imminent death) who "grew up among non-Jews and his directions were stated and written in a foreign language . . . that we follow the language of the people. . . ."

See also Rabad's critique of Maimonides' conclusion, *MT,* Malveh ve-Loveh 25:10, that where two persons have acted as surety for a debtor, the creditor may recover from either surety at his option. Rabad said: "I say that this is correct only on the basis of custom, and we learn from gentiles [how to decide] for Jews." There is, however, a difficulty here in regard to Rabad's position, for the subject is dealt with in *Tosefta* Bava Batra 11:15, where it is ruled that one may recover from both sureties; therefore, there is no lacuna in Jewish law and on Rabad's own theory no basis for applying *dina de-malkhuta dina.* This *tosefta* also raises a problem with regard to Maimonides' formulation of the rule. *See also Maggid Mishneh, ad loc.*

78. *See supra* pp. 56, 64.

79. *See infra* pp. 761–777, 942–944.

80. Maimonides, *MT,* Gezelah va-Avedah 5:14. This principle of nondiscrimination had already been discussed by Ri Migash in his novellae to Bava Batra 54b, s.v. Dina de-malkhuta dina, and was accepted by all authorities as law. *See also Tur* ḤM 369:14 and Sh. Ar. ḤM 369:8. The halakhic authorities refer to a discriminatory law as *gazlanuta de-malkhuta lav dina* (robbery by the government is not [valid] law). *See also* Landsman v. Ha-Va'adah le-Har Ẓiyyon, 1 *P.D.R.* 169, 172 (1954), which concerned an ornamental Torah crown that had been taken away from its owner in World War II. An argument based on *dina de-malkhuta dina* was rejected, since the law of the state was discriminatory. For an additional example of a conflict between state law and a basic principle of Jewish law—that the people's rights may not be abrogated—*see infra* pp. 134–135.

> The penalty the king imposed against all the Jews was utter robbery, as far as we are concerned. Is he permitted, because two or three people were guilty of debasing coinage, to give vent to his wrath against all the Jews by expelling them forcibly from his land so that they were forced to appease him by some thousands of gold coins? In regard to such situations, Abraham, our father (may he rest in peace), said to God: "Far be it from You to do such a thing, to bring death upon the innocent as well as the guilty, so that the innocent and the guilty fare alike. Far be it from You! Shall not the Judge of all the earth do justice?"[81] And Moses, our teacher (may he rest in peace), said:[82] "When one man sins, will You be wrathful with the whole community?" And the frequently used Aramaic expression[83] is also apropos here: "Tuvya sins, and Zigud is punished?" Therefore, this decree is utter robbery.[84]

One can point to additional instances when halakhic authorities refused to accord binding force to the law of the land.[85] It is precisely this critical attitude that enabled the doctrine of *dina de-malkhuta dina* to become at various times a vehicle not only for recognizing certain non-Jewish laws as binding without their becoming part of Jewish law, but also for incorporating other non-Jewish laws into the Jewish legal system.[86] At times, indeed, the authorities debated whether a particular legal rule should

81. Genesis 18:25. As is usual in responsa, only the opening words of the verse are quoted in the responsum itself.

82. Numbers 16:22.

83. TB Pesaḥim 113b.

84. *Resp. Ribash ha-Ḥadashot* #9. As to the prohibition of punishing one person for someone else's crime, *see further* Deuteronomy 24:16 and II Kings 14:6; *see also infra* pp. 303–304, 1025–1026. As to the author of the responsa in the collection *Resp. Ribash ha-Ḥadashot, see* Gerstein, *Ohel Mo'ed,* I, 1928, pp. 89–95, and *see infra* n. 85.

85. *See, e.g.,* a similar case to that of *Resp. Ribash ha-Ḥadashot*—in connection with collective punishment—in *Resp. Maimuniyyot,* Kinyan, #2; *Resp. Asheri* 18:16 (when a general rule fixing the time within which an appeal may be taken is considered valid); *Resp. Tashbeẓ,* I, #158 (a law of the government is invalid if it results in completely depriving anyone of the right to file a claim before a court); *see also infra* pp. 133–135.

86. In addition to all the examples cited, *see further* Rema to Sh. Ar. ḤM 259:7 (one who retrieves property deposited by ebbing tidewaters must return it because of *dina de-malkhuta dina*); and Rema to Sh. Ar. ḤM 356:7 and Sh. Ar. ḤM 368:1 (a stolen article must be returned to its owner even after the latter has abandoned hope of its recovery and after it has undergone a change of possession); *see also Shakh,* Sh. Ar. ḤM 356, subpar. 10, and 73, subpar. 39; *Keẓot ha-Ḥoshen,* Sh. Ar. ḤM 259, subpar. 3; and the case of Landsman v. Ha-Va'adah le-Har Ẓiyyon, *supra* n. 80. The rule that a found article must be returned even after there has been a change of possession and the owner has despaired of getting it back appears as early as in geonic responsa, *Teshuvot ha-Geonim, Sha'arei Ẓedek,* Part IV, Sha'ar I, #20, ed. Salonika (1792), p. 32a, and in a communal enactment from the period of Rabbenu Gershom Me'or Ha-Golah, *Resp. Rabbenu Gershom* #67 (ed. Eidelberg, pp. 155–156). *See also infra* pp. 686–688 and n. 35 and p. 894 n. 61; *Ḥazon Ish,* Bava Kamma 23:2, s.v. Ve-khol zeh be-leka minhag; ET, VII, pp. 295–308, s.v. Dina de-malkhuta dina; Z. Falk, *De'ot,* IX (Passover, 1959) and XI (Sukkot, 1959).

be accepted as a part of the Jewish legal system or should be recognized as binding only under the doctrine of *dina de-malkhuta dina.*[87]

The doctrine of *dina de-malkhuta dina* has been extensively discussed in the decisions of the Supreme Court[88] and the rabbinical courts[89] of Israel in connection with the problem of the relation between Jewish law and the legal system of the State of Israel.[90] This problem is discussed in detail in Volume IV of this work, which deals with the subject of Jewish law in the State of Israel.[91]

87. An interesting recent example is the subject of copyright, *i.e.,* the protection of legal rights in a literary or artistic creation. Joseph Saul Nathanson (*Resp. Sho'el u-Meshiv,* Mahadura Kamma, Part I, #44) concluded that such a right exists and relied, *inter alia,* on the fact that the right is accorded by the general law, quoting the adage, "Let not our perfect Torah be [thought of] as not being at least equal to their idle conversation; that is something that reason rejects." Isaac Schmelkes (*Resp. Bet Yiẓḥak,* YD, II, #75) distinguished between copyright of a general intellectual creation and copyright of a work of Torah study, for the teaching of which it is forbidden to take payment; but he concluded that there is also copyright for a creation in the field of Torah studies, since such a copyright exists under general law and is applicable pursuant to *dina de-malkhuta dina.* This represents a distinction between recognizing a principle of non-Jewish law and incorporating it into the Jewish legal system (after the manner of Joseph Saul Nathanson), on the one hand and, on the other hand, recognizing such a principle without incorporating it into Jewish law, but accepting it only on the ground of *dina de-malkhuta dina* (after the manner of Isaac Schmelkes). For a general view, *see* the sources cited *supra* n. 86. On the subject of *dina de-malkhuta dina, see further infra* pp. 132–137.

88. Wiloszni v. Rabbinical Court of Appeals, 36(ii) *P.D.* 733, 740ff. (1982).

89. *See* the rulings of the rabbinical courts cited in Wiloszni v. Rabbinical Court of Appeals, *supra* n. 88.

90. *See supra* n. 46, as to applicability of *dina de-malkhuta dina* to a Jewish government.

91. *See infra* pp. 1819–1826.

Chapter 3
THE SCIENTIFIC STUDY OF JEWISH LAW

I. Classification in Jewish Law
   A. Classification and Definition of the Fields of Law
   B. Substantive Changes in Various Subject Areas
      1. Law of Obligations
      2. Public and Administrative Law
      3. Conflict of Laws
II. The Concreteness of Jewish Legal Terminology
III. The Need for Research into All Periods of Jewish Law; The Historical-Dogmatic (also called Historical-Analytical) Method

Many problems arise in the course of research in Jewish law. We shall highlight here a few worthy of particular attention.

I. CLASSIFICATION IN JEWISH LAW

A. Classification and Definition of the Fields of Law

Classifying the law, *i.e.*, delineating the different fields or areas of the law, such as acquisitions, obligations, civil law, criminal law, etc., is neither easy nor uncontroversial in any legal system; and in the Jewish legal system particularly, such classification requires a great deal of careful consideration. For example, great care is necessary when Hebrew terms defining specific fields of law—such as *dinei mamonot* (civil law, lit. "monetary laws," *i.e.*, contracts, property, and the like), *dinei nefashot* (laws of capital cases; sometimes, more generally, criminal law), and *dinei kenasot* (laws of fines and penalties)—are sought to be carried over to legal fields that have similar names in other legal systems.[1]

Classification is also difficult because throughout the many eras during which the rules of Jewish law were crystallizing and becoming established, classification was quite general and rudimentary. This was the situation in

1. *See infra* pp. 108–109. *See also* Gulak, *Yesodei,* II, pp. 14–15 and notes thereto.

the Mishnah, the rest of halakhic literature in the period of the *tannaim*, and the two Talmuds.[2] The earliest attempts at a more detailed and systematic classification of Jewish law were in the *Mishneh Torah* of Maimonides in the twelfth century and in some of the later codes, such as the *Turim* and the *Shulḥan Arukh*.[3] Even those more elaborate attempts at classification preserved the specific character of the Jewish legal institutions. One must be careful, therefore, not to force Jewish legal institutions artificially into the institutional structure of other legal systems. Conversely, classifications generally accepted in any other legal system cannot be automatically applied to Jewish law, especially in view of the fact that different legal systems have different approaches to legal classification.[4]

B. Substantive Changes in Various Subject Areas

Particular attention should be given to two important factors affecting classification in Jewish law, namely, the substantive changes during the history of Jewish law in certain areas of the law, and the creation of entirely new legal fields. Let us briefly examine some examples.

1. LAW OF OBLIGATIONS

In the course of the history of Jewish law, the law of obligations underwent substantial changes in both content and character. From the beginning, it was a fundamental and unequivocal principle of Jewish law that the body of the debtor could not be subjected to the enforcement of the rights of the creditor.[5] Jewish law was thus required to develop an alternative remedy with enough power to secure payment from the debtor's property. This was accomplished by giving the creditor a lien on the property of the debtor that automatically attached as soon as the obligation arose.[6] "Obligation" in Jewish law thus had a clear property orientation, *i.e.*, the

2. *See infra* pp. 1038–1040 and index, s.v. Classification in Jewish law.

3. *See infra* pp. 1195–1203, 1287–1302, 1323–1327.

4. In *Yesodei*, Gulak organized the structure of the Jewish legal system according to that of Roman law. However, he himself noted that there are essential differences in structure between the two systems. *See, e.g.*, Gulak, *Yesodei*, I, pp. 18–19, 170ff.; *id.*, "Hashva'ah Kelalit bein Ru'aḥ Dinei Mamonot ha-Ivriyyim ve-Ru'aḥ Dinei Mamonot ha-Roma'im" [A General Comparison of the Spirit of Jewish Civil Law with That of Roman Civil Law], *Madda'ei ha-Yahadut* I (1926), pp. 45–50. These and other differences are sufficient to raise serious doubt as to whether the organization and classification of Roman law are suitable paradigms for organizing and classifying Jewish law.

5. *See* Elon, *Ḥerut*, and *infra* p. 589.

6. *See infra* p. 590.

creditor had a property right in the debtor's assets. Consequently, many laws relating to acquisitions became applicable to obligations.[7]

However, in the course of time, a substantial change—manifested in the gradual adoption of many important new principles—occurred in the character of contractual obligations in Jewish law. The law of obligations diverged from the law of acquisitions. It became possible to create an obligation even as to an object not yet in existence and therefore not capable of being "acquired." It was also established that an obligation could be created even when the debtor had no property to serve as security for the obligation. These and many other changes and developments[8] transformed the Jewish law of contractual obligations from an essentially property orientation to a basically personal one; the property aspect was subordinated to the personal.[9] Obviously, this important change in content also exerted a strong influence in effecting changes in legal classification; various legal matters were removed from the category of acquisitions and classified instead as part of the law of obligations.

2. PUBLIC AND ADMINISTRATIVE LAW

As a result of far-reaching social changes, substantial changes also occurred in almost all of the core subject matter of certain areas of the law. This was true, for example, with regard to public and administrative law, which was almost completely transformed as a result of fundamental changes that occurred in Jewish communal government during the course of Jewish history. In the early periods, public law defined the legal relationship between the people, on the one hand, and the individual who was the head of the people—such as the king, the *nasi,* or the exilarch—on the other.

By way of contrast, the new communal situation produced an elaborate system of public and administrative law to regulate collective leadership, whether elected or appointed. The local government of the Jewish community—and of associations of different communities—and the representative and elected institutions of that government were based upon the provisions of Jewish law. The halakhic authorities (and the leaders of the community, by means of communal legislation)[10] were required to de-

7. *See infra* p. 580. *See also* M. Elon, EJ, XI, pp. 227–232, s.v. Lien (reprinted in *Principles,* pp. 287–294); XII, pp. 1310–1316, s.v. Obligations, law of (reprinted in *Principles,* pp. 241–246).

8. *See* M. Elon, EJ, V, pp. 923–933, s.v. Contract (reprinted in *Principles,* pp. 246–256).

9. *See id.*

10. *See infra* pp. 681ff.

cide many questions of public and administrative law: matters dealing with the relation between citizens and the public authority, and between the public authority and its employees; the composition of communal institutions; the method of electing and appointing officials of communal institutions and other public officials; the procedure for communal legislation and the legal administration of communal agencies; the procedure for tax assessment and the methods of collection; and many other problems concerning the legal aspects of the economic and fiscal relationships in the community. Such problems gave rise to thousands of responsa and hundreds of communal legislative enactments by means of which the halakhic authorities and the communal leaders developed a whole new legal system of Jewish public law. This enormous development also required decisions as to how to classify these subjects in Jewish law.[11]

3. CONFLICT OF LAWS

Sometimes in the development of the law, areas open up that are virtually new creations. One prime example is the area of conflict of laws, which developed primarily as a result of social and geographic changes that took place in the course of time. The conventional view is that conflict of laws should not be regarded as a separate subject area of Jewish law. This view follows from the character of Jewish law as personal, *i.e.*, Jewish law purports to be binding on every Jew, no matter whether he is located within or beyond the territorial boundaries of Jewish sovereignty or autonomous jurisdiction. Consequently, the fact that a contract between two Jews is entered into in State A to be performed in State B—a situation which creates many problems in the field of conflict of laws—would have no legal significance in Jewish law.

Nevertheless, Jewish law was not without many important conflict-of-laws problems. These problems arose because: (a) notwithstanding the existence of Jewish juridical autonomy during much of Jewish history, Jews were subject to the overriding sovereignty of the various governments within whose boundaries they lived, each having its own legal system; and (b) even more importantly, the various centers of Jewish life were scattered among different sovereign states. Because of this dispersal of Jewish com-

11. For example, Maimonides' *MT* contains almost no discussion of these questions and therefore, naturally, did not classify them. On the other hand, they were discussed later to some extent in the *Turim* and in the *Shulḥan Arukh. See also* M. Elon, EJ, VIII, pp. 279–287, s.v. Hekdesh (reprinted in *Principles*, pp. 701–708); XIII, pp. 1351–1359, s.v. Public authority (reprinted in *Principles*, pp. 645–654); XV, pp. 837–873, s.v. Taxation (reprinted in *Principles*, pp. 662–701).

munities, many *takkanot*[12] and customs[13] with reference to the same legal subject differed from place to place.

This situation, it is true, existed to some extent even in the Talmudic period. However, it intensified immensely from the tenth century C.E. onward when, instead of a single center with hegemony over all of the Jewish diaspora, different Jewish population centers were created alongside one another, so that different local enactments were promulgated and local customs and local decision making proliferated. Thus, although there was no problem of choice between Jewish and non-Jewish law, if some of the events in a particular case occurred in place A and others in place B, choice-of-law problems did arise as to which of the different customs and *takkanot* of the different places within the Jewish legal system should govern in any particular case. In addition, because of the close contact between Jewish law, on the one hand, and, on the other, the non-Jewish law generally applicable in each of the different places of dispersion where the Jewish people lived, the doctrine of *dina de-malkhuta dina*[14] crystallized and developed, and in turn generated various principles in the area of conflict of laws.[15]

II. THE CONCRETENESS OF JEWISH LEGAL TERMINOLOGY

There is an additional reason why great caution is necessary in any attempt to translate the terminology of Jewish law into the abstract legal concepts that are commonly used today in various other legal systems. Jewish legal terminology is taken from actual life situations and is remarkably concrete—for example, "horn" (*keren*), "tooth" (*shen*), "foot" (*regel*), and "pit" (*bor*) are terms for major categories of torts in Jewish law. A Jewish legal term may have various meanings, so that careful and thorough analysis is necessary in order to fix the exact meaning of the term in a particular context. For example, the term *ḥazakah* has at least four different meanings: (1) a mode of acquisition of property, (2) a legal presumption, (3) possession, and (4) the rule (characterized by Jewish law as procedural) that pos-

12. *See infra* pp. 666–677.
13. *See infra* p. 936.
14. *See supra* pp. 64–74.
15. For specific examples, *see* M. Elon, EJ, V, pp. 882–890, s.v. Conflict of laws (reprinted in *Principles*, pp. 715–723). *See also* the discussion there of litigation between parties, one of whom is Jewish and one not. For creativity and developments in the field of criminal law, *see supra* pp. 10–11; p. 47 and n. 1 and the sources there cited.

session of real property for three years under claim of right is equivalent to a deed as proof of ownership.

Similarly, the term *kinyan* is used to refer to a mode of acquisition, *i.e.*, a method of acquiring property (or establishing an obligation), but it also means ownership. The term *o'nes* could mean "force" or "coercion," *i.e.*, duress; or it could mean "superior force," *i.e.*, *vis major;* or it could mean "the use of force against a woman," *i.e.*, rape.

Conversely, common terms in other legal systems may be translated by a number of Hebrew legal terms. For example, "contract," which in current legal Hebrew is *ḥozeh*,[16] is referred to in Jewish legal sources by various names such as *ḥiyyuv, kinyan, shetar,* and in a later period, *hitkashrut* (from the root "to bind"; *cf.* "obligation," from a Latin root, *ligare,* with the same meaning). These same terms, moreover, could also be used for meanings other than "contract." For example, *ḥiyyuv* may mean a debt that is not the result of a contract, and *shetar* may simply mean a "document."

It should be pointed out that much of the recent research in Jewish law, as well as the considerable analysis of Jewish law contained in the opinions of the Israeli courts, has helped appreciably to clarify problems in Jewish legal classification and terminology. A significant example of such a contribution is the *Digest of the Responsa Literature,*[17] which, in addition to setting out the substance of the "case law" component of Jewish law, classifies this material into specific topics, and divides each topic into sections and subsections, all arranged according to a clear and useful system of terminology.[18]

III. THE NEED FOR RESEARCH INTO ALL PERIODS OF JEWISH LAW; THE HISTORICAL-DOGMATIC (ALSO CALLED HISTORICAL-ANALYTICAL) METHOD

A fundamental question relating to the scope of Jewish legal study deserves to be considered in greater detail, because this question is critical to the way

16. This term appears only once in the Bible, but there it has no legal significance: "For you have said, 'We have made a covenant with Death, concluded a pact (*ḥozeh*) with Sheol'" (Isaiah 28:15). Apparently, it was J.S. Ẓuri (*Mishpat ha-Talmud* [Talmudic Law], V, p. 1) who first used the word in the sense of "contract," for which it is now the accepted Hebrew legal term.

17. *See Digest of the Responsa Literature of Spain and North Africa, Legal Digest,* 2 vols., 1986; *Digest of the Responsa Literature, Responsa of Asheri,* 1965, Introduction, pp. 7–12. For full discussion of these references, *see infra* pp. 1525–1528. These publications have greatly refined and crystallized the classification and terminology of Jewish legal institutions.

18. On these problems of Jewish legal research, *see* Gulak, *Yesodei,* I, pp. 3–19, II, pp. 5–6; Elon, *Ḥerut,* pp. XI–XIV, p. 1 n. 1; *Digest (Asheri), supra* n. 17.

in which Jewish law is understood and to how Jewish law is received into the legal system of the State of Israel.

Almost up to the present, the literature of scientific research into Jewish law has been mainly devoted to the Biblical and Talmudic periods. This was the approach taken by scholars such as John Selden, a seventeenth century pioneer in the scientific research of Jewish law;[19] Johann David Michaelis,[20] in the second half of the eighteenth century; Eduard Gans,[21] Joseph Levy Saalschütz,[22] Samuel Mayer,[23] and Joseph Salvdor,[24] in the nineteenth century; and in the twentieth century in the books of J.S. Ẓuri,[25] the enlightening and exhaustive studies of Asher Gulak on property[26] and contract[27] law in the Talmudic period, and the two volumes of essays by Boaz Cohen on Jewish and Roman Law.[28]

19. For details of the research of John Selden, *see* S. Eisenstadt, *Ein Mishpat* [A Bibliography of Jewish Law], p. 102, doc. 884; p. 126, doc. 1136; p. 151, doc. 1449; p. 207, doc. 2207; p. 337, doc. 3718; p. 359, doc. 4002.

20. J.D. Michaelis, *Mosaisches Recht* [Mosaic Law], 2nd ed., Reutlingen, 1785–1793; *id., Mosaisches Peinliches Recht nebst einer Vergleichung des heutigen Peinlichen Rechtes mit demselben* [A Comparative Study of Mosaic and Contemporary Penal Law], Braunschweig u. Hildesheim, 1778; *id., Abhandlungen von dem Ehegesetzen Mosis, welche die Heyrathen in die nahe Freundschaft untersagen* [Studies in Mosaic Marriage Laws Forbidding Incestuous Marriages], Goettingen, 1768.

21. E. Gans, "Die Grundzüge des mosaisch-talmudischen Erbrechts" [Basic Elements of the Mosaic-Talmudic Law of Succession], *Zeitschrift für die Wiss. des Jud.* (Zunz), B.I. (1823), H. III, pp. 419–471.

22. J.L. Saalschütz, *Das Mosaisches Recht mit Berücksichtigung des spätern Jüdischen* [Mosaic Law in the Light of Later Jewish Law], Berlin, 1846–1848.

23. S. Mayer, *Die Rechte der Israeliten, Athener und Römer, mit Rücksicht auf die neuen Gesetzgebungen* [Israelite, Athenian, and Roman Law in the Light of Modern Legislation], I, *das Öffentliche Recht* [Public Law], Leipzig, 1868, II, *das Privatrecht* [Private Law], Leipzig, 1865.

24. J. Salvdor, *Histoire des Institutions de Moïse et du Peuple Hébreu* [A History of Mosaic and Hebrew Institutions], Paris, 1828.

25. J.S. Ẓuri, *Mishpat ha-Talmud* [Talmudic Law], in twelve parts: Kodemot [Introductions]; Mishpat ha-Nefashot [Capital Crimes]; Mishpat ha-Mishpaḥah [Family Law]; Mishpat ha-Yerushah [Law of Succession]; Mishpat ha-Nekhasim [Property Law]; Mishpat ha-Hitḥayyevut [Law of Obligations]; Mishpat ha-Onshin [Penal Law]; Mishpat ha-Din [Judicial Proceedings]; Mishpat ha-Medinah [Public (State) Law]; Mishpat ha-Ḥevrah [Law of Associations]; Mishpat ha-Kohanim [Law of Priests]; Mishpat ha-Mikdash [Law of the Temple], Warsaw, 1921–1922; *id., Toledot ha-Mishpat ha-Ẓibburi ha-Ivri, Shilton ha-Nesi'ut ve-ha-Va'ad* [A History of Jewish Public Law, The Rule of the Patriarchate and the Council], Paris, 1931, *et al.*

26. A. Gulak, *Le-Ḥeker Toledot ha-Mishpat ha-Ivri bi-Tekufat ha-Talmud* [Studies in the History of Jewish Law in the Talmudic Period], I, Dinei Karka'ot [Law of Real Property], Ha-Sifriyyah ha-Mishpatit, Jerusalem, 1929.

27. A. Gulak, *Toledot ha-Mishpat be-Yisra'el bi-Tekufat ha-Talmud, ha-Ḥiyyuv ve-Shi'budav* [A History of Jewish Law in the Talmudic Period: Obligations and Their Associated Liens], 1939.

28. B. Cohen, *Jewish and Roman Law,* New York, 1966.

The post-Talmudic period, extending over some 1300 years, fared not nearly as well as a subject for Jewish legal research. Some scholars, including the majority of those mentioned up to this point, did not even deal with this period. Others dealt with it only perfunctorily, merely mentioning the basic laws as they are found in major codes such as *Sefer ha-Halakhot* of Alfasi, the *Mishneh Torah* of Maimonides, the *Turim* of Jacob b. Asher, and the *Shulḥan Arukh* of Joseph Caro. Examples of such treatment may be found in the research of Hirsch Fassel,[29] Zacharias Frankel,[30] Leopold Auerbach,[31] and Moses Bloch[32] in the nineteenth century, and of Mordecai Rapaport in the beginning of the twentieth century.[33] Not only did these scholars not concern themselves with the historical development of Jewish law in its various stages during the post-Talmudic period (either chronologically or according to particular geographical centers of Jewish life), but even from the purely dogmatic (analytical) point of view they did not mention most of the material on Jewish law contained in the unexplored treasures of commentaries and novellae, the codificatory literature, the collections of legislative enactments and of legal forms, the books of principles of decision making, the reports of travels, the books on Jewish thought, and—most importantly—the massive treasure of the responsa literature.

Even in Gulak's work, *Yesodei ha-Mishpat ha-Ivri* [The Foundations of Jewish Law], which was the first comprehensive scientific work on Jewish law in Hebrew, the attention to post-Talmudic halakhic literature was relatively minimal. The four volumes of Gulak's work cover the substantive

29. H. Fassel, *Das Mosaisch-Rabbinische Strafgesetz und strafrechtliche Gerichts-Verfahren* [Mosaic-Rabbinic Penal Law and Criminal Proceedings], Gross-Kanisza, 1870.

30. Z. Frankel, "Über manches Polizeiliche des talmudischen Rechts" [On Various Talmudic Police (Criminal) Laws], *MGWJ*, I (1851–1852), pp. 243–261; *id.*, *Der gerichtliche Beweis nach mosaisch-talmudischen Rechte: Ein Beitrag zur Kenntniss des mosaisch-talmudischen Criminal und Civilrechts* [Legal Proof in Mosaic-Talmudic Law: A Contribution to Knowledge of Mosaic-Talmudic Criminal and Civil Law], Berlin, 1846.

31. L. Auerbach, *Das jüdische Obligationenrecht nach den Quellen und mit besonderer Berücksichtigung des römischen und deutschen Rechts, systematisch dargestellt* [The Jewish Law of Obligations Systematically Presented According to the Sources, with Special Regard to Roman and German Law], Berlin, 1870. A reprint of Auerbach's book was published by M. Shalom, Ltd., Gedera, Israel, 1976, with an introduction and supplementary notes (in English) by Abraham M. Fuss.

32. M. Bloch, *Das mosaisch-talmudische Polizeirecht* [Mosaic-Talmudic Criminal Law], Budapest, 1879; *id.*, *Das mosaisch-talmudische Straftgerichtsverfahren* [Mosaic-Talmudic Criminal Proceedings], Budapest, 1901; *id.*, *Das mosaisch-talmudisch Besitzrecht* [The Mosaic-Talmudic Law of Possession], Budapest, 1897; *id.*, *Der Vertrag nach mosaische-talmudischen Rechte* [The Mosaic-Talmudic Law of Contract], Budapest (Leipzig), 1893; *id.*, *Das mosaische-talmudische Erbrecht* [The Mosaic-Talmudic Law of Succession], Budapest, 1890; *id.*, *Die Vormundschaft nach mosaisch-talmudischen Recht* [Fiduciary Relations in Mosaic-Talmudic Law], Budapest, 1882.

33. M.W. Rapaport, *Der Talmud und sein Recht* [The Talmud and Its Law], Berlin, 1912.

principles of Jewish civil law as well as the law of procedure and evidence,[34] and embody the author's attempt to expound the principles of Jewish law and the Jewish legal order in a form consistent with modern juristic thought. From this point of view, the work is a basic text for Jewish legal research regardless of whether one agrees with all of its hypotheses.[35] Gulak successfully accomplished "the scientific organization of the substance of Jewish law";[36] but, considering the state of research into Jewish law in his time, he limited himself to the outlines and the basic material in the Talmud, the codes and their ancillary literature (*nos'ei kelim*, lit. "armor bearers," *i.e.*, commentaries and glosses).[37]

Only recently has there been some change in the direction of emphasizing dogmatic (analytical) historical research in Jewish law in the post-Talmudic period, reflected in the research of several scholars such as Simḥah Assaf,[38] Abraham Ḥayyim Freimann, and Isaac Herzog.[39]

What is the explanation for the astonishing fact that in the study of a legal system extending over 3000 years, most attention has been centered on only slightly more than the first half of this period, and the last 1300 years have been investigated only in a cursory manner? There is even more reason for wonder if we consider that although the Biblical and Talmudic periods are more significant in terms of spiritual values and authority, the post-Talmudic period has vastly more significance from the standpoint of

34. The first volume, which treats the laws of acquisition, was published in Warsaw, 1913; *see* S. Eisenstadt, *Ẓiyyon be-Mishpat*, p. 167. In 1923, a second edition of the first volume appeared together with three additional volumes. In 1967, a facsimile edition was published by Devir, Tel Aviv.

35. *See, e.g.*, the criticism of Rabbi A.A. Kaplan, *Be-Ikvot ha-Yir'ah*, Jerusalem, 1960, pp. 67–74. On several matters where his critique is directed at the substantive contents, his criticism is justified. *See also supra* n. 4. However, his overall objection to the need for scientific and methodical research into Jewish law is astonishing. When Gulak wrote his book, there was a pressing need for such research; and there still is such a need, notwithstanding the existence of Maimonides' *Mishneh Torah* and the *Bet Yosef*, etc. Scientific legal research does not purport to supplant the great creations of the halakhic masters. Rather, its aim is to search out and arrange Jewish law—including those great creations—in a scientific and systematic form. Such research was, as Gulak put it, "a forgotten and deserted landscape," and engaging in such research involves no denigration of anyone. On Gulak's method of research in Jewish law, *see also* M. Elon, "More about Research into Jewish Law," *Modern Research in Jewish Law* (ed. B.S. Jackson), Leiden, 1980, pp. 66, 72–83; *id.*, "In Memory of Asher Gulak," *Shenaton ha-Mishpat ha-Ivri* [Annual of the Institute for Research in Jewish Law, The Hebrew University of Jerusalem] (hereinafter, *Shenaton*), IX–X (1982–1983), pp. 3–10.

36. Gulak, *Yesodei*, I, p. 4.

37. As to *nos'ei kelim*, *see infra* p. 1173 and n. 85.

38. *See, e.g.*, his books, *Battei ha-Din* and *Onshin*.

39. Freimann, *Kiddushin ve-Nissu'in*. Isaac Herzog's *Institutions* is another analytical study that emphasizes the post-Talmudic period.

thoroughness, number and range of legal decisions, and quantity of legal and quasi-legal material.

It is submitted that this phenomenon can be explained by three factors—two are subjective and one, which will be discussed last, is objective. These factors have sometimes all been operative at the same time, but at other times only one or two of them influenced any particular scholar.

The first factor is manifest in the indifferent and sometimes even negative approach of some of the scholars toward the halakhic *oeuvre* of the post-Talmudic period. Some saw in it barren scholasticism and casuistic subtlety for its own sake. Others saw it as a creation whose horizon reached only to the walls of the ghetto. Still others saw it not merely as a legal system that was lacking the pulse beat reflecting the great vitality of real life, but as a system in which the lifeblood had completely congealed to the point that there was no place for any innovative developments in its study halls. This approach was an aspect of how more than a few scholars viewed Jewish history and intellectual creativity during most of the medieval period, namely, as "a period that the builders rejected."[40]

The second factor is related to the purpose that animated research in Jewish law. The objective was pure research; there was no attempt to reach legal conclusions for practical application in the real world. This research, which extended from the end of the eighteenth century through the nineteenth century, was carried on at a time when Jewish juridical autonomy in the diaspora was gradually being reduced to the point of extinction. Not only did the scholars in the field therefore fail to see any practical relevance to their research in Jewish law, but to a considerable extent they actively opposed even such limited practical application of Jewish law in the life of the Jewish community as may have been possible at that time.

The purposes of research in Jewish law in those days varied. They included: (a) comparison with other legal systems, (b) study of the ethical and philosophical values expressed in Jewish legal institutions, and (c) study of the historical and literary themes contained in the sources of Jewish law. The common denominator of these scientific approaches was the insistence that investigation and study were for their own sake, embellished by a greater or lesser measure of apologetics; but there was no purpose to satisfy the actual legal needs of the Jewish community. Whereas during the time that Jewish law was a living system the traditional method of study and analysis of the *Halakhah* was to a considerable extent intended to satisfy the actual needs of the entire people in regard to its legal relationships,

40. H.H. Ben-Sasson, *Perakim be-Toledot ha-Yehudim bi-Mei ha-Beinayim* [Chapters in the History of the Jews in the Middle Ages], Introduction, p. XI. The allusion is to Psalms 118:22 ("The stone that the builders rejected has become the chief cornerstone").

the goal of the systematic scientific researchers was merely to satisfy the needs of the narrow circle of researchers themselves. Research with this purpose could allow itself to isolate for study one or another period from the total spiritual-legal order, so as to extract its ethical, philosophical, literary, and historical conclusions or to compare it to other ancient legal systems.

The third factor is connected not to the outlook or the purposes of the scholar but rather to the objective circumstances of the subject of the research. It is known to all those who have even limited knowledge of post-Talmudic halakhic literature that that literature is difficult. Although considerable effort is certainly necessary to understand all the details and latent implications of the *Halakhah* contained in the Talmud itself, nevertheless this material in the final analysis is fixed and finite, and there are guidebooks such as introductions, books on principles of decision making, and, more recently, many concordances to the literature of the *tannaim* and *amoraim*.

Post-Talmudic halakhic literature, by contrast, is much more diffuse. It includes immense and massive material, consisting of three principal types: commentaries and novellae, responsa literature, and codificatory literature. Collections of *takkanot* and legal forms and other quasi-legal historical literature are also important for research in post-Talmudic Jewish law. The major sources of guidance through this vast material are the commentaries and novellae that follow the sequence of the discussions (*sugyot*) in the Talmud, and also the major code-books—of Alfasi, Maimonides, Jacob b. Asher and Joseph Caro—and their ancillary literature. Even full use of those resources will not reveal to the researcher a considerable part of the post-Talmudic halakhic material, especially the pertinent material hidden in the vastness of the responsa literature.

The first two factors appear to have lost any force they may have had: the first factor (denigration of the value of post-Talmudic halakhic literature), because it is based on an erroneous premise; and the second (the purely academic character of the enterprise), because of the essential change in the condition of life of the Jewish people in the twentieth century. The indifferent or negative attitude to the Jewish legal development of the post-Talmudic period is wrong both because it fails to give due regard to the extent of juridical autonomy of the various Jewish centers up to the eighteenth century (and in North Africa and the Near East even afterwards) and because it ignores the creativity and the continuous development of the institutions of the Jewish legal system in civil, administrative, public, and to a certain extent even criminal law, until very shortly before the Emancipation. This creativity and development took place because Jewish law was a living law that was applied in practice to the solution of real-life problems.

Increasingly, contemporary scholars of Jewish history are stressing the need to adopt a different perspective on the history of the Jewish people during its dispersion in the Middle Ages. They are pointing out that this history was one of activity and not passivity, that it was abundantly creative and rich in spiritual power and tenacity notwithstanding the constraints on the Jewish people at that time. Certainly, one of the clearest, if not the clearest, of the manifestations of originality and creativity in the history of the Jewish people in the Middle Ages was the creativity in the Jewish legal system.[41]

As to the second factor, the Jewish national reawakening added another purpose to scientific research in Jewish law. From then on, it became the task of the scholar, above and beyond the scholarly purposes that we have discussed, to direct scientific research to preparing Jewish law for adaptation into a living and working legal system, *i.e.*, the legal system of the future Jewish state. This objective was discussed in detail in the program of the Ha-Mishpat Ha-Ivri Society, which was organized in 1918;[42] in studies and plans appearing throughout the various issues of the periodical *Ha-Mishpat Ha-Ivri*, in 1918 and from 1926 to 1936,[43] and in the five compilations of materials from that periodical; in the four volumes of the periodical *Ha-Mishpat*, which appeared from 1927 to 1931; and in additional sources.[44] Indeed, at the opening of the School of Law and Economics in Tel Aviv in 1935, this objective was explicitly declared to be one of the goals

41. *Id.* at 10–16; *see also* the quotation from Y. Kaufmann, *supra* pp. 38–39.

42. As to the Ha-Mishpat Ha-Ivri Society, *see infra* pp. 1588–1591.

43. Gulak presented an interesting plan in his article, "Tokhnit le-Avodat Ḥevrat Ha-Mishpat Ha-Ivri" [A Program for the Ha-Mishpat Ha-Ivri Society], *Ha-Mishpat Ha-Ivri*, II (1927), pp. 195–204.

44. Several issues of *Ha-Mishpat* appeared after 1931. See also the correspondence between Chaim Tchernowitz (Rav Ẓa'ir) and Chaim Weizmann, who was the head of the Zionist Executive in London, regarding the proposal to establish an academy for research in Jewish Law in Jerusalem. (This unpublished material is in the Aḥad Ha-Am Archive in the National Library at the Hebrew University in Jerusalem, File 33/3). The correspondence is from October 1921–January 1922. Tchernowitz proposed that the Zionist Organization establish in Jerusalem an academy for research into Jewish law, the purpose of which would be, *inter alia*, "to prepare the law for life in a sovereign state when the time is ripe and the nations of the world agree to recognize [our right to] our political freedom in our land." In his letter to Weizmann, written during the intermediate days of the Sukkot festival, 1921, Tchernowitz included a detailed plan and even a budget. In a letter of January 3, 1922, Weizmann stated that the proposal "was received by the Zionist Executive with enthusiasm and we have decided to begin the realization of this project in the course of the coming months." He also informed Tchernowitz that Tchernowitz had been chosen to be the director of the academy. The latter responded, accepting the appointment and discussing various details involved in getting the project started. Apparently, however, nothing further came of this. (I am grateful to my good friend, Prof. S. Ettinger, who drew my attention to the correspondence.)

of the Ha-Mishpat Ha-Ivri Society, and it was also one of the goals of the study of Jewish law in the Talmud department of the Hebrew University.[45]

Despite growing recognition of the need to study Jewish law with a view to preparing it for practical application, most of the scholars did not sufficiently understand that such study required research into every period from the very beginning of Jewish law up to the present. It seems obvious, however, that scientific research and elaboration of any legal principle can be accomplished only by reviewing all of the various stages of development of the principle throughout its history. No principle of Jewish law can be established on the basis of the Talmud alone, without reference to the subsequent development of the principle, any more than the "Jewish law" on any point can be definitively established solely from the writings of one of the later authorities (*aḥaronim*) without considering the nature and character of the controlling principle earlier in its history. In either case, one would not be setting forth the position of Jewish law on the particular subject involved but rather pointing to only a single early or late link in the chain of Jewish law.

It may perhaps be true that a rabbi deciding a point of Jewish law fulfills the obligation of his office when he finds and follows an opinion of one of the great *aḥaronim;* but the legal scholar who wishes to present the essence and character of a particular principle, especially when he wishes to draw conclusions with regard to adapting that principle for practical application, must know: (a) what were the various stages of this principle throughout all the periods of Jewish law, (b) what were the economic and social factors that brought about these various stages, (c) how Jewish law absorbed the changes during the various stages and incorporated them as an integral part of its legal system, and (d) what were the legal methods Jewish law employed to integrate the new developments into existing law.[46]

As has been pointed out, an important reason for lack of comprehensiveness in Jewish legal research was the failure to appreciate sufficiently the enormous development that each principle of Jewish law underwent in

45. Similarly, Jewish law was taught, to a limited extent, in the governmental law classes in Jerusalem. *See* S. Eisenstadt, "Al Hora'at ha-Mishpat ha-Ivri be-Vet ha-Sefer le-Mishpat Shel Memshelet Ereẓ Yisra'el" [On Teaching Jewish Law in the Law School of the Palestine Government], *Ha-Mishpat,* II (1927), pp. 209–216.

46. The methods of integration included interpretation, legislation, custom, and other similar legal sources, which will be discussed in this volume, chs. 8–12 and in Volume II of this work. For the importance of this approach to research in Jewish law, *see* Elon, *Ḥerut,* pp. 261ff.

the post-Talmudic period.[47] Now that the extent of this development is more generally understood, it is beyond dispute that conclusions as to any particular principle of Jewish law cannot be properly reached without full research into the status of the principle after, as well as before, the completion of the Talmud. A.H. Freimann has well described this dynamism that existed in the post-Talmudic period:[48]

> The living *Halakhah* that was applied in practice during the last generations before the Emancipation was far different in most of the branches of the law not only from the Talmudic *Halakhah* but also from the *Halakhah* laid down in the *Shulḥan Arukh.* This will not surprise the legal historian, because he is accustomed always to keep in view the social function that rules and principles are designed to fulfill in governing relationships in the society and among the people according to the needs of the particular time and place.[49]

47. *See, e.g.,* the plan "Sha'arei Ha-Mishpat Ha-Ivri" [The Gates of Jewish Law], prepared by the Ha-Mishpat Ha-Ivri Society immediately after its organization (*Ha-Mishpat Ha-Ivri,* Moscow, June–August 1918, pp. 122ff., written by P. Dikstein on the basis of the Society's discussions and précis). *Inter alia,* the plan refers to the material on Jewish law in the Talmudic and post-Talmudic periods, and in this connection states (p. 129):

> When we divide all of our legal material into two periods, as mentioned, we find that the first period [until the close of the Talmud] is the creative period, which in importance and inherent value is greatly superior to the second and also has great significance as a unit in and of itself. The second period [from the close of the Talmud onward] is poorer in creativity and in new ideas, but quantitatively exceeds the Talmudic period at least tenfold. Under the approach of the members who wish to delete from the Talmud the debates as well as those matters that have little inherent value, much of the responsa, the codes, and the commentaries, both on the Talmud and on the codes, should also be abridged or deleted. Moreover, most of the material should be deleted under this view, and only the few places that have some new idea or reasoning or reform suitable for contemporary needs should be selected [for retention].

Similarly, Tchernowitz, in setting forth his proposal for an academy for research into Jewish law (*supra* n. 44), could still argue that "almost from the completion of the Talmud and especially after the legal power of the *geonim* ended, our national law has lost its creative power and can now only explain and interpret." Even Gulak, in the introduction to his study of the law of obligations, implies that in his opinion the main creativity in Jewish law was in the Talmudic period and that subsequently Jewish law merely refined what the Talmudic period had created. *See also* H. Cohn, "Da'agah le-Yom Maḥar" [Concern for Tomorrow], *Ha-Praklit,* 1946, p. 43, proposing that all that has been added to Jewish law since the loss of political sovereignty after the Second Jewish Commonwealth be discarded. This is a strange view, which its author apparently later retracted. *See also* the opinion of M. Silberg, *Talmudic Law and the Modern State,* discussed *infra* p. 181 n. 360.

48. A.H. Freimann, "Dinei Yisra'el be-Ereẓ Yisra'el" [Jewish Law in the Land of Israel], *Lu'aḥ ha-Areẓ,* 1946, pp. 120–121.

49. Research into how a given legal subject was dealt with in the various Jewish centers in the diaspora and throughout all periods of the exile is of special significance, because differences in the economic and social conditions in each center also affected the shaping, in each of the different centers, of the legal institution dealing with that subject matter. *See supra* pp. 46–51. It is especially worth noting that to a great and significant extent the teachings and enactments of the halakhic authorities and communal leaders in Turkey,

Undoubtedly, an equally important cause impeding sufficient research into the post-Talmudic period is the third factor that we have discussed—the difficulty of making any headway into this enormous legal storehouse and of finding the relevant material. This difficulty is especially great in that portion which constitutes the great bulk of post-Talmudic halakhic literature, namely, the responsa literature, the case law of the Jewish legal system, estimated to contain as many as 300,000 responsa.[50] Dealing with almost any part of this massive material, even for one who devotes himself exclusively to the study of Jewish law, requires vast knowledge and effort, and even one so equipped will not know what percentage of all the responsa on a particular subject he has succeeded in finding.

Failure to find pertinent material contained in the responsa literature has more serious consequences than does lack of knowledge of some particular law contained in some other type of post-Talmudic halakhic literature. This is not only because the responsa literature makes up the dominant part of post-Talmudic halakhic literature in terms of quantity, but also because, in terms of subject matter and quality, the differences between it and the other forms of Jewish legal literature make it the prime source of research into every question in Jewish law.

Commentaries and novellae are fundamentally of an abstract, hypothetical character and not intended for practical application; and the codificatory literature generally indicates only the substance of legal conclusions without explaining how the conclusions were reached. Only in the responsa literature is the researcher in the midst of a real-life legal situation, listening to the facts and the arguments of the parties, and accompanying an authoritative halakhic decisionmaker during each stage of his legal analysis.

The student and the researcher studying a responsum find themselves inside the laboratory. They share in experimentation and creation. They are participants in a comprehensive and penetrating legal analysis. They hear an objective and candid description of the economic and social background

---

North Africa, and other eastern countries from the seventeenth century onward were unknown in the various Ashkenazic centers. As we shall see (*infra* pp. 1584–1586), it was specifically in those eastern lands that Jewish juridical autonomy continued even after it ceased to exist in Europe.

50. It is estimated that these responsa are contained in more than seven thousand volumes (it should be remembered that one "book" of responsa can sometimes have several volumes, such as those of Rashba, Maharashdam, etc.). Boaz Cohen, in his *Kuntres ha-Teshuvot* [Pamphlet of Responsa], Budapest, 1930, and its supplement, listed nearly two thousand printed books of responsa; but, as he pointed out in his Introduction (p. 2), the list is far from complete. Even today, the responsa literature is still growing. *See also infra* p. 1524.

as part of the legal discussion; and they can discern clues, some more apparent than others, to the arduous search of the halakhic authority for a decision based on a legal solution anchored in the past yet satisfying the manifold needs of his own generation. In addition, the fact that the legal principles contained in the responsa, whether established or innovative, were the product of deliberation and analysis of legal problems that arose out of actual life situations entitles them not only to greater authority than conclusions contained in the literature of commentary and novellae but also, according to most halakhic scholars, to superiority over principles in the codificatory literature.[51]

Obviously, the difficulty in exploring the enormous material in the responsa literature cannot justify allowing research in Jewish law to remain incomplete and stunted to the point that any subject studied is plumbed to no more than a fraction of its depth. An important step toward removing this difficulty is the project undertaken by the Institute for Research in Jewish Law of the Hebrew University in Jerusalem, which is preparing a digest of the responsa literature. The digest has three parts: a legal digest, a historical digest, and an index of sources. The most important part is the legal digest, which contains all the legal material found in each responsum, and classifies the material alphabetically according to major topics and subtopics under a modern legal classification system that nevertheless preserves the original Hebrew terminology.

The Institute has completed digests of all of the more than ten thousand responsa of the Spanish and North African authorities from the eleventh to the fifteenth centuries. These digests are planned for publication in seven volumes, of which five have already appeared.[52] As additional digests of responsa literature are published, more and more of the secrets of this great unexplored storehouse will be open for full, methodical research into the principles and rules of Jewish law.

This method of researching each legal institution in Jewish law in all its periods will make it possible for the scholar of Jewish law to accomplish the two great tasks of scholarship incumbent upon him in every age, and especially in the State of Israel today. The first is to examine the changes and modifications undergone by each Jewish legal institution in its historical stages and in the various geographical centers,[53] while identifying the economic and social factors that brought about these changes. This investigation will lay bare the central concept that is the basis of that legal institution—a concept that was preserved during all of the periods and through-

51. *See Resp. Maharil* #72; *Resp. Meshiv Davar,* I, #24; and *see infra* pp. 975–978, 1457–1459.

52. For full particulars as to the digests, *see infra* pp. 1525–1528. *See also supra* n. 17.

53. *See supra* nn. 46–49 and associated text.

out the various places of Jewish life and that constituted the central core of the institution through all its stages. The second task is to examine the legal methods that Jewish law employed to absorb these changes and modifications and integrate them into its legal structure. These methods constitute the legal sources of Jewish law, *i.e.*, those sources that the *Halakhah* itself recognizes as the instruments for creating and developing the rules of the Jewish legal system.[54] A considerable portion of the present work will be devoted to a detailed study of these sources.[55]

The research methodology here outlined not only presents the substance of Jewish law in all of its comprehensiveness but also enables Jewish law to be properly absorbed into the legal system of the Jewish State.[56] Only such an approach will enable the legal scholar to know when and how to make appropriate connections between the economic and social needs to which the law responded in the various stages of any given legal institution and the economic and social needs of contemporary society.[57]

54. For an example of this methodology, *see* Elon, *Ḥerut,* particularly the Introduction (pp. XI–XIV) and the Summary and Conclusions (pp. 255–269). As to research in Jewish law and its method of development, *see supra* pp. 46–51 and *infra* pp. 1588–1591.

55. *See* ch. 6 and chs. 8–24.

56. For a full discussion, *see infra* Volume IV.

57. For more on this subject, *see* M. Elon, "Ha-Mishpat ha-Ivri be-Mishpat ha-Medinah, Keiẓad?" [Jewish Law in the Legal System of the State—What Is the Way?], *De'ot,* X, pp. 16ff. As to Jewish legal research generally, *see also* I. Englard, "Research in Jewish Law: Its Nature and Function," *Modern Research in Jewish Law* (ed. B.S. Jackson), Leiden, 1980, pp. 21–65; M. Elon, "More about Research into Jewish Law," *id.* at 66–111; B. Schieber, "The Albeck System in Talmudic Research," *id.* at 112–122; the essays of S. Albeck, Ḥaim Cohn, and Bernard Jackson, *id.;* M. Elon, "Im ha-Shenaton" [On the Appearance of the *Shenaton*], *Shenaton,* I (1974), pp. 7–13.

Chapter 4

MISHPAT IVRI: DEFINITION AND NATURE

I. The Concept of *Halakhah*
II. The Reciprocal Relationship between *Halakhah* and *Aggadah*
III. The Term *Mishpat Ivri*
  A. The Terms *Mishpat* and *Din*
  B. The Term *Ivri*
IV. Common Features of "Religious" *Halakhah* and "Legal" *Halakhah*
  A. Common Thought Patterns and Terminology
  B. Common Legal Principles
  C. Dependence of "Religious" Precepts on "Legal" Precepts
  D. Common Fictions
  E. Interaction between Different Parts of the *Halakhah*
    1. The Obligation of Child Support
    2. "The Payment of a Debt is a Religious Obligation"
    3. The Creation of an Obligation by Vow, Ban, or Oath
    4. The Nature of a Divorce Judgment
V. Distinction between "Religious" and "Legal" *Halakhah*—"*Issur*" and "*Mamon*"
  A. Freedom of Contract—"Contracting Out of a Law Contained in the Torah"
  B. Illegal Contracts
  C. Legislation (*Takkanot*)
  D. Custom (*Minhag*)
  E. Different Rules for Decision Making, and Other Distinctions
  F. Distinction between Matters of *Issur* and Matters of *Mamon* with Regard to *Dina de-Malkhuta Dina* ("The Law of the Land Is Law")
  G. Logic and Legal Reasoning as the Major Creative Source of Law in the Area of *Mamon*
VI. Law and Morals in the Jewish Legal System
  A. Reciprocal Relationship between Law and Morals—Recourse by the Legal System to the Moral Imperative
  B. "Exempt by Human Law but Liable by Divine Law"
  C. The Imprecation "He Who Punished" (*Mi she-Para*)
  D. "Fulfillment of Duty in the Sight of Heaven" (*Lazeit Yedei Shamayim*)
  E. "The Sages are Displeased with Him," and Other Forms of Moral-Religious Sanctions
  F. *Lifnim Mi-Shurat Ha-Din*—Acting More Generously than the Law Requires
  G. Law, Justice, and Equity
    1. "Judge Your Neighbor Fairly"
    2. Justice as a Supplement to Law
    3. Justice as a Primary Norm
    4. Law and Equity—Rule and Discretion
  H. Good Faith (*Tom Lev*)

I. THE CONCEPT OF *HALAKHAH*

Mishpat ivri is a part of the corpus of the *Halakhah.*[1] Before defining *mishpat ivri* and discussing its nature, the meaning and content of the concept of *Halakhah* must be briefly examined.

The term *Halakhah* is used in a number of different senses. In its most general and usual sense, *Halakhah* refers to the normative portion of the Oral Law (*Torah she-be-al peh*). In this sense, *Halakhah* is used to contrast with *Aggadah* (or *Haggadah*), which denotes, *inter alia,* wise and ethical sayings, philosophical meditations, and admonitions. The *Halakhah* includes all of the precepts in Judaism—those laws involving the commandments concerning the relationship between people and God ("*bein adam la-makom*") as well as those laws applicable to relationships in human society ("*bein adam le-ḥavero*").[2]

The root of the word *Halakhah* is *halokh* ("to go"). As explained by Nathan b. Jehiel of Rome, the author of the *Arukh:*[3] "[It is] something that proceeds [lit. "*goes* and comes"] from beginning to end, or according to which Israel [*i.e.,* the Jewish people] conducts itself [lit. "the path in which Israel goes"]."[4] Perhaps a clue to the correct philological explanation of the term *Halakhah* is furnished by a *baraita*[5] that states:

1. *See supra* pp. 4–5.

2. At present, laws concerning the relationship between people and God are described—quite arbitrarily and without any basis in the conceptual framework of the *Halakhah*—as "religious" or "ritual," and laws applicable to relationships in human society are called "legal," in a manner reminiscent of the dichotomy in Roman law between *ius divinum* and *ius humanum,* between *Fas and Jus; see* F. Schultz, *History of Roman Legal Science,* pp. 30–31; I. Pokrovsky, *Toledot ha-Mishpat ha-Roma'i* [A History of Roman Law], pp. 24–26; S. Eisenstadt, *Ha-Mishpat ha-Roma'i* [Roman Law], pp. 17, 46–47, 49–50, 55, 70. The laws of the ancient East are also secular in character; *see* L. Finkelstein, *Enẓiklopedyah Mikra'it* [Encyclopaedia Biblica], V, pp. 588–614, s.v. Mishpat (ha-mishpat ba-mizraḥ ha-kadmon), and bibliography, *ad loc. See also* Levinstam, *id.* at 614, 620, s.v. Mishpat (mishpat ha-mikra). A later legal system, Moslem law, exhibits the same integration and unity of the "religious" and the "legal" as does Jewish law; *see* Goitein-Ben Shemesh, *Ha-Mishpat ha-Muslemi bi-Medinat Yisra'el* [Moslem Law in the State of Israel], pp. 20ff.

3. *See Arukh ha-Shalem,* III, p. 208, s.v. Halakh. As to the *Arukh* and *Arukh ha-Shalem, see infra* pp. 1564–1565.

4. *See also* Onkelos' Aramaic translation of Exodus 21:9: *Ka-mishpat ha-banot ya'aseh lah* ("he shall deal with her as is the practice [*mishpat*] with free maidens"): *ke-hilkhat benat Yisra'el ya'avid lah* ("he shall act towards her according to the practice [*hilkhat*] applicable to daughters of Israel"). *See also Arukh ha-Shalem, supra* n. 3.

5. TB Megillah 28b *et al.*

> It was taught in the school of Elijah: Anyone who studies *halakhot* is assured of a place in the world to come, as Scripture says: "His ways (*halikhot*) are everlasting."[6] Do not read it as "His ways" (*halikhot*) but read "His laws" (*halakhot*).[7]

The term *halakhah* was given additional meanings in Talmudic literature. (When used in this work in other than its general and usual sense, it is written with a small "h.") Sometimes, *halakhah* designates "the law" in the sense of a binding decision or ruling on a contested legal issue, as in the frequently used expression: "The law (*halakhah*) is in accordance with the opinion of R. Judah." Sometimes, *halakhah* refers not to the content of a particular precept but to its literary form. When a particular precept is stated as being derived from a verse in the Torah, it is called *midrash;* when it is presented on the basis of its own authority, in abstract form, it is called *halakhah.*[8] The word *halakhot* (plural of *halakhah*) is also used to indicate a collection of a particular category of normative, or even non-normative, rules.[9]

II. THE RECIPROCAL RELATIONSHIP BETWEEN *HALAKHAH* AND *AGGADAH*

As stated, *Halakhah* does not include non-normative matters; these are included in *Aggadah.* However, there is a persistent reciprocal relationship between *Halakhah* and *Aggadah* that finds expression in various ways.

A considerable portion of *Aggadah* consists of the philosophy behind the *Halakhah*—explaining the reasons for the *Halakhah.* These explanations are scattered throughout Talmudic *Aggadah* in connection with strictly

6. Habakkuk 3:6. The JPS *Tanakh,* 1985, has: "His are the ancient routes."

7. The concept of *halikhah, i.e.,* "going" or "walking," is frequently associated with fulfilling God's commandments; *see* Genesis 6:9, 17:1; Exodus 18:20; Deuteronomy 5:30, 13:5. For an alternative philological origin for the term *Halakhah, see* S. Lieberman, *Hellenism in Jewish Palestine* (hereinafter, *Hellenism*), p. 83 n. 3.

8. *See infra* pp. 1047–1049.

9. Such as *hilkhot rofe'im,* "rules relating to physicians" (*Sifrei,* Deuteronomy, Ki Teẓe, sec. 247, p. 276); *hilkhot yeẓirah,* "rules of creation" (TB Sanhedrin 67b). For additional meanings of *Halakhah, see infra* p. 718. For discussions of the concept and its various meanings, *see also* Z. Frankel, *Darkhei ha-Mishnah* [The Methodology of the Mishnah] (hereinafter, *Mishnah*), ed. Sinai, 1959, pp. 6ff.; M. Ish Shalom, *Hakdamah la-Mekhilta* [Introduction to the *Mekhilta*], pp. XXXVIIff.; Weiss, *Dor Dor ve-Doreshav,* I, pp. 67ff.; W. Bacher, *Erkhei Midrash* [Midrashic Terminology], s.v. Halakhah, pp. 30, 182–184; ET, IX, pp. 241–243, s.v. Halakhah; I.M. Guttmann, *Zur Einleitung in die Halacha* [An Introduction to the *Halakhah*], pp. 1–30; H. Strack, *Introduction to the Talmud and Midrash,* Atheneum, N.Y., 1974, p. 6; E.E. Urbach, *The Sages, Their Concepts and Beliefs* (hereinafter, *The Sages*), pp. 586–588.

"legal" norms as well as with commandments concerning human relationships with God. In fact, on appropriate occasions, aggadic material was the basis for normative rulings.[10] This reciprocal relationship is clear in Talmudic literature, where *Halakhah* and *Aggadah* are also intertwined from the literary point of view—*e.g.*, in a particular subject area, aggadic material appears side by side with legal argumentation—as well as in other ways.[11] The relationship also exists even in post-Talmudic literature, in which the division between these two parts of the Oral Law is more distinct.[12] Even in this later period, *Aggadah* continued to fulfill its function of explaining and providing background for various provisions of Jewish law;[13] and sometimes authoritative decisionmakers (*posekim*) and respon-

10. *See* the detailed discussion on this point in Z.H. Chajes, *Darkhei ha-Hora'ah* [Methodology of Decision Making], II (*Collected Writings of Maharaẓ Chajes*, 1958, I, pp. 250–252); Weiss, *Dor Dor ve-Doreshav*, III, ch. 21, pp. 220–223. *See also* Chajes, *op. cit.* (and also his *Imrei Binah* #1), regarding the statement of R. Ze'ira in the name of Samuel: "One may not derive [legal norms] from the *halakhot*, the aggadic passages (*haggadot*), or the *Tosefta* (*Tosafot*), but only from the Talmud" (TJ Pe'ah 2:4; Ḥagigah 1:8). The interpretation of this *dictum* is highly problematic because, among other reasons, the *dictum* places aggadic passages on the same level as the *halakhot* and the *Tosefta* and states that norms may not be derived from any of them. *See also Resp. Noda bi-Yehudah*, Mahadura Tinyana, YD, #161.

For various interpretations of the *dictum* in TJ, *see Tosafot Yom Tov* to M Berakhot 5:4 and *Gilayon R. Akiva Eger, ad loc.*; *Sefer Mayim Ḥayyim* (by the author of *Peri Ḥadash*) to Sh. Ar. OḤ 128, subpar. 20, and *Magen Avraham* to Sh. Ar. OḤ 128, subpar. 29; *Yad Malakhi*, I, Kelalei ha-Alef, #72; and *Resp. Noda bi-Yehudah, supra.* The *dictum* in TJ bears comparison with a *baraita* in TB Bava Batra 130b:

> Our Rabbis taught: One may not derive a legal norm from academic study (*talmud*) or from an actual case [*ma'aseh*; *see infra* ch. 23], unless they [the halakhic authorities involved] specifically state that the norm is intended to be applied in practice (*halakhah le-ma'aseh*). If he [the student] asks and they tell him that the norm is intended to be applied in practice, he may go and apply it in practice.

This means that no legal norm is to be taken as finally settled unless it is declared to be *halakhah le-ma'aseh* (the view of TB) or it is derived from the Talmud (the view of TJ). Regarding the *baraita* in TB, *see infra* pp. 963–964. A similar interpretation of the passage in TJ is implied by *Or Zaru'a*, III, Bava Batra #112, #113, #114; *Resp. Rashba*, I, #335; and *Resp. Radbaz* #647.

11. For example, the way in which interpretive methodology is employed; *see infra* p. 317 regarding the thirty-two canons of Biblical interpretation.

12. Several geonic sources stress that aggadic statements are not to be relied on (*Ha-Eshkol*, ed. Albeck, I, pp. 157–158, Hilkhot Sefer Torah; *Teshuvot ha-Geonim*, ed. Harkavy, #9, #353; *Teshuvat ha-Geonim, Ḥemdah Genuzah* #124). In the post-Talmudic period there is also less literary integration of *Halakhah* and *Aggadah* than in the Talmud. *But see infra* nn. 13, 14.

13. This was the case even in codificatory literature. For example, in his *Mishneh Torah*, Maimonides frequently integrated aggadic and ethical material by way of introduction, or as the rationale or background to many laws. *See* W. Bacher, "Die Agada in Maimunis Werken" [Aggadic Material in Maimonides' Works], *Sefer ha-Yovel la-Rambam* [Jubilee Volume in Honor of Maimonides], Leipzig, II, pp. 131–197. *See also infra* pp. 1150–1152, 1161–1163, 1191–1193 *et passim.*

dents base their legal rulings and responsa on materials or anecdotal incidents that are aggadic.[14]

The responsa of two leading halakhic authorities provide instructive examples. The details of the responsa will be given later at the appropriate points;[15] but we will consider the responsa here to the extent necessary for our present subject.

With the rise in the power of the local Jewish community (*kehillah*) and the increase in its internal governmental authority from the tenth century C.E. onward, the question arose whether a majority of the community has the power to obligate a dissenting minority to acquiesce in the majority's decision and to obey it. Most halakhic authorities held that the majority does have this power. Over the course of time, another fundamental question naturally arose: Does the quality of the majority have any significance? For example, does every vote have equal weight, regardless of whether the voter is rich or poor? Talmudic *Halakhah* is silent on this subject, and the halakhic authorities approached the answer in different ways.

A question submitted to Menahem Mendel Krochmal, a halakhic au-

14. *See, e.g.,* Maimonides, *MT,* Sanhedrin 4:7: "One authorized to ordain [rabbis] may ordain even one hundred at one time; King David ordained thirty thousand on one day." The source of this law is an incident involving R. Judah b. Bava, who ordained five scholars at the same time (TB Sanhedrin 14a), and the aggadic passage regarding King David in TJ Sanhedrin 10:2, 52b (17:2, 29a), which is given as an interpretation of II Samuel 6:1.

Similarly, Asheri drew from the incident involving R. Bena'ah in TB Bava Batra 58a support for his ruling that a judge may base his decision, in certain cases, on persuasive circumstantial evidence (*umdena de-mukhaḥ*) (*Resp. Asheri* 107:6). Simeon Duran (Rashbeẓ) drew on the story regarding Mar Zutra Ḥasida in TB Bava Meẓi'a 24a to conclude that it is permissible in specific circumstances to rule without the testimony of witnesses required by strict law (*Resp. Tashbeẓ,* III, #168).

See also Paltoi Gaon on the rule that when a defendant is summoned to a Jewish court but refuses to appear, the plaintiff may resort to a non-Jewish court. Paltoi Gaon derived the rule from the folk-saying quoted in TB Bava Kamma 92b: "There is a popular saying: 'If you draw the attention of your fellow [to warn him] and he does not respond, push down a large wall on him.'" That "derivation," however, is merely a makeweight argument (*asmakhta,* lit. "supportive device"). *See supra* p. 15 n. 43.

For many further examples, *see* Z.H. Chajes, *supra* n. 10; S. Lieberman, *Hilkhot Yerushalmi,* Introduction, p. 5. *See further* M. Elon, "Samkhut ve-Oẓmah ba-Kehillah ha-Yehudit; Perek ba-Mishpat ha-Ẓibburi ha-Ivri" [Authority and Power in the Jewish Community: A Chapter in Jewish Public Law], *Shenaton,* III–IV (1976–1977) (hereinafter, *Samkhut ve-Oẓmah*), pp. 7ff., particularly at pp. 13, 22–27; *id.,* "Darkhei ha-Yeẓirah ha-Hilkhatit be-Pitronan Shel Ba'ayot Ḥevrah u-Mishpat ba-Kehillah" [The Methodology of Halakhic Creativity in Solving Social and Legal Problems in the Jewish Community], *Y. Baer Memorial Volume* (*Zion,* XLIV [1979]), pp. 241ff., particularly at pp. 250–264.

See also Ch. Tchernowitz, *Toledot ha-Posekim* [History of the Jewish Codes], I, pp. 24–29, who exaggerates the opposition of the *geonim*—as compared to the attitude of the Talmud—to the reciprocal relationship between *Halakhah* and *Aggadah.* For *Halakhah* and *Aggadah* and the relationship between them, *see further* A.I. Kook, *Iggerot ha-Re'iyah* [The Letters of Rabbi Abraham Isaac Kook] #103.

15. *Infra* pp. 151–154, 721–723.

thority in Germany in the middle of the seventeenth century,[16] related to a proposal by some of the town notables to adopt a rule that not all taxpayers should have the right to vote, but only those who "have the distinction of paying a substantial tax. . . . Since the greater part of the community's business involves the expenditure of money, how can the opinion of a poor man be of equal weight with that of a rich man?" The counterargument appears in the question presented to Krochmal: "The poor, who are the mass of the people, protest: Since they are taxpayers and give their share, why should their rights be curtailed? Although the rich pay more, it is a greater burden for the poor to pay their small sum than it is for the rich to pay their greater amount."[17]

The response given by Krochmal on these fundamental issues between the rich and the poor was as follows:

> It is clearly not right to reject the poor who give a small amount. Proof of this is found in the Mishnah at the end of Tractate *Menaḥot:*[18] "Scripture refers to a sacrificial offering of an animal as 'an offering by fire of pleasing odor,'[19] and to a sacrificial offering of a bird as 'an offering by fire of pleasing odor,'[20] to teach that there is no distinction between those who give more and those who give less, etc."[21] It is thus expressly stated that a small amount given by the poor is equal to a substantial amount given by the rich.
>
> One might go further and say that the contribution of the poor has even greater weight. Scripture states in connection with a meal offering:[22] "When a person [in Hebrew, *nefesh,* lit. "a soul"] presents an offering of meal to the Lord. . . ." The Sages commented:[23] "The word 'soul' was not used in connection with any voluntary offering except the meal offering. Who usually offers a meal offering? A poor person. God said: 'I account it for him as if he offered his very soul.'" (This passage is quoted by Rashi in his commentary on the Torah in the first section of Leviticus).[24] The reason is that since a poor

16. *Resp. Ẓemaḥ Ẓedek* #2.

17. Another position of the town notables was that the right to vote should also be given to persons distinguished in their knowledge of Torah, even if they were not wealthy. As to this position, *see infra* pp. 726–727.

18. M Menaḥot 13:11; TB Menaḥot 110a.

19. Leviticus 1:9.

20. *Id.* 1:17.

21. M Menaḥot 13:11 reads in full:

> Scripture refers to a sacrificial offering of an animal as "an offering by fire of pleasing odor [to the Lord]" [Leviticus 1:9]; and to a sacrificial offering of a bird as "an offering by fire of pleasing odor [to the Lord]" [*id.* 1:17]; and to a meal-offering as "an offering by fire of pleasing odor to the Lord" [*id.* 2:2] to teach that there is no distinction between those who give more and those who give less, provided that one's intent is directed toward Heaven.

22. Leviticus 2:1.

23. TB Menaḥot 104b.

24. Rashi to Leviticus 2:1.

person must labor strenuously [lit. "with his soul"] to earn enough to bring a meal offering, Scripture uses the term "soul." Similarly, Scripture states in connection with a laborer's wages:[25] "For he is needy and urgently depends on it" [lit. "sets his soul upon it"]. This does not apply to a rich person who brings what he already has, and does not exert himself [to obtain it for the specific purpose of offering it].

The Mishnah states that there is no distinction between those who give more and those who give less; the one who gives less is accorded the same merit as the one who gives more. The matter can be viewed in two ways: It can be argued that the contribution of the rich man is more acceptable because it is greater, and it can also be argued that the poor man's gift, even though it is of less intrinsic value, is more acceptable, because it is more difficult for him [to give his lesser gift] than it is for the rich man [to give his greater gift]. The Mishnah therefore states that the offerings are in fact of equal weight, that the contribution of the rich man is not more acceptable on account of its amount, as might be thought, and that the contribution of the poor man is not, as might be thought, more acceptable on account of the effort that went into it, but both are of equal weight so long as the donor's intent is for Heaven.

Therefore, the argument of the poor is valid, since the little that they give is as difficult for them as the substantial amount is for the rich. A similar point is made in the fifth chapter of Tractate *Berakhot*[26] in connection with the dictum of R. Ḥanina, "Everything is predetermined by [lit. "in the hands of"] Heaven. . . . The matter may be compared to someone who is requested to give a vessel: If it is a large vessel but he has it, it seems to him like a small vessel; if it is a small vessel but he does not have it, it seems to him like a large vessel."[27]

25. Deuteronomy 24:15.

26. The source is actually TB Berakhot 33b, which reads as follows:

R. Ḥanina said: "Everything is predetermined by [lit. "in the hands of"] Heaven except reverence for Heaven, as it is written [Deuteronomy 10:12], 'And now, O Israel, what does the Lord your God demand of you? Only this: to revere the Lord your God. . . ."

Is reverence of God then such a minor matter? Did not R. Ḥanina say in the name of R. Simeon b. Yoḥai: "The Holy One, blessed be He, has no treasure in His storehouse but reverence for Heaven, as it is written [Isaiah 33:6], 'Reverence for the Lord—that is His treasure.'"

Yes! For Moses it was a minor matter; as R. Ḥanina said: "The matter may be compared to someone who is requested to give a vessel; if it is a large vessel but he has it, it seems to him like a small vessel; if it is a small vessel but he does not have it, it seems to him like a large vessel."

27. Further on in his responsum, Krochmal discussed *Resp. Asheri* 7:3, which implies that the majority should be reckoned according to wealth rather than the number of persons. In order to reconcile his own opinion with Asheri's view, he ruled that the correct criterion is a combination of the two, or, as he put it—a majority in both wealth and number (lit. "a majority of the structure and a majority in number [*rov binyan ve-rov minyan*]"). This interpretation does not accord with Asheri's plain meaning, but Krochmal adopted it in order to harmonize his own conclusion (that a poor man's vote is totally equal to that of a wealthy

The sources on which Krochmal based the principle that the votes of a poor man and a rich man are equal are all taken from the universe of *Aggadah;* and it goes without saying that these beautiful philosophic homilies which maintain that the toil and exertion of the poor are equal in weight to the large monetary contribution of the rich were not directed, when they were first expressed, to the concrete question that faced Krochmal, namely, What relative weights were to be given to the votes of the poor and the rich in the administration of communal affairs? However, Krochmal saw in these aggadic passages the philosophy of the *Halakhah* and consequently found in them his rationale for his ruling on the legal problem he was called upon to decide.

The responsum of the second halakhic authority goes even further in demonstrating the extent to which a purely legal question may be decided on the basis of aggadic passages.

Simeon b. Ẓemaḥ Duran (Rashbeẓ) was asked[28] about a certain wealthy woman who became ill and made a will in which she left her property "to the poor or to the synagogue." The woman had a poor relative who was her legal heir and who "had sons who were scholars of the Torah, and a daughter who was to be married, and he had to leave his town to beg in other communities to obtain funds sufficient for his daughter's marriage." The question asked of Rashbeẓ was:

> Do the halakhic authorities approve of the act of charity that this woman wishes to perform when it means disinheriting this relative?

The questioner knew that the will was legally valid, since under Jewish law one is free to make a will so long as it is properly drafted and executed.[29] The question thus was only whether the act here was morally deficient, *i.e.,* such that, as it is traditionally put in Jewish law, "the Sages are displeased with" the actor. The Mishnah uses this very expression when someone disinherits his lawful heirs and gives his property to someone else,[30] but this case raised a novel question because the purpose of the tes-

---

man), which is based entirely on aggadic sources, and the contrary ruling of Asheri, which is firmly based by way of analogical reasoning on Talmudic *Halakhah. See also infra* p. 723–725 and n. 185.

28. *Resp. Tashbeẓ,* III, #190. Rashbeẓ was an important halakhic authority in Majorca and Algeria at the end of the fourteenth and the first half of the fifteenth centuries.

29. *See infra* pp. 1673, 1877.

30. M Bava Batra 8:5 (TB Bava Batra 133b):

> If one bequeaths his property to others, disinheriting his sons, his act is legally effective, but the Sages are displeased with him. Rabban Simeon b. Gamaliel says: "If the sons were not conducting themselves properly, his act is praiseworthy [lit. "he should be remembered for good"]."

On the concept "the Sages are displeased with him," *see infra* pp. 149–154.

tatrix—giving charity to the poor and supporting the synagogue—was important and generally praiseworthy.

In the first part of his responsum, Rashbeẓ dealt with the halakhic sources concerning the moral wrong in disinheriting one's legal heirs in favor of someone else who is not an heir; and he concluded that since the legal heir in this case was a poor and upright individual, it was morally wrong to give the property to someone else, even the synagogue or the charity fund for the poor. We will examine that aspect of the discussion by Rashbeẓ later, when we deal with the subject of the relation between law and morals in Jewish law.[31] Rashbeẓ concluded this portion of his responsum by saying: "But all this does not nullify the will once it has been made; it establishes only that it should not be made" in the first instance. That is, the will, once made, may perhaps be legally valid; but it is not proper to make such a will, which is morally defective.

However, later in the responsum, Rashbeẓ reached the conclusion that the will was void and completely ineffective, and held that the poor relative inherited the estate. How did Rashbeẓ come to this unprecedented conclusion? He reasoned as follows:

> However, it [the will] can be nullified on the basis of a passage in the Jerusalem Talmud in the Order of *Zera'im* at the end of Tractate *Pe'ah* (8:8):[32] "R. Judah Ha-Nasi showed Rav the gate of a synagogue that he had built. He remarked, 'How much money my ancestors have invested in this place!' He [Rav] responded, 'On the contrary, how many lives have your ancestors sunk in this place! Was there no one who studied Torah [and needed financial support], or were there no sick people who were cast off into the ash heap?' He applied to him the verse: 'Israel has ignored his Maker and built temples' [Hosea 8:14]."
>
> Thus, it appears that there is greater merit in teaching students and supporting the poor than in building a synagogue; and some of the early authorities also so held.[33]

31. *Infra* pp. 151–154.

32. TJ Pe'ah 8:9, 21b (ed. Venice) and similarly in TJ Shekalim 5:6, 49b. In both these sources, the text is slightly different from that quoted in *Resp. Tashbeẓ; inter alia,* the protagonists are R. Ḥamma b. Ḥanina and R. Hoshaia rather than R. Judah Ha-Nasi and Rav. A version similar to that of *Resp. Tashbeẓ* is given in *Sefer Tashbeẓ* (by Samson b. Ẓadok) and *Resp. Maharik; see infra* n. 33. With regard to the textual variations, *see also* D.B. Ratner, *Ahavat Ẓiyyon vi-Yerushalayim* to TJ Pe'ah, p. 80, and to TJ Shekalim, pp. 34–35; and Z.W. Rabinowitz, *Sha'arei Torat Ereẓ Yisra'el* to TJ Pe'ah, pp. 32–33. However, the textual variations are not relevant to our discussion.

33. *Resp. Maharam of Rothenburg,* ed. Prague, #692; *Sefer Tashbeẓ* (by Samson b. Ẓadok) #533; *Resp. Maharik* #128. On the basis of these responsa, Sh. Ar. YD 249:16 held: "There is an opinion that the commandment [*miẓvah*] of [supporting] a synagogue takes precedence over that of giving charity to the poor; but the *miẓvah* of giving charity to aid

This case falls within the category of "Israel has ignored [his Maker and built temples]," and the law is that the will of a person dangerously ill or otherwise facing imminent death (*shekhiv me-ra*) who directs that his property be used to commit a transgression is to be disregarded, as Maimonides wrote in chapter 9 of *Hilkhot Zekhiyyah u-Mattanah* [Laws of Entitlement and Gifts].[34] This being so, this charitable bequest is void, and her relative will inherit from her.

A *midrash* also states:[35] "Solomon, in building the Temple, did not use any of the sacred funds left by David, his father. He said: 'There was a famine in the days of my father for three years, and he should have expended those funds to sustain the poor of Israel.'"

According to the strict law, the will, as has been pointed out, was valid. However, Rashbeẓ found a way of invalidating it so that the estate would pass to the poor relative who was the legal heir, whose sons were scholars of the Torah, and who urgently needed the money for the marriage of his daughter. Rashbeẓ determined that the objective of the will was the performance of a transgression. He made this determination on the basis of an *aggadah* in the Jerusalem Talmud, according to which whoever gives his money for the synagogue when scholars of the Torah or poor, sick people are in need of financial help is compared to someone who, as it were, committed the transgression of building a temple for idol-worship.[36] Consequently, the will of the woman leaving her estate to the synagogue at a time when there was a poverty-stricken relative whose sons were scholars of the Torah was a transgression,[37] and the case is governed by the rule that the

---

young students to study Torah or to help poor people who are sick takes precedence over the *miẓvah* of supporting the synagogue." *See also Be'ur ha-Gra, ad loc.*, subpar. 20.

34. Maimonides, *MT*, Zekhiyyah u-Mattanah 9:10. As to a will of a *shekhiv me-ra, see infra* pp. 1877–1878.

35. *Pesikta Rabbati*, sec. 6, end (ed. Ish-Shalom, pp. 25b–26a, and *see* subpar. 62).

36. This is indeed the plain meaning of Hosea 8:14. Rashbeẓ emphasized that earlier authorities had deduced on the basis of the aggadic passage in TJ the halakhic rule that the *miẓvah* of giving charity to facilitate Torah study or to aid the ailing poor takes precedence over giving to the synagogue (*see* sources *supra* n. 33), and he cited Samuel of Bamberg, the teacher of Maharam of Rothenburg, as authority. On this basis, Rashbeẓ concluded that this aggadic passage had already served as a source of *Halakhah* in earlier generations, thus reinforcing his own ruling in the matter of the will.

37. Although the bequest was for the poor or for the synagogue, so that the poor relative would appear to have no priority over other poor people, the law is that in giving charity to the poor there are different levels of priority; the governing principle is, "The poor of one's household have priority over the poor of one's town" (Sh. Ar. YD 251:3, following sources in *Sifrei* and TB; *see infra* p. 117 and n. 107). This being so, the poor relative had priority over the poor of the town. Rashbeẓ also emphasized that the poor relative had sons who studied Torah, and Torah study is, as we have seen, another factor weighing in favor of priority.

will of a *shekhiv me-ra* directing the performance of a transgression is null and void.[38]

To support his ruling that the case before him involved a transgression, Rashbeẓ cited an additional *midrash,* also aggadic, according to which Solomon made no use of the funds that his father David had prepared for the building of the Temple, because those funds should have been used by his father during the famine for the support of the poor; the failure to use them for this purpose was sinful, and rendered the funds inappropriate for use in building the Temple. On the basis of these passages, Rashbeẓ came to the conclusion that the will of the woman was void even as a matter of law, thus establishing the poor relative as the heir.

As mentioned, this reliance on *Aggadah* for the purpose of deciding a legal case is extremely far-reaching. On the basis of the principle that Rashbeẓ deduced from aggadic passages, he came to a conclusion contrary to the previously settled legal rule. This is undoubtedly an extraordinary ruling, which required judicial courage and statesmanship in order to do justice in that particular case. Nevertheless, the ruling demonstrates how *Aggadah* and *Halakhah* each provide resources for the other. It is an illustration of the practice of the halakhic authorities to base their decisions, when reason and justice require, on the philosophy of the *Halakhah,* which was heavily colored by the *Aggadah.*[39]

38. This rule, which is set forth by Maimonides, has no explicit source in the Talmud; *see Maggid Mishneh* to *MT,* Zekhiyyah u-Mattanah 9:10. *See also Mishneh la-Melekh, ad loc.,* explaining that a gift by a person dangerously ill or facing imminent death (*shekhiv me-ra*) is valid by rabbinic enactment, and the rabbis did not intend their enactment to apply if the result would be to permit what was prohibited by law. This follows the view of Ran, who so ruled in a similar matter involving a rabbinic enactment.

Mishneh la-Melekh raised an objection to Maimonides' ruling, on the basis of the rule that even though a person who advises a *shekhiv me-ra* to make bequests to others when the estate is not large enough to maintain his children is considered to be a "cunning rogue," the bequest is nevertheless legally effective. However, the objection fails since there is no inconsistency. The act of the "cunning rogue" is not a legal but a moral transgression, as indeed is obvious from *Resp. Tashbeẓ* regarding the case of the poor man sifting through leftover bread. (*See infra* pp. 153–154, where this passage of *Resp. Tashbeẓ* is discussed). In that case, too, whoever deprives the poor man of his find is considered a "rogue," but his act stands. Similarly, a bequest is not invalidated by a moral transgression that does not violate the law.

The rationale of Maimonides' rule is clear (*see Maggid Mishneh, ad loc.,* s.v. U-fashut hu): Even when a transaction is provided for by Biblical law, the court will not permit the transaction to take effect if doing so would result in the commission of an illegal act; a transaction that takes place in the course of a transgression is valid only if the transaction itself is lawful, and if enforcement of the transaction does not itself bring about an illegal act. *See* the discussion of illegal contracts, *infra* pp. 128–130.

39. Rashbeẓ's responsum reflects the reciprocal support provided by all parts of the *Halakhah*—"legal" and "religious"—to one another; in this case, a "religious" rule, *i.e.,* a prohibition derived from an aggadic exegesis of the verse, "Israel has ignored his Maker," is

Sometimes a general concept that is aggadic in nature serves as a basis for determining the substance of legal rules and may have great significance in the strictly legal area. An instructive example is found in the well-known doctrine that "A Jew—even one who has sinned—is nevertheless still a Jew." The origin of this doctrine was the aggadic dictum of R. Abba b. Zavda, an *amora* of the second and third generation in the Land of Israel, concerning the act of Achan, who appropriated property in Jericho that had been proscribed.[40] God's statement to Joshua,[41] "Israel has sinned! They have broken the covenant by which I bound them," was interpreted by R. Abba b. Zavda as follows: "Even though it has sinned, it is still 'Israel'";[42] *i.e.*, since God did not say "the people have sinned" but "Israel has sinned," one infers that even after they have sinned, they are still called Israel.[43] This concept, which is purely aggadic, was transformed in the eleventh century C.E. into one of the most powerful rationales (and, according to some halakhic authorities, even the single decisive rationale) for a long series of laws by which it was established that the same law that applies to a Jew also applies to an apostate in various matters, including marriage, *ḥaliẓah*, and inheritance. The halakhic authorities incorporated the aggadic concept into the *Halakhah*, and even extended the doctrine beyond its original aggadic scope; the Book of Joshua referred to the people of Israel collectively, but the laws based on the doctrine apply to every Jew individually.[44]

This reciprocal relationship between *Halakhah* and *Aggadah* is rooted in their common source and context. The halakhic Sages were at the same time also aggadic Sages; just as they debated and analyzed legal norms, they also sought to understand the ethical and philosophical impulses that help to shape the law. In the final analysis, *Halakhah* and *Aggadah* are both integral parts of the Oral Law, and each sustains and nourishes the other.[45]

---

utilized to support a purely "legal" ruling invalidating the will. *See* the discussion *infra* pp. 111–122. On the question of ruling in special circumstances in accordance with the requirements of equity, even though contrary to the normally accepted law, *see infra* pp. 176–181.

40. Joshua ch. 7.

41. *Id.* 7:11.

42. TB Sanhedrin 44a.

43. *See* Rashi, Sanhedrin 44a, s.v. Ḥata Yisra'el.

44. *See* J. Katz, "Af Al Pi She-Ḥata Yisra'el Hu" [A Jew, Notwithstanding He Has Sinned, Remains a Jew], *Tarbiẓ*, XXVII (1958), pp. 203–217.

45. By contrast, the main concern of Roman jurists was analysis of legal norms and definition of their legal nature. They did not devote any special attention to the philosophy of law. *See* Pokrovsky, *supra* n. 2 at 153.

This is how the Sages interpreted the verse in the Torah section of *Ha'azinu*,[46] "May my discourse come down as the rain":

> Just as the rain falls on the trees and gives sustenance to each one of them according to its nature—to the vine according to its nature, to the olive tree according to its nature, to the fig tree according to its nature—in the same way the teachings of the Torah are all one, encompassing Scripture, Mishnah, Talmud, *halakhot*, and *aggadot*.[47]

Consequently, just as a Jew is commanded to delve into the profundities of the *Halakhah*, so he is commanded to immerse himself in the world of *Aggadah:*

> So that one should not say, "It is enough that I have studied *halakhot*," Scripture states: "commandment," "the commandment," "all this commandment"[48] [stating "commandment" three times to teach that one must] study [all three]: Midrash, *halakhot*, and *aggadot*. Scripture also states:[49] "For man does not live on bread alone"—this means Midrash—but "man may live on anything that the Lord decrees" [lit. "on everything that issues from the mouth of the Lord"]—these are *halakhot* and *aggadot*.[50]

It appears that there is an additional reason for the use of *Aggadah* by the halakhic authorities. As we shall note in our discussion of the legal sources of Jewish law, one of the sources that create Jewish law is legal reasoning, *i.e.*, the reasoning process employed by the halakhic authorities by whom the *Halakhah* is carried forward. This reasoning process is nourished by penetrating insight into the essence of halakhic and legal principles, by an appreciation of human characteristics in social relationships, and by a careful study of the real world and its manifestations.[51] All these are as appropriate for *Aggadah* as for *Halakhah*, both of which formed the basis upon which the halakhic authorities' thought processes and their methods of reasoning were shaped. Reaching legal decisions on the basis of the principles and concepts taken from the world of the *Aggadah* is, in the final analysis, decision making on the basis of the *legal reasoning* of the halakhic authorities, which, as previously stated, is one of the legal sources for the creation of Jewish law.

46. Deuteronomy 32:2.
47. *Sifrei*, Deuteronomy, Ha'azinu, sec. 306.
48. Deuteronomy 11:22: "If, then, you faithfully keep all this instruction (*kol ha-mizvah*, lit. "all this commandment")."
49. *Id.* 8:3.
50. *Sifrei*, Deuteronomy, Ekev, sec. 48.
51. *See infra* pp. 987ff.

III. THE TERM *MISHPAT IVRI*

The term *mishpat ivri,* in its currently accepted meaning, includes only those parts of the *Halakhah* corresponding to what generally is included in the *corpus juris* of other contemporary legal systems, namely, laws that govern relationships in human society, and not the precepts that deal with the relationship between people and God.[52] An alternative and more specific definition of *mishpat ivri* as currently used is that it includes only those subjects covered in the parts of the *Shulḥan Arukh* titled *Even ha-Ezer* and *Ḥoshen Mishpat* (plus certain "legal" matters contained in the two other parts of the *Shulḥan Arukh,* such as the law of usury in the part titled *Yoreh De'ah*). It does not, however, include the other subjects dealt with in the parts *Oraḥ Ḥayyim* and *Yoreh De'ah.*[53]

Did the original meaning of the term *mishpat ivri* include only those matters now generally understood as being within the scope of this term? Let us briefly examine this question.

A. The Terms *Mishpat* and *Din*

There are a number of meanings of the Hebrew term *mishpat:*[54]

1. *Mishpat* may mean the act of judging, as well as the resulting decision: "You shall do no unrighteousness in judging (*ba-mishpat*); do not favor the poor or show deference to the rich";[55] "You shall not be partial in judgment (*ba-mishpat*): hear out low and high alike. Fear no man, for judgment (*ha-mishpat*) is God's. And any matter that is too difficult for

52. There is no inherent legal impediment precluding a legislature from legislating on "religious" or "ritual" issues; and, indeed, every legal system has such legislation whenever there is a perceived special national or social basis (as, for example, is the case with laws regarding the cessation of business on Sunday in England and even in the United States, where the First Amendment to the U.S. Constitution constitutes perhaps the most severe restriction on legislative power over religious issues). Such legislation also exists in Israel, *e.g.*, the prohibition against raising pigs. *See* M. Elon, *Ḥakikah Datit be-Ḥukkei Medinat Yisra'el u-vi-Shefitah Shel Battei ha-Mishpat u-Vattei ha-Din ha-Rabbaniyyim* [Religious Legislation in the Statutes of the State of Israel and in the Decisions of the General and the Rabbinical Courts] (hereinafter, *Ḥakikah*), pp. 14ff. However, in current liberal legal systems, the legislature, in general, voluntarily refrains from venturing into matters of religion or conscience.

53. For details of the subject matter of the four sections of *Shulḥan Arukh, see infra* pp. 1287–1302, 1323–1327.

54. In the Bible, the root of *mishpat* (*shafat*) also connotes ruling or leadership (Judges 3:10, 4:4 *et al.;* I Samuel 4:18 *et al.;* Ruth 1:1). The ruler generally also functioned in a judicial capacity.

55. Leviticus 19:15. The JPS *Tanakh* renders the first clause "You shall not render an unfair decision."

you, you shall bring to me and I will hear it";[56] "You shall not judge unfairly (*tatteh mishpat*); you shall show no partiality; you shall not take bribes";[57] "The Israelites would come to her for adjudication (*la-mishpat*)."[58] An illustration of the term as meaning "decision" is: "When all Israel heard the decision (*ha-mishpat*) that the king had rendered, they stood in awe of the king; for they saw that he possessed divine wisdom to execute justice" (*la'asot mishpat,* lit. "to reach just decisions").[59]

2. *Mishpat* may also mean a system of laws and precepts similar to the English concept "law" and the German term *Recht,* as in: "There He made for them fixed rules (*ḥok u-mishpat*) and there He put them to the test";[60] "These are the rules (*mishpatim*) that you shall set before them";[61] "What great nation has laws and rules (*ḥukkim u-mishpatim*) as perfect as all this Teaching that I set before you this day?"[62]
3. A third meaning of *mishpat* is legal right: "He must accept the first-born, the son of the unloved one, and allot to him a double portion of all he possesses; since he is the first fruit of his vigor, the birthright (*mishpat ha-bekhorah*) is his due";[63] "Buy my land in Anatot . . . for the right (*mishpat*) of succession is yours. . . ."[64]
4. A fourth meaning of *mishpat* is fixed custom, usage, or practice: "In three days Pharaoh will pardon you [lit. "lift your head"] and restore you to your post; you will place Pharaoh's cup in his hand as was your custom (*ka-mishpat*) formerly when you were his cupbearer";[65] "And

56. Deuteronomy 1:17.

57. *Id.* 16:19.

58. Judges 4:5. The JPS *Tanakh* renders *la-mishpat* as "for decisions."

59. I Kings 3:28. Similarly, the word *mishpat* also includes everything involved in the judicial process regarding a specific matter. *See, e.g.,* Numbers 27:5: "Moses brought their case [*mishpatan*] before the Lord." *See also infra* n. 70.

60. Exodus 15:25.

61. *Id.* 21:1.

62. Deuteronomy 4:8. It should be pointed out that in English the term "law" has two meanings. The first is as a general term for either part or all of a legal system, *e.g.,* "criminal law" or "English law." The second is as the term for a specific rule, as in "Congress has enacted a law." Other languages have separate terms for these two connotations. In German, for example, *Recht* refers to the legal system and *Gesetz* to a specific law. *See* J.W. Salmond, *Jurisprudence,* 12th ed., London, 1966 (hereinafter, Salmond), p. 48, n. b. For the meanings of the Hebrew term *ḥok, see infra* n. 64.

63. Deuteronomy 21:17.

64. Jeremiah 32:7–8. *Mishpat* in Deuteronomy 19:6 and Jeremiah 22:13 also has this meaning. The term *ḥok* also has this connotation (*see* Genesis 47:22; Leviticus 6:11) in addition to its usual meaning of a system of laws; *see infra* nn. 70, 76 and Deuteronomy 4:8.

65. Genesis 40:13.

they marched around the city in the same manner [*ka-mishpat ha-zeh,* lit. "according to this practice"] seven times."[66]

Among the four meanings of the term *mishpat,*[67] the most relevant to our discussion is the second meaning, *i.e.,* a system of legal rules and precepts. However, when we examine what is included in this sense of *mishpat,* we find that it includes not only laws that are "legal" but also laws that are "religious."[68] For example, the verse, "These are the rules (*mishpatim*) that you shall set before them,"[69] introduces a legal code that includes civil and criminal law, as well as a long series of religious laws such as the laws of the sabbatical year, the sabbath, and first fruits (*bikkurim*).[70]

66. Joshua 6:15; the word appears in the same sense in Judges 18:7 and I Kings 18:28.

67. The use of *mishpat* as a grammatical term meaning "sentence" is a much later development and does not appear in the Bible. *See Millon Ben Yehudah* [Ben Yehudah's Hebrew Dictionary], VII, pp. 3408–3411, s.v. Mishpat.

68. The terms "legal" and "religious" are arbitrary and are currently accepted to differentiate between matters concerning relationships in human society and matters concerning a relationship with God. These terms have no basis in the terminology or substance of the *Halakhah.* For the sake of convenience, the terms are used in this book in their currently accepted sense, but generally with quotation marks. *See also supra* n. 2.

69. Exodus 21:1.

70. *Id.* 23:10ff. Those verses in which *mishpat* is used in the sense of a judicial proceeding usually refer to legal matters involving relationships in human society; *see* the verses cited *supra* in which *mishpat* is used in this sense, and also Jeremiah 21:12, 22:3. Some Talmudic Sages interpret *mishpat* as referring to a portion of civil and criminal law. *See, e.g.,* R. Eleazar ha-Moda'i's interpretation of the verse, "There he gave them *ḥok u-mishpat*" (Exodus 15:25), in *Mekhilta de-R. Ishmael,* Be-Shallaḥ, Tractate De-va-Yassa, sec. 1 (p. 156): "'*Ḥok*' refers to [laws dealing with] prohibited sexual relationships, as it is written, '. . . that you should not engage in any of those abhorrent practices [*ḥukkot ha-to'evot*]' (Leviticus 18:30); '*u-mishpat*' refers to the laws of robbery, the laws of fines, and the laws of bodily injury." *But see* R. Joshua, *ad loc.:* "'*ḥok*' refers to the sabbath, '*u-mishpat*' refers to the honor due to parents."

Similarly, Naḥmanides in his commentary on Deuteronomy 7:12 ("And if you do obey these rules [*mishpatim*] and observe them faithfully, the Lord your God will maintain for you the gracious covenant that He made on oath with your fathers") interpreted the term *mishpatim* as referring to legal matters involving relationships in human society. Naḥmanides (Chavel, Hebrew ed.) commented:

> Rashi explained [it as meaning] that if you observe the minor commandments, which people usually take lightly, God will keep His promise to you. The verse mentions *ha-mishpatim,* perhaps in order to warn that one should not take lightly even the minor laws, such as civil laws. . . . The verse especially emphasizes that *mishpatim* must be enforced because it is impossible that an entire populous nation will keep all the commandments without anyone sinning at all, and it is only by observance of the *mishpatim* that the Torah can be kept viable, as it is written of the *mishpatim,* "And all Israel will hear and be afraid" [Deuteronomy 21:21]. Furthermore, many people will be too merciful to execute [lit. "to stone or burn"] a man after he has performed a transgression, as it is said [*i.e.,* as indeed the Torah saw necessary to admonish], "You must show him no pity" [*id.* 19:13]. And still further, people will be afraid of violent

Hebrew terminology also includes the term *dinim.* This term appears in Scripture[71] and is also found in many tannaitic and amoraic sources referring to various laws that are covered in the fourth Order of the Talmud, namely, *Nezikin.*[72] *Dinim* are divided into two main categories: *Dinei mamonot* (lit. "monetary law") and *dinei nefashot* (lit. "law of souls").[73] "*Dinei*

---

or deceitful men, as it is written, "Fear no man, for judgment is God's" [*id.* 1:17], and, with regard to a false prophet, "Do not stand in dread of him" [*id.* 18:22]. And with regard to the enticer it is written, "Do not assent or give heed to him. Show him no pity or compassion, and give him no protection" [*id.* 13:9]; [the verse] thus warns that you must not listen to him with regard to his enticements; that you must not pity him, because the soft-hearted may incline to compassion toward the convicted; and that you give him no protection—you should not be silent because of his power and your fear of his family.

Tur ḤM 1:1–2 cites a long array of Scriptural verses and Talmudic statements in which the term *mishpat* appears in its various senses (*see infra* pp. 1295–1299); the author of the *Turim* apparently used the term as encompassing those matters dealt with in *Ḥoshen Mishpat.* Similarly, Jacob Ḥazzan divided his book *Eẓ Ḥayyim* into two parts: one, called *Sefer ha-Torah,* which treats all matters of "ritual" and family law, and the other, called *Sefer ha-Mishpat,* which treats monetary matters, capital cases, corporal punishment, the laws concerning judges, and the laws concerning the king and his wars—*i.e.,* what we would classify as criminal law, public law, and civil law (with the omission of family law). *See infra* pp. 1255–1256.

71. *See, e.g.,* Deuteronomy 17:8: "If a case is too baffling for you to decide, be it a controversy *bein dam le-dam* [lit. "between blood and blood"], *bein din le-din* [lit. "between law and law"], or *bein nega le-nega* (assault)—matters of dispute in your gates [*i.e.,* where the courts sat]—you shall promptly repair to the place that the Lord your God will have chosen. . . ." "*Dam le-dam*" refers to homicide and other capital cases; "*din le-din*" refers to cases involving money. *See* commentators *ad loc.* and Hoffmann, *Commentary on Deuteronomy* 17:8–11 (Hebrew ed., pp. 301–307).

72. *See* M Ḥagigah 1:8; *Tosefta* Eruvin 11:24 (8:23), Ḥagigah 1:9, Avodah Zarah 8(9):4, Bekhorot 3:8; *Mekhilta de R. Ishmael,* Mishpatim, Tractate De-Nezikin, sec. 1, p. 246 ("R. Simeon b. Yoḥai says: Why were the *dinim* given before all the other commandments in the Torah?"); TB Kiddushin 35a; Sotah 41b, 47b; Bava Kamma 15a, 87a; Sanhedrin 56a. In these sources the term *dinim* is generally used for those areas of law covered by the current meaning of *mishpat.* M Ḥagigah and *Tosefta* Ḥagigah and Eruvin set forth terms designating the various areas in the *Halakhah* and reserve *dinim* for designation of those matters treated in the Mishnaic Order of *Nezikin. See also infra* p. 194 for an interpretation of *dinim* as it appears in the list of the Noahide laws. For the use of the term *din* in exegetical interpretation, *see infra* p. 277.

73. A third category is "laws of fines" (*dinei kenasot*), but this is really a branch of civil law (*dinei mamonot*), despite the usual meaning of the term "fines" in other legal systems. The "law of fines" in Jewish law is not a part of the criminal law. When the extent of monetary liability in tort or contract is objectively identical to the value of the contract or the amount of the loss to the injured party, it is called *mamon,* "money"; when, however, it is not identical, it is called *kenas,* "fine" (*see, e.g.,* TB Bava Kamma 15a/b). The lack of equivalence may be because the liability is greater than the actual damage (as in the case of theft, where the thief is liable for double the value of the article stolen or four or five times its value if he stole a sheep or an ox and slaughtered or sold it, Exodus 21:37, 22:3), or less than the actual damage (as in the case of an "innocent" ox—*i.e.,* an ox not in the habit of

mamonot" in the Talmudic sources does not completely coincide with "civil law." On the one hand, *dinei mamonot* includes more than civil law,[74] and on the other, it does not cover everything that civil law now includes—*dinei mamonot* does not include the law of usury or some of the laws prescribing limits of permissible conduct within family relationships. "*Dinei nefashot*" in the Talmudic sources, which includes a part of what is included in criminal law in contemporary legal systems, also includes matters solely involving commandments concerning relationship to God, such as violation of the sabbath laws, idolatry, etc., but excludes offenses that do not involve capital or corporal punishment.[75]

The conclusion to be drawn from our analysis is that the content of the concept *mishpat* in Hebrew terminology is not congruent with what is denoted by the term "law" as currently used in other legal systems. Even the term *din,* or *dinim,* which is much closer to what is denoted according to current usage by the term "law," has a broader meaning than "law": one speaks of *dinei issur ve-hetter* ("religious" regulations, lit. "laws of prohibition and permissibility") just as one speaks of *dinei mamonot,* which, as has been noted, is generally compared to "civil law."[76]

This lack of congruence is hardly surprising. What would be surprising would be complete congruence between any term of Jewish law and any generally accepted concept of contemporary legal systems. We have already seen and stressed—as we shall have occasion to do again—that conceptually the very idea of distinguishing "religious" from "legal" norms, as those terms are generally understood today, is foreign to Jewish law. All halakhic precepts, "legal" as well as "religious," include an aspect of divine commandment as the source of civil or criminal obligation.[77] One will therefore search in vain in the halakhic literature for a term or expression that denotes all, and only, that which is generally included in contemporary legal systems.

---

goring—which causes damage by goring, for which the owner of the ox is liable to pay only half [Exodus 21:35, TB Bava Kamma 15a]), or because the liability is for a prescribed amount (as in the case of slander of a newly wedded wife, Deuteronomy 22:19, and the case described in Deuteronomy 22:29). *See* M. Elon, EJ, XII, pp. 1310–1316, s.v. Obligations, law of (reprinted in *Principles,* pp. 241–246); ET, VII, pp. 376ff., s.v. Dinei kenasot.

74. Note the form in which the question is put in TB Sanhedrin 2b: "Are *gezelot* (robbery) and *ḥabalot* (personal injury) not *dinei mamonot?*" and the subsequent course of the discussion there. *See also* ET, VII, pp. 308ff., s.v. Dinei mamonot.

75. *See* ET, VII, pp. 353ff., s.v. Dinei nefashot. Another term, *dinei makkot,* refers to those offenses punishable by flogging (*malkot*); *see* TJ Shekalim 1:1, 2b (1:1, 46a); TB Sanhedrin 36a, 87a/b; Mo'ed Katan 14b.

76. The same applies to other terms, *e.g., ḥok; see supra* n. 64.

77. *See also supra* p. 4–5 and *infra* pp. 111–122.

the same approach, the same way of looking at things and the same system of classification.[86]

B. Common Legal Principles

Not only the definitional methods and thought patterns but also the substance of the entire halakhic *corpus juris* fully manifests the interweaving of the "legal" and the "religious" in the *Halakhah*. There is a long list of legal principles common to both categories of the *Halakhah*. Thus, laws of agency are applied, to the same extent and with the same postulates, to matters dealing with sacred objects, priestly tithes, and the sacrifice of the paschal lamb as they are to matters such as marriage, divorce, and the collection of debts. Moreover, the basic legal principle of the relationship of principal and agent, which applies in all these contexts, namely, that "the act of the agent is the act of the principal," was derived by the Sages from matters in the domain of "religious" *Halakhah*.

For example, the section of the Torah that deals with the paschal sacrifice says:[87]

> You shall keep watch over it until the fourteenth day of this month; and all the assembled congregation of the Israelites shall slaughter it at twilight.

On the basis of this verse, R. Joshua b. Korḥa stated:

> What is the source of the rule that action by an agent is equivalent to action by the principal? It is stated: "All the assembled congregation of the Israelites shall slaughter it at twilight." But does the entire congregation do the slaughtering? Is not the slaughtering done by only one person? We deduce from here that action by an agent is equivalent to action by the principal.[88]

In other words, since the verse cannot be understood in a literal manner (because it is not possible for the entire community to slaughter the sacrifice) we must interpret the verse on the basis that the act of one person is imputed to and considered to be the act of another person or even of an entire community.

Other Sages derive the principle that the act of an agent is the act of the principal from other subjects in the realm of religious *Halakhah* such as the laws of sacrificial offerings and tithes.[89] Indeed, the only reference to

86. Silberg, *Talmudic Law and the Modern State*, pp. 65–66. The quotation is our own translation from the original Hebrew.

87. Exodus 12:6.

88. TB Kiddushin 41b. With regard to this exegesis, *see also infra* p. 342.

89. For details, *see* H. Albeck, M Zera'im, pp. 333–335.

this principle in the Mishnah is in connection with the laws of prayer, which are quintessentially "religious."[90] Thus, the major source of the law of principal and agent, which has great significance in all areas of Jewish law, is clearly the "religious" portion of the *Halakhah.*[91]

C. Dependence of "Religious" Precepts on "Legal" Precepts

This interweaving of the "religious" and the "legal" throughout the entire *Halakhah* frequently results in instances where binding religious norms are dependent on and are supported by authoritative legal norms. For example, the Torah[92] commands that first fruits be brought to the priest in Jerusalem. The priest takes the basket and places it before the altar, and it is incumbent on the one who brings the first fruits to recite certain verses in the section of the Torah that narrates the history of the people of Israel until its return to the Land of Israel. The recitation includes the verse: "Wherefore I now bring the first fruits of the soil which you, O Lord, have given me."[93] Thus, this commandment is composed of two parts: the bringing of the first fruits and the recitation of the pertinent verses.

It was in connection with this commandment that one of the basic questions in the Jewish law of acquisition was discussed:

90. M Berakhot 5:5: "If the one who recites the *Tefillah* [*i.e.,* the *Amidah* prayer] falls into error, it is a bad omen for him [because his intention was not pure]; and if he was the agent (*shali'aḥ*) of the congregation, it is a bad omen for those who appointed him, because the act of an agent is the act of the principal." *See also Ginzei Schechter,* II, p. 548 n. 20, for the difference between the terms *shali'aḥ* and *shalu'aḥ.*

91. Similarly, *e.g.,* the general rule that "a benefit may be conferred upon a person in his absence, but a burden may not be imposed on anyone unless he is present," is applied in all areas of the *Halakhah.* A divorce is generally a burden on a woman since she loses the right to maintenance by her husband, whereas a gift is a benefit to its recipient (TB Bava Meẓi'a 12a). However, when a husband is childless and his wife would have to undergo levirate marriage upon his death, or when there is a great deal of family strife, a divorce is beneficial to the wife (TB Yevamot 118b).

In contrast, an *eruv ḥazerot* (which permits carrying objects in a courtyard on the sabbath) is always beneficial for the householder; he may therefore be included in the *eruv* without his prior knowledge. However, an *eruv teḥumin* (which doubles for a particular direction the usual limit of two thousand cubits beyond which one may not go outside a town on the sabbath) eliminates the possibility of traveling in a different direction; therefore, no one may set such an *eruv* for another person without his consent (M Eruvin 7:11, and *see* Maimonides, *MT,* Eruvin 1:20, 6:18). *See also* A. Schaky, "Ba'ayat ha-Ḥozeh le-Tovat Ẓad Shelishi" [The Problem of Third-Party-Beneficiary Contracts], *Sugyot Nivḥarot ba-Mishpat* [Selected Subjects in Law], I, pp. 470–508.

92. Deuteronomy 26:1–11.

93. *Id.* verse 10.

> It has been said: As to one who sells his field for its fruit [*i.e.*, the land itself remains under the ownership of the seller and the purchaser purchases only the fruit], R. Johanan said: "He brings and recites" [the purchaser brings the first fruit from these fruits and also recites the verses]; Resh Lakish said: "He brings but does not recite." R. Johanan said: "He brings and recites," [because] acquisition of the fruit is the same as acquisition of the underlying property [*i.e.*, with the acquisition of the fruit, one also acquires the property for purposes of cultivating the fruit, and therefore he may recite the statement, "I now bring the first fruits of the soil which you . . . have given me"]. Resh Lakish said: "He brings but does not recite," [because] acquisition of the fruit is not the same as acquisition of the underlying property [*i.e.*, he acquires only the fruit, but he has no rights in the property itself, and therefore he cannot say "the soil which you . . . have given me"].[94]

The law was settled in accordance with the latter view.[95]

Thus, the incidence of the commandment to recite the section on the first fruits depends upon first clarifying the concept of ownership, because the one who recites the verses must say that the land belongs to him, and he cannot make this declaration unless it is clear that legally the land does belong to him. This basic question raised in connection with the recitation of the verses concerning the first fruits,[96] *i.e.*, whether the acquisition of fruits is the equivalent of acquiring the underlying property, is dealt with in the same depth and by the same methods of analysis and proof as in other manifestly "legal" contexts, such as the law of gifts, wills, and the like, which also depend upon the meaning ascribed to the legal concept of acquisition of fruits.[97]

94. TB Gittin 47b.

95. Maimonides, *MT*, Bikkurim 4:6.

96. TB Gittin 47b–48b.

97. *See, e.g.*, TB Bava Batra 136a–137b, which provides a further example of the interdependency between a "religious" norm and a "legal" norm:

> Rava said: "[Where one says to his fellow,] 'You can have this citron (*etrog*) as a gift on condition that you return it to me,' and he [the donee] takes it and performs the ritual with it, if he returns it, he has fulfilled his obligation to perform the ritual, but if he does not return it, he has not fulfilled his obligation." This [ruling] teaches us that a gift given on the condition [that the donee] return it is a valid gift (fol. 137b).

A person may fulfill the commandment of taking the *etrog*, which is one of the four species taken on the festival of *Sukkot*, only with an *etrog* that belongs to him, because the Torah states, regarding the commandment of *etrog* and the rest of the four species, "You shall take for yourselves (*lakhem*) . . ." [Leviticus 23:40], which the Sages interpreted to mean "belonging to you" (TB Sukkah 41b; *see also* Rashbam, Bava Batra 137b, s.v. Ve-im lav lo yaẓa). Rava's ruling was that a person who does not own an *etrog* can fulfill his obligation if he receives an *etrog* as a gift from another person, even if the gift was given on condition that he return it (which is an understandable condition since the original owner still needs it). This is because there is an effective transfer of ownership until the *etrog* is returned, provided, of course, that the condition requiring it to be returned is complied with.

D. Common Fictions

We may deduce from the following example that even fictions, which are vital for all legal systems, operate to the same extent in both categories of the *Halakhah:*

> Two things are not legally subject to individual ownership, yet Scripture has treated them as if they were. These things are: a pit in the public domain and *ḥameẓ* (leaven) from the sixth hour and thereafter.[98]

The prohibition of the presence of *ḥameẓ* on the fourteenth day of the month of Nisan (the eve of Passover) after the sixth hour (counting from the beginning of the day) and the liability for injuries caused by a pit in the public domain have an element in common: even though neither the *ḥameẓ* nor the pit is owned by an individual (the pit because it was dug in the public domain, which is not subject to individual appropriation, and *ḥameẓ,* because the prohibition against any kind of use or enjoyment effectively divests the individual of all the prerogatives that give ownership its meaning), Biblical law treated them as if they were owned by the individual who in fact possessed them. Therefore, the "owner" of the pit is liable for damages caused by the pit and the "owner" of the *ḥameẓ* transgresses the commandments, "No leaven shall be found in your houses for seven days,"[99] and "No leavened bread shall be found with you, and no leaven shall be found in all your territory."[100]

The same necessity for finding a legal basis for imposing liability on the pit's "owner" for injuries even though the pit is located outside his zone of individual ownership also exists for providing sanctions against transgressing the prohibition of *ḥameẓ,* which is likewise not technically "owned" by the individual. The solution for both problems—the one in "legal" *Halakhah* (tort liability of one who digs a pit) and the other in "religious" *Halakhah* (the prohibition of *ḥameẓ*)—was to posit in each instance a fictional "ownership" by the party upon whom it was sought to impose liability.

This rule applies not only to the four species taken on *Sukkot* (*see* Maimonides, *MT,* Lulav 8:10–11; Sh. Ar. OḤ 658:4–9), but to all areas of the law:

> If a person gives a gift on condition that it be returned, it is a valid gift. Whether he stipulates that it be returned immediately, or after a fixed time, or after the death of one of the parties to the transaction, or after the death of a third party, it is a valid gift. Whether the subject of the gift is personalty or real property, he [the recipient] enjoys the income for the entire period of the gift. (Maimonides, *MT,* Zekhiyyah u-Mattanah 3:9; Sh. Ar. ḤM 241:6).

98. TB Pesaḥim 6b; Bava Kamma 29b.

99. Exodus 12:19.

100. *Id.* 13:7.

E. Interaction between Different Parts of the *Halakhah*

The common source of the two parts of the *Halakhah* brought about a synergistic interaction between them. There is even a mutuality of relationship between the *Halakhah* and completely nonhalakhic fields such as *Aggadah* and ethics.[101] Within the *Halakhah* itself, not only is there mutual interconnection between the "religious" and the "legal," but sometimes a precept of the "religious" part may fill a lacuna in the "legal" part. The following examples illustrate the point:

1. THE OBLIGATION OF CHILD SUPPORT

A father's obligation to support his children was originally not a legal norm but a religious obligation: "It is a [religious] commandment to support sons" and "It is a [religious] commandment to support daughters."[102] The family unit was stable and secure; and the religious obligation, the *mizvah*, was sufficient to assure paternal support of children. In the middle of the second century C.E., when the Jewish family structure seemed to be weakening after the Bar Kokhba rebellion and the Hadrianic edicts, the Sanhedrin, sitting at Usha, promulgated a series of enactments (*takkanot*) designed to strengthen the Jewish family unit, in regard to both the relationship between husband and wife and the relationship between parents and children.[103] One of these enactments provided that "a man must support his sons and daughters when they are young."[104] As the sources indicate, both the question whether this enactment was adopted as a binding legal norm and the precise age at which the obligation would cease were uncertain for a considerable time, until finally the age of six years was set as the age at which the legal obligation to support expired.[105] There was thus no legal norm requiring support for children above this age; and, from time to time, fathers in fact refused to support such children.

How, then, was it possible to enforce against these fathers the obligation of support when that obligation did not have the character of a legal norm? Here an important precept taken from the "religious" part of the *Halakhah* filled in the gap in the "legal" part. This religious precept was the commandment to give charity. The law prescribes that the giving of charity can be compelled,[106] *i.e.*, when a court is convinced that an individual is financially able to give charity and there are people dependent on charity

101. *See supra* pp. 94–104 and *infra* pp. 141–167.
102. TB Ketubbot 49a.
103. *See infra* pp. 566–569.
104. TB Ketubbot 49b.
105. *Id.* 65b and *Tosafot, ad loc.*, s.v. Aval zan ketanei ketanim.
106. *Id.* 49b; TB Bava Batra 8b; Maimonides, *MT*, Mattenot Aniyyim 7:10.

funds, the court, by the same methods that are normally used to enforce legal norms, may compel the individual to give charity in an amount that it determines he is able to pay.

The law relating to charity contains an additional rule that establishes priorities of entitlement for recipients. That rule states: "The poor of one's household have priority over the poor of one's town, and the poor of one's own town have priority over the poor of any other town."[107]

The combination of these two rules yielded the conclusion that a father could be subjected to legal sanctions for failure to support his children,[108] because such support constitutes the highest charity; there is no one closer to a father than his children, who are his own offspring and the poor of his own household.[109]

The obligation of a son to support his father likewise derives from the law of charity.[110] Thus, a principle taken from religious law, namely, the enforceability of the commandment to give charity, filled in a gap in the "legal" *Halakhah.*

2. "THE PAYMENT OF A DEBT IS A RELIGIOUS OBLIGATION"

In the second half of the fourth century C.E., there was a fundamental difference of opinion between two Babylonian *amoraim* concerning the nature of the personal obligation of a debtor to fulfill his obligation to pay his creditor. According to R. Huna b. R. Joshua, a debtor has a full legal obligation to pay the debt, similar to the obligation of a bailee to return a bailed chattel to its owner at the agreed time. According to R. Papa, the obligation to pay a debt is not "legal"; it is not like the obligation to return a bailed chattel. R. Papa reasoned that the obligation to return a bailed chattel is "legal" because title remains in the bailor, who has the legal right to demand what is his. Money, on the other hand, is lent to be spent ("the purpose of a loan is to make use of the money"), and the creditor's money is no longer in the hands of the debtor after it is spent. Therefore, R. Papa was of the opinion that "the payment of a debt is a religious obligation,"[111] *i.e.*, the obligation does not rest upon a legal basis of "duty" and "right" but on

107. Sh. Ar. YD 251:3, following *Sifrei,* Deuteronomy, Re'eh, sec. 116 (ed. Finkelstein, pp. 174–175), and TB Bava Meẓi'a 31b, 71a; *see also* Finkelstein's comments, *ad loc.*

108. Sh. Ar. EH 71:1.

109. In 1944, the Chief Rabbinate of the Land of Israel adopted an enactment mandating support of children up to the age of fifteen (*see infra* pp. 831–832). With the adoption of this enactment, the obligation to provide such support became a purely legal duty (which is more comprehensive than the requirement rooted in the obligation to give charity, since, in the latter case, sanctions can be enforced against a father only if the resources he would have left are enough to maintain himself). *See also infra* n. 121.

110. TJ Pe'ah 1:1, 4a (1:1, 15d); Maimonides, *MT,* Mamrim 6:3; Sh. Ar. YD 240:5.

111. TB Ketubbot 86a; Bava Batra 174a; Arakhin 22a.

miẓvah—a religious commandment to pay in order to fulfill one's promise and keep one's word.[112]

With regard to this position taken by R. Papa, R. Kahana asked him:

> According to your opinion that the payment of a debt is a religious commandment, suppose the debtor says, "I do not wish to perform the religious obligation," what is the rule?[113]

In other words, if the obligation to pay a debt is a matter of religious obligation rather than a legal duty enforceable by judicial sanction, what is the rule if the debtor says, "I find this religious obligation inconvenient and I do not choose to perform it"? Is the creditor without any redress?

The response of R. Papa was that just as a Jewish court may compel the fulfillment of a religious obligation such as *sukkah* (the booth or tabernacle erected for the festival of *Sukkot*) or *lulav* (the palm branch used on the *Sukkot* festival), so the court may likewise compel performance of the religious obligation to pay debts.[114] According to R. Papa, neither the obligation to pay debts nor the judicial enforcement of that obligation is based on any legal duty of the debtor to pay, or any right of the creditor to be paid. Rather, they are based on the religious obligation of the debtor to pay pursuant to the commandment "Your word shall be your bond" (lit. "Your 'yes' shall be honest and your 'no' shall be honest").[115] Here, too, a principle

112. *See* Rashi, Ketubbot 86a, s.v. Peri'at ba'al ḥov miẓvah: "He has a religious obligation to pay his debt and keep his word, as it is written, 'An honest *hin*' [a liquid measure] (Leviticus 19:36), [which means that] your 'yes' [*hen,* a play on the word *hin*] shall be honest and your 'no' shall be honest (TB Bava Meẓi'a 49a)." *Bet ha-Beḥirah,* Ketubbot, *ad loc.,* s.v. Kevar be'arnu (ed. Sofer, pp. 384–385), gives the same interpretation. Other commentators suggest another source for the rule that repayment of a debt is a religious obligation. *See* Elon, *Ḥerut,* p. 20 n. 44.

113. TB Ketubbot 86a.

114. On the nature of such compulsion and the circumstances under which it is applied, *see* Elon, *Ḥerut,* pp. 22–23.

115. Urbach (*The Sages,* pp. 337–339) distinguishes between an "optional precept" (*i.e.,* a precept that it is meritorious to perform but that carries no liability to punishment if not performed) and an "obligatory precept." He then disagrees with the interpretation given here, namely, that the basic issue between the *amoraim* was whether repayment of a debt is a religious obligation or a legal duty. He argues:

> Such a distinction was far from the minds of the *amoraim.* Undoubtedly, even Rav Kahana did not recognize an obligation under civil law that did not fall within the category of the commandments. That which is not a commandment (*miẓvah*) is certainly not obligatory, but optional; yet within this option it was possible, as we have seen, to upgrade and approximate certain acts to the status of commandment, even acts not included in the concept of "an obligation under civil law."

See also id. at n. 80: "But the restoration of a stolen article is also not a 'legal obligation' but a positive precept; *see* Maimonides, *MT,* Gezelah [va-Avedah] 1:1."

However, it would appear that Urbach is not correct. A fundamental distinction exists throughout *dinei mamonot* in Jewish law between the legal aspect and the religious element

taken from the religious part of the *Halakhah,* namely, that sanctions may be applied to compel the fulfillment of a positive religious commandment, was employed to fill a gap in the "legal" part of the *Halakhah* with respect to the payment of debts.[116]

3. THE CREATION OF AN OBLIGATION BY VOW, BAN, OR OATH

An interesting post-Talmudic example of the reciprocal relationship between the "legal" and the "religious" parts of the *Halakhah* is the creation of commercial obligations by means of vows, oaths, or bans; *i.e.,* the obligor makes a vow, or takes an oath under penalty of a ban, to pay a specific sum or to perform a particular act. This creates an obligation to perform the promise or declaration. The vow, oath, and ban—which create religious

---

of any matter. This is the premise of most of the *rishonim,* who explained that R. Huna b. R. Joshua regarded the obligation to repay debts as both legal—based on law—and religious. *See, e.g., Resp. Ribash* #484: "But R. Huna b. R. Joshua concluded that the lien [on the debtor's property for repayment of the debt] is Biblical (*shi'buda de-oraita*), that the court can execute against his [*i.e.,* the debtor's] property as a matter of law, and that repayment of a debt is more than a *mizvah.*" *See also* Elon, *Ḥerut, supra* n. 114.

Both Simeon b. Ẓemaḥ Duran (Rashbeẓ) (*infra* pp. 133–136) and Shimon Shkop (*infra* pp. 136–137) have explained this fundamental distinction very clearly. It is worthwhile to repeat the latter's remarks:

> Civil laws, which govern the relations among people, operate differently from the other commandments of the Torah. In respect of all other commandments—the positive and negative precepts enjoined by the Torah—our obligation to fulfill them rests on our duty to obey God's command. Matters of *mamon* [civil law], however, are different; there must be a legal duty before a religious obligation arises to pay damages or make restitution. . . .
>
> There is another basic principle here: When we deal with a legal right in a chattel or with a lien, the focus of our concern is not the observance of a religious commandment but rather the objective circumstances determining who has the legal ownership of the object or is legally entitled to its possession.

Thus, in a case of robbery, the first question to be addressed is whether, from the legal standpoint, the chattel taken was the property of the victim. Only when such ownership has been established must the religious commandment to return the property be carried out.

With regard to the matter discussed in the text, R. Papa held that the duty to repay is legal in nature in cases of robbery or bailment but not in the case of a loan, since the particular money lent no longer belongs to the lender; the borrower's only obligation is to perform the religious obligation that "your 'yes' shall be honest and your 'no' shall be honest." R. Huna b. R. Joshua, on the other hand, held that even in the case of a loan, the primary duty is legal, although there is also a corollary religious obligation (*mizvah*) involved. The distinction between religious obligations and legal duties leads to other distinctions and divergent conclusions, depending on how the obligation is categorized. *See infra* n. 121.

116. The law was settled in accordance with R. Huna b. R. Joshua's view that repayment of a debt is not only a religious but also a legal obligation; *see* Elon, *Ḥerut,* pp. 22–23 nn. 44, 45. Consequently, in this instance there is no need to invoke the reciprocal support that exists between the two parts of the *Halakhah,* but no halakhic authority denies the possible existence of such support even here.

duties and obligations as between human beings and God—were especially useful to create obligations that the "legal" *Halakhah* did not protect or enforce, such as where the object of the undertaking was not yet in existence at the time of the promise,[117] where a promise was legally defective because of *asmakhta,*[118] and in other cases.[119] Again, it was "religious" law that filled the gap in the "legal" law.[120] This recourse helped provide solutions to various practical problems that arose in Jewish law, although as a general rule it did not give this type of obligation the same legal status as an obligation stemming from a "legal" norm.[121]

4. THE NATURE OF A DIVORCE JUDGMENT

An interesting aspect of the reciprocal relationship among all parts of the *Halakhah* found expression in a decision of the Supreme Court of Israel on the nature of a judgment of divorce in Jewish law. Under Section 3 of the Rabbinical Courts Jurisdiction (Marriage and Divorce) Law, 1953, and the decisions of the Supreme Court, when an action for divorce brought in a rabbinical court also raises issues involving the couple's property, the rabbinical court has exclusive jurisdiction over both the complaint for divorce and the property issues as well; but this jurisdiction exists only when the rabbinical court renders a judgment on the claim for divorce. The question was, What kind of decision constitutes a "judgment" of divorce? Sometimes, depending on the circumstances of the case, the court determines

117. Rema to Sh. Ar. ḤM 209:4: "If he swore an oath to carry out the transaction, even though [it involved something] not yet in existence, he must fulfill his oath."

118. *Asmakhta* exists when a transaction is entered into without a deliberate and unqualified intention to enter into it. Examples are an obligation entered into on the assumption that it need not be fulfilled, or when the transaction involves a penalty or forfeiture, or the promised performance is grossly disproportionate to the consideration received. *See infra* p. 301 n. 51; p. 1604 n. 76; Sh. Ar. ḤM 207:19: "A vow, an oath, or a handshake is effective even in [transactions based on] *asmakhta.*" A handshake can create a legal obligation if it is the custom of merchants to use a handshake as a mode of acquisition (*see* Sh. Ar. ḤM 201:1–2); however, even where there is no such custom, a handshake can create a binding obligation similar to that created by a vow or an oath.

119. *See, e.g.,* Sh. Ar. ḤM 129:5. *See also* Gulak, *Yesodei,* II, pp. 52–56.

120. For the reciprocal relationship between the various parts of the *Halakhah, see further* the instructive responsum in *Resp. Tashbeẓ,* III, #190, discussed *supra* pp. 99–102 and n. 39 and *infra* pp. 151–154.

121. Generally, while there is reciprocal support between "religious" and "legal" obligations, there is still a difference between an obligation that originates in "legal" *Halakhah* and one that stems from "religious" *Halakhah.* Thus, as we have seen, where the obligation to support children is derived from the commandment to give charity, it is qualified by two conditions: (1) that the father has enough left to maintain himself, and (2) that the recipient is in need (*see supra* n. 109). Similarly, there is a difference between a legal obligation and one flowing from an oath or a vow. In the latter instance, the obligation is personal; it abates on the obligor's death and will not bind his heirs. The methods of enforcement of the two types of obligations are also different. *See* Sh. Ar. ḤM ch. 129; *Sema, ad. loc.,* subpar. 16.

that a divorce should be given, or even imposes sanctions to compel the divorce. However, there are occasions when the court does not state that a divorce is obligatory, but the language of the decision is that it is a *mizvah* (here, "religious or moral obligation") for the husband to give the divorce or that it is appropriate that the couple should be divorced. The members of the Supreme Court at one point disagreed on this question, and one justice was of the opinion that the latter form of decision is not a *judgment* on the claim for divorce:

> Even if the decision states that "it is desirable that the parties divorce" or "it is a *mizvah* that they divorce," I would not see in this language a judgment that obligates the parties or either of them from a legal, as distinguished from a religious or moral, point of view; the law is clear that so long as the decision does not obligate the parties to consummate a divorce, the rabbinical court does not have jurisdiction to decide issues concerning their joint property.[122]

This opinion was not accepted, and in a later unanimous decision it was said:[123]

> With all due respect, I cannot accept this argument that there is a distinction between the legal and the religious or moral character of a judgment of divorce by a rabbinical court under the Rabbinical Courts Jurisdiction (Marriage and Divorce) Law, 1953. The criterion for determining what is and is not included in the term "judgment of divorce" must be derived from the provisions of the legal system that the Legislature vested with jurisdiction in matters of divorce, and it is not reasonable that the nature and content of such a judgment should be determined by criteria rooted and developed and matured in the conceptual framework of another legal system. Consequently, inasmuch as the Legislature prescribed in the Rabbinical Courts Jurisdiction Law that the rabbinical courts have exclusive jurisdiction over matters of divorce, it follows that the nature and quality of a judgment of divorce is to be determined under the law governing matters of divorce in the rabbinical courts—namely, Jewish law. The outlook of Jewish law as to the distinction between law and religion or morals is different from that of other legal systems; and this difference, reflected in all areas of the law, also applies to the nature and content of judgments. This is not the place to go into this matter, which I have already examined elsewhere.[124] As to the particular issue before us, this type of divorce judgment, in which the rabbinical court rules that it is a *mizvah* for the parties to divorce, is a daily occurrence in the judgments of the rabbinical courts and has been accepted from ancient times in the Jew-

122. Haber v. Rabbinical Court of Appeals, 32(iii) *P.D.* 324, 333 (1978) (S. Asher, J.).

123. Gutman v. District Rabbinical Court, Tel Aviv–Jaffa, 34(i) *P.D.* 443, 447–448 (1979) (M. Elon, J.).

124. *See supra* pp. 111–119, *infra* pp. 141–167.

ish legal system. I will cite one example concerning the complaint for divorce on the ground that "he is detestable to me," which is similar to the case before us. Rabbenu Jonah (a Spanish authority of the thirteenth century) wrote:

> Although one does not compel (*i.e.*, by flogging) the giving of a divorce when the wife claims "he is detestable to me," the court declares to him that it is a *mizvah* for him to divorce her and advises him that he should divorce her.[125]

We thus see that where it is inappropriate to render a judgment compelling a divorce, the judgment will state ("the court declares to him") that it is a *mizvah* for him to divorce, and such a judgment also has halakhic-legal consequences.

In conclusion, the settled law in this court as to the interpretation of Section 3 of the Rabbinical Courts Jurisdiction (Marriage and Divorce) Law, 1953, is that a rabbinical court has jurisdiction to determine the allocation of the couple's property when it renders a judgment of divorce in the accepted sense of that term in Jewish law, *i.e.*, whether it states that the giving or receiving of the bill of divorcement is mandatory or obligatory or whether it states that it is a *mizvah* or that it is desirable to give or receive it. For all these various forms of decision constitute judgments of divorce according to Jewish law.

V. DISTINCTION BETWEEN "RELIGIOUS" AND "LEGAL" *HALAKHAH*—*"ISSUR"* AND *"MAMON"*

The pervasive qualitative similarity between the two parts of the *Halakhah* raises a question of fundamental importance in any study or consideration of Jewish law: Does the *Halakhah* make *any* distinction between these two basic categories of which it is composed?

Although all parts of the *Halakhah* are rooted in the same source, share the same principles and methods of analysis, and provide and receive reciprocal support, nevertheless, study of the halakhic sources reveals that the *Halakhah* did make very fundamental distinctions between its two major categories, namely, monetary matters (that part of the *Halakhah* included in the concept of *mamon*) and nonmonetary matters (that part of the *Halakhah* included in the concept of *issur*).[126]

It is undoubtedly true that these two categories, *issur* and *mamon*, do not coincide with contemporary concepts of "religion" and "law."[127] Never-

125. *Shittah Mekubbezet*, Ketubbot 64a *et seq.*

126. *See Tosefta* Kiddushin 3:8: ". . . a case which is a matter of *mamon* . . . a case which is not a matter of *mamon* . . ."

127. *See supra* nn. 2, 68.

theless, the basic distinction between *issur* and *mamon* had a decisive and far-reaching influence on the pattern of development of a large part of the *corpus juris* of *mishpat ivri.*

The beginning of this distinction between *issur* and *mamon* appears as early as the tannaitic period. The School of Shammai, in their debates with the School of Hillel, argued, "You have been permissive on a matter of forbidden sexual relations, a subject where great stringency is required; should you not therefore also be permissive on a monetary matter, which is not nearly so serious?"[128] As early as toward the end of the tannaitic period, a number of important distinctions were made between these two halakhic categories. A review of a number of legal issues will shed light on the nature of these distinctions.

A. Freedom of Contract—"Contracting Out of a Law Contained in the Torah"

One distinction involves the question of freedom of contract, to which every legal system has given extensive consideration. There are two methods of establishing the rules governing the legal relationship between the parties to a legal transaction. One method is to establish applicable legal rules and norms that are beyond the power of the parties to vary or to escape from by agreement. These rules are mandated by law and have the character of *jus cogens.* The other method is to prescribe legal rules that will govern the relationship between the parties to a transaction only when the parties have not agreed to a different legal relationship. Under this method, the legal rules are subject to change by agreement of the parties; the parties may prescribe their own rules to govern their relationship, and these rules may supplement or even conflict with the legal rules that would otherwise be applicable. Where this method prevails, the legal rules are merely *jus dispositivum.*

Some legal systems favor the first approach, while others follow the second; but, as a general rule, any given legal system uses both methods. The choice in any particular case depends on the nature and subject matter of the particular transaction, considered in light of the economic and social needs of the time. The technical term Jewish law uses to describe whether there is freedom of contract for a transaction is whether it is permissible "to

128. M Eduyyot 1:12; Yevamot 15:3. The response of the School of Hillel was that in the situation there under discussion the monetary dispute required greater stringency, since the attempt was to extract property from one who had possession; *see also infra* n. 166. For details of the law that was the subject of the discussion between the School of Hillel and the School of Shammai, *see infra* pp. 402, 521.

contract out of a law contained in the Torah" (*lehatenot al mah she-katuv ba-Torah*).

It appears that in the early *Halakhah,* the rule was that any stipulation to a result contrary to a Biblical norm, whether as to *mamon* or *issur,* was void.[129] It was on the basis of this doctrine that the Mishnah states:[130]

> If one says: "So-and-so, who is my firstborn son, shall not take a double share [in my estate]," or "my son shall not inherit with his brothers," he has said nothing [*i.e.,* his statement is ineffective], since he has stipulated out of a law contained in the Torah.

In other words, under this view, since the Torah states both that the firstborn takes a double share in the estate of his father and that all sons inherit from their father, the stipulation to the contrary is void.[131]

In the fourth generation of *tannaim,* some of the Sages limited the application of the doctrine prohibiting contracts varying Biblical norms and applied the prohibition only to nonmonetary matters. Thus, the Mishnah states:[132]

> If a husband writes to his wife, "I waive all rights to your property and to its usufruct during your lifetime and after your death," he has no claim to the usufruct during her lifetime; and, if she dies, he does not inherit from her. Rabban Simeon b. Gamaliel says: "If she dies, he does inherit from her because he has stipulated out of a law contained in the Torah [which prescribes that he does inherit], and any stipulation out of a law contained in the Torah is void."

According to the Sages, who disagreed with Rabban Simeon b. Gamaliel, the waiver of the husband with regard to inheritance is fully effective, notwithstanding that he has agreed to a result contrary to the Biblical norm.

The distinction between monetary matters and nonmonetary matters

129. M Bava Meẓi'a 7:11.

130. M Bava Batra 8:5.

131. Similarly, the *mishnah* continues: "If one [who has no son] says, 'So-and-so shall inherit me' when there is a daughter, or [one says] 'My daughter shall inherit me' when there is a son, he has said nothing, since he has stipulated out of a law contained in the Torah." These rules, according to their plain meaning, negate freedom of contract even in a monetary matter, namely, succession to the estate of a decedent. The distinction made in TB Bava Batra 126b, which interprets these rules as being consistent even with the view of R. Judah that in monetary matters a stipulation to contract out of a Biblical norm is valid, is not consistent with the plain meaning of the *mishnah.* For a fuller discussion of this question, *see infra* n. 140.

132. M Ketubbot 9:1. *See also* TB Ketubbot 83b–84a and TJ Ketubbot 9:1, 59a *et seq.* (9:1, 32d *et seq.*).

in regard to freedom of contract is even more pronounced in the following law in the *Tosefta:*[133]

> [If he says] "I hereby betroth you . . . on condition that if I die you shall not be subject to levirate marriage," she is betrothed, and the condition is void, as he has contracted out of a law contained in the Torah, and when anyone stipulates out of a law contained in the Torah, the condition is void. [If he says] "on condition that you have no claim against me for food, clothing, or conjugal rights,"[134] she is betrothed, and the condition is valid. This is the principle: Contracting out of a law contained in the Torah as to a monetary matter is valid, but as to a nonmonetary matter is void.

The stipulation that seeks to release the wife from the Biblical obligation of levirate marriage[135] is void, because that stipulation concerns a nonmonetary matter; and the principle voiding a stipulation for a result contrary to a Biblical norm applies. On the other hand, the stipulation that seeks to release the husband from his obligations for food, clothing, and conjugal relations is valid even though these obligations are prescribed by the laws of the Torah,[136] since these are monetary matters, as to which Biblical norms are subject to change by stipulation. A different *baraita*[137] teaches that this distinction between stipulations concerning *issur* and those concerning *mamon* was in accordance with the view of R. Judah,[138] but that according to R. Meir, the stipulation with regard to food, clothing, and conjugal relations is also void. R. Meir agreed with Rabban Simeon b. Gamaliel that the principle that one may not stipulate to a result contrary to a Biblical norm applies both to monetary and nonmonetary matters.[139]

133. *Tosefta* Kiddushin 3:7–8.

134. For a discussion of "food, clothing, and conjugal rights," *see infra* pp. 570–571.

135. Deuteronomy 25:5–6.

136. Exodus 21:10: "He must not withhold . . . her food, her clothing, or her conjugal rights." *See also infra* p. 571. As to agreements regarding conjugal rights, *see infra* n. 138.

137. TB Ketubbot 56a; Bava Meẓi'a 94a *et al.*

138. Rashi, Ketubbot 56a, s.v. Be-davar she-be-mamon, and Rashbam, Bava Batra 126b, s.v. Be-davar shel mamon, comment that even according to R. Judah, an agreement limiting conjugal rights is invalid because it involves not merely money but a person's body. This is also the view of Maimonides, *MT,* Ishut 6:9–10, and other *rishonim.* This basic distinction between monetary and personal rights in regard to the effectiveness of contracting out of the legal rules of the Torah is also made in TJ Ketubbot 9:1, 52b (9:1, 32d). *Tosefta* Kiddushin 3:7 implies that an agreement regarding conjugal rights is also valid, as does TJ Bava Meẓi'a 7:7, 29a (7:10, 11c). Rabbenu Hananel (*Oẓar ha-Geonim,* Ketubbot, collected commentary of Rabbenu Hananel, p. 45) also gives the same interpretation. *See also id.,* Responsa Section, p. 168, citing to the same effect *Sefer ha-Ma'asim li-Venei Ereẓ Yisra'el. See also Miẓpeh Shemu'el,* Letter *lamed; Minḥat Bikkurim* and *Ḥazon Yeḥezkel* to *Tosefta* Kiddushin 3:9.

139. The opinion of the Sages who limit to nonmonetary matters the applicability of the principle that a stipulation to contract out of a Biblical norm is invalid is also reflected

In the amoraic period,[140] the view became accepted that in monetary matters, contracting out of a law contained in the Torah would be given effect,[141] provided that the stipulation is made in the correct form;[142] and this became settled law in the post-Talmudic era.[143]

---

in M Bava Meẓi'a 7:10: "An unpaid bailee may stipulate to be exempted from taking an oath, a borrower [may stipulate] to be relieved of liability to pay, and a paid bailee or lessee [may stipulate] to be exempted from taking an oath and relieved of liability to pay." *See also* TB Bava Meẓi'a 94a: "Why is that so? Is he not stipulating out of a law contained in the Torah? . . . This [*mishnah*] reflects the view of R. Judah who holds that in monetary matters such a stipulation is valid. . . ."

140. In order to reconcile the conflict between the rule permitting freedom of contract as to monetary matters and the rule in M Bava Batra 8:5 that a father cannot by stipulation prevent his firstborn son from inheriting the Biblically prescribed double share in the father's estate and cannot entirely disinherit any son, the discussion in the Talmud (TB Bava Batra 126b) suggests that the question of inheritance is unique, because it may be presumed that the son does not agree to the stipulation that would deprive him of his right to inherit (Rashbam, *ad loc.*, s.v. Hatam), or—according to other commentators—the son lacks the legal capacity, or is otherwise unable to agree to the stipulation (*Yad Ramah, ad loc.*, par. 100, s.v. Beram; *Shittah Mekubbeẓet, ad loc.*, s.v. Hatam). However, the plain meaning of the *mishnah* is to the contrary; the *mishnah* explicitly states that the reason the stipulation is invalid is that it contravenes a Biblical norm, *i.e.*, the stipulation is inherently invalid as a matter of fundamental principle, whereas according to the rationale in TB Bava Batra 126b, the reason is that the party whose rights would be adversely affected by the stipulation does not or cannot agree to it. An indication that inheritance is no different from other monetary matters can be found in *Tosefta* Kiddushin 3:7–8, quoted *supra* at n. 133, which gives levirate marriage as an example of a nonmonetary matter as to which contracting out of a Biblical norm is invalid, but does not indicate that such a stipulation can also be invalid even as to a monetary matter, *e.g.*, inheritance.

141. *See, e.g.*, TB Ketubbot 83b–84a; Bava Meẓi'a 51a/b; TJ Ketubbot 9:1, 51a *et seq.* (9:1, 32c *et seq.*); Bava Batra 8:5, 24a (8:6, 16b), R. Jeremiah's statement in the name of Rav. In particular, freedom of contract was widely exercised with respect to the financial relationship between husband and wife because of social and economic changes that occurred in the course of time. *See, e.g.*, TJ Ketubbot 9:1, 53b (9:1, 33a) ("R. Yose said: A marital agreement that 'if she [*i.e.*, the wife] shall die without children, her property shall revert to her father's house,' is a monetary stipulation and is valid"). Similarly, TJ Ketubbot 5:8, 38a (5:10, 30b) ("R. Yose said: A marital agreement that if he [*i.e.*, the husband] comes to hate [the wife] or she comes to hate [him, she will be given an agreed sum of money] is a monetary stipulation and is valid"). *See also* TJ Bava Batra 8:8, 26b (8:10, 16c); J.N. Epstein, "Ma'asim li-Venei Ereẓ Yisra'el," *Tarbiẓ*, I, Book 2 (1930), pp. 33ff., at p. 40 and notes *ad loc.*

In the final analysis, the criteria for the existence of freedom of contract were established in light of the substantive importance of the legal institution involved, and it is possible that freedom of contract was denied with respect to a particular law, even though the law was not Biblical but was enacted by rabbinic legislation. Thus, even according to the view of R. Judah, which permits such stipulation in monetary matters, the husband cannot stipulate that his wife receive less than the prescribed minimum amount of the *ketubbah*, because "the *ketubbah* is rabbinic and the Sages gave this law greater force than Biblical law," in order to protect the institution of the *ketubbah*, which is vital for well-ordered matrimonial relations. On the other hand, the husband could agree that he would not have the usufruct of his wife's property, since the husband's usufruct is not a vital institution for matrimonial relations, in that it applies only in those cases where the wife brings her own

Thus, on the question of freedom of contract, Jewish law established a fundamental distinction based on whether the matter involved *issur* or *mamon.* In matters of *issur,* such as levirate marriage, the Biblical norms are obligatory and are not subject to change by the stipulation of an interested party. However, with regard to matters of *mamon,* "one may waive one's rights, inasmuch as the Torah established such obligations only if desired by the obligee."[144] The Torah itself did not prescribe these rules as mandatory, but made the rules subject to the will of the parties[145] to any particular legal transaction or relationship.[146]

---

property to the marriage, and there is consequently no reason to limit freedom of contract with respect to that right (TB Ketubbot 56a/b). *See also infra* pp. 215–217.

142. TB Makkot 3b:

> R. Anan said: "I can explain Samuel's opinion. [If one says, 'I will sell you the article] on condition that you will have no claim of overcharging against me,' he has no claim of overcharging [*i.e.,* the agreement is that the purchaser will waive his claim and that agreement is valid]; [but if he said,] 'on condition that the [rule against] overcharging will not apply to this transaction,' the rule against overcharging does apply. . . . [If he said, 'I make you this loan] on condition that you will not cancel it in the sabbatical year,' the sabbatical year does not cancel it; [but if he says,] 'on condition that the sabbatical year will not cancel it,' the sabbatical year does cancel it."

See Tosafot, ad loc., s.v. Al menat she-ein bo ona'ah (which is followed in the foregoing translation with respect to the claim of overcharging). Rashi, *ad loc.,* s.v. Le-didi mefarsha li, gives the passage a somewhat different meaning. *See also* Maimonides, *MT,* Shemittah ve-Yovel 9:10, Mekhirah 13:3–4; *Tur* ḤM 67:12; Sh. Ar. ḤM 67:9; *Tur* ḤM 227:24–26; Sh. Ar. ḤM 227:21.

143. Maimonides, *MT,* Ishut 12:7–9, Shemittah ve-Yovel 9:10, Mekhirah 13:3–4; *Tur* EH 38:12–13; Sh. Ar. EH 38:5; *Tur* ḤM 67:12; Sh. Ar. ḤM 67:9; *Tur* ḤM 227:24–26; Sh. Ar. ḤM 227:21.

144. Naḥmanides, Novellae to Bava Batra 126b, s.v. Harei zu mekuddeshet u-tena'o batel. *See also* B. Lipkin, "Hatna'at ha-Goremim bi-Devarim she-be-Mamonot" [Stipulation by the Parties in Monetary Matters], *Sinai,* XXXV (1954), pp. 111ff.

145. Matters concerning which a person is not free to contract include those that adversely affect his body or his personal freedom. Thus, no person can stipulate that another should cause him bodily injury (TB Bava Kamma 93a; TJ Bava Kamma 8:8, 37a [8:11, 6c]; *Resp. Ribash* #484). Nor can a creditor and his debtor agree that the debtor may be imprisoned for nonpayment notwithstanding that he does not have the means to pay the debt (*Resp. Ribash* #484; *see also* Elon, *Ḥerut,* pp. 140ff.). *See also supra* n. 138, regarding contracts concerning a person's body, as distinguished from money. A stipulation that is contrary to the public welfare or morals is invalid, even if it relates to a monetary matter; *see, e.g., Resp. Ḥavvot Ya'ir* #163. There are other instances with respect to which there are conflicting opinions as to whether freedom of contract exists, such as suretyship (*see* M. Elon, "Ḥofesh ha-Hatna'ah be-Dinei Arvut ba-Mishpat ha-Ivri" [Freedom of Contract in the Jewish Law of Suretyship], *Proceedings of the Fourth International Congress of Jewish Studies,* I (1967), pp. 197–208), and succession (according to Maimonides, *MT,* Naḥalot 6:1; for the source of Maimonides' statement, which is contrary to the plain meaning of the Talmudic discussion, *see Bet ha-Beḥirah* to Bava Batra 126b). *See also supra* n. 141; *infra* pp. 1672–1674; and M. Elon, EJ, V, pp. 923–933, s.v. Contract (reprinted in *Principles,* pp. 246–256).

146. The principle of freedom of contract as developed in Jewish law has been dealt with by the Supreme Court of Israel in two contexts: (1) the invalidation of contracts to

B. Illegal Contracts

Jewish law also distinguishes between *mamon* and *issur* in connection with legal transactions that involve violation of a "religious" law.

Different legal systems take divergent views on the subject of illegal contracts, *e.g.*, contracts that involve a violation of the criminal law or are made for illegal purposes. In some continental legal systems, such a contract is absolutely void. According to English law, the contract is not void, but the court refrains from lending any aid by way of enforcement. Two principles operate in the English law in such cases: *ex turpi causa non oritur actio* ("a tainted claim does not give rise to a right of action") and *in pari delicto melior est pars possidentis* ("if two parties are equally guilty, the party in possession has the better part [and his possession will not be disturbed]").[147]

The approach of Jewish law is fundamentally different. Although, according to Jewish law, an illegal contract may not be enforced if such enforcement carries out the illegal act itself, the mere transgression of a religious law is not enough to preclude the legal validity of the contract, or to prevent the court from enforcing it. Consequently, in the case of a usurious loan (as to which Biblical law prohibits the debtor from paying and the creditor from taking interest),[148] the creditor cannot claim the interest from the debtor on the basis of the contract, because this would result in the accomplishment of the prohibited act. However, a debtor who has paid interest may recover it from his creditor even though the debtor transgressed a Biblical rule when he paid the interest.

If the debtor gave the creditor a chattel instead of paying money as interest, the debtor may claim the return only of the amount of interest but not the chattel itself, as "the transfer is valid and it is no ground for voiding this transfer that the transfer was made in violation of a religious prohibition."[149] The same applies to a note that provides for interest: according to R. Meir, the creditor is penalized in that he recovers neither the principal

---

cause physical injury to a person, *see* Sharon v. Levi, 35(i) *P.D.* 736, 755 (1980), or to abridge personal freedom, *see* State of Israel v. Rivkah Abukasis, 32(ii) *P.D.* 240, 248 (1978), and State of Israel v. Tamir, 37(iii) *P.D.* 201, 207 (1983); and (2) the establishment of the principle of joint ownership of property by a married couple where the facts and circumstances of the particular situation give rise to a presumption of an implied agreement between the couple for the joint ownership of the property, *see* Azugi v. Azugi, 33(iii) *P.D.* 1, 15–17 (1979), and cases cited.

147. For a more detailed discussion, *see* Jacobs v. Kartoz, 9 *P.D.* 1401 (1955); M. Silberg, *Talmudic Law and the Modern State*, pp. 70ff. and bibliography.

148. TB Bava Meẓi'a 61a and the pertinent codificatory literature.

149. TB Bava Meẓi'a 65a; Rashi, *ad loc.*, s.v. Gelima lo mafkinan mineih; *Piskei ha-Rosh*, Bava Meẓi'a, ch. 5, #19.

nor the interest;[150] but according to the majority of the Sages, the creditor does not collect the interest, but he does collect the principal. The majority view of the Sages became settled law.[151] Only when the note is for a lump sum that includes both principal and interest, and it is therefore impossible to ascertain from the note how much of the obligation represents interest, does the lender recover nothing "because otherwise he would recover interest [which the Torah forbids]."[152] The same rule applies to any transaction that is illegal in part: the transaction is valid except for the illegal part.[153]

This basic approach produced the following rule in Jewish law: "Whoever sells, or gives a gift, on the sabbath (and, needless to say, the same rule applies to a festival)—even though he is flogged, his act is valid."[154] Similarly, a legal obligation results from the making of a contract on the sabbath: "If anyone performs an act of acquisition in due legal form [*i.e., kinyan sudar*][155] on the sabbath, the acquisition is valid and the deed is written and delivered after the sabbath."[156] The rule applies even if the acquisition is carried out in a manner that involves a violation of the Biblical law of the sabbath.[157]

Thus, Jewish law distinguishes between the part of the *Halakhah* that concerns *mamon* and the part that concerns *issur.* It gives full legal effect to a contract that involves a religious transgression as long as the enforcement of the contract does not itself result in the commission of the transgression. This sharp distinction makes for stability in the administration of the law and also is consistent with the reciprocal relationship between law and ethics in the Jewish legal system.[158] Jewish law takes the view that the law should not confer an additional benefit on the guilty party by treating the civil contract as void and leaving the guilty party with both the *quid* and the *quo.*[159] However, when it does appear in a particular situation that giving effect to a transaction would serve to encourage the commission of an

150. TB Bava Meẓi'a 72a.
151. Maimonides, *MT,* Malveh ve-Loveh 4:6.
152. Sh. Ar. ḤM 52:1, YD 161:11.
153. Sh. Ar. ḤM 208:1 and Rema, *ad loc.*
154. Maimonides, *MT,* Mekhirah 30:7.
155. For the nature of this mode of acquisition, *see infra* pp. 581–583.
156. Maimonides, *MT,* Mekhirah 30:7; Sh. Ar. ḤM 195:11, 235:28.
157. *See* TB Bava Kamma 70b: "If he says to him, 'Pluck off figs from my fig tree and transfer to me what you have stolen [in exchange for the figs]' . . . or if he says to him, 'Throw what you have stolen into my courtyard and [thus] transfer ownership in it to me.'" The transfer was accomplished on the sabbath by plucking the figs or by moving the stolen article from one domain to another, both of which actions are prohibited according to Biblical law. *See Piskei ha-Rosh,* Beẓah, ch. 5, #2, and *Korban Netanel, ad loc.,* subpars. 80, 90.
158. *See infra* pp. 141–167.
159. *See* Silberg, *supra* n. 147 at 80ff.

illegal act,[160] the *Halakhah* provides that the court should not lend its assistance to the enforcement of the contract.[161]

C. Legislation (*Takkanot*)

The distinction between *issur* and *mamon* also has a substantial bearing on the question of the power to promulgate legislative enactments (*takkanot*) in the halakhic system. While the halakhic authorities' power to enact legislation was limited to a certain extent in matters of *issur*, it has remained undiminished in matters concerning *mamon*.[162] The distinction was also material as to the authority of the community and its leaders to legislate: that authority never extended to matters of *issur* but encompassed only matters in the area of civil and criminal law and violations of police regulations.[163]

D. Custom (*Minhag*)

The distinction between *issur* and *mamon* is also an important factor in regard to the binding authority and creative power of custom, particularly with regard to the fundamental principle in this field that "custom overrides the law" (*minhag mevattel halakhah*), which applies exclusively to matters of *mamon* but not at all to matters of *issur*.[164]

160. As in the case where false witnesses are hired: the court will not grant relief to a litigant who has hired such witnesses and then claims his money back when the witnesses do not testify (*Resp. Shevut Ya'akov*, I, #145. *See also* Sh. Ar. ḤM 32:1 and *Ateret Ẓevi* and *Pitḥei Teshuvah, ad loc.*, subpar. 1). For different opinions with regard to this situation, *see Netivot ha-Mishpat*, Sh. Ar. ḤM 9, Be'urim, subpar. 1; J.L. Zirelson, *Ma'arkhei Lev*, Responsa, ḤM, #113; *Ḥukkat Mishpat*, Mekhirah 30:12, Be'urim u-Mekorot, pp. 255–256. Similarly, a decision of the Rabbinical Court of Appeals of Israel denied relief on a monetary claim arising from a transaction in foreign currency that had been prohibited by law in order to promote the public welfare. *See infra* pp. 1603–1604.

161. *See generally* as to the Jewish law concerning the effect of illegality on transactions, E. Shochetman, *Ma'aseh ha-Ba be-Averah* [Transactions Involving Illegality], Jerusalem, 1981. In 1973, the Knesset passed the Contracts Law (General Part), 1973. Sections 30 and 31 of this statute resolve the question of illegal contracts by means of an approach that differs not only from that of Continental law but also from the common law as theretofore adopted in Israeli law. The provisions of these two sections are based on the general approach of Jewish law, as described *supra*, although they are not identical to the position of Jewish law. This is an interesting form of incorporation of the approach of Jewish law into the law of the State of Israel, and has been extensively dealt with in the decisions of the Israeli Supreme Court. This subject will be discussed in our treatment of Jewish law in the State of Israel, *see infra* pp. 1716–1720.

162. *See infra* pp. 490, 846.

163. *See infra* pp. 707–712.

164. *See infra* pp. 903–911.

E. Different Rules for Decision Making, and Other Distinctions

In the amoraic period, many general rules and principles were established marking out the distinctions between matters of *issur* and *mamon*. Thus, it was laid down that "no analogy in a matter involving *issur* may be drawn from a matter involving *mamon*";[165] and conversely, "no analogy in a matter involving *mamon* may be drawn from a matter involving *issur*."[166] A basic distinction between matters of *issur* and matters of *mamon* was also established with respect to a large number of rules that rest upon the principle that the burden of proof is upon the claimant: this principle applies to matters of *mamon* but not to matters of *issur*.[167] This difference in regard to

165. TB Berakhot 19b; and *see* Rashi, *ad loc.*, s.v. Mamona; TB Bava Meẓi'a 20b: "R. Amram said to Rabbah: 'How can you resolve [a problem] in *issur* by [analogy] from *mamon?*'" *See also Tosafot, ad loc.*, s.v. Issura mi-mamona; TB Gittin 34a and Rashi, *ad loc.*, s.vv. Hakha mamona, and Hakha issura. The rationale for this general rule is that matters of *issur* are substantively more serious than monetary matters. *See infra* n. 167.

166. TB Ketubbot 40b, 46b; Kiddushin 3b. For example, a father may annul his daughter's vows as long as she still has the status of *na'arah, i.e.*, before she has reached the age of twelve years, six months, and one day. The Talmud sought by analogy to this rule to reach the conclusion that until she reaches that age, her father also has the right to her earnings. However, the analogy was rejected on the ground that since a father's right to his daughter's earnings is a matter of *mamon*, it cannot be derived by analogy from a law concerning annulment of vows, which is a matter of *issur*. As to monetary matters, the general rule applies that "the burden of proof rests upon the claimant," and thus when an attempt is made to extract property from the person in possession, the law as to a monetary matter is more stringent than in a matter of *issur*. *See also* the response of the School of Hillel to the School of Shammai in the matter of the woman who claimed that her husband died, to the effect that she may remarry (*i.e.*, her testimony is sufficient to obviate the religious prohibition), but she cannot recover her *ketubbah* (which is a monetary claim). M Eduyyot 1:12; M Yevamot 15:1–3.

167. According to Samuel, in monetary matters a statistical majority is not sufficient to establish a claim; *i.e.*, it may not be assumed that the parties have acted as the majority of people generally act (*ein holkhin aḥar ha-rov*), but the burden is on the claimant to prove all the elements of his particular case. In matters of *issur*, however, the ritual status of an object is determined according to the preponderance of probability as to whether it is prohibited or impure (*holkhin aḥar ha-rov*). TB Bava Kamma 27b, 46a/b; Bava Batra 92a/b. For an analysis of this subject, *see infra* p. 906. *See also Tosafot*, Bava Kamma 27b, s.v. Ka mashma lan de-ein holkhin be-mamon aḥar ha-rov.

For the same reason, when a ritually prohibited object is mixed with a greater amount of permissible objects to the extent that the prohibited object is no longer distinguishable, the prohibition is no longer operative (*batel be-rov*). No such principle operates in matters of *mamon* (TB Beẓah 38b). Thus, if coins belonging to A are mixed with a greater number of coins belonging to B, A's coins will not pass into B's ownership (Rashi, *ad loc.*, s.v. Amar lo), because the rule is that B is not entitled to the money unless he proves that it is rightfully his.

For this reason also, evidentiary requirements are not as strict in matters of *issur* as they are in monetary matters. For example, "a single witness is believed in matters of *issur*" when his testimony would make a prohibition inapplicable (TB Gittin 2b, 3a; Ḥullin 10b)

burden of proof was responsible for differences in the rules for decision making applicable in these two areas: as a general rule, "doubt in matters of *mamon* is to be resolved in favor of leniency, but doubt in matters of *issur* is to be resolved in favor of stringency"; *i.e.*, if a doubt arises in a case of *mamon*, the proper decision is the lenient one, while in a matter of *issur* the proper decision is the one based on the stricter view.[168]

F. Distinction between Matters of *Issur* and Matters of *Mamon* with Regard to *Dina de-Malkhuta Dina* ("The Law of the Land Is Law")

The distinction between *issur* and *mamon* is also important with respect to the question of the applicability of the doctrine of *dina de-malkhuta dina*. We have already extensively discussed the nature of this doctrine, its legal-halakhic foundation, and the scope of its application in the field of *mamon*.[169] However, it is universally agreed that the "law of the land" is *not* the law if it is inconsistent with a Jewish law in the area of *issur*.

It seems to have been so clearly settled that the doctrine of *dina de-malkhuta dina* does not apply to matters of *issur* that most of the recognized halakhic authorities do not discuss the question directly or in any detail, but mention it only incidentally.[170] One of the few sources in which this matter is discussed in detail is the responsa of Simeon b. Ẓemaḥ Duran (Rashbeẓ) in connection with the appointment of Isaac b. Sheshet Perfet (Ribash) as rabbi and judge for the community of Algiers. The facts of the

---

and "a person is believed if he says, 'My father told me that that family is [ritually] impure' or 'that that family is pure.' . . . However, the testimony of a single witness is not sufficient if he says, 'I remember that A owes B a *maneh*,' or 'a right of passage exists through A's field,' because these are matters of *mamon*" (*Tosefta* Ketubbot 3:3).

On the other hand, matters of *issur* are substantively more serious than monetary matters. *See, e.g.*, TB Bava Meẓi'a 30a ("A matter of *issur* takes precedence over monetary considerations"); *id.* 27b (with regard to identification marks, "the Sages adopted enactments in matters of *mamon*, but they did not adopt enactments in matters of *issur*"). *See also* TB Gittin 34a, 39b; Shevu'ot 30b, 36a/b; Yevamot 91a; Ketubbot 24a; Kiddushin 27b–28a; Bava Meẓi'a 119a.

168. The reason for this difference is that if a doubt exists, money cannot be extracted from the person in possession, because the burden of proof is on the claimant. TB Ketubbot 73b; Bava Batra 57a/b; Niddah 25a; Ḥullin 134a; Gittin 63b. Another rule of decision making is that "the law accords with Rav's views in matters of *issur* and with Samuel's in monetary matters (*be-dini*)" (TB Bekhorot 49b, and *see* TB Niddah 24b), *i.e.*, when Rav and Samuel disagree on a matter of *issur*, the law follows the opinion of Rav; when they disagree on a matter of *mamon*, the law follows Samuel's opinion.

169. *See supra* pp. 64–74.

170. *See, e.g.*, Maimonides, *MT*, Zekhiyyah u-Mattanah 1:15; Naḥmanides, quoted in *Sefer ha-Terumot*, gate 46, ch. 8, par. 5.

case were as follows: Ribash, who was one of the leading halakhic authorities of the fourteenth century and who had served as rabbi of various communities in Spain, arrived in Algiers, North Africa, in the last decade of that century. As a result of the efforts of one of the communal leaders, the government appointed him as rabbi and judge of the Jewish community of Algiers. Rashbeẓ, a younger contemporary who greatly respected Ribash (as did the Jews of Algiers generally), nevertheless opposed Ribash's agreement to accept an appointment by the government to the position of *dayyan* (halakhic judge). Rashbeẓ' responsa[171] discussed in detail the reasons for his opposition and devoted a substantial part of the discussion to the question of whether *dina de-malkhuta dina* provides any basis for the validity of such an appointment by the government.[172] Rashbeẓ' discussion is interesting in a number of respects in regard to the distinction between matters of *issur* and matters of *mamon,* and we shall examine some of his points as we conclude our consideration of this distinction.

According to Rashbeẓ, the doctrine of *dina de-malkhuta dina* is no authority for governmental appointment of a judge over the Jewish community.[173] Among other reasons[174] he advanced were these:[175]

> Another point must be considered with regard to this appointment, *i.e.,* the king commands that only this judge shall sit and no other, and, consequently, it follows that no judge other than this judge whom he has appointed may hear any case. This raises a problem: even if one could argue that *dina de-malkhuta dina* applies here [*i.e.,* to the appointment], the doctrine clearly cannot confer authority to hear every case. This is because it is clear that on any matter that concerns *issur,* a forbidden act cannot be made permissible

171. *Resp. Tashbeẓ,* I, #158–#162. Regarding Ribash's appointment and the ensuing controversy, *see* A. Hershman, *Rabbi Yiẓhak bar Sheshet (ha-Ribash), Derekh Ḥayyav u-Tekufato* [R. Isaac b. Sheshet, His Life and Times], 1956, pp. 34–38, 168–170; I. Epstein, *The Responsa of Rabbi Simon b. Zemah Duran,* pp. 18–26.

172. Ribash's own opinion on the validity of appointment by the general government can be inferred from a responsum he wrote some years before his appointment as the *dayyan* in Algiers, regarding the appointment of Jonathan b. Mattathias as the Chief Rabbi of France; *see Resp. Ribash* #271. *See also* Hershman and Epstein, *supra* n. 171.

173. *Resp. Tashbeẓ,* I, #158.

174. The first two reasons were: (1) *Dina de-malkhuta dina* applies only to settled and well-known laws but not to matters "which the king wants to introduce of his own desire"; and (2) The law did not apply generally throughout the kingdom of Algeria, but only in the city of Algiers and only in the particular case of Ribash, whereas *dina de-malkhuta dina* applies to laws of general applicability. *See* the first half of the responsum. As to these arguments, *see supra* pp. 69–73. Similarly, according to Rashbeẓ, the legal basis for *dina de-malkhuta dina* is that "the whole population willingly accepts what the king introduces throughout his whole kingdom and since they accept it, it becomes settled law." This is the rationale given by Rashbam, Bava Batra 54b, s.v. Ve-ha-amar Shemu'el dina de-malkhuta dina. *See supra* p. 66.

175. *Resp. Tashbeẓ,* I, #158.

> by virtue of *dina de-malkhuta dina.* As stated previously, only matters of *mamon* are within the scope of that doctrine, and no one has ever contended that the doctrine is applicable to matters of *issur.*
>
> This last proposition cannot be refuted by arguing that the case of theft is a counterexample, in that theft is forbidden as a matter of *issur* and yet the law of the land does govern in such a case. It is true that if the government cuts down palm trees [belonging to private individuals] and uses them to build bridges, the doctrine of *dina de-malkhuta dina* permits the public to use the bridges, which otherwise would be prohibited.[176] That case, however, is not a true case of *issur,* because the prohibition is based on [property rights, which are a matter of] *mamon,* to which the doctrine of *dina de-malkhuta dina* applies. Therefore, the public use of the bridges is permitted, since there has been no theft, inasmuch as the law of the land, which authorized the cutting of the trees, validly applies to matters of *mamon* such as property rights.
>
> However, in true cases of *issur,* which belong to an entirely different category, there is no basis for using *dina de-malkhuta dina* to permit what Jewish law forbids. This should be obvious even to a child, and there is no point in discussing it any further.
>
> This being so, this judge may not sit in judgment in a case involving his friend or his enemy. [According to Jewish law, a judge may not sit if a case involving a friend or an enemy comes before him.][177] This is a matter of *issur;* and since an *issur* is involved, one cannot apply *dina de-malkhuta dina.* Yet no other judge may sit, as the king has taken away authority from any other judge except the one he appointed. Then to whom can the case be brought? Shall the defendant retain what is in his possession and rejoice [because there is no judge before whom to bring the case]? It is a governmental error that would be a deprivation of a right of the people,[178] and the law [of the land] is not law in such a case.

Rashbeẓ' point is that the government did not foresee the results that would flow from such an appointment, *i.e.,* that since only the appointed judge, and no other, may sit, no friend and no enemy of the judge would be able to find anyone to adjudicate his case, and such a litigant would thus be completely deprived of any remedy. Such result would be an infringement of "a right of the people," and the doctrine of *dina de-malkhuta dina* does not apply to such a case where the "law of the land" involves an

176. This example is cited in connection with the principle of *dina de-malkhuta dina* in TB Bava Kamma 113b. *See supra* p. 68 and n. 61.

177. Sh. Ar. ḤM 7:7.

178. The concept "a right of the people" also appears in Maimonides, *MT,* Edut 11:6, with regard to the rule that persons incompetent as witnesses by rabbinic law are not considered incompetent until they have been so declared, in order "not to work a deprivation of a right of the people, who are unaware that a particular person is incompetent, where his incompetency is only by rabbinic law." The source of Maimonides' usage of the expression "deprivation of a right of the people" requires further investigation.

infringement of the basic principles of right and justice embodied in Jewish law.[179]

Rashbeẓ concluded:

> And if you respond that if there are no Jewish judges, then let the case be brought to the gentile judges, the consequence would be even more grave, because the Torah states [Exodus 21:1: "These are the rules that you shall set] before *them* [the judges]," which our Sages have ruled excludes gentiles. To resort to gentile judges would be to "uproot" a Biblical mandate on the strength of the "law of the land" (*dina de-malkhuta*)—something that should not happen among Jews.[180]

This responsum of Rashbeẓ helps us to understand some of the distinctions between *mamon* and *issur:*

1. The doctrine of *dina de-malkhuta dina* applies only to matters of *mamon* and not to *issur.* This distinction is obvious from the halakhic rationale for the doctrine of *dina de-malkhuta dina.* According to Rashbeẓ, the rationale of the doctrine is that the people have consented to accept the law of the land.[181] This consent, however, can be effective only for matters of *mamon,* because agreement of the parties may vary only those Biblical norms relating to monetary matters.[182] The same conclusion is also supported by the other halakhic rationales for the doctrine.[183]

2. Another interesting principle that follows from this responsum is the basic principle that a matter of *mamon* that also contains an element of *issur* does not thereby lose its status as *mamon.* The reason is that in every matter of *mamon* there is also, by the very nature of Jewish law, a matter of *issur;* for if a chattel belongs to A, and B refuses to give it to A but retains it for himself, he violates the prohibition "You shall not steal." This, however, leads to the following questions: Why is it that cases of doubt in monetary matters are resolved in favor of the more lenient result? In view of the fact that every case of doubt involving a monetary matter also involves the prohibition "you shall not steal," should we not be driven to conclude that doubts even as to monetary

179. *See supra* pp. 72–73. This is similar to the requirement that the king's law must apply equally to all and to the rule that a law imposing collective punishment is invalid.

180. *See supra* pp. 13–18.

181. *See supra* n. 174.

182. *See supra* pp. 123–127.

183. The rationale based on the notion of the existence of common legal principles—the Noahide laws—does not apply to matters of *issur,* which are unique to the Jews. As to the rationale based on identifying *dina de-malkhuta dina* with the king's law, the king has no authority in matters of *issur.* Similarly, *hefker bet din hefker* applies only to monetary matters (*see infra* pp. 507–511). For these rationales, *see supra* pp. 66–67.

matters should be resolved in favor of the more stringent result? Or, as Rashbeẓ put it in the responsum discussed above: Since the doctrine of *dina de-malkhuta dina* does not apply to a matter of *issur,* how can it apply to a matter of *mamon,* inasmuch as every matter of *mamon* also necessarily includes an element of *issur?*

Rashbeẓ's answer to these questions was that the element of *issur* invoked in a monetary matter comes into play only after the legal aspects of the monetary situation have been clarified. Consequently, if, as a matter of property law, it remains doubtful whether the chattel that is in B's possession belongs to him or to A, the legal principle applicable to this monetary issue is that the burden of proof is on the claimant who seeks recovery of property in the possession of another. The law thus provides a clear and definite solution: B is not required to give the chattel to A, and therefore it "belongs" to B, with the obvious result that B's retention of the chattel does not violate the negative commandment "you shall not steal." The same rationale underlies the application of the doctrine of *dina de-malkhuta dina* in monetary matters.

This important distinction, whereby the element of *issur* comes into play only after the monetary matter is clarified, was well stated in the writings of one of the leading Talmudic educators of the past generation, Shimon Shkop, the head of the *yeshivah* (academy) in Grodno. The following is a portion of his instructive and cogent explanation:

> Civil laws, which govern the relations among people, operate differently from the other commandments of the Torah. In respect of all other commandments—the positive and negative precepts enjoined by the Torah—our obligation to fulfill them rests on our duty to obey God's command. Matters of *mamon* [civil law], however, are different; there must be a legal duty before a religious obligation arises to pay damages or make restitution. . . .
>
> There is another basic principle here: When we deal with a legal right in a chattel or with a lien, the focus of our concern is not the observance of a religious commandment but rather the objective circumstances determining who has the legal ownership of the object or is legally entitled to its possession.
>
> Therefore, the general principles governing cases of doubt on monetary matters that our Sages laid down were surely arrived at by logical reasoning leading to the conclusion that according to law a particular result was proper. . . . However, the religious commandment prohibiting theft is that one should not steal whatever legally belongs to one's fellow. Similarly, the rule that one may not withhold a worker's wages refers to wages that, according to Torah law, one is obligated to pay. But where the law of the Torah gives the right to withhold the money, how can there be any concern with a possible violation of the commandment against theft? If the money is his [*i.e.,*

in the hands of the one entitled to it] according to the law of the Torah, how can the prohibition of theft be involved?[184]

3. A third point is exemplified by this responsum, namely, that from the viewpoint of Jewish law, we are dealing with an issue that is both "legal" (*mamon*) and "religious" (*issur*), whereas from the viewpoint of conventional legal classification, the issue is entirely "legal." The question whether or not a judge may sit in a case where one of the parties is his friend or his enemy is a legal and not a religious question in other legal systems; but as appears from Rashbeẓ' discussion, in Jewish law the question has two aspects. First, the appointment of a judge is not a matter of *issur,* and therefore there is no objection to applying the principle of *dina de-malkhuta dina* to judicial appointments. At the second stage, however, where the issue is whether the judge may rule on a matter involving his friend or his enemy, the question is one of *issur,* and the principle of *dina de-malkhuta dina* cannot be applied to permit the judge to sit in such a case.

We have already stressed that the concepts of *mamon* and *issur* do not coincide with the concepts of "law" and "religion"; there are many "legal" areas such as family law and criminal law that are classified as *issur* in Jewish law. Nevertheless, there is still a rough correspondence, even if not complete congruence, between *mamon* and "law," as there is also between *issur* and "religion." The distinction between *mamon* and *issur* is recognized as being of critical importance in the creative development of Jewish law, since it is in the area of *mamon* that the *Halakhah* has the greatest latitude for such development.

G. Logic and Legal Reasoning as the Major Creative Source of Law in the Area of *Mamon*

To conclude this study of the distinction between *issur* and *mamon,* it is appropriate to point out an additional feature that is particularly significant in regard to the category of *mamon,* namely, the matter of the creative methods of the *Halakhah.* In our later discussion of the legal sources of Jewish law, by means of which its institutions and laws were continually developed, one of the sources we will consider is the legal reasoning of the

184. Shimon Shkop, *Sha'arei Yosher* 5:1. *See also id.,* the early chapters; M.A. Amiel, *Middot le-Ḥeker ha-Halakhah* [Principles of Halakhic Research], Middah 11, Meẓi'ut ve-Din (especially pars. 3–10). Shkop's reasoning has important implications for the absorption of *mishpat ivri* into the legal system of the State of Israel. *See infra* pp. 1906–1914.

halakhic authorities, which involves a deep and discerning probe into the essence of halakhic and legal principles, an appreciation of the characteristics of human beings in their social relationships, and a careful study of the real world and its manifestations.[185] Legal reasoning functions as a creative legal source in every part of all areas of *Halakhah.*[186] However, it was given special place in the area of *mamon;* and, consequently, the "legal" *Halakhah* had the benefit of a far greater capacity for creative development.

The following are the comments of Jacob Anatoly, a halakhic authority in southern France in the thirteenth century:[187]

> When God in His mercy chose His people Israel, He informed them of the mysteries of existence and the commandments that are the guardians of faith as they are embodied in the Ten Commandments, and He made known to them His laws and legal norms that are prerequisite for the political society necessary to meet the needs of mankind everywhere and at all times. This is the reason for the textual proximity of the section in the Torah that begins with "These are the rules"[188] to the Ten Commandments:[189] to teach that human perfection is not to be attained through wisdom and truth alone, but requires a system of laws enabling people to live with one another. . . .
>
> All the laws mentioned there are very much abbreviated, and many laws were completely omitted from the Torah and not mentioned even indirectly or by allusion; they are mentioned in the Talmud without any question being raised as to a possible Scriptural source, and there is no indication that they were taught as part of the oral tradition. This is so, because the rules of civil law are more ancient and are different from the other commandments of the Torah. When the descendants of Noah were commanded to keep the law,[190] the essence of that commandment was that they should establish and maintain a functioning legal order, since the world depends on law, as has been shown above in the Torah portion of *Noah.* Even after the Torah had been given, this continued to be the case with regard to matters for which the Torah did not explicitly provide. It was for the judges to establish rules of law for the proper conduct of society, as is still the custom today among the nations.
>
> Tradesmen and merchants were also entitled to enact laws to govern the relationships among themselves. The Sages noted[191] that donkey drivers may agree among themselves to replace a donkey lost by any driver, and boatmen

185. *See infra* p. 987.
186. *See infra* pp. 987–1014.
187. *Malmad ha-Talmidim* [A Goad to Scholars], Mishpatim (ed. Mekiẓei Nirdamim, 1866), pp. 71b–72b.
188. Exodus 21:1.
189. *Id.* 20:1–14.
190. TB Sanhedrin 56a; *see also infra* p. 194.
191. TB Bava Kamma 116b.

may agree among themselves to replace a boat lost by any one of them.[192]. . . All such laws are regarded as if written in the Torah, and those who transgress them transgress the Torah, which commands us to obey "the judge (*shofet*) of that time."[193]

Also relevant to this point is the rule of *dina de-malkhuta dina.*[194] Since the rules of civil law are ancient and impossible to list in detail, and since new developments among men are endless, any law adopted by the king ruling in a country is entitled to recognition if it does not conflict with the Torah, and should be regarded as obligatory; and judgments should be rendered in accordance with it. . . .

In conclusion, some of the laws adopted at the time of the Talmudic Sages were formulated according to these principles, through the use of legal reasoning as to what they thought desirable conduct in society, even where there was no Scriptural support for or against it. . . . Since most of these laws were arrived at by legal reasoning and were not derived from the Written or Oral Law, Jehoshaphat had to admonish the judges: "Consider what you are doing, for you judge not on behalf of man, but on behalf of the Lord."[195] He meant by this that a legal system appropriate for human society should be modeled on the ways of God, Who upholds existence by law and justice, for all His ways are based on law and justice, as He told us earlier, "That [upholding the rights of the poor and needy] is truly heeding Me,"[196] and since this is so, "The Lord is with you when you pass judgment" [II Chronicles 19:11]. . . . Moses, too, sat in judgment in this manner, and he did not need to inquire of the Lord in every decision. He then designated judges, and they judged the lesser matters that they were capable of deciding through legal reasoning, as it is written, "They exercised authority over [lit. "judged"] the people at all times; the difficult matters they would bring to Moses, and all the minor matters they would decide themselves";[197] and this passage[198] appears in the Torah before the Ten Commandments.

192. *See infra* pp. 680–681.

193. Deuteronomy 17:9; *Sifrei,* Deuteronomy, Shofetim, sec. 153, p. 206. The JPS *Tanakh,* 1985, translates *shofet* as "magistrate." The statement that ". . . such laws are regarded as if written in the Torah, and those who transgress them transgress the Torah" is not precise, since these laws are rabbinic. Apparently the statement has reference to the Torah's delegation of authority to the rabbis (*see infra* pp. 230–232, 478–481), as expressed in TB Shabbat 23a regarding the kindling of the *Hanukkah* lights: "Where did He command us? R. Avia said: 'In the verse "You must not deviate."'" For a detailed discussion, *see infra* pp. 481–483.

194. TB Nedarim 28a and parallels.

195. II Chronicles 19:6.

196. Jeremiah 22:16.

197. Exodus 18:26.

198. *I.e.,* "they judged the people at all times . . . ," which, as stated *supra,* means in accordance with their own legal reasoning. The passage in Exodus precedes the giving of the Ten Commandments and appears before the pericope *Mishpatim,* in which the laws were given; thus, it can only mean that they judged according to their own legal reasoning.

About three hundred years later, Maharal of Prague, a great halakhic scholar and thinker, discussed the difference in the manner in which "civil laws between man and his fellow," on the one hand, and the rest of the laws of the *Halakhah,* on the other, are interpreted and created:[199]

> The first [category] relates to civil laws between man and his fellow; the second, to the [other] laws of the Torah. . . .
>
> Civil laws are not like the [other] laws of the Torah. Civil laws [and] the [other] laws of the Torah . . . are . . . separate categories.
>
> With regard to civil laws, one must understand the root of the law so as not to impose liability on one who should not be liable or to absolve one who should be held liable, and this depends on legal reasoning that penetrates to the very depths of the law. This differs from the approach to the [other] laws of the Torah in that it involves legal reasoning exclusively, even as to matters as to which the Torah is silent. The civil laws that were written in the Torah are only general principles, and not every matter that arises between man and his fellow was covered there.

The comments of Israel Lipschutz, the author of *Tiferet Yisra'el,* and one of the leading commentators on the Mishnah in recent generations, are also instructive. The last *mishnah* of Tractate *Bava Batra* states:

> R. Ishmael says: "He who wishes to become wise should study civil laws (*dinei mamonot*), for there is no other subject in the Torah more significant; they are like a flowing spring."

Lipschutz commented:[200]

> There is not a single law in the Torah relating to *issur* in respect to which the Torah gave human wisdom the leeway to soar to the maximum, to penetrate, to investigate, and to decide as it sees fit, as it did in respect of *dinei mamonot.* With regard to *dinei mamonot,* the Torah opened up for man an inexhaustible legacy to weigh, judge, and carefully ponder by the exercise of reason, to such an extent that most of the law concerning civil disputes, which is as loaded down with legal rules as a straw-laden wagon, is included in the Torah in a few words of a single verse, namely: "Judge your neighbor fairly."[201]
>
> It is only because the web of the law is so fine, making it so easy for the human mind to fall into error, that our Sages of the Mishnah and the Talmud, who were the leaders of the nation, gathered in their multitudes and laid down for us foundations and sources for all of these [rules of *dinei mamonot*]. Even with all that they have done, there nevertheless remains room for judicial flexibility [lit. "for a judge to move to the right or to the left"] to draw an

199. *Derekh Ḥayyim* to M Avot 1:1, s.v. Hem hayu omerim sheloshah devarim.
200. *Tiferet Yisra'el* to M Bava Batra 10:8.
201. Leviticus 19:15.

analogy between one case and another or to make distinctions, sometimes exceedingly fine. Therefore, in dealing with civil law matters, human wisdom must carefully reflect, so that the exact truth will be attained.

Furthermore, the search for truth in matters of *mamon* is obligatory, in that it is simply impossible to ease the burden of that search by applying the same rule that governs in cases of Biblical *issur,* namely, that all doubts are to be resolved in favor of the strict result. In a matter of *mamon,* the doubt cannot be resolved by ruling stringently, for what is stringent for one party will be lenient for his adversary. There is therefore no escape from the heavy labor of striving to attain the result that precisely accords with truth and justice.

To summarize: The *Halakhah* is of one piece in that every aspect of it is rooted in religion; the "religious" and "legal" aspects of the *Halakhah* share the same methods of thought and analysis, and the same general rules and principles; and the *Halakhah*'s "religious" commandments and its "legal" precepts support and reinforce each other. Nevertheless, the *Halakhah,* as it has been crystallized in its different periods, has recognized the essential and fundamental distinction, as to both substance and creative methods, between *issur* and *mamon*—the latter generally corresponding to most of what is included in the *corpus juris* of contemporary legal systems. This basic distinction has given to the "legal" part of the *Halakhah*—the part particularly sensitive to the effects of constant changes in economic and social life—its great flexibility and extraordinary potential for development.

VI. LAW AND MORALS IN THE JEWISH LEGAL SYSTEM

The existence of the extraordinary interrelationship between the two parts of the *Halakhah* leads to consideration of a problem much discussed in the literature of jurisprudence: the relation between legal commands and moral imperatives. Many theories and a variety of opinions have been expressed on this question. The accepted distinction appears to be that what distinguishes legal command from moral imperative is more procedural than substantive. The failure to perform a legal norm is subject to judicial sanction, and a court will enforce compliance; not so, a moral imperative—this is a matter for the individual himself, his God, and his conscience. The legal order does not involve itself in the performance or lack of performance of purely moral obligations and certainly does not enforce compliance. Consequently, there is no objective criterion for determining the nature of legal norms or the content of moral imperatives; rather, the distinction depends on the intent and objective of each legal system in light of the particular factors and conditions under which it operates. That intent or objective may sometimes limit and at other times increase the number of obligations regarded as proper to be encompassed in the legal system.[202] What is the relation between law and morals in the world of *Halakhah?*

A. Reciprocal Relationship between Law and Morals—Recourse by the Legal System to the Moral Imperative

It is well known that just as the Written Law (*i.e.,* the Torah) commands the individual and the people to carry out commandments that are clearly legal in character, it similarly and quite as categorically commands the performance of precepts considered to be moral and ethical in nature. Thus, just as the commands "you shall not murder" and "you shall not steal"[203] are basic mandates contained in the Ten Commandments, the command "you shall love your neighbor as yourself, I am the Lord"[204] is a major principle basic to the entire Torah[205]—a moral principle which has served as the basis for rules of law in various fields.[206] This common source for

202. *See* H. Klinghoffer, *Mishpat Minhali* [Administrative Law], Jerusalem, 1957, p. 4: "The enforcement power is a characteristic of a normative legal system, for it is only on the basis of such a power that law is distinguishable from other normative systems (such as ethics, religion, etc.)." *See also* H. Kelsen, "On the Pure Theory of Law," 1 *Israel Law Review* 1, 3 (1966). The interdependency between social conditions and the transformation of ethical into legal norms and *vice versa* also exists in Jewish law; *see* the quotation from *Maggid Mishneh, infra* pp. 159–160, and the discussion of *lifnim mi-shurat ha-din* in the post-Talmudic period, *infra* pp. 157–159.

203. Exodus 20:13.

204. Leviticus 19:18.

205. "'You shall love your neighbor as yourself.' R. Akiva says: 'This is a great principle in the Torah.'" *Sifra,* Leviticus, Kedoshim 4:12; TJ Nedarim 9:4, 30b (10:3, 41c). *See also* TB Shabbat 31a for Hillel's answer to the would-be proselyte who wanted to learn the whole Torah while standing on one foot: "That which is hateful to you, do not do to your fellow—that is the whole Torah; the rest is commentary. Go and study it"; and Rashi, *ad loc.,* s.v. Da-alakh senei le-ḥavrakh la ta'aveid. *Avot de-R. Nathan* (ed. Schechter, 2nd version, ch. 26 [27:1]) attributes the story to R. Akiva, and the text reads: ". . . that is the general principle (*kelalah*) of the Torah." For the meaning of *kelal gadol* ("a great principle"), *cf.* Maimonides, *Commentary on the Mishnah,* Shabbat 7:21: "It says '*kelal gadol*' because the punishment for [the desecration of] the sabbath is by stoning, which is more severe than that prescribed for other prohibitions." *See also* H.Z. Reines, *Torah u-Musar* [Torah and Morals], pp. 234ff.

206. *See, e.g.,* TB Ketubbot 37b; Sanhedrin 45a, 52b, *et al.,* regarding execution of a death sentence in the least painful and least degrading manner possible: "'You shall love your neighbor as yourself'—choose a decent death for him." *See also* the responsum of Joseph Tov Elem (quoted in *Resp. Maharam of Rothenburg,* ed. Prague, #941) to the effect that taxes may be levied only on income, and even then only if they do not tend to erode capital. His rationale is:

> It is forbidden to be overly diligent to levy a tax that will erode the taxpayer's capital; rather, [you must behave] in the manner of "You shall love your neighbor as yourself." That is the Jewish way and the custom of the Jewish communities. They are careful [in the choice of communal] officials, as it is written, "And you shall search out from all the people . . . ," and they sit and examine [each case] carefully and levy

both law and morals has been the guide for the Jewish people in every age and generation.[207]

This basic phenomenon, of course, does not mean the obliteration of the distinction between law and morals. For example, the Torah, the Prophets, and the *Halakhah* are full of commands and warnings concerning the obligation to support the poor and to uphold their dignity. Certainly, the command that "You shall not subvert the rights of your needy in their disputes"[208] is a serious prohibition. But the Torah also adds two more proscriptions: "Nor shall you show deference to a poor man in his dispute"[209] and "You shall do no unrighteousness in judging; do not favor the poor or show deference to the rich; judge your neighbor fairly."[210] Why are all these instructions necessary? "So that you shall not say: 'This person is poor, and since both I and his wealthy opponent must support him, I will judge in his favor and he will thereby be supported in an honorable way'; it is therefore written, 'Do not favor the poor.'"[211]

While it is true that supporting the poor is an important obligation, that moral obligation does not justify twisting or corrupting the law. The method by which both these imperatives—the obligation to support the

---

> on each person justly, each one according to his labor, . . . and they judge their brethren as they would themselves in order to apply what [the Sages] said [TB Shabbat 31a]: "That which is hateful to you, do not do to your fellow."

See M. Elon, EJ, XV, pp. 837ff., s.v. Taxation, at 849 (reprinted in *Principles*, pp. 662ff. at 673). Similarly, the fact that a physician is entitled to perform invasive procedures on his patient when medically necessary (such as drawing blood or performing a surgical operation) is explained, not on the basis of the patient's explicit or tacit agreement, but rather on the basis of the verse, "You shall love your neighbor as yourself" (TB Sanhedrin 84b), which implies "that a Jew is forbidden to do to his fellow only that which he would not want done to himself" (Rashi, *ad loc.*, s.v. Ve-ahavta le-re'akha kamokha). *See also* Naḥmanides, *Torat ha-Adam*, pp. 42ff. (Kitvei ha-Ramban, ed. Chavel, II), and *Avot de-R. Nathan, supra* n. 205. This last principle was discussed in Sharon v. Levi, 35(i) *P.D.* 736, 755 (1980), and in State of Israel v. Tamir, 37(iii) *P.D.* 201, 206 (1983).

207. *See, e.g.*, Obadiah Bertinoro in his commentary to M Avot 1:1, s.v. Moshe kibbel Torah mi-Sinai:

> I say that this tractate is not based on the explanation of any of the commandments of the Torah, as are the other tractates of the Mishnah; it deals entirely with ethics and morals. The wise men of the nations have also written books containing their own notions of ethics [and] how a person should behave towards his fellow. Therefore the redactor (*tanna*) of this tractate began with "Moses received the Torah from Sinai," to make clear that the moral and ethical precepts in this tractate were not invented by the Sages of the Mishnah on their own, but were part of the revelation at Sinai.

See also infra p. 192.

208. Exodus 23:6.

209. *Id.* 23:3.

210. Leviticus 19:15.

211. *Sifra*, Leviticus, Kedoshim 4:2.

poor and the obligation to judge justly—can be accomplished simultaneously is described in the following quotation:[212]

> R. Simeon b. Lakish said, "What is the meaning of the verse, 'Vindicate the lowly and the poor'?[213] What does 'vindicate' mean? Can it refer to lawsuits [Rashi: 'that you must decide a case in the poor man's favor']? [This cannot be, for] does not the Torah also say, 'Nor shall you show deference to a poor man in his dispute'? It therefore means: favor him with your own property and give to him."

Thus, the halakhic system carefully distinguishes between normative rules that involve sanctions enforced by a court, and precepts not enforced by such sanctions. However, the fact that legal norms and moral imperatives both have a common source and background in the halakhic system has an important consequence: the legal system itself, functioning as such, from time to time invokes, even though it does not enforce, the moral imperative. The court does not refuse to decide a case brought before it even when the decision cannot be enforced. The author of a legal responsum or halakhic code and the court in its rulings all include the moral imperative, insofar as it is pertinent, as an integral part of their discussion:

> It is apparent from the Talmud that it is incumbent on a judge to declare what is proper conduct and to state that even where such conduct is not required by strict law, nevertheless good and upright people will act in that manner. The litigant [to whom the declaration is addressed] may then conform [to the guidance so given], but if he does not, no sanction is taken against him [by the court].[214]

212. TB Ḥullin 134a.

213. Psalms 82:3.

214. Jehiel Michal Epstein, *Arukh ha-Shulḥan*, ḤM 304:11; the quotation in the text refers to the incident of the porters in TB Bava Meẓi'a 83a; and, according to Epstein's interpretation, Rav told Rabbah bar bar Ḥanan that although by law the porters were liable for the damage they had caused, the principle of *lifnim mi-shurat ha-din* (*see infra* pp. 155–167) applied; and, accordingly, they were not required to pay damages and Rabbah bar bar Ḥanan was obliged to pay them their wages. *See infra* pp. 156–157 for discussion of that passage.

Inclusion of a discussion of a moral obligation in a judicial ruling is a common and accepted occurrence in Jewish law. The following are a few examples: *Resp. Maharaḥ Or Zaru'a* #222, quoted *infra* pp. 763–766; the responsum of Abraham b. Isaac of Narbonne, Provence (Southern France, first half of twelfth century C.E.), quoted in *Sefer ha-Terumot* (by Samuel Sardi), gate 35, ch. 1, par. 27 (the beginning reads, "He was asked further" and is a reference to Abraham b. Isaac, who was mentioned at the beginning of par. 25). This responsum discusses a person who stood surety for a gentile (the debtor) to a Jew (the creditor). The surety handed over to the creditor a pledge belonging to the gentile that he had in his keeping, and thus fulfilled his suretyship. The debtor wanted his pledge back and pleaded with the surety to reassume the personal responsibility of suretyship so that the debtor could retrieve his pledge. After much pressure, the surety agreed, but in terms not legally sufficient to create a suretyship relation. The creditor restored the pledge to the gentile, and Abraham

B. "Exempt by Human Law but Liable by Divine Law"

In Jewish tort law, it sometimes happens that one who injures another is not legally liable for damages, because of the absence of a direct causal relation between his act and the resulting injuries, or because he acted with the consent of the injured party, or because of other reasons. The doctrine

---

b. Isaac ruled that the new commitment of the surety was not valid because it was not expressed correctly. Legally, therefore, the surety was not liable. However, Abraham b. Isaac added: "Nevertheless, the surety is duty bound to assist him [*i.e.,* the creditor] to recover his loan from the gentile," since it was the surety who caused the creditor to return the pledge to the gentile. This is a moral obligation, since by law there was no valid suretyship. (The responsum is quoted in *Tur* ḤM 131:5 in the name of Alfasi, but, as stated, Abraham b. Isaac was the author. S. Assaf, *Sifran Shel Rishonim,* 1935, #15, also cites the responsum as being by Abraham b. Isaac, and it also appears in *Teshuvot ha-Rabi Av Bet Din* [Responsa of Abraham b. Isaac of Narbonne], ed. Kafaḥ, Jerusalem, 1962, #124. The responsum does not appear in any known collection of Alfasi's responsa.)

The ruling in the responsum is codified as law in Sh. Ar. ḤM 131:5 and *Arukh ha-Shulḥan,* ḤM 131:6, where the text reads:

> And they have ruled that the law is with the surety, because the creditor should have insisted that he undertake the suretyship explicitly. Nevertheless, the surety is obligated to assist the creditor in recovering the debt from the debtor [the gentile], for he [the debtor] will not be brazen against him [the surety], considering the favor [the surety] did for him [the debtor, *i.e.,* in procuring the return of the pledge].

Another example concerns the ruling in M Ketubbot 4:9 that a husband is liable to pay for his wife's medical treatment if she falls sick, but "if he said, 'Behold, here is her bill of divorcement and the amount of her *ketubbah:* let her heal herself,' he has the right to do so." The rationale for this rule is that medical treatment is considered part of maintenance, "and just as with regard to maintenance he can say to her, 'Here is your bill of divorcement and the amount of your *ketubbah,* from which you will be maintained,' so too may he do with regard to medical treatment" (*Bet ha-Beḥirah,* Ketubbot 51a). However, *Bet ha-Beḥirah* adds: "But that is a despicable practice and the court should censure it," which means that the court should include an official censure in the announcement of its ruling. Rabad's opinion (quoted in the course of the discussion in *Bet ha-Beḥirah, ad loc.*) is interesting. It is to the effect that the rule applies when "she is sick and not sick [*i.e.,* when the illness is not serious], but if she is seriously ill, *i.e.,* confined to bed, he has no right to say this. The proof for this is the statement in *Sifrei* (to Deuteronomy 21:14) regarding a woman taken as a war captive, 'You must release her outright [lit. "to herself"]'—this teaches that if she was sick he must wait until she recovers. And that most certainly applies to Jewish women."

Rashba (*see Shittah Mekubbeẓet,* Ketubbot, *ad loc.*) and Ritba (Novellae, Ketubbot, *ad loc.*) both agree with this ruling, and even *Bet ha-Beḥirah* (*ad loc.*) does not disagree, but merely states that "this is not a complete proof, because in that case [*i.e.,* of the captive woman] the rule expresses a moral obligation, whereas here we are speaking of a legal rule."

It is instructive to consider the efforts made by the halakhic authorities to overcome the ethical problem involved in the legal rule that a person may divorce his sick wife and, upon giving her the amount of her *ketubbah,* relieve himself of the responsibility to provide her medical treatment. At present, however, after Rabbenu Gershom's enactment that a woman cannot be divorced against her will, the problem no longer exists.

For an example of the inclusion of a moral directive in judgments of the rabbinical courts of the State of Israel, *see infra* n. 256.

was established with regard to a wide range of such injuries that "the party causing the injury is exempt by human law but is liable by divine law,"[215] or as the *Tosefta* puts it, "He is exempt by human law, and the question of his liability is committed to the decision of Heaven."[216]

An interesting example is the question of a physician's legal responsibility. A physician licensed to practice because of his expertise in medicine[217] is liable if he intentionally injures a patient—"if he intentionally inflicted a wound that was greater than necessary."[218] However, if he caused injury to a patient inadvertently, he is exempt from liability "for the welfare of society" (in spite of the doctrine that, for purposes of tort liability, "a human is deemed forewarned for all time," *i.e.*, is generally liable even for inadvertent harm), for otherwise, the physician will desist from practicing his profession.[219] However, this exemption for unintentional injuries is "by human law, and [the question of the physician's responsibility] is committed to the decision of Heaven."[220]

215. M Bava Kamma 6:4; TB Bava Kamma 55b–56a.

216. *Tosefta* Bava Kamma 6:16–17. These instances are so characterized in the codificatory literature, *see* Maimonides, *MT*, Nizkei Mamon 4:2, 14:14, Edut 17:7; Sh. Ar. ḤM 32:2, 396:4, 418:11, *et al.* For details, *see* ET, VII, pp. 382–396, s.v. Dinei shamayim. Gulak, *Yesodei*, II, p. 18, summarized the subject of liability by divine law as follows:

> Some obligations are not subject to judicial enforcement and are fulfilled only because of the good will of the obligor. No liability exists here according to the laws of man; for man's laws entail enforcement, and there is simply no basis for that here. The obligation here is only moral or religious, and the obligor is therefore "exempt by human law but liable by divine law."
>
> In Jewish law, liability under divine law exists wherever the case is too weak to justify liability as a matter of strict law but is sufficient to raise a moral obligation that should be fulfilled by an honorable person. We will clarify the special nature of liability under divine law by examples from the law of torts.
>
> A tortious act always brings some loss to the victim's property and, like everything in life, the damage has a cause that preceded and produced it. The imposition of liability for an act that caused damage requires that there be a relationship of cause and effect between the act and the damage—that the act be a necessary cause, but for which the damage would not have occurred. If this relationship exists but is remote and indirect, liability under divine law arises.
>
> The relation of cause and effect between a person's act and the ensuing damage exists [and gives rise to liability] when the damage is the direct, natural, and probable consequence of the act. If, in the ordinary course, the act would not result in the damage, but an unusual and unforeseeable circumstance intervenes and combines with the act to cause the damage, the actor is liable only under divine law to compensate for the loss.

217. *Tosefta* Gittin 4(3):6, Bava Kamma 6:17, 9:11, Makkot 2:5.

218. *Tosefta* Gittin 4(3):6, Bava Kamma 9:11.

219. *Tosefta* Gittin 4:6; *Resp. Tashbeẓ*, III, #82.

220. *Tosefta* Bava Kamma 6:17; Sh. Ar. YD 336:1. Naḥmanides, himself a physician, explained a physician's responsibility for inadvertent injury caused to his patient as follows: "If he is unaware that he has made a mistake, he is exempt from liability both by human

What is the nature of this liability by divine law? According to one opinion, "Wherever the ruling is that there is liability by divine law, even though the court does not enforce payment, it should attempt without judicial sanctions to persuade him to pay."[221] However, most authorities apparently disapprove not only of judicial enforcement but even of strong judicial persuasion,[222] although even those who hold this opinion agree that it is the duty of the court to refer in its judgment to the liability under divine law:

> In any case presented to a court where there is liability by divine law, the court must inform a party so liable: "We will not apply sanctions against you, but you should fulfill your duty in the sight of Heaven, because Heaven will be your judge." The court should so declare in order that the party will consider the matter carefully, placate his neighbor, and so fulfill his obligation to Heaven.[223]

The announcement that there is an obligation to Heaven is thus given by the court, and the matter is not left solely to the conscience of the individual.[224] In the same way as the halakhic authorities, after careful consideration, either limited or broadened liability enforced by human agency, they similarly weighed the issue of liability when the only sanction was the decision of Heaven.[225]

---

and by divine law; but if he inadvertently made a mistake and subsequently became aware of it, then, although he is not liable by human law, he is liable by divine law" (*Sefer Torat ha-Adam, Kitvei ha-Ramban,* ed. Chavel, II, p. 42). A further interesting distinction was made in the fourteenth century by Simeon Duran (Rashbeẓ), the Rabbi of Algiers, who was also a physician. According to him, the liability by divine law in the case of an inadvertent mistake is only for injury caused in a surgical operation but not for an injury resulting from a mistaken prescription of drugs. *See Resp. Tashbeẓ,* III, #82. *See also* M. Elon, "Ha-Halakhah veha-Refu'ah ha-Ḥadishah" [*Halakhah* and Modern Medicine], *Molad,* XXI (1971), pp. 228ff.

221. A responsum quoted in *Yam Shel Shelomo,* Bava Kamma 6:6.

222. *See id.*

223. Raban to Bava Kamma 55b (p. 190); *Yam Shel Shelomo, supra* n. 221.

224. *See also* Meiri, *Bet ha-Beḥirah,* Bava Kamma 56a (ed. Sofer, pp. 171–172):

> Whenever we have written here that he is liable by divine law, the meaning is that he is obligated to make good his wrong for the damage caused (by restitution or compensation). However, even where he is not liable by divine law, he has still violated a prohibition, although he has no obligation to make payment. Thus, the great scholars of the generation [Meiri's appellation for Naḥmanides] have written that any person ruled liable by divine law is disqualified as a witness until he discharges his obligation to pay [just as in the case of a robber]. And that seems to be correct; since he must make payment, the law applicable to him until he does so is the same as that applicable to a robber.

See also Keẓot ha-Ḥoshen to Sh. Ar. ḤM 32, subpar. 1.

225. *See, e.g., supra* n. 220 and *infra* pp. 150–154.

C. The Imprecation "He Who Punished" (*Mi she-Para*)

A considerable number of the types of religious and moral sanctions discussed above have been established as part of the normative legal system in Jewish law. They vary according to subject matter and nomenclature, and also generally in the extent of their scope and severity. For example, where the purchase price for a chattel has been paid, but the buyer has not yet drawn the chattel into his possession—so that legally the transaction is incomplete and either party may withdraw[226]—the buyer or seller who does withdraw "has not behaved as an Israelite should and is subject to the imprecation 'He Who punished' (*mi she-para*),"[227] *i.e.*, the court declares: "He who punished the generation of the Flood, the generation of Babel which witnessed the confusion of languages, the people of Sodom and Gomorrah, and the Egyptians who drowned in the sea, He will punish whoever does not keep his word."[228]

D. "Fulfillment of Duty in the Sight of Heaven" (*Laẓeit Yedei Shamayim*)

The following is another example of a moral and religious sanction from which we can discern progressively ascending levels of obligations. The case, discussed in the Mishnah and Talmud,[229] is summarized by Maimonides:[230]

> A person steals from one of five people, but no one knows from which one, and each one of the five makes a claim against the thief and states: "You stole from me." Even though there are no witnesses to the theft, each of the claimants takes an oath that he was the victim, and the accused has to pay each of them. This is a penalty imposed by the Sages because he transgressed and stole. Under Biblical law [the burden of proof is on the claimant, and since the identity of the victim has not been established] the case is regarded as too doubtful for recovery.
>
> If one says to two people [voluntarily, as distinguished from the prior case where they first make claim against him], "I have stolen from one of you or from the father of one of you [the fathers have died and there is no evidence a claimant can produce] and I do not know which," if he wishes to

226. M Bava Meẓi'a 4:2; and *see infra* pp. 297–298, 576–580, 913–920 on modes of acquisition in Jewish law and their development over the course of time.

227. Maimonides, *MT*, Mekhirah 7:1, following M Bava Meẓi'a 4:2 and TB Bava Meẓi'a 44a *et seq.*

228. TB Bava Meẓi'a 48b and Maimonides, *supra* n. 227; Sh. Ar. ḤM 204:1,4. *See also* the dispute between Abbaye and Rava (TB Bava Meẓi'a 48b) on how the court brings the *mi she-para* imprecation to the attention of the blameworthy litigant.

229. M Yevamot 15:7; TB Yevamot 118b; M Bava Meẓi'a 3:3; TB Bava Meẓi'a 37a/b.

230. Maimonides, *MT*, Gezelah va-Avedah 4:9–10.

fulfill his duty in the sight of Heaven (*lazeit yedei shamayim*), he must pay to each one the amount stolen. However, his legal obligation is to restore only the amount stolen, and they divide it equally, as neither was aware that there was a theft, and it was the thief who volunteered that he had stolen it. [Therefore, there is no reason to retain the money in court until one of them admits that the theft was not from him; rather, they divide it immediately.] In such a case, the Sages did not prescribe any punitive damages, inasmuch as no claim was made [against the thief].

We are thus confronted by three levels. The first is Biblical law, according to which, even if the victims sue, the thief need not pay, since according to the law "A case can be valid only on the testimony of two witnesses . . .";[231] and here, although each one of the "doubtful" victims claims that the thief stole from him, he has no witnesses to prove it. The second level is the law whose source is legislation by the Sages.[232] They enacted that since the defendant is clearly a thief and a transgressor, and each of the plaintiffs positively asserts that he is the victim, the thief is obligated to pay to each plaintiff. The third level is an obligation "to fulfill one's duty in the sight of Heaven"; this is the case where there is no plaintiff, because none of the possible victims is aware that anything has been stolen, and it is the thief himself who first raises the issue. In this case, the Sages did not require that he must pay each possible victim, and the applicable law is the Biblical rule that requires restitution of only the amount stolen. However, if the thief wishes to fulfill his duty in the sight of Heaven, he must pay to each of the possible victims the full amount that was stolen.[233]

E. "The Sages are Displeased with Him," and Other Forms of Moral-Religious Sanctions

Another moral-religious sanction was established with regard to a person who does a particular act that is permissible under the law, yet "the Sages are displeased with him." Let us examine two illustrations:

231. Deuteronomy 19:15.

232. The phrase in *MT,* Gezelah va-Avedah 4:9, *kenas hu she-kansuhu ḥakhamim* ("This is a penalty imposed by the Sages") is synonymous with "This is an enactment that the Sages adopted." Similarly, Maimonides' statement (*id.* 4:1–2), *kenas kansu ḥakhamim legazlanin* ("The Sages imposed a penalty on robbers"), is a reference to the enactment of the Sages relating to the oath to be taken by the robbery victim (M Shevu'ot 7:1–2; TB Shevu'ot 44b *et seq.*).

233. These two laws of Maimonides are also found in Sh. Ar. ḤM 365:1–2. It is noteworthy that Sh. Ar. par. 1 quotes Maimonides' law of par. 9 with slight stylistic changes, but does not quote the concluding portion of that paragraph, "This is a penalty imposed by the Sages . . . ," because, as an enactment of the Sages, it has as much force as any other law. Maimonides, however, emphasized the origin of the law. The last part of par. 2 in Sh. Ar. is redundant and merely repeats par. 1. *See also Sema, ad loc.*, subpar. 5, and *see infra* Appendix B, example 1.

The Mishnah states:[234]

> When a person disinherits his sons and bequeaths his property to others, his act is legally effective, but the Sages are displeased with him. Rabban Simeon b. Gamaliel says: If the sons were not conducting themselves properly, his act is praiseworthy [lit. "he should be remembered for good"].

From the strictly legal point of view, a person may leave his property to whomever he wishes, whether by way of a gift or in the form of the will of a *shekhiv me-ra* (person facing imminent death), *i.e.*, so long as the will is properly phrased and certain circumstances and conditions exist.[235] However, the Sages viewed the order of inheritance established in the Torah as they interpreted it (*i.e.*, first the children of the decedent and then other relatives in the order of their kinship) as the appropriate and preferred method of distributing an estate; they considered the passing of the worldly assets of fathers to their children to be a reflection of the notion of continuity from generation to generation.[236] Consequently, a bequest of property to those other than one's relatives, although legally effective, falls short from the moral standpoint and is displeasing to the Sages—"the Sages do not have pleasure from his conduct, but it vexes them and they are angry at him for having deprived his Biblical heirs of their inheritance [lit. for uprooting a Biblical inheritance]."[237] The view of Rabban Simeon b. Gamaliel was that this moral blameworthiness exists only when the sons are conducting themselves properly.

Maimonides ruled in the *Mishneh Torah:*

> If one has come to an oral agreement, he should keep his word even though he [the seller] has taken no money,[238] the merchandise has not been marked [as the buyer's],[239] and he [the buyer] has not given a deposit. Whoever reneges, whether the seller or the buyer, although not subject to the imprecation "He Who punished," is lacking in trustworthiness, and the Sages are displeased with him.[240]

234. M Bava Batra 8:5; TB Bava Batra 133b.

235. For a more detailed discussion, *see infra* pp. 1673, 1877–1878.

236. *See infra* pp. 1672–1673.

237. Rashbam, Bava Batra 133b, s.v. Ein ru'aḥ ḥakhamim.

238. However, if the seller has accepted payment, the defaulting party is liable to the imprecation "He Who punished" (*mi she-para); see supra* p. 148.

239. The reference is to acquisition by *sitomta; see infra* pp. 914–915.

240. Maimonides, *MT,* Mekhirah 7:8. In the course of time, the modes of acquisition underwent extensive development in order to respond to the economic changes from period to period (*see supra* n. 226), and according to many halakhic authorities, oral declarations are sufficient to effect acquisition and create obligations; *see infra* pp. 913–916.

Under the strict law, as has been mentioned, the performance of a *kinyan* (a formal mode of acquisition or conveyance) is necessary for a transaction to be legally binding, but the Sages ruled that a person has a moral obligation to keep his word; and whenever anyone reneges, the Sages are displeased with him even though his conduct is within the law.[241] Here too, we find a hierarchial arrangement in these sanctions. As we saw above, if the purchase price of a chattel was given and only the buyer's act of taking formal possession is lacking, the sanction is the imprecation "He Who punished." However, if the purchase price had not yet been given, and no other acts had been performed, and the negotiations had reached the point of merely an oral understanding, the moral sanction does not go so far as the imprecation "He Who punished," but is to the effect that the Sages are displeased with the reneging party.

An additional moral and religious concept adverted to in the language of Maimonides quoted above is "lacking in trustworthiness" (*meḥusar amanah*). This sanction is applied in the Talmudic *Halakhah,* according to Maimonides, to a person who reneges on a transaction to which there has been only an oral agreement.[242] In the aphorism "that your 'yes' shall be honest and your 'no' shall be honest"[243] (*i.e.,* when you say "yes" or "no," keep your word and make it good)[244] and in many other *dicta,* the Sages emphasized the moral and religious obligation to do business with integrity.[245]

As stated, these moral and religious obligations are defined and ranked according to the nature and severity of the matter, and the Sages deliberated on them in the same way that they deliberated on sanctions subject to enforcement through legal means. An instructive instance in regard to a determination that the Sages are displeased with someone is the responsum of Simeon b. Ẓemaḥ Duran (Rashbeẓ), part of which has already been re-

241. M Shevi'it 10:9 formulates the same principle affirmatively: "All chattels may be [legally] acquired by *meshikhah* ["pulling," *i.e.,* taking possession], but the Sages are pleased with whoever keeps his word [even though the transaction is not legally binding]."

242. TB Bava Meẓi'a 49a.

243. *Id.; see also supra* pp. 117–119 for R. Papa's view that the obligation to repay debts is a religious, but not a legal duty.

244. Rashi, Bava Meẓi'a 49a, s.v. Ella she-yehei hen shelekha.

245. "If one is honest in his business dealings and people esteem him, it is accounted to him as though he had fulfilled the whole Torah" (*Mekhilta,* Be-Shallaḥ, Tractate De-va-Yassa, sec. 1, ed. Lauterbach, II, p. 96; ed. Horowitz-Rabin, p. 158). TB Shabbat 31a states: "Rava said: When a man is brought in [before the Heavenly Court] for judgment, they ask him: 'Were you honest in your business dealings? Did you set aside fixed times for Torah study?'" *See also* Sh. Ar. OḤ ch. 156; Roth v. Yeshufeh, 33(i) *P.D.* 617, 633–634 (1979), and the discussion of that case *infra* pp. 184–187 in connection with the concept of "good faith."

viewed in our discussion of the reciprocal relationship between the *Halakhah* and the *Aggadah*.[246] As previously discussed, Rashbeẓ was asked[247] about a woman who became ill and bequeathed her property to the alms fund and to the synagogue of the town, and in this way extinguished the legal right of her poor relative to inherit her property, although he had sons who were scholars of the Torah and he needed the money to marry off his daughter.

The question that Rashbeẓ was asked was, "Do the halakhic authorities approve of the act of charity that this woman wishes to perform when it means disinheriting this relative?" The nature of the question and the very manner in which the question was worded indicate the special quality of the relationship between law and morals in Jewish law. The question did not even raise an issue as to the legal validity of the bequest; this was not a matter of doubt for the questioner, since he knew that under Jewish law a person may bequeath his property as he sees fit, if the will is in proper legal form. The only issue raised by the question was on a religious and moral level, *i.e.*, whether a religious and moral sanction such as that "the Sages are displeased with him" was applicable to that case. Indeed, the first part of Rashbeẓ' responsum dealt with the question precisely on the level on which it was posed:

> We all know the statement in the Talmud:[248] "Do not be among those who transfer an inheritance, even from a bad son to a good son,[249] and even more so from a son to a daughter."[250] If they [the Sages] said this with regard to a

246. *Supra* pp. 99–102.

247. *Resp. Tashbeẓ*, III, #190.

248. TB Bava Batra 133b.

249. The law was settled in accordance with the view of the Sages and not in accordance with Rabban Simeon b. Gamaliel, who believed that in such a case the father is praiseworthy.

250. According to the section on inheritance in the Torah (Numbers 27:8; M Bava Batra 8:2), a daughter inherits only when the decedent leaves no sons or offspring of sons. However, in order to ensure the continued maintenance of a daughter after her father's death, the Sages adopted an enactment giving a daughter the right to maintenance from the estate until she reaches maturity or, according to another opinion, until she marries; *see infra* pp. 574–575.

As early as in Talmudic *Halakhah*, there is evidence of a trend to give daughters a share in their fathers' property and even to give them the status of heirs as to a certain portion of the estate; *see infra* pp. 575–580, 655–656. From the fourteenth century on, enactments were adopted to give unmarried daughters an equal share in the estate with the sons; *see infra* pp. 842–846. In the procedural enactments that were adopted by the Chief Rabbinate of the Land of Israel in 1943, the rabbinical courts undertook to distribute estates according to the provisions of the governmental law of inheritance that gave daughters equal status with sons as heirs; *see infra* pp. 828–829. When the State of Israel was established, a proposal was made to the Council of the Chief Rabbinate to adopt an enactment within the

transfer to those who are his rightful heirs, how much more so [does it apply] with regard to those who are not his heirs, such as the charity fund and the synagogue. The purpose of giving charity for the synagogue is to provide for its maintenance and to furnish oil for the lamp and other necessities. These are duties that rest on the community, and anyone who donates his property for such purposes only frees the rest of the community from their obligation for this charity. He thus disinherits his rightful heir in favor of those who are not his heirs. The same applies to one who bequeaths his property to the poor, for two reasons: first, he frees the community from its duty, and second, he disinherits his rightful heir in favor of the poor who are not his heirs. If the relatives who are his heirs are also poor, then it is like the case of a poor man who is sifting through left-over bread [and is on the point of taking some] when someone else comes along and takes it away from him, in which case the latter is called "wicked."[251] But all this does not nullify the will once it has been made; it establishes only that it should not be made [in the first instance].

Rashbeẓ relied on the statement in Tractate *Bava Batra* that the Sages are displeased with one who disinherits his legal heirs, whether the testator by this act prefers a more distantly related heir over one more closely related or prefers a person who is not a legal heir at all, as in the case here discussed. Although this case involved a transfer for communal purposes, the heir still had priority; the community had the obligation of seeing to the satisfaction of the needs of its institutions and of the needy, and may not be relieved of this obligation. For it is an important principle in the laws of charity in the *Halakhah* that "the poor of one's household have priority over the poor of one's town";[252] and since the case involved a poor relative, there was an additional moral flaw in supplanting the relative as distributee of the estate. This is the same moral shortcoming that characterizes one who

---

framework of the *Halakhah* to the effect that daughters and sons would have equal rights of inheritance, but the proposal was not adopted; *see infra* p. 1494 n. 124 and p. 1684 and n. 270. In the middle of the twentieth century, the Council of the Rabbis of Morocco legislated that the above-mentioned enactment pursuant to which unmarried daughters inherit their father's estates on an equal basis with sons should be effective in all the Jewish communities in Morocco. Similarly, the Council considered a proposal that the enactment should apply to married daughters as well. *See* M. Elon, "Yiḥudah Shel Halakhah ve-Ḥevrah be-Yahadut Ẓefon Afrika mi-le-Aḥar Gerush Sefarad ve-ad Yameinu" [The Exceptional Character of *Halakhah* and Society in North African Jewry from the Spanish Expulsion to the Present], *Halakhah u-Petiḥut, Ḥakhmei Morokko ke-Fosekim le-Doreinu* [*Halakhah* and Open-Mindedness: The Halakhic Authorities of Morocco as Authorities for Our Own Time], ed. Moshe Bar Yuda, Histadrut Center for Culture and Education, 1985 (hereinafter, *Yiḥudah Shel Halakhah*), pp. 15, 29–31.

251. TB Kiddushin 59a.

252. *See supra* p. 117 and n. 107.

sees a poor person sifting through left-over bread[253] and runs ahead and takes it for himself. Even though the interloper is legally entitled to keep it, because the poor person had not yet taken possession of it, the interloper is called "wicked" because "he torments [lit. "descends into the life of"] his fellow."[254] This was the situation in our case. Rashbeẓ' conclusion in this part of his responsum was that nothing said up to that point established any basis for invalidating the bequest on legal grounds but that the bequest should not have been made because it suffers from two moral deficiencies: "the Sages are displeased," and it partakes of "wickedness."[255]

As we have seen, Rashbeẓ subsequently decided that there was a basis for nullifying even the legal effectiveness of the bequest, because the bequest involved the performance of a transgression. But what is pertinent here is that even when Rashbeẓ had not yet found legal grounds for setting aside the bequest, it was nevertheless appropriate to rule on the question he was asked, and he ruled that the will was morally and religiously defective.[256]

253. "He was sifting through it in order to acquire it either as ownerless property or by gift from its owner"; Rashi, Kiddushin 59a, s.v. Ani ha-mehapekh be-ḥararah.

254. Rashi, *ad loc.*, s.v. Nikra rasha.

255. The concept of "wickedness" (*rish'ut*) also appears in TB Bava Batra 137a: "Abbaye said: 'Who is a cunning rogue [lit. "a sly, wicked person"]? One who advises another to sell property according to the ruling of Rabban Simeon b. Gamaliel.'" This statement was made with regard to a bequest that left property to A for life with the remainder to B. According to R. Judah Ha-Nasi, A cannot sell the property, since all he has in it is a life interest in the income; if he does sell it, B is entitled to recover it from the purchaser, by virtue of the terms of the will, when A dies. However, according to Rabban Simeon b. Gamaliel, B receives only what A leaves intact, because A has a right in the property itself, and B, in case of a sale by A, may not recover the property from A's purchaser. Abbaye held that the law accords with the view of Rabban Simeon b. Gamaliel, but that anyone who advises A to sell is a cunning rogue, because "he is interfering in a controversy in which he is not involved and he is defeating the intent of the testator, who said, 'My property should go to you [A] and after you to B,' and who did not intend that A should sell the property to a third party and thereby deprive B [of his legacy]" (Rashbam, Bava Batra 174b, s.v. Eizehu rasha arom). He is called "cunning" because "at any rate, he succeeds in that what he did is effective . . . because B receives only what A leaves intact, and A left B nothing." The term "cunning rogue" is also applied to a person who advises a poor man to divorce his wife so as to enable her to claim the amount of her *ketubbah* from one who guaranteed its payment, when the plan is that the couple will later remarry, and the sole purpose of the divorce is to collect the money from the guarantor (TB Bava Batra 174b).

256. Other types of moral-religious sanctions include: "He has a complaint against him" (TB Bava Meẓi'a 75b); and "the standard of pious behavior (*mishnat ḥasidim*)" (TJ Terumot 8:4, 44a [8:10, 46b]). *See* S. Federbush, *Ha-Musar ve-ha-Mishpat be-Yisra'el* [Jewish Law and Morals], 1950; Herzog, *Institutions*, I, pp. 381–386; M. Silberg, *Talmudic Law and the Modern State*, pp. 61ff.; Urbach, *The Sages*, pp. 329–335.

The position adopted by the Rabbinical Court of Appeals in this matter is interesting. In a case brought before it, Histadrut Po'alei Agudat Yisra'el, Reḥovot v. Histadrut Agudat Yisra'el, Reḥovot, 6 *P.D.R.* 202 (1966), the defendant bought a plot of land while the plain-

F. *Lifnim Mi-Shurat Ha-Din*—Acting More Generously than the Law Requires

Another type of religious and moral obligation that, in the course of time, underwent an interesting development from moral imperative to legal duty is the direction to act *lifnim mi-shurat ha-din* (lit. "on the inside of the line of the law"), *i.e.*, to act more generously than the law requires. In certain situations, the conduct contemplated by this extralegal obligation ultimately became enforced like any strictly legal duty. The Scriptural verse "Make known to them the way they are to go and the practices they are to follow"[257] was interpreted by R. Eleazar of Modi'in as follows: "'The practices' refers to the strict law; 'they are to follow' refers to *lifnim mi-shurat ha-din.*"[258] In terms of strictly legal rights and obligations, the direction to act *lifnim mi-shurat ha-din* does not carry with it any kind of sanction. The only function of this moral principle is to inform us that it is proper for an individual who is scrupulous in his behavior not to limit his acts to what is required by law, but to conduct himself according to a standard higher than

---

tiff was engaged in serious negotiations to purchase it. The plaintiff's main argument was that it had the right to buy the property pursuant to its legal right as an adjoining landowner, *see infra* pp. 621–622. The plaintiff also argued that it was in the position of the poor man sifting through left-over bread, which the defendant had snatched away from him (*see supra* n. 253). Both of the plaintiff's arguments were rejected, but at the conclusion of its judgment, the court addressed the defendant as follows:

> As an addendum to this judgment, although we have decided that the plaintiff's position is not that of a poor man sifting through left-overs, etc., and that [the members of defendant organization] cannot, Heaven forfend, be classified as wicked, the court finds it fitting to counsel the defendant's members, who are meticulously observant Jews and are accustomed to follow the stringent opinion and heed the words of the stringent authorities even when the law is not so strict. . . . Clearly, when the defendant will take the virtuous way and follow the just path and withdraw from this transaction, the plaintiff will be obligated to reimburse the defendant so that it should suffer no loss, Heaven forfend, for acting piously—which is something it is not required to do by law. . . . Then they will live together in affection, harmony, peace, and friendship, and peace will rule among them and in their abodes. Thus will the name of Heaven be sanctified by them.

After ruling that by strict law the plaintiff had no case, the court nevertheless saw fit to inform the defendant that as an act of piety it should accept the plaintiff's claim. *See further* S. Shilo, "Dinei Mamonot be-Vattei ha-Din ha-Rabbaniyyim" [Civil Law in the Rabbinical Courts], *Ha-Praklit,* XXVI (1970), pp. 523ff.; *id.*, "Hassagot al Pesikat Battei ha-Din ha-Rabbaniyyim be-Inyan Hassagat Gevul Misharit" [Critique of Rulings of Rabbinical Courts on the Question of Unfair Business Competition], *Mishpatim,* VI (1976), pp. 530ff., at p. 542.

257. Exodus 18:20.

258. *Mekhilta de-R. Ishmael,* Yitro, Tractate De-Amalek, sec. 2, p. 198; TB Bava Kamma 99b–100a; Bava Meẓi'a 30b. In the last two sources, the exegesis is quoted in the name of R. Joseph.

the law requires.[259] However, an incident recorded in the Talmud indicates a difference of opinion among the Sages as to whether the requirement of acting more generously than the strict law requires may sometimes be an enforceable legal norm. The incident was as follows:[260]

> A group of porters broke a barrel of wine belonging to Rabbah bar bar Ḥanan.[261] He seized their cloaks. They came before Rav and told him of the incident. Rav said to Rabbah bar bar Ḥanan: "Return the cloaks to them." Rabbah responded: "Is this the law?" [The porters have not shown that they were not negligent in their work.] Rav replied: "Yes, for it is written, 'So follow the way of the good.'"[262] He gave them their cloaks. The porters [then] said to Rav: "We are poor, we have worked all day, we are hungry and we have nothing to eat." Rav said to Rabbah bar bar Ḥanan: "Go give them their wages." He responded: "Is this the law?" He said to him: "Yes, as it is written, 'And keep to the paths of the just.'"[263]

In this incident, Rav ruled that the workers should not be made to pay for the damage and also ordered that their wages be paid, on the ground that one must do more than what the law strictly requires—one must follow the way of the good and keep to the paths of the just.[264] The question to which Rav responded was, "Is this the law?" He gave no indication to Rabbah that his response was intended to do anything other than state the law. As a result, many halakhic authorities in the post-Talmudic period concluded that Rav's ruling declared a norm fully legal in character:

259. *See, e.g.,* TB Bava Meẓi'a 24b, regarding the restoration of lost property to its owner when the law does not so require. Similarly, *see* TB Bava Kamma 99b, regarding payment of compensation for damage caused as a result of erroneous expert advice for which, by law, there is generally no liability. In certain circumstances the law may impose such liability. For a detailed discussion of the subject from the point of view of Jewish, English, and American law, *see* Amidar v. Aharon, 32(ii) *P.D.* 337 (1978), and the fine article on this case by D. Schonberg, "New Developments in the Israeli Law of Negligent Misrepresentation," 31 *Int. and Comp. L.Q.* 207 (1982).

260. TB Bava Meẓi'a 83a.

261. *See Dikdukei Soferim, ad loc.,* for v.l.

262. Proverbs 2:20.

263. *Id.* In many versions the word "*in*" ("yes") is omitted in Rav's response. *See* the parallel version of the incident in TJ Bava Meẓi'a 6:6, 27a/b (6:8, 11a). *See also* Urbach, *The Sages,* pp. 330–332.

264. *See* Rashi, *ad loc.,* s.v. Be-derekh tovim: "lifnim mi-shurat ha-din." *Tosafot,* Bava Kamma 100a and Bava Meẓi'a 24b, s.v. Lifnim mi-shurat ha-din, distinguishes between the principle of *lifnim mi-shurat ha-din* (which by itself was not sufficient to require Rabbah bar bar Ḥanan to refrain from claiming damages, since his loss was substantial) and the reason of "So follow the way of the good," according to which one should not claim damages even if his loss is substantial.

> It seems that Rav's ruling in Rabbah bar bar Ḥanan's case was binding and legally enforceable, for if not, why did he tell him that this was "the law" if it was not intended to be binding and enforceable?[265]

However, even if we take the view that Rav was only pointing out that this is the way of the righteous and the good rather than binding and enforceable law (which is the meaning of *lifnim mi-shurat ha-din* as a general rule in Talmudic *Halakhah*), nevertheless, in the post-Talmudic period, many halakhic authorities concluded from Rav's words that the principle of *lifnim mi-shurat ha-din* is legally enforceable in certain situations:

> Since we see that this rule was enforced, as stated at the end of chapter *Ha-Umanin* [TB *Bava Meẓi'a* 83a], we too enforce the performance of an obligation that is greater than what the law strictly requires if it is within the individual's capacity, *i.e.*, if he is wealthy.[266]

Others disagree and are of the opinion that the court does not compel a party to act more generously than the strict law requires,[267] but this view is not accepted by most of the authorities.[268] The view that the principle is judicially enforceable against wealthy obligors was confirmed by Joel Sirkes at the beginning of the seventeenth century:

> It is the practice in every Jewish court to compel the wealthy to perform their obligation where it is right and proper, even if the strict law does not so require.[269]

Here, then, is an example of a norm that originally had only moral and religious sanction but in the course of time became in certain situations a full, judicially enforceable legal norm.[270] To a great extent, this transforma-

265. *Bayit Ḥadash* to *Tur* ḤM 12:4. Urbach, *The Sages,* pp. 330–332, is of the opinion that the correct textual reading omits the word "*in*" ("Yes") in Rav's response, and therefore there is no proof that Rav believed that there was any legal force to the principle of *lifnim mi-shurat ha-din.* Urbach's conclusion does not necessarily follow. The text of the Talmud as quoted in *Bayit Ḥadash, supra,* does not contain the word "*in,*" yet the author of *Bayit Ḥadash* still drew the conclusion quoted in our text. With regard to the post-Talmudic period, it is extremely difficult to argue that acts *lifnim mi-shurat ha-din* are not legally required but are merely matters of piety (as argued by Urbach, *op. cit.,* pp. 331ff.), since, according to most early and late authorities (*rishonim* and *aḥaronim*), the court can, in certain circumstances, enforce obligations that are *lifnim mi-shurat ha-din. See* text accompanying nn. 266 *et seq.*

266. *Mordekhai,* Bava Meẓi'a, ch. 2, #257, and *see* the discussion there.

267. Asheri and others; *see Bayit Ḥadash, supra* n. 265.

268. Such as Raban, Raviah, the author of *Ha-Agudah,* and others. *See also Mordekhai* and *Bayit Ḥadash, supra* nn. 265 and 266, and Rema to Sh. Ar. ḤM 12:2.

269. *Bayit Ḥadash, supra* n. 265, *and cf. Derishah* to *Tur* ḤM 1, subpar. 2.

270. This, as well as the converse process, exists in other legal systems; but in Jewish law it has special significance. Similarly, in Jewish law, legal norms and decisions are not

tion is explained by the fact that all norms in the sphere of the Oral Law have a common source. Additional reasons arose out of the particular conditions under which the Jewish legal system operated in the various diasporas[271] and out of the need for the development of new legal norms.[272]

---

infrequently based on moral and philosophical principles. An example is the use of the guideline "Her ways are pleasant ways and all her paths, peaceful" in arriving at a solution of purely legal problems. For details, *see* M. Elon, "Ekronot Musariyyim ke-Normah Hilkhatit" [Moral Principles as Halakhic Norm], *De'ot,* XX (1962), pp. 62–67; *Digest of the Responsa Literature of Spain and North Africa, Index of Sources,* ed. M. Elon, 1981, Introduction, p. 25. *See also infra* pp. 387–390, 624–627.

271. Apparently, the need to raise the level of obedience to Jewish law within the Jewish community in the diaspora also led to giving full legal validity to norms previously carrying only moral sanction. *See supra* ch. 1.

272. An interesting example of this process can be found in a decision that Jewish law requires severance pay for employees. Ben-Zion Ḥai Uziel, the Chief Rabbi of Israel, grounded this rule on the case of the porters discussed above and concluded:

> A court has the authority to order the employer to make payments for the benefit of his employees whenever it sees that this will promote the goal of "follow[ing] the way of the good and keep[ing] to the paths of the just [Proverbs 2:20]." In exercising its discretion, it should take into account the manifest circumstances of the employer and employee, as well as the reasons why the employer dismissed the employee or why the employee stopped working for the employer."

The decision is quoted in M. Findling, *Teḥukat ha-Avodah . . . Lefi Dinei ha-Torah . . .* [Labor Law . . . According to the Torah . . .], pp. 132–133. For additional discussion of the question of severance pay, *see* EJ, VII, pp. 1003–1007, s.v. Ha'anakah (reprinted in *Principles,* pp. 315–319), and *infra* pp. 924–926 and pp. 1631–1634.

A further example of judicial enforcement of compliance with *lifnim mi-shurat ha-din* is presented by a decision of the Rabbinical Court of Appeals, rejecting a claim of privilege by the Ministry of Defense and ordering the production of various documents in the ministry's possession to clarify a matter of personal status involving a husband and wife. A. v. B., 5 *P.D.R.* 132 (1962). The court added that even according to the opinion that compliance with *lifnim mi-shurat ha-din* is ordinarily not legally enforceable, when a public body is a party to the suit "a court order should be sufficient to assure compliance, and woe to a generation whose leaders refuse to comply and whose compliance must be judicially enforced" (*id.* at 152). (*Cf.* the practice of American appellate courts to refrain from issuing the formal writ of mandamus against inferior court judges and instead to transmit the appellate opinion, confident that the lower court judges will do their duty as instructed by the opinion, without the necessity of a formal writ against them. *See, e.g.,* Anderson v. Sorrell, 481 A.2d 766 (D.C. App. 1984)).

A similar attitude was taken by the Rabbinical Court of Appeals in Friedman v. Savorai, 4 *P.D.R.* 239 (1962). The plaintiff had claimed priority in renting an unoccupied room adjacent to his apartment. The court rejected his legal arguments, but, toward the end of its judgment, expressed the view that "it is fitting, good, and right to rent to the plaintiff the vacant room adjacent to his apartment rather than to give preference to other prospective tenants." The last sentence of the opinion states: "The defendant must follow the way of the good and rent to the plaintiff the room adjacent to the plaintiff's apartment." This constitutes a decision with legal consequences, based on the principle "so follow the way of the good," just as it was in the matter concerning the porters, and is an application of the general principle that in certain circumstances conduct *lifnim mi-shurat ha-din* may be enforced by judicial sanctions. *See further* Shilo, *supra* n. 256; however, Shilo's critique to the effect that

The transformation of *lifnim mi-shurat ha-din* into a full legal norm was lucidly set forth in the following comments by Joshua Falk, a contemporary of Joel Sirkes:[273]

> What is meant by "a judgment that is completely and truly correct" [*din emet la-amito,* lit. "a true judgment to its very truth"—TB *Shabbat* 10a; *Sanhedrin* 7a] is that one should judge in accordance with the particular place and time, so that the judgment is in full conformity with the truth, rather than always inflexibly apply the law precisely as it is set forth in the Torah. For sometimes a judge's decision must go *lifnim mi-shurat ha-din* and reflect what is called for by the particular time and circumstances. When the judge does not do this, then even if his judgment is correct, it is not "a true judgment to its very truth." This is the meaning of the statement of the Sages: "Jerusalem was destroyed because they based their judgments on the law of the Torah and did not go *lifnim mi-shurat ha-din*" [TB *Bava Meẓi'a* 30b]. As to this, it was written, "You must not deviate from the verdict that they announce to you either to the right or to the left" [Deuteronomy 17:11], which the Sages interpret to mean that you may not deviate even if they tell you that right is left . . . and certainly if they identify the right as right. . . . When you are told sometimes by the judge that the law seems to lead to one result in a judgment, but he is deciding the opposite, this is the "right" for him under the circumstances of the particular matter.

The point is that sometimes a judge is obligated to decide *lifnim mi-shurat ha-din,* in accordance with the felt necessities of the time and the exigencies of the case; if he does not do so, his decision may be "true," but it does not reflect the essential truth of the law. When, in a particular case, a judge decides contrary to his view of what strict law requires, he is not deviating from the law but declaring it truly: he does not change left into right, but his decision is "right."[274]

The reciprocal relation between law and morals in the sphere of the *Halakhah* was summarized by Vidal of Tolosa, the author of *Maggid Mishneh:*[275]

> Our perfect Torah, in order to improve human character and conduct in the world, laid down principles such as "You shall be holy."[276] The intent was,

---

the court must demonstrate special reasons to justify judicial enforcement of conduct *lifnim mi-shurat ha-din* is not persuasive, since this type of decision is quite common and accepted in the rabbinical courts.

273. *Derishah* to *Tur* ḤM 1, subpar. 2.

274. As to the principle "Even when they say that right is left and left is right," *see* the discussion *infra* pp. 243–247 regarding rabbinic authority and *infra* pp. 176–181, 247–261 regarding the relationship between law and equity.

275. *Maggid Mishneh* to Maimonides, *MT,* Shekhenim 14:5.

276. Leviticus 19:2.

> as our Sages said: "Sanctify yourselves through that which is permitted to you,"[277] so that you shall not be swept away by your passions. The Torah also states: "Do what is right and good . . . ,"[278] the intent being that one should behave ethically and honestly toward one's fellow.
>
> Even so, it was not possible to give detailed directives, because the commandments of the Torah apply in all times and in all situations, and are obligatory, yet human mores and behavior vary according to the time and the society.
>
> The Sages wrote down some of the specific practical applications of these general principles; some they established as binding law, others as [ethical precepts for] proper and pious behavior, but all of it was laid down by the Sages. It was with respect to this that it was commented: "The words of the beloved (*dodim*) [this was understood as referring to the words of the Sages] are dearer than the wine of the [written] Torah,[279] as it is said,[280] 'For your love is more delightful than wine.'"

Taking into consideration "human mores and behavior [which] vary according to the time and the society," the Torah itself authorized the halakhic authorities to establish, from time to time, different rules having the basic purpose of doing what is right and good. Sometimes, the halakhic authorities gave these rules the sanction of a full legal norm,[281] and sometimes the rules were established only as a guide to proper and pious behavior.[282] But both these types of rules are rooted in the words of the halakhic authorities and are essential parts of the Oral Law. Consequently, the halakhic authority and the judge, in declaring the law and in deciding cases, have recourse to moral norms and may direct that such norms be complied with when there is no legal ground in the case before them for enforcement by judicial sanctions.

An interesting exchange of views on the policy of *lifnim mi-shurat ha-din* in a contemporary setting is contained in a decision of the Supreme

277. TB Yevamot 20a.

278. Deuteronomy 6:18.

279. The source is *Shir ha-Shirim Rabbah* 1, on Song of Songs 1:2. However, the reading in the generally current editions of *Shir ha-Shirim Rabbah* is: "The words of the *soferim* are dearer than the words of the Torah." That is also the version in TJ Berakhot 1:4, 8b (1:8, 3b) and TJ Avodah Zarah 2:7, 15a (2:8, 41c).

280. Song of Songs 1:2.

281. *E.g.*, the legislation regarding adjoining landowners and the principle that land taken in satisfaction of a debt may be redeemed by the debtor at any time, *see infra* pp. 623–628, and also, at particular times and in special circumstances, *lifnim mi-shurat ha-din*, discussed *supra* pp. 155–159.

282. The term *tov ve-yashar* (good and upright) is also used to characterize moral norms of the type classified as belonging to the category of *lifnim mi-shurat ha-din*. *See, e.g.*, Maimonides, *MT*, Gezelah va-Avedah 11:7; Sh. Ar. ḤM 259:5. *See also Sifrei*, Deuteronomy, Re'eh, sec. 79, p. 145.

Court of Israel.[283] The case dealt with the tort liability of a corporation whose employee, a security guard, killed the husband and father of the plaintiffs with a revolver that had been given to him in the course of his employment. The Supreme Court decided that although the negligence of the employer had been proved, in that the employer had not met its duty of care and did not properly supervise and control the dangerous weapons issued to the guards in its employ, the requisite causal connection between the employer's negligence and the killing of the deceased had not been proved. The plaintiffs' claims for damages from the employer were therefore rejected. A concurring opinion (Elon, J.) states:[284]

> It is true that the law supports the appellant [the employer], and under the law it cannot be compelled to compensate the respondents [the widow and children]. During the hearing before us, the appellant proposed to pay the respondents *lifnim mi-shurat ha-din,* more generously than the law requires, a sum in addition to what it had already paid to them, which would compensate for a large portion of the damages suffered by the respondents as a result of the death of their husband and father. I wish to commend the appellant for this, for it is a Jewish tradition and a fundamental principle in Jewish law that, along with strict legal liability, there is the additional obligation to act *lifnim mi-shurat ha-din.* It is of particular significance here that this obligation found one of its chief expressions in Jewish law in the field of torts, in a case precisely in point with the instant case.[285]
>
> As the principle of *lifnim mi-shurat ha-din* developed, many halakhic authorities took the position that, in certain circumstances, the principle is legally enforceable. . . . [286] This approach rests on the wider outlook of Jewish law, and it is expressed, among other places, in the well-known rule that "the giving of charity may be compelled."[287] This rule, too, is applicable only under specific conditions and circumstances. As is known, this rule constituted the basis for the duty in certain circumstances to support children and relatives, even when this duty did not exist under strict law.[288]
>
> In our current legal system [in the State of Israel], we do not compel anyone to act more generously than the law requires; such action is left to the initiative and will of the party involved. However, the expression by the judge of such an aspiration in certain circumstances would seem to be appropriate. I base this also on the tradition of Jewish law. . . . [289]
>
> For myself, I would hope that the appellant, whom the strict law sup-

283. Kitan v. Weiss, 33(ii) *P.D.* 785 (1979).
284. *Id.* at 809.
285. *See supra* pp. 155–157.
286. *See supra* pp. 156–159.
287. TB Ketubbot 49b.
288. *See supra* pp. 116–117.
289. *See supra* p. 144.

> ports, will act more generously than the law demands, and compensate the respondents as it originally proposed to do. This will fulfill what the wisest of men taught us: "So follow the way of the good and keep to the paths of the just,"[290] this being the source for the principle of acting *lifnim mi-shurat ha-din.*

Justice (later Court President) Shamgar had the following to say about this question:[291]

> My distinguished colleague, Justice Elon, at the end of his opinion, discussed the possible payment of compensation *lifnim mi-shurat ha-din.* In the course of the argument before us, the appellant did indeed make an offer to pay compensation beyond what the law would require, in consideration of the tragic circumstances of this case. The respondents, however, categorically refused to accept this offer in spite of the recommendation of the court, and insisted on a decision based strictly on the law. This is their right, and they should not be criticized for this.
>
> However, I strongly dissent from the objective revealed between the lines of the opinion of my distinguished colleague, that seeks to elevate payment of compensation *lifnim mi-shurat ha-din* to the status of a settled general principle of the law of torts. It may be immediately pointed out that such a notion would be a promise made to the ear but broken to the hope, considering that it is raised in the framework of a legal system which, much to our distress, deals in the year 1979 with an injury that occurred in 1965, the claim for which was filed in 1971. The legal decision in this case has indeed been much delayed. It is also superfluous to add that such an approach will necessarily bring about the filing of frivolous appeals and thus add to the difficulties with which the courts are struggling; for if one is not required to rely on arguments that rest on the law alone in order to obtain compensation, why not take every case up through the court system to the very highest court possible? My concern here is not for the time of the court, but for the resulting consequence, namely, the adverse effect on those appellants whose appeals have merit and who will have to wait even longer for a decision in their cases.
>
> Moreover, a legal system that deliberately chooses to abandon the boundary lines marked out in the substantive law and to add, as an additional and alternative stratum and as an established part of the system, a recommendation for the payment of compensation beyond what the law requires, necessarily acts according to impossibly vague standards, which ultimately depend on the fortuity of which particular judge sits when the case is reached. Such a system will, over the course of time, bring about confusion in the law and adversely affect the rights of the parties. The absence of clear standards may also often actually produce inconsistent results. A nonlegal recommendation which, in view of its inherent character, can be made only in excep-

290. Proverbs 2:20.
291. 33(ii) *P.D.* at 805.

tional circumstances should not, in a system such as ours, be turned into a principle of general applicability, because this would be contrary to its essential nature.

These two opinions thus present the question whether it is proper to recommend in a judgment, in particular and appropriate circumstances, that a party should act more generously than the law requires; and they thereby raise the broader question of the relationship between morals and law within the legal system. On this broader issue, the first-mentioned opinion went on to state:[292]

> My distinguished colleague, Justice Shamgar, fears that my statements, and the wish that I expressed to the appellant, contemplate a *system* of recommending the giving of compensation *lifnim mi-shurat ha-din.* My concern is not with a *system.* I believe that it is fitting, as I emphasized, that in certain circumstances the court should make such a request. As to the effect of that request, I completely agree with the following statement of my distinguished colleague, Justice Witkon, for whom I have the utmost respect: "I too will be happy if the respondents receive some measure of compensation, but the matter is entirely in the discretion of the appellant, and I would not propose to obscure the boundary between liability and nonliability."
>
> What are the particular circumstances in the matter before us? The District Court found the appellant liable, under the law, to compensate the respondents. The appellant believed—and, it turned out, correctly—that, under the law, it was not liable to compensate the respondents; but it proposed, in consideration of the circumstances of the case, that it pay a certain sum *lifnim mi-shurat ha-din.* The majority of this court held that, in fact, the negligence of the appellant was proved, but that the causal connection between this negligence and the death of the respondents' decedent was not proved; and we therefore absolved the appellant, under the law, from liability to compensate the respondents. Why should we now refrain from expressing the request that the appellant, which started to perform the *miẓvah* [lit. "commandment" and also in colloquial usage "good deed"] of *lifnim mi-shurat ha-din,* continue and complete what it has begun? These are the specific circumstances of the matter before us, and the court should consider whether it is proper under the special circumstances of each case coming before it to express such a request. It need not be pointed out that appellants who think they can submit frivolous appeals will soon discover that not only will there be no suggestion by us that respondents do more than the law requires of them, but such appellants will also incur appropriate costs for conducting vexatious litigation against the respondents and for wasting the court's time.
>
> I do not share the apprehension that it will bring about confusion in the law if we express our view and make the parties aware that in certain circum-

292. *Id.* at 810–811.

stances one should act more generously than the law requires. Courts regularly make decisions based on considerations of justice, equity, good faith, public welfare, equal protection, and *locus standi* in matters on which property and life itself depend. They are not deterred by fear that these standards are vague or, Heaven forbid, that on occasion they may reach an unfair result. It should, therefore, be presumed that the courts will find their way in this matter where law and morals intersect, and will be able to weigh well, in the light of the circumstances of each case, whether to request—and it would be only a request—that the injured party be compensated *lifnim mi-shurat ha-din*.

If we are apprehensive about the danger of combining morality with law, why should we not be concerned with the manner in which the law itself is applied? My colleague points out that, in the case before us, the injury occurred in 1965 and the final judgment was given in 1979. How does the judgment look to the parties and to us when it is given—and to our sorrow this is not a rare occurrence—after the passage of two full sabbatical cycles [fourteen years], and we see [the injustice] yet are powerless to afford any remedy? Perhaps when parties recognize the value of acting *lifnim mi-shurat ha-din* in appropriate circumstances, there will even be a decrease in the innumerable legal actions for strictly legal relief, which are not always necessary, thus possibly reducing somewhat the heavy burden on the courts.[293]

In another case,[294] a unanimous Supreme Court followed the view of Jewish law and incorporated in its judgment a request to the successful party to pay *lifnim mi-shurat ha-din*. The case concerned a contract between the plaintiff and the Ḥevrat Shikkun Ovedim (Workers Housing Authority) that was entered into in 1943 for an apartment to be obtained by the Authority through the Keren Kayemet le-Yisra'el (Jewish National Fund). The plaintiff made a deposit of sixty Israeli pounds, which was held by the Jewish National Fund. The apartment was never provided, but the deposit was not returned. Following sporadic negotiations, suit was brought in 1978, thirty-five years after the contract was entered into, claiming (1) specific performance of the contract, (2) in the alternative, damages for the value of an apartment, and (3) in any event, the return of a sum equivalent to the real value of the sixty Israeli pounds as of the date of the deposit. After rejecting all claims on the ground that the period of limitations had expired, the court stated with respect to the third claim:[295]

293. This call for conduct more generous than the law requires was repeated in other cases. *See* Proper v. General Custodian, 35(ii) *P.D.* 561, 564 (1981); Ness v. Golda, 36(i) *P.D.* 204, 220–221 (1981).

294. Boyer v. Shikkun Ovedim, 38(ii) *P.D.* 561 (1984) (Opinion of Elon, J.; Court President Shamgar and D. Levin, J., concurring).

295. *Id.* at 569–570.

The learned attorney of Keren Kayemet le-Yisra'el conceded before us that the sum of sixty Israeli pounds was still recorded in the books of Keren Kayemet to the credit of the appellant, and Keren Kayemet, going beyond its legal duty, was willing to refund this sum to the appellant, linked [*i.e.*, partly, to the rate of inflation]; and after linkage, this sum, at the time of the hearing before us, came to 30,000 Israeli pounds, *i.e.*, 3000 *shekalim*. When we compare the real value of sixty pounds in 1943 (and in this connection we heard from the appellant's attorney that the appellant earned a wage of seventeen and a half *grushim* per day in those distant times, as a construction worker [one pound was 100 *grushim*]) to the value of 3000 *shekalim*, this proposal by the attorney of Keren Kayemet is a poor joke. The appellant's money was not set aside "like an unturned stone," but it was used by Keren Kayemet, and our Sages had this to say about such a case: "How can one person make profit from another person's cow?"[296] This is a classic case where it is fitting and correct to act *lifnim mi-shurat ha-din*[297] and to refund to the appellant a sum equivalent to the value of sixty pounds in those days. It has already been said in this court, by President Shamgar, in a matter in which both the claim and the appeal were rejected under the law: "I would therefore recommend that, notwithstanding the passage of time, the insurance company should act more generously than the law requires and re-examine the matter so that the owner of the insured property does not sustain a total loss."[298]

Such conduct is certainly in order for a distinguished public body, such as Keren Kayemet, "for the public, like the individual, and perhaps *even more so*, should do what is good and right, and not stand on strict law."[299] As [aptly] concluded by a halakhic responsum holding that, under strict law, a community was not obligated to pay compensation to one of its employees because it had acted under *force majeure*: "All of this is the strict law; nevertheless, even though the community acted under *force majeure* in this matter and is legally exempt from paying, it is proper and correct that it act toward him more generously than the law requires, for he is a poor man and has dependent children."[300]

This applies even more so in the case before us, for Keren Kayemet reaped a benefit from money that does not belong to it but belongs to the appellant. We proposed to the attorney for Keren Kayemet that it choose an arbitrator. The appellant's attorney accepted this suggestion, but the attorney for Keren Kayemet did not see fit to agree to even this proposal. We can only express our surprise at this and request that Keren Kayemet will reconsider the matter, and compensate the appellant in a suitable fashion.

296. TB Bava Meẓi'a 35b.

297. TB Bava Meẓi'a 30b, 83a; *see also* Kitan v. Weiss, *supra* n. 283 at 809ff.; Ness v. Golda, *supra* n. 293 at 220.

298. Biton v. Ḥalamish, 36(ii) *P.D.* 706, 712 (1982).

299. A. v. B., *supra* n. 272 at 151.

300. *Resp. Mayim Ḥayyim*, ḤM, #6, cited in *Pitḥei Teshuvah*, Sh. Ar. ḤM 333, subpar. 3. *See also* Lev v. Siegel, 3 *P.D.R.* 91, 95–96 (1958).

> In conclusion, we have been compelled, to our sorrow, to reject the appellant's claims, and we are unable to aid him in any of them, from the aspect of strict law. But it seems to us, in view of what has been stated at the end of our opinion, that it is fitting and proper that the appellant should not be obligated to pay the respondents' costs, even though he did not win his case. We have therefore decided to reject the appeal, except for the District Court's order that the appellant pay the respondents' costs in that court. In order to express our disapproval of the respondents' behavior, we have decided that the appellant shall also be relieved from payment of respondents' costs for this appeal.

There are occasions when the Israeli legislature itself gives the status of law to a provision whose basic and original significance involves acting *lifnim mi-shurat ha-din*. These instances include all those provisions where the legislature gives the court discretion to act in certain instances not according to the formal letter of the law but "as appears to it to be just, and subject to such conditions as it deems appropriate."[301] The Supreme Court has dealt with such a provision in the Tenants Protection Law (Consolidated Version), 1972. This law provides that a tenant protected by the law is not to be evicted, even though there is no lease between the tenant and the landlord, except upon certain grounds explicitly set forth in the statute.[302] The statute also contains the following provision:[303]

> Notwithstanding the existence of a ground for eviction, the court may refuse to render a judgment of eviction if it is satisfied that in the circumstances of the case a judgment of eviction would be unjust.

With regard to the meaning of this provision, the Supreme Court stated:[304]

> In this provision, the Legislature determined that if, in the circumstances, it would not be just to subject the tenant to the strict letter of the law and to evict him from the property of which he is a tenant, it is proper to deal with him *lifnim mi-shurat ha-din* and not evict him. Acting in this manner with regard to the eviction of a tenant under the Tenants Protection Law (Consolidated Version) is thus part of the law, in the broad sense of "law," since it is based upon an explicit statutory provision. This is similar to what we have

301. Land Law, 1969, sec. 19; secs. 24 and 37(b), as well as a number of other laws, contain a similar provision. *See, e.g.*, Contracts Law (General Part), 1973, secs. 14(b), 31; Contracts Law (Remedies for Breach of Contract), 1970, secs. 3(4), 7(b), and 18(b), and other statutes.

302. Tenants Protection Law (Consolidated Version), 1972, sec. 131.

303. *Id.*, sec. 132(a).

304. Marcus v. Hammer, 37(ii) *P.D.* 337, 352 (1983) (Elon, J.).

found in Jewish law; there, too, in certain circumstances, acting *lifnim mi-shurat ha-din* is part of what the "law" itself requires.[305]

G. Law, Justice, and Equity

As has been pointed out, the Jewish legal system makes a sharp distinction between judicially enforceable legal norms and nonenforceable moral norms. Nevertheless, although moral norms have no effect as law, Jewish courts, functioning as such, deal with them, analyze them, rank them, and declare their conclusions about them to the parties. As we have seen, sometimes a particular norm enters the halakhic sphere backed only by a religious and moral sanction, but in the course of time, under certain circumstances, it becomes a full legal norm that a court is required to apply and enforce. This is exemplified by the judicial enforcement of certain conduct *lifnim mi-shurat ha-din,* where such conduct is "right "right and proper even if the strict law does not so require" (as stated by Joel Sirkes in his *Bayit Ḥadash*). In the words of the *Derishah,* by Joshua Falk, it is incumbent on a judge to rule on a matter "in full conformity with the truth, rather than always inflexibly apply the law precisely as it is set forth in the Torah. For sometimes a judge's decision must go *lifnim mi-shurat ha-din* and reflect what is called for by the particular time and circumstances."

These words, and the conceptual principle they reflect, lead to the discussion of another subject, namely, the relationship between law, on the one hand, and justice and equity, on the other. This relationship is very similar to the relationship between law and morals in that equity and morals share common goals, but equity and morals differ in that the norms of equity have the full force of law.

The term *ẓedek* ("justice"), when used in Scripture as well as in Talmudic and post-Talmudic literature in connection with adjudication, has many and various meanings, which researchers and scholars have already dealt with.[306] Philosophers and scholars have also labored to define the term

305. The court here cited: Rema to Sh. Ar. ḤM 12:2; *Bayit Ḥadash* to *Tur* ḤM 12; Kitan v. Weiss, *supra* n. 283; and the discussion *supra* pp. 155–160. The *Marcus* case also discussed the standards for determining when the court will act *lifnim mi-shurat ha-din:* The court should weigh the severity of the consequences of the eviction against the adverse effects of not enforcing the specific statutory grounds for eviction in the particular circumstances; the court should also consider the statutory policy in favor of protection of the tenant and the fact that the policy is generally subject to the conditions expressly laid down in the statute, giving more weight to the interest of tenants of residential property than to the interest of commercial or industrial tenants.

306. For the meaning of the term *ẓedek* (justice) in the Bible, *see Enẓiklopedyah Mikra'it* [Encyclopaedia Biblica], VI, pp. 678ff., s.vv. Ẓedek, Ẓedakah, Ẓadik, particularly pp. 681ff., and bibliography there cited. *See also* M. Weinfeld, *Mishpat u-Ẓedakah be-Yisra'el u-va-Amim* [Law and Equity in Israel and among Other Peoples], Jerusalem, 1985.

"justice," both generally and with particular reference to jurisprudence.[307] In the framework of our discussion, we will point to two basic meanings of the term "justice" in Jewish law, as they are found in the teachings of the halakhic authorities.

1. "JUDGE YOUR NEIGHBOR FAIRLY"

One meaning of doing justice in adjudication relates to the method of conducting litigation and the procedure for administering the law. An example of this is found in the verse "Judge your neighbor fairly" (lit. "with justice"),[308] from which the Sages deduced, "One party should not sit while the other party stands; one party should not be permitted to speak at length while the other party is admonished to be brief."[309]

Maimonides summarized this meaning of a just adjudication as follows:[310]

> A judge is positively commanded to adjudicate justly, as it is said, "Judge your neighbor fairly." What is a just adjudication? It is treating both parties impartially in all respects. One party should not be permitted to speak at length while the other party is admonished to be brief. The judge should not speak softly and courteously to one party and harshly and irascibly to the other.
>
> If one of the parties is wearing expensive garments and the other is wearing shabby clothing, the judge must say to the well-dressed litigant: "Either dress him like yourself before the trial is held, or you dress like him, and when that has been done, the trial may proceed."
>
> One party should not sit while the other stands, but both should be standing. If the court wishes to permit both to sit, it may do so. But one should not occupy a higher seat than the other; they are to be seated side by side on the same level.

Later, Maimonides stated another rule, which is also included in the concept of doing justice:[311]

> It is forbidden to act as a judge for a friend, even though not a close or most intimate friend. It is also forbidden to act as a judge for a person whom one

307. *See* H. Perlman, *Al ha-Ẓedek* [On Justice] (Hebrew trans. from the French), Jerusalem, 1962, and bibliography there cited; K. Kahana Kagan, *The Case for Jewish Civil Law in the Jewish State,* London, 1960, pp. 71ff.; *id., Three Great Systems of Jurisprudence,* London, 1955, pp. 127ff.

308. Leviticus 19:15.

309. TB Shevu'ot 30a.

310. *MT,* Sanhedrin 21:1–3. *See also* Sh. Ar. ḤM 17:1; *Shakh, ad loc.,* subpar. 1; *Bayit Ḥadash* to *Tur, ad loc.; Or ha-Ḥayyim* to Deuteronomy 1:16 ("A judge should not encourage one party by demeanor expressing approval and avert his gaze from the other, but his demeanor should be impartial as he hears the case").

311. *MT,* Sanhedrin 23:6.

dislikes, even though the dislike is not to the point of enmity or wishing any harm. Both parties must be regarded and esteemed alike by the judges. Adjudication is most just when the judge is not acquainted with either party and has no knowledge of their past conduct.

This type of justice involves the *procedure* for hearing a case—the *method* of adjudication. The classic illustration of just adjudication in this sense is, in the language of the title of chapter 17 of the *Shulḥan Arukh,* "Both parties are to be treated alike in all respects." The goal of justice in this sense is to prevent any discrimination, and a just judge is one whose attitude to all of the parties is exactly the same.

2. JUSTICE AS A SUPPLEMENT TO LAW

A different meaning of the term "justice," which is concerned not only with the procedure for the application of the law but with the *actual* determination of the law itself, was found by some of the Sages in the verse "Justice, justice shall you pursue."[312] In the following *baraita,* these Sages noted the difference between this aspect of justice, and justice in the procedural sense:[313]

> Resh Lakish contrasted [two verses]: It is written, "Judge your neighbor fairly" [lit. "with justice"], and it is also written, "Justice, justice shall you pursue." How is this to be explained?[314]
>
> As was taught, the Torah states, "Justice, justice shall you pursue." One [mention of justice] refers to [a decision based on] law and the other to compromise.
>
> How so? When two boats sailing on a river meet, if both attempt to pass simultaneously, both will sink; but if one makes way for the other, both can pass. Similarly, when two camels meet each other on the heights of Bet Ḥoron,[315] if both proceed on their course, they will both fall, but if one makes way for the other [by going back until there is enough room to move to the side], they can pass [safely].

312. Deuteronomy 16:20.

313. TB Sanhedrin 32b.

314. In the first verse, the demand for justice is stated once, but in the second it is repeated: "Justice, justice shall you pursue." *See* Rashi, *ad loc.,* s.v. Be-ẓedek tishpot.

315. Bet Ḥoron is located in the mountains of western Samaria, on the border of the territory of the tribe of Ephraim, close to the territory of the tribe of Benjamin. It lies between two settlements, Upper Bet Ḥoron, atop the mountain, and Lower Bet Ḥoron, in the foothills. Both settlements are mentioned as early as in Joshua (16:3–5, 18:13–14) and are well known as sites of historic military events up to Israel's Six-Day War in 1967. They figured particularly in the wars of Joshua (Joshua 10:11). For details, *see* Z. Vilnay, *Ariel, An Encyclopaedia of the Land of Israel,* I (A-B), pp. 717–722, s.v. Bet Ḥoron. Ma'alot [Heights of] Bet Ḥoron, as the name implies, was a path on the mountain with a steep drop on each side. In ancient times, the path was extremely narrow, and two camels could not go abreast without danger that one would fall into the abyss.

> How should they act? If one is carrying a load, and the other is not, the one without the load should give way to the other; if one is nearer than the other, the nearer one should give way to the farther.[316] If both are equally near or far, place a compromise before them whereby payment is to be made for the privilege of going first.[317]

What is the law with regard to the right of passing in a narrow mountain passage where there is room for only one camel, and two camel drivers meet each other going in opposite directions? Who has priority? As we have seen, the *baraita* speaks of two types of solutions: One, when those who wish to pass each other are in different circumstances, *i.e.*, carrying or not carrying a load or at different distances, and the other, when the circumstances are the same or similar, *i.e.*, when both are equidistant and carrying a load. Each one of the two solutions fulfills the obligation of reaching a decision as a result of the pursuit of justice.[318]

The Talmudic commentators dealt with the nature of these two solutions and the element of justice in each of them. Their comments are of great interest in the study of our present subject. We will note, very briefly, two different basic approaches.

The first approach, found in the commentaries of Meir ha-Levi Abulafia[319] and Menahem Meiri,[320] is that when the circumstances of the camels are not the same, the law is that "the one from which less effort is required [in that it has less distance to travel], or which can more easily wait [because it is not carrying a load], must give way."[321] However, when the circumstances of both camels are the same, an attempt must be made to compromise.

What is the nature of this compromise? Some commentators do not discuss the substance of the compromise but only its outcome, *i.e.*, the one who obtains priority by means of the compromise must compensate the other.[322] The compromise itself is something "that strict law does not gov-

316. Some commentators interpret the terms "nearer" and "farther" as referring to the place of origin or destination. *See Bet ha-Beḥirah*, Sanhedrin 32b; *Perishah* to *Tur* ḤM 272:18. *Yad Ramah* (Sanhedrin, *ad loc.*, s.v. Tanya ẓedek ẓedek tirdof) explains: "This [camel] is close to the pass and this camel is not close to the pass," *i.e.*, the terms "nearer" and "farther" in the Talmud refer to the distance from the point where it is too narrow for both of them to pass. This interpretation seems more reasonable.

317. The passage quoted is also found in *Tosefta* Bava Kamma 2:10, with slight v.l.

318. *See Yad Ramah* and Rashi, Sanhedrin 32b.

319. *Yad Ramah, ad loc.*, s.v. Tanya ẓedek ẓedek tirdof.

320. *Bet ha-Beḥirah, ad loc.*, s.v. Yesh devarim.

321. *Yad Ramah, ad loc.; Bet ha-Beḥirah, ad loc.*, has: "The one who can better bear the delay must give way to the other."

322. Apparently, this is the interpretation of *Bet ha-Beḥirah* and also seems to be that of Rashi, *ad loc.*, s.v. Aval kera'ei: ". . . [One reference to] justice [*ẓedek*] is for your law and

ern. Therefore, one must attempt to arrive at the most appropriate solution to obligate one of the parties to do through compromise and superior character what the law does not require."[323] At the same time, compromise also has an element of principled decision and does not depend merely on the good will of the parties: "whoever pays more will pass first."[324]

A fundamentally different approach is taken in the commentaries of two leading *aḥaronim,* one from the middle of the seventeenth century and the other much closer to our own time. Abraham Ḥayyim Schor, the author of *Torat Ḥayyim,*[325] at the beginning of his comments, focused on the nature of the query in the *baraita:* "How so?" (*I.e.,* What are examples of compromise?) Shor asked: "But did we not already know what is law and what is compromise?" His response to this question was:[326]

> One may say that the obligation to pursue [justice] rests on the judge, *i.e.,* that the Torah instructs the judge *to persevere and achieve a compromise even if a party objects,* just as the Torah directs that adjudication take place notwithstanding the wishes of the defendant.
>
> One may ask: This may be true of law, but can this be said of compromise, which does not depend on the judge, since he does not have the power to achieve a compromise unless both parties agree?
>
> It is therefore stated: "How so? When two boats. . . ." The meaning of the verse is that when the law cannot solve the problem, since the law cannot distinguish between them (such as where both are equally near or far or both are equally weighed down), there is no alternative but to make a compromise between them. In such a circumstance, Scripture directed the judge to persevere in arriving at a compromise, and made it incumbent on the judge to estimate how much one should compensate the other for giving way. If one of them agrees to accept compensation, so much the better; but if not, the judge should cast a lot between them to determine which one will take compensation and give way.

The position of the author of *Torat Ḥayyim* is that the pursuit of justice by way of compromise, in circumstances such as the one here discussed, where it is impossible to reach a decision on the basis of strict law, is expressed in terms of a duty placed on the judge to propose a compromise by

---

the other is for your compromise *as you deem appropriate,* and you should not pursue the one more than the other."

323. *Bet ha-Beḥirah, ad loc.*

324. *Yad Ramah, ad loc.*

325. Schor, who served as president of the rabbinical courts in Belz and Satanov in Poland, also wrote *Ẓon Kodashim* on the Order of Kodashim. He died in 1632 (*see* D. Halaḥmi, *Ḥakhmei Yisra'el* [The Sages of Israel, Rabbinical Biographies], 1980, pp. 60–61).

326. *Torat Ḥayyim,* Sanhedrin 32b, s.v. Eḥad le-din ve-eḥad li-fesharah.

determining the amount of compensation to be given to the party who relinquishes his right to pass first on the ascent to Bet Ḥoron and *to enforce this recommendation* through the casting of a lot between the parties if neither party is prepared to give up his claim to go first.[327] In such a situation, justice requires that a compromise be imposed on the parties, and the compromise is thus a part of the law under the circumstances.

A point of departure similar to that of the *Torat Ḥayyim* is taken by Naphtali Ẓevi Judah Berlin (Neẓiv), a halakhic master of the late nineteenth and early twentieth centuries; but his comments are even more far-reaching from the standpoint of both the meaning of the Talmudic discussion itself and the conclusions to be drawn from it. Neẓiv[328] dealt with the elements of adjudication and of the legal process, namely, truth, law, and peace, which are set forth by the prophet Zechariah[329] ("Render true and perfect justice [*mishpat shalom* (lit. "judgment of peace")] in your gates"), by the *mishnah* in Tractate *Avot*[330] ("The world exists on the basis of three things: law, truth, and peace"), and by the comment on this *mishnah* in the Jerusalem Talmud[331] ("When there is law, there will be truth and peace"). Neẓiv continued:

> But if the law cannot bring about peace, there *must* be a compromise. This is what is taught in Tractate *Sanhedrin:* "'Justice, justice shall you pursue'—one [mention of justice] refers to [a decision based on] law, and the other to compromise. How so? When two boats. . . ."
>
> There is a difficulty here. Why the question, "How so?" Do we not know what a compromise is? However, the point is that a directive to compromise can refer only to a situation where the compromise is imposed. For in the case of every compromise made with the consent of the parties, they certainly are confident of the arbitrators' impartiality; and if the parties have no concern about this, they accept any loss voluntarily, so no Biblical command is necessary. Thus, the verse must refer to a situation where a compromise is

327. *See also* the ensuing discussion in *Torat Ḥayyim:* "And this is why the formulation is, 'Place a compromise before them,' and not, 'Make a compromise between them,' because the judge does not have the power to force either of them to accept compensation and give up his right of passage. Instead, the judge must estimate the amount that would constitute adequate compensation and suggest the compromise to the parties, who will reach an agreed settlement or cast a lot to determine which of them should receive the compensation." This is a most instructive ruling. Since it is a compromise, the judge does not force his opinion on the parties but presents to them his estimate of the appropriate compensation. If the parties cannot agree as to which one will waive his right of way, the judge should cast a lot and thereby compel the parties to accept his proposal and thus solve the impasse.

328. *Resp. Meshiv Davar,* III, #10. Both *Torat Ḥayyim* and *Resp. Meshiv Davar* are quoted in R. Margaliot, *Margaliot ha-Yam* to Sanhedrin 32b.

329. Zechariah 8:16.

330. M Avot 1:18.

331. TJ Megillah 3:6, 26a (3:7, 74b).

> imposed and it is impossible to decide the case on the basis of the law. Consequently, the *tanna* asks, "How is a compromise imposed?" He then explains, "When two boats. . . ." There is no basis in the law upon which to force the camel without a load to be destroyed; but under the law, both may proceed and both will perish, or one of them will overcome the other and be saved at the other's expense.
>
> But this is not a judgment of peace. This is why there is a mandate not to apply strict law, but to force a compromise.
>
> This seems to be what the Sages had in mind when they said in chapter *Ha-Po'alim*[332] that the Temple was destroyed because, when disputes arose, they insisted on the strict law of the Torah, *i.e.*, they refused to waive their legal rights in the interest of peace when only compromise can bring about peace, because the strict law cannot do so.

Law that does not bring about peace is not proper and desirable law, for the very definition and essence of law is to produce a judgment that resolves a dispute peaceably (*mishpat shalom*). Pursuit of justice in such a case requires the compulsion of a peaceful result by way of "compromise." In Neẓiv's view, the law is that even when one camel is carrying a load and the other is not, the one with the load has no claim for priority over the other, since each has an equal right to pass; and the greater loss that one of them will incur on account of the delay in reaching its destination does not constitute a consideration that under the law gives it the right to go first.[333] However, since the result of insisting on legal rights is strife and contentiousness between the parties, a peaceful "compromise" is compelled. When one is carrying a load and the other is not, the one that will suffer a greater loss by waiting is given priority; and when both are carrying loads, one pays the other for the privilege of going first.[334] According to Neẓiv,

332. TB Bava Meẓi'a 88a. *See also id.* 30b.

333. As we have seen, according to *Yad Ramah* and *Bet ha-Beḥirah*, in the case of a loaded camel and an unloaded one, the one likely to suffer the greater loss actually has a *legal* right to go first. *See also infra* n. 334.

334. Neẓiv apparently interprets the phrase in the *baraita*, "one [mention of justice] refers to [a decision based on] law and the other to compromise," as referring to two separate verses: "Judge your neighbor fairly" for decision according to law, and "Justice, justice shall you pursue" for compromise. The repetition of "justice" (*ẓedek*) in the second verse relates to each of two situations, *i.e.*, one where the factual circumstances of the parties are equivalent and the other where they are not. *Yad Ramah*, Sanhedrin *32b*, also gives such an explanation as his first interpretation: "One refers to law—'Judge your neighbor fairly'. . . . And the other to compromise—'Justice, justice shall you pursue'. . . ."

Yad Ramah's explanation of this interpretation is interesting:

> The reason why justice is mentioned only once with regard to a decision based on law, but twice with regard to compromise, is that to decide according to law requires less consideration and perspicacity; all that has to be done is to decide the case according to the *Halakhah*, and there is less reason to fear that a mistake will be made. Compromise, however, requires more consideration, investigation, and careful discre-

both the principle favoring the party who will suffer the greater loss when the situation of each party is different and the principle that one party will pay the other for the privilege of going first when each would suffer equally by waiting are based on the obligation to do justice—an obligation which supplements the law when the law, alone and unaided, cannot bring about peace.[335]

The concept of justice contained in the verse "Justice, justice shall you pursue" is thus different in its nature and goal from the justice referred to in the verse "Judge your neighbor fairly" (lit. "with justice"). The pursuit of justice in the sense contemplated by the first-quoted verse focuses on a change in *the substance of the decision* and not merely on *the procedure for reaching the decision.* According to the commentaries of Abulafia and Meiri, when it is impossible to decide under the law (*i.e.,* when both parties are in the same situation and their losses would be equal), *justice* requires that the dispute be resolved through compromise, namely, payment of compensation by the one who is accorded the right to go first. The *Torat Ḥayyim* takes the view that in such circumstances, on the strength of the obligation to do justice, the "compromise" by payment of compensation to the one who lets the other go first is *imposed* by the casting of lots. According to Neẓiv, the rule of "compromise" that favors the party likely to suffer the greater loss when there is a dispute over the right to go first is based on the duty to pursue justice. It is not based on strict law, because the strict law does not accord any relevance to the comparative losses likely to be suffered. Consequently, in the view of *Torat Ḥayyim* and Neẓiv, "compromise" in this instance has a meaning different from the usual and accepted meaning of the term: compromise in the generally accepted use of the term is not *imposed;* its implementation depends on the consent of the parties. However, in a situation such as the one here discussed, where strict law is

---

tion to establish which of the parties is telling the truth and which should be made to bear the heavier burden.

Neẓiv's statement, *supra* p. 173, "There is no basis in the law upon which to force the camel without a load to be destroyed," is problematic; when the unloaded camel yields the right of way to the loaded one, the unloaded one is not destroyed.

335. From a wider perspective, the question here discussed involves the policy guidelines for decision making in Jewish law. Thus, for example, the verse in Proverbs, "Her ways are pleasant ways and all her paths, peaceful," is such a guideline (*see infra* p. 387 n. 375 and accompanying text; *Digest of the Responsa Literature of Spain and North Africa, supra* n. 270 at Introduction, pp. 24–25). So is the concern that the law should seek to prevent enmity (*see infra* pp. 628–630, 1715–1716). Similarly, a fundamental principle for Neẓiv is the desire that the law bring about peace. What is noteworthy in the instance here discussed is that Neẓiv saw the verse requiring *justice* to be done and pursued as the source for changing the strict legal norm (lit. changing "the depth of the law").

ineffective and incomplete, "compromise" *is imposed* in order to enable the judges to do and pursue justice.[336]

3. JUSTICE AS A PRIMARY NORM

The principle of justice was used by the halakhic authorities as a primary legal norm in all cases where Jewish law recognized the possibility of judicial decision on a basis other than the accepted rules of Jewish law. As we have seen, the Jewish legal system gives effect to legal rules of other legal systems through the doctrine of *dina de-malkhuta dina.*[337] However, this recognition is subject to the qualification that the legal rule of the non-Jewish system must not contravene the principles of justice and equity basic to Jewish law. Thus, a legal rule of another system is not given effect when it is discriminatory and does not apply equally to all residents of the country,[338] or inflicts collective punishment, or punishes one person for the transgressions of another:

> In regard to such situations, Abraham, our father (may he rest in peace), said to God, "Far be it from You to do such a thing, to bring death upon the innocent as well as the guilty, so that the innocent and the guilty fare alike. Far be it from you! Shall not the Judge of all the earth do justice?"[339]

To punish one person for the transgression of another, even if a rule of a non-Jewish legal system provides for such punishment, is inconsistent with the very idea of "law," which, in the Jewish legal system, is founded upon justice; the Jewish legal system therefore does not recognize such a rule. The halakhic authorities established a similar doctrine with regard to communal enactments. In our discussion of that extensive subject,[340] we

336. It should be pointed out that the law is settled to the effect that once litigants agree to compromise their dispute, the role of the courts of the Jewish legal system in fashioning the terms of the compromise is governed by detailed provisions purely legal in nature. "Even compromise requires making a considered decision" (TJ Sanhedrin 1:1). "Just as [a judge] is admonished not to pervert the law, he is also warned not to fashion a compromise unfairly favoring one party over the other" (Sh. Ar. ḤM 12:2). Moreover, if one of the parties is denied the opportunity to present his arguments fully, even if the judge is perfectly well acquainted with the facts of the case and aware of all the arguments that party wishes to make, the decision with respect to compromise is null and void (*Resp. Leḥem Rav* #87, by Abraham di Boton, a halakhic authority in Salonika in the sixteenth century). For a detailed discussion of the nature of compromise in Jewish law, *see* Sobol v. Goldman, 33(i) *P.D.* 789, 799ff. (1979); M. Elon, EJ, V, pp. 857–859, s.v. Compromise (reprinted in *Principles*, pp. 570–573). *See also Yad Ramah*'s remarks on law and compromise, *supra* n. 334.

337. *See supra* pp. 64–74.

338. Maimonides, *MT,* Gezelah va-Avedah 5:14; *see supra* p. 72.

339. *Resp. Ribash ha-Ḥadashot* #9, quoting Genesis 18:25. For details, *see supra* pp. 72–73.

340. *See infra* pp. 678ff.

shall learn that the community has the authority to enact civil, criminal, and public legislation containing provisions contrary to the existing rules of Jewish law, but these enactments may not violate the general principles of justice and equity in Jewish law. Consequently, the halakhic authorities invalidated retroactive enactments, enactments arbitrarily discriminating among the community's members, enactments subverting sound administrative procedures (such as an enactment eliminating the position of comptroller of communal affairs), and enactments arbitrarily infringing basic minority rights, *e.g.*, by taxing the poor, or imposing double taxation on the rich.[341] The same approach was taken to the king's law and to law based on custom: their validity was made subject to the principles of equity and justice basic to Jewish law.[342]

The halakhic authorities thus established the principles of justice and equity in Jewish law as primary norms that determined the substance of judicial decisions—principles to which all other rules were required to yield, however legally valid such rules might otherwise be. In essence, this was the basic concept in the case of the narrow mountain passage where the commandment "Justice, justice shall you pursue" overcomes the strict law even if that law is Jewish law. *A fortiori,* when the source of a legal rule is a foreign legal system, the rule is subordinate to the principles of justice and equity basic to Jewish law.

4. LAW AND EQUITY—RULE AND DISCRETION

The relationship between law and justice also involves another topic, ordinarily referred to in the writings of jurists and legal philosophers as "law and equity." This subject deals with the situation where a legal rule is generally appropriate but, in the particular circumstances of an individual case, turns out to be unfair and inappropriate. Such cases will inevitably occur because the essential characteristic of a legal norm is its generality. The legal norm aims at doing justice in the general run of circumstances, and therefore it is almost a natural corollary that there will be some cases where the norm will not produce a just result.

The problem is that the very idea of a legal norm involves an inherent inconsistency: a legal norm achieves justice, but only by and large—which necessarily means that it causes injustice in some cases to certain individuals. The question, then, is whether it is possible within the framework of the legal norm (*i.e.,* as a part of the binding force of the legal norm itself) to prevent this injustice in individual cases, and if so, how? The one who most keenly feels the tension of this inconsistency is the presiding judge

341. For details, *see infra* pp. 760–777.
342. *See supra* pp. 55–57 and *infra* pp. 942–944.

who directly encounters the litigant caught between the pressures of the generality of legal rules, on the one hand, and the demand of justice for a fair result in the individual case, on the other. What may a court do, and what should judges properly do, when presented with a case in which a decision applying a law aimed at a general situation would result in injustice, and yet any ruling the judge makes will itself establish a norm with legal consequences?

Philosophers and jurists have disagreed on this problem from ancient times. One view is that only the legislature may relieve injustice to individuals resulting from the unfairness of legal rules in particular cases. According to this view, judges may not bend the law to make it more equitable in hard cases; they may only apply the law as it stands. Others take the opposite view and hold that a judge does have authority to avoid injustice to an individual in a particular case. Still others developed a separate judicial system designed to do equity to individuals to whom the rigid application of general rules of law would be unfair; and in the course of time the two systems of law and equity tended to merge so that the same judges administered both law and equity, with law subordinate to equitable principles.[343]

The different approaches are grounded on two legitimate and vital objectives common to all legal systems. First, two fundamental qualities of every legal system are uniformity and stability, which are reflected in the generality of legal rules and in the predictability of the way they operate. Secondly, the goal of every proper and legitimate adjudication, the very soul of the law, is to do justice in each individual case presented for adjudication. These two objectives seem, at first blush, to conflict whenever the generality of the law would lead to an unjust result in a particular case. The question is, Which objective should be given priority in the unusual case where there seems to be such a conflict, or can they both be satisfied by striking a proper

343. A rich and extensive literature exists on this subject, which is discussed in all the basic studies of jurisprudence. *See* R.A. Newman, *Equity and Law: A Comparative Study,* New York, 1961; *id.,* "The Hidden Equity," 19 *Hastings L.J.* 147 (1967); *id.,* "Equity in Comparative Law," 17 *Int. and Comp. L.Q.* 807 (1968); A. Ross, *On Law and Justice,* London, 1958; H. Perlman, *Al ha-Ẓedek* [On Justice] (Hebrew translation from the French), Jerusalem, 1962, particularly pp. 63ff.; D. Even, "Samkhuto ha-Tevu'ah shel Bet ha-Mishpat: Makor le-Sa'adei Yosher" [The Inherent Authority of the Court: A Source for Equitable Relief], *Mishpatim,* VII (1976), pp. 490ff.; S. Rosenthal, "Al Derekh ha-Rov" [On the Way of the Majority], *Perakim, The Schocken Institute for Judaic Research Annual,* I, 1967–1968, pp. 183ff.; S. Rosenberg, "Ve-Shuv al Derekh ha-Rov" [More About the Way of the Majority], *Sefer Manhigut Ruḥanit be-Yisra'el, Morashah ve-Ya'ad* [The Book of Spiritual Leadership in Israel—Tradition and Objective], ed. A. Belfor, 1982, pp. 87ff.; A. Kirschenbaum, *Equity in Jewish Law: Halakhic Perspectives in Law,* Ketav/Yeshiva University Press, New York, 1991; H. Shein, "Al Derekh ha-Rov—Maḥaloket Medummah?" [On the Way of the Majority—A Pseudo-Controversy?], *Da'at,* 1984, pp. 55ff. *See also infra* n. 360, regarding Justice Silberg's position on this subject.

balance between the requisite generality of law and the requirement of flexibility in individual cases? A recent decision of the Supreme Court of Israel contains an instructive discussion of this issue, in which various points of view were expressed that are also found in general jurisprudence and are reflected in the stance of Jewish law.[344]

The case[345] concerned an individual who became an apprentice to a lawyer, with a view to being certified as an attorney. During his second year of apprenticeship, he transferred to another preceptor but failed to notify the Bar Association office of the transfer. It was undisputed that he served as an apprentice for the full second year and that the failure to notify was inadvertent and without any fraudulent intent. However, the Association refused to give any credit for the applicant's second year of apprenticeship and relied on its well-established regulation that no credit was to be given for any period of apprenticeship before the receipt of the notice. Generally, this regulation is fair; it serves the purpose of enabling the association to investigate whether the applicant did in fact serve an apprenticeship with a particular lawyer. However, in this case, when it was clear that he did so serve for a full year with the second preceptor, and that his failure to notify the association was due solely to oversight, the refusal to recognize his apprenticeship and to certify him as an attorney caused him serious loss of time and money.

The Supreme Court did not set aside the Association's action in this case. However, prior to the judgment, the Association had amended its regulation so as to permit notice to be effective if received within three months, rather than fifteen days, of the actual commencement of the apprenticeship. In its decision, the court recommended that the Association further amend the regulation to confer discretion to grant, where appropriate, a complete waiver of any delay in giving notice.

A concurring opinion discussed this question as follows:[346]

> It is accepted that a legal provision, by its very nature, prescribes standards and fixed measures, and that we may not and cannot challenge it even if a particular case falls short of the required standard or measure and even if we believe, and correctly, that an injustice has thereby been caused to a particular person because something took place one day early or one day late or involved either a lesser or a greater weight than the law requires. This is the nature of law, which establishes general standards that sometimes do not do justice in a particular case; and this is the character of legal norms, which aspire to do justice in the majority of cases but cannot succeed in every case.

344. For earlier cases on this question, *see* Ben Shaḥar v. Maḥlev, 27(ii) *P.D.* 449 (1973), and 28(ii) *P.D.* 89 (1974), and the cases there cited. *See also* D. Even, *supra* n. 343.

345. Minẓer v. Central Committee of Israel Bar Association, 36(ii) *P.D.* 1 (1982).

346. *Id.* at 13ff. (Elon, J., concurring).

This is well known and is one of the enigmas of legal philosophy. The scholar C.K. Allen has this to say on the subject:[347]

> But there are many circumstances in which, though the lot of the individual litigant seems hard, it is neither possible nor desirable to abrogate the general rule. It is impracticable to avoid such unfortunate incidents without abandoning uniformity in favour of mere caprice. In such circumstances, the law and lawyers often have to bear hard words. Too frequently, the layman, loud in his condemnation of "flagrant injustice," will not attempt to look beyond the particular to the general, which it is exactly the business of the lawyer to do, and which must be done by somebody, if society is to maintain its discipline. Repeatedly, law is denounced in the same manner as the whole science of surgery might be denounced because a single patient died under the knife. It must be admitted—and it is a source of genuine regret to every lawyer who respects his profession—that the law, like surgery, "loses" a certain number of patients; but its instrument is not, as some seem to think, that of the butcher, but of the healer.

Truly, not a joyful vision!

The opinion then outlines the position of Jewish law on this subject:

The approach of Jewish law to this subject of standards and measures, and of law and justice, is instructive. . . . Standards and measures, which are an essential feature pervading all aspects of the law, are certainly part of Jewish law, which clearly and unequivocally sets them forth. We find this in the teaching of the Sages, where the matter is most clearly emphasized in the well-known story about R. Jeremiah:[348] "A fledgling bird that is found within fifty cubits [of a dovecote] belongs to the owner of the dovecote; [if it is found] beyond fifty cubits, it belongs to its finder. . . . R. Jeremiah asked: 'What is the law if one foot [of the bird] is within fifty cubits and the other foot is beyond fifty cubits?' On account of this, they excluded R. Jeremiah from the study-hall" ["for he caused them bothersome annoyance"—Rashi]. Why was that necessary? Because: "This is the character of all measurements established by the Sages. A ritual bath must contain forty *se'ah* of water to be fit for immersion; if it contains forty *se'ah* less one *kurtov* [a very small liquid measure], it cannot be used for immersion."[349]

However, this basic approach of Jewish law to the need for fixed and stable standards and measures generally, did not prevent the law from requiring judges to search for a suitable solution for the exceptional case, should such a solution be required by justice and reason. This demand on the judge is cogently and succinctly expressed in the definition of the duty of the judge,

347. C.K. Allen, *Law in the Making,* Oxford, 1964 (7th ed.), pp. 385–386.
348. TB Bava Batra 23b.
349. TB Ketubbot 104a.

that it is incumbent upon him to give "a judgment that is completely and truly correct" [lit. "a true judgment to its very truth"].[350] What is "a true judgment to its very truth"? Is there something true that is not true "to its very truth"? . . . [351] On this, Elijah, the Gaon of Vilna, made an additional point:

> Judges must also be experts in worldly matters so that they do not rule erroneously; for if they are not expert in such matters, then even if they are expert in Torah law, the result will not be "a completely and truly correct" judgment; *i.e.*, even if the judge renders a true judgment, it will not be so in the fullest sense of truth. . . . Therefore the judge must be an expert in both fields . . . , namely, wise in the matters of Torah, and . . . astute with regard to worldly affairs.[352]

The Sages coined the expression "a judge can rule only in accordance with what his eyes see."[353] What is the nature of this "seeing of the eyes"? "That he must strive to apply the law both justly [lit. "in its justice"] and truly [lit. "in its truth"]."[354] Consider the matter carefully, for that is the way to reach a judgment that is completely and truly correct.

There should be no apprehension that the softening of the strictness of the law, in special cases where it is appropriate, will be detrimental to the stability of legal norms in their character as standards and measures. For in Jewish law, the exercise of discretion to judge *lifnim mi-shurat ha-din* is also a judicial determination that is subject to many rules and constraints, and the judge may not exercise his discretion except within that framework. . . .

This approach to adjudication is based on the perspective of Jewish law as to the relationship between law and morals, as to standing on the strict law and acting *lifnim mi-shurat ha-din,* and as to the nature of law and of the world in which the law is employed. This approach requires that when demanded by circumstances of the case and the times, all these strands be interwoven in the act of adjudication. To return to the words of C.K. Allen quoted above, it is indeed possible that the layman will be "loud in his condemnation of 'flagrant injustice,'" for he has not learned "to look beyond the particular to the general." But the full force of the condemnation is the "silent" heritage of all jurists, and even more so the heritage of the judge sitting in judgment, for the flagrant injustice being done to the litigant before him confounds his outlook on the nature and essence of rendering a just judgment.

350. TB Shabbat 10a; Sanhedrin 7a.

351. Here the opinion quotes the comment of Joshua Falk, the author of *Derishah,* quoted *supra* p. 159, to the effect that a judgment that stands on strict law, rather than adjudicating *lifnim mi-shurat ha-din* when the times and the case so require, is "a true judgment" but not "a true judgment to its very truth."

352. Commentary of Elijah, Gaon of Vilna, to Proverbs 6:4 (*Mikra'ot Gedolot,* Pardes).

353. TB Sanhedrin 6b.

354. Rashi, Sanhedrin 6b, s.v. Ella.

> There is nothing in the placid statement that this flagrant injustice constitutes "a source of genuine regret to every lawyer who respects his profession" that can minimize the injustice being done to the individual; and this sentiment is not even a small consolation for the lawyer or judge, trained as he may be "to look beyond the particular to the general." If the art of surgery and the rendering of a judgment can be fairly compared, it seems that the opposite conclusion should be reached, for the surgeon does not "lose" a number of patients, Heaven forbid, in order to uphold some purpose transcending successful surgery on his patient, to whom he owes the legal and ethical duty to do all in his power to heal.[355] It seems that the approach of Jewish law toward arriving at a judgment can bring us to a happier prospect, and perhaps can also save particular litigants, at whose door the hazard of flagrant injustice threatens, from being "lost" during the process of adjudication.[356]

This method of reaching decisions as it concerns the subject of equity and law—which is a part of the general subject of the relationship of justice and law in the Jewish legal system—is anchored, according to many halakhic authorities, in the basic nature of decision making and law-determination in Jewish law generally, and is part of the inherent jurisdiction of the court. As appears from the language of the *Derishah* previously quoted,[357] the judicial duty to go beyond the strict law and to rule on occasion *lifnim mi-shurat ha-din* in order to arrive at a judgment "true to its very truth" is based on the doctrine that the *Halakhah* is entrusted to the Sages and the halakhic authorities in each generation. This doctrine is based on verses in Deuteronomy,[358] and was put by the Sages into the form of an aphorism: "Even if they say that right is left and left is right, you must obey them."[359] The nature and extent of this delegation to the halakhic authorities is treated at length in Chapter 7.[360]

355. *See infra* p. 252 n. 56 for Maimonides' opinion that judgment must be based on law of general applicability and cannot be compared to the practice of medicine, which is directed solely to the particular patient the physician is treating. For aspects of this question as arising from the *Minzer* case, *see further* I. Englard, "The Example of Medicine in Law and Equity on a Methodological Analogy in Classical and Jewish Thought," 5 *Oxford Journal of Legal Studies* 238 (1985).

356. The court's recommendation that the general rule be amended to provide that in every case the Bar Association be given the discretionary power, even beyond the three-month period, to recognize the period of apprenticeship in special circumstances such as in the case in question, has not yet been implemented.

357. *See supra* p. 159.

358. Deuteronomy 17:8 *et seq.*

359. *See infra* pp. 243–244.

360. To complete this discussion of the relation of justice, morals, and equity in Jewish law, note should be taken of the position of the late Justice M. Silberg in his book, *Talmudic Law and the Modern State*, pp. 61–92 (law and morals), and pp. 93–130 (law and equity). With all respect, Justice Silberg's classification and his substantive discussion of some of the

subjects he treats seems flawed. He classifies as part of the subject of law and equity such matters as "the Sages are displeased," "pious behavior" (*mishnat ḥasidut*), and others, which really should be classified under law and morals, especially in view of the fact that he himself distinguished between law and morals, on the one hand, and law and equity, on the other, and he devoted a separate chapter to each. Silberg's classification of *lifnim mi-shurat ha-din* as part of the subject of law and equity is also subject to the same criticism. Silberg does not discuss at all the development of *lifnim mi-shurat ha-din* into a legal principle. (As to such development, *see supra* pp. 155–159, discussing rulings in *Mordekhai, Bayit Ḥadash,* and *Derishah.*) He treats the principle only as it is discussed in various Talmudic passages, which treat it as a moral and religious rule, and on that basis it is not pertinent to the subject of law and equity.

On the other hand, Silberg includes under the heading of law and equity, according to the principle "Do what is right and good," the enactments relating to adjoining landowners and the perpetual redeemability of a debtor's land taken by a creditor in satisfaction of a debt. This, too, lacks precision. These two matters involve legislative enactments, the ultimate source of which is the overarching principle "Do what is right and good," which serves as a guiding legislative principle and is discussed in the present work in that proper context (*infra* pp. 623–628). Silberg's contention (p. 95) that doing what is right and good "is an obligating category of law, a category made obligatory by the Sages—without any formal *takkanah,*" because "we were not told by whom, where, and when [such an enactment] was established, nor was it [expressly] designated as a *takkanah*" (n. 8, *ad loc.*) is difficult to understand. The verse "Do what is right and good" (Deuteronomy 6:18) served the Sages as an overarching principle on various subjects and as a legislative principle; and the laws regarding adjoining landowners and the redeemability of a debtor's property were incorporated in the *Halakhah* as *enactments* of the Sages (*see infra* pp. 625–628). Apparently Silberg, too, was aware of the difficulty of his position, since he added: "The distinctions [*sic*] between this [*i.e.,* a law made obligatory by the Sages without any formal *takkanah*] and a *takkanah* enacted by the Sages is very subtle and it has not yet been fully explored" (p. 95). With respect, there is no distinction—what we are dealing with is *takkanot* enacted by the Sages.

One further note on the matter at hand: Silberg explained the close relationship of the legal and the moral elements of Jewish law in part on the basis that from the end of the tenth century C.E. and the beginning of the eleventh

> there is no longer Jewish self-governing authority in the Jewish street throughout the Jewish dispersion, except for certain meager concessions, limited and of little significance, granted from time to time by the local ruler. In this atmosphere, in the dark walls of the ghetto, without judges and police authority authorized by an agency of government, our national law continues to develop through only one factor: the free consent of the people (p. 85).

The internal discipline of the Jewish people undoubtedly did play a most important role in the practical application of Jewish law until the end of the eighteenth century (as has been extensively discussed, *supra* ch. 1). However, Silberg's description of the situation ignores the historical reality that the Jewish legal system operated as a living system in the areas of civil, criminal, and public law, enforced by sanctions, including imprisonment, as has already been demonstrated at length (*see id.*). Silberg's view of history was generally accepted in the past even among scholars engaged in Jewish legal research (who believed that that view was accurate for the entire period after the completion of the Talmud), but it will not withstand scrutiny. *See supra* pp. 14–18, 82–86. Jewish juridical autonomy, with its court system and all that was associated with it, and, as a result, the constant development of Jewish law as a living and operating legal system, continued until the end of the eighteenth century—until the Jewish Emancipation. The special relationship between law and morals in Jewish law is based primarily on the common source and intertwining of all parts of the

H. Good Faith (*Tom Lev*)

We conclude our discussion of the relationship between law and morals in Jewish law with an explication of the concept of good faith (*tom lev*).

The term *tom lev* ("purity of heart") appears in five places in the Bible.[361] Its literal meaning implies uprightness, integrity, and truth. In Genesis and in Kings, the Aramaic translation of Onkelos translates this term as "with truth of heart," and in Psalms the translation is "with blameless heart." The term "good faith" is a synonym for wholeheartedness, and thus it appears in I Kings 9:4: "If you walk before Me as your father David walked before Me, wholeheartedly and with uprightness, doing all that I have commanded you [and] keeping My laws and My rules. . . ."

The substantive content of the term *tom lev,* namely, equity, truth, and integrity, is indeed the same as the substantive content of the various other principles and concepts dealt with above in the discussion of the relationship between law and morals. However, while these other principles acquired well-understood and accepted forms of expression in Jewish law (*e.g.*, "fulfilling one's duty in the sight of Heaven" [*lazeit yedei shamayim*], "acting more generously than the law requires" [*lifnim mi-shurat ha-din*]), there is no distinct term in Talmudic literature specifically corresponding to "good faith."

In Israeli legislation, the concept of "good faith," together with an associated concept of "usual and customary practice," first appeared in the Sale Law, 1968,[362] and afterward in the Hire and Loan Law, 1971,[363] and in greater detail in the Contracts Law (General Part), 1973. Section 12 of the last cited statute states: "Contract negotiations must be conducted in the usual and customary manner and in good faith," and Section 39 states: "A contractual obligation shall be performed and a right arising out of a contract shall be exercised in the usual and customary manner and in good faith." Under Section 61(b) of the Contracts Law above referred to, this principle, "so far as appropriate and *mutatis mutandis,*" is applicable not only to contractual obligations and rights, but to legal transactions and obligations throughout the legal system, such as obligations imposed and rights conferred by law, compliance with rules of procedure, and perform-

---

Halakhah, as well as of *Halakhah* and *Aggadah,* as has already been extensively discussed. These, as well as other factors Silberg correctly points to, explain the close connection between law and morals in Jewish law. However, Silberg's attempt to explain the connection on the basis of lack of juridical autonomy from the tenth century C.E. onward is not consistent with historical reality.

361. Genesis 20:5, 6; I Kings 9:4; Psalms 78:72, 101:2.

362. Sec. 6.

363. Sec. 4.

ance of legal obligations and of transactions in the area of administrative law.[364]

The Israeli courts have had occasion to consider the definition and scope of the concept of good faith. As more fully explained below, some of the justices of the Supreme Court of Israel are of the opinion that all value-laden terms—such as public welfare, justice, and the like—are to be construed according to the basic world-view deeply rooted in the Jewish consciousness through the moral and cultural outlook of Jewish law.[365] This approach has led to the exposition of the concept of good faith in accordance with the basic ideas that have evolved in the Jewish legal system on the subject of law and morals. This was the position taken by the Supreme Court of Israel in one of the leading cases on the subject:[366]

> The basic element in the term "good faith" [in Jewish law] is therefore uprightness, or acting with full integrity;[367] and it constitutes an integral part of a norm of first rank in the *Halakhah,* expressed in such terms as "Do what is right and good" [Deuteronomy 6:18]. This overarching norm served as a guiding principle for the halakhic authorities, a kind of royal command throughout the realm of the *Halakhah.* The concept has been applied in either of two ways. At times, doing "what is right and good" is only a religious and moral requirement to act more generously than the law requires—an act of piety—not enforceable by law; and at other times it is the fountainhead for the creation of rules having full legal force, all depending on the circumstances and the matter. Thus, for example, the law giving a property owner the right of first refusal in the event of a sale of adjoining property entered Jewish law on the basis of this principle, because the Torah states: "Do what is right and good." The Sages said: "Since any sale is the same [to the seller, who is, by hypothesis, in the same position no matter who the buyer is], it is good and right that the adjoining owner, rather than someone more remote, should buy this property,"[368] and this law has full legal force.
>
> On the other hand, in the view of various halakhic authorities, this principle is the source for a moral duty, involving no legal consequences, to act in a manner not required by the law. [Naḥmanides expressed this view as follows]:

364. For details, *see* Amrani v. Rabbinical Court of Appeals, 37(ii) *P.D.* 1, 9–10 (1982).

365. For a summary of these opinions, *see* Roth v. Yeshufeh, 33(i) *P.D.* 617, 630–634 (1979).

366. *Id.* at 635. There was no dissent as to the point covered by the quoted portion of the majority opinion. *See also infra* pp. 1736, 1738–1739.

367. The Hebrew expression *tom lev* is thus defined in the dictionaries of Ben Yehuda and Even Shoshan: "In uprightness of heart, out of complete integrity and sincerity." G. Shalev expresses the idea nicely in her *Tenayot Petor be-Ḥozim* [Exculpatory Clauses in Contracts], p. 174 n. 24. For an additional Hebrew expression involving a similar use of the word *tom, see* the third Hebrew edition of the present work, p. 165 n. 367.

368. Maimonides, *MT,* Shekhenim 12:5. *See also infra* pp. 625–626.

> He [God] first says that you should obey His laws and precepts that He commanded you, and immediately afterward He says that even in regard to matters as to which He did not command you, you should be scrupulous to do what is right and good in His eyes [Deuteronomy 6:17–18] because He loves goodness and equity. This is a matter of great consequence. Inasmuch as it is impossible for the Torah to mention explicitly all the ways in which people relate to their neighbors and fellows and to cover all the types of business transactions and all the things necessary for the proper ordering of society and government, it mentioned a great many such things . . . and then stated generally that in all things one should do what is right and good. This is the basis for compromise (*pesharah*), for behaving more generously than the law requires (*lifnim mi-shurat ha-din*), and for what has been set forth in connection with giving a preemptive right to adjoining property owners. . . .[369]
>
> Elsewhere, Naḥmanides coined an apt and pointed term that illuminates the meaning of "doing what is right and good": A person who acts according to the technical and formal sense of the Torah's laws, *i.e.*, who carefully follows only the explicit rules but not those implicit from the general spirit of the text, is "a scoundrel within the bounds of the Torah" (*naval bi-reshut ha-Torah*). Therefore, "The Torah's method is to particularize and generalize; for after stating the specifics of the law relating to all dealings between men—you shall not steal, you shall not rob, you shall not cheat, and the other prohibitions—it states in general terms: 'Do what is right and good,' in order to establish an affirmative commandment to behave with uprightness and fairness and all that is involved in the concept of *lifnim mi-shurat ha-din*, for the good of one's fellow man."[370]

The Supreme Court opinion proceeds to quote Vidal of Tolosa (the author of the commentary *Maggid Mishneh* on Maimonides), quoted above,[371] who pointed out that some of the "detailed directives" that flow from the principle of "Do what is right and good" were made "binding law," while others were ethical precepts for "proper and pious behavior." This principle operated throughout the history of the Jewish legal system to produce one or another of these results.

The term *tom lev* should thus be given meaning by analogical reasoning from the basic ideas that infuse the various principles applicable to the relationship between law and morals in Jewish law. This type of exposition is familiar in Jewish law, as the opinion proceeds to demonstrate:[372]

369. Naḥmanides, *Commentary on Deuteronomy* 6:18. *See also* his *Commentary on Deuteronomy* 12:28.

370. *Id.* on Leviticus 19:2.

371. *Supra* pp. 159–160.

372. Roth v. Yeshufeh, *supra* n. 365 at 636.

The matter is summarized by Asher b. Jehiel (Asheri), a halakhic authority in Germany and Spain at the end of the thirteenth and the beginning of the fourteenth centuries, in one of his instructive responsa:[373]

> We see from all of these instances, that whenever anyone sought to fraudulently evade any prescription of the Sages and to scheme against his fellow, he was thwarted by the ingenuity of the Sages, who took action against him to frustrate his plan and nullify his evil design. And we shall draw inferences and reach conclusions by analogy from one case to another [*i.e.*, from the action taken by the Sages]. For the Sages of the Talmud were not able to specify everything that would happen in the future or all the new developments that would daily arise. Those who come after them follow in their footsteps and draw parallels from one case to another [when necessary to fashion new rules].[374]

After an analysis of the sources of Jewish law on the question of good faith, the opinion stated:

> What arises from this collection of sources is this: By incorporating the principle of good faith in Section 39 as an integral part of the general principle of "Do what is right and good" in Jewish law, the Legislature has given the judiciary a powerful instrument, and consequently also a great responsibility. This has two results: Sometimes the lack of good faith does not conform to "pious behavior" but has no legal effect, and the court has no enforcement power; at other times, the lack of good faith reaches a level where one must intercept the deceiver in his trickery and stand up against him "to frustrate his plan and nullify his evil design." The result depends on the particular issue and circumstances, and how one case compares with another.
>
> The court, in its use of the principle of "good faith," must act with the utmost care, in accordance with the circumstances of each case brought before it. On the one hand, when the conduct of a party constitutes the behavior of a "scoundrel within the bounds of the law," the court should compel the contractual obligation to be performed or the contractual right to be exercised in the usual and customary manner and in good faith. On the other hand, when the conduct of a party constitutes only a shortcoming in "pious behavior," the court should refrain from giving full legal force to the principle of good faith.
>
> The comments by Professor U. Yadin, who was in charge of legislative drafting for the Knesset, in his instructive article, "The Principle of Good Faith in the New Legislation,"[375] are correct and well stated. After considering other principles in Israeli legislation (such as the principle of justice, which

373. *Resp. Asheri* 78:3.

374. For further discussions of Asheri's responsum, *see* Elon, *Ḥerut,* pp. 125ff.; *infra* pp. 416–418 and pp. 1891–1894.

375. *Proceedings of Judges' Seminar,* Jerusalem, 1975, pp. 30ff., at p. 56.

also originates in the precept "Do what is right and good"), he concludes: "Thus the precept 'Do what is right and good' is a type of overarching doctrine above and beyond the principle of good faith. It gives a special character to the new Israeli law, and perhaps it constitutes a revival of Jewish law in its most exalted and sublime character."

As is true with regard to judicial recommendations for action *lifnim mi-shurat ha-din,* as well as with regard to other issues discussed in this chapter, the principle of good faith raises fundamental issues of the tension between stability and flexibility, between rule and discretion, and between predictability and uncertainty in the law. These issues are highlighted in another opinion in a case decided by the Supreme Court of Israel:[376]

> We have a paramount principle, namely, that the legal system cannot be nourished by the corpus of the law alone. The body of the legal system needs a soul, and sometimes even an "additional soul" [*neshamah yeterah* (a reference to the "additional soul" that tradition says Jews are endowed with on the sabbath)]. Such a soul can be found for the legal system in the form and guise of various value-laden norms, which are based on the primary principle of doing what is right and good. The principle of good faith is an important and special example of these value-laden norms. And if anyone should have misgivings that the operation of this value-laden norm will destroy legal stability, since there is as yet no measuring rod with which to correctly gauge the dimension of good faith, the answer to his fears is that this is the way of a legal system in which law, equity, and justice join together; and the net result, in the final analysis, is that the increase in the general stability of a legal system produced by the principle of good faith outweighs any possible damage to legal stability that may be caused in one or another specific case by the application of the principle of good faith.
>
> However, the standard of good faith is not meant to replace or to substitute for the legal standard. The legal system cannot exist with the instability that would result from imposing obligations never contemplated by the parties. . . . One may discern in the Jewish legal system, in which morals and law combine into a unique pattern of decision making,[377] the utmost care that the principle of good faith should not extend the limits of legal enforceability further than is desirable and practicable.[378]

Thus, the concept of good faith in Israeli law has not been extended to the point where it would be the basis for creating obligations in addition to those for which the parties had contracted. The good faith contemplated by the Contracts Law (General Part), 1973 is the doing of "right and good" to

376. Laserson v. Shikkun Ovedim, 38(ii) *P.D.* 237 (1984).
377. *See supra* pp. 141–167.
378. Laserson v. Shikkun Ovedim, *supra* n. 376 at 262ff. (Opinion of Elon, J.).

carry out the intent of the parties to the contract in accordance with the spirit of the obligation and not solely according to its technical and formal wording; but the principle of good faith does not create new obligations, not mentioned in the contract, which the parties had no intention of undertaking.[379] To extend the principle that far would mean that "even a person of good faith would never know what obligations he has undertaken and how far they extend."[380]

The proper scope of the principle of good faith in the law of contracts was well expressed by Professor R. Powell:[381]

> The common man, however much he may pray for miracles, does not really expect them to happen. If the judge gives him more than he expects, he can do so only by taking away more from the other party. To justify that action, he is driven to exaggerate the standards of conduct that can be expected from the parties. It could be said, perhaps, that that is necessary in order to protect the common man against the uncommon man—against the impersonal giant company, the tycoon, or even the criminal. Certainly, in England, the early chancellors may have felt constrained to resort to some higher level of conscience in order to protect petitioners against the overmighty subjects of those days. But this straining of morality is, to my mind, unnecessary. When I read of a lawyer trying to tread daintily in the china-shops of ethics, I wish that someone would lead him back into the streets where walk all manner of men. Plato wrote that "Good judges are those who have mixed with all sorts of people." And seeking the happy man among all sorts of people, I would be content with the common usages of the common man. In the Hebrew language there is a simple phrase that satisfies that requirement. It is *Derech Eretz*. It means the "way of the land," but it also means "good manners."[382]

The relationship between law and morals and between justice and equity constitute an important subject in Jewish law, as in every other legal system. Even those who view law solely as a technical discipline, as an instrument to attain practical social ends, to regulate daily activities, and to promote the stability of transactions, acknowledge that a legal system must perforce give attention to the issues of morals, justice, and equity, to which every civilized society must be sensitive. These issues have particular importance if the view is taken that law reflects the values of society and

379. *Id.*

380. *Id.* at 265. *See also* Roth v. Yeshufeh, *supra* n. 365 at 635–638.

381. Powell, "Good Faith in Contracts," 9 *Current Legal Problems* 16, 37–38 (1956), quoted in Laserson v. Shikkun Ovedim, *supra* n. 376 at 265–266.

382. For case law elaborating the concept "good faith," and the divergent opinions of the justices of the Supreme Court of Israel on the question, *see infra* p. 1734 n. 432 and pp. 1871–1874.

expresses the fundamental cultural and spiritual outlook of the society in which it functions.[383] This is the view of Jewish law, as the discussion in this chapter has sought to demonstrate.

383. On these various approaches, *see infra* pp. 1918–1920. The divergent opinions of the justices of the Supreme Court of Israel on the question of value-laden principles will be more fully discussed *infra* pp. 1736–1737, 1871–1874.

Chapter 5

THE ORAL LAW: DEFINITION AND GENERAL PRINCIPLES

I. The Concept of the Oral Law
II. The Antiquity of the Oral Law
  A. Noahide Laws
  B. Legal Practices Antedating the Sinaitic Revelation
    1. The Purchase of the Cave of Machpelah
    2. The Liability of a Paid Bailee
  C. Biblical Law Modifies Earlier Legal Practices
    1. Levirate Marriage—The Account of Judah and Tamar
    2. The Murderer Who Takes Hold of the Corners of the Altar
  D. The Oral Law Elucidates and Supplements the Written Law
III. *Divrei Kabbalah* ("Matters of Tradition")
IV. *Halakhah Le-Moshe Mi-Sinai* ("Law Given to Moses at Sinai")
V. Biblical Law (*De-Oraita*) and Rabbinic Law (*De-Rabbanan*)
  A. Classification into Biblical Law and Rabbinic Law
  B. Differences in Legal Consequences of Classification as Biblical or Rabbinic
    1. Leniency in Regard to Rabbinic Law
    2. "The Sages Gave Their Laws the Same Force as Biblical Law"
    3. "The Sages Gave Their Laws Greater Force than Biblical Law"
    4. Legal Enforcement of Rabbinic Laws
VI. Reduction of the Oral Law to Writing
  A. The Nature of the Prohibition Against Reduction to Writing and the Reasons Therefor
  B. Dating the Reduction of Talmudic Literature to Writing

I. THE CONCEPT OF THE ORAL LAW

The term "Oral Law" (*Torah she-be-al peh*) includes all of Jewish law that is not explicitly set forth in the Written Law, *i.e.*, in Scripture. Specifically, it includes all of the rules deriving from any of the legal sources[1] of the *Halakhah*. In its broadest sense, it includes not only Talmudic *Halakhah*, *i.e.*, the *Halakhah* found in the Mishnah, in the books of halakhic midrash, in the

1. As to the term "legal sources," *see* ch. 6.

Tosefta, in the *baraitot,* and in the two Talmuds—but also the entire corpus of the *Halakhah* in all its forms throughout its history.[2]

At the outset, it should be made clear that these concepts, "Written Law" and "Oral Law," are not the same as two apparently similar concepts similarly labeled in other legal systems. For example, Roman law uses the terms *jus scriptum* (written law) and *jus non scriptum* (unwritten law), which at first glance might seem to be the same as "Written Law" and "Oral Law" as used in the Jewish tradition. However, the term *jus non scriptum* refers to law that has its source in custom and has not been reduced to writing; it is sometimes equated with the idea of *jus naturale, i.e.,* law whose source is "in nature" and not in legislation or in authoritative decisions. Jewish "Oral Law" is different, in that it includes legislation, *i.e., takkanot* and *gezerot,* as well as laws that have been arrived at through the process of interpretation and similar methods; the only part of Jewish law not included in the "Oral Law" is the law explicitly written in Scripture. Therefore, the terms "Written Law" and "Oral Law" in the Jewish legal system are not really comparable to the "written law" and "unwritten law" of other legal systems.[3]

We find the term "Oral Law" as early as in the well-known incident involving Hillel and Shammai, who lived at the end of the first century B.C.E. and the beginning of the first century C.E.:

> A gentile once came to Shammai and asked, "How many Torahs do you have?" Shammai said to him, "Two—a Written Law and an Oral Law." The gentile responded, "I trust you with respect to the Written Law but I do not trust you with respect to the Oral Law. I wish to be converted on the understanding that you will teach me the Written Law." Shammai rebuked him and angrily sent him away. The gentile [then] came to Hillel, who agreed to convert him [on the gentile's terms]. On the first day he taught him the alphabet in correct order. The following day he taught him the alphabet in reverse order. The gentile said to him, "Did you not teach me differently yesterday?" Hillel responded, "Did you not put your trust in me [to learn the Written Law]? Depend on me also with regard to the Oral Law."[4]

2. "Law" in "Written Law" and "Oral Law" is the conventional and generally accepted English rendering for the Hebrew word *Torah,* but it is inaccurate and conveys less than the Hebrew. The Hebrew terms *Torah* and *Torah she-be-al peh* ("Oral Torah") encompass the entire universe of Judaism and not merely the normative *Halakhah, i.e.,* the "law"; *see also* Urbach, *The Sages,* pp. 286ff. Nevertheless, the terms "Written Law" and "Oral Law" are so entrenched in both lay and scholarly usage that they are used here.

3. *See* R.W. Lee, *The Elements of Roman Law,* pp. 37, 41; H.F. Jolowicz, *Historical Introduction to the Study of Roman Law,* p. 363; Salmond, p. 190; F. Schultz, *History of Legal Science,* pp. 73, 137.

4. TB Shabbat 31a. In *Avot de-R. Nathan* (1st version, ch. 15, p. 31a) the story is told somewhat differently. It does not involve a gentile, and the ending is "Just as you have accepted the one on faith, so accept also the other on faith."

Why was the term "Oral Law" used to designate virtually the entire corpus of the *Halakhah?* There are two reasons:

First, according to the beliefs of the halakhic authorities throughout history, the Oral Law was given to Moses at Sinai along with the Written Law, and included all of the "subtleties of Biblical exegesis, and the new interpretations of the *soferim* (scribes), and everything that the *soferim* would later establish."[5] The *Halakhah* is the manifestation of this law that was given orally to Moses at Sinai.

Secondly, the *Halakhah* was studied and transmitted orally from generation to generation, and up to a certain juncture it was forbidden to reduce it to writing for the purpose of public study.

Let us examine both of these explanations.

II. THE ANTIQUITY OF THE ORAL LAW

The doctrine that the Oral Law was given at Sinai is stated in the first *mishnah* in Tractate *Avot:*[6]

> Moses received the Torah[7] at Sinai and transmitted it to Joshua, Joshua transmitted it to the elders, the elders transmitted it to the prophets, and the prophets transmitted it to the men of the Great Assembly.

In the *Avot de-Rabbi Nathan* the chain is given in greater detail:

> The elders to the judges; the judges to the prophets; and the prophets to Haggai, Zechariah, and Malachi; and they transmitted it to the men of the Great Assembly.

The *mishnah* in *Avot* then lists the recipients of the tradition after the men of the Great Assembly: Simeon the Just, who was one of the last of the men of the Great Assembly; Antigonos of Sokho; the five *Zugot* ("pairs"); and the *tannaim.* In so doing, the *mishnah* points out the unbroken chain of Jewish tradition. In many statements, the halakhic authorities expressed their fundamental belief that divine revelation ("Torah from

5. TB Megillah 19b.

6. M Avot 1:1.

7. "Torah" here means both the Written Law (*Torah she-bi-khetav*) and the Oral Law. However, the reference may possibly be only to the Oral Law, because Deuteronomy 31:9 states with regard to the Written Law that "Moses wrote down this Torah and gave it to the priests . . . and to all the elders of Israel." *See also* H. Albeck's commentary to M Avot, *ad loc.*, his Introduction to Tractate Avot (p. 347), and his *Mavo la-Mishnah* [Introduction to the Mishnah] (hereinafter, *Mavo*), p. 24.

Heaven") includes not only the Written Law but the entire *Halakhah.* The verse "These are the laws, rules, and instructions (*torot*) [pl. of *torah*] the Lord established, through Moses on Mount Sinai, between Himself and the Israelite people"[8] was interpreted as follows: "'The *torot*'—this teaches that two Torahs were given to Israel, one written and the other oral; 'through Moses on Mount Sinai'—this teaches that the [entire] Torah, including its laws, its subtleties of exegesis, and its interpretations, was given to Moses at Sinai."[9]

The Sages thus recognized the distinction between that part of the Oral Law that has its basis in the personal transmission of the tradition extending back to God's revelation to Moses and that part of the Oral Law committed to the halakhic authorities to fashion and develop.[10] This recognition involved no conflict with the belief of the Sages that the Oral Law was given by God and that in every generation an additional part of what was revealed at Sinai is transformed from potential into actual and explicit law.[11]

The origin of the Oral Law in the Sinaitic Revelation is a matter of faith to the same extent as it is a basic tenet of faith that the Written Law is the product of Revelation. These two articles of faith are one in the teaching of the halakhic authorities and in Jewish belief: "Just as you have accepted the one [the Written Law] on faith, so accept also the other [the Oral Law] on faith."[12] Nevertheless, the existence of the Oral Law as a supplement to the Written Law can be ascertained by an examination of the Written Law itself. Such an examination will reveal a number of phenomena: the existence of legal practices before the Revelation that were confirmed and continued in the Torah; the existence of legal practices before the Revelation that were partly confirmed and partly nullified or changed by the Torah; and the inescapability of the conclusion that there was a structure of law

8. Leviticus 26:46.

9. *Sifra,* Beḥukkotai, sec. 2, 8:12.

10. *See infra* pp. 240–242.

11. *See infra* pp. 240–242. On this subject, *see* N. Krochmal, *Moreh Nevukhei ha-Zeman* [A Guide for the Perplexed of the Time], pp. 189–190; Z.H. Chajes, *The Student's Guide Through the Talmud,* ch. 3; Weiss, *Dor Dor ve-Doreshav,* I, pp. 9–10, 45; Ch. Tchernowitz, *Toledot ha-Halakhah* [History of the *Halakhah*], I, pp. 31, 67–123; Urbach, *The Sages,* pp. 286ff. The Sages particularly emphasized the importance of the Oral Law:

> R. Johanan said: The Holy One, blessed be He, made His covenant with Israel only for the sake of the Oral Law [*devarim she-be-al peh,* lit. "words that are oral"], as it is written (Exodus 34:27), "For in accordance with [Hebrew *al pi,* lit. "by the mouth of"] these commandments I make a covenant with you and with Israel" (TB Gittin 60b).

See infra pp. 233–234.

12. *Avot de-R. Nathan,* 1st version, ch. 15, p. 31a. *See also supra* n. 4.

that explains and completes the laws contained in the Written Law. Let us briefly examine these three phenomena.

A. Noahide Laws

Every society, in every stage of its life, adheres to certain fundamentals of a legal order; and it is clear that even at the very beginning, before the Torah was given, such legal norms existed in Jewish society.

This notion of fundamentals of a legal order appears in Jewish law in connection with the Noahide laws. A *baraita* states:[13]

> The Rabbis taught: Seven commandments were given to the descendants of Noah: [to establish] a legal order, [and to refrain from] blasphemy, idolatry, incest, bloodshed, robbery, and eating flesh of a live animal.

Thus, the social and moral life of human society before the Revelation at Sinai[14] followed many established norms.[15]

The concept of "a legal order," set forth as the first of the seven Noahide laws, is explained in various ways by the halakhic authorities. The following comments of Naḥmanides are typical:[16]

> In my opinion, the legal order enjoined upon the descendants of Noah in their seven commandments not only includes the requirement of maintaining judges in every district, but they were also given laws relating to theft, overreaching, extortion, the payment of wages, bailees, rape and seduction, torts and personal injuries, loans and commercial transactions, etc., corresponding to the laws that were given to Israel.[17]

Thus, the halakhic authorities have noted that the Written Law was not given in a legal vacuum, but was introduced into a particular legal environment.[18] By examining the Written Law, it is possible to ascertain the legal environment to which the Torah related in various ways.

13. TB Sanhedrin 56a.

14. That society is called "descendants of Noah" because everyone after the Flood was a "descendant of Noah."

15. For an explication of the Seven Noahide Commandments, *see* ET, III, pp. 348ff., s.v. Ben Noaḥ.

16. Naḥmanides, *Commentary on Genesis* 34:13.

17. Maimonides was of the opinion that the obligation to maintain judges in every district was the only requirement of the legal order that the first Noahide commandment mandated. Maimonides, *MT*, Melakhim 9:14.

18. The Talmudic Sages saw in the Noahide commandments a kind of universal natural law. *See, e.g.*, the view of Rashi, who found in the Noahide commandments a basis for acceptance of the doctrine of *dina de-malkhuta dina*, Gittin 9b, s.vv. Kesherin and Ḥuẓ mi-gittei nashim. *See also supra* p. 67 and *Resp. Ḥatam Sofer*, OḤ, #208, quoted *supra* p. 61 n. 37.

B. Legal Practices Antedating the Sinaitic Revelation

As early as the patriarchal period, the Torah speaks of doing right and justice and observing commandments and laws. With reference to Abraham, it is stated: "For I have singled him out, that he may instruct his children and his posterity to keep the way of the Lord by doing what is just and right, in order that the Lord may bring about for Abraham what He has promised him."[19] It is similarly stated: "Inasmuch as Abraham obeyed Me and kept My charge: My commandments, My laws, and My teachings."[20] According to the comment of Rashbam on the words "My laws and My teachings":[21]

> The plain meaning is that all laws consonant with human reason [*ha-miẓvot ha-nikarot*, lit. "the recognized laws"],[22] such as those concerning robbery, incest, covetousness, the establishment of a legal system, and the offering of hospitality, were observed before the Torah was given, but were renewed and explicated to Israel, which entered a covenant to observe them.[23]

Thus, the Jewish people accepted and followed many laws even before the Revelation at Sinai, and these were renewed and confirmed by the Torah, whose authority established them as binding.[24]

The existence of legal norms and institutions in the patriarchal period can also be seen from incidents in the lives of the patriarchs, such as the following two examples.

1. THE PURCHASE OF THE CAVE OF MACHPELAH

The Book of Genesis[25] tells of Abraham's detailed legal negotiations with the Hittites, and later with Ephron the Hittite, concerning the purchase of the cave of Machpelah. This incident sheds light on certain legal practices. The negotiations and the purchase were carried on in public at the gate of the city:

> So Ephron the Hittite answered Abraham in the hearing of the Hittites—all who entered the gate of his town . . . and Abraham bowed low before the people of the land (*am ha-areẓ*).[26]

19. Genesis 18:19.
20. *Id.* 26:5.
21. Rashbam on Genesis 26:5, s.v. Ḥukkotai ve-torotai.
22. This is the correct reading (*see* Rashbam, *Commentary on the Torah*, ed. David Rosin, Breslau, 1882, p. 29); and it means "the commandments for which the reasons are apparent," *i.e.*, rational commandments.
23. To similar effect, *see* Rashbam on Exodus 18:13, s.v. Lishpot et ha-am, and *Resp. Rema* #10.
24. On these observations of Rashbam, *see infra* p. 234.
25. Genesis 23:3–20.
26. *Id.* 23:10–12. For other interpretations of *am ha-areẓ, see* EJ, II, p. 833, s.v. Am ha-areẓ; Hertz, *Pentateuch and Haftorahs* (2d ed., 1977), pp. 80–81.

This is a practice that is familiar to us from the laws of other ancient peoples. Abraham, the purchaser, made an offer to Ephron and the Hittites, which they accepted. The field of Ephron became Abraham's after Abraham acquired it by paying money, which he counted out and put in Ephron's hands. Thus, from the incident of the purchase of the cave of Machpelah we can discern some of the methods by which property was acquired in that period. We can also deduce here that the property that Abraham purchased was described precisely and in detail:

> So Ephron's land in Machpelah, facing Mamre—the field with its cave and all the trees anywhere within the confines of that field—passed to Abraham as his possession. . . .[27]

The Sages based various legal rules on this incident. R. Judah Ha-Nasi based on this last verse the law that "the seller of a field must write a description of the field and its monuments and markers"; *i.e.*, the property that is being sold must be described in detail according to its various identifying characteristics.[28] An additional rule, as to what is included in a sale, was also supported by this verse.[29] Other Sages deduced from this incident general principles governing acquisition of property.[30]

2. THE LIABILITY OF A PAID BAILEE

An additional illustration is furnished by the argument between Jacob and Laban concerning the liability of a paid bailee.[31] Jacob argued that throughout all the years of his labor he compensated Laban for all damages sustained by the cattle in his charge, whether stolen by day or night, and even if killed by beasts: "That which was torn by beasts I never brought to you; I myself made good the loss; you exacted it of me, whether snatched by day or snatched by night."[32]

If we examine the section on the laws of bailees in the Torah, we may understand the legal implications of Jacob's words:

> When a man gives to another an ass, an ox, a sheep, or any other animal to guard, and it . . . was stolen from him, he shall make restitution to its owner.

27. Genesis 23:17.
28. *Midrash Rabbah,* Genesis, Ḥayyei Sarah, 58:11.
29. TB Bava Batra 69a/b.
30. TB Kiddushin 2a, 3a, 11b: *gamar kiḥah kiḥah mi-sedeh Efron* (we derive the meaning of "taking" from [the story of the purchase of] the field of Ephron). As to the purchase of the cave of Makhpelah generally, *see* E.Z. Melamed, "Keniyyat Me'arat ha-Makhpelah" [The Purchase of the Cave of Machpelah], *Tarbiz,* XIV (1943), pp. 11–18 and references cited; N. Leibowitz, *Studies in Bereshit* (Genesis), 3d rev. ed., 1976, pp. 207–213.
31. Genesis 31:1ff.
32. *Id.* 31:39.

> If it is torn by beasts, he shall bring it as evidence; he need not replace what has been torn by beasts.[33]

The Torah in its discussion of the paid bailee provides that such a bailee is liable for damage even if the animal was stolen from him, but he is not liable if the animal is torn by beasts; however, in such a case, he must produce as evidence those parts of the torn animal that he succeeded in saving.[34]

This rule that a bailee is not liable in the case of attack by a beast was operative even before the Torah was given, and Jacob therefore argued that not only in the case of robbery did he compensate Laban for the damage as the law required, but because of loyalty to Laban he acted more generously than the law required and compensated him even for torn animals.

The same legal rule is also found in the Code of Hammurabi in approximately the same period as the patriarchs:

> If a visitation of a god happens to an animal fold or if a lion kills, the shepherd shall show himself innocent before the god and the owner of the fold shall bear the loss.[35]

The exemption of a bailee from liability in the event of *force majeure* is thus an ancient legal rule that the Torah endorsed and adopted, and which thus became accepted as part of the Torah.

C. Biblical Law Modifies Earlier Legal Practices

We can also perceive through the Torah the existence of legal practices preceding the Revelation that were not accepted in their preexisting form but were modified by the Torah.

1. LEVIRATE MARRIAGE—THE ACCOUNT OF JUDAH AND TAMAR

From the account concerning Judah and Tamar,[36] it follows that the institution of levirate marriage existed before the Revelation. Judah's son,

33. Exodus 22:9–12.

34. This is the meaning of the words in Exodus 22:12, *yevi'ehu ed* ("he shall bring it as evidence"). *See also* Amos 3:12: "Thus said the Lord: As a shepherd rescues from the lion's jaws two shank bones or the tip of an ear . . ."; M.D. Cassuto, *Exodus* (Hebrew ed.), p. 200.

35. Laws of Hammurabi, par. 266. *See also* Cassuto, *supra* n. 34, and D.H. Müller, *Die Gesetze Hammurabis und ihr Verhältnis zur mosaischen Gesetzgebung sowie zu den XII Tafeln* [The Laws of Hammurabi and their Relationship to Mosaic Legislation and the Twelve Tables], pp. 68, 170–172.

36. Genesis 38:6–26.

Er, who was the husband of Tamar, had died. "Then Judah said to Onan: Join with your brother's wife and do your duty by her as a brother-in-law and provide offspring for your brother."[37] When Onan also died, Judah delayed the marriage of his daughter-in-law, Tamar, to his third son, Onan's younger brother Shelah, until Shelah matured; and when Shelah grew up and Judah did not give Tamar in marriage to him, Tamar disguised herself as a prostitute and became pregnant by Judah. When Judah was informed that his daughter-in-law—who, being a childless widow, was prohibited from marrying a stranger—had become pregnant by prostitution, he ordered: "Bring her out and let her be burned";[38] but when she demonstrated that Judah himself had made her pregnant, he vindicated Tamar, saying: "She is more in the right than I, inasmuch as I did not give her to my son Shelah."[39]

We learn from this episode that in that period the duty of levirate marriage fell first on the brothers of the deceased husband; and if there were no brothers, or if the brothers could not marry the deceased's widow, the duty of marriage was imposed on the father of the deceased husband. Therefore, when Judah learned that Tamar had become pregnant by him, he acknowledged that she had acted properly, inasmuch as he had not given her to Shelah, her husband's brother; he himself was therefore obligated to marry her, and consequently her child by him was not conceived in harlotry. Both the institution of levirate marriage and the rule that the father of the deceased husband may be obligated to marry his daughter-in-law are found in various ancient legal systems.[40] The Sages deduced from this episode that the institution of levirate marriage was practiced before the Revelation: "Judah had already fulfilled the requirement of levirate marriage [before the Torah was given]."[41]

The Torah approved the basic principle of levirate marriage,[42] but introduced a number of important changes. On the one hand, it limited levirate marriage to brothers of the deceased husband; the husband's father may not marry the widow: "When brothers dwell together and one of them

37. *Id.* 38:8.

38. *Id.* 38:24.

39. *Id.* 38:26.

40. *See* M. Segal, *Sefer ha-Zikkaron le-Gulak u-le-Klein* [Memorial Volume to Gulak and Klein], pp. 128–129.

41. *Genesis Rabbah*, Va-Yeshev, 85:6. *See also* the observation of Abraham, son of Maimonides, in the name of his father and grandfather, that in ancient times the custom was that all the relatives could perform the levirate duty. *See* R.S. Offenstein, *Sefer ha-Yovel la-Rambam, 700 Shanah le-Mitato* [Maimonides' Jubilee Volume: The Seven Hundredth Anniversary of His Death], 1908, p. 415; Naḥmanides, *Commentary on Genesis* 38:8 (tracing in detail the development of the levirate law from the customs before the revelation of the Torah through the law as established by the Torah).

42. Deuteronomy 25:5–10.

dies and leaves no son, the wife of the deceased shall not be married to a stranger outside the family. Her husband's brother shall unite with her and take her as his wife, performing the *levir*'s duty."[43] On the other hand, the Torah includes an additional provision enabling the widow to be released from the obligation of levirate marriage by means of *ḥaliẓah* (loosening of the shoe): "If the man does not want to marry his brother's widow, . . . his brother's widow shall go up to him in the presence of the elders, pull his shoe off his foot, and spit before him [lit. "in his face"] and declare: 'Thus shall be done to the man who will not build up his brother's house.'"[44] If the possibility of release by *ḥaliẓah* had existed at the time of Judah, he could have released Tamar and freed her, so that his failure to marry her to his son Shelah, or to marry her himself, would not have prevented her from remarrying.

2. THE MURDERER WHO TAKES HOLD OF THE CORNERS OF THE ALTAR

An additional illustration of a legal practice that the Torah changed is found in the verse "When a man schemes against another and kills him treacherously, you shall take him from My very altar to be put to death."[45]

The ending of the verse—"you shall take him from My very altar to be put to death"—can be understood only against the background of the accepted custom and practice of the time that presence in a holy place protected the murderer against the punishment prescribed by the law for his crime. The Torah abolished this practice and established that the holiness of the sanctuary does not have priority over the sanctity of human life.[46] The practice of holding on to the corners of the altar to escape judgment as a murderer is also evident in a later period from the incident in which David instructed Solomon to kill Joab, for "what he did to the two commanders of Israel's forces, Abner son of Ner and Amasa son of Jether: he killed them. . . ."[47] When news of this reached Joab, "Joab fled to the Tent of the Lord and grasped the horns of the altar."[48] In this way Joab hoped to save himself from death; but when Joab refused to leave the sanctuary, Solomon instructed Benaiah, son of Jehoiada, to kill Joab in the sanctuary because Joab had committed premeditated murder: "Thus the Lord will bring his [Joab's] bloodguilt down upon his own head because . . . he struck down

43. *Id.* 25:5.
44. *Id.* 25:7–9.
45. Exodus 21:14.
46. *See* Cassuto, *supra* n. 34 at 181–182, 188.
47. I Kings 2:5.
48. *Id.* 2:28.

with the sword two men more righteous and honorable than he."[49] In so doing, Solomon acted according to the law of the Torah and contrary to the preexisting practice.

We learn from the examples given—and additional ones can be adduced—that the Torah was not given in a legal vacuum; even before the Revelation, the people had legal norms that they observed. The Torah, which originated many new laws, sometimes adopted preexisting practices, supporting them with its own authority and sanctions, and sometimes prescribed specific modifications or even total abolition of preexisting practices.[50]

D. The Oral Law Elucidates and Supplements the Written Law

One may conclude from even a cursory examination that Biblical commandments and laws were accompanied by many explanations and detailed rules—given orally or preexisting in practice—which supplement and give meaning to what is written in the Torah. The following are a few illustrations.

With regard to the law of the Hebrew slave it is stated:[51]

> When you acquire a Hebrew slave, he shall serve six years; in the seventh year he shall be freed, without payment.

The basic intent of this and the ensuing verses is to limit the number of years of work and to establish the law applicable to a slave who enters his master's service either with or without a wife.[52] Scripture postulates that

49. *Id.* 2:32.

50. *See also* Weiss, *Dor Dor ve-Doreshav,* I, pp. 5ff; A.V. Aptowitzer, "Emdat ha-Ubar be-Dinei ha-Onshin Shel Yisra'el" [The Status of the Fetus in Jewish Criminal Law], *Sinai,* XI (1942), pp. 9, 13 n. 10; *Resp. Ribash* #328 (before the giving of the Torah, ownership of something not yet in existence could be transferred; only after the Torah was given did it become settled that such a conveyance could not be effective).

51. Exodus 21:2.

52. The Scriptural passage deals with two possibilities, namely, that the slave was married when he came into his master's service or that his master provided a wife for him. The text, however, does not indicate whether the slave has the right to bring his wife with him and obligate the master to maintain her or whether the master must agree before this can be done. *See also Mekhilta de-R. Ishmael,* Tractate De-Nezikin, sec. 1 (ed. Lauterbach, III, p. 9):

> "Then his wife shall go out with him" [Exodus 21:3]. R. Isaac says: "But who brought her in with him that Scripture should say she shall go out with him? Why then does Scripture say: 'Then his wife shall go out with him?' To tell us that the master is obligated to provide food for the wife of his slave. He must also provide food for the slave's children. For it is said: 'Then shall he go out from thee, he and his children

it is possible to acquire a Hebrew slave and that how to do so is known, even though the Torah itself gives no details as to how such a slave may be acquired.

Later in the same passage it is said:[53] "When a man sells his daughter as a slave, she shall not be freed as male slaves are," and also[54] "if he [the buyer] designated her for his son, he shall deal with her as is the practice with free maidens." What is "the practice with free maidens" to which the verse refers? Neither this verse nor any other part of the Torah explains the nature of this legal institution. It necessarily follows, therefore, that these were laws that were known and accepted by the people, and the Torah's provisions were additions and refinements.

Divorce is another illustration of the same point. The Torah states:[55]

> A man marries a woman and lives with her. She fails to please him, because he has found something obnoxious about her, and he writes her a bill of divorcement, hands it to her, and sends her away from his house. . . . [Then, if the woman marries a different man and that man divorces her or dies, her first husband] who divorced her first shall not take her to wife again.

The thrust of the passage is to prohibit remarriage to one's former wife after she has married someone else. The passage is premised on certain legal assumptions: that the woman was married to the first man; that he divorced her with a bill of divorcement, which he handed to her; and that she then married someone else. The Torah is silent as to any details concerning how marriage is effected, the nature of a bill of divorcement, etc. If no Oral Law existed to explain and give content to these legal institutions, it would have been impossible in practice to carry out the provisions that are stated in this Scriptural passage.

The Book of Deuteronomy provides still another illustration:[56]

> When there is a dispute between men and they go to law and a decision is rendered declaring the one in the right and the other in the wrong; if the guilty one is to be flogged, the judge shall have him lie down and be given lashes in his presence, by count, as his guilt warrants. He may be given up to forty lashes but not more, lest being flogged further, to excess, your brother be degraded before your eyes.

---

with him' [Leviticus 25:41]. From the law about the going out, you learn about the coming in."

53. Exodus 21:7.
54. *Id.* 21:9.
55. Deuteronomy 24:1–4.
56. *Id.* 25:1–3.

The point of this section is to teach us that if the accused is adjudged to undergo flogging, the rule is "He may be given up to forty lashes but not more." But when is a person to be sentenced to flogging? How does the court declare the one in the right and the other in the wrong? This, too, was necessarily law that was customary or transmitted orally, and the Torah builds on this law and merely complements it.

Finally, many commandments by their very nature require at least some explanation in order to understand their meaning and delineate their scope. For example, the prohibition of work on the sabbath is repeatedly stated in very general terms: "You shall not do any work,"[57] "And on the seventh day you shall cease from labor,"[58] etc.[59] But what manner of work is prohibited? The Torah lists only three: plowing, harvesting,[60] and the kindling of fire.[61] However, is there any logic to prohibiting only these forms of labor and not others that are similar and even more onerous? From the Torah itself we learn that these three forms of labor were not the only ones prohibited. The Book of Numbers states:[62]

> Once, when the Israelites were in the wilderness, they came upon a man gathering wood on the sabbath day. Those who found him as he was gathering wood brought him before Moses, Aaron, and the whole community. He was placed in custody, for it had not been specified what should be done to him.

Thus, the people that found the man knew that he was violating the sabbath, in that this was one of the forbidden labors, but they did not know what punishment was destined to be prescribed for him.

In short, the existence of oral laws necessarily follows from what is revealed by examination of the Written Law.[63] The undefined terms and

57. Exodus 20:10, and *see generally id.* 20:8–11.
58. *Id.* 23:12.
59. *E.g., id.* 16:22–26, 29–30; 31:12–17.
60. *Id.* 34:21.
61. *Id.* 35:3.
62. Numbers 15:32–34.
63. *See further* Maimonides' Introduction to his *Commentary on the Mishnah,* beginning with: "Know that every commandment which the Holy One, blessed be He, gave to Moses . . ." (ed. Kafaḥ, p. 1). *Kuzari,* Essay 3, 35ff. states:

> For the subject is broader than the [bare] words. . . . When [God] said to them [Exodus 12:2], "This month shall mark for you the beginning of the months," the people did not have any doubt whether He meant the months of the Egyptians (among whom they were living) or the months of the Chaldeans (who had been contemporaries of Abraham at Ur Kasdim), or solar months, or lunar months . . . ; or whether *zeviḥah* [the method of slaughtering an animal that makes it permissible as food] means slaughter by piercing or by some other method . . . ; or whether in Exodus 16:29, "Let no man leave his place on the seventh day," "his place" means his house, his courtyard, or his domain; or as to the definition of *melakhah* (work) that is prohibited on

vague references in the Written Law simply cannot be understood, and therefore the Written Law cannot be carried out, without the Oral Law, which provides the necessary explanation and complementation.[64]

III. *DIVREI KABBALAH* ("MATTERS OF TRADITION")

In connection with the first reason for the term "Oral Law," *i.e.*, that the *Halakhah* is the manifestation of the law given orally to Moses at Sinai, we must examine the meaning of some additional terms. The first is the term *divrei kabbalah* (matters of tradition).

The Sages deduced many specific legal rules from the words of the Prophets and the Hagiographa (*Ketuvim*), which were called *divrei kabbalah*.[65] For example, from the verse in Jeremiah[66]—"Fields shall be purchased and deeds written and sealed and witnesses called . . ."—they deduced that signature of witnesses on a deed is required by Biblical law.[67]

> the sabbath. . . . Even what is explicitly stated in the Torah requires explanation; how much more so is this true where the Torah's language is obscure because they were relying completely on the Oral Law.

See further Hoffmann, *Commentary on Deuteronomy* 21:15–17, Part II, p. 419 (Hebrew ed.) ("The laws of succession are not given in the Torah in prescriptive form; Scripture rather assumed these laws to be familiar through usage or as a result of their status as settled law); *id.*, *Commentary on Leviticus*, pp. 3–8; H. Albeck, *Mavo*, pp. 3–4; *id.*, M Shabbat, Introduction, pp. 9–12; A.I. Kook, *Eder ha-Yekar*, pp. 42ff.

64. On *Halakhah* in Scripture, *see infra* pp. 1020–1027.

65. *See, e.g.*, M Ta'anit 2:1: "And in *kabbalah* it is stated: 'And rend your hearts rather than your garments,'" which is a reference to Joel 2:13. In TB Sotah 37a, the term *kabbalah* is applied to a verse in Psalms, and in Niddah 25a, to a verse in Job. *See also* Rashi, Bava Kamma 2b, s.v. Divrei kabbalah: "*Divrei kabbalah*, which are the Prophets and the Hagiographa."

The writings of the Prophets and the Hagiographa are called *divrei kabbalah* because "they have been a continuously accepted tradition from the days of Joshua" (*Maḥzor Vitry*, p. 462), and "because they all received their prophecy from Moses" (*Shittah Mekubbeẓet*, Bava Kamma 2b, s.v. Mi-divrei kabbalah, second explanation). Also interesting is the first explanation in *Shittah Mekubbeẓet*, according to which *divrei kabbalah* is the appropriate name for these writings "because the prophets complain [the Hebrew root of *kabbalah* (*kbl*) can also mean "complain"] and cry out against the calamities appearing to them in their visions." *See* ET, VII, pp. 106–107, s.v. Divrei kabbalah; W. Bacher, *Erkhei Midrash*, pp. 113–114, s.v. Kabbalah.

"Mysticism" is a very much later meaning of *kabbalah* or *divrei kabbalah*. *See* Bacher, *supra*. Another meaning that *kabbalah* acquired in the course of time is "the tradition transmitted orally from one person to another" (Maimonides, *MT*, Mamrim 1:2). *See also infra* p. 238. For the various meanings of *kabbalah* generally, *see Millon Ben-Yehudah* [Ben-Yehudah's Hebrew Dictionary], XI, pp. 5696–5704 and the editor's notes there.

66. Jeremiah 32:44.

67. TB Gittin 36a: "Witnesses sign the *get* (bill of divorcement) for reasons based upon public policy. [To which the query was raised:] Why talk of public policy? It [the require-

And from the verse in the Book of Ezra[68]—"Anyone who does not come in three days, as required by the officers and elders, will have his property confiscated and himself excluded from the congregation of the returning exiles"—they deduced the important principle of *hefker bet din hefker* (the court has the power to expropriate property),[69] which is basic to many areas of Jewish law.[70]

Later, when we discuss the authority of the Sages and of the subsequent halakhic authorities, it will be noted that in a number of connections the Babylonian Talmud states the additional principle that "statements from the non-Pentateuchal Scriptures are not a valid basis for determining the meaning of the text of the Torah" (*divrei Torah mi-divrei kabbalah lo yalfinan*).[71] It seems that this principle stems from a different approach taken by some of the Sages toward law transmitted by the prophets.[72] However, the fact that there are differences in approach concerning the nature of *divrei kabbalah* cannot change the fact, evident from Talmudic literature, that the words of the Prophets and the Hagiographa—*i.e.*, the non-Pentateuchal books of the Hebrew Bible—are sources from which various halakhic rules have been derived.

IV. *HALAKHAH LE-MOSHE MI-SINAI* ("LAW GIVEN TO MOSES AT SINAI")

An additional term whose meaning we must explore is *halakhah le-Moshe mi-Sinai* ("law given to Moses at Sinai"). This term is used in Talmudic literature to refer to a certain number of laws; and there are a number of other laws, not specifically so designated, but referred to in various other ways, that are also properly classifiable as *halakhah le-Moshe mi-Sinai*.[73] This

---

ment of witnesses' signature] is based on Scripture, for it is written (Jeremiah 32:44), 'and deeds written and sealed [the word for "and sealed" in Hebrew is *ve-ḥatom;* in the Talmud it means "and signed"].'" *See also infra* pp. 208–212, 220–221.

68. Ezra 10:8. Our translation differs from the JPS *Tanakh,* in the interest of greater consonance with the Talmudic understanding of the verse.

69. TB Yevamot 69b, Gittin 36b.

70. *See, e.g., infra* pp. 507–514 and 685–690. For additional examples, *see* ET, VII, pp. 110–114; A. Karlin, *Sinai,* XXIX (1941), pp. 141–145.

71. TB Bava Kamma 2b.

72. For a detailed discussion, *see* E.E. Urbach, "Halakhah u-Nevu'ah" [*Halakhah* and Prophecy], *Tarbiẓ,* XVIII (1947), pp. 12ff.

73. Such as *hilkheta gemiri* (an accepted or traditional rule); *halakhah; be-emet amru* (truly, they [the Sages] have said); and others. The Sages differed as to whether some of these terms are properly classifiable as *halakhah le-Moshe mi-Sinai; see* ET, IX, pp. 383–386, s.v. Halakhah le-Moshe mi-Sinai; J. Levinger, *Darkhei ha-Maḥashavah ha-Hilkhatit Shel ha-Rambam* [The Halakhic Methodology of Maimonides], pp. 52ff., 206–209.

category consists of a relatively small number of rules concerning such matters as standards of measurement (*shi'urim*) in connection with religious requirements or with ritual purity and impurity (such as the measure of an "olive-size" [*ke-zayit*] for solids or a "quarter" [*revi'it*] of a *log* for liquids), and various laws relating to the scroll of the Torah, phylacteries, *mezuzot*, ritual slaughter, the "corners" (*pe'ot*) of the field (the produce of which is to be left for the poor), tithes, torts, and crimes.[74]

The first question that naturally arises when considering *halakhah le-Moshe mi-Sinai* is: If the basic postulate of the entire Oral Law is that its principles and explanations were given at Sinai, why are only certain laws, and not others as well, referred to as "law given to Moses at Sinai"? The halakhic authorities and scholars have dealt at length with this question,[75] and we will review the solution formulated by Maimonides.

According to Maimonides,[76] "only those laws not hinted at or alluded to in Scripture and not deducible from the Biblical text by means of one of the authoritative canons of interpretation are labeled *halakhah le-Moshe mi-Sinai*"; and the term is further limited to those laws unanimously accepted by the Sages.[77] For example, the Torah states:[78] "On the first day [of the festival of *Sukkot*] you shall take the product of *hadar* trees (*peri eẓ hadar*)"; and the *Halakhah* then specifies that "the product of *hadar* trees" is the citron (*etrog*).[79] This explanation of "the product of *hadar* trees" was certainly given to Moses at Sinai; however, in Talmudic literature it is not designated as *halakhah le-Moshe mi-Sinai*, because its source and derivation is from the Torah itself and there was therefore no need to designate it specifically as being from Sinai. Laws classified as *halakhah le-Moshe mi-Sinai*, on the other hand, either have no source in Scripture, or their connection with Scripture is weak and tenuous; and since they are unanimously accepted, their authority is emphasized by designating them as *halakhah le-Moshe mi-Sinai*.

The Sages were well aware that it is not always possible to translate *halakhah le-Moshe mi-Sinai* literally as "law given to Moses at Sinai." Sometimes, they used this term even if they meant that only the basic principle

74. *See Resp. Ḥavvot Ya'ir* #192; ET, *supra* n. 73 at 365–387. For a complete list and a bibliography, *see* Levinger, *supra* n. 73 at 190–209.

75. *See Resp. Ḥavvot Ya'ir* #192; Z.H. Chajes, *Torat ha-Nevi'im*, ch. 4, *Ma'amar Torah She-be-al Peh* [Essay on the Oral Law]; Krochmal, *supra* n. 11 at 213; Frankel, *Mishnah*, p. 20; Weiss, *Dor Dor ve-Doreshav*, I, pp. 67ff.; Tchernowitz, *supra* n. 11, at 29–36; H. Albeck, *Mavo*, pp. 26–29; Y. Baer, "Ha-Yesodot ha-Historiyyim Shel ha-Halakhah" [The Historical Foundations of the *Halakhah*], *Zion*, XXVII, pp. 128–129.

76. Maimonides, Introduction to *Commentary on the Mishnah* (ed. Kafaḥ), p. 10.

77. *Id.* at 9–10.

78. Leviticus 23:40.

79. *Leviticus Rabbah* 30:15; TB Sukkah 35a. *See also* Maimonides, *supra* n. 76 at 9.

embodied in a particular rule was given to Moses at Sinai.[80] Moreover, sometimes the meaning of this term is only that a particular law is as clear and accepted as a law given to Moses at Sinai—"a matter as well settled as if given to Moses at Sinai"[81]—even though it actually originated later.

An instructive example of the nonliteral use of the expression is the law that requires the residents of Ammon and Moab to give the poor-tithe even during the sabbatical year. This rule is referred to in the Mishnah as *halakhah le-Moshe mi-Sinai.*[82] The basic rule imposing an obligation during ordinary years to give tithes from the produce grown in countries adjacent to the Land of Israel has its source in ancient legislation; and the additional *takkanah* that the residents of Ammon and Moab must give the poor-tithe even in the seventh year (and so provide sustenance to the poor of the neighboring Land of Israel, where there are no tithes of any kind during the sabbatical year) certainly cannot be attributed to a tradition going back to Moses. Nevertheless, the Sages described this law as "given to Moses at Sinai" because they wished to make clear that this law, although its source is a later enactment, is binding and indisputable to the same extent as if it had been given to Moses at Sinai.[83]

This sense of *halakhah le-Moshe mi-Sinai* was familiar to the Talmudic Sages themselves, as indicated by the following *aggadah:*[84]

> R. Judah said in the name of Rav: "When Moses went on high, he found the Lord sitting and fastening crownlets to the letters of the Torah. Moses said to Him, 'Master of the universe, why are you delaying [the giving of the Torah by taking the time to fasten the crownlets]?' God responded, 'There will be a man who will live many generations from now, whose name is Akiva, son of Joseph, who will deduce myriads of laws from every jot and tittle of every letter.' Moses said to God, 'Master of the universe, allow me to see him.' God replied, 'Turn around.' He [Moses] went and sat behind eight rows [of students] and did not understand what was being said, and he felt faint. But

80. M Eduyyot 8:7 and Maimonides' commentary, *ad loc.*, s.v. Lo nishma mi-Moshe.

81. *Piskei ha-Rosh,* Hilkhot Mikva'ot (end of Tractate Niddah) #1.

82. M Yadayim 4:3.

83. *See* commentary of Samson b. Abraham of Sens, M Yadayim 4:3, s.v. Halakhah le-Moshe mi-Sinai; Asheri, Commentary on M Yadayim 4:3, s.v. Halakhah le-Moshe mi-Sinai. What is interesting about this explanation of the term *halakhah le-Moshe mi-Sinai* is that the *mishnah* that is the subject of the explanation uses the term in a literal sense. What the *mishnah* says in *Yadayim* is this: "[R. Eliezer said,] 'I have received a tradition from Rabban Johanan b. Zakkai, who heard it from his teacher, and his teacher from his teacher, reaching back as far as a *halakhah le-Moshe mi-Sinai,* that Ammon and Moab must give the poor-tithe in the seventh year.'" Since what we know about when and how the poor-tithe in the sabbatical year was established makes it impossible to take R. Eliezer's statement literally, the statement is taken to mean that the matter is as clear as if it had been given to Moses at Sinai.

84. TB Menaḥot 29b.

when the discussion reached the question [of the source of the law], R. Akiva's students said to him, 'Rabbi, what is your authority?' R. Akiva answered, 'It is a law given to Moses at Sinai.' Then Moses was at ease."[85]

Moses himself was not familiar with the laws that were being discussed in the academy of R. Akiva; however, in spite of this, these laws were "given to Moses at Sinai," *i.e.*, they were affirmed and accepted as if given to Moses at Sinai.[86]

V. BIBLICAL LAW (*DE-ORAITA*) AND RABBINIC LAW (*DE-RABBANAN*)

Two additional terms essential to an understanding of the halakhic system are *de-oraita* (Biblical law, lit. "Torah law") and *de-rabbanan* (rabbinic law). All of the *Halakhah*, "religious" as well as "legal," is divided into two categories: (a) laws that are Biblical (in Aramaic—*de-oraita*),[87] and (b) laws that are rabbinic (in Aramaic—*de-rabbanan*), also sometimes referred to as "from the words of the Scribes" (*mi-divrei soferim*),[88] "their words," "rabbinic enactments," and the like.

85. This *aggadah* is further discussed *infra* p. 382.

86. In the field of *mishpat ivri*, as defined for our purposes (*see supra* p. 105), there are very few laws classified as *halakhah le-Moshe mi-Sinai;* and even as to those, there is dispute among the Sages as to whether they are properly so classified. In the law of torts, the payment of half the loss as compensation for damage caused by an animal kicking up pebbles as it goes along its way is designated in the Talmud as *hilkheta gemiri lah* (an accepted or traditional *halakhah*) (TB Bava Kamma 3b, 15b, 17b), which is explained by Rashi (*ad loc.*, 3b, s.v. Be-ḥaẓi nezek ẓerorot) as *halakhah le-Moshe mi-Sinai,* and by Maimonides (*MT*, Nizkei Mamon 2:3,7) as "from tradition" (*mi-pi ha-kabbalah*) or "which is a *halakhah*" (*she-hu halakhah*). *See also Resp. Ḥavvot Ya'ir* #192; *Kidmat ha-Emek,* Neẓiv's Preface to the *She'iltot,* ch. 1, subpars. 1–3 (to the effect that in the view of Maimonides this is not to be classified as *halakhah le-Moshe mi-Sinai*).

Another rule of tort law identified as a law given to Moses at Sinai is that "an eye for an eye" means monetary compensation; *see* Maimonides, *MT,* Ḥovel u-Mazzik 1:6. In connection with the criminal law, it is stated in TB Sanhedrin 53a: "The four methods of capital punishment by the court are derived by tradition (*gemara gemiri le-hu*)"; *see also* Maimonides, *MT,* Sanhedrin 14:1. The penalty of incarceration is classified by Rashi (Sanhedrin 81b, s.v. Ve-heikha remiza) as *halakhah le-Moshe mi-Sinai.* Other *rishonim* do not agree, and Rashi's position is problematic in light of TB Sanhedrin 82b. *See also* Elon, *Ma'asar,* p. 178 and n. 5.

87. At times, Biblical laws are also referred to as *divrei Torah* (words, or matters, of Torah) or *devar Torah* (a word, or matter, of Torah).

88. The term *mi-divrei soferim* is explained in the Talmud in two senses: (1) A matter essentially rooted in the written Torah but explained by the Oral Law (*e.g.*, TB Sanhedrin 88b: "R. Eleazar said in the name of R. Oshaia: 'He [the Sage who rejects the decision of the Sanhedrin] is liable only when the matter is one essentially rooted in the Torah but explained by *divrei soferim* . . . '"; and *see also* the continuation of that discussion); and (2)

A. Classification into Biblical Law and Rabbinic Law

Classification of halakhic rules as Biblical or rabbinic is not a simple matter; the halakhic authorities and scholars have struggled mightily with this subject.[89] Certainly, those laws that are explicit in the Torah are Biblical; laws that are clearly the product of legislation by the halakhic authorities are rabbinic.[90] This, however, is of little help in classifying laws that fall in the doubtful area between the two categories, such as laws whose source is *divrei kabbalah*[91] or which are *halakhah le-Moshe mi-Sinai.*[92]

A synonym for rabbinic law (*de-rabbanan*) (as in M Yevamot 2:4: "The [extension of the prohibition of incest from the first to the] second degree of consanguinity is *mi-divrei soferim," i.e.,* marriage to certain relatives, which would not constitute incest according to the Torah, was forbidden by the Sages as an extra safeguard; *see* TB Yevamot 20a). *See also* Maimonides, commentary on M Kelim 17:12:

> For all that does not emerge clearly from the language of the Torah is called *mi-divrei soferim,* including even matters that are *halakhah le-Moshe mi-Sinai,* for the term *mi-divrei soferim* means the tradition of the *soferim,* such as all the commentaries and *halakhot* traditionally harking back to Moses, as well as the legislation of the Scribes, such as all the *takkanot* and *gezerot. . . .*

Maimonides' use of the term *mi-divrei soferim* has occasioned much discussion, especially in connection with the rule that marriage is effected by the groom's giving money to the bride, which Maimonides characterizes as *mi-divrei soferim* (*MT,* Ishut 1:2), although it is in fact Biblical (*de-oraita*). *See Maggid Mishneh* and *Kesef Mishneh* to Maimonides, *ad loc.;* J. Neubauer, *Ha-Rambam al Divrei Soferim* [Maimonides on *Divrei Soferim*], Jerusalem, 1957; ET, VII, pp. 91ff., s.v. Divrei soferim. For a detailed and interesting discussion, *see* J. Levinger, *supra* n. 73 at 46ff. The usual and generally accepted meaning of *divrei soferim* is synonymous with *de-rabbanan.*

89. *See* Z.H. Chajes, *supra* n. 75; H. Albeck, *Mavo,* pp. 49–53; B. De Vries, *Toledot ha-Halakhah ha-Talmudit* [A History of Talmudic *Halakhah*], pp. 69–95; Herzog, *Institutions,* I, pp. 2–7.

90. *See infra* pp. 477–478.

91. *See supra* n. 67 and accompanying text, regarding the classification of the rule requiring signatures by the witnesses on a deed. *See also infra* p. 221, where *Resp. Radbaz,* I, #503 is quoted to the effect that a law derived from *divrei kabbalah* is rabbinic law.

92. *See supra* pp. 204–207. In TB Eruvin 4a it is stated:

> R. Ḥiyya b. Ashi said in the name of Rav: "*Halakhah le-Moshe mi-Sinai* includes [the laws relating to] *shi'urim* [standards of measurement in connection with religious requirements or with ritual purity and impurity]; interpositions [between the *mikveh* (ritual bath) water and the body of the bather that render the immersion invalid]; and [the dimensions of] partitions [necessary to create a private domain (*reshut ha-yaḥid*) and thus permit carrying within that enclosure on the sabbath]."

Thereupon, in the Talmudic discussion, the question is raised, "But surely *shi'urim* are Biblical, as it is written [Deuteronomy 8:8], 'A land of wheat and barley . . .'"; and the Talmud then proceeds to demonstrate how each of the species of foods mentioned in this verse is used as a standard of measurement. This discussion indicates that if a law is *de-oraita* it is not *halakhah le-Moshe mi-Sinai.* On the other hand, TB Sukkah 44a appears to reason that the very fact that taking the willow branch in the Sanctuary on the festival of *Sukkot* (Tabernacles) is *halakhah le-Moshe mi-Sinai* makes it Biblical and not rabbinic. *See also* Z.H.

Moreover, the definition of Biblical law is itself not sufficiently clear. What is the meaning of "laws that are explicit in the Torah?" Is a law considered Biblical if it is deduced from a verse in the Torah by one of the canons of interpretation?[93] And if so, is it invariably so? Two great halakhic authorities, Maimonides and Naḥmanides, were in fundamental disagreement on this question. Maimonides took the following position:[94]

> Not everything that is deduced by means of one of the thirteen canons of Biblical interpretation or by other interpretive methods that expand the text[95] can be considered Biblical. We have already explained at the beginning of our commentary on the Mishnah that most of the laws of the Torah are deduced by means of the thirteen canons of Biblical interpretation and that a law that is deduced by using these rules is sometimes the subject of disagreement. There are also settled laws for which support is found through one of the thirteen canons of interpretation but which are really elaborations based on oral tradition from Moses. . . . This being so, not every law that the Sages are said to have deduced by means of one of the thirteen canons can be said to have been told to Moses at Sinai.
>
> At the same time, however, it cannot be said that everything that the Talmudic Sages buttress by means of one of the thirteen canons is rabbinic, as it is possible that it is an elaboration based upon a universally accepted tradition. We therefore conclude: Anything not explicit in Scripture, but deduced in the Talmud by means of one of the thirteen canons, is *de-oraita* if the Talmudic Sages specifically so state or state that it is essentially Biblical. In such a case, it is entitled to Biblical status because the receivers of the tradition have stated it to be Biblical; but if they have not made a clear and specific statement designating the rule as Biblical, then it is considered *de-rabbanan,* since there is no verse that teaches it.

Maimonides, in other words, was of the view that even those laws deduced by means of the thirteen canons of Biblical interpretation should be considered rabbinic and not Biblical unless the interpretation is based on tradition dating back to Moses at Sinai and the Talmud states specifically that the rule is Biblical.

Naḥmanides, in his critical commentary on Maimonides' Book of the Commandments (*Sefer ha-Miẓvot*), disagreed with Maimonides and sub-

---

Chajes, *supra* n. 75; J. Levinger, *supra* n. 73 at 36. It should be borne in mind that at times the meaning of *halakhah le-Moshe mi-Sinai* is that the *halakhah* is as clear as if it had been given to Moses at Sinai. *See supra* p. 206.

93. *See infra* pp. 318–319.

94. *Sefer ha-Mizvot,* Second principle (trans. Kafaḥ, p. 11).

95. *See infra* p. 373.

stantiated his view with extensive references to Talmudic literature. He summarized as follows:[96]

> Thus, it is proper to say that just the opposite is true, *i.e.*, that every matter deduced in the Talmud by means of one of the thirteen canons is Biblical unless the Talmudic sages have specifically stated that the textual connection is *asmakhta* [lit. "something to lean on," *i.e.*, a supportive device].[97]

Thus, according to Naḥmanides, everything deduced by means of the thirteen canons of Biblical interpretation is regarded as Biblical; only where the Talmudic Sages have specifically stated with reference to a particular law that its Biblical derivation is merely *asmakhta* is the law considered rabbinic.

Most halakhic authorities accept the view of Naḥmanides that all laws deduced by means of the thirteen canons of Biblical interpretation are Biblical unless the Talmud specifically labels the exegesis as *asmakhta*.[98] However, even this view does not provide a completely accurate or comprehensive definition, because there are laws that are regarded as Biblical even though their connection to a verse of the Torah is by way of *asmakhta*,[99] and, in addition, there are many other laws classified as Biblical even though their legal source is not in Scriptural interpretation at all.[100]

The difference of opinion as to whether a law deduced from a verse in the Torah is classified as Biblical or rabbinic is not related to the important question of the nature of midrash (exegetical interpretation) in Jewish law, *i.e.*, whether midrash constitutes a creative legal source or whether its function is simply to validate and to integrate with a Scriptural verse an already existing law stemming from a different legal source.[101]

> Historical fact does not necessarily coincide with the conclusions to be drawn from the Talmud as to whether a particular law is Biblical or rabbinic. There are instances when the Sages proved a familiar law by Scriptural interpretation; and because they regarded the proof as conclusive, they determined the law to be Biblical. Yet, from the historical perspective, the law had been in effect well before discussion of its rationale and source. . . .[102] Also, a law that is stated to be rabbinic and for which a supportive Biblical verse is stated to

96. Naḥmanides, *Hassagot ha-Ramban al Sefer ha-Mizvot* [Critical Commentary on Maimonides' Book of the Commandments], ed. Pardes, p. 40 (end).

97. On the concept of *asmakhta* in interpretive exegesis, *see infra* pp. 300–305.

98. It is the general tendency of the halakhic authorities to construe Maimonides narrowly so that his views and those of Naḥmanides would not be basically different. *See Megillat Esther* and *Marganita Tava, Sefer ha-Mizvot,* p. 40; *Shakh,* Sh. Ar. ḤM 33, subpar. 1.

99. *See* examples in ET, II, pp. 105–106, s.v. Asmakhta.

100. *E.g.*, laws based on *sevarah* (legal reasoning) as their legal source; *see infra* pp. 988–990.

101. *See infra* pp. 283–286.

102. H. Albeck, *Mavo,* p. 50.

be an *asmakhta* may, in point of historical fact, have been enacted and prescribed by the rabbis because they found support for it in the Torah, and thus there was a connection between Scriptural interpretation and the law.[103]

In addition, if one follows the opinion of Maimonides, then even where a law was clearly created by means of Biblical interpretation, it is not regarded as "Biblical" unless the Talmud specifically so states. Thus, classification of a law as "Biblical" or "rabbinic" is not an indication of how far back that particular law dates. A law designated as "rabbinic" may be an ancient enactment, while a law designated as "Biblical" (according to Naḥmanides' view, for example, because it is deduced from a verse in the Torah) may be a later development.

The halakhic authorities in various periods were uncertain whether to designate various important laws as "Biblical" or "rabbinic." The legal institution of the *ketubbah* (marriage contract), according to Rabban Simeon b. Gamaliel, is Biblical, but according to the other Sages, it is rabbinic.[104] Rabban Simeon b. Gamaliel and R. Meir took the view that the law that a husband inherits from his wife is Biblical, while R. Eleazar's opinion was to the contrary, *i.e.*, that the husband's right of inheritance is rabbinic.[105] Similarly, the *tannaim* disagreed as to whether the obligation of a husband to support his wife is Biblical or rabbinic.[106]

Such disagreements were particularly frequent in the period of the *amoraim*. Thus, they disagreed as to whether acquisition of property by *meshikhah* ("pulling," or taking possession) is a Biblical rule or a rabbinic enactment,[107] as to whether the law requiring the return of a lost object when there are no witnesses but the object has identifying marks is Biblical or rabbinic,[108] and as to the Biblical or rabbinic character of many other laws. In the post-Talmudic period, classification of laws as Biblical or rabbinic continued to be a subject of disagreement among the halakhic authorities, with regard both to laws as to which the question had already been discussed in the Talmud[109] and laws as to which the point had not been dealt with in the Talmud but was being raised as a fresh question.[110]

103. *Id.* at 52, and *see also id.* at 53.

104. TB Ketubbot 10a, and *see* discussion there. *See also id.* 110b. In TJ Ketubbot 13:11, 72a (13:11, 36b), the opinions are recorded differently. *See infra* n. 120.

105. TB Ketubbot 83a *et seq.* (also explaining that Rav's view was that the husband's right of inheritance is rabbinic); TB Bekhorot 52b.

106. TB Ketubbot 47b. This difference of opinion persisted in post-Talmudic times. *See infra* pp. 570–571.

107. TB Bava Meẓi'a 47b. *See also infra* pp. 297–298.

108. TB Bava Meẓi'a 27a *et seq.* *See also infra* pp. 298–300.

109. *E.g.*, the obligation to support one's wife. *See supra* n. 106.

110. *See, e.g.*, on the question of whether acquisition by putting a mark (*sitomta*) on a barrel of wine (*see infra* pp. 914–915, for a discussion of this mode of acquisition) is Biblical

To summarize: When seeking to classify a law in the Jewish legal system as "Biblical" or "rabbinic," we do not have completely clear and all-inclusive principles. In addition, classification is not assisted by inquiry into legal history; and, conversely, classification of a law as "Biblical" or "rabbinic" does not itself indicate when the law came into being. Even scrutiny of the legal sources of a particular law will not always be helpful. The only way to determine whether any particular law is Biblical or rabbinic is to examine both Talmudic and post-Talmudic literature to see how that law was categorized and classified in the writings of the Talmudic Sages and of the post-Talmudic halakhic authorities.

B. Differences in Legal Consequences of Classification as Biblical or Rabbinic

Whether a law is classified as Biblical or rabbinic makes for important differences in legal consequences in all parts of the *Halakhah.* The following sections discuss some of these distinctions, particularly as they concern the area of *mishpat ivri.*[111]

1. LENIENCY IN REGARD TO RABBINIC LAW

A basic distinction between Biblical and rabbinic law is the tendency to strictness with regard to Biblical law and to leniency with regard to rabbinic law. This distinction comes into play mainly when there is doubt as to what the law is. In such cases, the principle was established that "all cases of doubt as to a Biblical law are resolved in favor of the stringent result; all cases of doubt as to a rabbinic law are resolved in favor of the lenient result."[112] Similarly, if a doubt arises as to the resolution of a dispute among the Sages as to a particular law, the principle was established: "If it is a matter of Biblical law, follow the more stringent opinion; and if it is rabbinic law, follow the more lenient."[113]

Sometimes, the tendency to be lenient with regard to rabbinic law was not confined to cases where there was doubt as to what the law was, but extended even to cases where the law was clear. The Sages would prescribe certain leniencies in the application of such a law, whenever they saw a

---

or rabbinic, *Kesef ha-Kodashim,* commentary on Sh. Ar. ḤM 201, subpar. 1. There are a great many such instances.

111. For definition of *mishpat ivri, see supra* p. 105. As to the consequences of whether a matter of *issur* ("ritual" or "religious" law) is Biblical or rabbinic, *see* ET, II, pp. 74–75, s.v. Issur de-oraita, and pp. 76–77, s.v. Issur de-rabbanan.

112. TB Beẓah 3b.

113. TB Avodah Zarah 7a.

need to do so, in consideration of the fact that the law was rabbinic. Let us consider one example. The *Tosefta* says:

> If one produces . . . a promissory note that states it was written in Babylonia, he collects in Babylonian money. If the note states that it was written in the Land of Israel, he collects in money of the Land of Israel.[114]

The case concerns a note that requires payment in a certain coin that is used in both Babylonia and Israel. However, in one of the places the value of the coin is greater than in the other, and the note is presented for payment in the country other than where it was made. The question arises, According to the value of which coin should the note be paid—the value of the coin where the obligation was entered into, *i.e.*, the place of making of the note, or the value of the coin at the place of payment? The principle set down in the *baraita* is that the place of the making of the note, where the obligation arose, is determinative.[115]

The same question was debated in connection with the payment of the *ketubbah:*[116]

> If a man marries a woman in the Land of Israel and divorces her there, he pays [her *ketubbah*] according to the money of the Land of Israel. If he marries a woman in the Land of Israel and divorces her in Cappadocia,[117] he pays her according to the money of the Land of Israel. If he marries a woman in Cappadocia and divorces her in the Land of Israel, he pays her according to the money of the Land of Israel. Rabban Simeon b. Gamaliel says: He pays her according to the money of Cappadocia.

In the discussion in the Babylonian Talmud,[118] the objection is raised that the opinion of the first *tanna* (*tanna kamma*) contains an inherent contradiction: in his opinion, a man who marries a woman in the Land of Israel and divorces her in Cappadocia must pay the *ketubbah* according to the money of the Land of Israel. Thus, his opinion is that the place where the

114. *Tosefta* Ketubbot 12:6 (ms. Erfurt, ch. 13) and *Tosefta* Bava Batra 11:3, following the reading in TB Ketubbot 110b.

115. Toward the end of the *baraita* an additional rule is stated: If the note does not indicate the place where it was made, the face amount should be paid according to the value of the coin in the place where the note is presented for payment. Halakhic authorities differ as to the rationale for this ruling. For a fuller discussion, *see* M. Elon, EJ, V, pp. 882–890, s.v. Conflict of laws (reprinted in *Principles*, pp. 715–723).

116. M Ketubbot 13:11. *See also Tosefta* Ketubbot and Bava Batra, *supra* n. 114.

117. A country in Asia Minor, famous in the Middle East for its mintage of coins. *See* S. Lieberman, *Tosefta ki-Feshutah*, Ketubbot, p. 389. The value of Cappadocian money was higher than that of money of the Land of Israel. *See also infra* n. 120.

118. TB Ketubbot 110b.

obligation arose is determinative. That being so, why in the reverse situation does he state that one who marries a woman in Cappadocia and divorces her in the Land of Israel also pays her according to the money of the Land of Israel? Was not Cappadocia the place where the obligation arose?

The Talmud answers:

> Rava states: "This law concerns one of the lenient aspects of the *ketubbah;* he [the first *tanna*] is of the opinion that the *ketubbah* is rabbinic in origin."

In other words, since the Sages held that the institution of the *ketubbah,* which imposed various obligations on the husband, is rabbinic, they established a lenient rule and permitted the husband in every case to pay according to the less valuable money; in such a case the place of the obligation is not determinative.

However, Rabban Simeon b. Gamaliel disagreed with the first *tanna* and held that if one marries a woman in Cappadocia and divorces her in the Land of Israel, he must pay the *ketubbah* according to the more valuable money of Cappadocia; Rabban Simeon b. Gamaliel regarded the *ketubbah* as being the same as any other promissory note, and he would always make the place where the obligation arose determinative. The reason is that "in his opinion the *ketubbah* is Biblical in origin."[119] He therefore saw no reason to be lenient to the husband with regard to collection of the *ketubbah,* since according to his view the law applicable to the *ketubbah* is no different from the law applicable to any other promissory note.[120]

2. "THE SAGES GAVE THEIR LAWS THE SAME FORCE AS BIBLICAL LAW"

The Sages prescribed leniencies with respect to rabbinic law, even where there was no doubt as to what the law was, only if they saw a particular need to do so;[121] however, as a general rule the Sages gave to a law enacted by them the same legal consequences as those of a Biblical law. The general principle is, "All that was enacted by the Sages was enacted to have

119. *Id.*

120. In TJ Ketubbot 13:11, 72a (13:11, 36b), the views of the Sages are reported as being the reverse of those reported in TB. According to TJ, the value of coinage in the Land of Israel was higher than that of Cappadocian coinage, and it was the majority of the Sages, and not Rabban Simeon b. Gamaliel, who held that rights conferred upon a woman by her *ketubbah* are of Biblical origin; therefore, the Sages were careful always to award her payment according to the worth of the more valuable currency, namely, that of the Land of Israel, even if the marriage had taken place in Cappadocia.

121. For social and economic reasons, a number of leniencies toward the husband were prescribed with regard to the collection of the *ketubbah.* It was, for example, assumed that "more than the man wants to marry, the woman wants to be married," TB Ketubbot 86a; *see also* Rashbam, Bava Batra 132b, s.v. U-mi-kulei ketubbah shanu kan.

the same effect as Biblical law,"[122] or, as another version puts it, "The Sages gave their laws the same force as Biblical law."[123]

3. "THE SAGES GAVE THEIR LAWS GREATER FORCE THAN BIBLICAL LAW"

Sometimes, when the Sages saw a special need to give particular force to a law enacted by them, they would give to that rabbinic law even greater force *(i.e.,* more stringent prescriptions regarding its observance) than that accorded to a Biblical law. The following is an illustration, once again concerning the *ketubbah:*

> R. Judah says: "If a husband wishes, he may write a *ketubbah* for his virgin bride in the amount of 200 *zuz,* and she writes: 'I have received 100 *zuz* from you.' In the case of a widow, he may write a *ketubbah* in the amount of 100 *zuz,* and she writes: 'I have received 50 *zuz* from you.'" R. Meir says: "Whoever undertakes to give less than 200 *zuz* to his virgin bride and less than 100 *zuz* to a widow actually engages in harlotry [since she does not possess a valid *ketubbah*]."[124]

According to R. Judah, a husband and wife may agree that he will not give her the entire prescribed minimum *ketubbah* amount (200 *zuz* to a virgin and 100 *zuz* to a widow), but they can accomplish this only by means of a fiction: He writes a *ketubbah* to her in the full amount, and she gives him a receipt for half the amount (leaving only the other half still owing). R. Meir disagreed and held that it is absolutely prohibited for the amount of the *ketubbah* to be less than the minimum of 200 *zuz* to a virgin and 100 *zuz* to a widow; the amount may not be reduced to any extent, even by agreement or waiver.

The Talmud proceeds to the following query on the position of R. Judah:[125]

> He [R. Judah] held that she must write [a receipt] to him, but an oral stipulation is insufficient. Why is this so? Is it not a monetary matter and do we not have the tradition that according to R. Judah, "A stipulation is effective as to a monetary matter"?[126] As stated in a *baraita,* "It is R. Meir's opinion

122. TB Gittin 64b–65a.
123. TB Ketubbot 84a.
124. M Ketubbot 5:1.
125. TB Ketubbot 56a.
126. In other words, according to R. Judah an agreement to limit a wife's *ketubbah* is effective when her husband writes the *ketubbah* for the full sum and she writes a receipt for half the sum entered in the *ketubbah;* in that case, there exists, at least formally, a *ketubbah* for the full sum as demanded by the law. But if he marries her subject to a condition (and even an oral agreement generally suffices to create conditions) that her *ketubbah* will be for no more than 100 *zuz,* then even R. Judah would concede that such a condition is not valid.

> that if a man says to a woman: 'You are betrothed to me on condition that you have no claim against me for food, clothing, or conjugal rights,' she is betrothed and the condition is void; R. Judah holds: Where the matter is monetary, the condition is valid."[127]

The question thus is: Since R. Judah holds that one may enter into an agreement on a monetary matter, such as the property rights of a couple about to marry, why may they not also agree with respect to the amount of the *ketubbah* (which is also a monetary matter) that instead of 200 *zuz* the amount should be 100? And why is there a need for the fiction of the writing of the *ketubbah* by the husband for the full amount and the writing of a receipt by the wife?

The Talmud responds: "R. Judah is of the opinion that the *ketubbah* is rabbinic, and the Sages gave this law greater force than Biblical law." In other words, in R. Judah's opinion the law of the *ketubbah* was enacted by the Sages; therefore, the usual rule that the parties are free to make their own contracts, which generally applies to all monetary matters—even those otherwise governed by Biblical law—does not apply, because the Sages gave to their requirement of a minimum amount for the *ketubbah* greater force than a Biblical rule, in order to make certain that the institution of the *ketubbah* would be adhered to in every family.

The succeeding portion of the Talmudic discussion is of interest. The question is asked: If, according to R. Judah, the Sages gave their laws greater force than Biblical law, why did he hold that the husband may effectively agree with his wife to waive his rights to the usufruct of her *melog* (lit. "plucked") property (the principal of which remains in the wife's ownership while the income is given to the husband)? Is his right to the usufruct of the wife's *melog* property not also an enactment of the Sages![128]

The response was:

The query of the Talmud is: Why should such a condition not be effective, inasmuch as it involves a monetary matter, as to which parties are free to contract out of a law contained in the Torah? R. Judah's statement that "she writes" is thus understood as not excluding an oral waiver on her part but as requiring her waiver (which may be either written or oral) of a part of her *ketubbah*, although the *ketubbah* had to be in the first instance for the full amount. Similarly, "an oral stipulation" is understood as referring to any agreement, whether oral or written, to reduce the basic amount of the *ketubbah*. "Oral" stipulation is mentioned by the Talmud to indicate that such a stipulation generally suffices to create conditions. *See also* Rashi, *ad loc.*, s.v. Aval al peh; Ritba, Novellae, *ad loc.*, s.v. Amar Rabbi; and *Shittah Mekubbeẓet, ad loc.*, particularly s.vv. Ve-zeh leshon ha-Ritba z"l, Ta'ama de katvah leih, Aval al peh lo.

127. *See* the discussion of this *baraita, supra* p. 125 and n. 138.

128. *See infra* p. 572.

> Abbaye said: "There is a *ketubbah* for every marriage but not everyone has usufruct. The Sages gave particular force to laws concerning matters that occur in the normal course of events. They did not give such force to laws relating to unusual occurrences."

Abbaye's point was that every couple, no matter how poor, has a *ketubbah,* but the question of usufruct of a wife's property is not applicable to every couple, because not every couple has such property. Therefore, with regard to matters of common occurrence the rabbis gave their law greater force than Biblical law in order to enable their doctrine to gain a strong hold in actual life. Usufruct of the wife's property, however, is not as common as the *ketubbah;* therefore, in the matter of usufruct, the Sages allowed the parties the freedom of contract usual in monetary matters and saw no need to take any special measures to strengthen their enactment.[129]

What has been said demonstrates the great vitality possessed by laws classified as rabbinic. The guiding principle is: "All that was enacted by the Sages was enacted to have the same effect as Biblical law"; however, at different times and with respect to particular rabbinic laws, the Sages would incline in one direction or another according to the need and the issue involved.

Thus, we have seen that with regard to the *ketubbah,* the Sages adopted various approaches. First, in connection with the collection of the amount of the *ketubbah,* the Sages adopted a practice (namely, payment of the amount in the less valuable currency) more lenient toward the husband than the Biblical law applicable to the payment of debts. Second, the Sages accorded the basic obligation of the *ketubbah* greater force than Biblical law; they prohibited an agreement for the payment of an amount less than the minimum that they prescribed, notwithstanding the doctrine that there is generally freedom of contract as to monetary matters. Finally, their enactment concerning the right of the husband to the usufruct of the wife's property was given the same force as Biblical law.

The approach depended on whether a particular legal institution needed to be strengthened or whether it was feasible to treat it leniently, which in turn depended on how frequently it was applicable in the normal course of events, as well as on other similar factors.

4. LEGAL ENFORCEMENT OF RABBINIC LAWS

Any significant distinction between Biblical law and rabbinic law tending to reduce the legal effect of a rabbinic law would have brought about far-reaching consequences in all areas of *mishpat ivri,* since most laws of

129. On this subject, *see also supra* p. 126 n. 141.

mishpat ivri are classified as rabbinic. For this reason, while there were distinctions for various purposes between Biblical law and rabbinic law,[130] the halakhic authorities generally accorded to both types of law the same effectiveness in point of obligatory character and enforcement. We find this approach taken as early as in the Talmud itself, and an additional instructive illustration is found in a responsum of David Ibn Zimra (Radbaz), the Chief Rabbi of Egypt and one of the leading halakhic authorities of the sixteenth century. The responsum of Radbaz dealt with what Jewish law terms "rabbinic-law theft" (*gezel mi-divreihem*). This term refers to a prohibition by the Sages against various acts as constituting "theft," although those acts did not constitute theft under Biblical law and were not even prohibited by Biblical law at all.[131] An example is gambling:

> Who are gamblers? Those that play with blocks of wood or stones or bones or similar objects and agree that whoever wins over his fellow in the game will take a certain sum of money from him—this is theft by rabbinic law. Even though the taking was by consent of the loser, yet inasmuch as the winner takes money by means of game or sport without giving anything in return, it is thievery. Similarly, those who play with a domestic or wild animal or with birds and agree that the owner of the animal that wins or runs faster will take from his fellow a certain amount of money, and all similar cases—this is all forbidden and is theft by rabbinic law.[132]

Biblical law does not regard as theft (*gezel*) the winnings from a game of chance, since the winner of the game receives the money with the previous consent of the loser.[133] However, it is theft according to rabbinic law because the winner receives the money without a *quid pro quo* and without working for it. The earnings come by means of a game in which the result is a gamble, and there is therefore no unreserved consent and unqualified intent to give up the money in case one loses.

There is an important difference between rabbinic-law theft and Biblical-law theft in regard to the sanctions against the thief. "If one has in

130. Examples, in addition to those already mentioned, are: the distinction between an oath required by the Torah and one required by rabbinic law (TB Shevu'ot 41a); and the priority of Biblical-law debts over rabbinic-law debts in regard to enforcement against property of the debtor (*see Nimmukei Yosef* to Bava Meẓi'a, ch. "Ha-Mekabbel," following the *mishnah, Ha-malveh et ḥavero lo yemashkenennu,* s.v. Aval lo le-ishto u-vanav [in our editions, 69b]; *Bet Yosef* to *Tur* ḤM 104:15, s.v. Katav ha-Ra'avad; *Leḥem Mishneh* to Maimonides, *MT,* Malveh ve-Loveh 1:8).

131. The various examples in the Talmud are summarized in Maimonides, *MT,* Gezelah va-Avedah 6:7–16.

132. *Id.* 6:10. *See also* Sh. Ar. ḤM 370:2–3 (concerning a gambler who also has another vocation).

133. Under Biblical law, forcible taking without the consent of the owner is a basic element of the offense of *gezel; see* Maimonides, *MT,* Gezelah va-Avedah 1:3.

his possession what has been 'stolen' by rabbinic-law theft, it cannot be taken from him by a court of law."[134] Thus, while a court will restore the proceeds of a Biblical-law theft, execution of judgment according to the usual course of the law is unavailable for rabbinic-law theft; the court, for example, has no power to restore, by execution against property, the money won in a game of chance.

David ibn Zimra (Radbaz) was asked the following two questions concerning this distinction between rabbinic-law theft and Biblical-law theft:[135]

> [W]hether, in view of the rule accepted by most authorities that the proceeds of a clear case of rabbinic-law theft cannot be recovered in a court of law, the thief can be put under a ban, and also whether this rule applies to all cases where the obligation to pay money is based on rabbinic and not Biblical law.

The questions, in other words, were: (a) Does rabbinic-law theft completely escape legal sanctions, or may a relatively light sanction be imposed, such as a ban, which was in the past a common sanction?[136] and (b) more fundamentally, Does it necessarily follow that the usual methods of judicial enforcement are not available for any obligations in Jewish law that are rabbinic?

Radbaz' answer to the first question was that rabbinic-law theft is subject to the sanction of a ban, as it is to other religious and moral sanctions. In his response to the second question, he laid down some basic principles applicable to all laws characterized as rabbinic in Jewish law. His response is therefore worth studying in some detail. Radbaz wrote:

> It is certainly not the case that this rule is applied to all obligations based on rabbinic law. There are many matters concerning which legislation by the Sages is fully enforced.
>
> For example, liability for *garmi*[137] exists only by rabbinic law, yet execution is levied against the best of the defendant's property.[138] The verbal as-

134. *Id.* 6:16, following TB Gittin 61a.

135. *Resp. Radbaz,* I, #503.

136. *See supra* pp. 11–12.

137. This term includes various types of loss other than direct damage to property itself, *e.g.*, where a coin is thrown into the sea and is not damaged as such but represents a loss to the owner, or where a promissory note is burned and the only direct physical damage is to the paper, which is intrinsically of minimal value, but the loss to the owner is the amount of the note. Biblical law imposes no liability on the person causing the harm in such cases, but rabbinic law does. *See* Maimonides, *MT,* Ḥovel u-Mazzik 7:7–12; Sh. Ar. ḤM ch. 386; Gulak, *Yesodei,* II, pp. 206ff., p. 208 n. 7.

138. Literally, "execution is levied like a beam of wood used for decorative purposes," for which only the best quality was used. This is a Talmudic expression (TB Ketubbot 86a) that means that just as the best quality wood is used for decorative purposes, compensation for tortious harm may be recovered from the best property.

signment of rights or obligations through a "meeting of the three"[139] is valid only by rabbinic law, yet is enforced by a court. There is the case involving Issur Giora ("the Proselyte") and Rava,[140] and other cases that constantly arise. Similarly, the sale of a promissory note,[141] according to Alfasi and Maimonides and most of the authorities, is valid only by rabbinic law, and yet is enforceable even against subsequent purchasers of the debtor's property.[142] *A fortiori,* the court will collect the debt from the property in the hands of the debtor himself for the benefit of the purchaser of the note. The rule that a chattel may be acquired by *meshikhah* ("pulling," or taking possession) is also rabbinic in origin;[143] according to Biblical law, the transfer of a chattel is effected by payment of money, and it was the Sages who substituted *meshikhah* for the payment of money. Yet if the purchaser has taken possession of the chattel and the seller comes and seizes the chattel from him, the court will take the chattel from the seller; and if, before the court has done so, the chattel is lost or consumed, the court will enforce the buyer's claim [for the value of the chattel] against the seller's property.

What is the rationale for this? Could not the seller argue that the acquisition is only by rabbinic law and that by Biblical law the buyer had not acquired it? We must therefore conclude that the Sages gave this enactment the same force as Biblical law. The same rationale applies to the wife's *ketubbah,* according to those who maintain that the *ketubbah* is a rabbinic enactment.[144] How else is it possible for the court to enforce a husband's obligation under the *ketubbah* against his property [if his obligation under the *ketubbah* is rabbinic]? The same applies to the symbolic act of acquisition by means of

139. "A meeting of the three" (*ma'amad sheloshtan*) is one of the ways to transfer property rights or obligations; the creditor-assignor, in the presence of the debtor, assigns to the assignee the right to collect the debt. This form of transfer requires no writing, but the three parties must be present. *See* TB Gittin 13a; Sh. Ar. ḤM ch. 126; Gulak, *Yesodei,* II, pp. 97–99; *infra* p. 584.

140. The reference is to the incident involving Issur Giora and Rava reported in TB Bava Batra 149a.

141. Promissory notes are sold by transferring from the assignor to the assignee the debtor's obligation represented by the note. This is effected by written assignment and delivery. The assignor, by endorsement on the note or by a separate instrument, writes: "I, [name], assign to you the promissory note of [name of maker] together with the full lien rights thereto appertaining." The assignor then delivers the note to the assignee together with the assignment, if separate from the note; and this concludes the transaction. This sale of instruments of indebtedness is, according to the majority of halakhic authorities, also "rabbinic." *See* TB Bava Batra 76a; Sh. Ar. ḤM ch. 67; Gulak, *Yesodei,* II, pp. 100–101.

142. If, after the debt arises, the debtor sells his property to a third party, the creditor is entitled to seize the property from the buyer, because it was charged with a lien for the payment of the debt. For a detailed discussion, *see infra* pp. 590–591.

143. The act of "pulling" (*meshikhah*) is one of the methods of acquisition and, according to some Talmudic Sages, was originated by legislation. *See infra* pp. 297–298 and 581.

144. *See supra* pp. 211, 214, 216; *infra* p. 560 and n. 66.

> *sudar,*[145] which, it seems to me, is rabbinic in origin, as it arises out of the case of barter (*ḥalifin*),[146] and barter is derived from *divrei kabbalah,*[147] since we deduce it from the verse:[148] "One man would take off his sandal and hand it to the other." Yet it is a fact that all our current property transfers are accomplished by means of *sudar,* and the court enforces them and executes against property and there is no one who objects to this! I do not propose to list them all, like a peddler listing his wares, in order to demonstrate that there are many types of acquisitions by rabbinic law that are judicially enforced.
>
> The essence of the matter is that all of those acts which under rabbinic law constitute acts of acquisition have the force of Biblical law; for it is on this basis that the general public engages in business transactions, and this [rabbinic legislation] can in no way be inferior to custom, which, according to the generally accepted opinion of Rabban Simeon b. Gamaliel, overrides the law. Thus, whoever transacts business or buys or sells merchandise or marries a woman acts with the intention that the transaction will be valid on the basis of the law of the Rabbis, and therefore a court may enforce judgments based on these transactions, and execute against property on such judgments, as if the transactions had been directly governed by Biblical law.

This being the case, why does the court not execute against the property of a thief when the theft is only by rabbinic law? Radbaz next addressed this question:

> But in connection with robbery, theft, and usury,[149] did the Sages give their laws the same force as Biblical law? [No]. The foregoing reasoning does not

145. Acquisition by *sudar* (kerchief) is one of the methods instituted by the Sages for effecting a transfer of property. It became the most widely used method, on account of its efficiency and convenience. For a detailed discussion, *see infra* pp. 582–583.

146. *See infra* pp. 581–582.

147. *I.e.,* from the Prophets and the Hagiographa, *see supra* pp. 203–204. In the view of Radbaz, what is derived from *divrei kabbalah* is only rabbinic and not Biblical. *But see supra* p. 203 and n. 67, pointing out that the rule requiring the signature of witnesses on a deed, which is derived from *divrei kabbalah,* was characterized in the Talmud as being Biblical.

148. Ruth 4:7. The full text of the verse is: "Now this was formerly done in Israel in cases of redemption or exchange: to validate any transaction, one man would take off his sandal and hand it to the other. Such was the practice in Israel." *See also infra* p. 582.

149. The laws of prohibited interest differentiate between two main types: (1) *ribbit keẓuẓah,* fixed-rate interest, which is forbidden by the Torah; and (2) *avak ribbit,* "dust of interest," not prohibited by the Torah, but forbidden by the Sages. An example of the former is where lender and borrower agree when the loan is made that the borrower must add a fixed sum to the principal amount of the loan at the time of repayment, such as when the loan is for $100 and the borrower obligates himself to pay $120, or when the borrower agrees at the time the loan is made to augment the principal by any valuable consideration other than money. Some *rishonim* held that if the borrower seeks an extension of time to repay and the lender consents on condition that the borrower pay something more than the principal of the loan, the excess over the principal, even though not agreed upon at the time the loan was made, nevertheless also constitutes *ribbit keẓuẓah.*

> apply, because the robber, thief, or usurer does not act with the intent of following the law of the Sages; on the contrary, he transgresses those laws.[150] Thus, the result is obvious: the Rabbis have ordained that these acts should not be done; however, if they are done, the outcome is determined under Biblical law and the proceeds are not recovered. In the case of the robber who takes property from his victim by force, the Sages established the severe penalty of "banning" him until he returns the property, and the same applies to rabbinic-law theft where the property is taken without the knowledge of the owner; however, in the case of a usurious loan, in which the forbidden interest is taken with the consent of the borrower, the Sages were not severe. That is the sum and substance of the matter.

Radbaz demonstrated in this responsum that entire segments of the law of obligations and property acquisition are rabbinic in origin and that, even so, both as a matter of law and in actual practice, the full range of the usual and customary methods of judicial enforcement are available against the property of the obligor to the same extent as in the case of an obligation created by Biblical law.

The legal basis, the "essence of the matter," consists of two rationales that in the final analysis coalesce into one:

1. The Sages gave to laws originating in rabbinic legislation binding force equal to that of Biblical law;
2. Since the Sages enacted and laid down these laws, all who engage in a legal transaction do so on the basis of these legal rules and with full knowledge of them. These rules are therefore similar to customs, which have the full effectiveness of law and, in matters of monetary law, even override a Biblical rule.[151]

The concept of *avak ribbit,* "dust of interest," includes, among other things, any type of benefit that the borrower confers on the lender, regardless of whether or not it was expressly agreed upon at the time the loan was made.

Ribbit keẓuẓah is recoverable by court action, *i.e.,* if the borrower has paid this form of interest to the lender, the court will order the lender to return it. *Avak ribbit* is not recoverable by legal proceedings; if the borrower has conferred any form of benefit on the lender, the court cannot order the lender to return it, but it is the lender's moral obligation to do so, *laẓeit yedei shamayim* ("to fulfill his duty in the sight of Heaven"). *See supra* pp. 148–149; TB Bava Meẓi'a 63b *et seq.;* Maimonides, *MT,* Malveh ve-Loveh, chs. 4–6; Sh. Ar. YD, chapters 160 *et seq.;* Gulak, *Yesodei,* II, pp. 172–177.

150. *I.e.,* rabbinic-law theft and "dust of interest."

151. *See infra* pp. 896–907. Radbaz was not saying that all legislation by the halakhic authorities is effective only by virtue of the force of custom. Custom and legislation are two distinct legal sources, and legislation operates in its own right. *See infra* ch. 13–20 on legislation and ch. 21–22 on custom. Radbaz himself stressed that rabbinic legislation is "in no way . . . inferior to custom," and his manifest purpose was to develop this legal notion. Since it can be assumed that every legal transaction is made in light of the applicable legal rules,

It is thus clear that with regard to all legal transactions, including those governed by rabbinic law, all the methods of execution of judgments are available. However, it follows as a corollary of this very rationale that where it cannot be assumed that a legal transaction is entered into in reliance on rabbinic law (*e.g.*, violations of prohibitions against acts such as robbery, theft, and usury, where the actor does not rely on the law or conform his conduct to it but rather transgresses it), there is no enforcement against the obligor's property, inasmuch as the tacit agreement between the parties to engage in the transaction in reliance on rabbinic law is lacking.

There is therefore no execution against the property of one who is a thief according to rabbinic law or of one who takes interest prohibited by rabbinic law. These transgressions are not within the rationale for enforcement of rabbinic law and, of course, they are not violations of Biblical law.

Consequently, there is no legal right to recover the fruits of these transgressions—the property that rabbinic law considers to have been stolen or the "interest" that rabbinic law deems usurious—by means of judicial enforcement. In these cases, there is only a prohibition by rabbinic law; and the transgressor is subject to different sanctions, depending on his conduct. In those cases of rabbinic-law theft that involve serious misconduct on the part of the transgressor—acting without the victim's consent and contrary to his will[152]—the sanction of the ban may be imposed against the wrongdoer until the property is returned. In the case of rabbinic-law usury, where the transaction is less serious in that the borrower consented, the Sages did not apply the sanction of the ban against the lender, but contented themselves with establishing that the lender is obliged to return the forbidden interest to the debtor if the lender is to "fulfill his duty in the sight of Heaven."[153]

---

the parties are deemed to have incorporated those rules as a part of their agreement, and such a stipulation is fully effective. According to Radbaz, the principle that "custom overrides the law" (*minhag mevattel halakhah*) is an example of such an implied agreement; the principle is based on the premise that the whole community has agreed to conduct their transactions in accordance with existing custom and usage, and such a stipulation is valid and effective even if its terms are contrary to the substantive rules of the *Halakhah*. *See infra* pp. 905–907. What custom and rabbinic legislation have in common, according to Radbaz, is that we presume that they are both incorporated, by public consensus, into juristic transactions. This presumption is in fact generically common to both rabbinic legislation and custom. *See infra* pp. 881–882 and 885–886.

152. This rationale does not seem to cover every case of rabbinic-law theft. It does not, for example, seem to fit the facts of gambling; however, it is possible to view the loser as in a sense paying against his will, since his "consent" is not fully given, but is given in the context of a sporting game; *see supra* p. 218. It may also be the case that a ban is not placed on gamblers just as it is not placed on one who receives the "dust of interest."

153. As to "fulfilling one's duty in the sight of Heaven," *see supra* pp. 148–149.

VI. REDUCTION OF THE ORAL LAW TO WRITING

Let us briefly examine the second reason for the use of the term "Oral Law," namely, the prohibition against reducing the *Halakhah* to writing.

A. The Nature of the Prohibition Against Reduction to Writing and the Reasons Therefor

The verse in the Book of Exodus,[154] "And the Lord said to Moses: 'Write down these commandments for, in accordance with these commandments, I make a covenant with you and with Israel,'" was interpreted in the School of R. Ishmael as follows: "'Write down these commandments' [lit. "words"]—these shall you write, but you shall not write the *halakhot* (Oral Law)."[155] In the following century (the third century C.E.), R. Judah b. Naḥmani, the spokesman (*meturgeman*) for Resh Lakish, an *amora* of the Land of Israel, interpreted this verse from the Book of Exodus in a dual manner: "Matters that are written you are not at liberty to recite orally; matters transmitted orally you are not at liberty to recite from a writing."[156]

From many Talmudic sources, we learn of Sages who had in their possession, for reference use when necessary, private scrolls containing newly adopted laws.[157] The object was to prevent the contents from being forgotten.[158] There is also evidence of discussion of halakhic matters by letter and by other means of communication.[159] Consequently, we may conclude that individuals were permitted to put laws in writing for their own use, and that the prohibition was aimed only at the writing of laws for the purpose of teaching them in public directly from the text.[160] This nicely explains the parallelism in the words of R. Judah b. Naḥmani quoted above: The Written Law should be taught only from the text and not orally from memory; conversely, the Oral Law should be taught only orally from memory and not from written texts; and this was true even when there were laws that had been put in writing.

154. Exodus 34:27.

155. TB Temurah 14b; Gittin 60b.

156. TB Gittin 60b; likewise in TB Temurah 14b, where it is stated in reverse order; "matters transmitted orally . . . , etc."

157. TB Shabbat 6b; Bava Meẓi'a 92a.

158. Rashi, Shabbat 6b, s.v. Megillat setarim.

159. TB Ketubbot 49b, 69a *et al.*

160. *See* J.N. Epstein, *Mavo le-Nusaḥ ha-Mishnah* [Introduction to the Text of the Mishnah] (hereinafter, *Mavo*), pp. 699ff.; H. Albeck, *Mavo*, pp. 113ff. The accuracy of such notes, written for the personal purposes of the Sages, was sometimes questioned ("They do not have the signature of Mar b. Ravana upon them"—TB Yevamot 22a), and "they had no more weight than their statements and they did not carry the authority of written documents"—Lieberman, *Hellenism*, pp. 87ff.

The Sages and the authorities in the various periods of the *Halakhah* gave a number of different explanations for the prohibition against reducing the Oral Law to writing. R. Judah b. Shalom, an *amora* of the fifth generation in the Land of Israel, perceived in this prohibition the uniqueness of Israel among the nations and a proof that the halakhic Sages are the true heirs and preservers of Biblical revelation:

> R. Judah b. Shalom said: "When God told Moses, 'Write down,' Moses sought to have the Mishnah reduced to writing. But God foresaw that in the future the nations of the world would translate the Bible and read it in Greek and they would say: 'We are Israel!—and now the scales are balanced.' God said to the nations: 'You say that you are My sons. I recognize only those to whom I have confided My secret mystery—they are My sons; and what is My secret mystery? It is the Mishnah, which was given orally.'"[161]

There is an echo here of Judaism's debate with Christianity. Christianity adopted Scripture and attempted to prove from its verses that it was Christianity that discovered and maintains the Scriptural teachings. Therefore, the Oral Law, which was also given to Moses at Sinai to clarify and explain the Torah, was not put in writing; it was to remain secret between the Jewish people and its Maker, to prove and identify Israel as the children of God.[162]

In later times, Jewish scholars viewed the prohibition against putting the *Halakhah* in writing as an indication of the character and aim of the *Halakhah* itself. The Written Law is sacred in every letter and crownlet, and from them innumerable legal rules have been derived. The essence of the Oral Law, on the other hand, is the content of its rules and not the form, and it is especially the fact that it is not committed to writing that gives it its great flexibility. "Therefore, general principles, which the Torah only

161. *Tanḥuma,* Ki Tissa, 34. *See also* the continuation of the quotation:

> R. Judah b. Shalom said: "The Holy One, blessed be He, said to Moses, 'Why do you request that the Mishnah be set down in writing? What, in that event, will be the difference between Israel and the other nations? For, as it is said, "The [lit. "My"] many teachings I wrote for him" [Hosea 8:12]; therefore [*i.e.,* because they were in writing], they "have been treated as something alien." [*Id.*] Instead, present to them Scripture in writing, but Mishnah orally.'" "Write down these commandments" [Exodus 34:27] refers to Scripture; "for in accordance with [*al pi,* lit. "by the *mouth* of"] these commandments" [*id.*] refers to Mishnah transmitted orally.

See also Tanḥuma, Va-Yera, 5, for an additional *dictum* of the same *amora:*

> . . . Mishnah is the mystery of the Holy One, blessed be He, Who would not entrust His mysteries to any but the just, as it is said, "The secret of the Lord is for those who fear Him" (Psalms 25:14).

162. *See* Epstein, *Mavo,* p. 694; H. Albeck, *Mavo,* pp. 114–115; Urbach, *The Sages,* p. 305; *id., supra* n. 72 at 1, 6–8; Baer, *supra* n. 75 at 118–130. *See also infra* n. 167.

briefly suggests, were revealed orally to Moses at Sinai, so that the halakhic authorities of every generation would use them to derive new laws."[163]

Careful deliberation and oral discussion also strengthen the creative power of the *Halakhah:*

> [T]hey should not depend on a written text to which they are less likely to give the same careful consideration that must be given to what is taught orally: oral instruction requires constant thought to keep the material in mind, and as a result, many laws will be brought into being out of the deliberations and reasoning process involved in studying the Oral Law.[164]

Permission to reduce the Oral Law to writing is connected in the Talmudic tradition with the difficulty of remembering the material of the *Halakhah* and transmitting it orally; putting it in writing became necessary to prevent the Torah from being forgotten. In justifying the elimination of this prohibition, the Sages interpreted the verse in Psalms,[165] "It is a time to act for the Lord, for they have violated your Torah," to mean, "When it is time to act for the Lord, Your Torah may be violated," *i.e.*, that "It is better that one letter of the Torah should be uprooted so that the [entire] Torah will not be forgotten by Israel."[166]

163. *Sefer ha-Ikkarim* 3:23. *See also infra* pp. 240–242.

164. Introduction of Joshua Falk to his *Sema* on Sh. Ar. ḤM. Earlier, he quoted the reason stated in *Tanḥuma:*

> The Sages [lit. "ancients"] wrote that the reason was so that sectarians (*minim*) would not transform the Oral Law into heresy, as they did to the Written Law, and as it is written: "The many teachings I wrote for him have been treated as something alien."

He later presented an interesting reason, illustrating it with what happened while he was studying on the day he wrote:

> I say that for the following reason did God [lit. the One-Whose-Name-is-to-be-blessed] not want the Oral Law to be written down, for a text that is before us in written form is subject to a variety of interpretations, as is the case with the passage we are studying today in ch. "Lulav ha-Gazul" of Tractate *Sukkah*. . . . And if that be the case with a simple *halakhah*, how much more is it true of difficult trends of thought (*shittot*), discussions (*sugyot*), and subjects (*inyanim*). If the *Halakhah* had never been set down in writing, but had continued to be orally transmitted with its explanations from scholar to scholar, mouth to mouth, there would not have arisen diversity of interpretation, and we would not have been required to spend our days in perplexity and in explication of the *Halakhah* but could have used those hours for other study.

See also Maimonides, *Guide for the Perplexed,* Part I, beginning of ch. 71.

165. Psalms 119:126.

166. TB Gittin 60a, Temurah 14b. *See further* on this subject *infra* pp. 503–504, 534, and especially p. 503 n. 39 as to how the Sages derived this conclusion from the verse.

B. Dating the Reduction of Talmudic Literature to Writing

When was Talmudic literature put in writing? Halakhic authorities and scholars have disagreed on this question from the time of Saadiah Gaon in the tenth century C.E. up to the present, and there is an extensive and detailed literature on the subject.[167] The majority view is that the Mishnah was put in writing contemporaneously with its redaction by R. Judah Ha-Nasi,[168] and that, similarly, the two Talmuds were written contemporaneously with their redaction.[169] The opposing view is that the Mishnah was not put in writing at the time of its composition by R. Judah Ha-Nasi, and the *amoraim* did not have a written Mishnah; according to this view, both the Mishnah and the Talmud were first reduced to writing at the time of the *savoraim*, in the sixth century C.E.[170]

167. For details, *see* Epstein, *Mavo*, pp. 692ff. (which includes an extensive bibliography, to which should be added H. Albeck, *Mavo*, pp. 111–115, and Lieberman, *Hellenism*, pp. 83–99).

168. In this connection, *see* the Preface of the *Levush* to OḤ (first page, column 1):

> Rabbenu ha-Kadosh [R. Judah Ha-Nasi] came and expounded in his holiness, "It is a time to act for the Lord, for they have violated Your Torah [as meaning "When it is a time to act for the Lord, Your Torah may be violated"], and he made for us garments of skins (*kotnot or*) by the clarity of his light (*be-or behirato*) [a play on the Hebrew word *or*, which, spelled with the letter *ayin*, means "skin," and with the letter *alef*, means "light"] and wrote it all down in true record—the numerous commentaries and traditions in his possession that he skillfully wielded as a double-edged sword. Taking an example from him, the outstanding disciples who followed him made their own private scrolls.

169. Even if the Mishnah was put in writing as soon as it was redacted by R. Judah Ha-Nasi, study in public and in the academy (*yeshivah*) continued to be conducted orally and not from the written text. The written Mishnah was consulted only when necessary, in case of doubt or inability to remember. *See* Epstein, *Mavo*, p. 703, and the bibliographic references, *supra* n. 167.

170. For a unique approach, *see* Lieberman, *Hellenism*, pp. 83ff.

Chapter 6

THE BASIC NORM AND THE SOURCES OF JEWISH LAW

I. The Three Meanings of the Term "Sources of Law"
II. The Basic Norm of a Legal System
III. The Basic Norm of Jewish Law
IV. The Sources of Jewish Law
  A. The Literary Sources
  B. The Historical Sources
  C. The Legal Sources

Before dealing with the basic norm and the sources of Jewish law, let us briefly examine the meaning of these terms as understood in general jurisprudence.

I. THE THREE MEANINGS OF THE TERM "SOURCES OF LAW"

The study of any legal system requires probing into the system's sources of law (Latin, *fontes juris;* German, *die Quellen des Rechts*).

There are three principal meanings to the term "sources of law":

a. The literary sources of law[1] (German, *die Erkenntnisquellen des Rechts,* "the sources of knowledge of the law"). This term refers to the authoritative compendia of the statutes, decisions, and regulations in a legal system, *e.g.,* the volumes of statutes found in every legal system, from which we can discover and ascertain the various norms of that system.
b. The historical sources of law (German, *die historischen Quellen des Rechts*). This term refers to those sources that are the foundation for a particular norm as a matter of historical fact. For example, we can point in various legal systems to many laws for which Roman law is the historical source. Legal history for the most part consists of research into the historical

1. For the Hebrew term *mekorot rishumiyyim,* coined for this concept, *see infra* n. 25.

roots of legal norms in different legal systems in order to discover, *inter alia,* the various influences of one legal system upon another. "Historical sources of the law" in its broadest sense includes every factor—economic, social, and moral—which has contributed to the formulation of a given legal norm. For example, if a particular economic or social condition caused the enactment of certain statutes to respond to the needs of the time, then the historical source of those statutes is the economic or social condition that shaped that result.

c. The legal sources of law (German, *die Entstehungsquellen des Rechts,* "the sources through which laws come into being"), *i.e.,* those sources which directly produce and create law. The term "sources" in this sense refers to those processes and methods recognized by the legal system itself as giving binding effect to a particular legal norm.

The meaning of "legal source of law" is essentially different from the meaning of "historical source of law," and the distinction must be carefully kept in mind. When we search for the legal source of a particular norm, we aim to find the legal constitutive source, *e.g.,* legislation or precedent, which gives binding force to the legal norm; we are not looking for the source that in point of historical fact brought about that legal norm, *e.g.,* adoption of the norm from a different legal system or development of the norm as the result of a particular social or economic situation. As stated by Salmond:

> This is an important distinction which calls for careful consideration. In respect of its origin, a rule of law is often of long descent. The immediate source of a rule of English law may be the decision of an English court of justice. But that court may have drawn the matter of its decision from the writings of some lawyer, let us say the celebrated Frenchman Pothier; and Pothier in his turn may have taken it from the compilations of the Emperor Justinian, who may have obtained it from the praetorian edict. In such a case all these things—the decision, the works of Pothier, the corpus juris civilis, and the edictum perpetuum—are the successive material sources of the rule of English Law. But there is a difference between them, for the precedent is the legal source of the rule and the others are merely its historical sources. The precedent is its source, not merely in fact, but in law also; the others are its sources in fact, but obtain no legal recognition as such.[2]

The historical sources of the law consequently operate only indirectly in the development of a legal system, as factors that constitute a model (as in the case of the absorption of a legal principle from a different legal system) or that produce the need for a certain development in the legal system

2. Salmond, p. 109.

(*e.g.*, particular economic or social conditions). On the other hand, the direct development of any legal system comes about by means of the legal sources, which constitute the only channels through which change, repeal, or introduction of new doctrine becomes effective as law in that legal system.[3]

II. THE BASIC NORM OF A LEGAL SYSTEM

The concept of the legal sources of a legal system thus denotes the sources recognized by that legal system as constituting the method or process that gives every legal norm its binding effect as law. The obvious question at this point is, of course: Where did these legal sources themselves receive their binding nature and authority, *i.e.*, who recognized them as competent to effect the prescription or reception of legal norms as part of the legal system? Salmond has given this answer:

> There must be found in every legal system certain ultimate principles, from which all others are derived, but which are themselves self-existent. Before there can be any talk of legal sources, there must be already in existence some law that establishes them and gives them their authority. . . . These ultimate principles are the grundnorms or basic rules of recognition of the legal system.[4]

Every legal source of a legal system receives its recognition and authority from what Salmond called an ultimate principle, which he compared to the term *Grundnorm*—"basic norm"—in the well-known theory of Kelsen. According to Kelsen, the *Grundnorm* is the highest principle in the scale of principles of that legal system, *i.e.*, the principle which by its power directly or indirectly gives to all legal norms in that legal system their binding effect.[5]

For example, suppose there is a regulation in a particular city prohibiting a store from being open for business after 7:00 P.M. What is the source of authority of this regulation? The immediate source may be a city ordinance. But where did the city obtain the authority to pass ordinances?

3. Our discussion concerning the various meanings of the term "sources of law" is based upon Salmond. For additional discussion of this subject, *see* C.K. Allen, *Law in the Making*, pp. 268ff.; R. Cross, *Precedent in English Law*, pp. 147–156, and Cross's observation (p. 147 n. 1) that in "historical sources" one ought to include the personality and *Weltanschauung* of the judge to the extent that these influence his decision. *See also* Cross, *op. cit.* at 45–49; Elon, *Ḥakikah*, pp. 69ff.

4. Salmond, pp. 111–112.

5. On Kelsen's theory, *see* Salmond's comments, pp. 48–49.

From a law enacted by a state or national legislature conferring upon cities the authority to pass such ordinances. And where did the legislature obtain its authority to pass such a law? From the primary norm that confers upon the legislature competence to enact laws binding in the particular legal system. The highest legal principle, or the basic norm, from which the regulation requiring the store to be closed receives its binding effect is therefore this primary norm; the authoritative power of the city ordinance is on a lower level and derives its own force from the authority flowing down to the city from the ultimate legal principle.[6] In every legal system there is thus found a chain of delegation of power or authority, descending from the ultimate legal principle of that legal system.

It should be pointed out that a change in the basic norm from which a legal rule derives its force does not necessarily require a change in the content of the rule itself. It is very possible that the same legal rule may receive its authority from one basic norm until a particular political or legal event, and thereafter may be just as authoritative by virtue of the successor basic norm. This was the situation, for example, when the British Mandate was succeeded by the State of Israel. In the period of the British Mandate, the basic norm of the legal system was the norm that established the binding legal authority of the British Parliament. When the State of Israel was proclaimed, the norm that established the ultimate legal authority of the Provisional Council of State became the basic norm of the legal system of Israel,[7] although the overwhelming majority of the legal rules in the

6. In every legal system there is necessarily at least one ultimate legal principle (although there may be more than one). *See* Salmond, pp. 48–49:

> Where there is a written constitution, the grundnorm will be that the constitution ought to be obeyed. Where there is no written constitution, we must look to social behaviour for the grundnorm. The English legal system would seem to be based on several different such basic rules, one of which concerns parliamentary legislation, others of which deal with the binding force of judicial precedents.

Salmond's reason for classifying precedent as a separate "basic rule" is that precedent does not derive its force as binding authority in England from legislation by Parliament. *See further* Salmond, pp. 111–112. In the State of Israel, by contrast, precedent derives its binding effect from Section 33 of the Courts Law, 1957; hence, precedent in Israel is merely a derivative source of law, deriving its authority from legislation by the Knesset.

7. *See* H. Klinghoffer, "Die Entstehung des Staates Israel" [The Birth of the State of Israel], *Jahrbuch des Öffentlichen Rechts der Gegenwart,* Neue Folge, X, pp. 458–459 (the sovereign power of the Provisional Council of State is necessarily implied, albeit not stated explicitly, from the Declaration of Independence: "That passage [in the Declaration of Independence] stating that the People's Council shall function as a Provisional Council of State is to be regarded, in terms of Kelsen's *Grundnorm* theory, as the basic norm of the State of Israel"). The binding authority of the Knesset is thus not merely theoretical, but is the positive result of legislation by the Provisional Council of State. *See also* B. Akzin, *Torat ha-Mishtarim* [Theories of Government], I, pp. 27–34, 102–109, 120–143; M. Sternberg, "Ha-Normah ha-Basisit Shel ha-Mishpat be-Yisra'el" [The Basic Norm of the Law in Israel], *Ha-Praklit,* IX (1953), pp. 129ff; *infra* n. 9.

legal system itself remained unchanged and continued to have the force of law.[8]

At this point, an additional question arises: Who gives authority and force to the ultimate legal principle, the basic norm? The answer requires transcending the bounds of legal thought and entering the domain of history, ideology, and philosophy:

> But whence comes the rule that Acts of Parliament have the force of law? This is legally ultimate; its source is historical only, not legal. The historians of the constitution know its origin, but lawyers must accept it as self-existent. It is the law because it is the law and for no other reason that it is possible for the law itself to take notice of.[9]

III. THE BASIC NORM OF JEWISH LAW

Let us now examine how these ideas of general jurisprudence apply to Jewish law.

What is the basic norm of Jewish law? It is the fundamental norm that everything set forth in the Torah, *i.e.*, the Written Law, is binding on the Jewish legal system. The basic norm of Jewish law is thus more than the source of a chain of authority. It is also intertwined with the substantive content of the Written Law as the permanent constitution of the Jewish legal system—a constitution not subject to modification, either by addition or subtraction.[10] This norm is the source of authority and the starting point for the entire Jewish legal system in all its periods, changes, and developments; it authorizes the legal sources of Jewish law to serve as effective means for continued creativity and development.[11]

For example, there is a rule that ownership of chattels is acquired by

8. Law and Administration Ordinance, 1948, Sec. 11. *See infra* p. 1620.

9. Salmond, p. 111. For the jurist, the basic norm is conceived as an incontrovertible axiom: "Such basic rules are to a legal system what axioms are to geometry; they are the initial hypotheses from which all other propositions in the system are derived" (Salmond, p. 49). B. Akzin, *supra* n. 7 at 32ff., notes, with some reservations, that the network of legal norms is separate from other normative networks. *See* Section III of this chapter, where this point is discussed as regards Jewish law.

10. *See infra* pp. 496–502. Such integration of the basic norm with substantive content is also called for when a constitution expressly provides that one or more of its provisions are not subject to amendment: *e.g.*, the constitutions of France and Italy, with regard to the republican form of the government; of Brazil, with regard to the republican–federal form of government; and of Norway, with regard to the "basic principles" of the constitution. *See* B. Akzin, *supra* n. 7 at II, 44; H. Klinghoffer, *Ha-Enẓiklopedyah ha-Ivrit*, XVII, pp. 867–871, s.v. Ḥukkah. Such provisions can be amended only by a revolutionary change that breaks the framework of constitutional continuity and thereby effects a change in the basic norm.

11. *See infra* pp. 236–238.

meshikhah—"pulling" (taking physical possession). What is the source for the binding nature of this rule? It was legislated as a *takkanah.*[12] When we continue to ask, What is the basis for the binding effect of this *takkanah?* the answer is: the halakhic authorities enacted it. Where is the authority for them to enact the *takkanah?* The answer is: the Torah confers on them the authority to enact *takkanot,*[13] and there is a basic norm that whatever the Written Law provides is binding on the Jewish legal system.

What is the source for the authority and the binding force of this basic norm? With this question we leave jurisprudence and pass into the sphere of faith: a basic article of the Jewish faith is that the source for the authority of the Torah is the Ruler of the universe—He who gave the Torah, which reflects His will and His commandments. When we consider the question from the perspective of Judaism in its full and most inclusive sense, we must conclude that Judaism cannot be perceived merely as a collection of legal norms, separate and independent from its other normative categories such as religious or ethical. All of these have one basic norm and one single supreme value: the command of God as embodied in the Torah given to Moses at Sinai.[14]

The halakhic authorities understood well the conceptual implications of this basic norm as a binding source for everything included in the Jewish legal system. Let us quote two examples. Maimonides drew the following conclusion from what the Mishnah[15] says concerning the prohibition of the eating of the sinew of the thigh[16] of an animal:[17]

> Note well the basic principle expressed in the statement in this *mishnah:* "It was prohibited at Sinai."[18] The principle is that you should know that everything we are prohibited or permitted to do today is only because of the command of God given to Moses, and not because God commanded it to prophets before Moses.
>
> As an example, we do not eat a limb torn from a living animal. This is not because God forbade the descendants of Noah to eat a limb from a live animal. The prohibition against eating a limb from a live animal remains in force because Moses prohibited it to us, having been so commanded at Sinai. Similarly, we do not practice circumcision because Abraham circumcised

12. *See infra* pp. 297–298, 510–511, 580.

13. *See infra* pp. 476–478.

14. *See also* our discussion of the basic concept of *Torah min ha-shamayim* ("Torah from Heaven"), *supra* pp. 192–194 and *infra* pp. 240–242.

15. M Ḥullin 7:6.

16. Genesis 32:32–33.

17. Maimonides' commentary on M Ḥullin 7:6.

18. Maimonides' text is *ne'esar* ("it was prohibited"). Another reading is *ne'emar* ("it was said"). *See also Dikdukei Soferim, ad loc.,* and H. Albeck, *ad loc.,* and in his Hashlamot, p. 379.

> himself and his household, but because God, through Moses, commanded circumcision just as Abraham had practiced it. The same applies to the eating of the sinew of the thigh; that prohibition is not the consequence of the prohibition to Jacob our father, but of the command of Moses our teacher. This is the import of the statement:[19] "Six hundred and thirteen commandments were given to Moses at Sinai," and all of these constitute the commandments.

The source for the binding force of both the positive and negative commandments in the halakhic system—even of commandments that existed before the Sinaitic Revelation—is that they are "the command of God given to Moses" when the Torah was revealed at Sinai.

This idea is also expressed in the comments of Rashbam on the verse in Genesis:[20] "Inasmuch as Abraham obeyed Me, and kept My charge: My commandments, My laws, and My teachings." Rashbam said:[21]

> "My laws and My teachings": the plain meaning is that all laws consonant with human reason,[22] such as those concerning robbery, incest, covetousness, the establishment of a legal system, and the offering of hospitality, were observed before the Torah was given, but were renewed and explicated to Israel, which entered a covenant to observe them.

Even commandments and laws required by reason and nature—the *jus naturale*—have their source and binding effect in the covenant that Israel made with God[23] at the time of the Revelation to fulfill and observe them.[24]

19. TB Makkot 23b.

20. Genesis 26:5.

21. Rashbam's Commentary on the Torah, *ad loc.*, s.v. Ḥukkotai ve-torotai (ed. Rosin, Breslau, 1882, p. 29).

22. The Hebrew is *ha-mizvot ha-nikarot* (lit. "the recognized laws"), which include all the laws for which the reasons are apparent, namely, the rational commandments. *See also supra* p. 195, discussing Rashbam's comment.

23. The idea that the acceptance of the Torah was on the basis of a covenant, a consensual agreement between God and the Jewish people, is very often referred to in Scripture. *See, e.g.*, Genesis 17:13 and Exodus 31:15ff., with regard to particular commandments; Exodus 34:27 and Deuteronomy 29:11, 13, and 14, with regard to the Torah in general. The idea also appears in many Talmudic sources. *See, e.g.*, TB Nedarim 25a, Gittin 60b. *Cf.* the detailed Talmudic discussion in TB Shabbat 88a, with regard to the degree of consent that existed in that covenant, and *Tosafot, ad loc.*, s.vv. Kafah aleihem har ke-gigit, and Moda'a rabbah le-oraita. The concept of consent as the basis for the binding force of legal rules appears in Rashbam in additional contexts as well. *See supra* p. 66 and *cf. also* p. 59 n. 32.

24. Sternberg, *supra* n. 7 at 141, notes the change effected by the establishment of the State of Israel in the basic norm for provisions of Jewish law enacted as legislation by the Knesset. Previously, the basic norm had been "the will of [God,] the universal Sovereign (*ribbon ha-olam*)," but now it became "the will of the sovereign nation (*ribbon ha-le'um*)." This clearly highlights the problem created by the intersection between the *Halakhah* and the State of Israel. *See* an interesting example of a similar problem in C.K. Allen, *supra* n. 3

IV. THE SOURCES OF JEWISH LAW

The three types of sources of law—*i.e.*, literary, historical, and legal—all exist in the Jewish legal system, as well as in other systems.

A. The Literary Sources[25]

The literary sources of Jewish law include all the authoritative sources containing the various provisions of Jewish law, such as the Torah, the Mishnah, the books of halakhic *midrashim*, the *Tosefta*, the two Talmuds, the commentaries and novellae, the responsa, and the codificatory literature. The Jewish legal system, like other legal systems, also has additional secondary sources (akin to what is called "the literature of the law"), as well as general literature containing useful and instructive information about the legal system. This type of general literature, however, is not recognized by the legal system as an authoritative source in which the law is to be found.

---

at 447 n. 1, with regard to various prohibitions enacted in English law against incest because such conduct offended divine commandments. A statute (25 Hen. VIII c. 22, sec. 3) provided, for instance: "No man, of what estate, degree or condition soever he be, hath power to dispense with God's laws, as all the clergy of the realm in the said convocations, and the most part of all the famous universities of Christendom, and we also, do affirm and think." This section was interpreted in the case of Brook v. B., [1861] 9 H.L.C. 193, 226, where Lord Granworth said:

> We do not hold the marriage to be void because it is contrary to the law of God, but because our law has prohibited it on the ground of being contrary to God's law. It is our laws which makes [*sic*] the marriage void, and not the law of God."

See also the additional material on this question in the cases referred to by Allen.

Two observations are in order at this point: First, the establishment of the State of Israel was not the first time there was such a change in the basic norm validating the provisions of Jewish law. In matters of personal status in Jewish law, the basic norm in the period of the British Mandate had been the authority of the British Parliament. The point Sternberg apparently intended to make, and correctly so, was that this was the first time there had been such a change within the legal system of a Jewish state.

Secondly, this change in the basic norm takes place only in the legal system of the state; in the legal system of Jewish law, no change has taken place in the basic norm validating any of its rules, even after one or more of its rules has been incorporated into another legal system. From the point of view of Jewish law, the basic norm remains, as it has always been, the binding authority of the Written Law (*Torah she-bi-khetav*). *See infra* pp. 1906–1908; Elon, *Ḥakikah*, pp. 59ff.

25. For the Hebrew edition of this work, a special term, *rishumiyyim*, was coined for "literary" sources, as applied to Jewish law. The accepted Hebrew for "literary" is *sifruti*, which is too closely associated with *belle-lettres* to be an accurate description of the written Torah, the Mishnah, the Talmuds, or the codificatory and kindred literature. The German *Erkenntnisquellen* ("the sources of knowledge of the law") is even more appropriate than the English "literary." I am grateful to my friend Prof. H. Rabin for his help in coining the Hebrew term. For a fuller and more technical discussion, *see* p. 209 n. 25 of the third Hebrew edition of the present work.

All these types of literature are discussed in detail in Volume III of this work.[26]

B. The Historical Sources

Much work and effort is involved in discovering the historical sources of the various norms of the Jewish legal system; and there is always great danger of being misled by insufficiently proved, and sometimes completely unfounded, hypotheses. Therefore, before any suggestion as to the historical source of any given law is accepted, it must be carefully tested. Identification of economic, social, and moral conditions as the foundation for the creation and development of a legal norm is most feasible for norms whose legal source is legislation[27] or custom,[28] because such norms are often accompanied, either expressly or by implication, by an explanation of the background that gave rise to their creation. Sometimes it is possible to discern the influence of a different legal system upon particular legal rules.[29] Research into the historical sources of Jewish law has been done in various works that treat the general history of the *Halakhah*,[30] as well as in specific studies dealing with this subject.[31] In a later discussion of various legal norms, we point out from time to time, to the extent possible, the historical sources of those norms.

C. The Legal Sources

As previously noted, the Written Law recognizes and gives binding effect to the legal sources of Jewish law, which are the Biblically sanctioned methods for according binding authority to every norm in the legal system.

The halakhic authorities found the grant of such authority in many sections and verses in the Torah.[32] The main passage is the following in the Book of Deuteronomy:

26. *Infra* pp. 1017–1019, 1027–1037.
27. *See infra* pp. 477ff. concerning various enactments.
28. *See infra* pp. 880ff. concerning various customs.
29. *See supra* pp. 62–64.
30. *E.g.*, Frankel, *Mishnah;* Weiss, *Dor Dor ve-Doreshav;* Tchernowitz, *Toledot ha-Halakhah* [History of the *Halakhah*]. *See* bibliography *infra*. *See also* the critique of G. Alon in *Meḥkarim*, II, pp. 181–247.
31. *See* Y. Baer, *Yisra'el ba-Ammim* [Israel among the Nations], 1955; *id.*, "Ha-Yesodot ha-Historiyyim Shel ha-Halakhah" [The Historical Foundations of the *Halakhah*], *Zion*, XVII, pp. 1–55; XXVII, pp. 117–155.
32. On this point, *see* pp. 275ff. in this volume, and Volume II of this work, at the beginning of the discussion of each of the legal sources.

> If a case is too baffling for you to decide, be it a controversy over homicide [*bein dam le-dam,* lit. "between blood and blood"], civil law [*bein din le-din,* lit. "between law and law"], or assault [*bein nega le-nega,* lit. (according to one meaning) "between blow and blow"]—matters of dispute in your gates [*i.e.,* where the courts sat]—you shall promptly repair to the place that the Lord your God will have chosen and appear before the priests the Levites, and the judge of that time, and present your problem. When they have announced to you the verdict in the case, you shall carry out the verdict that is announced to you from that place that the Lord chose, observing scrupulously all their instructions to you. You shall act in accordance with the instructions given you and the ruling handed down to you; you must not deviate from the verdict that they announce to you either to the right or to the left.[33]

In these and in additional verses the halakhic authorities found not only the general authority to solve problems that would arise from time to time[34] but also the methods, *i.e.,* the legal sources, according to which these problems were to be solved and by means of which the authorities were to

33. Deuteronomy 17:8–11. The translation of *bein dam le-dam,* etc., follows Ibn Ezra and Naḥmanides. Rashi, however, has a different interpretation.

34. As early as in the written Torah itself, we find problems that arose as a result of new situations for which existing law provided no solution. The man who pronounced the name of God in blasphemy was placed in custody "until the decision of the Lord should be made clear to them" as to what his sentence should be (Leviticus 24:10–16). Similarly, the men who were ritually impure and could not offer the Passover sacrifice on the fourteenth day of the first month "appeared before Moses and Aaron and said, 'Unclean though we are by reason of a corpse, why must we be debarred from presenting the Lord's offering at the set time with the rest of the Israelites?' Moses said to them, 'Stand by, and let me hear what instructions the Lord gives about you.' And the Lord spoke to Moses, saying . . ." (Numbers 9:1–14).

Similarly, the man who was found gathering wood on the sabbath day was placed in custody, "for it had not been specified what should be done to him" (Numbers 15:32–36). Again, the daughters of Zelophehad came before Moses with the plea, "Our father died in the wilderness . . . and has left no sons. Let not our father's name be lost to his clan because he had no son. Give us a holding among our father's kinsmen" (Numbers 27:3–4). Whereupon, the rules of succession were given, *i.e.,* that in the absence of a son, the daughters shall inherit (*id.* 6–11). Then, the Torah continues, the heads of one of the Josephite clans, to whom the daughters of Zelophehad belonged, argued to Moses that letting the daughters inherit could mean that the ancestral holding would pass to another tribe if the daughters married out of their own tribe. Thereupon, an additional rule was laid down whereby "Every daughter among the Israelite tribes who inherits a share must marry someone from a clan of her father's tribe, in order that every Israelite may keep his ancestral share" (*id.* 36:5–9). Regarding the manner of solving these new problems, the Torah states, "Moses brought their case [that of the daughters of Zelophehad] before the Lord" (*id.* 27:5). Similarly, all the other rules and solutions mentioned were promulgated by Moses, who received them from the Lord by divine revelation. In the passage in Deuteronomy 17:8–11 quoted in the text, authority for solving new problems arising after the Torah was given is conferred upon the halakhic authorities of each generation. For a detailed discussion of this point, *see infra* ch. 7.

continue to explicate, develop, and create the law. Maimonides summarized the subject as follows:[35]

> The High Court (Sanhedrin) in Jerusalem is the main institution of the Oral Law. The members thereof are the fount of instruction; from them issue statutes and judgments to all Israel. The Torah bids us repose confidence in them, as it is said: "[You shall act] in accordance with the instructions given you." This is a positive command. Whoever believes in Moses our teacher and his law is bound to follow their guidance in the practice of religion and to rely on them.
>
> It is immaterial whether the direction given by them concerns the Oral Law [in the narrow sense], *i.e.*, matters learned by tradition [handed down from person to person going back to Moses at Sinai], or whether it concerns interpretations that seem correct to them as a result of deduction by means of any of the canons by which the Torah is interpreted,[36] or whether it concerns decrees, enactments, and practices—measures devised by them to serve as a fence around the law, and designed to meet the needs of the time. Obedience to the directions given by them in all of these three categories is a positive commandment, and whoever disregards any of them [also] transgresses a negative commandment.[37]
>
> Scripture says: "In accordance with the instructions given you"—this refers to the enactments, decrees, and practices as to which they instruct the people in order to strengthen religion and improve the social order. "And [in accordance with] the ruling handed down to you"—this refers to laws derived through interpretation[38] by means of any of the canons by which Scripture is expounded. "From the verdict that they announce to you"—this refers to matters of tradition transmitted orally from person to person.

Analysis reveals that there are six legal sources of Jewish law:

1. *Tradition (kabbalah)*.[39] Chronologically, the first of the legal sources is "matters of tradition transmitted orally from person to person," tracing back to their reception by Moses from God. A legal rule derived from

35. Maimonides, *MT*, Mamrim 1:1–2.

36. *See infra* pp. 318–319.

37. Namely, the commandment that "you must not deviate from the verdict that they announce to you either to the right or to the left" (Deuteronomy 17:11); *see* TB Berakhot 19b. *See further* the critique of Naḥmanides in *Sefer ha-Mizvot*, Shoresh Rishon #4; *Kiryat Sefer* and *Leḥem Mishneh* commentaries to *MT*, Mamrim 1:1–2.

38. The Hebrew term used here by Maimonides for interpretation is *din*. For the use of the term *din* to refer to interpretation, *see infra* p. 277.

39. This term *kabbalah* is used in the sense given it by Maimonides, *MT*, Mamrim 1:2. *See also infra* n. 40. The terms *kabbalah* and "matters of *kabbalah*" are also used in different senses; *see supra* p. 203 n. 65 and accompanying text.

this legal source is transmitted from generation to generation.[40] This legal source is fundamentally different from the other legal sources of Jewish law in that it is inherently not amenable to development; it does not change but remains fixed—a static source of Jewish law. In contrast, the other legal sources are inherently dynamic; in fact, a significant aspect of their function is to continue the creativity and development of Jewish law.

2. *Interpretation* (*midrash*). This includes the interpretation of Scripture and of the *Halakhah* in its different periods, and also, to a certain extent, other types of interpretation.
3. *Legislation* (*takkanah* and *gezerah*). This includes legislation by the halakhic authorities and by competent public bodies.
4. *Custom* (*minhag*). This includes various forms of custom and usage.
5. *Case* or *Incident (ma'aseh)*. This refers to legal decisions and also to the personal conduct of halakhic authorities in particular real-life situations.
6. *Legal Reasoning* (*sevarah*). This is the process of legal and practical reasoning by the halakhic authorities.

All of the last five legal sources serve as the recognized methods of the Jewish legal system for solving new legal and social problems, creating new legal rules, and changing existing legal rules where necessitated by changes in mores or in economic and social conditions. In Part Two of this work (the second part of this volume and all of Volume II), each of these five legal sources is studied in detail. We indicate the basis of each source in the Written Law; describe the distinctive characteristics of each source, as well as its major principles and limitations; and show, taking specific laws as examples, how each source has operated in the Jewish legal system and how the bulk of this system was developed by means of these legal sources.[41]

40. M Avot 1:1; *Avot de-R. Nathan* 1:1; Maimonides, *MT*, Mamrim 1:2; Maimonides' Introduction to his *Commentary on the Mishnah*. For additional discussion of this legal source, *see supra* ch. 5.

41. Any of these legal sources may sometimes also be a historical source. This is true, for instance, of custom, which, apart from its function as a legal source validating legal norms, sometimes serves as the historical source of a norm that subsequently receives its legal force from one of the legal sources. *See infra* pp. 880–882 and n. 8.

Chapter 7
THE PREROGATIVES OF THE HALAKHIC AUTHORITIES

I. "The Torah Is from Heaven" and "The Torah Is Not in Heaven"
II. No Suprahuman Authority in Halakhic Determinations
  A. "A Prophet Is No Longer Authorized to Innovate"
  B. The Torah Was Entrusted to the Halakhic Authorities
  C. Law and Equity—"Right" That Is "Left" and "Left" That Is "Right"
  D. The Oven of Akhnai
  E. Differences of Opinion with Regard to Suprahuman Influences in the Determination of the *Halakhah:* The Accepted View
III. The Prerogatives of the Halakhic Authorities as Existing in Every Generation
IV. The Principle that "The Law Is in Accordance with the Views of the Later Authorities" (*Hilkheta ke-Vatra'ei*)

I. "THE TORAH IS FROM HEAVEN" AND "THE TORAH IS NOT IN HEAVEN"

As has been noted in the preceding chapter, the Sages based the binding force of the legal sources of the law on statements in Scripture—the Written Law. Close examination reveals that, rather than providing specific support for one or another particular legal source, the Torah delegates to the halakhic authorities the overall responsibility for establishing the ultimate form of the halakhic system. The halakhic authorities in different periods—both Talmudic and post-Talmudic—used this authority as a powerful instrument for continuing the creativity and development of the *Halakhah*.

Our previous discussion emphasized tradition—the doctrine that the Oral Law was handed down from person to person, beginning with Moses, who received it from God—as the basis of the Oral Law. We found this characteristic of the *Halakhah* attributed to the entire *corpus juris* of the *Halakhah* in all of its details and provisions: the halakhic authorities describe the totality of the *Halakhah* as making manifest what had already been given and declared at Sinai.[1]

1. *See supra* pp. 192, 225–226.

Statements by many of the halakhic authorities nevertheless indicate that they distinguished carefully between two parts of the Oral Law: (1) the part originating in "tradition handed down from one person to another," going back to Moses, who received it from God, and (2) the part that the halakhic authorities had the responsibility to create and develop. The distinction is made in a comment of the Sages on a verse in Exodus.[2] According to the verse:

> When He finished speaking with him on Mt. Sinai, He gave Moses the two tablets of the Testimony, stone tablets inscribed with the finger of God.

The Sages commented:

> But did Moses learn the entire Torah? It is written in Scripture:[3] "Its measure is longer than the earth and broader than the sea." Did Moses really learn something so vast in just forty days? The answer is, God taught Moses the general principles. . . .[4]

Together with the Written Law, Moses was given principles whereby the Written Law was to be interpreted and understood; and it was according to these principles that new laws were generated, so as to render explicit what had previously been only implicit in Scripture. The thought expressed in the comment quoted above was further developed by Joseph Albo, the Spanish Jewish philosopher, at the end of the fourteenth century:

> It is impossible for the Torah of God to have covered all possible cases that may ever arise, because the new situations that constantly arise in human affairs, in law, and as a result of human enterprise are so manifold that a book cannot encompass them. Therefore, general principles, which the Torah only briefly suggests, were revealed orally to Moses at Sinai, so that the halakhic authorities of every generation would use them to derive new laws.[5]

Thus, when we examine the views of many of the halakhic authorities, we will find that as clearly and unequivocally as they emphasized the suprahuman and divine quality of the Source of the entire *Halakhah*, in the very same way and with the same emphasis they also stressed the human factor—the exclusive prerogative of the halakhic authorities in regard to the ongoing development and creation of the *Halakhah*. The dual character of the *Halakhah* is expressed in two fundamental maxims pervading the

2. Exodus 31:18.
3. Job 11:9.
4. *Exodus Rabbah*, Ki Tissa, 41:6.
5. *Sefer ha-Ikkarim* 3:23.

halakhic ambiance. On the one hand, it is a basic article of faith that "the Torah is *from* Heaven"; and on the other, it is also a basic principle that "the Torah is not *in* heaven."[6] The source of the *Halakhah* is Heaven, but the place of the *Halakhah*, and its life and development, are not in heaven but in human society.

The halakhic authorities saw no contradiction between "the Torah is from Heaven" and "the Torah is not in heaven"; they firmly believed that each halakhic authority's interpretations, enactments, new perceptions, and writings merely actualize what was already included *in potentia* in the Revelation at Sinai and designated from the very beginning for the needs of his particular generation: "Not only did all the prophets receive their prophecy from Sinai, but every halakhic authority of every generation received his [portion in the *Halakhah*] from Sinai."[7]

II. NO SUPRAHUMAN AUTHORITY IN HALAKHIC DETERMINATIONS

A. "A Prophet Is No Longer Authorized to Innovate"

The Sages concluded from the previously quoted passage in Deuteronomy[8] that the determination of every question that will arise in any area of law in connection with the commandments involving human relationships with God, as well as those involving relationships within human society, must be sought from the priest, the Levite, and the judge, who will sit in judgment in the appointed place and declare the law in accordance with the circumstances of the time and place. The Sages explained that the composition of this group—priest, Levite, and judge—was to ensure that the law would be determined and established by teachers and judges whose decisions are guided solely by their own wisdom and learning—the function of the priest and the Levite being to guide and teach the people.[9] For this reason, when in the course of time the priests and the Levites ceased to function as the exclusive religious teachers,[10] we are told:[11]

6. TB Bava Meẓi'a 59a/b, Temurah 16a; TJ Mo'ed Katan 3:1, 10b (3:1, 81d)—based on Deuteronomy 30:12; Maimonides, *MT*, Yesodei ha-Torah 9:4.

7. *Exodus Rabbah*, Yitro, 28:4; *Tanḥuma* (printed eds.), Yitro, 11. *See also* Urbach, *The Sages*, pp. 304ff.

8. *Supra* p. 237.

9. Deuteronomy 33:10. The blessing of Moses to the tribe of Levi was: "They shall teach Your laws to Jacob and Your instructions to Israel"; similarly, Ezekiel 44:23–24; Malachi 2:7. *See also infra* n. 15.

10. *See infra* p. 309.

11. *Sifrei*, Deuteronomy, Shofetim, sec. 153 (p. 206).

"To the priests [and] the Levites"—the requirement is that a court should include priests and Levites. Shall we conclude that the requirement is mandatory, so that if a court is without them it has no authority? Therefore Scripture states: "And [to] the judge"—even though a court does not include any priests or Levites, it is a competent court.

The prophet, on the other hand, who has a suprahuman function as the bearer of heavenly vision, may not participate in the determination of the law. The *Sifra* comments[12] as follows on the last verse in the Book of Leviticus[13] (namely, "These are the commandments that the Lord gave Moses for the Israelite people on Mt. Sinai"): "'These are the commandments'—a prophet is no longer authorized to introduce anything new."

A law that has been forgotten may be recalled by means of logic and careful study, not by intervention of the Divine Spirit.[14] This is because of the principle summarized by Maimonides as follows:

> God did not permit us to learn [the law] from the prophets but from the halakhic authorities, men of reason and knowledge. The Torah does not state "you shall go to the prophet who will be in those days" but "you shall . . . appear before the priests the Levites, and the judge. . . . [Deuteronomy 17:9].[15]

B. The Torah Was Entrusted to the Halakhic Authorities

This basic doctrine that the halakhic authorities have the exclusive prerogative to interpret the Torah and to carry on the creation and development of the *Halakhah* was expressed by the Talmudic Sages in an extreme but

12. *Sifra,* Beḥukkotai, 13:7.
13. Leviticus 27:34.
14. TB Temurah 16a.
15. Maimonides, Introduction to the *Commentary on the Mishnah. See also* Josephus, *Antiquities,* IV, 8:14 (describing the composition of the court referred to in Deuteronomy 17:9 as ". . . the High Priest, the Prophet, and the Council of the Elders." His addition of "the Prophet" is contrary to the plain meaning of the text. *Cf.* Schor's translation, p. 198 n. 5, and that of Shalit, nn. 127, 127a). The statement in TJ Berakhot 1:4, 3b is also instructive:

> The statements of the Elders [Sages] have greater weight than those of the Prophets. . . . To what may the Prophet and the Elder [respectively] be likened? To a king who sent two representatives to a province; with regard to one of them, he wrote, "Place no credence in him unless he shows you my signature and my seal," and with regard to the other, he wrote, "Even if he does not show you my signature, place your credence in him without signature or seal." Thus, it is written with regard to the Prophet, "And he gives you a sign or a portent" [Deuteronomy 13:2], whereas here [with regard to the Sage], "You shall act in accordance with the instructions given you" [*id.* 17:11].

compelling manner. They interpreted the verse in Deuteronomy [17:11]: "You must not deviate from the verdict that they announce to you either to the right or to the left" as follows:[16]

> "To the right or to the left"—even when it appears to you that they are saying that right is left and left is right, you must obey them.[17]

The *Halakhah* is thus identified with those to whom it is entrusted, to the point that even an error of the halakhic authorities is still *Halakhah*. This idea was clearly expressed by Naḥmanides:

> Even if you think that they [the halakhic authorities] are mistaken and the matter is as clear to you as the difference between your right hand and your left, you shall do as they direct. You shall say: "The Lord, who is the source of the commandments, has commanded me to perform all of His commandments in accordance with the instructions of those who stand in His presence in the place that He will choose. He gave me the Torah to carry out according to their opinion as to its meaning, even if their opinion is erroneous. . . ." [Their opinion controls] as to all of their interpretations of the Torah, whether they received the interpretation by transmission from person to person extending back to Moses, [who received it] from God [*i.e.*, by tradition], or whether they base their views upon the sense of Scripture [*i.e.*, exegesis] or on their own objectives [according to a different text: its objective]. This is because He gave the Torah to us with the understanding that the ultimate

16. *Sifrei*, Deuteronomy, Shofetim, sec. 154 (p. 207).

17. With variations in style, this is also the version in *Midrash Tannaim*, pp. 102–103; *Shir ha-Shirim Rabbah* #1 (the third), par. 2; *Midrash Lekaḥ Tov*, Shofetim, 17:11; and *Yalkut Shim'oni*, Shofetim, 911. TJ Horayot 1:1, 2b (1:1, 45d), however, has a version expressing a diametrically opposite meaning:

> It might be thought that if they say that right is left and left is right, you must still obey them. [To forestall such an interpretation,] Scripture therefore states that you must not deviate . . . "either to the right or the left," *i.e.*, [you must obey them only] when they declare the right to be right and the left to be left.

This version presents a difficulty: By what criterion is the correctness of their ruling to be judged? This difficulty is raised by Abrabanel in his commentary on Deuteronomy, *ad loc.*, and by David ha-Levi, author of the *Taz*, in his commentary, *Divrei David*, on the Pentateuch, *ad loc. See further* Ḥayyim Joseph David Azulai (Ḥida), *Sha'ar Yosef*, on Tractate *Horayot*, *ad loc.*; D.Z. Hoffmann, *Der Oberste Gerichtshof* [The Supreme Court], Berlin, 1878, pp. 9–13; Hoffmann, *Commentary on Deuteronomy*, *ad loc.* (Hebrew trans. p. 315).

Presumably, the two versions express two different basic approaches regarding the extent of the prerogative of the halakhic authorities. One can find a hint of the two approaches in the difference of opinion between R. Kahana and R. Eleazar in TB Sanhedrin 88a regarding the "rebellious elder" (*zaken mamre*) who rejects a decision of the Sanhedrin, where R. Kahana takes the same view as the TJ version and R. Eleazar takes the view of the other sources. According to most authorities, the version, with its attendant conclusions, that should be accepted as correct is that of the majority of sources and not that of TJ. *See also infra* n. 18.

prerogative to construe it is entrusted to the halakhic authorities, and their construction is binding even if they appear to be changing right into left.[18]

There is no inconsistency in the statement of Naḥmanides: "Since He who commanded the observance of the Torah and what is prohibited and what is permissible also commanded that 'you must not deviate from the verdict that they announce to you,' it follows that whatever they direct may properly be done because that is what God commanded."[19]

Even if the decision of the halakhic authorities in a particular case is erroneous, "it is better to suffer one error and generally let everything be governed by their sound judgment than to allow each individual to act according to his own judgment, which would result in the ruination of [the Jewish] religion, the spread of schism, and the destruction of the [Jewish] people. It was also commanded that a minority of the halakhic authorities should always defer to the majority."[20]

Nissim Gerondi explained further:[21]

18. Naḥmanides, *Commentary on Deuteronomy* 17:11. *See also* Naḥmanides' critical glosses on Maimonides' *Sefer ha-Mizvot,* First Principle (p. 14 in Pardes ed.), and the difficulty he presents from TB Horayot 2b (which to some extent is similar to the difficulty from TJ Horayot, *see supra* n. 17). The remarks of Nissim Gerondi are also pertinent:

> We have been commanded to obey their decision whether it represents the truth or its opposite . . . for the [power of] decision has been entrusted to the halakhic authorities of each generation. Whatever they decide is what God has commanded (*Derashot ha-Ran* #7).
>
> For the Lord, Who is to be blessed, has entrusted these decisions entirely to the halakhic authorities of our generation and has commanded us to obey them, so that whatever they decide is what Moses was commanded by the Almighty. Even if we are informed by a heavenly voice or a prophet that their decision is the opposite of the truth, we may still not deviate from it . . . for God has not entrusted the decision on doubtful matters of Torah to a prophet or to a heavenly voice but to the halakhic authorities of the generation. This is what R. Joshua [was saying when he] stood up and declared: "It is not in heaven" [Deuteronomy 30:12]. (*Derashot ha-Ran* #11).

Various aspects of this concept may be found in Talmudic literature. *See, e.g.,* the incident when R. Joshua went, staff and money in hand, on the day that was Yom Kippur according to his own reckoning of the calendar, to visit Rabban Gamaliel (M Rosh ha-Shanah 2:9, cited by Naḥmanides, *Commentary on Deuteronomy* 17:11); TB Ḥagigah 18a ("From this it follows that Scripture has entrusted exclusively to the Sages [the authority] to declare to you on which day labor is prohibited and on which day it is permitted, which types of work are prohibited and which are permitted"); Bekhorot 26b ("Scripture has referred you solely to the Sages"); Rashi, *ad loc.,* s.v. Lo mesarekha ha-katuv ella la-ḥakhamim; Rashi, Sotah 19a, s.v. Ve-Rabbi Yehudah; Rashi, Kiddushin 11b, s.v. U-tenan shevu'at ha-dayyanim; Rashi, Shevu'ot 7b, s.v. Mi-tum'ot ve-lo kol tum'ot.

19. Maharal of Prague in *Gur Aryeh* on Deuteronomy 17:11.

20. *Sefer ha-Ḥinnukh,* ed. Chavel, Commandment #508. With regard to the author of that work, *see infra* p. 1265.

21. *Derashot ha-Ran* #11.

> The Torah took pains to prevent an ever-threatening misfortune: schisms and dissension that would cause the Torah to become two Torahs. It forestalled this constantly threatening misfortune when it entrusted the decision of doubtful cases to the halakhic authorities of each generation. In most cases, the result will be desirable and their decisions will be just; for the Masters of the *Halakhah* will err much less frequently than persons of lesser wisdom. This is certainly true for the Sanhedrin, who stand before God in His Temple and in the Divine Presence, which abides among them. And if it happens that on an extraordinary and unusual occasion they may err in some matter, the Torah was not apprehensive about the remote possibility of such mischance, because it is worthwhile accepting that risk, it being outweighed by the beneficial results over the long run, and no other solution exists [which can reduce the risk].[22]

Other halakhic authorities have a different explanation of the doctrine of the binding force of the pronouncements of the halakhic authorities even when those pronouncements declare that "right" is "left" and "left" is "right." In their view, it should not be thought that the doctrine contemplates that the halakhic authorities indeed erred in their ruling and that the doctrine commands obedience to rulings in fact erroneous. Isaac Abrabanel, one of the leading Biblical commentators and Jewish thinkers who lived at the time of the expulsion from Spain, wrote:[23]

> My mind is not at ease, because both as a general matter and in any particular case we cannot believe that evil will result from divine commandments, and God will not command that we should ever believe a false thing. Far be it from the Sages to intend this! The Torah does not contemplate that the perception of one who observes the divine commandments will be such that he will think that what is pure is impure, what is permissible is prohibited, and what is helpful is injurious, for the Torah of God embodies the pursuit of absolute justice, and the Lord God is true and His Torah is true.

This line of reasoning led some halakhic authorities and thinkers to a different explanation of the substance and intent of the doctrine: "right" and "left" are not identical to truth and nontruth, to right and wrong. *Both* "right" and "left" are elements of the *correct* law, in the broad sense of the meaning of the law. Both are *correct* decisions in that they both contain elements of truth and justice. Furthermore, the doctrine pertains primarily to the prerogative of the halakhic authorities and to their duty in particular circumstances to reach a decision that what appears to be right is left and vice versa. The doctrine does not refer to an error where the right was

22. *See,* to similar effect, Naḥmanides, *Commentary on Deuteronomy* 17:11, citing the same rationale for the prerogative of the halakhic authorities, *i.e.,* to minimize dissension.

23. Abrabanel, *Commentary on Deuteronomy* 17:8 *et seq.*

actually mistaken for the left or the left for the right, but to a purposeful and intentional decision that what appears to be left is in fact right and what appears to be right is in fact left. For in the world of the *Halakhah,* as in all other legal systems, there are particular circumstances when such a ruling is the desirable and correct decision. We have already touched on such decision making to the extent required in connection with the subject of law and equity.[24] The more extensive discussion in the following section is now appropriate for purposes of the subject at hand.

C. Law and Equity—"Right" That Is "Left" and "Left" That Is "Right"

There are times when a particular norm, generally satisfactory and desirable overall, is the cause of injustice when applied in the special circumstances of a particular case. The problematics of this situation are the central topic in the subject of law and equity, which has already been discussed. Some take the view that only the legislator may protect against individual injustice and the court must apply the strict law, so as to preserve the stability and uniformity of the law.[25] According to the basic approach of equity, however, the protection of the individual is a judicial function: just as courts must adjudicate according to justice as expressed in the general rules of law, they must see to it that these general rules do not cause harm or injustice in the special circumstances of an individual case. This obligation to do equity is part of the inherent jurisdiction of a court.[26] Many halakhic authorities found this fundamental principle to be the meaning of the doctrine that obedience is required even when they say that right is left and left is right.

This interpretation is discussed, extensively and in great detail, by Abrabanel's contemporary, Isaac Arama, in his book, *Akedat Yiẓhak.*[27] Isaac Arama discussed the subject in its various aspects, from the philosophic-

24. *Supra* pp. 176–181.

25. *See supra* pp. 176–178. *See also infra* n. 56 for the approach of Maimonides as explicated by Isaac Arama.

26. The king's law was also meant to rectify the deficiencies resulting from the application of strict law, which cannot always succeed in promoting the social welfare and in meeting contemporary needs. *See supra* pp. 56–57 for Nissim Gerondi's comments on this subject; however, he was referring primarily not to the specific problem of injustice resulting from the application of a general rule in a particular case, but to harmonizing the requirements of the general law with the contemporary needs of society. Even with regard to the latter objective, Nissim Gerondi himself remarked that the Talmud indicates that to some extent this is properly a function of the legal system itself. *See supra* p. 57 n. 27.

27. *Akedat Yiẓhak,* Yitro, gate 43 (ed. H.J. Pollack, Pressburg, 1849), pp. 85b–86b. The author (1420–1494) lived in Spain and Italy.

theoretical and the practical-legal perspectives, while comparing the views of other thinkers on the subject. It is worthwhile to quote him, albeit at some length:

> Scripture states: "He [God] is just (*ẓaddik*) and equitable (*yashar*)."[28] This is a marvelous statement. You will understand it when I remind you what the philosopher [Aristotle] wrote in chapter 13 in the above-mentioned essay of the *Book of Ethics*,[29] where he distinguishes between the equitable person and the just person. He poses the following query: Since the just and the equitable are both species of that genus of virtue called justice, the question inevitably arises: If the just man is the best in that category, then the equitable man cannot be thought good, because he goes to excess, which is the opposite of his praiseworthy reputation among all men. If, on the other hand, the equitable man is the best in that category, then the just man cannot be thought good, for he falls short, which is contrary to what is explicated and affirmed in that entire essay.
>
> He [Aristotle] resolves this quandary by stating that the just man excels with respect to the prevailing laws, *i.e.*, the general principles that are for the most part just, for he obeys them and is careful not to stray from them to the right or the left. But the equitable man is the one who perfects and refines the prevailing laws by making exceptions to these general rules, to the extent necessary, when, for whatever reason, the legislator, if then present, would not have applied the prevailing laws himself.
>
> This is the import of the statements [by the Sages]: "Thus we will judge you and all your violent companions"[30] [*i.e.*, when the defendant is a violent man and the plaintiff's witnesses are afraid to testify, the burden of proof, contrary to the usual rule, is placed on the defendant] and "Judgment is reached both according to the law and not according to the law (*ka-din ve-she-lo ka-din*), as the needs of the time require."[31]
>
> Thus, we see that the just person is good with respect to conventional law, which is generally just, but the fair and equitable person is superior, in that he perfects and refines that law in situations in which the prevailing law does not succeed in achieving justice. The law cannot encompass the endless number of atypical cases. A result fair in one case may not be fair in another. This is the very notion the Psalmist had in mind in the expression, "He is equitable (*ḥasid*) in all his works."[32] This means that although He is just in promulgating rules of law, which are generally just and are to be followed in all matters where their application is appropriate, "He is equitable in all his works," since in actual practice he does not desire these general rules to be

28. Deuteronomy 32:4. The JPS *Tanakh*'s translation of *yashar* as "upright" does not give the true sense of the argument here.

29. Aristotle, *Ethics*, 5:13.

30. TB Ketubbot 27b; Bava Meẓi'a 39b. *See also infra* p. 1715; *Resp. Ribash* #170.

31. TB Yevamot 90b. *See also infra* pp. 515–519.

32. Psalms 145:17. JPS *Tanakh* translates: "He is faithful in all His works."

always followed. Instead, each judgment should fit the unique situation whenever it is realized that the general rule is inconsistent with true justice. In such cases, it is not the conventional law but peace and equity that should govern.

This very notion is expressed by the words of the chief of the prophets [Moses]:[33] "He [God] is just (*ẓaddik*) and equitable (*yashar*)." For the immediately preceding statement, "All His ways are just, a faithful God, never false,"[34] becomes questionable when it is realized that even His judgments will result in confusion and perplexity when the general rules do not fit particular cases. For example, there is an important rule of civil law that the burden of proof is on the claimant,[35] and another rule that it is presumed that a person does not repay a debt before its due date.[36] It can happen, for example, that a plaintiff has a meritorious claim but can furnish no proof, or that a debtor in fact prepaid his debt with no witnesses present. The judge is then faced with a dilemma: either he must decide according to the truth of the particular case, thus doing violence to the general rule, or he must apply the general rule and do violence to the truth of the particular case; and there are other similar instances [presenting this dilemma]. The solution to this difficulty is: "He [God] is just (*ẓaddik*) and equitable (*yashar*)," *i.e.,* He is the Just One who promulgates the law and He is also the Equitable One who refines and perfects it when necessary, so that He may be truly called "a faithful God" in Whom there is no unfairness whatsoever.

This kind of fairness is commanded and insisted upon to an extraordinary degree in the Torah: "If a case is too baffling for you to decide . . . you shall . . . appear before the priests the Levites . . . you shall carry out the verdict that is announced to you . . . in accordance with the instructions given you. . . . Should a man act presumptuously and disregard the priest . . . or the judge. . . ."[37] The passage talks about cases that, for any reason, are too baffling for them. For the most part, this will occur when they realize that the general rules do not fit the case being litigated and they are uncertain whether to apply the general rules or to decide on some other basis. Such a case should be decided by the High Court, for God has given its members full authority to refine and adjust the law as they see fit for that particular case.

Furthermore, God commanded that one may not deviate from their ruling to the right or to the left because even if their judgment does not accord with the letter of the general law, it is the essential truth for this particular case. This is the meaning of the statement of the Sages,[38] "Even when they say that right is left, and that left is right, and certainly if they tell you that right is right and left is left [you should follow their ruling]." Even though

33. Deuteronomy 32:4.
34. *Id.*
35. TB Bava Meẓi'a 2b; Bava Kamma 46b; *see also infra* pp. 385, 992–993.
36. TB Bava Batra 5a/b; *see also infra* p. 996.
37. Deuteronomy 17:8–13.
38. *Sifrei,* Deuteronomy, Shofetim, sec. 154.

under the general rules it would at first sight seem that they are declaring right to be left and left to be right, yet for that specific case they are in fact judging right to be right and left to be left. The purpose of Scripture's statement, "Should a man act presumptuously and disregard the . . . judge, that man shall die. Thus you shall sweep out evil from Israel,"[39] is to strengthen their authority and eliminate all hostile objections based on the written laws.

This is the source of authority for the courts in every generation to judge and to inflict a punishment that will be both "according to the law and not according to the law." "According to the law" means according to the requirement of the particular case; "not according to the law" means not applying the general rules. As the Sages said,[40] "not that this is the law, but the times demand it," *i.e.,* that this is not the general law, but that the specific case, as put to them, requires it. Thus, the Torah encompasses all types of people and all of their individual activities, as is to be expected from a perfect Torah and divine law that includes within its vast insight all the details of matters and events pertaining to everything that exists. As the Psalmist wrote,[41] "He . . . fashions the hearts of them all . . . [and] discerns all their doings."

This notion is what the Sages had in mind in saying,[42] "All who give judgments that are completely and truly correct [lit. 'true to their very truth' (*din emet le-amito*)] become partners with God in the creation of heaven and earth," because all mankind will thereby be maintained in the nature and manner in which they were created, in accordance with their very essence. Because of this partnership, judges are called *elohim*[43] [which usually means "God"] throughout Scripture. Similarly, the serpent said, "You will be like God, who knows good [and bad],"[44] on which the Sages commented,[45] "[You will be] creators of worlds."

Indeed, judges who always decide only according to the general rules, although they give a true judgment, [do not give a judgment "true to its very truth" and in fact they] destroy the world, as it was said,[46] "Jerusalem was destroyed because they gave true judgments," *i.e.,* their judgments were based on general truth, which they did not adjust even when necessary; but they said "Let the law cut through the mountain" [*i.e.,* "Let the law be applied no matter how unjust the result"].[47] Concerning them, did the Psalmist say,[48] "They neither know nor understand, they go about in darkness; all the

39. Deuteronomy 17:12.
40. TB Yevamot 90b.
41. Psalms 33:15.
42. TB Shabbat 10a.
43. Exodus 21:6, 22:7–8.
44. Genesis 3:5.
45. *Genesis Rabbah,* sec. 19.
46. TB Bava Meẓi'a 30b; this Talmudic discussion should be given careful consideration.
47. *Cf.* TB Sanhedrin 6b, and the Latin maxim *Fiat justitia, ruat caelum* (let justice be done though the heavens fall).
48. Psalms 82:5.

foundations of the earth totter." This group is the most dangerous of all the types of harmful judges mentioned earlier, as will be explained in the commentary[49] on "And you shall choose from among the people" [Exodus 18:21].

All of this thought-provoking subject is included in the complete explanation of "He [God] is just (*ẓaddik*) and equitable (*yashar*),"[50] for otherwise he could not be "The Rock . . . [Whose] deeds are perfect, yea, all His ways are just" [Deuteronomy 32:4]. As the Master Teacher (*ha-rav ha-moreh*)[51] wrote in chapter 49 of section 3:

> You will be exceedingly amazed by the contents of God's laws as you are at His deeds. Scripture says:[52] "The Rock!—His deeds are perfect, yea, all His ways are just," which means that just as His deeds are absolutely perfect, so, too, are His judgments perfectly fair.

Although from chapter 34 in that section[53] it might appear that he was discussing the general principles of the Torah and not their specific applications, examine his statement carefully, because what we have written is the correct conclusion that necessarily follows from the perfection of the divine Torah, as we have stated.

This quotation is instructive: There exists the general truth of legal rules and the individual truth of specific cases. A judge does not discharge his obligation if he decides only according to general truth; he must render not only a "true judgment" but one "true to its very truth," *i.e.*, the perfect truth of the specific case. This same point, with the very same formulation, has been noted in the previous discussion of *lifnim mi-shurat ha-din*, and of how obligations *lifnim mi-shurat ha-din* became legal obligations.[54]

According to Isaac Arama, the thrust of the verse "If a case is too baffling for you to decide," which begins the section of the Torah that is the Scriptural basis for the creative legal sources of Jewish law,[55] is directed to the "kind of fairness" that is called for when "general rules" do not produce a fair result under the circumstances of a particular case. In such instances, the crucial issue is whether "to apply the general rules or to decide on some other basis" (lit. "to judge within or outside them"). It is the High Court

49. *See Akedat Yiẓḥak, supra* n. 27, continuation of gate 43.

50. Deuteronomy 32:4.

51. Maimonides, *Moreh Nevukhim* [The Guide for the Perplexed], Part III, ch. 49. Note the play in the Hebrew on *moreh*, "teacher," in *ha-rav ha-moreh* and *Moreh* in the title of Maimonides' work.

52. Deuteronomy 32:4.

53. Maimonides, *supra* n. 51, ch. 34.

54. *Supra* p. 159. Joshua Falk also explained the statement by the Sages regarding left that is right and right that is left on the basis of this fundamental idea. *See* his further comments, *supra* p. 159.

55. *See supra* pp. 236–238.

that has the authority "to refine . . . the law," and one must not deviate either right or left from its judgments.

"Right" and "left" are thus relative and not absolute concepts. From the perspective of general truth, the fairness to the individual in his particular case that comes from bending the strict law is "left"; but from the perspective of individual truth, this "left" is actually not left but right. From the perspective of "truth," it is left, but from the perspective of perfect truth ("a judgment true to its very truth"), it is right. Isaac Arama proves that this is the method of the *Halakhah:* where a defendant is a violent person, the court deviates from the general rule that the burden of proof is on the plaintiff. Similarly, in a case of a particular social need, the court is authorized to impose punishment for which the law does not provide. In every such situation, it cannot be said that the court is calling "right" what is in fact left; rather, the court is rightly calling "right" what is really right. Not only is the court acting within its authority in deciding in this manner, but it is obligated to decide in this way—"to refine and adjust the law as . . . [it sees] fit for that particular case." Every court that bases its judgment "on general truth which . . . [it does] not adjust even when necessary" and that says, "Let the law cut through the mountain," carries on blindly, abuses its judicial function, and causes the very foundations of the earth to totter.[56]

56. At the conclusion of his comments, Isaac Arama emphasized that his view conflicts with that of Maimonides in *The Guide for the Perplexed,* Part III, ch. 34; this assessment seems correct. Maimonides' statement is directly connected with our subject and merits quotation here:

> It is also important to note that the Torah does not take into account exceptional circumstances; it does not deal with conditions that rarely occur. Whatever the Torah commands, whether it be of an intellectual, moral, or practical nature, is directed to common, and not exceptional circumstances; it ignores the injury that might be caused to a particular individual through any given law or particular divine precept. For the Torah is a divine institution; and [in order to understand its operation] we must consider how, in nature, the various forces produce general benefits, but in some individual cases they also cause injury. This is clear from what we ourselves [Part III, ch. 12] as well as others have said.
>
> We must consequently not be surprised when we find that the Torah does not achieve its objectives in the case of every individual; there must, naturally, be people whom the rules of the Torah do not fully make perfect. . . . From this consideration, it also follows that the commandments cannot be like medical prescriptions, specially compounded for a particular individual at a given time. They cannot vary with the different conditions of persons and times, but the divine guidance contained in the Torah must be certain and general, although its effect may be beneficial for some but not for others. If the precepts of the Torah varied with each individual, they would be imperfect in their totality, each precept being uncertain. For this reason, it would not be right to make the fundamental principles of the Torah dependent on time or place. On the contrary, legal rules must be absolute and general, in accordance with the divine words: "There shall be one law for you and for the resident stranger" [Numbers 15:15]; they are intended, as has been stated before, to produce results that are generally beneficial.

The comments of Isaac Abrabanel on the section of the Book of Deuteronomy that begins "If a case is too baffling for you to decide . . ."[57] also seem to take this same basic approach. Some of Abrabanel's comments and proofs are even identical to what has been quoted from Isaac Arama.[58] It is worthwhile reviewing some of the comments of Abrabanel that Arama did not cover or that more fully explain points that Arama did make. Such a review suggests a somewhat different approach from that taken by Arama in *Akedat Yiẓḥak.*

After Abrabanel dealt with the general rules of law, "which are essentially just and fair," and demonstrated in the same way as Arama that at certain times and in particular circumstances they are neither just nor fair, he added:

> This is what we learned in chapter *Hayu Bodekin* in Tractate *Sanhedrin*[59]—that witnesses in murder cases were questioned: Do you recognize the defendant? Did you forewarn him? Did he accept the forewarning? Did he commit the murder immediately thereafter? For all this is required by general justice and the constraints of the law, so that no one will be executed unless he is aware that he will be subject to the death penalty for what he is about to do. Thus, the judges acting pursuant to justice under law will not execute a murderer unless there were witnesses, there was a forewarning, the murder was committed immediately thereafter, and all the other requirements mentioned have been fulfilled.
>
> However, if that degree of technicality will always be insisted on, the number of murderers will increase, and the body politic will be destroyed, as the Sages, of blessed memory, said in chapter *Eillu Meẓi'ot:*[60] "Jerusalem was destroyed because they judged according to the law of the Torah," *i.e.,* according to the general law, which they did not adjust to the needs of the times, maintaining instead, "Let the law cut through the mountain." It is therefore sometimes necessary to decide a matter contrary to the general provisions of the law, depending on the time and place. This is not for the purpose of violating the laws of the Torah, but to meet temporary exigencies. Because such power and capacity—to inflict punishment not provided by law and to deviate from the laws and rules of the Torah—should not be given to everyone,

---

For a discussion of this passage in Maimonides, as compared to other passages in his *Mishneh Torah* and *Guide for the Perplexed, see* the articles by S. Rosenthal, S. Rosenberg, A. Kirschenbaum, and H. Shein, *supra* p. 177 n. 343.

57. *See supra* p. 237.

58. On the relationship between Abrabanel's commentary and Arama's book, *Akedat Yiẓḥak,* both of which were written by members of the same generation of Spanish exiles, *see* B. Netanyahu, *Don Isaac Abravanel: Statesman and Philosopher,* Philadelphia (2d ed., 1968), p. 296 n. 92.

59. TB Sanhedrin 40b.

60. TB Bava Meẓi'a 30b.

> but only to the few called upon by God, God commanded that the local judges in each city should always judge according to law and should not have the power to deviate in any way from the general rules of the Torah.
>
> However, should a case become too baffling for them (which would mostly occur when it becomes clear that the general principles of the Torah are inconsistent with what their reasoning indicates would be appropriate for the particular case before them . . .) and they are uncertain whether to decide according to the fixed general rules of the law that would lead to an unfair and unsuitable result, considering the times and the other circumstances of the case, or whether to decide according to the essential truth of the particular case, and they lack the power to reach the desired result, then they shall go up to the Temple and inquire of the Sanhedrin, to whom God has given the authority and the capacity to temper the laws of the Torah with equity and adjust them as they deem appropriate in the particular case.
>
> It was concerning such a case that Scripture cautioned that one should not deviate either right or left from the verdict that they will announce. The meaning is that even when they depart from the letter of the general law and take the matter to the left, or if the generally just law is to the left and they decide the matter to the right, they must be obeyed, because, whatever they decide (even if from the standpoint of the general rules they have determined that right is left and left is right), they are really declaring right to be right and left to be left, according to the particular truth and the nature of the specific matter, because the decision they have reached is the only appropriate one. In this way, through the power God entrusted to the Sanhedrin, He enabled the Torah to encompass all types of people and all of their individual activities.
>
> It is thus clear that the Sanhedrin will not declare that what appears to be right is left and what appears to be left is right when it decides on the basis of a received tradition, or on a matter of Scriptural interpretation, for in such matters they will not, God forbid, willfully and knowingly say that right is left and left is right. To do so would not only be contrary to the truth but also even contrary to the view of the questioner.
>
> The reference, therefore, is to what the Sages decree (*she-yigzeru*) for the needs of the time (*kefi ẓorekh ha-sha'ah*) [*i.e.,* to do justice in the individual case]; for such decrees are faithful to the root values and basic principles of the Torah. This is the true meaning of "right is left and left is right."

Abrabanel emphasizes another aspect of the tension between law and equity, in a different and even perhaps diametrically opposite direction, namely, in the area of individual rights in criminal law. "General justice and the constraints of the law" prescribe that a criminal may not be punished unless he has been warned before the commission of the crime and is clearly shown to have known that he was committing a crime.[61] The law

61. *See* TB Sanhedrin 41a; Maimonides, *MT,* Sanhedrin 12:1–3.

also provides that no proof that the accused committed the offense is sufficient unless there are at least two witnesses who so testify. This general justice is for the *benefit of the individual;* but, in a particular social situation, it is contrary to the public interest—"the number of murderers will increase, and the body politic will be destroyed." In this particular situation, adjudication according to the general law is indeed for the benefit of the individual, but it is unfair to the public interest. The statement that Jerusalem was destroyed because cases were decided according to the Torah underscores the failure to consider the needs of the time in light of the increase in crime. The judges at that time proclaimed "Let the law cut through the mountain" and decided on the basis of the law of general justice, which is liberal and benefits the individual, but did not give due weight to the needs of the general society. This, too, according to Abrabanel is part of the subject of the relationship between equity and law and of the need to reconcile the two.[62]

Abrabanel and Arama thus both rejected the possibility of interpreting the statement "Even when they say that right is left and left is right" as referring to a situation where there was an error in a decision by the halakhic authorities. Even when the halakhic authorities "depart from the letter of the general law and take the matter to the left, or if the generally just law is to the left and they decide the matter to the right," and "from the standpoint of the general rules they have determined that right is left and left is right," nevertheless, "they are really declaring right to be right and left to be left, according to the particular truth and the nature of the specific matter, because the decision they have reached is the only appropriate one."

It is possible to conclude from Abrabanel's discussion that in his opinion "the particular truth and the nature of the specific matter" cannot be achieved through legal interpretation in the course of adjudication[63] but

62. Isaac Arama also very briefly mentioned the passage in TB Yevamot 90b, which states that if the times so demand, the strict law also need not be followed with regard to criminal punishment; however, it is difficult to determine from this reference Arama's attitude with regard to this question.

63. At the conclusion of his discussion, Abrabanel states: "The reference [concerning right and left], therefore, is to what the Sages decree (*she-yigzeru*) for the needs of the time (*kefi ẓorekh ha-sha'ah*) [*i.e.,* to do justice in the individual case]." The terms *she-yigzeru* and *ẓorekh ha-sha'ah* are strongly suggestive of legislative enactments. *Gezerah* is a legislative enactment, *see infra* pp. 490–492, and *ẓorekh ha-sha'ah* is a term commonly used in connection with *takkanot; see infra* pp. 519–520. However, the matter is not completely certain; it is still possible that Abrabanel meant that one should not decide cases according to the general truth of Torah, but rather according to the particular truth of the specific case. *Cf.* Maimonides' statement in *MT,* Mamrim 2:9 regarding the prohibition "You shall not add anything to what I command you or take anything away from it," in connection with legislation by the halakhic authorities; *see infra* pp. 499–502.

only through the promulgation by the court of a legislative enactment (*takkanah*). As we have seen, Abrabanel emphasized that this authority to follow the particularized truth of the individual or of the community is vested only in the High Court, but "the local judges in each city should always judge according to law and should not have the power to deviate in any way from the general rules of the Torah." Abrabanel's emphatic restriction of this authority to the High Court seems explicable on the basis that he was referring to legislation in the narrow sense of formal adoption of enactments that are contrary to existing law, and not to *interpretation*, in the course of the normal judicial process.[64]

An important and vital point necessary to an understanding of the approach of both Arama and Abrabanel is made in the comments of a halakhic thinker and authority of Polish Jewry of the same period, Solomon Ephraim of Luntshitz.[65] As we shall presently see, his basic and fundamental concept is firmly anchored in the age-old outlook of the *Halakhah*, but what is especially relevant to our subject is his integration of this concept with the principle here discussed, namely, "Even when they say that right is left and left is right—you must obey them."[66]

Solomon Ephraim's remarks are a gloss on Deuteronomy 17:11: "You must not deviate from the verdict that they announce to you either to the right or to the left":

> Rashi comments, "Even if they say that right is left, etc. . . ." It would appear that Rashi deduced his comment from the fact that Scripture does not read, "You must not deviate either to the right or to the left from the verdict. . . ." Since "either to the right or to the left" is placed *after* "the verdict that they announce to you," his conclusion was that the verse means that even when "right" and "left" are not actually so, their verdict makes it so, and is to be obeyed.
>
> The commentators found it difficult to accept this, and they have given many different reasons. Actually, I do not see any difficulty in the matter, for our Sages have already said:[67] "One might say, 'Since some authorities pro-

64. Even so, the vesting of this authority exclusively in the Sanhedrin raises a difficult problem inasmuch as in all generations enactments were adopted by various courts, and not only by the Sanhedrin or the highest court of the generation. Perhaps Abrabanel meant that what he described was the ideal situation—which might have existed in the early *Halakhah*—but not later, when other courts obtained legislative authority.

65. Solomon Ephraim also was active in Prague during the second half of the sixteenth century and is known particularly for his commentary on the Torah, *Keli Yakar*, from which the ensuing passages are taken.

66. Abrabanel, like Arama, saw in the combination of general truth and individual truth an exemplification of the doctrine of "right that is right and left that is left." In this respect, *Keli Yakar* is consistent with Abrabanel even if we interpret Abrabanel as referring only to the adoption of legislative enactments, *see supra* n. 63.

67. TB Ḥagigah 3b.

nounce ritually pure the same object that others pronounce impure, and some prohibit the very thing others permit, how, in these circumstances, can one learn Torah?' Scripture therefore states: 'All of them are given by one Shepherd; one God gave them all.'" Yet one may still object that this is not really an answer, and the difficulty persists, "How can one really learn Torah?"

The explanation of the matter is that in every case where the question arises as to whether an object is pure or impure, there are some arguments for declaring it pure and others for declaring it impure. If the Torah declares it to be pure, that is because the arguments in favor of purity are stronger than those pointing the other way; and the converse is true when the Torah declares an object impure. The same explanation applies when the question is whether an act is permitted or prohibited, or whether something is fit (*kasher*) or unfit (*pasul*) to be used.

For this reason, our Sages, of blessed memory, said at the end of chapter *Dinei Mamonot*[68] that no one is appointed to sit on the Sanhedrin unless he has the capacity to prove from Biblical verses that a creeping insect [which unquestionably is impure] is pure. The reason is that when an emergency requires a ruling inconsistent with the law of the Torah in a situation where "it is a time to act for the Lord" [Psalms 119:126], the Sage or prophet, following the example of Elijah at Mount Carmel,[69] will be able to add to the weight of the consideration that it is "a time to act for the Lord" [*i.e.*, that there is an urgent need for action] the weight of the minority view, which had originally been rejected by the majority. But this can never happen if the Sage or prophet is ignorant of the grounds for the opposing view; in that case, he will never declare it pure even as an emergency measure, whereas it is his duty to do so by combining the need for emergency action with the force of the minority opinion to overcome the power of the contrary ruling by the majority.

If an earthly court pronounces pure an object that is impure under the laws of the Torah, then, since arguments can also be found for declaring it pure, the weight of the majority ruling of the earthly court can be added to the weight of the hitherto insufficient reasons for declaring it pure, and the combined weight of both these factors is sufficient to outweigh the reasons for holding it impure. For God has vested authority even in an earthly court to reason to either conclusion, and in this instance the grounds for purity were stronger. The Sages stated this well:[70] "Turn your ear into a funnel and develop a mind receptive to both sides of the argument—both in favor of and opposed to declaring the object pure." For, in truth, everyone must understand all the arguments; otherwise, he could not be a member of the Sanhed-

68. TB Sanhedrin 17a.

69. I Kings 18:19–46; *Sifrei*, Deuteronomy, Shofetim, sec. 175; TB Yevamot 90b. Elijah's action on Mount Carmel is discussed *infra* p. 520. For the exegesis of Psalms 119:126, *see infra* p. 503 n. 39.

70. TB Ḥagigah 3b.

> rin. For this reason, their ruling that [what appears to be] right is left must be accepted because of those grounds that tend to the conclusion that "left" is the proper ruling. This is truly the correct explanation.
>
> If you take the view that the Sages were speaking with reference to civil law (as to which "a judge must be guided only by what his own eyes see," as it is said:[71] "He is with you when you pass judgment") and that this verse [referring to "right" and "left"] relates to civil-law matters that Scripture spoke of at the beginning of the passage (*"bein din le-din"*), *i.e.*, that it all depends on how the judge views the matter, then it [the exegesis of "right" and "left"] is perfectly clear: the judge decides [civil cases] by the exercise of his understanding and judicial discretion (as it is said:[72] "Render true and perfect justice [lit. "a judgment of truth, justice, and peace"] in your gates"). This judgment must encompass all three elements [truth, justice, and peace], and *sha'ar* (gate) has the same root letters as *shi'ur* (appraisal). For all three elements require rational appraisal, understanding, and judicial sagacity, according to the time, the place, and the matter. Sometimes, one must make one of these elements yield to another, *i.e.*, truth must give way to peace. On the other hand, peace is also not always for the best, for an assembly of the wicked does harm to those who participate and to the world at large.[73] Judgment, likewise, requires judicious appraisal and evaluation, as has been explained.

Every case has more than one side, and there is no clear line dividing the pure from the impure, or the permitted from the prohibited. The theoretical possibility of more than one result in any case is characteristic of the *Halakhah*. The judge must turn "his ear into a funnel," hear and understand all aspects of every case, and rule accordingly in matters brought to him for decision. In any event, Solomon Ephraim of Luntshitz states, this is true in the area of civil law, the "legal" part of the *Halakhah*, which must be decided on the basis of "rational appraisal, understanding, and judicial sagacity, according to the time, the place, and the matter." The conclusion that flows from this is that there is no absolute "right" nor is there an absolute "left"; it is only the judge's decision, fortified by all the possible arguments for it, that is indeed the "right," and the correct decision. The judge has the authority and the duty to bring both law and equity to bear in rendering a decision.

As stated, this view of the nature of the *Halakhah* is anchored in the world of the Sages from ancient times, and it is expressed in their statement, "The words of both are the words of the living God." During a certain period, in connection with the disputes between the schools of Shammai and

71. II Chronicles 19:6.
72. Zechariah 8:16.
73. M Sanhedrin 8:5; TB Sanhedrin 72a.

Hillel, the *Halakhah* even recognized pluralism in practice, *i.e.*, variant decisions as to the conduct of practical affairs, but when the Sages saw that this situation was untenable, they declared: "The words of both are the words of the living God, but the law is in accordance with the School of Hillel."[74] In theory, both are the words of the living God; but for purposes of practical action, one from among the set of legitimate opinions is the law.

This quality of the *Halakhah* in the Talmudic period is dealt with later in the discussion of the many differing opinions recorded in the Mishnah of R. Judah Ha-Nasi.[75] From the time of the Mishnah, this quality of the *Halakhah* has been basic to the halakhic decision-making process. The question was asked even with regard to the form of the text of the Mishnah: Why is the minority view recorded if the majority decision settles the law to the contrary? One of the answers given is that if a later court concludes that there is good reason to decide according to the minority, it is free so to decide.[76] The explanation for this given by Samson of Sens, a leading halakhic authority in France and in the Land of Israel at the end of the twelfth and beginning of the thirteenth centuries, is substantially the same as the comments of Solomon Ephraim of Luntshitz:

> Although the minority opinion was not initially accepted, and the majority disagreed with it, yet if in another generation the majority will agree with its reasoning, the law will follow that view. For the entire Torah was given to Moses in this manner, with grounds for considering [an object] to be impure and other grounds for considering it to be pure. When the people said to Moses, "How long shall we take to clarify the matter?" he replied that the majority view is to be accepted, but the words of both are the words of the living God.[77]

74. TJ Berakhot 1:4, 9a.

75. *See infra* pp. 1061–1072.

76. M Eduyyot 1:5.

77. Commentary of Samson of Sens on M Eduyyot 1:5. A similar view is expressed by Rashi, Ketubbot 57a, s.v. Ha kamashma lan:

> [Whenever there are two versions], we ignore the version according to which two *amoraim* are in dispute as to what another said, and we accept the version according to which they themselves differ on the question involved. For when two disagree over what a third authority said . . . one of them is making a misstatement of fact; but when two *amoraim* disagree over a civil or a religious law, each one says what seems to him to be correct and no misstatement is involved. Each one offers his own reasoning: One will show why the matter should be permitted and the other will show why it should be forbidden; one will make one analogy and the other will make a different one. In such a case it can be said that "both are the words of the living God" [TB Eruvin 13b, Gittin 6b]. Sometimes, the reasoning of one is apposite and sometimes the reasoning of the other, because [the force of] the reasoning changes with the slightest change in the circumstances of the case. . . .

See also TJ Sanhedrin 4:2, 21a/b (11:2, 22a), quoted *infra* p. 383.

The essence of this concept and the conclusions to be drawn from it were subjects of deliberation among the halakhic authorities in every generation and era. This quality of the *Halakhah* was the basis of the various approaches taken by the halakhic authorities throughout history to the question of the nature and method of codification of Jewish law, as will be more fully discussed in a later part of this work.[78]

Certainly, it should be obvious that these strongly worded statements of Samson of Sens and Solomon Ephraim of Luntshitz to the effect that there is no absolute and unequivocal answer to legal questions, but that every legal question involves arguments both pro and con, do not alter the basic nature of the *Halakhah,* which distinguishes between the law and what is beyond the law, between what is permitted and what is prohibited, and between liability and nonliability. The boundary lines between these categories are neither ill defined nor broken, but are clear and firm. The purpose of the instructive and profound comments of these halakhic masters is to underscore clearly the prerogative and duty of the halakhic authorities to reconcile, when necessary, in exceptional cases and in special circumstances, the conflicting demands of law and equity, of the public good and individual justice. They emphasize that such reconciliation and balancing do not change the law or declare right to be left or left to be right, but such reconciliation and balancing *constitute* the law, in view of the special circumstances of the case and the time; and the judgment so arrived at is a judgment correctly declaring right to be right and left to be left.

To summarize: Neither a prophet nor any suprahuman power has the authority to decide a matter of *Halakhah.* This prerogative is exclusively vested in the halakhic authorities, to whom the Torah was entrusted. They alone are authorized to interpret it and to continue to fashion and develop it.

This authority is expressed in two directions: On the one hand, it imposes a duty of absolute compliance on those to whom the law is addressed—a duty which exists even with respect to decisions that appear to be erroneous to the point of declaring left to be right and right to be left. On the other hand, it imposes on the halakhic authorities the duty to keep the law sufficiently flexible so as not to cause injustice in special circumstances through overrigidity. It is the duty and the "inherent jurisdiction" of the halakhic authorities to interweave law and equity, and to decide what is right and what is left on the basis of a "rational appraisal, understanding, and judicial sagacity, according to the time, the place, and the matter."

As manifold as are the possibilities implicit in this prerogative and duty

78. *See infra* pp. 1222–1229, 1273–1287, 1311–1319, 1378–1379, 1451–1452. On pluralism and uniformity in *Halakhah, see further* A.I. Kook, *Eder ha-Yekar,* pp. 13ff.

of the halakhic authorities to consider every legal rule in all its diverse aspects and all the various circumstances in which the rule may apply, so correspondingly great is the care they must take to exercise this broad prerogative in accordance with the outlook and the spirit of the *Halakhah.* Of course, the exercise of this discretion itself constitutes judicial decision making and is governed by the principles applicable to all adjudication. Indeed, many rules have been formulated constraining the exercise of discretion in regard to the subject at hand. Some have already been discussed and are further dealt with later.[79] It is sufficient here to point out that a judge's discretion is not free and untrammeled, but may be exercised only on the basis of these rules and within the framework of their constraints.

D. The Oven of Akhnai

This dual principle—on the one hand, the absolute prerogative of the halakhic authorities, and, on the other hand, the rejection of the influence of any suprahuman factor on the determination of the *Halakhah*—is emphasized in a wonderfully graphic form in the well-known story of the dispute between R. Eliezer b. Hyrcanus and R. Joshua and his colleagues about the oven of Akhnai,[80] which, according to R. Eliezer, was ritually pure but, according to R. Joshua, was impure. A *baraita* states:[81]

> It has been taught: On that day R. Eliezer brought forward every imaginable argument, but they did not accept them. He said to them: "If the *Halakhah* is in accord with me, let this carob tree prove it." Thereupon, the carob tree was uprooted 100 cubits out of its place—others state 400 cubits. They responded: "No proof can be brought from a carob tree."

79. *See particularly infra* pp. 1138–1148, for a discussion of codification and the problems of the methodology of reaching a decision in connection with codification when the authorities are in conflict.

80. M Kelim 5:10. The meaning of "of Akhnai" is "belonging to a person named Akhnai." This is the view of Elijah, the Gaon of Vilna, in *Eliyahu Rabbah* on M Kelim 5:10; it is also suggested as a possible explanation by *Tosafot,* TB Bava Meẓi'a 59b, s.v. Zeh tannur shel akhnai. In the Talmudic discussion in TB Bava Meẓi'a, the name is taken as a derivative of *naḥash* (snake) "because they encompassed him with arguments like a snake." But in TJ Mo'ed Katan 3:1, 10b (3:1, 81d) the reading is *Ḥakhinai,* a well-recognized name. *See further* L. Ginzberg, *Perushim ve-Ḥiddushim ba-Yerushalmi* [A Commentary on the Palestine Talmud] (hereinafter, *Perushim*), I, p. 81. In TJ, *loc. cit.,* a midrashic play is made on the word *ḥakhinai:* "Great friction (*ḥakhakh*) took place on that day. Whatever R. [E]liezer looked at was destroyed," *i.e.,* a great catastrophe struck on that day. *See Korban ha-Edah, ad loc.* Ginzberg's remark on TJ, *loc. cit.,* "and by way of midrashic license the two Talmuds [TJ and TB] gave the explanation that they encompassed him with arguments like a snake," does not appear to be accurate, since TJ gives no such explanation.

81. TB Bava Meẓi'a 59b; TJ Mo'ed Katan 3:1, 10b (3:1, 81d). The quotation in the text follows TB.

> Again he said to them: "If the *Halakhah* is in accord with me, let the stream of water prove it." Whereupon, the stream of water flowed backward. "No proof can be brought from a stream of water," they rejoined.
>
> Again he urged: "If the *Halakhah* is in accord with me, let the walls of this study hall prove it." Whereupon the walls leaned at an angle as if to fall. But R. Joshua rebuked them, saying: "When scholars are engaged in halakhic disputation, what business have you to interfere?" Hence, out of respect for R. Joshua they did not fall; but out of respect for R. Eliezer they did not right themselves either, and thus they are still standing aslant.
>
> Again he said to them: "If the *Halakhah* is in accord with me, let it be proved from Heaven." Whereupon, a heavenly voice cried out: "Why do you dispute with R. Eliezer, seeing that in all matters the *Halakhah* is in accord with him?" R. Joshua arose and exclaimed: "It is not in heaven."[82] What did he mean by this? R. Jeremiah said: "The Torah has already been given at Mt. Sinai. We pay no attention to a heavenly voice because You [God] have already written in the Torah at Mt. Sinai, 'Follow the majority.'"[83]

The story reaches its climax with this conclusion:

> R. Nathan met Elijah [the prophet] and asked him: "What did the Holy One, blessed be He, do at that time [during the discussion between R. Eliezer and R. Joshua]?" Elijah replied: "He smiled, saying, 'My children have bested Me, My children have bested Me.'"

The carob tree, the stream of water, the walls of the study hall, and even the heavenly voice—a divine revelation—cannot interfere in the determination of the law, because the Torah, once having been given, is "not in heaven." The decision in that very instance was determined according to the Torah's own statement that "one must follow the majority."

The full scope and force of the principle go even further: God Himself, the Giver of the law and its Source, Who made known, as it were, by means of a heavenly voice, that R. Eliezer, although in the minority, was correct as to what the Torah actually intended to say, concedes that those of His children who believe otherwise, but are in the majority, are entitled to prevail even over Him. Objective truth was on the side of the dissenter; the majority were in effect stating that "left was right and right was left." Legal truth, however, follows the majority because the *Halakhah* was entrusted to the halakhic authorities, and the Giver of the Torah Himself, as it were, accepts their decision.[84] It would be difficult to picture a more telling illustration of

82. Deuteronomy 30:12.

83. Exodus 23:2.

84. For a detailed discussion of the possibility of divergence between legal truth and historical and factual truth in jurisprudence generally, *see* Alon v. Government of Israel,

the exclusive prerogative of the halakhic authorities to declare the law and of the absolute rule of law, even, as it were, over the divine Legislator Himself.[85]

36(iv) *P.D.* 449, 456–463 (1982) (Ben-Porat, J.) and 464–475 (Elon, J.). The latter also discusses the question from the point of view of Jewish law as herein set forth.

85. *See further* M. Silberg, *Talmudic Law and the Modern State,* pp. 63ff.; I. Englard, "Tannuro Shel Akhnai—Perushah Shel Aggadah" [Akhnai's Oven—An Interpretation of an *Aggadah*], *Shenaton,* I (1974), pp. 45–56.

For another interesting instance, *see Tanḥuma* (printed eds.), Vayeshev, sec. 2, concerning Joseph, after his brothers had cast him into the pit:

> They resolved, "Let us bind ourselves on oath that none of us tell our father Jacob. . . ." What did they do? They included God in that ban so that He should not tell their father. . . . And God, notwithstanding that Scripture says that "He declares His word to Jacob" (Psalms 147:19), did not tell him what happened because of the ban.

Similarly, in *Pesikta Rabbati,* beginning of #3 (ed. Ish-Shalom, p. 7b):

> Let no person say, "I will not fulfill the instructions of the Elders, since they are not from the Torah." God declares to such a person, "No, My son. You must fulfill everything they decree upon you, as it is written, 'You shall act in accordance with the instructions given you' [Deuteronomy 17:11]. Why [should this be so]? For they issue decrees even upon Me, as it is said, 'You will decree and it will be fulfilled'" [alternate translation: "and He will abide by it for you"] [Job 22:28].

A similar passage appears in *Tanḥuma* (printed eds.), Naso, sec. 29, where the text reads:

> Let no person say, "I will not fulfill the instructions of the Elders, since they are not from the Torah." God declares to such people, "My children, you are not allowed to speak thus, but you shall fulfill whatever they decree upon you, as it is written, 'You shall act in accordance with the instructions given you.' Why [should this be so]? For I, too, agree to [obey] their commands, as it is written, 'You will decree and He will abide by it for you.'"

See further TB Bava Meẓi'a 86a, Gittin 6b; and *Derashot ha-Ran* #7:6–11, discussing at length the conclusion to be drawn from the incident involving the oven of Akhnai and from other Talmudic sources.

It is interesting to compare this absolute prerogative of the halakhic authorities "to whom the Torah has been entrusted even if they are in error," with a different theory, prevalent in English law in the sixteenth and seventeenth centuries, when the supreme value was the "divine law." *See* Allen, *Law in the Making,* p. 446:

> But the absolutely unlimited sovereignty of statute has not been admitted in the theory of law until comparatively recent times. In the sixteenth and seventeenth centuries it would have required considerable audacity on the part of any lawyer to deny that the only ultimate, supreme authority lay in a law higher than any man-made ordinance—the eternal dictates of natural justice, reason, or equity; or, in its theological aspect, the law of God. "There is no law in England," said Keble J. in 1653, "but is as really and truly the law of God as any Scripture phrase, that is by consequence from the very texts of Scripture; for there are very many consequences reasoned out of the texts of Scripture; so is the law of England the very consequence of the very Decalogue itself; and whatsoever is not consonant to Scripture in the law of England is not the law of England . . . : whatsoever is not consonant to the law of God in Scripture, or to right reason which is maintained by Scripture, whatsoever is in England, be it acts of Parliament, customs, or any judicial acts of the Court, it is not the law of England, but the error of the party which did pronounce it; and you, or any man else at the bar, may so plead it."

E. Differences of Opinion with Regard to Suprahuman Influences in the Determination of the *Halakhah:* The Accepted View

Some halakhic authorities conceded to suprahuman power some measure of influence on the determination of the *Halakhah.* This was particularly so in the case of the words of the prophets, whose halakhic statements about law are interpreted by the same methods as the Torah itself. There were also some halakhic authorities who accorded a particular influence to suprahuman factors in the determination of the *Halakhah* even after prophecy ceased—*e.g.,* R. Eliezer, who turned to a heavenly voice to prove the truth of his opinion. The Sages even reported a tradition that the well-known dispute between the schools of Shammai and Hillel was decided by a heavenly voice that "emerged and declared: 'the words of both are the words of the living God, but the law is in accordance with the School of Hillel.'"[86] However, it appears that those who held the view that suprahuman factors played a part in determining the *Halakhah* were very few; the prevailing opinion, with which the overwhelming majority of post-Talmudic halakhic authorities concurred, was evidently that of R. Joshua, who said: "We pay no attention to a heavenly voice."[87]

We shall quote the words of two such authorities, one from the beginning of the rabbinic period and the second from a period much closer to our own time. Maimonides, in the introduction to his code, the *Mishneh Torah,* assigned an important role to the prophets and the courts on which they served; he held that they are links in the chain of the tradition of the *Halakhah;* but in this role the prophets were acting as Sages like all the other Sages, and not as prophets, for "if a man will arise, whether from among the gentiles or among the Jews, and make a sign or wonder and say that God sent him to add or delete a commandment or to give any of the commandments an interpretation that we have not heard from Moses . . ., he is a false prophet."[88]

Not only if he wishes to add or delete, but even if he states that "God

86. TB Eruvin 13b; TJ Berakhot 1:4, 9a (1:7, 3b), Kiddushin 1:1, 4b (1:1, 58d). *See also infra* pp. 1061–1070, 1375–1379.

87. TB Berakhot 52a; Pesaḥim 114a. *See* Z.H. Chajes, *Torat ha-Nevi'im,* ch. 1, "Elleh ha-Miẓvot"; E.E. Urbach, "Ha-Halakhah ve-ha-Nevu'ah" [*Halakhah* and Prophecy], *Tarbiẓ,* XVIII (1947), pp. 1–27; *id., The Sages,* pp. 304–314; *see also infra* p. 520 n. 117 on the subject of a prophet's authority to suspend temporarily a Biblical law; on this subject, *see Bet ha-Beḥirah,* Ketubbot 9a (ed. Sofer, p. 45), regarding the adultery of Bathsheba and David, to which there were no witnesses: "There is no stronger testimony than a disclosure by a prophet"; *see* the editor's note, *ad loc.,* subpar. 6 and the statement quoted there from *Resp. Ḥatam Sofer,* OḤ, #208: "It is clear that if a prophet declares a person tainted [apparently as to his genealogy], we will not render judgment on that basis."

88. *MT,* Yesodei ha-Torah 9:1.

commanded him concerning one of the laws of the Torah that the rule is such and such or that the law is in accordance with the opinion of a particular Sage—he is a false prophet . . . as he has come to deny the Torah that stated 'It is not in heaven.'"[89] Prophecy has no role in the determination of the *Halakhah;* the prophet "comes not to establish a rule of conduct but to exhort the people to obey the words of the Torah and to admonish the people not to violate them, just as the last of the prophets (Malachi) said: 'Be mindful of the Teaching (*Torah*) of my servant, Moses.'"[90]

The role of the prophet in the determination of the *Halakhah* is, therefore, the same as that of any other halakhic authority:

> When a prophet and one who is not a prophet both engage in legal reasoning, and the prophet contends that God told him that his reasoning is correct, you shall pay no heed to him. If a thousand prophets—all of them as great as Elijah and Elisha—all agree on a particular result to which their legal reasoning has led them, and 1001 halakhic authorities who are not prophets are of the opposite opinion, "one must follow the majority"; and the law follows the view of the 1001 authorities who are not prophets, and not that of the thousand distinguished prophets.[91]

About seven hundred years after Maimonides, the nature of the power of the halakhic authorities to determine the methods and the content of the *Halakhah* was summarized by the author of *Kezot ha-Hoshen,* Aryeh Leib ha-Kohen, as follows:

> Certainly, one should be fearful of stating matters of Torah erroneously, and human wisdom falters in the search for truth. . . . However, the Torah was not given to ministering angels but to mankind, who are endowed with human reason. . . . God gave us the Torah to administer as human understanding determines it to be, even if that determination falls short of objective truth. Thus, if one brings forth a completely new idea, it need only be true by the measure of human reasoning. . . . Truth should sprout forth from the earth; and the truth is what the halakhic authorities, exercising their human intelligence, agree is true.[92]

89. *Id.* 9:4.

90. *Id.* 9:2. The quotation is from Malachi 3:22.

91. Maimonides, *Commentary on the Mishnah,* Introduction.

92. Preface to *Kezot ha-Hoshen* to Sh. Ar. ḤM. In this statement, Aryeh Leib ha-Kohen extensively relied on the writings of Nissim Gerondi in *Derashot ha-Ran,* quoted *supra* n. 18. *See also Nahal Yizhak* by Isaac Elhanan Spektor, Rabbi of Kovno in the second half of the nineteenth century (Part I, Vilna, 1972, in the first paragraph of the Introduction): ". . . He entrusted to us His Torah, which will stand as determined by human reason. Heaven itself will agree with us. . . ." *See also* the instructive remarks of M. Feinstein, *Iggerot Moshe,* Introduction to OḤ; A.I. Kook, *Iggerot ha-Re'iyah,* I, #103; *and cf. Kuzari,* Ma'amar #3, pars. 39–41.

III. THE PREROGATIVES OF THE HALAKHIC AUTHORITIES AS EXISTING IN EVERY GENERATION

This basic principle in the *Weltanschauung* of the halakhic authorities, which is discussed above, was translated into practical terms by means of the legal sources of the *Halakhah;* this principle guided the path of the *Halakhah* during all of its long periods, in the course of which, from time to time, new spiritual centers were established for the Jewish people. The *Sifrei* comments on the verses mentioned previously (Deuteronomy 17:8ff.: "If a case is too baffling for you to decide . . . you shall . . . appear before the priests the Levites, and the judge of that time and present your problem. When they have announced to you the verdict in the case . . .").[93] The *Sifrei* says: "'You shall appear'—this includes the court at Yavneh,"[94] which became the spiritual center of the people after the destruction of the Temple. R. Yose the Galilean, who lived in the first half of the second century C.E. and was one of the leading Sages at Yavneh, added: "Can it be conceived that a person will appear before a judge who is not of his own time? Rather, the meaning is: a judge who is worthy and is so recognized at that time."[95]

It may indeed be true that the authorities of a later generation are not equal in their wisdom to the authorities of a prior generation. However,

> The generation of your day and the halakhic authority of your day should be in your eyes the equal of the past generation and of the earlier Sages who lived before you. . . . Scripture considered three judges of insubstantial quality to be equal to three who were the greatest authorities, in order to teach you that the court of Jerubaal is of equal stature and worth before God as the court of Moses; that Samson's court is equal to that of Aaron; that the court of Jephthah is equal to the court of Samuel; that, in short, even if the most insignificant person is chosen as a leader of the community, he should be considered the equal of the mightiest of the ancient masters, for it is stated: "You shall . . . appear before the priests the Levites, and the judge of that time." This teaches that the judge of your generation is in his time the equal of a judge who lived in the very earliest times.[96]

Furthermore:

> Do not ask, Why is it that former days were better than these days? For this is not a wise question.[97]

93. Deuteronomy 17:8–9.
94. *Sifrei,* Deuteronomy, Shofetim, sec. 153 (p. 206).
95. *Id.*
96. *Kohelet Rabbah* 1:4; *Tosefta* Rosh ha-Shanah 2(1):3; TB Rosh ha-Shanah 25b.
97. Sources cited *supra* n. 96, following Ecclesiastes 7:10.

The continuity and vitality of the *Halakhah* require and demand that the halakhic authorities of every generation use the prerogative conferred on them in a way that furthers halakhic creativity and development; and it is not wise either to refrain from using this prerogative, or to challenge it on the ground that later generations are not so endowed with wisdom as their predecessors.

IV. THE PRINCIPLE THAT "THE LAW IS IN ACCORDANCE WITH THE VIEWS OF THE LATER AUTHORITIES" (*HILKHETA KE-VATRA'EI*)

The basic prerogative of the halakhic authorities to continue to fashion and determine the *Halakhah* was supplemented in the post-Talmudic era by an important principle as to the method for ascertaining the law—"The law is in accordance with the views of the later authorities."

In the history of the *Halakhah*, the term *rishonim* (early authorities) is used to refer to the halakhic authorities who were active from the middle of the eleventh century C.E. until the sixteenth century, and the term *aḥaronim* (later authorities) refers to the halakhic authorities who were active from the sixteenth century onward.[98] These two terms, *rishonim* and *aḥaronim,* not only indicate the period when halakhic authorities were active, but also connote the greater authority that the halakhic system confers on the earlier *rishonim* as compared to the later *aḥaronim.*

This attitude applies not only to these two periods. The same distinction and even the identical terms—*rishonim* and *aḥaronim*—are characteristically applied to all halakhic periods and not only to the rabbinic period (which commenced in the eleventh century C.E.). The halakhic system always attributed to earlier halakhic authorities greater weight and authority than it did to the authorities who succeeded them. R. Johanan, one of the leaders of the *amoraim* of the Land of Israel in the third century C.E., stated:[99] "The minds [lit. "hearts"] of our ancestors were as wide as the entrance to the outer chamber of the Temple; those of the later generations were as wide as the entrance to the inner chamber; and ours are like the eye of a fine needle." Abbaye, Rava, and R. Ashi, who were among the leading Babylonian *amoraim* in the fourth and fifth centuries C.E., considered themselves much inferior to the Sages of the previous generations.[100]

98. *See supra* p. 44 and *infra* p. 1101.

99. TB Eruvin 53a.

100. *Id. See also* TB Yoma 9b: "R. Johanan said: 'The fingernail of the earlier generations is better than the whole body of the later ones.'"

The *amoraim* had no authority to dispute the views of the *tannaim*,[101] and similar deference was also shown by the *geonim* towards the *amoraim*. Similarly, the early authorities in the rabbinic period (the *rishonim*) accorded special veneration to the *geonim*, and the *aḥaronim* showed the same respect toward the *rishonim*. Each preceding period enjoys a priority in that its authority is greater and more compelling than that of later periods.[102]

This great veneration for the views of earlier authorities did not prevent Jewish law from establishing, over a period of time, a fundamental principle for determining the law—a principle that, on the surface, seems contrary to the principle of priority of the earlier over the latter, but which was essential in order to empower the authorities of later generations to make legal rulings responsive to contemporary problems and consonant with contemporary conditions. This important principle is that "the law is in accordance with the views of the later authorities" (*hilkheta ke-vatra'ei*), and it has existed since the geonic period. The *geonim* established the rule that until the days of Abbaye and Rava, if there were differences of opinion among the *amoraim* on a particular law, the view of the Sages of the earlier generation prevailed over the contrary view of the later Sages. However, if there were differences of opinion among *amoraim* from the time of Abbaye and Rava (middle of the fourth century C.E.) or among halakhic authorities after the redaction of the Talmud, the view of the later authorities was accepted.[103] The principle that the views of the most recent authorities are accepted applies even in the case of a dispute of a "disciple against his own

101. Concerning Rav, who was of the first generation of *amoraim*, it was said, "Rav [ranks as] a *tanna* and hence has authority to differ" (TB Eruvin 50b), *i.e.*, with the *tannaim*, for he, too, is in this respect regarded as a *tanna*.

102. These two terms, *rishonim* (early authorities) and *aḥaronim* (later authorities), in a connotation generally similar to that used here, are found even in Scripture; *see, e.g.*, Ecclesiastes 1:11. It should be noted that in all periods (including the period of the *rishonim*, *i.e.*, the early rabbinic period), the terms *rishonim* and *aḥaronim* were, in fact, used with regard to preceding ages. *See, e.g.*, the comment of Vidal of Tolosa (fourteenth century) in his *Maggid Mishneh* to Maimonides, *MT*, Malveh ve-Loveh 25:3: "This rule is in accord with the views of most of the authorities, *rishonim* and *aḥaronim*, of blessed memory." *See similarly* Rema (who lived at the end of the period of the *rishonim* and the beginning of the period of the *aḥaronim*) to Sh. Ar. ḤM 25:2, quoted *infra* p. 271, where he speaks of "a responsum by a *gaon*" and of *aḥaronim*. Many more examples of this usage are to be found. In contemporary usage, the halakhic authorities until the sixteenth century are considered *rishonim* and those who lived after that century, *aḥaronim*.

103. *Piskei ha-Rosh*, Bava Meẓi'a, ch. 3, #10 and ch. 4, #19, #21 (*see* the gloss of Isaiah Pick [Berlin], *Haggahot ha-Grip*, to #19); Shabbat, ch. 23, #1 (and *Korban Netanel*, *ad loc.*, subpar. 4); Kiddushin, ch. 2, #7–#8. Alfasi's statement, referred to by Asheri, indicates that this rule applies also to the period prior to Abbaye and Rava. The correctness of Alfasi's statement is supported by the geonic responsum quoted by L. Ginzberg in *Geonica*, II, p. 32 (responsum 17); *see also id.* at 21–22.

teacher"[104] and even in the case of the "single individual against the many," *i.e.*, where a single individual later in time disagrees with the views of a number of earlier authorities.[105]

This principle has been extensively discussed in the writings of the halakhic authorities from the time of the geonic period, and different rationales for the principle have been advanced. Asheri explained it as follows:[106]

> Certainly, whoever has erred in failing to follow the decisions of the *geonim* as a result of ignorance of their views, and then accepted the geonic decision as being correct when it was called to his attention, has committed the equivalent of an error on a law of the Mishnah [*i.e.*, he has erred on a matter of law that was clear and well settled, and it is as if his error concerned a law expressly set forth in the Mishnah];[107] and it goes without saying that this is true not only for such error in matters decided by the *geonim* but also in matters decided by the authorities in all succeeding generations, who, after all, are not simply reed-cutters in a bog [*i.e.*, they are not ignorant and untutored].[108] In all these cases, if an authority has rendered a decision contrary to earlier views and, upon being made aware of the earlier rulings, accepts those rulings as being correct and acknowledges that he has erred, it is as if his error concerns a matter stated in the Mishnah, and he must retract his decision.
>
> However, if he disagrees with the earlier opinions and brings proof for his own position acceptable to his contemporaries, then Jephthah in his generation has as much authority as Samuel in his generation—at any given time, there is only "the judge of that time," and he may choose not to follow the views of his predecessors. For as to all questions that were not definitively decided in the Talmud as compiled by R. Ashi and Ravina, one may "demolish and create" even to the point of disagreeing with the views of the *geonim* . . . just as the later *amoraim* sometimes disagreed with the earlier ones. Indeed, we consider the views of those later in time to have greater authority, since they were aware of the reasoning of the earlier authorities as well as

104. *Resp. Maharik* #84; *Yad Malakhi* #17. However, when the disciple is still studying with his teacher, and discusses with him the law in question, the view of the teacher is accepted. *Yad Malakhi* #169.

105. *Yad Malakhi* #169. *See also Pitḥei Teshuvah*, Sh. Ar. ḤM ch. 25, subpar. 8, where the query is raised: Is it not the rule that we follow the opinion of the majority? To which the reply is:

> Since the later authorities saw the statements of the earlier ones but gave reasons for rejecting them, we assume, as a matter of course, that the earlier authorities would have agreed with the later ones. Consequently, this principle applies even to the view of a single [later authority] against [the view of] the many [earlier authorities].

106. *Piskei ha-Rosh*, Sanhedrin, ch. 4, #6.

107. *See also infra* pp. 982–983.

108. *See* TB Sanhedrin 33a.

their own, and they reached their decision on the basis of choice from among all views and after fully deliberating in order to get to the heart of the matter.[109]

Joseph Colon added:[110]

It seems, in my humble opinion, that the reason that from the time of Abbaye and Rava the law follows the views of the later authorities is that the later ones know the views of the earlier, but the earlier did not know the views of the later. Since we see that the later authorities chose not to reach the same conclusion as the earlier, it is apparent that they concluded that what the earlier authorities said on a particular matter did not provide a sufficient basis on which to rely.[111]

109. *See further Resp. Asheri* 55:9 in his reply to R. Israel:

With regard to the statement in your letter that since the venerable scholar, Jacob b. Shushan, was fully skilled in [the exercise of] those two faculties [*i.e.*, soundness of reasoning and knowledge of Arabic; the subject there being the interpretation of certain enactments], no one should entertain doubts about him or set aside his interpretation—that is not a valid position. What greater man was there than Rashi, of blessed memory, who with his commentaries enlightened the minds of the whole diaspora? Yet in many instances his descendants, Rabbenu Tam and R. Isaac, of blessed memory, differed with him and refuted his views. For the Torah is a Torah of truth, and we do not adulate any man. As to the two faculties he possessed, I apply to him, in the matter of sound reasoning, and to you, on the point of linguistic competence, the well-known adage, "Jephthah in his generation is as authoritative as Samuel was in his"; and in my decision I relied on your grasp of the meaning and your skill as a translator. Furthermore, the *geonim* declared that from [the time of] Abbaye and Rava onwards, the law is in accordance with the views of the later authorities; therefore our view [*i.e.*, that of the later authorities] is to be preferred.

On Asheri's statement in *Piskei ha-Rosh* on Sanhedrin, *see further infra* pp. 980–982. *See also infra* p. 981 n. 140 for the discussion of Asheri's statement by the Supreme Court of Israel in connection with the binding force of precedent.

110. *Resp. Maharik* #84.

111. The halakhic authorities understandably sought to find an explanation of why the principle that the views of the later authorities are accepted as the law applies only to a dispute arising after the time of Abbaye and Rava. Maharik, *supra* n. 110, suggests that up to the time of Abbaye and Rava a student studied only the views of his own teacher; hence, there is no sense in following the view of the successor, the student, because it was assumed that his teacher was his superior in knowledge. However, from the time of Abbaye and Rava, students also studied other viewpoints and had before them both their teachers' opinions and the opinions of others. A student's opinion, therefore, is superior to his teacher's, for the student's final decision is arrived at on the basis of the wide halakhic material at his disposal, whereas his teacher very likely may have followed just one view and may not even have been aware of the existence of another view. For details, *see* Maharik's statement. *Tosafot*, Kiddushin 45b, s.v. Havah uvda, explains the point thus:

Whenever there is a difference of opinion between teacher and student, the teacher's opinion is accepted as the law when it concerns the early *amoraim* up to the time of Abbaye and Rava, but from that time onward we rule in accordance with the later authorities because they were more meticulous than their predecessors to establish the law correctly. . . .

From these explanations, it follows that the principle that "the law is in accordance with the views of the later authorities" does not apply if the later authority reached his decision *per incuriam* (inadvertently), *i.e.*, without being aware of the views of his predecessors. For this reason, it became authoritatively established that the principle applies only if the later authority refers to and discusses the earlier opinion and shows by proofs acceptable to his contemporaries that, although contrary to the position of the earlier authority, his own view is sound.[112] This principle, which was accepted as a guideline in ascertaining and declaring the law, was formulated by Moses Isserles in his glosses to the *Shulḥan Arukh* as follows:[113]

> In all cases where the views of the earlier authorities are recorded and are well known and the later authorities disagree with them—as sometimes was the case with the later authorities who disagreed with the *geonim*—we follow the view of the later, as from the time of Abbaye and Rava the law is accepted according to the later authority. However, if a responsum by a *gaon* is found that had not been previously published, and there are other [later] decisions that disagree with it, we need not follow the view of the later authorities (*aḥaronim*), as it is possible that they did not know the view of the *gaon*, and if they had known it they would have decided the other way.[114]

Thus was established and accepted the fundamental principle of decision making in Jewish law—"The law is in accordance with the views of the later authorities."[115] It should not be thought that this principle diminished in any way the respect that later generations accorded to the earlier generations. It was precisely this respect that induced the later authority responsible for declaring the law to ponder his own decision earnestly, fearfully, and humbly, because he was aware that he was dealing with a question already considered by the earlier authorities. Nevertheless, when he finally reached his conclusion, his view, and not the view of the earlier authorities, became the law.[116]

112. *Piskei ha-Rosh, supra* n. 106; *Resp. Maharik* #94, #210. *See also Pitḥei Teshuvah, supra* n. 105.

113. Rema to Sh. Ar. ḤM 25:2.

114. Some halakhic authorities, mainly *aḥaronim,* set further limitations to the application of the principle that the law is in accordance with the views of the later authorities. *See, e.g., Resp. Maharam Alshekh* #39; Sh. Ar. ḤM 25:2; *Netivot ha-Mishpat, ad loc.,* subpar. 20; *Sema, ad loc.,* subpar. 19; *Shakh, ad loc.,* subpar. 21. *See also* ET, IX, pp. 341–345, s.v. Halakhah ke-vatra'ei.

115. On the meaning of the principle that "one court may not overrule another unless greater than the other in wisdom and number," and the conclusions that follow from it, *see infra* pp. 541–543.

116. The principle that the law is in accordance with the views of the later authorities performs an important function in connection with many central issues in the halakhic system, *e.g.*: the question of *ma'aseh* (a case or incident) as a binding precedent, *see infra* pp.

To summarize the nature of the prerogative of the halakhic authorities to determine and create *Halakhah,* as shown in this chapter: The task of determining and fashioning the *Halakhah* was entrusted to the halakhic authorities of every generation, to perform according to the tradition possessed by them and according to their human reason and intelligence. The halakhic authorities, who constituted an integral part of the general community and whose own lives were affected by the problems of their generation, were authorized to examine the previously existing *Halakhah* in the light of their own later circumstances; and their decisions established the law.[117] In this way, the *Halakhah* continued and developed. Linked to and interwoven with current life and problems, it guided and at the same time was shaped by contemporary life.

In exercising their vast power, the halakhic authorities faced a dual task. On the one hand, they were constantly concerned about carrying forward the creativity and development of the *Halakhah;* on the other hand, they carried the enormously heavy responsibility for preserving the spirit and maintaining the direction and continuity of the *Halakhah.* The halakhic authorities carried out this twofold obligation by using well-defined ways—endorsed by the halakhic system itself—of responding to the need for continued creativity and development, *i.e.,* by means of the legal sources of the *Halakhah,* which are discussed in detail in the rest of this volume and in Volume II.

983–984; the rule that the law is in accordance with TB when it differs from TJ, *see infra* pp. 1098 and 1130–1132; and the various approaches to codification. *See also* the subject index herein, s.v. Hilkheta ke-vatra'ei.

117. We do not here deal with the part played by the community and communal leadership in the shaping of the *Halakhah.* For this, *see supra* pp. 54–61 and *infra* pp. 538–541, 678ff., 880ff.

PART TWO

The Legal Sources of Jewish Law:

SECTION 1

Exegesis and Interpretation

Chapter 8
EXEGESIS AND INTERPRETATION (MIDRASH AND *PARSHANUT*): INTRODUCTION

I. Explanation of the Terms *Midrash* and *Parshanut*
II. Interpretation of the *Halakhah,* of Documents, and of Communal Enactments
III. Scriptural Authority for Biblical Exegesis

I. EXPLANATION OF THE TERMS *MIDRASH* AND *PARSHANUT*

The first legal source,[1] in point of time as well as importance, for the development of Jewish law is Midrash, or, as it was also later called, *parshanut.* The root of the word *midrash* is the verb *darosh,* which connotes study and investigation penetrating to the inner and logical meaning of a particular passage, a superficial reading of which may well indicate a different conclusion. The word *darosh* has the same general thrust when it is used in the context of laying bare the actual and objective truth of some occurrence. For example, we read in connection with the people of an "idolatrous town": "You shall investigate (*darashta*) and inquire and interrogate thoroughly. If it is true, the fact is established—that abhorrent thing was perpetrated in your midst. . . ."[2] In this sense, *darosh* connotes an investigation into all of the facts and circumstances of the event, beyond what is apparent on cursory initial inspection.

When we speak, therefore, of the midrash (exegesis or interpretation) of a particular verse in the Bible, we refer not merely to a statement of the plain meaning of the verse but to an investigation into its deeper content and thrust. As is written in the Book of Ezra: "For Ezra had dedicated himself to interpret (*lidrosh*) the Torah of the Lord so as to observe it, and to

1. For the meaning of "legal source," *see supra* pp. 229–230, 236–239.
2. Deuteronomy 13:15; *see also id.* 17:4.

teach laws and rules to Israel."[3] In order to "observe [the precepts of the Torah] and to teach laws and rules," Ezra searched and investigated the inner content and essential purpose of the Torah's text.[4]

In the *Halakhah,* midrash (sometimes also called *talmud*[5]) is similar to *interpretatio* in Roman law and "interpretation" in the common law. Etymologically, midrash and *perush* or *parshanut* have different meanings, comparable to the difference between their English equivalents, "interpretation" and "commentary." Midrash and "interpretation" denote penetration to the inner meaning, to the spirit of the text and the law, while *perush* and "commentary" refer to explanation, which as a general rule is a recasting of the text into simpler and more understandable language.[6] In the course of time, the technical distinction between these terms in halakhic terminology became blurred, and the term *parshanut* began to be used even where the intent was not merely to explain a particular law by paraphrasing it, but to interpret the law and delve into its content.[7] Because *parshanut* is still also used to refer to explanatory paraphrasing of the law, the term now is used to denote both what was included in the term midrash and what was covered by the term *perush.*[8]

3. Ezra 7:10. The 1985 JPS *Tanakh* translates *lidrosh* as "to study." This fails to convey the full meaning of the verse as set forth here.

4. *See* Segal, "Derash, Midrash, Bet Midrash," *Tarbiẓ,* XVII, p. 194; J.N. Epstein, *Mevo'ot le-Sifrut ha-Tanna'im* [Introduction to Tannaitic Literature] (hereinafter, *Tannaim*), pp. 501–504; Lieberman, *Hellenism,* pp. 47–50. In the opinion of J. Heinemann and E.E. Urbach, the verb *darosh* in Scripture does not denote inquiry by way of exegesis but rather an effort to see that precepts are observed in practice. *See* Urbach, "Ha-Derashah ki-Yesod ha-Halakhah u-Va'ayat ha-Soferim" [Exegesis as a Foundation of *Halakhah* and the Question of the *Soferim*], *Tarbiẓ,* XXVII, pp. 166, 171–173. According to this view, the word *darosh* was not used in the sense it now generally has until the time of Shemaiah and Avtalyon. *See also infra* pp. 311–314.

5. As in *le-talmudo hu ba* ("it is cited [not for its literal meaning, but] for its *talmud,* [*i.e.,* its deeper meaning yielded by interpretation]"); or *talmud lomar* ("the text teaches by *talmud* [*i.e.,* implication derived by exegesis]"). *See also* M Avot 4:13: "R. Judah says: 'Be heedful of *talmud* [interpretation], for an unwitting error in *talmud* is accounted as willful transgression.'"

6. Thus, Rashi's explanatory notes to the Pentateuch and the TB are called "Rashi's Commentary" (*Perush Rashi*).

7. *See Tanḥuma,* ed. Buber, Ḥukkat, 16, quoting Ecclesiastes 8:1: "'And who knows the meaning (*pesher*) of the matter (*davar*)?' This refers to the Holy One, blessed be He, who interpreted (*peresh*) the Torah to Moses." Incidentally, during the British Mandate in Palestine, and in Israel until 1981, the Interpretation Ordinance encompassed both interpretive and explanatory matter. The Hebrew name of the ordinance was *Pekudat ha-Parshanut.* The current Israeli statute, the Interpretation Law, 1981, is called in Hebrew *Ḥok ha-Parshanut. See further* Salmond, pp. 132ff. *See also* Idah v. Sasson, 11 *P.D.* 1100, 1103–1104 (1957), for Justice Cheshin's discussion of the distinction between "interpretation" and "construction."

8. The term *midrash* has usually been applied to interpretation of the Torah, and to the earlier stages of interpretation of the *Halakhah* and of documents. Later, the term *parshanut* became more widely used for the interpretation of the *Halakhah* and of documents.

The task of interpretation, *i.e.*, the search for the inner meaning of the text or of a law, is often carried out by means of fixed and known principles that guide the interpreter. Thus, we speak, for example, of the "canons of interpretation," *i.e.*, the principles and methods of investigation and inquiry into the Torah and its verses.

In Talmudic literature, we find additional terms to express the act of interpretation, one of the familiar ones being the term *din* (lit. "law"). According to various scholars, each different term refers to a distinct type of interpretation: *din* is confined to analogical or syllogistic interpretation (such as reasoning *a fortiori*), and midrash is sometimes confined to investigation into content by way of explication of the text.[9]

II. INTERPRETATION OF THE *HALAKHAH*, OF DOCUMENTS, AND OF COMMUNAL ENACTMENTS

The interpretive function and the rules of interpretation are not limited to the elucidation of the Written Law. The Mishnah, too, is interpreted; and in a broad sense the interpretive function was employed, in various forms and by means of various principles, as a major legal source in all of the different periods of Jewish law. This work describes in later chapters not only how Biblical verses were interpreted but also how later authorities interpreted prior statements of the Talmudic Sages by means of precisely the same methodology and approach that the Talmudic Sages themselves had applied to the Biblical verses. In the same way, the *rishonim* interpreted the statements and legal formulations of the *geonim*, and the *aḥaronim* interpreted the statements and formulations of the *rishonim*.

Together with interpretation of *Halakhah*, there developed in an early period in Jewish law the interpretation and elucidation of different types of legal documents that were used on a daily basis, such as the *ketubbah* (marriage contract setting forth obligations of the husband to his wife), bills of sale, contracts, and wills. Interpretation of documents also made use of the methods of Biblical and halakhic interpretation and even expanded on them to take account of the special needs of documentary interpretation.

An additional type of interpretation in Jewish law, which is connected in theory to the interpretation of documents, is the interpretation of com-

---

The doctrines relating to interpretation of communal enactments did not come into being until after the tenth century C.E., and the term *parshanut*, and not *midrash*, was applied to this type of interpretation from the start.

9. *See* Epstein, *Tannaim*, pp. 501–504; L. Finkelstein, "Midrash, Halakhot ve-Haggadot" [Midrash, Laws, and *Aggadot*], *Jubilee Volume for Y. Baer*, pp. 28, 35.

munal enactments. As early as the Talmudic period, there is evidence of enactment of legislation by townspeople or their representatives. However, such legislation became significant in Jewish legal history beginning with the tenth century C.E., when the Jewish communities in various diasporas obtained increased power and adopted communal enactments (*takkanot ha-kahal*). These *takkanot* were enacted by the community or by its representatives and elected officials. The process corresponds to the legislative activity of the public and its representatives in other legal systems. The promulgation of these enactments was a wide-ranging and fruitful legislative achievement of Jewish communities for hundreds of years, and covered many broad areas of civil, public, and criminal law. Like statutes, regulations, and ordinances in every legal system, these enactments in the course of their application to actual life also led to the development of an extensive and noteworthy system of interpretive methods.

The following chapters examine the fundamental principles of Biblical interpretation and the major outlines of the interpretation of the *Halakhah*, of documents, and of communal enactments. All of these areas, throughout their history, were cross-fertilized and became interlinked. In the course of our investigation, we note what is unique in each of these areas and what they share in common.

III. SCRIPTURAL AUTHORITY FOR BIBLICAL EXEGESIS

The halakhic authorities sought in the Written Law, which is the ultimate basis of authority for all Jewish legal sources, support and sanction for exegetical interpretation of the Torah. There were several verses relied on for such support.

The Sages inferred the practice of exegetical interpretation of the Torah (*midrash ha-Torah*) from a statement in the episode involving Jethro. To Jethro's question, "Why do you act [lit. "sit" (as judge)] alone while all the people stand about you from morning until evening?" Moses responded: "It is because the people come to me to inquire (*lidrosh*) of God. When they have a dispute, it comes before me and I decide between one person and another and I make known the laws and teachings of God" (Exodus 18:14–16). This last verse is explained by R. Joshua: "'The laws' (*ḥukkim*) are the interpretations (*midrashot*), and 'the teachings' (*torot*) are the directives (*hora'ot*)."[10] Moses informed the people of both the written text of the Torah and the pertinent interpretations of the text.

10. *Mekhilta de-R. Ishmael,* Yitro, Tractate De-Amalek, sec. 2, pp. 196–197, where *hora'ot* is taken to mean "matters that are written down in fixed form." *See* M. Ish-Shalom, *Mekhilta de-R. Ishmael,* Introduction, ch. 2; Epstein, *Tannaim,* p. 502.

In addition, the Sages explicated the statement in Deuteronomy (11:32): "Take care to observe all the laws and rules that I have set before you this day":

> "Take care" refers to study, "to observe" refers to practice, "all the laws" refers to the interpretations (*midrashot*), "and rules" refers to the legal rules (*dinim*), "that I have set before you this day" [is to tell you that] they should be as dear to you as if you had just received them this very day at Mount Sinai.[11]

The Sages also found a source for Biblical exegesis in Deuteronomy 17:8–11, which is the central prescription of the methodology for maintaining the creativity of the *Halakhah*. The *Sifrei*[12] comments as follows on the verse (Deuteronomy 17:8) "If a case is too baffling for you to decide . . .":

> "A case" refers to the law; "to decide" refers to the *din* [*i.e.*, "interpretation," which is sometimes called *din* or *dinim*].[13]

The same passage is cited by Maimonides in his discussion of the authority of the High Court in Jerusalem and of the sources for the development of the Oral Law:

> Scripture says [Deuteronomy 17:11]: ". . . and [in accordance with] the ruling handed down to you"—this refers to laws derived through interpretation by means of any of the canons by which Scripture is expounded [*i.e.*, the rulings and conclusions that the High Court will reach by application of midrashic methods, namely, the canons of Biblical interpretation].[14]

The following is the comment of Naḥmanides as to the meaning of this Scriptural passage:[15]

> Scripture laid down the requirement that we obey the High Court (which stands before God at the place that He chooses) as to all of their interpreta-

11. *Sifrei*, Deuteronomy, Re'eh, sec. 58 (p. 124).

12. *Sifrei*, Deuteronomy, Shofetim, sec. 152 (p. 205); TB Sanhedrin 87a and Rashi, *ad loc.*, s.v. La-mishpat.

13. *See further* TJ Berakhot 1:4, 9a (1:7, 3b): ". . . whereas in this instance, 'In accordance with the instructions given you . . . ,'" where the quoted language refers to *Halakhah* derived by midrash. *See also* Alon, *Meḥkarim*, II, p. 239.

14. Maimonides, *MT*, Mamrim 1:2. The full quotation from Maimonides appears *supra* at p. 238. *See also* Maimonides, *MT*, Introduction, describing the course of the *Halakhah* up to the time of the redaction of the Mishnah:

> In like manner did every [Sage], according to his ability, write down for himself [notes of] what he had heard [from his teachers] by way of explanation of the Torah and its *halakhot*, as well as [notes of] new legal developments in each generation that had not been handed down by word of mouth as part of the oral tradition but were derived through one of thirteen canons of interpretation and approved by the High Court.

15. Naḥmanides, *Commentary on Deuteronomy* 17:11. *See also supra* pp. 244–245.

tions of the Torah, whether they received the interpretation by transmission from person to person extending back to Moses, [who received it] from God [*i.e.,* by tradition], or whether they base their views upon the sense of Scripture [*i.e.,* exegesis] or on their own objectives [according to a different text: its objective]. This is because He gave the Torah to us with the understanding that the ultimate prerogative to construe it is entrusted to the halakhic authorities, and their construction is binding.

Chapter 9

EXEGETICAL INTERPRETATION OF THE TORAH

I. Nature and Function of Exegesis of the Torah
  A. Creative Interpretation (*Midrash Yoẓer*) and Integrative Interpretation (*Midrash Mekayyem*)
  B. Midrash as a Creative Source in Jewish Law
  C. Comparison with Other Legal Systems
  D. Differences in Legal Rules Resulting from Differences in Methods of Interpretation
  E. Integrative Interpretation
II. *Asmakhta* (Supportive Interpretation) in Midrash
III. Different Literary Forms for Creative and Integrative Interpretation
IV. Development of the Use of Midrash
  A. Antiquity of Exegetical Activity
  B. Exegetical Interpretation from Ezra the Scribe until the *Zugot* ("Pairs")
  C. Exegetical Interpretation in the Period of the *Zugot*
  D. Exegetical Interpretation in the Academies of R. Akiva and R. Ishmael
V. The Thirteen Canons (*Middot*) of Interpretation
VI. Explicative Exegesis
  A. Terms and Expressions—Generally
  B. Terms and Expressions—Conjunctive and Disjunctive, Masculine and Feminine
    1. The Letter *Vav*—Conjunctive or Also Disjunctive?
    2. Masculine and Feminine
  C. Generalization and Specification
    1. Inference from a Generalization Followed by a Specification (*Kelal u-Ferat*)
    2. Inference from a Specification Followed by a Generalization (*Perat u-Khelal*)
    3. Inference from a Generalization Followed by a Specification Followed in Turn by a Generalization (*Kelal u-Ferat u-Khelal*)
    4. The Relation between the Canons on Generalization and Specification and the Other Canons
    5. A Generalization that Requires a Specification or a Specification that Requires a Generalization
      a. A Generalization that Requires a Specification
      b. A Specification that Requires a Generalization
  D. A Matter Included in a Generalization and Also Specifically Mentioned (*Davar she-Hayah bi-Khelal ve-Yaẓa Min ha-Kelal*)
  E. An Ambiguous Word or Passage Is Explained from Its Context or from a Subsequent Expression (*Davar ha-Lamed me-Inyano, ve-Davar ha-Lamed mi-Sofo*)
    1. Explanation on the Basis of a Subsequent Expression
    2. Explanation on the Basis of Context
  F. Two Contradictory Passages
    1. Contradiction between Two Passages in Two Sections
    2. Contradiction between Two Passages in the Same Section
    3. Contradiction between Two Parts of the Same Verse
VII. Logical Interpretation
  A. Violation of a Betrothed Girl
  B. The Law of Pledges

C. Damage Due to a Pit
D. The Law of Agency
VIII. Analogical Exegesis
A. Scriptural Analogy (*Hekkesh ha-Katuv*)
1. Explicit Analogy
2. Analogy by Implication
B. Inference *A Fortiori* (*Kal va-Ḥomer*)
1. Inference from the More Lenient to the More Stringent
2. Inference from the More Stringent to the More Lenient
3. "It Is Enough for the Conclusion That It Be like the Premise"
C. Inference from the Similarity of Words or Phrases (*Gezerah Shavah*)
D. Application of a General Principle (*Binyan Av*)
1. Application of a General Principle Derived from a Single Verse
2. Application of a General Principle Derived from Two Verses
3. Application of a General Principle Derived from Three Verses
4. Application of a General Principle Derived from Four Verses
E. Order of Priority in the Use of the Analogical Canons
IX. Restrictive Interpretation
A. Acceptance of Proselytes from National Groups with Whom Marriage Was Forbidden
B. The Rebellious Son
1. Halakhic Interpretation with Regard to the Son
2. Halakhic Interpretation with Regard to the Parents
C. The Idolatrous Town
1. How an Idolatrous Town Comes into Being
2. Towns That Cannot Become Idolatrous Towns
D. Opposition to Drastically Restrictive Interpretation
X. The Methods of Interpretation of R. Ishmael and R. Akiva
A. The Principal Differences in the Methods of Interpretation by the Academies of R. Ishmael and R. Akiva
B. The Dispute Related Mainly to the Methods of Integrating the Law with Scripture, Not to the Substance of the Law
C. Criticism by the Sages of Symbolic Methods of Interpretation
XI. Exegetical Interpretation of the Torah in the Amoraic Period
A. Decline in the Use of Exegetical Interpretation of the Torah
B. Dispensing with the Need for Integrative Interpretation
C. General Guidelines for Use of Interpretive Methods
XII. Biblical Exegesis in the Post-Talmudic Period
A. Consecration of Something Not Yet in Existence
B. "Moving a Landmark" (*Hassagat Gevul*)
C. "Scheming Witnesses" (*Edim Zomemim*)

I. NATURE AND FUNCTION OF EXEGESIS OF THE TORAH

A. Creative Interpretation (*Midrash Yoẓer*) and Integrative Interpretation (*Midrash Mekayyem*)

To say that interpretation is a source for the creation and development of Jewish law is already to have taken a categorical position on a fundamental question that is a matter of controversy among the students of the *Halakhah.* Let us briefly examine the question.

When we study halakhic literature, we find a substantial number of laws expressed in the form of midrash, *i.e.,* the law is not in the form of an abstract rule stated prescriptively, such as the style generally used in the Mishnah, but is connected and interwoven with a verse from the Torah. There is no question about the basic midrashic style, which is well known; the midrashic form of these laws is beyond dispute.[1] The question, however, is: Is this solely a literary form for pedagogic purposes, whereby existing rules of law were learned by being connected with supportive Scriptural verses? Or is this much more than just a literary form, in that the verse with which a particular rule of law is connected and with which it is interwoven is actually the source of that law, *i.e.,* the law owes its existence to the analytical study of the verse and if not for the interpretation of the verse would not exist at all?

Let us clarify this problem with an illustration. Leviticus 5:1 states:

> [A] person incurs guilt [lit. "sins"]: when he has heard a public imprecation [against one who withholds testimony] and—although able to testify as one who has either seen or learned of the matter—does not give information, so that he is subject to punishment. . . .

In this verse, the principle was established in Jewish law that every person who has knowledge of relevant facts has a duty to testify, and if he withholds his testimony he is guilty of a transgression. According to the plain meaning of the verse, this obligation applies to all factual information acquired in any manner, whether as an eyewitness or by any other means, and the words "who has either seen or learned of the matter" and "give

1. As to when this literary form began, and as to the collections of the halakhic and aggadic midrashim, *see infra* pp. 1047–1049.

information" cannot be viewed, according to their plain meaning, as defining the qualifications of a witness or establishing standards to determine competency to testify.[2]

But in the *Tosefta* (Shevu'ot 3:8) we read:

> "And—although able to testify"—he must be a competent witness. "When he has heard"—this excludes the deaf. "Who has . . . seen"—this excludes the blind. "Or learned"—this excludes the idiot. "[He] does not give information, so that he is subject to punishment"—this excludes the mute. These are the views of the early [Sages] (*rishonim*).[3] R. Akiva states: "You shall investigate and inquire and interrogate thoroughly" [Deuteronomy 13:15]. Does one inquire from the deaf, or does one interrogate an idiot?

The *Tosefta,* according to both the early Sages and R. Akiva, declares the basic rule of law that an idiot or one who is deaf, blind, or mute is not a competent witness. But the *Tosefta* does not formulate this law as an abstract, black-letter legal proposition. The rule could have been succinctly stated: "The idiot, the deaf, the blind, and the mute are incompetent to be witnesses." Instead, the rule was formulated by the early Sages as being connected to and intertwined with the verse in Leviticus 5:1, while according to R. Akiva the rule is deduced from the already settled requirement that witnesses must be interrogated thoroughly, which is impossible in the case of the types of witnesses listed in the *Tosefta.*

This poses the question that is the subject of our discussion: Should we view this *midrash* as telling us that the Sages deduced the law on the necessary qualifications for a competent witness from the specific language of the verse? Is this *midrash* an expansive and contextual interpretation—penetrating into the essence of the various terms in the text and their connection to the subject of the verse—which led the Sages to the conclusion that the Torah also prescribes the necessary attributes for every witness (namely, the ability to hear, see, speak, and understand), so that someone without these qualifications is not competent to be a witness and, therefore, is not subject to punishment if he does not testify? Or should we perhaps view the purpose of this *midrash* as being only to connect preexisting and familiar law on the qualifications of a witness to a verse in the Torah so that, in fact, the law on the competency of witnesses was not deduced from an interpretation of the verse, but rather was already preexisting, on the basis of either tradition or an ancient enactment or custom? According to this latter view, the *midrash* would be only a literary device used by the scholars to study and teach this law, interweaving it with and supporting it by the

2. *See* commentaries of Ibn Ezra and Naḥmanides, *ad loc.*

3. For the meaning of *rishonim* as used here, *see* Epstein, *Tannaim,* p. 507. *See also supra* p. 267.

verse in Leviticus 5:1. Such use of the midrashic form served two purposes: first, to make it easier to learn and remember the laws (which, as is known, were studied orally) by connecting them with a Biblical verse; and second, to emphasize the link between the Oral Law and the Written Law.[4]

If we accept the first hypothesis—that the law on incompetent witnesses represents genuine interpretation that rendered explicit what was already implicit in the Biblical verse—then interpretation is a source for the creation of the law, and we may properly say that the Sages fashioned the law by means of creative interpretation (*midrash yoẓer*). On the other hand, if we accept the second hypothesis—that the law on incompetent witnesses was already in existence and the Sages merely sought by their "interpretation" to support the existing law by connecting it with a Biblical verse—then we reach the conclusion that the *midrash* was not a source for the creation of the law, but merely an exercise in integrating existing law with the Biblical text (*midrash mekayyem*).

As stated, the halakhic authorities and scholars disagreed at various times on this question of the nature of midrash. Among the recent scholars, J.N. Epstein represents the view that midrash merely attributes an existing law to a source in a Biblical verse. "Midrash supports law but does not create law; the law is buttressed by the text but not extracted from the text by means of interpretation."[5] On the other hand, Ḥanokh Albeck asserts that midrash not only supports the existing law but is also a source for deducing new rules of law from Biblical verses:

> In ancient times, when the High Court was in existence, whenever a problem came before it for which there was no tradition, they undoubtedly debated and discussed the interpretation of the Torah and on that basis alone they derived their legal conclusion.[6]

Midrashic interpretation, according to Albeck, performed this creative function in all periods—even during the time of the *amoraim*.[7] Yet, even those who argue for the creative function of midrash do not contend that every law stated to be deduced from a Biblical verse was an instance of creation of new law by interpretation. The halakhic authorities themselves occasionally emphasized that the "interpretation" of a verse was merely *asmakhta* (lit. "something to lean on," *i.e.*, a supportive device);[8] and in many other instances there are laws stated in midrashic form where, although the interpretations of the Biblical verses were not specifically la-

4. On this point, *see further infra* p. 1047.
5. Epstein, *Tannaim*, p. 511.
6. H. Albeck, *Mavo*, p. 42.
7. *Id.* at 54; *see also infra* pp. 383–384.
8. *See infra* pp. 300–305.

beled as *asmakhta,* there is reason to believe that the legal source of the law was not interpretation but rather tradition or some other halakhic source.[9] In any case, a large and significant proportion of the laws owe their existence to the midrashic process of interpreting Biblical texts.

The accepted view of most students of the *Halakhah* is that midrash simultaneously performed both the function of creating *Halakhah* and the function of integrating preexisting *Halakhah* with Scripture. Some of these scholars divide these two functions of midrash into different historical periods. According to E.E. Urbach,[10] in the earlier period the function of midrash was to connect the law with Scripture; the actual development of the *Halakhah* in this period was accomplished by other methods such as legislation (*takkanot*), custom (*minhag*), and *ma'aseh* (a case or incident); and midrash did not become an additional source for creating the *Halakhah* until just prior to the destruction of the Temple, when Jewish autonomy waned. On the other hand, J. Neubauer[11] believed that it was precisely in the earlier period that the midrashic method flourished as a creative force, whereas in the later periods its major task was to integrate existing law with Scripture.

B. Midrash as a Creative Source in Jewish Law

Of all the numerous and sharply divergent views as to the function of midrash, the most satisfactory is that midrash, from the earliest period and throughout the entire history of the *Halakhah,* operated as a force for creation and development[12] (although, of course, as is discussed later, more so in some periods than in others). For in every period, from the earliest days of the *Halakhah,* halakhic authorities were confronted with the need to resolve difficulties that came to light on close analysis of Biblical passages and to solve problems that arose in the course of actual life, especially as a result of changes in the times and in social conditions. The use of midrash to resolve difficulties in Biblical explication necessarily produced new laws,

9. On *asmakhta, see infra* pp. 300–305 and references in subject index. *See also* Maimonides, *Commentary on the Mishnah,* Introduction (ed. Mosad ha-Rav Kook, pp. 32–33), regarding the interpretation of "the product of *hadar* trees" (Leviticus 23:40) as referring to the *etrog* or citron (TB Sukkah 35a).

10. E.E. Urbach, "Ha-Derashah ki-Yesod ha-Halakhah u-Va'ayat ha-Soferim" [Interpretation as the Basis of the *Halakhah* and the Problem of the *Soferim*], *Tarbiẓ,* XXVII, pp. 166ff.

11. J. Neubauer, "Halakhah u-Midrash Halakhah" [*Halakhah* and Halakhic Midrash], *Sinai,* XXII (1948), pp. 49ff. (particularly pp. 75–76), reprinted in Neubauer, *Ha-Rambam al Divrei Soferim* [Maimonides on *Divrei Soferim*], 1957, pp. 101ff.

12. *Cf.* Maimonides' clear statement to this effect in his Introduction to the *Mishneh Torah* and in *MT,* Mamrim 1:2. *See also supra* p. 279 n. 14.

and midrashic creativity increased especially when the authorities sought to use midrash to solve new problems.

Of course, the halakhic authorities possessed other methods for finding solutions to these new problems, *e.g.*, by adopting enactments (*takkanot*), *i.e.*, legislation. This method, however, was neither convenient nor easy, because it is explicitly and designedly legislative and clearly intended to add to, derogate from, or modify the existing sanctified *Halakhah*. In the case of midrash, on the other hand, new law flows naturally out of the existing law; midrash does not purport to add to existing law, and the law created by midrash is certainly not contrary to existing law. The connection between the Written Law and the new law is the natural connection between antecedent and consequence: The "new" law is deduced from the Torah on the assumption that it was always included in the Torah itself. It therefore seems likely that when the halakhic authorities searched for solutions to emerging new problems, their first resort was to midrash; only when this did not provide an adequate and satisfactory solution for their problem did they turn for an answer to other creative legal sources in the *Halakhah*, such as legislation.

This view as to the creative function of midrash, even in the earliest periods of the *Halakhah*, finds support in the halakhic sources.[13] We cite two prime illustrations.

Tractate *Sanhedrin* discusses the law of the "rebellious elder" who issues a legal ruling contrary to the decision of the Sanhedrin, the High Court located in the Chamber of Hewn Stone at the Temple. The Mishnah[14] describes the various levels of judicial tribunals that hear and determine a controversy between a single Sage and his colleagues until the dispute comes for final resolution to the High Court:

> There were three courts there [in the Temple in Jerusalem], one sitting at the entrance to the Temple Mount, one sitting at the entrance to the Temple courtyard, and one in the Chamber of Hewn Stone. They [the Sages who disagreed on a matter of law] come to the court that is at the entrance to the Temple Mount and he [the dissenting Sage] says: "This is my interpretation and this is the interpretation of my colleagues; this is what I taught and this is what my colleagues taught."
>
> If they have heard [if the court possesses information on the matter, *i.e.*, a tradition as to how to determine the question], they tell them, and if not,

13. H. Albeck, *Mavo*, pp. 42–43. Early in the history of the *Halakhah*, many statements of the law were couched in the midrashic style. However, in most cases it is impossible to prove from the law itself whether it was created by midrash or whether it already existed and was merely connected by midrash with the Biblical text. In order to prove that the midrash was creative, it is necessary to find a separate halakhic source that so indicates.

14. M Sanhedrin 11:2.

> they come with them to the court that is at the entrance to the Temple courtyard and he says: "This is my interpretation and this is the interpretation of my colleagues; this is what I taught and this is what my colleagues taught."
>
> If the members of that court have heard [a tradition], they tell them, and if not, they all come to the High Court at the Chamber of Hewn Stone whence Torah issues to all Israel, as is said: "From that place that the Lord chose" [Deuteronomy 17:10].
>
> When he returns to his town, if he merely continues to teach in the same way that he previously taught, he is innocent; but if he instructs that his ruling be applied in actual practice, he is guilty, as is stated: "Should a man act presumptuously . . ." [Deuteronomy 17:12]. He is not guilty until he instructs that his view of the law be carried out in practice.[15]

The question that provoked the dispute between the dissenter and his colleagues was one that: (a) required a decision in an actual case (as is indicated by the statement at the end of the Mishnah "until he instructs that his view of the law be carried out in practice"), and (b) involved an elder who analyzed and taught (*limmed* [from the root *lamod,* whence Talmud], used here in the sense of "interpreted")[16] a Biblical verse in one way, while his fellow Sages analyzed and interpreted the verse in a different way.[17]

A different source[18] describes the private conference of the judges leading to a final decision after the prosecution and defense witnesses have all been heard in a criminal case:

> The most senior judge begins by arguing in his [defendant's] favor, and any colleague may support him. If they find in his favor, they acquit him, and if not, they delay it [they postpone a decision until the next day to let the matter rest and to give the judges additional time to consider the question]. On the next day, they [the judges] gather together in pairs. They eat little, they drink no wine, and they debate the question throughout that night. If he was a murderer [*i.e.,* if he was accused of murder], they discuss the section [of the

15. An individual was permitted to persist in maintaining his own opinion, to teach it in public, and to express opposition to the position of the Sanhedrin; however, in making rulings for practical application, he was obligated to follow the Sanhedrin's ruling. *See also infra* pp. 1061–1070.

16. *See supra* p. 276 and n. 5.

17. The plain meaning of the *mishnah* is that the decision of the Sanhedrin was "either on the basis of tradition or on the basis of a Scriptural interpretation that they arrived at in the specific case" (Maimonides, *MT,* Mamrim 1:4 and *Commentary on the Mishnah, ad loc.*). It was only regarding the other courts on the Temple Mount that the *mishnah* states that they ruled according to the traditions they possessed; no such limitation was applied in the *mishnah* to the Sanhedrin. *See* H. Albeck, *Mavo,* p. 42. This answers Urbach's objection to the argument that this *mishnah* proves the existence of creative interpretation as a legal source in early tannaitic times. *See* Urbach, *supra* n. 10 at 180 n. 49.

18. *Tosefta* Sanhedrin 9:1.

> Torah] dealing with murder, and if he was accused of incest, they discuss the section dealing with incest; and the next day they arrive early at court.

Thus, when the judges deliberated to determine whether a crime was committed and whether to convict the accused, they discussed the section of the Torah that deals with the particular subject matter before them, and they arrived at their decision as the outcome of the discussion of that section.[19] This discussion of the section of the Torah necessarily involved the interpretation of its verses; in a case of murder they reached their decision on the basis of the interpretation of the section dealing with murder, and in a case involving incest they reached their decision by interpreting the section on that subject.[20]

The following example provides a clear and pointed illustration of the essence of creation of law by means of interpretation. Numbers 27:8–11 contains a section on inheritance that lists the order of the heirs: son, daughter, brother, father's brother:

> If his father had no brothers, you shall assign his property to his nearest relative in his own clan and he shall inherit it. This shall be the law of procedure for the Israelites, in accordance with the Lord's command to Moses [verse 11].

In this order of inheritance, the father is not mentioned as an heir of his son. But the Mishnah[21] says:

> The following inherit . . . : a father from his sons and sons from their father.

A father inherits from his son if the son did not leave either a son or a daughter, and this is so even though the decedent leaves a surviving brother. This rule that the father of a decedent is entitled to priority of

19. The chronology of the procedure stated in the *Tosefta* indicates that the case was decided on the basis of the conclusions reached in the analysis of the relevant section in the Torah. The *Tosefta* goes on to state that on the day after they had discussed that section, the judges arrived at the court early, and the court officials read out the decision of each of them. There is no indication of any further discussion. Urbach, *supra* n. 10, relies on this passage of the *Tosefta* in arguing against Albeck's view as to the very early existence of creative interpretation. Urbach reasons that the *Tosefta* does not state "that they decided the case according to the results of their study of the Torah section (*parashat ha-Torah*), but only that they discussed the relevant issues (*parashat ha-inyan*)." In view of the *Tosefta*'s description of the chronology of the procedure, Urbach's contention seems unjustified.

20. There are many additional proofs that later in the tannaitic period the law was determined on the basis of exegetical interpretation of Scriptural verses. *See, e.g.*, R. Ishmael's retort to R. Akiva (TB Sanhedrin 51b): "Should we put her to the fire because you interpret [the words] '*and* if the daughter'?"; *see infra* p. 380. For further proofs, *see* H. Albeck, *Mavo*, pp. 43ff.

21. M Bava Batra 8:1.

succession over the decedent's brother is arrived at by interpretation: "'You shall assign his property to his nearest relative.' 'Nearest'—the nearer relative has priority," and a father is closer to his son than a brother to his brothers. The Sages thus applied the principle stated at the end of the section on inheritance—that the nearest relative is entitled to inherit—not only to the specific case upon which it immediately follows, *i.e.*, where the father has no brothers, but as a general principle that prevails even over the order of succession specifically mentioned in the text.[22]

This broad authority to determine the law through interpretation is stated in the *Sifrei* in the following manner:[23]

> "This shall be the law of procedure for the Israelites": The Torah gave wisdom (*da'at*) [according to a variant version: it gave permission (*reshut*)] to the Sages to interpret and to say [that] whoever is the nearest relative has priority in inheritance.

The Torah gave authority to the Sages to create law on the basis of the interpretation of the verse and thus to establish that in *every* case the nearest relative is first in the order of succession to a decedent's estate.[24]

C. Comparison with Other Legal Systems

This conclusion with regard to the creative function of interpretation and the origins of its use for this purpose can also be reached by examining the parallel phenomenon in the history of other legal systems that accorded special authority to their earliest and most authoritative legal code. This, for example, was the origin of the development of Roman law. R. Sohm, in his discussion of the crucial function that *interpretatio* performed in this development, states:

> Formal repeal of the laws of the Twelve Tables and substitution of a different code was simply inconceivable to the Romans of that period. For fully 1000 years, until the *Corpus Juris Civilis* of Justinian marked the end of the growth of Roman law, although not so much as a shred of the laws of the Twelve Tables remained in effect as law, those laws remained in theory the authoritative source of the entire Roman law. This theory fitted the conservative and cautious outlook of the Romans on everything relating to law. On one hand, it was forbidden to change even one letter of the Twelve Tables; on the other hand, it was also necessary to introduce a new spirit into the ancient letters. Consequently, subsequent to the Twelve Tables, mention is made of the inter-

22. *See* TB Bava Batra 108b and 109a: "The verses are not written in sequential order."
23. *Sifrei,* Numbers, Pinḥas, sec. 134 (p. 179).
24. This method of creating law was particularly prized. *See* TB Bava Batra 108b: "Since it comes from an interpretation, it is very dear to him."

pretation of the law, *interpretatio,* which developed the law and even changed it without touching as much as a single letter of the written law.[25]

If this was the function of interpretation from the beginning of Roman law, how much more so did midrash serve this purpose from the very beginnings of Jewish law. The feeling that the halakhic authorities of every generation had for the sanctity of the Written Law as God's Revelation at Sinai was much greater and more powerful than the attitude of the Romans toward the Twelve Tables, conservative and cautious as that was. Moreover, Roman law could much more easily and readily employ legislation and other methods in addition to *interpretatio* to solve new problems than could Jewish law. The rules of interpretation and their use in Jewish law, therefore, developed to a much greater extent than in Roman law.[26]

The nature of interpretation as described by scholars of Roman law is also of interest. Is interpretation of the law a device for imposing on a text a legal conclusion that is contrary to the original intent of the text, or does interpretation extract from between the lines of the text the law's basic and original intent and purpose? H. Dernburg responds to this question:

> Surely the content of the law should be expressed in the document that contains it. . . . But the content of the law need not be derived directly from its words. Often the general tenor of the law impels us to arrive at conclusions that are not expressed in its individual words but nevertheless undoubtedly reflect the legislative intent. *Interpretatio* therefore must recognize that a legally proper reading of a statute involves more than merely what the statute explicitly and directly states. It also requires attention to what the text alludes to only indirectly; one may term this "the hidden content" of the law.[27]

Why is this so?

> Because law is a phenomenon that has the quality of being able to supply from within itself what is missing in it.[28]

25. R. Sohm, *Institutionen,* 17th ed., 1949, p. 54.
26. *See infra* n. 29 for bibliographical references.
27. H. Dernburg, *Pandekten,* 5th ed., 1896, I, p. 76.
28. *Id.* at 86, and *see* pp. 75–88 for a description of *interpretatio* in Roman law. For trends in interpretation in contemporary legal systems, *see* H. Black, *Handbook on the Constitution and Interpretation of the Laws* (1986); G. Calabresi, *A Common Law for the Age of Statutes* (1982); Cardozo, "Law and Literature," in *Law and Literature and Other Essays* 10 (1931); Cox, "Judge Learned Hand and the Interpretation of Statutes," 60 *Harv.L.Rev.* 370, 372 (1947); Curtis, "A Better Theory of Legal Interpretation," 3 *Vand.L.Rev.* 407, 409 (1950); Frankfurter, "Some Reflections on the Reading of Statutes," 47 *Colum.L.Rev.* 527 (1947); O.W. Holmes, "Theory of Legal Interpretation," in *Collected Legal Papers* 207 (1921); Jackson, "The Meaning of Statutes: What Congress Says or What the Court Says," 34 *A.B.A.J.* 535 (1948) (advocating adoption of uniform principles of statutory construction in federal courts); R. Keeton, *Venturing to Do Justice* (1969); Landis, "Statutes and the Sources of Law,"

This self-completion is carried out by means of interpretation, which penetrates to the internal substance, the hidden content of the law. If the laws of the Twelve Tables were viewed by the Roman legal scholars not as a code whose content may be ascertained directly from its words but as law that completes itself from within itself, and indirectly yields up its hidden meaning, then how much more so did the halakhic authorities see the Written Law, the word of God, as being a complete and perfect Revelation, able to answer every new question from within itself, out of the hidden content embodied in its verses and sections![29]

D. Differences in Legal Rules Resulting from Differences in Methods of Interpretation

It has been seen from the three illustrations above that midrash was used to solve a specific problem that faced the halakhic authorities or to establish a halakhic principle. The following two illustrations show how differences among the Sages as to methods of interpretation led to differences in legal consequences with respect to a particular issue.

1. Deuteronomy 24:1 states:

---

in *Harvard Legal Essays* 213 (1934) (reprinted in 2 *Harv. J. on Legis.* 7 [1965]); Landis, "A Note on 'Statutory Interpretation,'" 43 *Harv.L.Rev.* 886, 893 (1930); R. Leflar, *Appellate Judicial Opinions* (1974); Lehman, "How to Interpret a Difficult Statute," 1979 *Wis.L.Rev.* 489; P.B. Maxwell, *On the Interpretation of Statutes*, 12th ed., Bombay, 1969; Nutting, "The Ambiguity of Unambiguous Statutes," 24 *Minn.L.Rev.* 509 (1940); Note, "Intent, Clear Statements, and the Common Law: Statutory Interpretation in the Supreme Court," 95 *Harv.L.Rev.* 892 (1982); Salmond, pp. 132ff.; Sanders and Wade, "Legal Writings on Statutory Construction," 3 *Vand.L.Rev.* 569, 580 (1950) (bibliography of articles on statutory construction); Sunstein, "Interpreting Statutes in the Regulatory State," 103 *Harv.L.Rev.* 405 (1989); Sykes, "A Modest Proposal for a Change in Maryland's Statutes Quo," 43 *Md.L.Rev.* 647 (1984); Tushnet, "Following the Rules Laid Down: A Critique of Interpretivism and Neutral Principles," 96 *Harv.L.Rev.* 781 (1983).

For additional material on statutory interpretation in the courts of the State of Israel, and for scholarly articles by Israeli commentators on statutory interpretation, *see infra* pp. 1731–1751, 1827–1838, 1861–1884, 1920–1923, 1934–1938.

29. Various scholars have discussed the similarity between several of the canons of interpretation in Jewish law and canons of interpretation in Roman law. *See* D. Daube, "On the Third Chapter of the Lex Aquilia," 52 *L.Q.R.* 253, 265 (1936); *id.*, Book Review, "F. Schulz, *History of Roman Legal Science*," *Journal of Roman Studies*, XXXVIII (1948), pp. 113ff.; *id.*, "Rabbinic Methods of Interpretation and Hellenistic Rhetoric," *HUCA*, XXII (1949), pp. 252ff.; B. Cohen, *Law and Tradition in Judaism*, p. 11 n. 32; S. Eisenstadt, *Ha-Mishpat ha-Roma'i* [Roman Law], pp. 119–122. For a comparison with Greek canons of interpretation, *see* Lieberman, *Hellenism*, pp. 47ff., and for a comparison with Moslem law, *see* Goitein-Ben-Shemesh, *Ha-Mishpat ha-Muslemi bi-Medinat Yisra'el* [Moslem Law in the State of Israel], p. 64.

> A man marries a woman and lives with her. She fails to please him, because he has found something obnoxious [*ervat davar,* lit. unchastity, foul thing, nakedness] about her, and he writes her a bill of divorcement, hands it to her, and sends her away from his house.

This verse was interpreted by the Sages to deduce various laws relating to divorce. One of the subjects in this area of the law was, What are the grounds for divorce?

In this period of the *Halakhah,* there was still a basic distinction between marriage, on the one hand, and divorce, on the other, with respect to whether both parties had to consent. Marriage required the voluntary consent of both parties, husband and wife. For divorce, however, the unilateral will of only one party, the husband, was determinative; consent of the wife was unnecessary. As is known, this law was changed about a thousand years ago through the noted *takkanah* of Rabbenu Gershom that prohibited divorce without the wife's consent. But even in the Talmudic period, although only the husband could divorce his wife but not *vice versa,* it was held that only if certain specific grounds existed was a husband permitted to divorce his wife.

The Sages disputed the nature of these grounds for divorce:

> The School of Shammai says: A man may not divorce his wife unless he has found in her something sexually improper [*i.e.,* adultery or licentiousness], as is stated: "Because he has found something obnoxious (*ervat davar*) about her." The School of Hillel says: Even if she overcooked his food, as is stated: "Because he has found something obnoxious (*ervat davar*) about her." R. Akiva says: Even if he found another more beautiful than she, as is stated: "She fails to please him."[30]

In this *mishnah,* we find three different viewpoints in answer to the questions, (1) What are the grounds for divorce, and (2) When may a man divorce his wife? Each opinion was the result of interpretation of the very same verse (Deuteronomy 24:1) by various Sages, and we are thus called upon to consider how they reached three such different conclusions from the same verse (and in the case of the schools of Shammai and Hillel, even from the very same words).

The interpretation of the School of Shammai is a simple one, as the verse states explicitly: "Because he has found *ervat davar* about her," this apparently referring to sexual promiscuity (which is a primary connotation of the term, the root meaning of *ervah* being "nakedness") and being in all

30. M Gittin 9:10.

likelihood the reason why a man would write a bill of divorcement to his wife.

The School of Hillel also deduced from the verse that the ground for divorce is the existence of *ervat davar,* but sought to construe that term by looking to its meaning when used elsewhere in the Torah. Indeed, the term does appear elsewhere in the Torah, in the context of the duty of enforcing cleanliness and hygiene in a military camp when the nation goes to war against the enemy:

> There shall be an area for you outside the camp, where you may relieve yourself. With your gear you shall have a spike, and when you have squatted you shall dig a hole with it and cover up your excrement. Since the Lord your God moves about in your camp . . . let your camp be holy. Let Him not find anything unseemly (*ervat davar*) in you and turn away from you.[31]

In this passage, *ervat davar* does not connote immorality, but rather anything that is shameful and that violates acceptable standards of sanitation. On this basis, the School of Hillel drew upon an analogy to determine the meaning of the term *ervat davar:*

> It is stated here [in the passage on divorce] "*ervat davar,*" and it is stated afterward [in the chapter on the hygiene of a military camp] "*ervat davar*"; just as *ervat davar* in the later passage refers to shamefulness, so also *ervat davar* stated here [in the passage on divorce] refers to shamefulness.[32]

The conclusion thus reached is that anything unseemly about the wife constitutes a ground for divorce—even causing food to spoil is enough.

Contrary to these two opinions, R. Akiva took the view that the ground for divorce is stated at the beginning of the verse, which emphasizes the subjective element—"she fails to please him." According to R. Akiva, the additional clause spelled out in the verse—"because he has found something obnoxious about her"—is only one example, but certainly not the sole or exclusive instance, of the major ground, *i.e.,* that she failed to please her husband. On this theory, we cannot conclude that the finding of something obnoxious is the only ground for divorce, because the words "she fails to please him" would then be superfluous and the verse should have read: "A man marries a woman and lives with her, and he finds something obnoxious about her and he writes her a bill of divorcement. . . ."

This illustration shows us concretely how each one of the Sages created and deduced a different legal-halakhic principle by relying on a different interpretive approach to the verse. The School of Shammai used the

31. Deuteronomy 23:13–15.
32. *Midrash Tannaim,* Deuteronomy 23:15 (p. 148).

interpretive approach that explains a term appearing in a particular context solely on the basis of its relation to that particular legal context; therefore, when the text speaks of *ervat davar* in the context of divorce, it is fair to infer that the term is intended to refer to sexual promiscuity.[33] The School of Hillel used a method of interpretation that explains a particular term by analogy to the meaning of that term as used throughout the Torah—the entire Book of Laws—and not only in the particular section giving rise to the question of interpretation at issue; therefore, it interpreted *ervat davar* to refer to anything involving shamefulness or unpleasantness.[34] R. Akiva used a method of interpretation that distinguishes between what is primary and what is secondary in the particular verse being construed; and on the basis of this approach he concluded that the primary point is that the wife has failed to please her husband and that the reference to *ervat davar* is of only secondary importance and by way of example.[35]

2. Chapter 24 of Deuteronomy deals with the right of a creditor to take a pledge as collateral for the payment of a loan. In verses 12 and 13, the Torah prescribes how a creditor who takes a pledge from a poor debtor must conduct himself:

> If he is a needy man, you shall not go to sleep in his pledge; you must return the pledge to him at sundown, that he may sleep in his own cloth and bless you; and it will be to your merit before the Lord your God.

Later on, verse 17 states: "You shall not take a widow's garment for a pledge," *i.e.*, if the debtor is a widow, taking a pledge from her is completely prohibited. What is covered by the term "widow"? The Mishnah states:

> One may not take a pledge from a widow, whether she is poor or rich, as it is stated: "You shall not take a widow's garment for a pledge."[36]

From a different source,[37] we learn that there was a difference of opinion among the *tannaim* about this law:

> The Rabbis taught: One may not take a pledge from a widow, whether she is poor or rich; this is the opinion of R. Judah. R. Simeon holds: If she is rich, one may take a pledge from her; but if she is poor, one may not take a pledge from her, because you must return it to her, and in this way you cause her to have a bad reputation among her neighbors.

33. This is similar to *interpretatio grammatica* in Roman law with the purpose of *interpretatio restricta* (narrow interpretation).

34. This is similar to *interpretatio grammatica* in Roman law with the purpose of *interpretatio extensa* (broad interpretation).

35. This is similar to *interpretatio logica* in Roman law.

36. M Bava Meẓi'a 9:13.

37. TB Bava Meẓi'a 115a.

R. Simeon's position was that since the creditor is required to return the garment to a poor debtor every evening and to retrieve it again in the morning, the creditor, by going each evening and morning to the house of a poor widow who owes him money, will cause her to have a bad reputation among her neighbors.

What is the background for this difference of opinion between R. Judah and R. Simeon? The answer to this question is contained in a Talmudic discussion:[38] R. Simeon "interprets the logic of Scripture," *i.e.*, he seeks to discover the rationale and objective of the verse, and not just its literal meaning; R. Judah, in contrast, "does not interpret the logic of Scripture," *i.e.*, he does not seek to discover the rationale and objective of the verse but explains it according to the literal meaning of its words.

What underlies the difference of opinion between R. Simeon and R. Judah is that in R. Simeon's view we must examine the logic and intent of the rule prohibiting the taking of a pledge of a garment from a widow, as indicated by the overall approach of this section of Scripture. Since the beginning of the section states the general rule that one must return a pledge to a poor debtor every evening, it is logical to assume that the rule stated later in the section—that one must not take a pledge of a garment from a widow—is an extension of the same concept. On this basis, one may not take any pledge from a poor widow, because the creditor would have to return it to her each evening, thereby giving her a bad reputation among her neighbors. Therefore, if the debtor is a rich widow and there is no need to return the pledge to her home each evening, there is no reason to prohibit taking a pledge from her.

R. Simeon's view was that the term "widow" in this passage should not be interpreted literally, *i.e.*, a woman whose husband has died, but is to be construed as meaning a woman alone and destitute—a poor widow. On the other hand, R. Judah took the view that we should interpret the term in its literal sense. On this interpretive approach, the term "widow" refers to any woman whose husband has died; consequently, the prohibition "You shall not take a widow's garment for a pledge" applies to all widows, rich and poor alike.

In this instance, too, we note that different legal conclusions result from the use of different methods of interpretation—methods that have their parallels in other legal systems. R. Simeon's method of interpretation is similar to the Roman principle of *interpretatio logica*, *i.e.*, logical interpretation, according to which one must examine the legislator's logic and intent as it is expressed in the overall context of the legal institution involved. The method of interpretation of R. Judah is close to the Roman principle of

38. *Id.*

interpretatio grammatica, i.e., literal interpretation, according to which one must place major emphasis on the literal meaning of the language of the legal text.

E. Integrative Interpretation

We may conclude from the illustrations discussed above that midrash served as a source for the creation of new legal rules. As to a substantial proportion of the midrashic interpretations, we are unable to determine whether the interpretation preceded the law or the law preceded the interpretation. However, there are a considerable number of instances where it is possible to establish that the interpretation did not create the law but only supported it—*i.e.*, that the law already existed on a basis such as tradition, enactment, or custom, and interpretation merely served the purpose of connecting or "integrating" the law with a verse of the Torah. One can point to such examples from the interpretations of the *tannaim* and the *amoraim*.[39] We cite here two examples from the civil law area of the *Halakhah*.

1. One of the modes of acquisition of personal property in Jewish law is *meshikhah* (taking possession, lit. "pulling"),[40] *i.e.*, the buyer takes into his possession the chattel that he wishes to buy and by this act acquires ownership of it. The *amoraim* R. Johanan and Resh Lakish differed as to whether this mode of acquisition should be classified as Biblical or only rabbinic in origin.[41] Their difference of opinion is described as follows:[42]

> R. Johanan said: According to Biblical law, the payment of money effects acquisition [of personal property, *i.e.*, according to Biblical law only the payment of money transfers ownership, and taking possession (*meshikhah*) does not result in the transfer of title]. So why did the Sages say that taking possession effects acquisition? It is an enactment in case a fire breaks out accidentally [and not as a result of anyone's fault]. If we give him [the buyer] ownership of the chattel [upon taking possession], he will go out of his way and attempt to save it [because the chattel belongs to him]; but if not, he will not go out of his way and attempt to save it. [*I.e.*, if the rule is that taking possession without payment is insufficient to transfer title to the buyer, he will not care whether the chattel is destroyed, because the chattel is not his but the seller's.]

39. *See supra* pp. 285–286; H. Albeck, *Mavo*, p. 47.

40. *See* M Kiddushin 1:5; Bava Meẓi'a 4:2. For the modes of acquisition of property in Jewish law, *see infra* pp. 580–584, 913–920.

41. For a discussion of the terms "Biblical" and "rabbinic," *see supra* pp. 207–212.

42. TB Bava Meẓi'a 47b.

According to R. Johanan, acquisition by taking possession is a legislative enactment of the Sages for the reason stated, whereas under Biblical law, only the payment of money results in a transfer of ownership. Resh Lakish disagreed:

> Resh Lakish said: "*Meshikhah* as a means of acquisition is a Biblical rule." What is the reasoning of Resh Lakish? Scripture states [Leviticus 25:14]: "When you sell property to your neighbor or buy any from your neighbor" [lit. "from your neighbor's hand"]; this refers to things that are acquired by transfer from hand to hand.

Resh Lakish interpreted the words "from your neighbor's hand" to mean that a purchase is made "from the hand" of the seller when he delivers the chattel into the hand of the buyer—in other words, a transfer of possession by *meshikhah*.

From this discussion, we learn that acquisition by taking possession, which was one of the early methods of transferring ownership,[43] was known to both R. Johanan and Resh Lakish, and both of them recognized that it was one of the legally effective methods of transferring title. But to R. Johanan the source of this mode of acquisition is a specific *takkanah* of the Sages, whereas to Resh Lakish this method is Biblical, *i.e.*, it is validated by the interpretation of a verse in the Torah. The interpretation that Resh Lakish used thus serves to integrate an existing law with a verse in the Torah and not to create the law, since it is clear that the law was previously known and accepted.

2. A rule in the law of lost property provides that one is obligated to return a lost object when a claimant describes certain identifying characteristics, and it is not necessary for a claimant who furnishes such a description to bring witnesses to prove his ownership. In this connection, the following question was raised in the Talmud:[44]

> Are identification marks Biblical or rabbinic? [Is the rule that allows the return of a lost object on the basis of identification marks without witnesses Biblical in origin, or is it an enactment of the Rabbis?]
>
> What is the difference? [What is the difference whether this rule has its source in the Bible or in a rabbinic enactment?] Whether to return a *get* [bill of divorcement] on the basis of identification marks. [The difference is in the case where a husband sends an agent to deliver a *get* to his wife and the *get* is lost by the agent; the question is whether or not the document should be

43. *See supra* n. 40.
44. TB Bava Meẓi'a 27a/b.

> returned to the agent in order to effectuate the divorce by its subsequent delivery.]
>
> If the rule is Biblical, one should return it. [If the return of an object on the basis of identification marks has its source in the Torah, it is proper to return the *get* and to use it to effectuate the divorce.] But if it is rabbinic, then the rabbinic enactment would affect only monetary matters, since the rabbis did not intend their enactment to apply to a matter of "religious" commandment (*issur*) [and since marital status is a "religious" rather than a monetary matter, the Biblical rule requiring witnesses to prove ownership would apply].[45]

After a long debate, the discussion concluded:[46]

> Rava stated: The use of identification marks is Biblical, as it is written, "It shall remain with you until your fellow claims it" [lit. "searches it out"].[47] Can it enter your mind that you will give it back before he claims it? Rather, this means "search him out"—see whether he is attempting to deceive you or not.[48] How [should you search him out]? Through identification marks.

The theory is that it is so obvious that the finder will not return the lost object before someone claims ownership that the words "until your fellow searches it out" must mean more than their plain meaning; otherwise, there is no reason for them to be in the text, since the text would have

45. The rationale for an enactment allowing return of a lost object on the basis of nothing more than identification marks is explained in TB Bava Meẓi'a 27a/b. Under the view that the rule that allows the return of a lost object on the basis of identification marks is rabbinic, Biblical law does not permit return of the lost object except on the testimony of witnesses, because the object does belong to someone and if the finder returns it on the basis of identification marks alone, he may be giving it to one who is not its rightful owner, thus causing loss to the true owner. However, the Sages enacted that lost objects should be returned on the basis of nothing more than identification marks, because they assumed that the true owner would so desire, in view of the fact that it is generally difficult to find witnesses to identify an object. This consideration outweighed the risk that occasionally the object may be given to someone who has managed to come forward with the correct identification marks, but who is not the owner.

In the case of a lost *get,* because a mistake could lead to involvement of the wife in an adulterous "remarriage" (a *get* is valid only if it is written with explicit intention to be used by a particular man to divorce a particular woman), the Sages did not enact that the *get* be returned to the agent on the basis of identification marks; therefore, witnesses are required to identify the *get.*

46. TB Bava Meẓi'a 28a.

47. Deuteronomy 22:2, from the section dealing with lost property.

48. This very *midrash* ("can it enter your mind . . .") appears as early as *Sifrei,* Deuteronomy, Ki Teẓe, sec. 223 (p. 256), and in a *baraita* (TB Bava Meẓi'a 27b); similarly, the idea "until you search out your fellow . . ." is found in M Bava Meẓi'a 2:7.

the same meaning without them. Therefore, the true meaning of the text is not "until your fellow searches it out," but "until you search out your fellow" by investigating to see whether the lost object is his. How can one investigate? By identification marks—the owner of the lost object must give identifying characteristics to prove that the object is his.[49]

Here, too, we see that the rule requiring the return of a lost object on the basis of identification marks was accepted and known. However, when the question arose, either in an actual case or in a theoretical discussion, whether it is permitted to return a bill of divorcement to the husband's agent on the basis of identifying characteristics, the Sages sought out the source of the law and asked whether it is Biblical or rabbinic; and through interpretation it was found that the rule has support in the Torah itself. What is clear, however, is that interpretation did not create the law, but rather connected existing law to a verse in the Torah.

It is indeed possible that at a time before the era of Rava, R. Johanan, and Resh Lakish, this rule concerning lost property was in fact created by interpreting Scripture, just as it is also possible that it had its source in *takkanah,* custom, or the like; we simply cannot be sure. What is clear is that the interpretation of Rava concerning identification marks and of Resh Lakish on taking possession (*meshikhah*) did not create the law, but integrated a law then already known with a Biblical verse.

II. *ASMAKHTA* (SUPPORTIVE INTERPRETATION) IN MIDRASH

As stated, we cannot determine whether a substantial proportion of laws that were expressed in midrashic form were instances of creative or integrative interpretation; and it is, therefore, impossible to reach any definite conclusion as to how much of the *Halakhah* reflects creative and how much merely integrative interpretation.

However, the Sages specifically identified a certain number of laws expressed in midrashic form as instances of integrative rather than creative interpretation. These instances are termed *asmakhta* (lit. "something to lean on," *i.e.,* a supportive device).[50] We note that in such instances the Sages

49. *See* the discussion in TB Bava Meẓi'a 27b, where the question is posed whether the intention of Scripture might not be that the claimant is to be "searched out" to see whether he can produce witnesses rather than merely provide identification marks. Rava here assumed that identification marks are what was intended, but later in the discussion (*id.* 28a: *Im timẓi lomar . . .*) it seems that Rava himself was in doubt whether that is so.

50. *Asmakhta be-alma* ("Mere *asmakhta*")—TB Berakhot 41b and many other places. Similarly, the statement "they are *hilkhata* [*i.e.,* traditional laws] and the Sages supported

took pains to make clear that interpretation was not the source for a particular law even where it would have been possible to attribute the creation of that law to interpretation. To clarify the matter, let us briefly analyze the meaning of *asmakhta*.[51]

I. M. Guttmann established in a comprehensive study of this subject[52] that the use of the term *asmakhta* does not imply (as many scholars and researchers have thought it does[53]) that the law in question cannot be connected with the verse in a logical and rational manner. It indicates rather that the halakhic authorities knew that the creative source of the particular law was not interpretation but one of the other legal sources, such as tradition or legislation. Guttmann reached this conclusion on the basis of two findings he made as a result of his study: (a) On the one hand, there are midrashically expressed laws that can be derived rationally and logically from the plain meaning of the verse, yet the Sages declared the interpretation of the verse to be merely *asmakhta;* and (b) on the other hand, there are other midrashically expressed laws that do not have a rational connection with the verse, yet the Sages viewed the interpretation as the actual source for the creation of the law, and not merely as *asmakhta*.

Two examples illustrate the point:

1. Exodus 22:4 states:

---

them by verses"—TB Eruvin 4b; Sukkah 28a; Kiddushin 9a; Niddah 32a/b. In texts from the tannaitic period and in TJ, only the verb form (*samakh*) is used; *see, e.g., Tosefta* Ketubbot 12:2: "*Samkhu al ha-mikra* (they supported [the law] with the verse)"; TJ Gittin 5:1, 26b (5:1, 46c): "*Somekhin otah la-mikra* (they connect it to the verse)"; TJ Shevi'it 10:2, 29b (10:3, 39c): "*Samekhuhu li-devar Torah* (they connect it to the law of the Torah)."

51. The term *asmakhta* has an additional connotation in an entirely different area of law, namely, the law of acquisition and obligations. There, it signifies the transfer of ownership or the incurring of an obligation in a manner that indicates absence of serious, deliberate, and unqualified intention (*gemirut da'at*). *See* Gulak, *Yesodei*, I, pp. 67ff.; and *see supra* p. 120 n. 118; *infra* p. 1604 n. 76.

52. I.M. Guttmann, *Mafte'aḥ ha-Talmud* [Key to the Talmud], III, appendix at end of Part I.

53. *See* Tchernowitz, *Toledot ha-Halakhah* [History of the *Halakhah*], I, pp. 63–64:

> The sum and substance of the matter is that the difference between an *asmakhta* and interpretive exegesis (*derashah*) is one of degree only, *i.e.*, it depends on the extent to which the Sages thought the interpretation reflected what the verse really meant to say. When they thought that a particular legal interpretation reflected the intended meaning of Scripture, they regarded the interpretation as part of the Torah itself, but when they saw that it was impossible to regard it as actually intended by Scripture, they deemed it an *asmakhta*.

Tchernowitz (*id.* at 66 n. 1) alludes to Guttmann's view but maintains his own opinion that *asmakhta* involves only far-fetched Scriptural "hints" to a law. However, his argument is insufficient to overcome the clear proofs for Guttmann's thesis. Alon (*Meḥkarim,* II, p. 237) has criticized Tchernowitz's position on this subject.

> When a man lets his livestock loose to graze in another's land, and so allows a field or a vineyard to be grazed bare, then according to the best of his field or the best of his vineyard he must make restitution.

There is a difference of opinion in tannaitic literature as to whether the payment that the owner of the animal must make is to be measured by the best of his own property, *i.e.*, the best owned by the wrongdoer, or by the quality of the choicest field of the victim. According to the *Tosefta*[54] and the Jerusalem Talmud,[55] R. Akiva's opinion is that the Biblical verse refers to the highest quality of land owned by the victim, but that the Sages enacted a *takkanah* that the compensation should be measured by the value of the wrongdoer's best land.

The Jerusalem Talmud states:

> What is the source of R. Akiva's opinion that compensation is to be measured by the value of the [wrongdoer's] best land?
>
> It is not based on the Torah, but on an enactment.

At this point, the Jerusalem Talmud quotes the *Tosefta:*

> Why did they enact that compensation is to be measured by the value of the [wrongdoer's] best land?
>
> Because of robbers, so that a person should say: "Why should I rob and why should I do damage? Tomorrow [when I will become obligated to pay back the theft or the damage] the court will pick out my best field and take it from me."
>
> They [the Sages] support this with the verse: "According to the best of his field or the best of his vineyard he must make restitution."[56]

We have here an interesting phenomenon. The Biblical verse can be interpreted with equal reason to refer either to the best land of the wrongdoer or to the best land of the victim. R. Akiva's opinion was that the original intendment of the verse referred to the best land of the victim. However, it subsequently became necessary to change the Biblical law for reasons of public policy, and it was then established that the wrongdoer

54. *Tosefta* Ketubbot 12:2.

55. TJ Gittin 5:1, 26b (5:1, 46c). The 1985 JPS *Tanakh* renders Exodus 22:4 ". . . he must make restitution for the impairment of that field or vineyard." This translation has not been followed in this discussion because it obscures the entire basis for the halakhic argument.

56. The text of the *Tosefta* itself is slightly different: "Why did they enact that compensation is to be measured by the value of [the wrongdoer's] best land? Because of robbers and predators, so that everyone should say: 'Why should I rob and why should I use violence? Tomorrow the court will assess [the damage] out of my best field.' They [the Sages] supported [the law] with the verse: 'According to the best of his field or the best of his vineyard he must make restitution.'"

must pay from the best of his own lands. Although the text of the Torah was fully amenable to an interpretation that would have yielded the same rule as the enactment of the Sages, the Sages did not make such an interpretation, but made clear that the evaluation of the measure of damages according to the field of the wrongdoer was merely an *asmakhta*, a rule that is supportable by Scripture but that actually had its source not in the verse but in an enactment of the Sages.[57]

This is an example that confirms the hypothesis that the concept of *asmakhta* does not connote difficulty in connecting the law with the verse but turns on the purpose of the Sages to designate with precision the source for the creation of the law. From the perspective of the plain meaning of the text, the halakhic authorities could have interpreted the verse to have yielded the same rule as their enactment. However, since they knew the original interpretation and also that the actual source of that particular law was an enactment of the Sages, they made it clear beyond peradventure of doubt that the connection of this law with the verse was merely an *asmakhta*.[58]

2. Deuteronomy 24:16 states:

> Parents [lit. "fathers"] shall not be put to death on account of children, nor children put to death on account of parents; a person shall be put to death only for his own crime.

According to the plain meaning of the words, the interpretation of this verse is that a parent is not responsible for the offenses of his child and a child is not responsible for the offenses of his parent, each one being responsible only for his own offenses. This was the understanding of the verse at the time of Amaziah (the son of Joash, the King of Judea), who killed

57. TB (Gittin 48b–49b) explains R. Akiva's position differently:

> The Mishnah states the view of R. Akiva, who says that it is Biblical law that we measure compensation according to the wrongdoer's [best land], and it [*i.e.*, the explanation in the Mishnah that this rule is based on the furtherance of public welfare] accords with the approach of R. Simeon, who interprets Scripture to give effect to its underlying objective and rationale. The Mishnah gives the rationale: "Why is compensation measured by the value of the [wrongdoer's] best land? For the public good" (*id.* 49b).

The above-mentioned *Tosefta* is then quoted.

Thus, according to TB, R. Akiva was of the opinion that the verse refers to the best of the wrongdoer's property and that the explanation "Because of robbers . . ." was a rationale given for the Scriptural provision. TJ did not so understand the *Tosefta*, but emphasized that the law was rabbinically legislated, as indicated by the language of the *Tosefta* itself, "They supported this with the verse" (*samkhu al ha-mikra*), which connotes *asmakhta*. *See further* H. Albeck, *Mavo*, p. 51, and his introduction to Tractate Bava Kamma, p. 406; Lieberman, *Tosefta ki-Feshutah*, Ketubbot, p. 370.

58. *See also* Guttmann, *supra* n. 52 at 2–3 and 39 n. 2. For laws originating in enactments and then connected to Biblical verses, *see further infra* p. 513 n. 86 and p. 526 n. 140.

the men who conspired against his father, but "did not put to death the children of the assassins, in accordance with what is written in the Book of the Torah of Moses where the Lord commanded, 'Parents shall not be put to death on account of children, nor children put to death on account of parents: a person shall be put to death only for his own crime.'"[59]

The *tannaim* used midrash to deduce a basic rule of evidence from this verse:

> "Parents shall not be put to death on account of children." What does the verse teach us? That parents shall not be put to death because of [the crimes of] their children, nor shall children be put to death because of [the crimes of] their parents? But does not the verse already say, "a person shall be put to death only for his own crime" [and hence the reference to parents and children would be superfluous if it meant only that neither should be punished for the transgressions of the other]? Rather, it means that a parent shall not be put to death on the basis of his children's testimony, nor children on the basis of their parents'.[60]

This *midrash* deduces the rule from the apparent redundancy of the verse. If we assume that the plain meaning expresses the only intent of the verse, then the last phrase of the verse, "a person shall be put to death only for his own crime," would be sufficient. The beginning of the verse must therefore intend something more, namely, that in no way should a parent bring about the death of his child nor a child bring about his parent's death, whether by reason of transgressions by one of them or by reason of testimony of one concerning the other. Such was the explanation of the verse in the Aramaic translation of Jonathan b. Uzziel:

> Parents shall not be put to death on the basis of the testimony or on account of the crimes of their children, and children shall not be put to death on the basis of the testimony or on account of the crimes of their parents; each man shall be put to death because of his own crime and on the basis of the testimony of competent witnesses.[61]

This law was created by interpretation; yet it is not labeled *asmakhta,* even though it strains the text much more than does the interpretation of the verse "According to the best of his field or the best of his vineyard he

59. II Kings 14:6. *See also* Redak and Ralbag, *ad loc.,* who pointed this out. The point is also especially emphasized in *Resp. Rashba,* I, #1185, and in *Resp. Rashba Attributed to Naḥmanides* #125.

60. *Sifrei,* Deuteronomy, Ki Teẓe, sec. 280 (p. 297).

61. *See also* TB Sanhedrin 27b; Maimonides, *Sefer ha-Miẓvot,* Negative Commandment #287 (ed. Mosad ha-Rav Kook, p. 300); Maimonides, *MT,* Edut 13:15.

shall make restitution" as the Scriptural basis for the rule of compensation from the best lands of the wrongdoer.

In summary, the term *asmakhta* is used to distinguish between a law developed through interpretation and a law derived from one of the other legal sources (such as tradition or legislation), for which interpretation merely provides a link to a Scriptural verse. According to those who hold that a prerequisite of *asmakhta* is that the "interpretation" is too far-fetched to be the real source of the law, it is clear that in every instance of *asmakhta,* interpretation is not the source of the law but merely provides linkage to the supportive verse. Guttmann, on the other hand, takes the view that whether an interpretation is an *asmakhta* turns exclusively on whether or not the interpretation, rather than some different legal source, was the actual source of the law.[62]

It also bears repeating that one should not conclude from what we have said that every instance where a particular interpretation is not labeled as *asmakhta* involves a law whose source is interpretation. It is only occasionally that there is extant a declaration by the halakhic authorities that a particular interpretation is *asmakhta,*[63] but the absence of such a declaration with regard to other laws is not in itself a sufficient basis for a valid conclusion as to the original source of those laws.

III. DIFFERENT LITERARY FORMS FOR CREATIVE AND INTEGRATIVE INTERPRETATION

We have seen that there are two types of interpretation in Jewish law: one, whose purpose is to explain and clarify what is stated in the Torah or to create new laws, and the other, whose purpose is to support concededly preexisting law by integrating it with the Torah.

There is a corollary to this proposition: explanatory-creative interpretation and integrative interpretation differ in both form and style. When the interpreter seeks to explain the Torah or to create new law out of the Torah, his approach must be constrained by logic and by the text; for it is the Scriptural verse that the interpreter seeks to explain, and it is the Scriptural verse that is the source for the new law. However, the interpreter who

62. According to both views, the current Hebrew usage of *asmakhta* as meaning a proof of a claim or a basis for an argument is in error; *asmakhta* connotes the absence of proof. The correct term for proof of a claim or a basis for an argument is *simukhin*.

63. Occasionally, this is not stated by the Talmud, but the commentators declare an interpretation to be a mere *asmakhta,* or disagree as to whether it is an *asmakhta*. *See* ET, II, pp. 105–108, s.v. Asmakhta (1) (particularly p. 108).

merely integrates an already existing law with a verse has wide latitude to expand beyond the confines of the verse and to take liberties in the course of his interpretation.

Guttmann[64] describes the essential literary distinction between these two types of interpretation:

> With regard to the Written Law, interpretation is subservient to the text and may not depart from its basic intent even in the slightest. In this category of interpretation, the law is not connected to the letters of the verse by means of thin threads of overstrained subtlety, but it has a logical, inherent relationship to the text and is in a sense the soul of the verse.[65]
>
> By contrast, the rules of the Oral Law [*i.e.*, those laws with sources such as tradition, custom, or legislation] exist independently; and, as a result, the function of the interpreter is entirely different. He comes to the text with the law already in hand, and he uses the language and even the letters of the text as a mechanism to connect to the text—by way of a passing reference, a hint, or a sign—something that has already been taught or transmitted to him. He knows beforehand that his interpretations are not the plain meaning of the text and is well aware that the connection is only artificial, but he is not concerned by this. He himself concedes that some laws are like "mountains hanging by a hair."[66]

This distinction is significant for understanding the methods of interpretation of Jewish law. Often we get the impression that interpretation in Jewish law is some sort of magical sleight-of-hand completely at odds with the plain meaning and simple sense of the text, and this shakes our confidence in the legal conclusions to which such interpretation has led. This impression, however, is the result of failure to distinguish between the two types of interpretation in Jewish law.

Explanatory-creative interpretation observes the principles and keeps within the bounds of legal logic and genuine interpretation; it is the pre-

64. *Supra* n. 52 at III, Appendix re *Asmakhta*, p. 7.

65. *Compare* this concept *with* Dernburg's "hidden content," discussed *supra* p. 291.

66. *See also* Lieberman, *Hellenism*, pp. 47ff. Lieberman has shown that such artificial linkages were an accepted literary form at that time, and summarized his conclusions as follows (p. 78):

> The Rabbis applied comparatively few rules to the elaboration of the legal part of the Torah. They were the result of choice, discrimination, and crystallization out of many ways for the exposition of texts. In the *Aggadah*, however, and in the *asmakhtot* ("supports") for the *Halakha*, the Rabbis resorted to well established devices which were current in the literary world at that time. Had the Rabbis themselves invented these artificial rules in their interpretations, the "supports" from the Bible would be ineffective and strange to the public. But as the utilization of such devices was accepted all over the civilized world of that time, their rules of interpretation of the *Aggadah* (and their "supports" for the *Halakha* from Scripture) were a literary affectation which was understood and appreciated by their contemporaries.

ponderant type of interpretation in Jewish law. But interpretation that aims solely to connect an existing law to some Scripturally supportive text seizes upon the verse, its letters, and even the crownlets of its letters, with full awareness that it is not extracting the true meaning of the verse. This type of interpretation is justified because its only purpose is to create a bridge between the Oral Law and the Written Law, and use of such an extravagant literary device for such a purpose was accepted and understood in the entire civilized world in the Talmudic period.[67]

It should be pointed out that there are indeed possibly more than a few exceptions, in both directions, to this generalization about literary style. There are laws deduced from Scripture by accepted and logical methods of interpretation, and yet the source of these laws is not the Torah. A good example is the law previously discussed[68] to the effect that damages are collectible from the best of the lands belonging to the wrongdoer; this law's historical source was legislation, and its link to the verse in the Torah was merely supportive. The converse is also true; laws were created, particularly in the School of R. Akiva, by interpretation based solely on single letters and redundancies—an approach that R. Ishmael and his school vehemently opposed.[69] However, these instances do not destroy the validity of the general principle that attributes the difference in literary style between these two types of interpretation to the difference in their respective goals and functions.[70]

The difference between these two literary forms of interpretation can also be explained on the basis that they were produced in different historical periods. At first, midrash was mainly explanatory interpretation—legal contextual explanation and exposition based on logic and analogy, and carefully confined to the fair intendment of the Scriptural verse. The more fanciful styles of interpretation did not develop until later; particularly in R. Akiva's time a type of interpretation developed that rested on signs and hints in the Torah.

These later methods of interpretation developed because of the increase in the number of laws contained in the Oral Law. More and more laws were added by means of various legal sources, including legislation, custom, legal reasoning, and adjudication (*ma'aseh*); and in order to prevent these numerous laws from becoming a separate body of law indepen-

67. *See* Lieberman, *supra* n. 66. Guttmann, *supra* n. 52, calls the latter kind of midrash "symbolic and figurative interpretation."

68. *See supra* pp. 301–303.

69. *See infra* pp. 379–382.

70. The differences of opinion between R. Akiva and R. Ishmael regarding midrashic methodology in the main concerned integrative interpretation and not creative interpretation. *See infra* pp. 374–380.

dent of the Written Law, the halakhic authorities sought to connect these new laws with the Written Law even if in a symbolic and strained manner, out of a sense that "there is nothing that is not at least hinted at in the Torah."

In later generations, Jewish scholars attempted to ground even symbolic interpretations more firmly in Scripture. Meir Leibush Malbim[71] did much work in this area and wrote a commentary on the Torah and on halakhic midrash.[72] However, this method, as many halakhic authorities have pointed out, is not "midrash in the ordinary sense of that term."[73]

IV. DEVELOPMENT OF THE USE OF MIDRASH

A. Antiquity of Exegetical Activity

Interpretation was not only the most important source for the expansion and development of the *Halakhah,* but also the first source in point of time. The nation's Sages and judges necessarily made use of various methods of interpretation to explain the Torah and solve new problems as they administered the Written Law, the Jewish national code. It is probable that, at the beginning, interpretation was used to explain unclear parts of the Written Law and to reconcile different passages in the Written Law that seemed at first blush to be inconsistent; there was no way the Written Law could be understood or used in actual life without resort to interpretation and interpretive methods. Some Biblical terms required detailed explanation, and some laws seemed to contain internal inconsistencies either in the same verse, in two verses in the same section, or in one section as compared with another on the same subject.[74] The methods of interpretation were elaborated and crystallized over a period of time into different canons and rules; however, the process of interpretation itself began as soon as the Written

71. Malbim (1809–1879) served as rabbi in various communities, including Bucharest, Leczyca, and Kremenchug.

72. *See* the rules Malbim laid down in his introduction to his *Ayyelet ha-Shaḥar,* printed at the beginning of his commentary to Leviticus.

73. *See* S.I. Finn, *Kiryah Ne'emanah,* pp. 153–154, as to Elijah, Gaon of Vilna's approach to the plain meaning of a text and to interpretive exegesis. *See also* Guttmann, *supra* n. 52 at 84, quoting additional statements in the Gaon of Vilna's name:

> These people who exert themselves to explain the Sages' midrashic interpretations (*derashot*) so as to make them coincide with the plain meaning (*peshat*) of the Scriptural text are mistaken. Although their intention is commendable, their course is not correct, because such interpretation (*derash*) is far removed from plain meaning, and the two can never coincide.

74. In midrashic terminology, such Scriptural provisions are called "two Biblical passages that contradict each other," and rules were established for interpreting and explaining them. *See infra* pp. 335–339.

Law was given, since every dispute decided according to the Torah, the Book of Laws of the people, necessarily involved a certain measure of interpretation, whether because of the need to clarify and explain or the need to find solutions to practical problems.

B. Exegetical Interpretation from Ezra the Scribe until the *Zugot* ("Pairs")

The first written records extant definitively evidencing exegesis of the Torah date from the time of Ezra the Scribe. Ezra, son of Seraiah the Priest, returned from the Babylonian exile to the Land of Israel in the year 458 B.C.E. (about eighty years after the first wave of returnees during the reign of Cyrus, King of Persia). He was responsible for a fundamental change in studying and teaching the Torah—a change which laid particular emphasis on the function of Biblical exegesis.

Although the commandment to study the Torah had always been addressed to the people as a whole,[75] major responsibility for disseminating the Torah and for teaching the people was first committed to the priests and the Levites, who were the nation's teachers and judges. Often, however, the priests did not properly carry out this task with which they were charged, and the prophets severely rebuked them on this account. The prophet Malachi, the last of the prophets and a contemporary of Ezra the Scribe, addressed them: "And now, O priests, this charge is for you." Describing the special responsibility of the priests as the nation's teachers, he concluded (Malachi 2:7): "For the lips of a priest guard knowledge and men seek rulings (Torah) from his mouth; for he is a messenger of the Lord of Hosts."[76] So the situation should have been, but the reality was different:

> But you have turned away from that course: You have made the many stumble [through your instruction] in the Torah; you have corrupted the covenant of the Levites—said the Lord of Hosts. And I, in turn, have made you despicable and vile in the eyes of all the people, because you disregard My ways and show partiality in your rulings.[77]

75. "Moses charged us with the Torah as the heritage of the congregation of Jacob" (Deuteronomy 33:4); "Impress them [*i.e.*, the words of Torah] upon [lit. "You shall teach them diligently to"] your children" (*id.* 6:7). *See also* Joshua 1:8: "Let not this Torah cease from your lips, but recite it day and night"; Hoffmann, *Commentary on Deuteronomy* (Hebrew ed.), pp. 309ff.

76. Malachi 2:1–7. An alternative reading of v. 7 is: "For the lips of a priest are observed; knowledge and ruling are sought from his mouth." The Hebrew is susceptible to either reading. *See* JPS *Tanakh*, 1985, p. 1102 and note *c*.

77. Malachi 2:8–9.

This state of affairs had its effects on the development of Jewish law. It is an important principle that the development and creative power of a legal system depends on the extent to which the law of that system is nurtured and applied in practice. Thus, if those responsible to be the nation's teachers do not adequately safeguard the paths of the Torah and its law, the development of the law is inhibited; and, as a result, the way is open for legal institutions to take root that are foreign to the spirit and principles of the nation and therefore unacceptable for reception into the Jewish legal system.

The books of the Prophets and the Hagiographa contain many examples of such aberrant development. It is sufficient here to review one example that concerns the personal freedom of debtors. Deuteronomy 24:10–13 states:

> When you make a loan of any sort to your countryman, you must not enter his house to seize his pledge. You must remain outside, while the man to whom you made the loan brings the pledge out to you. If he is a needy man, you shall not go to sleep in his pledge; you must return the pledge to him at sundown, that he may sleep in his own cloth and bless you; and it will be to your merit before the Lord your God.

The logic of this law, which prohibits even entering the debtor's home, certainly prohibits subjecting one who does not pay his debt to involuntary servitude, such as by making him a slave.

From various passages in the Prophets and the Hagiographa, however, we learn that servitude for debt did in fact exist; it was practiced by the people for a long period of time and applied not only to the debtor himself but also to his family.[78] This practice was especially harsh in the days of Ezra, and there was a great outcry at that time by a segment of the people against their fellow Jews and especially against their leaders (the nobles and rulers) who exacted satisfaction of debts by enslaving the debtors' children.[79]

This practice of enslaving a debtor for the payment of his debt has its root in law prevailing at that time in the ancient Near East. The Code of Hammurabi, the Assyrian Code, and other codes specifically provided for the enforcement of a debt by execution against the person of the debtor and his family.[80] The Roman law of the Twelve Tables, in the period approximate to that of Nehemiah, established rules that were even harsher and

78. II Kings 4:1; Isaiah 50:1; *see also* I Samuel 22:2.
79. Nehemiah 5:1–13.
80. *See* Elon, *Ḥerut,* pp. 3–8.

more severe than those of the ancient Near East.[81] These laws were directly contrary to the laws of the Torah on the relation of creditor and debtor; Nehemiah rebuked the Jewish nobles and rulers for their harmful conduct, which gave "our enemies, the [pagan] nations, room to reproach us."[82] The Jews agreed to desist from the practice, and from then on this practice was eradicated from the Jewish legal system.[83]

Ezra and Nehemiah had the people renew their covenant to observe the Torah. Because the priests—the teachers of the people—were responsible for breaking the link between the people and the laws of the Torah, Ezra, who himself was one of the leading priests, deprived the priests of their position as chief students, interpreters, and teachers of the Torah, and placed these functions in the hands of the entire people, namely, the Sages of the Torah from all the tribes of Israel. The first such Sages, the *Soferim* (Scribes),[84] included many priests and Levites because of their proficiency in the laws of the Torah; however, from this time on, priests who became teachers of the people did so not because they were priests but because of their knowledge of the Torah.

This act of Ezra gave a tremendous impetus and élan to Jewish law, and his work paved the way for the uninterrupted development and creativity reflected in the extensive Talmudic literature. The Talmudic Sages expressed the importance of this great historic event in their *dictum* that "at the beginning, when the Torah had been forgotten in Israel, Ezra went up from Babylonia and established it,"[85] and in their comparison of the work of Ezra to the deeds of Moses, who received the Torah and transmitted it to the people.[86]

This transfer of the pedagogic and judicial functions in Jewish law from the priestly class to the people as a whole may be appropriately contrasted with a similar occurrence in Roman law. In Rome, at an early period, the knowledge and interpretation of the law was concentrated in the *pontifices*, the priestly caste who were the originators of Roman legal interpretation. According to Roman tradition, the *pontifices* concealed their knowledge and legal acumen from the people and turned it into a caste monopoly, thus impeding the proper development of the law. In approximately 300 B.C.E., Flavius, the son of a freed slave, took away from the *pontifices* the book containing the laws and the pleadings for the various

81. *See id.* at 11–12.
82. Nehemiah 5:9.
83. *See* Elon, *Ḥerut,* p. 9.
84. Regarding the term "the period of the *Soferim,*" *see supra* p. 41.
85. TB Sukkah 20a.
86. TB Sanhedrin 21b–22a.

forms of action (*legis actiones*) and publicized the book's contents.[87] This act ended the monopoly of the *pontifices* over Roman law.[88]

It is interesting to note the similarities and the differences in these parallel phenomena in Jewish and Roman law. In Roman law, the act of a member of a lower class, the son of a freed slave, ended the monopoly of the priests, the *pontifices,* over the legal system. In Jewish law, the parallel event occurred approximately 150 years before the Roman "revolution" and was effected not by a member of the lower class who succeeded through trickery in taking the law away from the priests, but by Ezra, a leading priest himself, who ended the special prerogative of the priesthood to teach the Torah and thus made learning and disseminating Torah the task of the entire people.

The return of the people to the law of the Torah, and the transfer of the function of teaching the Torah to the people as a whole, naturally generated a great and powerful upsurge in Biblical exegesis. Both the study of the Torah and the fact that economic and social life were conducted under the guidance of the legal principles of the Torah gave rise, as time went on, to ever-new questions, for the solution of which Biblical exegesis was the primary instrument.

The Book of Ezra confirms the truth of these propositions. Ezra was "a scribe expert in the Torah of Moses."[89] It seems likely that Ezra was called "the Scribe" not because of his skill in writing and copying, but because he knew the Torah and taught it to the people.[90] This scribal function is delineated in the description of Ezra's activities:[91]

> The entire people assembled as one man in the square before the Water Gate, and they asked Ezra the scribe to bring the scroll of the Torah of Moses with which the Lord had charged Israel. On the first day of the seventh month, Ezra the priest brought the Torah before the congregation, men and women and all who could listen with understanding. He read from it, facing the square before the Water Gate, from the first light until midday, to the men and the women and those who could understand; the ears of all the people were given to the scroll of the Torah. . . . And the Levites explained the Torah

87. Thus the name of the volume, *Jus Flavianum.*

88. *See* Pokrovsky, *Toledot ha-Mishpat ha-Roma'i* [A History of Roman Law], pp. 86–87.

89. Ezra 7:6.

90. In Aramaic, Ezra is called *safar data* (Ezra 7:12), "the scribe of the religion," *i.e.,* the sage of the religion. *See* Epstein, *Tannaim,* p. 502; Lieberman, *Hellenism,* pp. 47ff.; Urbach, *supra* n. 10 at 166ff, 172ff.

91. Nehemiah 8:1–8.

to the people, while the people stood in their places. They read from the scroll of the Torah of God, translating it and giving the sense; so they understood the reading.

The study of the scroll of the Torah, which continued from the first day of the month of Tishri until the twenty-fourth,[92] was not confined to reading and explaining the Torah, but involved application of intelligence and discernment, and analytical study of sections and verses through midrashic interpretation. Scripture characterizes Ezra, who filled this important role: "For Ezra had dedicated himself to interpret (*lidrosh*) the Torah of the Lord so as to observe it, and to teach laws and rules to Israel,"[93] *i.e.*, to study the Torah using methods of interpretation (midrash)[94] in order to teach the people the Torah's laws and rules.

The return of the people to the study of Torah, and the conduct of practical and communal life according to the laws of the Torah, necessarily invigorated the use and development of the methods of Biblical interpretation that made it possible to understand the contents of the Torah and to solve the new problems that periodically arose. The particular preoccupation of the Sages of this period with midrash is emphasized in Talmudic *Agaddah:* "The early Sages (*rishonim*) are called Scribes (*soferim*) because they would count (*hayu soferim*) every letter in the Torah,"[95] *i.e.*, they examined every detail and every fine point in the sections and verses of the Torah to interpret their content and their implications.[96]

The interpretive approach of the Scribes was not academic or theoretical (*interpretatio doctrinalis*), *i.e.*, interpretation for its own sake, with conclusions that have no legally binding effect. Rather, it was an authoritative interpretation (*interpretatio authentica*); its conclusions became an essential and binding part of the *Halakhah* itself, even if the interpretation was not occasioned by the need to decide an actual case.[97] Thus, Ezra and his associates, who expounded and interpreted the Torah each day for twenty-four days, developed the *Halakhah* and the legal system according to which the people were to conduct themselves.

It is fair to assume that the significant activity of Ezra the Scribe in the field of legal interpretation laid the foundations for continually increasing

92. *Id.* 9:1.

93. Ezra 7:10. *See supra* p. 276 n. 3.

94. *See supra* p. 276 n. 4.

95. TB Kiddushin 30a; *see also* TB Ḥagigah 15b. The statement is a word play. The root *safor,* from which *sofer* (scribe) is derived, also means "count."

96. *See also* Lieberman, *Hellenism,* p. 47.

97. For interpretation in the course of decision making, *see infra* pp. 945ff.

involvement in Biblical exegesis, although we have too few written records from this period to verify this thesis with certainty. In the Septuagint translation of the Bible (ca. middle of the third century B.C.E.) we learn of some laws whose source is Biblical exegesis.[98] The Apocryphal Book of Ben Sira (third century B.C.E.) speaks of academies of study that engaged in Biblical exegesis and of scribes who understood the Torah and interpreted it according to the wisdom of the early Sages.[99] It seems likely that, as a result of the persecution by Antiochus Epiphanes, the exact source and derivation of many laws previously arrived at by interpretation were forgotten, and a considerable number of them may have been lost. Consequently, there are few extant examples of interpretation that can be definitely identified as the product of this period. Some scholars have attempted to assign to this period a number of midrashically derived laws on the basis of various literary characteristics. For example, some midrashic laws attribute their origin to "the early Sages" (*zekenim rishonim*) or simply to "the early" (*rishonim*),[100] and it is conceivable that these titles refer to the Sages of this Scribal period.

In any event, in light of present knowledge about the Sages' involvement in Biblical exegesis from the period of Ezra and thereafter, we may assume that, as Epstein put it,[101] "Those interpretations that are contained in the halakhic Midrash without specific attribution of source, and even those that are attributed to later *tannaim*, may be very ancient, and the *tannaim* in whose name the interpretation is reported may have simply repeated and transmitted it."[102]

C. Exegetical Interpretation in the Period of the *Zugot*

In the second century B.C.E., the era of the great controversies between the Pharisees and the Sadducees, the methods of interpretation underwent further development. The Pharisees, in their struggle with the Sadducees about the validity of certain Pharisaic traditions embodied in the Oral Law, substantiated the validity of these traditions through exegesis connecting the laws in the tradition to Biblical verses. The Talmud refers to Shemaiah and Avtalyon, the fourth *Zug* (pair) in the period of the *Zugot*, as "two great

98. *See* Epstein, *Tannaim*, pp. 516–517; p. 517 discusses midrashic exegeses in the works of Philo of Alexandria.

99. Ben Sira 39:1–3.

100. *See, e.g., supra* p. 284, *Tosefta* Shevu'ot 3:8.

101. Epstein, *Tannaim*, p. 513.

102. For *tanna* in this sense, *see infra* p. 1042.

men of the generation . . . who are great Sages and *darshanim* [exegetes, experts in midrashic interpretation]," *i.e.*, they were renowned for their exegesis and interpretations of the Torah.[103] Thus, the heads of the Sanhedrin, the highest legal body charged with final determination of every halakhic question, were two people who were particularly expert in midrash and were given the title *darshan*. This fact indicates the crucial role of midrash in solving legal problems and creating new laws.

In the generation after Shemaiah and Avtalyon, the heads of the Sanhedrin were the fifth and last "pair," Hillel and Shammai. Halakhic literature attributes to Hillel—who helped fashion and shape the *Halakhah* by his enactments (*takkanot*)[104] and his ethical views—the crystallization of a significant part of the interpretive methods, namely, the Canons of Biblical Interpretation:[105]

> Hillel the Elder expounded (*darash*) seven canons (*middot*) before the elders of the Sons of Bathyra:
> 1. *Kal va-ḥomer*—inference *a fortiori*.
> 2. *Gezerah shavah*—inference from the similarity of words or phrases.
> 3. *Binyan av*—application of a general principle.
> 4. *Shenei ketuvim*—[inference from the relation between] two passages.
> 5. *Kelal u-ferat*—[inference from the relation between] a generalization and a specification.
> 6. *Ka-yoẓe vo mi-makom aḥer*—[inference from] a similar case in a different place.
> 7. *Davar ha-lamed me-inyano*—inference from the context.
>
> These are the seven canons that Hillel the Elder taught before the elders of the Sons of Bathyra.

Underlying these seven canons of interpretation are two general notions: (a) drawing an analogy from a topic other than the one under discussion and (b) reasoned contextual explication of the text on the specific topic. The canons were not originated by Hillel. From the very nature of these methods of interpretation there can be no doubt that Sages before Hillel made use of them; indeed, there is evidence of this use in the halakhic literature itself.[106] These canons are attributed to Hillel only because Hillel

103. TB Pesaḥim 70b.

104. *See infra* pp. 511–513, 561–562.

105. *Baraita de-R. Ishmael*, Foreword (*Petiḥta*) to *Torat Kohanim*, p. 3a, according to the version of Rabad (as indicated in *Masoret ha-Talmud, ad loc.*, letter *ẓadi*). *See also Tosefta* Sanhedrin 7:11; *Avot de-R. Nathan*, ch. 37 (p. 110).

106. *See* Epstein, *Tannaim*, p. 510; Lieberman, *Hellenism*, pp. 53ff. *See also Yad Malakhi*, I, Kelalei ha-Dalet #144 in regard to the canons and interpretive methods as having been part of the tradition since Sinai.

crystallized them and grouped them together; he may also have given some of them the labels by which they have become known.

D. Exegetical Interpretation in the Academies of R. Akiva and R. Ishmael

At the end of the first century C.E., two of the disciples of R. Johanan b. Zakkai, namely, R. Neḥunya b. ha-Kanah[107] and R. Nahum of Gimzo,[108] developed different approaches to the methodology of Biblical exegesis. The differences between these two *tannaim* directly concerned the canon "[inference from the relation between] a generalization and a specification," which is discussed later;[109] indirectly, they influenced the overall approach to the whole methodology of midrash.

According to R. Neḥunya b. ha-Kanah, the Torah should be interpreted in terms of "general and particular,"[110] *i.e.*, by drawing inferences that are reasonably similar to the particular specifically mentioned in the Torah—"similar to the particular," but not extending beyond it. On the other hand, R. Nahum of Gimzo held that one should interpret the Torah in terms of "inclusion and exclusion,"[111] *i.e.*, by drawing more expansive inferences from the text even though the conclusions so reached may occasionally not be of the same general character as the particular and may not even be similar to what is stated explicitly in the Torah.

R. Nahum of Gimzo went even further and attached legal consequences to the connectives that are found in the Bible. He said: "The words *et* [the sign of the accusative case, placed before the direct object of a verb] and *gam* ["also," "moreover"] are expansive, while the words *akh* ["however," "surely"] and *rak* ["only," "but"] are restrictive";[112] *i.e.*, wherever the Torah uses the words *akh* and *rak* it is to be viewed as intending to limit and confine, while wherever *et* and *gam* are used, the intent is to expand and be more inclusive.

These two approaches to interpretation reached the height of their development in the time of R. Ishmael (the disciple of R. Neḥunya b. ha-

107. A native of Kanah, a village in Lower Galilee.

108. A native of Gimzo, a town near Lydda; *see* II Chronicles 28:18. In later generations, the name was given an aggadic interpretation as meaning "this too" (*gam zo*), because he would always react to misfortune by saying "this too is for the best" (*gam zo le-tovah*).

109. *See infra* pp. 323–330.

110. TB Shevu'ot 26a.

111. *Tosefta* Shevu'ot 1:7; TB Shevu'ot 26a.

112. TJ Sotah 5:5, 25b (5:7, 20c). *See also infra* pp. 372–373.

Kanah)[113] and R. Akiva (the disciple of R. Nahum of Gimzo),[114] each of whom followed the view of his teacher. R. Ishmael and R. Akiva founded two academies representing two different schools of thought on Biblical exegesis, and we possess complete works from these two schools containing their respective interpretations.[115]

Although R. Ishmael opposed methods of interpretation that departed from a logical reading of the text of the Torah, he elaborated the canons that Hillel had established, and fixed their number at thirteen. In essence, the thirteen canons of R. Ishmael are included in the seven of Hillel, but R. Ishmael developed Hillel's canons with additional detail and subdivided them. For example, Hillel's canon "[inference from the relation between] the general and the particular" was divided by R. Ishmael into four canons covering four different situations: (1) a generalization followed by a specification, (2) a specification followed by a generalization, (3) a generalization followed by a specification that is in turn followed by a generalization, and (4) a generalization that requires a specification or a specification that requires a generalization.[116]

A *baraita* containing thirty-two canons (fixing at that number the canons of Biblical interpretation) is attributed to R. Eliezer b. R. Yose the Galilean (of the generation after R. Ishmael and R. Akiva). However, this enumeration was made mainly for purposes of homiletical and not legal interpretation.[117] The accepted number of canons for legal interpretation remains thirteen, although various other methods of interpretation not encompassed by the thirteen canons exist even with respect to the *Halakhah.*[118]

From the time of R. Akiva and thereafter, integrative interpretation became progressively more frequent than creative interpretation. In amoraic times, the great bulk of the exegesis was integrative. The need for even integrative interpretation progressively declined; the Mishnah, edited by R. Judah Ha-Nasi, became the authoritative book of laws and the basis for legal decisions in everyday life, and there was no longer a felt need to enhance a law's authority by connecting it with the Biblical text. After the completion of the Talmud, the only Biblical interpretation that continued to be used was integrative, and even that was used on relatively rare occasions.

113. TB Shevu'ot 26a.

114. *Id.*

115. For a description of those works, *see infra* pp. 1047–1049.

116. For these thirteen canons, *see infra* pp. 318–319.

117. In printed eds. of TB, the *baraita* is included following Tractate Berakhot. *See also* Samson of Chinon, *Sefer ha-Keritut,* ch. "Netivot Olam."

118. *See infra* pp. 319, 339–347.

V. THE THIRTEEN CANONS (*MIDDOT*) OF INTERPRETATION

As stated previously, Hillel crystallized the principles of interpretation and formulated them as seven canons (*middot*);[119] and R. Ishmael elaborated the canons of Hillel and formulated them as thirteen.[120]

> R. Ishmael says: The Torah is to be interpreted by means of thirteen canons:
>
> 1. Inference *a fortiori* (*kal va-ḥomer*).
> 2. Inference from the similarity of words or phrases (*gezerah shavah*).
> 3. Application of a general principle derived from one or two Biblical verses (*binyan av*).
> 4. Inference from a generalization followed by a specification (*kelal u-ferat*).
> 5. Inference from a specification followed by a generalization (*perat u-khelal*).
> 6. Inference from a generalization followed by a specification that is in turn followed by a generalization, in which case one must be guided by what the specification implies (*kelal u-ferat u-khelal*)
> 7. Inference from a generalization that requires a specification or from a specification that requires a generalization (*kelal she-hu ẓarikh li-ferat u-ferat she-hu ẓarikh li-khelal*).
> 8. Whatever is included in a generalization, and is also specifically mentioned to teach us something new, is stated not only for its own sake [lit. "to teach about itself"] but to teach something additional concerning all the matters included in the generalization (*kol davar she-hayah bi-khelal ve-yaẓa min ha-kelal le-lammed*).
> 9. Whatever is included in a generalization, and is also specifically mentioned to add another provision similar to the general law, is specified in order to alleviate and not to increase the severity of that particular provision (*kol davar she-hayah bi-khelal ve-yaẓa min ha-kelal lit'on to'an aḥer she-hu ke-inyano*).
> 10. Whatever is included in a generalization, and is also specifically mentioned to add another provision that is not similar to the general law, is specified in order to alleviate in some respects and to increase in other respects the severity of that particular provision (*kol davar she-hayah bi-khelal ve-yaẓa min ha-kelal lit'on to'an aḥer she-lo ke-inyano*).
> 11. Whatever is included in a generalization, and is also specifically mentioned to deal with a new matter, can no longer have the terms of the general law apply to it unless Scripture expressly declares that they do apply (*kol davar she-hayah bi-khelal ve-yaẓa min ha-kelal lidon ba-davar he-ḥadash*).

119. As to the Hebrew term *middah, see* W. Bacher, *Erkhei Midrash,* Tannaim, s.v. Middah; *see also infra* p. 1048 nn. 39–40.

120. *Baraita de-R. Ishmael,* Foreword to *Torat Kohanim,* p. 1a; our division of the canons follows Rabad, *ad loc.*

12. An ambiguous word or passage is explained from its context or from a subsequent expression (*davar ha-lamed me-inyano ve-davar ha-lamed mi-sofo*).
13. When two Biblical passages contradict each other, they may be harmonized by a third passage (*shenei ketuvim ha-makḥishin zeh et zeh*).

These canons basically pertain to two general categories of exegesis: (a) explicative, which aims at explaining and clarifying the verses and sections of the Torah; and (b) analogical, which relates one subject to another to broaden Jewish law and find solutions to new problems.[121]

The first category, explicative exegesis, is the subject of the last ten canons in the listing in the *baraita* of R. Ishmael. These can be subdivided into the following groups: (1) the general and the specific (canons 4 through 7), (2) a matter that is included in a generalization and is then specifically mentioned (canons 8 through 11), (3) a word or passage that is explained from its context or from a subsequent expression (canon 12), and (4) two passages that contradict each other (canon 13).

The second category, analogical exegesis, includes the first three canons—the inference *a fortiori,* the inference from the similarity of words or phrases, and the application of a general principle—and it also includes the canon called "analogy" (*hekkesh*),[122] which is not included among the thirteen canons but is considered in the Talmud as a separate canon.

There is a third category that should be added to these two, namely, "logical interpretation."[123] It plays an important role in the methods of interpretation in Jewish law, although it, too, is not listed as one of the thirteen canons.

VI. EXPLICATIVE EXEGESIS

Explicative exegesis is the primary method of Biblical interpretation and the most important for understanding the meaning of the verses and sections of the Torah. The direct and most important function of this type of interpretation is to explain the verse so that its content may be understood. However, there are instances when an explanation broadens the scope of a law by making additions to the law as a by-product of the exegesis.

There are two types of explicative exegesis: (a) explication of terms and expressions contained in a verse, and (b) explication of the content or scope of a legal rule stated in the Torah. We examine both of them.

121. Explicative midrash is similar to *interpretatio grammatica* in Roman law, but far wider and more comprehensive. Analogical Midrash is similar to the Roman *analogia*.
122. TB Zevaḥim 49b.
123. Similar to *interpretatio logica* in Roman law.

A. Terms and Expressions—Generally

Exodus 21:2 states: "When you acquire a Hebrew slave, he shall serve six years; in the seventh year he shall be freed, without payment."

The term "seventh" may be interpreted in two ways: (a) the seventh year after he was sold into servitude; and (b) the seventh year in the cycle of years, *i.e.*, the sabbatical year, which elsewhere in the Torah is called "the seventh year."[124]

The *Mekhilta*[125] explains this term as follows:

> "In the seventh"—the seventh following the sale. You say the seventh following the sale, but perhaps it is the seventh year in the cycle of years? Scripture therefore states: "He shall serve six years"; thus, it is the seventh year following his sale and not the seventh in the cycle of years.

The *Mekhilta* thus explains the term "seventh" at the end of the verse as a continuation of the "six years" first referred to in the verse as the period of the servitude. Consequently, the number "seventh" should also be understood as relating to the period of the servitude, *i.e.*, as referring to the seventh year after the sale into bondage, and not to the sabbatical year, as it does in another section of the Torah.

In the foregoing explicative interpretation, there was complete consensus about the result. However, there are occasions when different interpretive approaches produce conflicting views as to the correct legal conclusion.

The passage in the Torah containing the *Shema* reads:

> Hear (*Shema*) O Israel, the Lord is our God, the Lord is one! You shall love the Lord your God with all your heart and with all your soul and with all your might. Take to heart these words with which I charge you this day. Impress them upon [or, "teach them diligently to"] your children. Recite them when you stay at home and when you are away [lit. "when you walk by the way"], when you lie down and when you get up.[126]

The Mishnah deals with the manner of reciting the *Shema:*[127]

> The School of Shammai says: In the evening one should recline and recite [recline on one side in the manner of lying down and recite the *Shema*], and in the morning one should stand [one should recite the *Shema* while stand-

124. For example, Leviticus 25:4: "But in the seventh year the land shall have a sabbath of complete rest, a sabbath of the Lord: you shall not sow your field or prune your vineyard."

125. *Mekhilta de-R. Ishmael,* Mishpatim, Tractate De-Nezikin, sec. 1 (p. 249).

126. Deuteronomy 6:4–7.

127. M Berakhot 1:3.

ing], as is stated: "When you lie down and when you get up" [*i.e.*, in the evening one must lie down and in the morning one must stand].

The School of Hillel says: One should recite as one wishes [in the way that he is accustomed to recite, whether lying down or standing], as is stated: "When you walk by the way" [this indicates that one may recite while walking]. If so, what is the purpose of the clause "when you lie down and when you get up"? This refers to the time that people lie down and the time that people get up.

The question raised here is, How should one interpret the expressions, "when you lie down" and "when you get up"? Should they be interpreted precisely and literally to refer to the supine and standing positions, or should they be given a broader and more contextual interpretation, referring to the time of lying down and the time of getting up? The School of Shammai employed a restrictive and precise interpretation, similar to the *interpretatio restricta* of Roman law, while the School of Hillel employed a broader interpretation, similar to the *interpretatio extensa* of Roman law. This difference in the method of interpretation produced two different and divergent halakhic conclusions.

B. Terms and Expressions—Conjunctive and Disjunctive, Masculine and Feminine

Explicative exegesis of terms and expressions also includes various rules of interpretation relating to conjunctive and disjunctive words and letters, to the question of whether the masculine form also includes the feminine, and to the like. These rules of interpretation are indispensable for explaining the text and understanding its laws, and Talmudic literature contains many discussions on this subject.[128] The following are two illustrations.

1. THE LETTER *VAV*—CONJUNCTIVE OR ALSO DISJUNCTIVE?

Leviticus 20:9 states:

If anyone reviles his father (*et aviv*) and his mother (*ve-et immo* [the Hebrew for *ve* is the letter *vav*]), he shall be put to death; he has reviled his father (*aviv*) and his mother (*ve-immo*)—his bloodguilt is upon him.

128. Some explicative *midrashim* dealing with the scope or content of legal rules (as distinguished from terms and expressions), which will be discussed later, also provide examples of *midrashim* very similar to those that explain terms and expressions. *See, e.g., infra* pp. 328–330 (inference from a generalization that requires a specification or from a specification that requires a generalization). The division of explicative *midrashim* into two categories is, therefore, general and not precise.

The *Sifra* comments on this verse:[129]

> "If anyone reviles his father and his mother"—this tells us only that the law applies if one curses both his father and his mother. From where is the rule derived that this also applies when one curses only one's mother or only one's father? It is for this that the Torah continues: "he has reviled his father and his mother"—to teach that the law should be interpreted expansively.[130] This is the view of R. Josiah. R. Jonathan states: It [the letter *vav*] means both together ["and"] as well as each one separately ["or"] unless the Torah specifically states that it means only both together.[131]

The question of interpretation is whether the letter *vav,* which normally means "and," is used only conjunctively, or whether it is possible to give it an additional disjunctive meaning (*i.e.,* "or").

This difference of opinion gave rise to an additional dispute concerning the function of the word "or" (*o*) in the Torah. According to R. Josiah, the letter *vav* is conjunctive only, and always means "and"; therefore, if the Torah wishes a verse to apply in the case of either of two alternatives, it must use the word *o,* which always signifies the disjunctive. According to R. Jonathan, there is no need to use *o,* since the letter *vav* is sufficient to cover the disjunctive, and thus when the word *o* is used it must have an additional purpose beyond signifying the disjunctive.[132]

2. MASCULINE AND FEMININE

As a general rule, "the Torah is written in the masculine gender,"[133] but laws stated in this form also apply to women. For example, Exodus

129. *Sifra,* Leviticus, Kedoshim 9:5 (p. 91b); TB Sanhedrin 66a (the quotation is according to *Sifra*).

130. In other words, since the second part of the verse repeats (and here the translation is precisely literal and differs from the more idiomatic translation in our text) "his father and his mother has he reviled," and in this part of the verse, "mother" is the closer direct object of "reviled," whereas in the first part of the verse "father" is the closer direct object, the inference is that one who curses either his father or his mother violates the law stated in this verse. *See* Rashi, Sanhedrin 66a, s.v. Aviv she-lo immo.

131. *I.e.,* the letter *vav* is not only conjunctive, but also disjunctive, for when the intention is exclusively conjunctive, the Torah uses the word *yaḥdav* ("together") in addition to the *vav,* as in Deuteronomy 22:10: "You shall not plow with an ox and an ass together," and *id.,* v. 11: "You shall not wear *sha'atnez*—wool and linen together." *See* Rashi, Sanhedrin 66a, s.v. R. Yonatan omer. *Tosafot, ad loc.,* s.v. Ad she-yefaret, explains that R. Jonathan's opinion was not based on proof from the verses regarding mixed species (*kilayim*), but on his interpretive logic.

132. *See, e.g.,* TB Bava Meẓi'a 94b–95a; Shevu'ot 27a/b. *See also* ET, I, pp. 112–113, s.v. O leḥalek; *id.,* XI, pp. 400–412, s.v. Vav (2); A. Karlin, "Midrash Halakhah," *Sinai,* XXXI, pp. 163, 169ff.; and *cf.* sec. 7 of the Israeli Interpretation Law, 1981, with regard to interpretation of words such as *o* ("or"). As to interpretation of the letter *vav, see also infra* pp. 407–408 n. 23 in connection with halakhic interpretation (*midrash ha-Halakhah*) and pp. 440–442 in connection with interpretation of documents.

133. *See Tosafot,* Kiddushin 2b, s.v. Litni sheloshah; *Kesef Mishneh* to *MT,* Edut 9:2.

21:1 states: "These are the laws (*mishpatim*) that you shall set before them." Even though the gender of "before them" (*lifneihem*) here is masculine, the principle is that "Scripture equated men and women for all laws in the Torah."[134]

When a verse uses the word *ish* ("man"), however, the reference is only to men and not to women[135] unless there is a specific indication that women are also included;[136] and the same applies to the term *ben* ("son").[137]

C. Generalization and Specification

As has been pointed out, the thirteen canons of R. Ishmael include ten canons for explaining the substance or scope of a Biblical law. These ten canons can be subdivided into four groups. We examine each of these groups and their canons and give examples of each canon.

The first group involves general and specific terminology and includes four canons: (1) a generalization followed by a specification, (2) a specification followed by a generalization, (3) a generalization followed by a specification that is in turn followed by a generalization, and (4) a generalization that requires a specification or a specification that requires a generalization.[138]

The central question basic to the first three of these four canons is a question common to every legal system. When a statute or document specifically enumerates the instances to which a stated rule applies but also

134. TB Bava Kamma 15a. *See also* Rashba, *ad loc.; Tosafot, ad loc.*, s.v. Hishvah ha-katuv, and the discussion in TB Temurah 2b. Similarly, the word *adam* ("man") includes women as well. *See* ET, I, p. 73, s.v. Adam (p. 76). *See also infra* n. 136, and *Resp. Rashba Attributed to Naḥmanides* #93. *Cf. also* sec. 6 of the Israeli Interpretation Law, 1981, as to use of the masculine form as also including the feminine.

135. TB Sanhedrin 46a: "A man may be hanged but not a woman, as it is written, 'If a man (*ish*) is guilty of a capital offense . . . and you hang him on a tree' [Deuteronomy 21:22]—'a man' but not a woman."

136. As there is, for example, in the matter of respect due to parents, about which it is stated, "You shall each revere his mother and his father" [lit. "each man (*ish*) shall revere"] (Leviticus 19:3). The commandment is applied to women by a special inclusive interpretation in *Sifra*, Kedoshim, sec. 1 (p. 86b): "The only reference in the verse is to males. On what basis can it be said that it also applies to females? The verse states, '*Tira'u* (you [plural] shall revere).' This refers to two [*i.e.*, both a son and a daughter]." The same interpretation is set forth in TB Kiddushin 30b. *See also* ET, I, pp. 343–345, s.v. Ish; *id.*, II, pp. 242–257, s.v. Ishah. *See also* Maimonides, *MT*, Edut 9:2, which derives a woman's incompetence to be a witness from the verse (Deuteromy 17:6) "on the testimony of two witnesses (*edim*)," which is stated in the masculine form; and the query of *Kesef Mishneh, ad loc.*

137. *See* ET, III, pp. 346–348, s.v. Ben, and the discussion there as to whether grandchildren are to be included in the term *ben* ("son"). *See also Resp. Rashba*, III, #335.

138. All four of these canons are included in the fifth of Hillel's seven canons, "[inference from the relation between] a generalization and a specification." *See supra* p. 317.

includes a general classification covering not only the specifically enumerated instances but others as well, there seems to be an internal inconsistency, which raises this question: Should the law be applied only to those instances that are explicitly mentioned and the scope of the general class be limited to those instances alone? Or, should the law apply to the entire class generally described and the particulars mentioned be regarded merely as illustrative rather than exhaustive? There are three possible solutions to this problem; and which one is applicable, under Jewish law, in any particular case depends on the sequence of the general and specific terms in the legal provision in question. The following three illustrations, one for each of the first three canons, will make the point clear.

1. INFERENCE FROM A GENERALIZATION FOLLOWED BY A SPECIFICATION (*KELAL U-FERAT*)

The first canon teaches that where a generalization is followed by a specification, the generalization is no broader than the specification. Thus, if a generalization is stated first and then followed by particular instances, the particulars are deemed to be exhaustive rather than merely illustrative of the generalization; therefore, the generalization covers only the enumerated specific instances that follow it in the text.

For example, Leviticus 1:2 states:

> Speak to the Israelite people and say to them: When any of you presents an offering to the Lord, he shall choose his offering from the animals (*min ha-behemah*), from the herd or from the flock.

This verse, which designates the animals that may be brought as a sacrificial offering, first states a generalization—"from the animals"—a term which includes both domesticated and wild animals.[139] After this general class, the text specifies "from the herd or from the flock," which are examples of domesticated animals only, and not of wild beasts. Because the specification follows the generalization, we conclude that the intent of the verse is to particularize the general statement and to indicate that only an animal that is from the herd or from the flock can be brought as a sacrificial offering.

139. *See* Deuteronomy 14:4–5 regarding animals whose meat it is permissible to eat: "These are the animals that you may eat: the ox, the sheep, and the goat; the deer, the gazelle, the roebuck, the wild goat, the ibex, the antelope, the mountain sheep." The verse begins "These are the animals" (*ha-behemah*), which is the same general term used in Leviticus 1:2, and then lists as included in that term "the deer, the gazelle, the roebuck," which are wild animals. *See also* TB Zevaḥim 34a.

The verse is thus interpreted:[140]

> We draw an inference from a generalization followed by a specification. In what way? "From the animals" is a general class. "From the herd or from the flock" are specifications. When a generalization is followed by a specification, the generalization is no broader than the specification.

2. INFERENCE FROM A SPECIFICATION FOLLOWED BY A GENERALIZATION (*PERAT U-KHELAL*)

The second canon teaches that when a specification is followed by a generalization, the generalization broadens the specification. Thus, if a specification is followed by a generalization that includes, but is broader than the specification, the specification is deemed merely illustrative, and the full scope of the generalization applies.

For example, Exodus chapter 22, beginning with verse 9, deals with a bailee's legal responsibility when property entrusted to him has been stolen or destroyed. In some circumstances, the bailee is responsible for the loss suffered by the owner and must compensate him. In other circumstances, the bailee is not liable, but must take an oath that he did not misappropriate the property. To what kinds of property do these rules apply? On this subject, Exodus 22:9 tells us that they include "an ass, an ox, a sheep or any other animal" (lit. "any animal"). This is the same phenomenon—specific enumeration together with a general class—as in the previous example concerning the sacrificial offerings; but here the order is reversed—the enumerated particulars "an ass, an ox, a sheep" come first and are followed by the general class "or any animal." In this case, we conclude that the particulars are only illustrative and the full scope of the general term applies. Thus, the laws of that section of the Torah apply to a bailee who has been given any animal and not just an ass, an ox, or a sheep.

And so the verse was interpreted:[141]

> We draw an inference from a specification followed by a generalization. In what way? "If a man gives to another an ass or an ox or a sheep" is a specification, "or any animal to guard" is a general class. Where a specification is followed by a general classification, the generalization broadens the specification.[142]

140. *Baraita de-R. Ishmael,* Foreword to *Torat Kohanim,* p. 2a.

141. *Id.*

142. *See also* TB Bava Meẓi'a 57b, where this verse is also interpreted by applying the canon of inference from a generalization followed by a specification that is in turn followed by a generalization (*kelal u-ferat u-khelal*), discussed immediately *infra. See Torah Temimah,* commentary on the Torah, *ad loc.*

3. INFERENCE FROM A GENERALIZATION FOLLOWED BY A SPECIFICATION FOLLOWED IN TURN BY A GENERALIZATION (*KELAL U-FERAT U-KHELAL*)

The third canon teaches that where a generalization is followed by a specification that is in turn followed by a generalization, one must be guided by what the specification implies. In this case, the sequence is: first a general statement, then particulars included in but not exhaustive of the general statement, and finally a general statement that includes more than the specific examples that precede it.

Here we have a combination of the two prior canons. On the one hand, we have "a generalization followed by a specification," as to which the first canon teaches that the generalization should be read restrictively, *i.e.*, "the generalization is no broader than the specification." On the other hand, we also have here "a specification followed by a generalization"—the specification in the middle and the second generalization that follows—and as to this, the second canon teaches that the generalization should be expansively construed, *i.e.*, "the generalization broadens the specification." The Sages resolved this internal inconsistency by drawing the line at a point between the two canons, so that the generalization is construed more broadly than if the first canon governed, but more narrowly than if the second controlled. They concluded that where a generalization is followed by a specification that is in turn followed by a generalization, the intent of the verse is not to include all that is implied in the generalization but also not to limit the verse to only the specific examples given; the intent is to include more than, but only so much more as is comparable in nature and quality to, the specific examples.

For example, the Torah states that a thief must pay double damages—compensatory damages to make good the value of the property he stole, plus punitive damages in the same amount as the compensatory damages. This law is stated with regard to both a thief and a bailee who claims that the bailed property was stolen from him and who is later found to have stolen it himself.[143]

To what kinds of property does this rule of double damages apply? The answer is deduced from a verse in that section:[144]

> In all charges of misappropriation—pertaining to an ox, an ass, a sheep, a garment, or any other loss, whereof one party alleges, "This is it" [*i.e.*, identifies the property as having been misappropriated]—the case of both parties shall come before the judges: he whom the judges declare guilty shall pay double to the other.

143. Exodus 22:3, 6–8.
144. *Id.* 22:8.

The situation presented here is this: The beginning of the verse states, "In all charges of misappropriation," *i.e.*, a generalization that includes all property. This is followed in the middle of the verse by "an ox, an ass, a sheep, a garment"—*i.e.*, specifications of particular examples; and at the end of the verse, after these particulars, there is again a generalization—"or any other loss"—which again includes all property.

Here is how the verse was interpreted:[145]

> The Rabbis taught: "In all charges of misappropriation" is a generalization. "Pertaining to an ox, an ass, a sheep, a garment" is a specification of particulars. "Or any other loss" is again a generalization. Where a generalization is followed by a specification in turn followed by a generalization, one must be guided by what the specification implies. Since the particulars specified consist of property that is movable and has intrinsic value, the law includes all property that is movable and has intrinsic value. This excludes real estate [there is no double payment for the theft of realty], which is not movable; and it excludes slaves, who are treated like real estate [according to the *Halakhah,* the laws as to the method of acquisition, etc., that apply to non-Jewish slaves are the same as those that apply to real estate]. It also excludes bills and notes that, even though movable, have no intrinsic value [the documents themselves are only evidence of a claim for money].

On the one hand, the obligation to pay double is not applied to every charge of misappropriation; on the other hand, it is not limited to an ox, ass, sheep, or garment. The incidence of the obligation is between these two extremes, *i.e.*, the obligation applies with respect to any property of the same type as the particulars mentioned in the verse, in that it shares certain fundamental characteristics with them, namely, movability and intrinsic value.[146]

4. THE RELATION BETWEEN THE CANONS ON GENERALIZATION AND SPECIFICATION AND THE OTHER CANONS

One may well ask with regard to the three canons concerning "a generalization followed by a specification," "a specification followed by a generalization," and "a generalization followed by a specification followed in turn by a generalization": What is the purpose of the portions of the text that are disregarded? For example, in the case of a specification followed by a generalization we include all that is in the generalization and we dis-

145. TB Bava Kamma 62b.

146. The same approach is taken in the case of "a specification followed by a generalization that is in turn followed by a specification," where the rule is also that the interpretation must follow the tenor of the specific limitation, but somewhat differently than in the case of "a generalization followed by a specification that is in turn followed by a generalization." *See* TB Nazir 34b.

regard the particulars except as illustrations. Why were these particulars mentioned at all? The same applies to the converse: In the case of a generalization followed by a specification, why was the general statement made at all?

The answer given to this question is that the literary form of the verse teaches us that we should interpret it by searching for its meaning within the confines of the verse itself and not make use of other canons of interpretation, such as inference *a fortiori,* application of a general principle (*binyan av*), etc.[147] Thus, if the verse contained only the general statement or only the specification, it might have been interpreted on the basis of an inference *a fortiori* or an inference based upon the application of a general principle. However, once faced with a verse in a form such as a generalization followed by a specification, the exegete should not resort to any other canon.[148] The principle is, therefore, that where it is possible to use the methods of interpretation based upon the canons relating to generalization and specification, those canons alone are to be employed.[149]

5. A GENERALIZATION THAT REQUIRES A SPECIFICATION OR A SPECIFICATION THAT REQUIRES A GENERALIZATION

The fourth canon, dealing with "a generalization that requires a specification or a specification that requires a generalization," covers those in-

147. For example, the case of a generalization followed by a specification in Leviticus 1:2: ". . . from the animals, from the herd or from the flock." Had the verse stated only "from the herd or from the flock," it might have been possible to find an inference *a fortiori* (*kal va-ḥomer*) or a general principle (*binyan av*) to the effect that the terms "herd" and "flock" include other animals. Inasmuch, however, as the general term "from the animals" precedes the more limited "from the herd or from the flock," there is a generalization followed by a specification, which necessarily requires the interpretation that only the animals specified, *i.e.,* from the herd or from the flock, are fit sacrifices, and it is not permissible to utilize other methods of interpretation that might change that conclusion.

148. *See Tosafot,* Nazir 35b, s.v. Ika.

149. The interpretive problem involved in canons relating to the sequence of generalizations and specifications in Biblical verses is similar to the familiar *ejusdem generis* ("of the same kind") canon in the common and civil law. Thus, in English law, when a list of specific terms is followed by a more general term, the *ejusdem generis* canon calls for construing the general term to include only items having the characteristics of the specific terms and nothing else. (Jewish law reaches the same result in the case of "a generalization followed by a specification that is in turn followed by a generalization.") As to the English *ejusdem generis* canon, *see* Chitty on Contracts, I, 21st ed., p. 155–157; Odgers, *The Construction of Deeds and Statutes,* 4th ed., pp. 133ff.; Salmond, p. 135. *See also* Boehm v. Mayor of Tel Aviv, 3 P.M. 98, 104–106 (1948).

On the other hand, the Israeli Supreme Court has ruled that in the case of "a specification followed by a generalization" the generalization adds to the specification and includes items that are not of the same nature as those specifically listed. *See* Lazarowitz v. Supervisor of Food Products, 10 *P.D.* 40 (1956). The legal situation in Israel regarding "a specification followed by a generalization" is, therefore, similar to that of Jewish law.

stances where the generalization and the specification do not broaden or narrow the scope of the text, but explain each other; the particular and the general are each in need of and are dependent on the other. We examine the two parts of this canon in the following sections.

a. A GENERALIZATION THAT REQUIRES A SPECIFICATION

There are instances in the Torah where a general statement is subject to two interpretations or is not clear. In such instances, "you cannot understand what the generalization means until the specific explains it";[150] and thereupon a specification follows and explains the meaning of the general term. For example, the Torah commands that both human and animal firstborns must be redeemed from the priests. This command is contained in the verse: "Consecrate to Me every firstborn; man and beast, the first issue of every womb among the Israelites is Mine";[151] and in the verse: "You shall consecrate to the Lord your God all male firstlings that are born in your herd and in your flock."[152]

These verses were interpreted as follows:

> "Consecrate to Me every firstborn" [Exodus 13:2]—Does this include the female? Scripture states: "Male" [Deuteronomy 15:19]. If it includes only males, does it also apply if a female was previously born? Scripture states: "The first issue of every womb" [Exodus 13:2]. If it applies to "the first issue of every womb," does it also apply after a previous caesarean birth? Scripture states: "Every firstborn" [Exodus 13:2]. This is a case of a generalization that requires a specification and a specification that requires a generalization.[153]

The word "firstborn," even when clarified to include only males, can still have two meanings: (a) the first male child, *i.e.,* the first male even if a female was born previously; (b) the firstborn child, but if, and only if, that child is a male (so that the first male is not a firstborn of his mother if born after a female). From the text "the first issue of every womb," we deduce that the intended reference is to the first to be born; the specification "the first issue of every womb" thus clarifies that the general term—"firstborn"—has the second of the two possible meanings rather than the first.

150. Rashi, Bekhorot 19a, s.v. Kelal ha-ẓarikh li-ferat. *See also Shittah Mekubbeẓet, ad loc.,* Letter *tet:* "And you cannot understand what the generalization means. . . ."

151. Exodus 13:2.

152. Deuteronomy 15:19.

153. *Baraita de-R. Ishmael,* Foreword to *Torat Kohanim,* p. 2a/b; TB Bekhorot 19a. The quotation in the text is from the version in the *Baraita de-R. Ishmael.*

b. A SPECIFICATION THAT REQUIRES A GENERALIZATION

This canon refers to a specification that is explained by a generalization in a certain manner, whereas the text, if it contained only the specification without the generalization, could have been interpreted differently.

As we have seen in the last sentence of the *midrash* quoted just above,[154] the verse there interpreted also provides an example of a specification that requires a generalization. The relevant passage is that part of the *midrash* that states, "If it applies to 'the first issue of every womb,' does it also apply after a previous caesarean birth? Scripture states: 'Every firstborn.'" If Scripture stated only "the first issue of every womb," it would have been possible to reach the conclusion that one must consecrate the first issue of the womb even if there had been a previous offspring by a caesarean birth. However, since the verse states "firstborn," we deduce that the reference is to the first to be born, and one born after a prior caesarean birth is not the first to be born. The specification, "first issue of every womb," is thus explained by the generalization, "firstborn."

D. A Matter Included in a Generalization and Also Specifically Mentioned (*Davar she-Hayah bi-Khelal ve-Yaẓa Min ha-Kelal*)

The following group of canons in the thirteen canons of R. Ishmael includes the eighth, ninth, tenth, and eleventh, and can be subsumed under the single heading: "A matter included in a generalization and also specifically mentioned." The basic question common to these four canons, as expressed in the terminology of other legal systems, is: What is the relationship between a general rule (*lex generalis*) and a specific rule (*lex specialis*) that deal with a common subject? In the terminology of Jewish law, the situation is described as a matter included in a generalization (*i.e.*, included in a law stated generally in the Torah) and also specifically mentioned (*i.e.*, reiterated as a specific and separate rule).

The difference between the four canons subsumed under "a matter included in a generalization and also specifically mentioned" and those canons that are grouped under "generalization and specification" is this: In the canons of "generalization and specification" there is a single law that the text applies explicitly to a general class (the generalization) and also to a particular member or instance included in the class (the specification). The question arises: Why did the text include both the general and the specific? By contrast, in the canons concerning "a matter included in a gen-

154. The last sentence reads: "This is a case of a generalization that requires a specification and a specification that requires a generalization."

eralization and also specifically mentioned," there are two separate laws: one, a general statement of a law (the generalization) that covers the specific instances subsumed under it, and the other, a specific statement of that law with regard to a particular instance already contained in the class ("and also specifically mentioned"). In such a case, the problem arises: Why was the specific statement made? (The distinction will become clear in the following two illustrations.) Since the canons concerning "a matter included in a generalization and also specifically mentioned" involve two separate statements of a law, the difference crucial to the canons of "generalization and specification," namely, whether the generalization comes before the specification or after it, is immaterial; the fact that there are two separate statements negates the importance of the question of which of the two statements comes first.

The nature and character of the specific rule (the singling out from the general for specific mention) differs in each one of the canons in this group, with the result that there are four principles that cover the question. The most significant principle, and the one which is most common, is the eighth canon—"Whatever is included in a generalization, and is also specifically mentioned to teach us something new, is stated not only for its own sake [lit. "to teach about itself"] but to teach something additional concerning all the matters included in the generalization"; and we will confine ourselves to the examination of this canon.[155]

This canon concerns the case where there is a law stated in general terms and there is also a specific statement of that law with regard to a particular matter obviously included in the general statement, and the purpose of the specific statement is to disclose ("to teach") a new rule that could not be known from the general statement. The principle is that the specification is added not only "for its own sake" but also for the sake of the general rule, *i.e.*, "to teach something additional concerning all the matters included in the generalization."

We examine two illustrations.

1. In connection with the sabbath, the Torah states at one point:

> Six days you shall labor and do all your work, but the seventh day is a sabbath of the Lord your God: you shall not do any work—you, your son or daughter,

155. For detailed treatment and examples of the ninth, tenth, and eleventh canons, *see Baraita de-R. Ishmael*, Foreword to *Torat Kohanim*, p. 2b; ET, VI, pp. 728–738, s.vv. Davar she-hayah bi-khelal ve-yaẓa min ha-kelal lidon ba-davar he-ḥadash; Davar she-hayah bi-khelal ve-yaẓa min ha-kelal lit'on to'an aḥer she-hu ke-inyano; Davar she-hayah bi-khelal ve-yaẓa min ha-kelal lit'on to'an aḥer she-lo ke-inyano; M. Ostrowsky, *Mavo la-Talmud* [Introduction to the Talmud], pp. 163–172.

your male or female slave, or your cattle, or the stranger who is within your settlements.[156]

The Torah states elsewhere:

You shall kindle no fire throughout your settlements on the sabbath day.[157]

The Midrash comments on this:

The kindling of fire was within the generalization [the prohibition of the labor of the kindling of fire on the sabbath was included in the general rule of "you shall not do any work"]. Then why was it specifically mentioned [*i.e.*, why was it written as a specific rule]? To create an analogy in order to teach that just as the kindling of fire is a principal category of work (*av melakhah*) for which there is separate culpability, similarly, for all other principal categories of work there is separate culpability.[158]

Since the Torah established a specific prohibition against the kindling of fire, in addition to the general rule of the prohibition of all labor on the sabbath, we learn a new law that also applies to the general rule: Just as there is a specific and separate prohibition against the kindling of fire on the sabbath, there is also a separate prohibition against each of the other principal categories of work on the sabbath ("[it] is stated not only for its own sake but to teach something additional concerning all the matters included in the generalization"); hence, we deduce that if one performs several principal categories of work on the sabbath he is culpable for each category separately, *i.e.*, he has not merely committed the single offense of violating the general prohibition.

2. In connection with the command of returning lost property, the Torah says:

If you see your fellow's ox or sheep gone astray, do not ignore it; you must take it back to your fellow. If your fellow does not live near you or you do not know who he is, you shall bring it home and it shall remain with you until your fellow claims it; then you shall give it back to him. You shall do the same with his ass; you shall do the same with his garment; and so too you shall do with anything that your fellow loses and you find; you must not remain indifferent.[159]

156. Exodus 20:9–10.

157. *Id.* 35:3.

158. *Mekhilta de-R. Ishmael,* Va-Yakhel, Tractate De-Shabbata, sec. 1 (p. 347), following the text in TB Shabbat 70a.

159. Deuteronomy 22:1–3.

Here we have an example of two rules that appear in the same section and, indeed, in the very same verse. The general rule is "so too you shall do with anything that your fellow loses," *i.e.,* you must return every lost object—which includes, of course, an ass or a garment. But the same verse also contains two specific rules: "You shall do the same with his ass," and "you shall do the same with his garment"; *i.e.,* since the verse reiterates the statement "you shall do" three times, we have here "a matter included in a generalization and also specifically mentioned."[160]

The Sages interpreted this as follows:

> The garment was included among all of these [in the general rule of returning "anything that your fellow loses"]. Why was it specifically mentioned [why was it written as a special rule, "you shall do the same with his garment"]? To create an analogy in order to teach that just as a garment is unique in that it has identification marks and claimants [owners who have not abandoned it], so for anything that has identification marks and claimants, the finder must publicly announce [that he has found it].[161]

In other words, the fact that a garment was singled out for specific mention was meant to indicate that the same rule that applies to garments should apply to all lost objects, and to teach that only in the case of a lost article that has identification marks and claimants (*i.e.,* every lost object similar in these respects to a garment) is the finder required to make a public announcement that he has found it.

E. An Ambiguous Word or Passage Is Explained from Its Context or from a Subsequent Expression (*Davar ha-Lamed me-Inyano ve-Davar ha-Lamed mi-Sofo*)

Another canon in the category of explicative exegesis is the twelfth among the canons of R. Ishmael—"An ambiguous word or passage is explained from its context or from a subsequent expression." This canon means that if there is doubt concerning the content of a rule, one should seek to resolve

160. Had the verse read, "You shall do the same with his ass, with his garment, and with anything that your fellow loses," we would be faced with a matter of two specifications and one generalization, since the one verb "you shall do" governs both the specification and the generalization. In that case, the appropriate canon would be "a specification followed by a generalization." As it is, however, the verb in the Hebrew is repeated before each of the particulars and also before the generalization. The verse thus gives two specific rules and one general rule and must be treated as a case of "a matter included in a generalization and also specifically mentioned."

161. M Bava Meẓi'a 2:5. For the restitution of lost property on the basis of identification marks, *see also supra* pp. 298–300.

the doubt on the basis of the general context of the subject matter where the rule is found. The difference between the two parts of the canon is this: "From a subsequent expression" indicates that the true content of the rule should be ascertained from the subsequent text of that law itself;[162] "from its context" indicates that the content of the rule may be deduced not only from the subsequent text of that law but also from a different law if the subject is related.

1. EXPLANATION ON THE BASIS OF A SUBSEQUENT EXPRESSION

In the section in Leviticus on forbidden marriages, it is first stated: "None of you shall come near to anyone of his own flesh [*i.e.*, a blood relative] to uncover nakedness, I am the Lord."[163] This verse itself can be interpreted to prohibit marriage to all blood relatives of whatever degree—"anyone of his own flesh." However, further in this same section[164] there is a detailed list of the marriages forbidden, and from this subsequent passage we learn what the initial prohibition does and does not include.[165]

2. EXPLANATION ON THE BASIS OF CONTEXT

It is stated in the Ten Commandments:[166] "You shall not steal." From these words alone we cannot know whether the reference is to the theft of property or to kidnapping, which is called in the Torah "the theft of human beings."[167] This ambiguity was resolved by means of the following interpretation:[168]

> The Rabbis taught: The Scriptural verse "You shall not steal" refers to kidnapping. You say that the reference is to kidnapping, but perhaps it refers to the theft of property? You can find the answer from the thirteen canons of Biblical interpretation—this is a matter that is explained from its context. What is the general subject of the text? Capital offenses. Thus, our verse too refers to a capital offense.

162. Despite the reference in the canon to "a subsequent expression," language anywhere in the relevant passage—before or after the ambiguous expression—may be resorted to when using this canon. *See* Rabad's commentary on *Baraita de-R. Ishmael,* Foreword to *Torat Kohanim,* p. 3a; ET, VI, pp. 556–557, s.v. Davar ha-lamed mi-sofo.

163. Leviticus 18:6.

164. *Id.* 18:7ff.

165. This example is given in Abudarham's commentary on the thirteen canons in the daily morning prayer service; *Baraita de-R. Ishmael,* Foreword to *Torat Kohanim,* pp. 2b–3a, offers a different example from the law of houses afflicted with a leprous plague, *see* Leviticus 14:34ff.

166. Exodus 20:13; Deuteronomy 5:17.

167. Exodus 21:16; Deuteronomy 24:7.

168. *Mekhilta de-R. Ishmael,* Yitro, Tractate De-ba-Ḥodesh, sec. 8 (p. 233), following the text in TB Sanhedrin 86a.

In the Ten Commandments, immediately preceding the prohibition of theft, there are the commandments "You shall not murder" and "You shall not commit adultery," violations of which constitute capital offenses. Consequently, we may conclude that the prohibition of theft, mentioned in the same context, also involves an offense that carries the death penalty. Since this is true only for kidnapping,[169] the commandment must refer only to kidnapping. The scope of the prohibition against theft in the Ten Commandments is thus deduced from the general context.

By using the same canon, we deduce that the reference in Leviticus 19:11, "You shall not steal; you shall not deal deceitfully or falsely with one another," is to the theft of property and not to kidnapping.

> It is also taught: The Scriptural verse "You shall not steal" refers to the theft of property. You say that the reference is to theft of property, but perhaps it refers to kidnapping? You can find the answer from the thirteen canons of Biblical interpretation—this is a matter that is explained from its context. What is the general subject of the text? Property. Thus, our verse too refers to property.[170]

The section in Leviticus discusses offenses against property. For example, Leviticus 19:13 states: "You shall not defraud your fellow. You shall not commit robbery. The wages of a laborer shall not remain with you until morning." From the context of those subjects, we may conclude that "you shall not steal" also refers to theft of property.

F. Two Contradictory Passages

The last canon in the category of explicative exegesis that is included in the thirteen canons of R. Ishmael is: "When two Biblical passages contradict each other, they may be harmonized by a third passage." The purpose of this canon is to resolve the uncertainty that arises when we find a contradiction between two Biblical passages on the same subject. Such a contradiction may occur between two verses contained in two different sections, between two verses in the same section, or between two parts of the same verse. In these situations, the principle was established that we should find the harmonization of the contradiction in a third verse; if there is no such possibility, the resolution will be arrived at by the Sages according to their understanding of the subject.

169. Exodus 21:16; Deuteronomy 24:7. These verses prescribe the death penalty for *gonev ish* or *gonev nefesh* (lit. "one who steals a person"), *i.e.*, a kidnapper.

170. *Mekhilta de-R. Ishmael, supra* n. 168 at 233–234; TB Sanhedrin 86a. Our text follows the latter.

Thus, the Jerusalem Talmud states:[171] "One verse states . . . [A]. Another verse states . . . [B]. Take your position between the two." Rabad, in discussing this canon, states: "This teaches us that we must clarify and reconcile each of two verses that seem to contradict each other, and that we should not reject either of them. We should not presume that there is an error in the Torah,"[172] *i.e.*, the halakhic authorities must find the way to reconcile the verses.

We examine one illustration for each of the three ways in which two passages may contradict each other.

1. CONTRADICTION BETWEEN TWO PASSAGES IN TWO SECTIONS

The law against delaying the payment of a laborer's wages appears in the Torah in two different places. One is Leviticus 19:13:

> You shall not defraud your fellow. You shall not commit robbery. The wages of a laborer shall not remain with you until morning.

The second is Deuteronomy 24:14–15:

> You shall not abuse a needy and destitute laborer, whether a fellow countryman or a stranger in one of the communities of your land. You must pay him his wages on the same day, before the sun sets, for he is needy and urgently depends on it; else he will cry to the Lord against you and you will incur guilt.

On a first reading of these two verses, we find the following difficulty: According to the verse in Leviticus, one must pay the wages of a laborer before the morning following the workday, but there is no obligation to pay the laborer immediately after the completion of his work. However, according to the passage in Deuteronomy, one must pay the wages on the day of the work itself and not retain it even until sunset.

The contradiction between these two passages is reconciled on the basis that each verse applies to a different factual situation. The verse in Leviticus refers to a day laborer, in which case the employer may pay his wages until the morning of the following day, whereas the verse in Deuteronomy applies to a night laborer, in which case the employer may pay his wages at any time during the entire next day until sunset. Through this interpretation of the two verses, the contradiction between them is resolved, and a uniform legal principle is fashioned concerning delay in the payment of a

171. TJ Ḥagigah 1:1, 3a (1:1, 76a).

172. Rabad's commentary on *Baraita de-R. Ishmael*, Foreword to *Torat Kohanim*, p. 1b.

laborer's wages, *viz.*, that in all situations the employer is given twelve hours after the work is finished in which to pay the laborer for his work.

And so we read:[173]

> The Rabbis taught: Whence do we deduce that a day laborer may be paid during the entire night? Scripture tells us, "The wages of a laborer shall not remain with you until morning." And whence do we deduce that a night laborer may be paid during the entire day? It is stated, "You must pay him his wages on the same day."[174]

2. CONTRADICTION BETWEEN TWO PASSAGES IN THE SAME SECTION

Exodus 23:4 states:

> When you encounter [*tifga*, lit. "meet"][175] your enemy's ox or ass wandering, you must take it back to him.

Verse 5 states:

> When you see the ass of your enemy prostrate under its burden and would refrain from raising it, you must nevertheless raise it with him.

The first verse states "when you meet," and the second verse states "when you see." "When you see" is much broader than "when you meet," because "seeing" includes even seeing from a distance. We find, therefore, that with regard to the same rule, *i.e.*, the requirement of preservation of

173. *Sifrei*, Deuteronomy, Ki Teẓe, sec. 279 (p. 296), following the text in TB Bava Meẓi'a 110b.

174. This method of harmonizing these two contradictory verses generates an additional rule, namely, that the right to compensation does not arise until all the work has been completed. Were the law otherwise (if the right to compensation accrues "from the beginning to the end," *i.e.*, as the work proceeds—TB Kiddushin 48a *et al.*), the verses could have been harmonized in a converse fashion: "The wages of a laborer shall not remain with you until morning" would have been interpreted as referring to a night worker, in which case payment would have to be made immediately at the conclusion of the work and not thereafter. The verse "You must pay him his wages on the same day" would be interpreted as referring to a day worker, who also would have to be paid the instant he completes his work. However, since the rule is that the right to compensation does not arise until the work has been completed, the obligation to pay likewise does not exist until the work is completed; and the verse "The wages . . . shall not remain with you until morning" cannot be taken as referring to a night worker, since the obligation to pay arises only after the night is ended, and conversely with the day worker. *See* TB Bava Meẓi'a 110b: "But can I not say the reverse? [No.] The right to compensation does not arise until after the work is completed." *See also* Rashi, *ad loc.*

175. *Cf.* Genesis 28:11: "He came upon [*va-yifga*, lit. "met"] a certain place and stopped there for the night. . . ."

the property of others, there are two different criteria as to when the rule applies.

The two verses were harmonized as follows:[176]

> "When you meet." I take this to have its ordinary meaning [involving an actual encounter], but Scripture states: "When you see" [*i.e.*, seeing is sufficient to impose the obligation and an actual meeting is unnecessary]. "When you see." Should I take this to mean even from a mile away? But Scripture states: "When you meet." How can these two verses be harmonized? The Sages estimated [the distance sufficient to impose the obligation to be] two-fifteenths of a mile.[177]

The Sages harmonized the contradiction between the two passages—"encountering," on the one hand, and "seeing," on the other—and resolved it by taking an intermediate position that the intent here was not to require an actual encounter but only visibility from a specified fixed distance.

3. CONTRADICTION BETWEEN TWO PARTS OF THE SAME VERSE

Exodus 21:20–21 states:

> When a man strikes his slave, male or female, with a rod, and he [the slave] dies there and then [lit. "under his hand"], he must be avenged. But if he survives for a day or two [lit. "for one day or for two days"], he is not to be avenged, since he is the other's [his master's] property.

Upon reading the second sentence, the following question immediately arises: How should we interpret the phrase "for a day or two" (lit. "for one day or for two days")? There is an internal inconsistency here, whichever time period is interpreted to be controlling. If we say that the words "one day" are decisive, then if the servant remains alive for only one day after his master has struck him, the master should not be punished. However, if the words "two days" are decisive, the legal conclusion follows that only if the servant remained alive for at least two days after his master struck him should he not be avenged; thus, even if the servant survived more than one day but died before two days had fully elapsed, vengeance may be had against the master.

176. *Mekhilta de-R. Ishmael,* Mishpatim, Tractate De-Kaspa, sec. 20 (pp. 323–324). *See also* the parallel *midrash* on v. 4, *id.* at 325.

177. The measure in the *Mekhilta* is a *ris,* an accepted measure in Talmudic times, which was about 2/15 of a mile; *see* M. Jastrow, *A Dictionary of the Targumim, The Talmud Babli and Yerushalmi, and Midrashic Literature,* Philadelphia, 1903 (New York, 1950), s.v. Ris.

The contradiction in this verse was resolved as follows:[178]

> "For one day." Should I understand this literally? But Scripture states: "Or for two days. . . ." Should I understand this literally? But Scripture states: "For one day." How can these two verses both be given effect? It means a day that is similar to two days and two days that are similar to one day, *i.e.*, a twenty-four-hour period.

Out of the contradiction that arises from the two terms—"for one day or for two days"—in the same legal rule, the Sages determined that the correct interpretation of the verse is a middle ground between the two. There are here two extremes: "two days" may be forty-eight hours and "one day" may be twelve hours; we therefore adopt an intermediate position between these two extremes: a twenty-four-hour period, which falls between "one day" (of twelve hours) and "two days" (of forty-eight hours). According to this determination, the word "day" means a full day, *i.e.*, twenty-four hours, and the words "two days" refer to two minimal days, *i.e.*, two days of twelve hours each, which also total twenty-four hours.

VII. LOGICAL INTERPRETATION

Before examining the types of analogical exegesis included among the thirteen canons, it is appropriate to discuss another type of interpretation—logical interpretation (*interpretatio logica*)—which, although not included among the thirteen canons of R. Ishmael, plays a large and important role in the methods of interpretation of Jewish law. In its essence and purpose, logical interpretation is similar to explicative exegesis. The function of each is, first and foremost, to explain and clarify so as to be able to understand the content of the Torah with the aid of logic, in accordance with the various forms and methods of that discipline. Logical interpretation also—even more than explicative exegesis—creates new legal rules and principles. We here examine some examples and forms of this method of interpretation.

A. Violation of a Betrothed Girl

Deuteronomy 22:25–27 deals with the punishment for one who rapes a betrothed girl. (By reason of her betrothal, she is forbidden by Jewish law to any man other than her betrothed.) The Torah states:

178. *Mekhilta de-R. Ishmael,* Mishpatim, Tractate De-Nezikin, sec. 7 (p. 274).

> If the man comes upon the betrothed girl in the open country and the man lies with her by force, only the man who lay with her shall die, but you shall do nothing to the girl. The girl did not incur the death penalty, for this case is like that of a man attacking another and murdering him. For he came upon her in the open; though the betrothed girl cried for help, there was no one to save her.

Evidently, the girl is innocent only if the incident takes place in the open country; this is a point emphasized twice in the passage. Correspondingly, where the girl is guilty, Scripture twice states that the incident took place in the city—verses 23–24.

However, the Sages interpreted this verse as follows:

> "For he came upon her in the open." Shall we take this to mean that she is guilty [if the incident occurred] in the city but is innocent [if it occurred] in the open country? But does not Scripture state: "Though the betrothed girl cried for help, there was no one to save her"? This implies that if there was someone there to save her, whether in the city or in the open country, she is guilty, and that if there was no one to save her, whether in the city or in the open country, she is innocent.[179]

This interpretation searches out the logic and the rationale for declaring the girl innocent. The rationale is that she resisted and sought help, but there was no one there to help her. Therefore, the fact that the event took place in a field is neither determinative of nor necessary for the girl's innocence, but only illustrative, since the open country is the kind of isolated place where assistance would normally not be available. Consequently, the factor that determines innocence or guilt is not geographical location but whether or not the girl objected.[180]

B. The Law of Pledges

In the section on loans, the Torah states:[181]

> A handmill or an upper millstone shall not be taken in pawn, for that would be taking someone's life in pawn.

A creditor may not take a handmill or upper millstone as a pledge from his debtor, because the debtor needs these vitally important implements to make his bread and sustain his life.

The Sages reasoned:[182]

179. *Sifrei*, Deuteronomy, Ki Teẓe, sec. 243 (p. 273).
180. Philo had reached this same halakhic conclusion earlier; *see infra* pp. 1030–1031.
181. Deuteronomy 24:6.
182. M Bava Meẓi'a 9:13; *Sifrei*, Deuteronomy, Ki Teẓe, sec. 272 (p. 292).

> Not only a handmill or upper millstone,[183] but anything useful in sustaining life, as it is stated: "For that would be taking someone's life in pawn."

In other words, because the logic and rationale of the prohibition against the taking of a handmill or upper millstone is that the debtor needs these implements to prepare the food he needs to keep alive, the references to the handmill and the upper millstone are merely illustrative; the creditor may not take as a pledge anything useful in sustaining life, including, *e.g.*, scissors or the yoke for a pair of heifers.[184]

C. Damage Due to a Pit

Exodus 21:33–34 states:

> When a man opens a pit, or digs a pit and does not cover it, and an ox or an ass falls into it, the one responsible for the pit must make restitution; he shall pay the price to the owner and the dead animal shall be his.

What is the meaning of "and the dead animal shall be his"? From a first reading, it would seem that the dead animal should go to the wrongdoer, inasmuch as he is compensating the victim for the animal that was killed. However, the *Mekhilta* states:[185]

> "And the dead animal shall be his." This means that it belongs to the victim. You say that it belongs to the victim, but perhaps it belongs to the wrongdoer? If so, what is the point of "and the dead animal shall be his"? [If we interpret the verse according to its plain meaning and say that the dead ox belongs to the wrongdoer, then what need is there for the verse specifically to state this? If the wrongdoer pays the full monetary equivalent to the victim for the loss of the animal, it is obvious that the dead animal should belong to the wrongdoer, as the victim should not reap a windfall as a result of the accident]. It tells us that the value of the carcass is assessed and deducted from the damages [the carcass remains the property of the victim and not of the wrongdoer, and the wrongdoer need not pay the victim the full value of

183. In the printed editions, the word *amru* (they said) appears after "upper millstone," but it does not appear in the more accurate texts. *See* H. Albeck's commentary, *ad loc.*

184. *Tosefta* Bava Meẓi'a 10:11.

185. *Mekhilta de-R. Ishmael,* Mishpatim, Tractate De-Nezikin, sec. 11 (p. 289). In line 10, *ad loc.*, the word *la-nizak* ("the victim's") appears for the third time. We have followed the textual variants there noted, which omit it at that point.

Our translation of Exodus 21:34 differs from the 1985 JPS *Tanakh,* which is "but shall keep the dead animal." The JPS translation, as will be seen, is contrary to the traditional resolution of the ambiguity as to who is referred to by "his" in the clause "and the dead animal shall be his."

> the ox but only the additional amount over and above the value of the dead ox to compensate the victim for the loss of the ox's life].

Here we have a legal conclusion formed from a deeper penetration into the logic of the words of a verse.

D. The Law of Agency

Sometimes, the logic relied on in this type of interpretation is based upon situation-sense—the practical possibilities inherent in the situation—which forms the basis for deducing a particular legal principle from a Scriptural verse.

For example, Exodus 12:6, in the section concerning the paschal sacrifice, states:

> You shall keep watch over it until the fourteenth day of this month; and all the assembled congregation of the Israelites shall slaughter it at twilight.

The Sages interpreted this verse to yield the following legal principle:

> R. Joshua b. Korḥa said: "What is the source of the rule that action by an agent is equivalent to action by the principal? It is stated: 'All the assembled congregation of the Israelites shall slaughter it at twilight.' But does the entire congregation do the slaughtering? Is not the slaughtering done by only one person? We deduce from here that action by an agent is equivalent to action by the principal."[186]

This interpretation is the product of a practical insight into the nature and circumstances of the situation. The verse cannot be given the literal interpretation that the entire Israelite community should slaughter the sacrifice, inasmuch as this would be factually impossible. Therefore, the verse must be construed to mean that the act of one person is, in effect, the act of another person or even of an entire group. This is the source of the doctrine of principal and agent—that action by an agent is equivalent to action by the principal.[187]

186. *Mekhilta de-R. Ishmael,* Bo, Tractate De-Pisḥa, sec. 5 (p. 17), following the text in TB Kiddushin 41b, which also appears in TJ Kiddushin 2:1, 23a (2:1, 62a). *See also Mekhilta, op. cit.,* sec. 3 (p. 11), where the principle is derived from "Each of them shall take a lamb to a family" (Exodus 12:3); the same derivation also appears in TJ Kiddushin, *supra.* For a fuller discussion, *see* H. Albeck, Hashlamot, Berakhot, pp. 333–335.

187. *See also supra* p. 112 and *compare* this method of interpretation *with* the method *rerum natura* (the nature of things) of Roman law.

From the few illustrations that we have mentioned,[188] we see how the Sages used logical analysis of the content of a Biblical law, both for purposes of explication and for deducing new legal principles.

VIII. ANALOGICAL EXEGESIS

The two types of Scriptural interpretation that we have discussed, namely, explicative exegesis and logical interpretation, were means by which the study and analysis of the meaning and explanation of the Torah expanded and developed the *Halakhah.* The need to clarify and explain the laws of the Torah resulted both from the fact that people occupied themselves in studying the Torah and from the need to know how to conform daily life to the Torah.

Practical life, however, gave rise to questions beyond those involving the meaning and explanation of the laws. Often, new questions arose for which the Torah had no explicit solutions, and the Sages had to search for solutions in accord with its laws. The methods of explicative exegesis and logical interpretation were not always sufficient to answer these questions, and it became necessary to make use of the methods of analogical exegesis, *i.e.*, an approach that makes analogical comparisons between different matters and subjects, and is used primarily to create new law in order to solve new problems.

Analogical exegesis includes mainly the first three canons of the thirteen canons of R. Ishmael: inference *a fortiori,* inference from the similarity of words or phrases, and application of a general principle. These three canons have a single common denominator—the analogical approach (*analogia*):

a. The canon of inference *a fortiori* draws an analogy from one subject to another on the basis of logic;
b. The canon of inference from the similarity of words or phrases draws an analogy from one subject to another on the basis of similarity in form of expression;
c. The canon of application of a general principle draws an analogy from one or more matters, leading to a particular conclusion on the basis of comparable features.

A further instance of analogical exegesis is an additional canon not included among the thirteen canons of R. Ishmael, but often found in Tal-

188. Examples of logical interpretation are abundant. *See, e.g.*, ET, VI, pp. 553–555, s.v. Dibber ha-katuv ba-hoveh.

mudic literature. This is the canon of "Scriptural analogy" (*hekkesh ha-katuv*), sometimes called simply "analogy" (*hekkesh*),[189] or "Scriptural comparison" (*hishvah ha-katuv*),[190] etc.[191] This interpretive approach also rests on analogy, as its title indicates; but it differs from the prior three analogical canons in that the Sages used those three canons to compare one subject to another, whereas this canon applies when the Torah itself explicitly or implicitly makes a comparison between different matters.

This additional canon is basic to the theoretical foundation of midrash: the Sages discerned that the Torah itself drew inferences from one subject to another, and this fact provided explicit support for their own use of analogy in order to draw legal conclusions. Therefore, we begin our study of the methods of analogical interpretation with the canon of "Scriptural analogy," which constitutes the source and foundation of the other analogical canons.

A. Scriptural Analogy (*Hekkesh ha-Katuv*)

Scriptural analogy is sometimes explicit and sometimes implicit.

1. EXPLICIT ANALOGY

In Deuteronomy 22:25–27, in connection with the rape of a betrothed girl,[192] the Torah states that the girl, although betrothed to another, is completely innocent:

> But you shall do nothing to the girl. The girl did not incur the death penalty, for this case is like that of a man attacking another and murdering him.[193]

The rationale for holding the girl innocent is based on comparing rape to murder. Thus, the Torah itself based the innocence of the ravished girl on an analogy from a legally and conceptually similar, though factually distinct, situation—the case of a murderer who pursues a victim. Indeed, the Sages expanded on the analogy between murder and rape, and thereby arrived at new legal rules taken from one and applied to the other.

189. TB Zevaḥim 49b; Sanhedrin 73a, and *see* Rashi, *ad loc.*, s.v. Hekkeisha hu, to the effect that this canon is superior to the *kal va-ḥomer; but see* TJ Pesaḥim 6:1, 39a (6:1, 33a), where the term *hekkesh* is applied to a different canon.

190. TB Kiddushin 35a.

191. *See* ET, X, pp. 557–575, s.v. Hekkesh.

192. This subject is discussed *supra* pp. 339–340.

193. Deuteronomy 22:26.

Thus, a *baraita* states:[194]

> It was taught, Rabbi [R. Judah Ha-Nasi] says: "This case is like that of a man attacking another and murdering him." But what is it that we have learned from the reference to the case of murder?[195] We deduce that although the case of murder is cited to teach us about a different case [*i.e.*, rape], its citation here also teaches something about the case of murder itself. Murder is compared to [the rape of] a betrothed girl: Just as in the case of [the rape of] a betrothed girl one may save her at the cost of his [the rapist's] life[196] [if there is no other way to prevent the rape], similarly, in the case of murder, one may save the victim at the cost of the life of the attacker.
>
> And [the rape of] a betrothed girl is compared to murder: Just as in the case of murder one should rather let himself be killed and not perpetrate the act [the principle is that if a person is ordered to kill someone else on pain of death if he fails to carry out the order, he must allow himself to be killed rather than commit murder], similarly, the betrothed girl should permit herself to be killed rather than transgress.[197]

The Sages thus adopted the method of analogy that they found in the Torah itself, and they broadened the scope of new laws that could be deduced through this reciprocal analogy between murder and rape. As a result, they concluded that the following two principles apply in the case of rape of a betrothed or married woman as well as in the case of murder: (a) "One should permit oneself to be killed rather than commit a transgression"; and (b) one is permitted to rescue the victim even at the cost of the life of the pursuer, if there is no other way the victim can be saved.

194. TB Sanhedrin 74a.

195. In other words, the analogy to the case of a murderer cannot possibly have been stated merely to exempt the girl from capital punishment, since that exemption is explicitly stated in the verse "The girl did not incur the death penalty." The addition of the analogy must, therefore, have an additional purpose. *See also* Rashi, Sanhedrin 73a, s.v. Ve-khi mah lamadnu mi-roẓe'aḥ.

196. This is the reading in TB Sanhedrin 73a. Folio 74a has: *le-hazzilo be-nafsho* (lit. "to save him in his soul," *i.e.*, to save the pursuer from committing the sin). However, it appears that the correct reading is *le-hazzilah*, "to save her," *i.e.*, the girl, as we learn from the verse: "'There was no one to save her'—but if there was, he may save her any way he can" (TB Sanhedrin 73a). This is also the reading in *Yad Ramah* to Sanhedrin 73a, s.v. Matnitin ve-eillu she-maẓẓilin otan. *Yad Ramah* also has the reading in folio 74a (s.v. Arayot u-shefikhut damim): "One may save her (*le-hazzilah*) at the cost of the pursuer's life."

197. *See also Tosafot*, Sanhedrin 74b, s.v. Ve-ha Ester parhesiah havai, which has another reading: "Similarly, in the case of rape of a betrothed girl, *he* should rather be killed than commit a transgression." This refers to a *man* ordered on pain of death to rape the girl (a case similar to being so ordered to commit murder), where he should rather be killed than commit the transgression. In this view, the requirement to die rather than sin does not apply to the girl. As to the law requiring that one under duress to commit murder should rather let himself be killed than take the life of another, *see infra* pp. 990–991.

2. ANALOGY BY IMPLICATION

Deuteronomy 21:5 states:

> The priests, sons of Levi, shall come forward; for the Lord your God has chosen them to minister to Him and to pronounce blessing in the name of the Lord, and every disputed case and every plague spot (*nega*) is subject to their ruling.

Thus, the priests are the decisionmakers on all matters of dispute and on all matters involving "plague spots" (*i.e.*, whether a particular lesion in one's body is ritually impure or pure).[198]

The fact that the Torah includes in a single reference, in the same verse, the two priestly tasks—deciding civil controversies (monetary matters) and making rulings as to bodily lesions (matters of ritual impurity and purity) implies an analogy between these two subjects. This analogy was interpreted as follows:[199]

> "Every disputed case and every plague spot is subject to their ruling." This establishes an analogical relationship between monetary disputes and bodily lesions: Just as bodily lesions are to be examined during the day,[200] so monetary disputes are to be heard during the day; and just as monetary disputes cannot be decided by relatives [a judge is disqualified if he is related to any of the parties], so bodily lesions cannot be examined by relatives [of the afflicted].

The continuation of that *midrash* is interesting:

> Shall we say that just as monetary disputes are to be decided by three judges, so too bodily lesions are to be examined by three [*i.e.*, why should we not also draw an analogy in regard to the composition of the decision-making body: since for monetary disputes there must be three judges, should not the same number also be required for the examination of bodily lesions]? Is this not a valid inference *a fortiori*[201]—if monetary disputes are decided by three, should not matters pertaining to the human body certainly be decided by three [*i.e.*, is it not an *a fortiori* argument that the decision-making body for "lesions," which pertain to the human body, should not consist of fewer members than the one for "disputed cases," which are merely monetary matters]?

198. *See supra* pp. 309–312 for the function of the priesthood before and after Ezra. The 1985 JPS *Tanakh* translates the last part of the verse as "every disputed case of assault is subject to their ruling." The traditional sources interpret *nega* as "plague spot."

199. *Sifrei,* Deuteronomy, Shofetim, sec. 208 (p. 243).

200. Leviticus 13:14: "But on the day undiscolored flesh appears. . . ." (This is the literal translation. The 1985 JPS *Tanakh* has: "As soon as undiscolored flesh. . . .") *See* TB Sanhedrin 34b.

201. The Hebrew term used here for *a fortiori* is *din. See infra* n. 212.

> However, Scripture states [Leviticus 13:2]: "When a person has on the skin of his body a swelling, a rash, or a discoloration, and it develops into a scaly affection on the skin of his body, he shall be brought to Aaron the priest or to *one* of his sons, the priests." This teaches that a single priest may examine a bodily lesion.

Thus, the analogy could not be extended to cover the question of the composition of the tribunal, because there is a specific rule (*lex specialis*) on this point in the section on lesions that it is sufficient if "one of . . . the priests," *i.e.*, a single priest, examines the lesion. This specific rule precludes any possible broadening of the analogy to cover the question of the composition of the tribunal.[202]

B. Inference *A Fortiori* (*Kal va-Ḥomer*)[203]

The first reference to the canon of inference *a fortiori* is contained in the Torah itself, as pointed out in the *baraita* attributed to R. Ishmael,[204] who made this the first of his thirteen canons, just as it was the first in the seven canons of Hillel:

> It was taught by R. Ishmael: One of the ten examples of *a fortiori* inferences that are set forth in the Torah is: "Here we brought back to you from the land of Canaan the money that we found in the mouths of our bags."[205] Does it not then stand to reason, "How then could we have stolen any silver or gold from your masters's house?!"[206]
>
> [Other examples are:] "The Israelites would not listen to me." All the more so, "How then should Pharaoh heed me. . . ?"[207]
>
> "Even now, while I am still alive in your midst, you have been defiant toward the Lord." *A fortiori,* "How much more, then, when I am dead. . . ."[208]

The *baraita* goes on to list seven other examples, and there are many others as well.[209]

202. This is an interesting example of the integration of several methods of interpretation: analogy, inference *a fortiori,* and decisive effect of a specific provision of the verse. As to analogy, *see further* ET, II, p. 319–320, s.v. Ba le-lammed ve-nimẓa lamed; X, pp. 557–575, s.v. Hekkesh.

203. As to the correct pronunciation of the Hebrew name of this canon, *kal va-ḥomer, see* W. Bacher, *Erkhei Midrash,* Tannaim, s.v. Kal va-ḥomer.

204. *Genesis Rabbah* 92:7 (III, pp. 1145–1146).

205. Genesis 44:8; *see* the continuation of the *baraita, Genesis Rabbah, supra* n. 204 at 1146.

206. Genesis 44:8.

207. Exodus 6:12.

208. Deuteronomy 31:27.

209. *See* Bacher, *supra* n. 203.

In the cited examples, the method of drawing an inference from one subject to another is simple and self-evident because the compelling force of the inference is also simple and obvious. Thus, whoever discovers that money has come into his possession without his previous knowledge and returns the money to its owner is surely not the kind of person who will intentionally steal money from the same owner; and the other examples are similar in this respect.

From this basic notion, the canon of inference *a fortiori* was given a much broader application, *i.e.*, the deduction of one proposition from another even when the greater strength of one of the propositions is not obvious and must be proved before the deduction can be validated. In using the canon of inference *a fortiori,* we compare one matter to another when the two have a common subject; and we draw inferences in two directions: (a) from the more lenient to the more stringent, and (b) from the more stringent to the more lenient. In drawing inferences from the more lenient to the more stringent, we proceed from a point of strictness that we find in the generally more lenient rule to conclude that that degree of strictness certainly applies where the applicable rule is generally more stringent; and in the converse situation we reason that if a generally more stringent rule involves leniency in one aspect, then certainly that lenient aspect will apply where the applicable rule is generally more lenient.

We examine this canon by illustrating each of the two directions.

1. INFERENCE FROM THE MORE LENIENT TO THE MORE STRINGENT

Exodus 22:6–14 contains the section on bailments that delineates the responsibilities placed on each of the different types of bailees. The section states, with regard to a bailee who is paid for his services, that if an animal bailed to him is stolen or lost, he must pay compensation; however, if the animal was injured (*i.e.*, torn by a wild beast against which the bailee was powerless), or if it died a natural death, the bailee is not liable. In the case of a gratuitous borrower, *i.e.*, one who borrows an animal for his own use without paying the owner, the section states that he must pay compensation if the animal was injured or died a natural death, but the text is silent as to the rule applicable to the theft or loss of the animal while in the gratuitous borrower's possession. The rule applicable to this situation is deduced by the canon of inference *a fortiori:*

> "It is injured or dies" [this is a quotation from Exodus 22:13, which states that a borrower is liable when the animal is injured or dies]. This tells us only about the case of injury or death; what is the law if it is stolen or lost? This is an inference *a fortiori:* If a paid bailee, who is not liable for injury or death, is nevertheless liable for theft or loss, does it not necessarily follow that a gra-

> tuitous borrower, who is liable for injury or death, is certainly liable for theft or loss?[210]

We compare here two types of bailees. First, we establish the premise that the law is more lenient to a paid bailee than to a gratuitous borrower, inasmuch as the paid bailee is not responsible for injury by *force majeure*, whereas the borrower is. From this we deduce that since the paid bailee is liable to pay compensation for theft and loss, the gratuitous borrower should certainly also be liable. If liability is imposed upon the one to whom the law is more lenient, then the one to whom the law is more strict is *a fortiori* liable.

2. INFERENCE FROM THE MORE STRINGENT TO THE MORE LENIENT

The schools of Shammai and Hillel disputed whether an *olah* (a sacrificial "burnt-offering") may be brought by an individual on festivals. The School of Hillel permitted it, but the School of Shammai held that it was forbidden. The School of Hillel argued in support of its view as follows:[211]

> It was taught: The School of Hillel said to the School of Shammai: "If an act is prohibited for an individual yet permitted for [service of] the Almighty [*i.e.*, on the sabbath, a private individual may not do any labor, including even food preparation for consumption, but sacrificial offerings to God may be brought in the Temple on the sabbath], should not an act that is permitted for an individual certainly be permitted for [service of] the Almighty? [On festivals, a private individual may prepare food for consumption, so it should certainly be permissible to bring sacrificial offerings to God in the Temple.]"

Here, too, we compare the rules applicable on the sabbath to those applicable on festivals. We find that the rules applicable on the sabbath are more stringent, since food preparation is prohibited on that day but not on festivals. We also note that there is a lenient rule relating to the sabbath, namely, that sacrificial offerings may be brought in the Temple on that day. We therefore deduce that it necessarily follows that sacrificial offerings may certainly be brought in the Temple on festivals, since the law applicable on those days is generally less strict than the law relating to the sabbath.

3. "IT IS ENOUGH FOR THE CONCLUSION THAT IT BE LIKE THE PREMISE"

From the two foregoing illustrations of the nature of the canon of inference *a fortiori*, we have seen that there are two components in any such

210. TB Bava Meẓi'a 95a.
211. TB Beẓah 20b.

inference. The first is the case on which the inference is based (*e.g.*, the paid bailee in the first illustration), called "the premise" (*ha-nidon*); and the second is the case to which the inference applies (*e.g.*, the gratuitous borrower in the first illustration), called "the conclusion" (*ha-ba min ha-din*, lit. "what follows from the argument").[212] Sometimes the premise is called "the instructor" (*melammed*) and the conclusion is called "the lesson" (*lamed*).

There is an important doctrinal principle relating to inference *a fortiori* that is called "it is enough for the conclusion that it be like the premise" (*dayyo la-ba min ha-din liheyot ka-nidon*), *i.e.*, the conclusion we deduce can be as strict as the law applicable in the situation covered by the premise, but it should not be more strict, even if there is a sound basis in logic to argue otherwise.

The Sages arrived at this principle from an example of *a fortiori* reasoning found in the Torah:[213]

> What is an example of inference *a fortiori?* "The Lord said to Moses: 'If her father spat in her face, would she not bear her shame for seven days? Let her be shut out of the camp for seven days, and then let her be readmitted!' "[214] Is it not a logical *a fortiori* inference that she should be shut out of the camp for fourteen days, since she has been reproached by the Divine Presence, and not merely a human father? However, it is enough for the conclusion that it be like the premise; therefore, Miriam should be shut out of the camp for seven days and then readmitted.[215]

Logic would dictate that if, after a rebuke by her father, Miriam should have been excluded from the camp for seven days, then after a divine rebuke she should be excluded for fourteen days.[216] However, this conclusion

212. The term *din* has many meanings, *e.g.*, "judgment," "law," "lawsuit," etc. As here, it is also used for the analogical canons, particularly the *kal va-ḥomer; see supra* p. 277.

213. *Baraita de-R. Ishmael,* Foreword to *Torat Kohanim,* p. 1a/b; TB Bava Kamma 25a; Bava Batra 111a. The *kal va-ḥomer* itself is also set forth in *Genesis Rabbah* 92:7 (III, p. 1146) as being among those that appear in the Torah.

214. Numbers 12:14. Miriam and Aaron had slandered Moses regarding the Cushite woman he had married, and Miriam was punished with leprosy. Moses beseeched God to heal her, and He answered that if her father had reproved her, she deserved to be shut away for seven days; therefore, in this case she should certainly be shut away for seven days.

215. *Sifrei,* Numbers, Be-Ha'alotekha, sec. 106 (p. 105), has the reading: "If in the case of her father, who is flesh and blood, [she should be shut away] for seven days, in the case of Him Who spoke and the universe was created, [shouldn't she certainly be shut away for] fourteen days?! It is enough for the conclusion that it be like the premise. Just as for her father, who is flesh and blood, seven days, so too for Him Who spoke . . . , seven days."

216. As to why fourteen days, rather than some other number greater than seven, *see Tosafot,* Bava Kamma 25a, s.v. Kal va-ḥomer la-shekhinah. Naḥmanides' explanation (Novellae to Bava Batra 111a) that "it is the natural tendency of language to double [numbers] in every case [where intensification is intended]" seems reasonable. *See also* ET, VII, pp. 282–290, s.v. Dayyo la-ba min ha-din liheyot ka-nidon.

is not reached, because the conclusion reached by *a fortiori* reasoning cannot be more strict than the rule applicable in the situation on which the inference is based.

The canon of inference *a fortiori* is based on the fact that the law with regard to one matter is more lenient, or more stringent, than it is with regard to another. Consequently, we can destroy the argument by what in amoraic terminology (Aramaic) is called *pirkha* or "refutation," and in tannaitic terminology (Hebrew) is called *teshuvah* or "retort," which consists of proof that the matter in which the law is claimed to be more lenient is actually dealt with more stringently in some respect than the matter in which the law is claimed to be more strict. That proof destroys the possibility of any valid inference from one matter to the other, because the fact that each of them has an aspect more stringent than the other puts them both on the same level. Conversely, a refutation or retort can also be made by proving that the matter in which the law is claimed to be the more stringent actually has a lenient aspect not found in the matter in which the law is claimed to be more lenient.[217]

C. Inference from the Similarity of Words or Phrases (*Gezerah Shavah*)

The second analogical canon in the list of canons of Hillel the Elder and of R. Ishmael is the canon "Inference from the similarity of words or phrases." Halakhic authorities and scholars have labored long over the literal meaning of the Hebrew term for this canon of interpretation (*gezerah shavah*) and over its nature and scope.[218] Lieberman has explained the term as meaning "comparison with something equivalent."[219] Thus, the meaning of *gezerah shavah* was originally an analogy drawn between two equivalent or similar matters. Only later did the canon of *gezerah shavah* come to refer not to a comparison of matters of equivalent content but to a comparison based on identical forms of language, *i.e.*, linguistic similarity between words and phrases in different verses, even when there was no connection between their contents.

The Sages disagreed as to when use of this canon was appropriate. Some were of the opinion that a *gezerah shavah* is appropriate whenever a

217. *See, e.g.*, TB Ḥullin 114a–116a, and many other sources. For the rule that criminal punishment cannot be based on *a fortiori* inference, *see infra* pp. 373–374.

218. Lieberman, *Hellenism*, pp. 57ff. has dealt with this problem. *See also* H. Albeck, Hashlamot, Arakhin, pp. 403–404.

219. Lieberman, *Hellenism*, p. 58. In both Biblical and rabbinic Hebrew, the word *gezerah* means "a decision" or "a verdict." As Lieberman has noted, its Greek parallel also connotes analogy.

phrase in one verse is similar to a phrase found in a different verse. Others felt that a *gezerah shavah* is not appropriate unless the word or phrase in question is redundant in either of the two textual references (in Talmudic terminology, "open on one side").[220] The use of a *gezerah shavah* may be subject to challenge (see the illustration below). However, if it is "open on both sides," *i.e.*, if the word or phrase that is the basis for the inference is redundant in both places in the text, it is universally conceded that "the inference is made and is not to be rebutted," *i.e.*, the inference is valid and beyond challenge.[221] Let us examine some examples of the use of this canon.

As previously stated, the section in the Torah on bailments states that a gratuitous borrower is liable if the borrowed animal was injured (torn by a wild beast) or died. The Talmud states[222] that a borrower is also liable if the animal was carried off by force, and the question was raised as to the source of this law:

> Granted that the borrower is liable in case of injury or death, because Scripture states: "When a man borrows [an animal] from another and it is injured or dies";[223] however, from where do we know [that the borrower is also liable] when the animal is carried off?

The response was:

> Injury and death are mentioned in connection with a borrower, and injury and death are also mentioned in the case of a paid bailee; just as in the case of the paid bailee, carrying off is included in the text along with death or injury, so here it is also included.

The meaning is as follows: The Torah states that a paid bailee is not liable when an animal "dies or is injured or carried off";[224] in the case of a gratuitous borrower, the Torah states that he is liable when the animal "is injured or dies." We therefore draw an inference from the similarity of phrases; since in the case of both a paid bailee and a gratuitous borrower the text mentions the animal's injury or death, and since being carried off is explicitly associated with injury or death in the text on paid bailees, it follows that in the case of a gratuitous borrower, being carried off is implicitly included in the expression "it is injured or dies." To put it another way: In

220. TB Shabbat 64a; Niddah 22b.
221. TB Niddah 22b.
222. TB Bava Meẓi'a 94b.
223. Exodus 22:13.
224. *Id.* 22:9.

its reference to a gratuitous borrower, the Torah abbreviated its language and mentioned only "it is injured or dies," as a kind of briefer summary of the more detailed passage on paid bailees, which includes the case where the animal is carried off.

From the further discussion in the same Talmudic passage, we may note the method of refuting a *gezerah shavah:*

> The inference can be refuted as follows: The rule for a paid bailee is that he is not liable, so how can we draw the inference for a gratuitous borrower, who is liable?

That is to say, the Biblical equation of carrying off with injury and death in the case of a paid bailee is not a basis for an inference that the same equation should be made for a gratuitous borrower, because a paid bailee is not liable for injury or death and, therefore, certainly not liable for carrying off (as to which there is even less likelihood of culpability on his part). However, a gratuitous borrower is liable in case of injury or death; it is possible that he is liable only in these cases, since there may be an element of fault on his part, but that he is not liable where the animal is carried off, which is a matter of complete *force majeure*. It is therefore conceivable that the Torah deliberately did not mention carrying off in connection with a gratuitous borrower because it intended that there be no liability in that case.[225]

The following is an example of an analogy that is "open on one side." Deuteronomy 23:3 states:

> No *mamzer*[226] shall be admitted into the congregation of the Lord [*i.e.*, eligible to marry into the Jewish people]; none of his descendants, even in the tenth generation, shall be admitted into the congregation of the Lord.

The verse immediately following states:

> No Ammonite or Moabite shall be admitted into the congregation of the Lord; none of their descendants, even in the tenth generation, shall ever be admitted into the congregation of the Lord.

Two things stand out upon an examination of these two verses:

225. In the light of this refutation, a borrower's liability when the borrowed article is carried off is derived in a different way; *see* TB Bava Meẓi'a 94b.

226. A *mamzer* is the offspring of an incestuous or adulterous union that calls either for capital punishment to be imposed by a court or for extirpation by God (*karet*). Examples of such unions are one between a brother and sister or between a married woman and a man other than her husband.

a. The prohibition against marriage to a *mamzer* exists until the tenth generation, while the prohibition of marriage to a Moabite or Ammonite continues forever.
b. In the verse on Ammonites and Moabites, the words "even in the tenth generation" are superfluous, since the verse states "ever," and "ever" certainly includes the tenth generation.

The matter was interpreted as follows:[227]

> Since it is stated "ever," why does the verse also state "the tenth generation"? It is superfluous so as to enable us to analogize and to draw an inference through a *gezerah shavah* [the phrase "tenth generation" is unnecessary and superfluous so far as the plain meaning of the text is concerned, and it is therefore available for analogical use by way of *gezerah shavah*]. It is here stated "tenth generation" and it is stated above [in connection with the prohibition of marriage to a *mamzer*] "tenth generation." Just as "tenth generation" stated here [in regard to Ammonites and Moabites] means forever, "tenth generation" stated above [in connection with prohibition of marriage to a *mamzer*] also means "forever."

This is a *gezerah shavah* "open on one side." In one verse, concerning Ammonites and Moabites, the words "the tenth generation" are superfluous, and we therefore make an analogy between these words to the same words "the tenth generation" stated in connection with a *mamzer*. From this analogy, we deduce that just as in the case of Ammonites and Moabites the Torah has made clear that the words "the tenth generation" do not mean the specific number of ten, but rather a number of generations that will never end, so the meaning of the words "tenth generation" in connection with the prohibition against marrying a *mamzer* is not just ten generations but never. (This can be compared to a man who tells his friend: "Even if you ask me one hundred times, I will not give it to you," where the intent is not that on the one-hundred-and-first request he will relent; the number mentioned is not precise but simply rhetorical.)

This method of interpretation, which reaches halakhic conclusions by analogy based solely on similarity of language without regard to similarity of content, is likely at times to produce comparisons and analogies lacking any logical basis and thus to lead to strange and bizarre halakhic conclusions.[228] To prevent such results, Talmudic tradition established a general

227. *Sifrei,* Deuteronomy, Ki Teẓe, sec. 249 (pp. 275–276); *see* Finkelstein's comment, *ad loc.*, as to how the beginning of the passage should read.

228. *See* examples in TJ Pesaḥim 6:1, 39a (6:1, 33a).

principle that "no one may employ a *gezerah shavah* on his own authority"; a halakhic authority may use this method of interpretation only if he has received a tradition from his teacher that a particular word or phrase is appropriate for interpretation by way of *gezerah shavah*.[229] Without such a tradition he may not employ a *gezerah shavah*[230] on his own.[231]

D. Application of a General Principle (*Binyan Av*)

An additional analogical canon is "application of a general principle." This canon, as expressed in the canons of R. Ishmael, is divided into two parts: a general principle derived from one verse, and a general principle derived from two verses. Halakhic literature indicates that the use of this canon was further broadened to include general principles derived from three and even four verses.[232]

The approach of this canon is to make an analogy and draw conclusions from a single subject or from a common denominator of a number of similar subjects. The text out of which the conclusion is drawn is the *av* ("father" or premise) and the conclusion "built" on the premise is the *binyan* ("structure" or inference).

229. *Id.*; TB Pesaḥim 66a; Niddah 19b; *see also* Rashi, Niddah 19b, s.v. Ein adam: "No one may employ a *gezerah shavah* on his own authority. He must have received it from his teacher as a *halakhah le-Moshe mi-Sinai* (law given to Moses at Sinai), because the verse may be needed for some other purpose." *See also* Rashi, Sukkah 11b, s.v. Lo yalfeinan, and Sanhedrin 16a, s.v. Davar davar.

230. *See* Naḥmanides' commentary on Maimonides' *Sefer ha-Miẓvot*, Shoresh 2:

> For a *gezerah shavah*, an explicit tradition is required, because there is no end to what a person can do with it—one can contradict all the laws of the Torah through it. For words are repeated in the Torah many times, and no large book can possibly consist of words never used more than once. This was explained in the Talmud: one may employ a *kal va-ḥomer* on his own authority, but may not employ a *gezerah shavah* on his own authority. He must have received it as a tradition from his teacher.

See also ET, V, pp. 546–564, s.v. Gezerah shavah; S. Federbush, *Bi-Netivot ha-Talmud* [In the Pathways of the Talmud], 1957, pp. 118ff.

231. Rashi (Sanhedrin 73a, s.v. Hekkeisha hu, and Sukkah 31a, s.v. Lo makshinan) implies that even for the other canons, except the *kal va-ḥomer*, a tradition is required; *Tosafot*, Sukkah 31a, s.v. Ve-Ri savar lo makshinan, questions the validity of that view.

232. Hillel's canons include one called "[inference from] a similar case in a different place" that is similar to the one known in the Talmud as *mah maẓinu* ("just as we find"). Neither these canons, nor the canon known in the Talmud as *mah ha-ẓad* ("just as the common denominator"), is expressly included in R. Ishmael's list because in substance and content they are similar to the *binyan av* (application of a general principle) canon, under which R. Ishmael subsumed them all. *See* ET, IV, pp. 1–12, s.v. Binyan av; M. Ostrowsky, *Mavo la-Talmud*, pp. 103–106, 128–138.

1. APPLICATION OF A GENERAL PRINCIPLE DERIVED FROM A SINGLE VERSE[233]

Deuteronomy 19:15 states:

> A single witness [lit. "one witness"] may not validate against a person any guilt or blame for any offense that may be committed; a case can be valid only on the testimony of two witnesses or more [lit. "two witnesses or three witnesses"].

A *baraita* expounds:[234]

> It was taught: If it had stated "a witness may not validate," would I not know that it refers to one witness? Why then does Scripture state "one witness"? We deduce a general principle that in every verse that refers simply to "witness," the reference is to two unless Scripture specifies "one."

According to this *baraita,* we deduce from Deuteronomy 19:15 the principle that in Biblical terminology the word "witness," even in the singular, unless qualified by the adjective "one," does not refer to one person but to one evidentiary unit, which consists of two witnesses. Therefore, whenever the Torah uses the term "witness" it means an evidentiary unit—two witnesses; where Scripture intends to refer to one individual, it specifically says "one witness."[235]

This principle has provided the interpretation of many important passages in which the Torah uses the unqualified term "witness."[236]

2. APPLICATION OF A GENERAL PRINCIPLE DERIVED FROM TWO VERSES

Exodus 21:26–27 states:

> When a man strikes the eye of his slave, male or female, and destroys it, he shall let him go free on account of his eye. If he knocks out the tooth of his slave, male or female, he shall let him go free on account of his tooth.

233. For the meaning of "from a single verse," *see* ET, IV, pp. 1–12, particularly pp. 3–4, s.v. Binyan av.

234. TB Sanhedrin 30a; Sotah 2a/b; *Sifrei,* Numbers, secs. 7, 161; *Tosefta* Shevu'ot 3:8, TJ Shevu'ot 4:1, 19a/b (4:1, 35b/c).

235. Other verses are also thus interpreted: *e.g.,* Exodus 20:13 ("You shall not bear false witness against your neighbor." "False witness" is interpreted to mean "false testimony," *i.e.,* testimony by an evidentiary unit of at least two witnesses); Deuteronomy 31:21 ("Then this poem shall confront them as a witness [*le-ed*]." "As a witness" is understood to mean "as testimony").

236. For example, the verse concerning a wife suspected of infidelity (Numbers 5:13), "And she keeps secret the fact that she has defiled herself . . . and there is no witness . . . ," is interpreted to mean that there are not two witnesses to her defilement; if there is only one witness, she does not undergo the ordeal of drinking the bitter waters. *See* TB Sotah 2a/b.

With this law, the Torah deterred maltreatment of slaves on the part of their masters. These verses were interpreted as follows:[237]

> It would seem that the law should apply solely to a tooth and an eye [which are the only bodily parts mentioned in the Torah passage]. How do we know about other limbs and organs (*roshei evarim*)? [*I.e.*, how do we know that if a slave is injured in some other limb or organ he will then also be set free?] You draw an inference and deduce a general principle from both of the bodily parts that are mentioned: A tooth is different from an eye, and an eye differs from a tooth [each one of these parts of the body has its unique characteristics, so that if Scripture had mentioned, for example, only a tooth, we should not apply the same rule to an eye]. Their common denominator is that they are visible bodily parts that have suffered intentionally inflicted permanent injury, and they do not regenerate; in such case, the slave is set free. Similarly, in the case of all bodily parts that do not grow back again, the slave is set free.

From two verses—destruction of an eye and the knocking out of a tooth—we construct a common denominator, which is that they are bodily parts that cannot regenerate. We thus create a legal principle that considerably broadens what is explicitly stated in the Torah. Such bodily parts, as reckoned by the Sages, totaled twenty-four, and included, among others, fingertips, toes, tips of the ears, and tip of the nose; injury to any of them gives a slave his freedom.[238]

3. APPLICATION OF A GENERAL PRINCIPLE DERIVED FROM THREE VERSES

Numbers chapter 35 discusses the laws of intentional and unintentional homicide. In connection with intentional murder it states, *inter alia*:[239]

> Anyone . . . who strikes another with an iron object so that death results is a murderer; the murderer must be put to death. If he struck him with a stone tool [lit. "stone of the hand"] that could cause death, and death resulted, he is a murderer; the murderer must be put to death. Similarly, if the object with which he struck him was a wooden tool [lit. "wooden implement of the hand"] that could cause death, and death resulted, he is a murderer; the murderer must be put to death.

237. *Mekhilta de-R. Ishmael,* Mishpatim, Tractate De-Nezikin, sec. 9 (pp. 279–280).

238. TB Kiddushin 25a; *see also id.* 24b to the effect that this matter is derived from "a generalization followed by a specification that is in turn followed by a generalization" (*kelal u-ferat u-khelal*).

239. Numbers 35:16–18.

We learn from these three verses the law of murder in regard to three different dangerous weapons: iron, stone, and wood. There is no reference in this section or in any other place to the law of one who kills with any weapon other than the three specified here.

The problem was solved by the Sages through interpretation:[240]

> Since it states: "Anyone . . . who strikes another with an iron object so that death results," and "If he struck him with a stone tool" or with "a wooden tool," we might conclude that he is guilty only if he kills him with these. How do we know that it applies to any other object? We deduce a general principle from the three of them. Stone is different from wood, wood is different from stone, and neither is the same as an instrument of iron, which differs from both of them [each one of the three materials has unique characteristics]. The common denominator of the three is that they are able to kill. [The three implements mentioned are the basis of an inference that the rule applies to any object that may deal a lethal blow. With regard to wood and stone, it is specifically stated "that could cause death." This additional phrase is not used with regard to iron; but it goes without saying, since an instrument of iron is the most dangerous of the three, and "any iron instrument can kill"—see Sanhedrin 76b and Rashi to Numbers 35:16.] And just as the blood avenger is commanded to kill a murderer who has killed with any object made of these three materials, so the blood avenger must put to death anyone who has committed homicide with any implement that may be deadly.[241]

The rule as to the characteristics that an instrument used in a homicide must possess in order that the killer be guilty of murder is arrived at by constructing a general principle out of the three illustrations that the Torah gives in dealing with the law of murder. Each example—iron, stone, and wood—differs from the others. However, there is a feature common to all three, namely, that all of them can be deadly; and anyone who uses them for the purpose of killing is guilty of murder and is subject to capital punishment. It follows from this that anyone who intentionally commits homicide by means of any implement that can be deadly is a murderer and is subject to capital punishment.

4. APPLICATION OF A GENERAL PRINCIPLE DERIVED FROM FOUR VERSES

Exodus chapters 21 and 22 discuss the liability of one whose property has caused damage. In this section of the Torah, the four primary categories

240. *Sifrei*, Numbers, Mas'ei, sec. 160 (p. 218).

241. According to Biblical law, when it is clear that murder was committed deliberately, the execution of the judgment against the murderer is entrusted to the blood-avenger; *see* Numbers 35:19, 21. However, if the killing was unintentional, the killer is allowed to flee to one of the cities of refuge; and there the blood-avenger may not injure him (*id.* 35:22–25).

of causes of damage (*avot nezikin*) are listed. The first is "ox," which injures by goring or ramming;[242] the second is "pit" (uncovered or dug), into which an ox or an ass may fall;[243] the third is "grazing animal," which eats and destroys in fields belonging to others;[244] and the fourth is "fire," which, after being lit, spreads and causes damage to the property of others.[245]

The question naturally arose: What is the law if damage was caused by property in a manner not among the four categories specifically mentioned in the Torah?

This is the response given to this question:[246]

> There are four primary categories of causes of damage: the ox, the pit, the grazing animal,[247] and fire. The ox is different from the grazing animal, and the grazing animal differs from the ox. [In the case of an ox, in which the horn of a goring ox causes damage, there is a difference between the liability of the owner where the ox is "innocuous" (Hebrew *tam*—has gored not more than twice before) and where it "has given forewarning" (Hebrew *mu'ad*—has gored three times previously). In the case of an "innocuous" ox, the owner is liable for only half the damage, but the owner of an ox that "has given forewarning" is fully liable. In the case of grazing, *i.e.*, damage caused by an animal eating in the fields with its teeth, forewarning is considered as having been given by the very nature of the animal; and the owner of the animal must pay full compensation even when the animal causes damage for the first time.]
>
> Both the goring and grazing animal are living creatures, and are thereby different from fire, which is not a living creature; and all of these [*i.e.*, the ox, the grazing animal, and fire] are mobile and cause damage, and are thereby different from the pit, which is stationary [and the victim comes to it].
>
> The common denominator of all of them [the four primary categories of causes of damage] is that their nature is to cause damage, that the person responsible for them must prevent such damage, and that if such damage occurs, he must pay compensation for the damages out of the best of his land [*i.e.*, from his most valuable property].

From these four verses—relating to the ox, the pit, the grazing animal, and fire—we create a common denominator, namely, anything that is by

242. Exodus 21:28–32, 35–36.
243. *Id.* 21:33–34.
244. *Id.* 22:4.
245. *Id.* 22:5.
246. M Bava Kamma 1:1.
247. The Hebrew for the third primary cause of damage (the grazing animal) is *ha-mav'eh*. The Aramaic *ba'ah*, which is the root of *mav'eh* (the "b" and "v" are different forms of the letter *bet*), means the same as the Hebrew *ba'or*, *i.e.*, to consume, as in Exodus 22:4: "When a man lets his livestock loose (*shillaḥ et be'iro*) to graze (*u-vi'er*) in another's land, and so allows a field or a vineyard to be grazed bare (*yav'er*), . . . he must make restitution."

nature likely to cause damage. The person responsible must take precautions to prevent such damage, and if he fails to do so, he must pay compensation. The Sages deduced from this the general principle of Jewish law that if anything is by its nature likely to cause damage, the owner has the responsibility of guarding against such damage, even if the cause of the damage is not one of the four categories specified in the Torah, and if such damage occurs, the owner is liable to pay compensation.

E. Order of Priority in the Use of the Analogical Canons

There is an order of priority in use of the four canons of interpretation that we have just discussed. The highest ranking canon is the Scriptural analogy. An analogy that the Torah itself makes between two matters ranks higher than any other canon of interpretation; it is as if the rule had been stated explicitly in the Torah.[248] The second-ranking canon is *gezerah shavah,* the inference from the similarity of words or phrases, because one may make such inference only if he has received it as a tradition from his teacher.[249] Third in order of importance is the canon of inference *a fortiori,* which, as we have seen, is rooted in the Torah itself.[250] Fourth in order of rank is *binyan av,* the canon of the application of a general principle.[251]

IX. RESTRICTIVE INTERPRETATION

Just as interpretation served to expand the scope of the *Halakhah* by adding new laws, it also at times restricted, in greater or lesser measure, the scope of a particular law by what is called "restrictive interpretation." Examples are scattered throughout Talmudic literature; we cite a few here.

248. TB Sanhedrin 73a and Rashi, *ad loc.,* s.v. Hekkeisha hu; Zevaḥim 48a; *see* ET, X, pp. 557–575, s.v. Hekkesh (at p. 572).

249. TB Pesaḥim 66a, and *see* Rashi, *ad loc.,* s.v. Ve-khi me'aḥar de-gamiri; ET, V, p. 561, s.v. Gezerah shavah. *But see Tosefta* Sanhedrin 7:7 (if a question by a disciple in the Sanhedrin is based on a *kal va-ḥomer* and another question is based on a *gezerah shavah,* the question based on the *kal va-ḥomer* is responded to).

250. *See also* ET, IV, p. 11, s.v. Binyan av.

251. Certain restrictions, either grounded in logic generally or stemming from concerns about the validity of particular types of analogical reasoning, were prescribed in connection with the analogical canons: *e.g.,* the rule that "one may not derive the possible from the impossible" (*see* ET, I, pp. 283–284); the rule "Make the inference from it and leave it in place" (*Dan minah ve-okei ve-atra, i.e.,* only the basic principle is inferred from the premise, but the details are the rules of the case to which the inference is to be applied); and the rule "Make the inference from it and from it" (*Dan minah u-minah, i.e.,* both the basic principle and the details are inferred from the premise). As to the latter two rules, *see* ET, VII, pp. 235–238.

A. Acceptance of Proselytes from National Groups with Whom Marriage Was Forbidden

Deuteronomy 23:4–7 states:

> No Ammonite or Moabite shall be admitted into the congregation of the Lord; none of their descendants, even in the tenth generation, shall ever be admitted into the congregation of the Lord, because they did not meet you with food and water on your journey after you left Egypt, and because they hired Balaam, the son of Beor, from Pethor of Aram-naharaim, to curse you. But the Lord your God refused to heed Balaam; instead, the Lord your God turned the curse into a blessing for you, for the Lord your God loves you. You shall never concern yourself with their welfare or benefit as long as you live.

Nevertheless, the Mishnah says:

> "Ammonite or Moabite"—[they] are forbidden and the prohibition is forever. But their women are permitted immediately.[252]

Thus, only males, even if they convert, are forbidden to marry into the Israelite community, but females who convert are permitted to marry into the Israelite community immediately.

What is the source of this fundamental distinction? We find the answer to this in the following interpretation:[253]

> "No Ammonite or Moabite shall be admitted into the congregation of the Lord." Scripture speaks of males and not females: "Ammonite," but not Ammonitess; "Moabite," but not Moabitess. This is the view of R. Judah. The Sages say:[254] "Because they did not meet you with food and water." Who comes forward to approach a traveler? Men, not women.

Restricting the prohibition to males was thus arrived at through two methods of interpretation: (a) the method of R. Judah, *i.e.*, precise grammatical definition of the word "Ammonite" (a masculine noun in the Hebrew) as intending to denote only males and not females;[255] and (b) the method of the Sages, namely, interpreting "the logic of Scripture,"[256] *i.e.*,

252. M Yevamot 8:3.

253. *Sifrei*, Deuteronomy, Ki Teẓe, sec. 249 (p. 277); TB Yevamot 77a, and other sources.

254. TB Yevamot 77a reads: "R. Simeon says." *See infra* n. 256.

255. *See also* TB Yevamot 76b (where the question is raised, Why are women not excluded from the prohibitions relating to *mamzerim*, Egyptians, and others, which are also stated in the masculine?); M Yevamot 8:3; *Sifrei*, *supra* n. 253. *See also supra* pp. 322–323, pointing out that the whole Torah is written in the masculine, but its laws apply also nonetheless to women.

256. *See supra* pp. 295–296, pointing out that this second method was R. Simeon's. *See also supra* n. 254, pointing out that, according to the reading in TB Yevamot, the opinion there expressed (based on the logic of the verse) is also R. Simeon's.

the Torah explained the prohibition as being based on the Ammonites' failure to meet the children of Israel with food and water. This rationale applied only to men, who would have been the ones to come forward and bring food and water, but not to women, because it was not womanly to come out and do such a thing.[257]

The Talmud directs us to the background of this law.[258] The Book of Samuel tells of the conversation between King Saul and Abner, the commander of the army:

> When Saul saw David going out to assault the Philistine, he asked his army commander, Abner: "Whose son is that boy, Abner?" And Abner replied: "By your life, Majesty, I do not know."[259]

Afterward Abner brought David to Saul, and David responded to Saul's question:

> [I am] the son of your servant Jesse the Bethlehemite.[260]

The Sages saw this conversation that took place in the setting of David's victory over Goliath as being in the nature of a conference of Saul and his close advisers on the possibility of David's becoming king of Israel in the future. Doeg the Edomite, David's enemy,[261] also participated in this conference, and the Sages attributed to him a basic objection to David's right to become king:

> Before you ask whether or not he is worthy of becoming king, you should ask whether he can be a member of the Israelite community. Why so? Because he is a descendant of Ruth the Moabitess.

Doeg the Edomite thus contended that it was unnecessary to investigate whether David had the personal qualities that would make him worthy to be the king of Israel, because David was descended from a Moabitess, and the Moabites are forbidden to enter the Lord's congregation forever. To this, Abner responded that the law applies to an "'Ammonite' [masculine form], but not an Ammonitess, to a 'Moabite' but not a Moabitess."

257. The beginning of the discussion (TB Yevamot 76b) raised a question about this reason too: "Should not the men have come forward to approach the men and the women to approach the women?" The answer was given (*id.* 77a) that women would not come forward even for that.

258. TB Yevamot 76b–77a.

259. I Samuel 17:55.

260. *Id.* 17:58.

261. *See id.* 21:8ff., 22:9ff; Psalms 52.

Later in the Talmudic discussion, it is stated that Amasa[262] also took part in the discussion and expressed the same view with great asperity:

> Whoever does not heed this law should be cut through by the sword! I have the tradition from the court of Samuel of Ramah: "'Ammonite,' but not Ammonitess; 'Moabite,' but not Moabitess."

It was the tribunal of Samuel, who crowned David as king of Israel,[263] that interpreted the verse prohibiting Moabites from being admitted into the community of Israel as applying only to males and not females.[264] Consequently, Ruth the Moabitess was permitted to marry into the Jewish community, and there was therefore no defect in David's lineage.[265]

It is instructive to review the tradition of the Sages as to how in the course of time even Ammonite males were permitted to marry into the Jewish people. This permission was at first the subject of a dispute among the Sages in the generation of Rabban Gamaliel of Yavneh:[266]

> On that day,[267] Judah, an Ammonite proselyte, came and stood before them in the academy. He said to them: "May I become admitted into the congregation?"
>
> Rabban Gamaliel told him: "You may not"; R. Joshua told him: "You may."
>
> Rabban Gamaliel said to him: "Scripture states [Deuteronomy 23:4]: 'No Ammonite or Moabite shall be admitted into the congregation of the Lord . . . even in the tenth generation.'"
>
> R. Joshua responded: "But are Ammonites and Moabites in their original location? Has not Sennacherib, King of Assyria, come upon them and

262. II Samuel 17:25.

263. I Samuel 16:13.

264. Maimonides, *MT,* Issurei Bi'ah 12:18, calls this lenient ruling "a law given to Moses at Sinai," perhaps because it is attributed to the court of the prophet Samuel of Ramah and is thus a clear, undisputed law, as though it had been given to Moses at Sinai. *See supra* pp. 205–206 for the two meanings of "given to Moses at Sinai."

265. *See also* TB Yevamot 77a:

> Rava made this exegesis: What does "You have undone the cords that bound me" mean? [Psalms 116:16; the beginning of the verse, "O Lord, I am Your servant, the son of Your maidservant," suggests an association with David's mother.] David said before the Holy One, blessed be He: "Master of the universe, the two cords [the Hebrew term refers to the straps binding the yoke on oxen] that were on me You have loosened [by the exemption of females from the prohibitions]—Ruth the Moabitess and Na'amah the Ammonitess [who was the mother of Rehoboam]."

266. M Yadayim 4:4; *Tosefta* Yadayim 2:17–18; TB Berakhot 28a. Our quotation follows the text of the Mishnah.

267. The day when R. Eleazar b. Azariah was installed as head of the academy following the dispute between Rabban Gamaliel and his colleagues. For details of the incident, *see* TB Berakhot 27b–28a.

> mixed together all the nations, as is stated [Isaiah 10:13]: 'I have erased the borders of peoples, I have plundered their treasures, even exiled their vast populations'?"
>
> Rabban Gamaliel said to him: "But does not Scripture state [Jeremiah 49:6], 'But afterward I will restore the fortunes of the Ammonites,' thus indicating that they [the Ammonites] have returned [to their original location]?"
>
> R. Joshua responded: "But does not Scripture state [Amos 9:14], 'I will restore my people Israel [and Judah back from captivity]'? Still they have not yet returned [and thus the Ammonites, too, of whom it is stated: 'I will restore the(ir) fortunes,' have likewise not yet returned to their original location]."

This halakhic-historical debate was concluded with the acceptance of the viewpoint of R. Joshua:

> Judah, the Ammonite proselyte, said to them: "What is my status?" They responded: "You have already heard from the elder—you are eligible to be admitted into the congregation."[268]

Moreover, proselytes from other nations originally forbidden to marry into the Jewish community and then not yet eligible to do so[269] were later declared eligible,[270] and the *Halakhah* was settled as follows:[271]

> When Sennacherib, King of Assyria, came, he mixed together all the nations, obliterated their distinctiveness, and exiled them from their original locations. The Egyptians who today inhabit the land of Egypt are not the same people as the original Egyptians, and the same applies to the Edomites in the land of Edom. Since the four national groups who were prohibited have become intermingled among all the nations of the world who are eligible, all are now eligible, as the presumption is that whoever among them wishes to convert is a member of the majority. Therefore, any proselyte anywhere who presently wishes to convert—whether Edomite, Egyptian, Ammonite, Moabite, or Ethiopian, or from any other nation, and whether male or female—is immediately eligible to be admitted into the community of Israel.[272]

268. *Tosefta* Yadayim 2:18; similarly in M Yadayim 4:4: "They declared him eligible to be admitted into the congregation."

269. *Tosefta* Yadayim 2:18, concerning an Egyptian.

270. *Tosefta* Kiddushin 5:4.

271. Maimonides, *MT,* Issurei Bi'ah 12:25.

272. For other opinions on this matter, *see* Sh. Ar. EH 4:10; *see also* S. Lieberman, *Tosefet Rishonim,* on the above cited paragraphs of *Tosefta* Kiddushin (II, p. 88) and Yadayim (IV, pp. 158–159).

B. The Rebellious Son

Sometimes, restrictive interpretation was employed so drastically that in certain cases it rendered the law a completely dead letter in actual practice. We examine two illustrations.

Deuteronomy 21:18–21 states:

> If a man has a wayward and defiant [trad. "stubborn and rebellious"] son, who does not heed his father or his mother and does not obey them even after they discipline him, his father and his mother shall take hold of him and bring him out to the elders of his town at the public place of his community. They shall say to the elders of his town, "This son of ours is disloyal and defiant; he does not heed us. He is a glutton and a drunkard." Thereupon, the men of his town shall stone him to death. Thus, you will sweep out evil from your midst: all Israel will hear and be afraid.

In this section, the Torah limited the absolute life-and-death power of the father, the head of the family, over his son—a power widely known and accepted in the laws of ancient nations. It transferred the decision-making power over the stubborn and rebellious son to the judges of the locality, the elders of the town. The Sages, through interpretation, further restricted the possibility of carrying out the death penalty against such a son to the point where they made it completely impossible in actual practice to carry out the law stated in this section.

1. HALAKHIC INTERPRETATION WITH REGARD TO THE SON

> "If a man has a . . . son"—a son and not a daughter, a son [*i.e.*, a boy] and not a[n adult] man. A minor is exempt, as he has not reached the age of responsibility for [fulfilling] the commandments.[273]

The passage therefore applies neither to a minor under the age of thirteen nor to one who is already an adult but to "a son who is near to adulthood,"[274] and the *amoraim* therefore concluded that "the time during which the law of the stubborn and rebellious son applies is only three months."[275] Moreover, if a decision had not yet been made in his case by the time the three-month period expired, the son was exempted from punishment.[276]

> If he ate any food but not meat, if he drank any drink but not wine—he does not become a stubborn and rebellious son until he eats meat *and* drinks wine,

273. *Sifrei*, Deuteronomy, Ki Teẓe, sec. 218 (pp. 250–251); M Sanhedrin 8:1.
274. TB Sanhedrin 68b; *see* Maimonides, *MT*, Mamrim 7:5–6.
275. TB Sanhedrin 69a.
276. M Sanhedrin 8:4; Maimonides, *MT*, Mamrim 7:7, 9.

> as it is stated: "He is a glutton and a drunkard." Even though there is no proof for this interpretation, it is suggested in the verse [Proverbs 23:20]: "Do not be of those who are drunk from wine or glut themselves on meat."[277]
>
> **2. HALAKHIC INTERPRETATION WITH REGARD TO THE PARENTS**
>
> "His father and his mother shall take hold of him." This teaches that he is not guilty unless he has a father and mother.[278] If one of them [of the parents] was maimed, lame, mute, blind, or deaf, he cannot become a stubborn and rebellious son, as is stated: "His father and his mother shall take hold of him"—thus, they cannot be maimed; "and bring him out"—thus, they cannot be lame; "they shall say"—thus, they cannot be mute; "this son of ours"—thus, they cannot be blind; "he does not heed us"—thus, they cannot be deaf.[279]

The most extreme of all is the interpretation by R. Judah:

> R. Judah says: If his father and his mother are not the same in voice, appearance, and height, he cannot become a stubborn and rebellious son. What is the reason for this? Scripture states: "He does not heed us" [lit. "heed our voice"]. Since the voices must be the same [as the words "our voice" are interpreted to mean that the voices of the mother and father are equivalent and identical], their appearance and height must also be the same.[280]

A tannaitic tradition states the inescapable conclusion from these legal interpretations:

> The law of the rebellious son was never and will never be applied in practice. Why was it written? To tell us, "Study and you will be rewarded."[281]

277. M Sanhedrin 8:2.
278. *Sifrei,* Deuteronomy, Ki Teẓe, sec. 219 (p. 252).
279. *Id.;* M Sanhedrin 8:4.
280. TB Sanhedrin 71a.
281. *Tosefta* Sanhedrin 11:6; TB Sanhedrin 71a. In fact, this section of the Torah did serve as an admonition to parents and educators in various periods. *See, e.g.,* the comment of Samuel Edels (Maharsha, Poland, 1555–1631), in his novellae to this passage of the Talmud:

> Why then was it written? So that his father and mother should study it . . . and thus they will reprove and chastise their children, and for that they will be rewarded, as it has been said, "What is the merit of these women? It is that they rear their sons to [engage in] Torah study" (TB Berakhot 17a; *see also* Sotah 21a). But nowadays people pay no attention to this and each one protects his son . . . and does not reprove him. Thus, the youths spend most of their time neglecting the study of Torah, and it was said (TB Shabbat 119b): "Jerusalem was destroyed because the school children did not study Torah. . . ." Consider this carefully.

C. The Idolatrous Town

Deuteronomy 13:13–17 states:

> If you hear it said, of one of your towns that the Lord your God is giving you to dwell in, that some scoundrels from among you have gone and subverted the inhabitants of their town, saying, "Come let us worship other gods"—whom you have not experienced—you shall investigate and inquire and interrogate thoroughly. If it is true, the fact is established—that abhorrent thing was perpetrated in your midst—put the inhabitants of that town to the sword and put its cattle to the sword. Doom it and all that is in it to destruction: gather all its spoil into the open square, and burn the town and all its spoil entirely, for the Lord your God. And it shall remain an everlasting ruin, never to be rebuilt.

In this passage, the Torah sets forth the law concerning a town the majority of whose inhabitants were enticed and incited to idol worship. A town such as this is called "an idolatrous town" (lit. "a town that has been led astray"). A collective punishment is imposed against the town—the destruction of all its inhabitants and animals and the burning of all its property.

The possibility of actual existence of an idolatrous town was limited by various halakhic interpretations.

1. HOW AN IDOLATROUS TOWN COMES INTO BEING

"'If you hear it said of one of your towns.' But not if you are the source yourself,"[282] *i.e.*, only if the report comes to your attention unbidden should you investigate and inquire. But you are not to investigate on your own initiative whether such a town exists.

The same idea is expressed in the following halakhic interpretation:[283] "'If you hear it said of one of your towns.' But not by one who roams around to eavesdrop," *i.e.*, the judges are not to travel to different places to investigate and play detective.[284]

There is therefore no obligation to become inquisitors, to search out and to dig for something that may be improper; only if a report actually reaches you should you begin to investigate and inquire into the matter.

2. TOWNS THAT CANNOT BECOME IDOLATROUS TOWNS

"Jerusalem cannot have the status of an idolatrous town, for the Torah says 'your towns'—and Jerusalem was not allocated among the [Israelite]

282. *Midrash Tannaim*, Deuteronomy, ed. D.Z. Hoffmann, p. 66.

283. *Sifrei*, Deuteronomy, Re'eh, sec. 92 (p. 153).

284. The word *meẓotet* ("listens"), in the same sense of "eavesdrop," occurs in TJ Sotah 9:1, 40a (9:1, 23b). *See also Midrash Tannaim, supra* n. 282; Hoffmann, *Commentary on Deuteronomy*, p. 201; *Sifrei, supra* n. 283.

tribes."[285] In contrast to the remainder of the Land of Israel, which was allocated among the Israelite tribes, Jerusalem was not so allocated, but belonged to the entire nation. It is therefore not included in the term "your towns."[286]

"'From among you'—and not from the border."[287] Thus, a town that is on the border cannot have the status of an idolatrous town—"Even a single town that is near the border should not be declared idolatrous, so that foreign nations would not be able to break into and destroy the Land of Israel."[288]

"'Of one of your towns.' A single town can have the status of an idolatrous town, but three towns cannot."[289] The reason is that "One may not declare three towns in the Land of Israel to be idolatrous towns, so that the Land of Israel will not be destroyed; but one or two towns can be so declared."[290]

The following interpretation restricts as tightly as any interpretation can the possibility that an idolatrous town could actually exist:

> R. Eliezer says: Every town that contains even one *mezuzah* [parchment scroll containing Biblical verses affixed to doorposts] cannot have the status of an idolatrous town, since it is written: "Burn the town and all its spoil entirely." This, however, is not possible where there is a *mezuzah*, for it is written: "You shall not do so to the Lord your God" [Deuteronomy 12:4].[291]

285. TB Bava Kamma 82b.

286. The exposition in *Sifrei*, Deuteronomy, Re'eh, sec. 92 (p. 154), is: "'To dwell in'—this excludes Jerusalem, which is not allotted for dwelling." *See also* Rabbenu Hillel's commentary to *Sifrei*, *ad loc.*, explaining "which is not allotted for dwelling" as meaning "was not included in the allocation [of the land] among the tribes but constituted a lodging-place for all Israel when they come on pilgrimage." *See also* Hoffmann, *Commentary on Deuteronomy*, p. 201.

287. *Sifrei*, Deuteronomy, Re'eh, sec. 93 (p. 154); TB Sanhedrin 16b, 111b.

288. *Tosefta* Sanhedrin 14:1; TB Sanhedrin 16b, where the reading is: "This is the view of R. Simeon, who interprets the logic of Scripture."

289. *Sifrei*, Deuteronomy, Re'eh, sec. 92 (p. 154).

290. *Tosefta* Sanhedrin 14:1; TB Sanhedrin 16b reads: "Because of *karḥah* [lit. baldness, *i.e.*, desolation]," which is another way of stating the same reason. *See also* Hoffmann, *Commentary on Deuteronomy*, *ad loc.*, for another reason: "When sin is too widespread, when there are so many [bad] examples to mislead, the transgression becomes permitted in the sight of the people, and therefore punishment should not be meted out. Those who transgress can no longer be accounted as willful and knowing violators."

291. TB Sanhedrin 71a, 113a (the quotation in our text follows the latter). Our translation of Deuteronomy 12:4 is literal. The 1985 JPS *Tanakh* has: "Do not worship the Lord your God in like manner."

See Rashi, Sanhedrin 71a, s.v. Va-afillu mezuzah aḥat: "Even one *mezuzah*, and how much more so one of the books of the Torah or one of the books of the Prophets in which God's name is written; to such we cannot apply [the verse] 'and burn the town and all its spoil.'"

Since it is forbidden to burn the *mezuzah* contained in the town, it is impossible to carry out the requirement of the verse to burn everything in the town, and it necessarily follows that the law of the idolatrous town cannot be applied to it.[292]

Indeed, there is a tradition of the Sages with regard to these restrictive interpretations:

> An idolatrous town never existed and never will exist. Why was it written? To tell us, "Study and you will be rewarded."[293]

D. Opposition to Drastically Restrictive Interpretation

At times, this propensity to use exegesis to make it impossible to carry out a particular law in practice met opposition from some Sages. There is an interesting debate in this connection with regard to the laws of ritual purity and impurity. Various laws are set forth in the Torah on the subject of impurity resulting from a bodily issue (*zav*),[294] and the Mishnaic Order of *Tohorot* (Purities) contains a specific tractate devoted to this subject, entitled *Zavim* (Bodily Issues).

The Mishnah enumerates seven contingencies that should be kept in mind in examining an individual who has had a bodily issue; if it is ascertained that one of these seven contingencies occurred before the person saw the issue, he is not impure, because it is presumed that the issue resulted from such occurrence. Among the seven contingencies listed is "eating and drinking."[295]

In the course of time, the Sages disagreed as to the scope of this term, "eating and drinking." "R. Eliezer b. Phinehas said in the name of R. Judah b. Bathyra: 'Milk, cheese, fatty meat, old wine, powdered beans, eggs, and pickles cause a bodily issue,'"[296] and if someone eats one of these and the issue comes soon thereafter, he is not impure. R. Akiva disputed this view: "R. Akiva holds: Even if he has eaten any kind of food, whether harmful or beneficial, or has drunk any kind of liquid";[297] *i.e.*, whatever food was eaten or liquid was drunk, we attribute the issue to that account, and he is not impure.

292. For further restrictive interpretations in regard to idolatrous towns, *see Sifrei*, Deuteronomy, Re'eh, sec. 93 (p. 154); TB Sanhedrin 16b, 111b.

293. *Tosefta* Sanhedrin 14:1; TB Sanhedrin 71a.

294. Leviticus 15:1–15.

295. M Zavim 2:2.

296. *Tosefta* Zavim 2:5; TB Yoma 18a.

297. M Zavim 2:2; *Tosefta* Zavim 2:5 has: "We attribute the issue to any type of food."

The Mishnah records the following debate between R. Akiva and the other Sages on this point:[298]

> They said to him [to R. Akiva]: "From now on there will never be impurity from a bodily issue!" He said to them: "You are not responsible to see that impure bodily issues exist!"

The Sages were saying to R. Akiva that according to his interpretation it would be almost impossible for impurity to arise from a bodily issue, since the issue would always be attributed to the person's having eaten or drunk before the issue was discovered.[299] However, this result did not daunt R. Akiva, who took the view that the Sages had no responsibility to make sure that impure issues actually exist: "If there will never be an impure bodily issue, why are you concerned? You were not charged with responsibility for seeing that impure bodily issues exist."[300]

The foregoing discussion of restrictive interpretation has included some far-reaching examples. In general, however, restrictive interpretation was not carried to such a point; it was limited to some specific detail of a particular law and did not render the entire law impossible to apply.[301]

298. M Zavim 2:2.

299. *See* Maimonides, *Commentary on the Mishnah, ad loc.* (ed. Kafaḥ, p. 668), as to when, according to R. Akiva, a case of *zav* is possible.

300. Obadiah Bertinoro, *Commentary on the Mishnah, ad loc.* This is an example of halakhic interpretation (*see infra* pp. 400ff.) and not Biblical exegesis. However, this interpretation contributed to depriving the law of bodily issues, which is explicitly set forth in the Torah, of virtually all practical relevance. *Cf. Shittah Mekubbeẓet,* Ketubbot 3a, s.v. Vekhen katav ha-Ra'ah z.l. talmido (ed. Ziyyoni, p. 49): "Rashi raised the objection that if this is so, *mamzerim* can be freed of taint [*i.e.,* by retroactive annulment of the marriages of their mothers]. . . . To which my teacher replied: 'It does not bother me that *mamzerim* can be freed of taint. Would that they be freed of taint. . . .'"

301. M Keritot 1:7 provides an interesting example of the employment of midrash to supply an urgent solution to a practical problem. The law is that a woman must bring a sacrifice for each birth and for each bodily issue she emits.

> Once in Jerusalem [doves became very expensive and] a pair of doves cost a golden *denar* [= twenty-five silver *denars*]. Rabban Simeon b. Gamaliel [the Elder, who lived at the end of the period of the Second Temple] said: By this Temple! I will not rest this night until their price is only one [silver] *denar!* He went into the court and taught [*limmed, i.e.,* expounded midrashically, *see supra* pp. 276, 288], "If a woman had five definite miscarriages or five bodily issues as to which there was no doubt, she need bring but one offering, and she may then eat of the animal-offerings, and she is not bound to offer anything further." On the same day the price of a pair of doves dropped to a quarter of a [silver] *denar* each.

The details of Rabban Simeon b. Gamaliel's exegesis have not survived, but the purpose it served is clear from the *mishnah.* Rashi's comment on the *mishnah* (TB Keritot 8a, s.v. Nikhnas le-vet din lilmod) is instructive: "Although he relaxed a law of the Torah, it was a time to act for the Lord, for otherwise they would have ceased bringing even one and would have eaten holy things in a state of impurity." Rabban Simeon b. Gamaliel's example also served as a precedent for the rabbis who stood fast against outrageous prices for sabbath

X. THE METHODS OF INTERPRETATION OF R. AKIVA AND R. ISHMAEL

As previously mentioned,[302] midrash reached its apogee in the time of R. Ishmael and R. Akiva. These two *tannaim* established large academies in which the study of exegetical interpretation occupied an important place, and these academies have left a wide-ranging and many-faceted literature of halakhic *midrashim.*[303]

The academies of R. Ishmael and R. Akiva developed two different schools of halakhic interpretation, following the differences in approach of their teachers, R. Neḥunya b. ha-Kanah and R. Nahum of Gimzo.[304] R. Ishmael and his school attempted to confine the methods of interpretation within the bounds of the legal and logical implications of the verse, whereas R. Akiva and his school expanded the methods of interpretation far beyond these limitations.

Often, the two schools did not disagree about the legal principle itself, but only about how to connect the principle with the Scriptural text. R. Ishmael connected the law with the text by means of the thirteen canons and the other methods of Biblical interpretation. R. Akiva connected the same law to Scripture by interpretations based on redundancy in expression and even by using the letter *vav* when it appears to be superfluous in the verse.

Thus, when R. Ishmael found it impossible to connect an existing law with a verse through interpretation, he would forgo such a connection; but R. Akiva would connect that law to Scripture by methods of interpretation based on redundancy of language and letters. There were even instances when R. Akiva and his school created *Halakhah* through these extravagant interpretive methods—a practice strongly opposed by R. Ishmael and his school.

A. The Principal Differences in the Methods of Interpretation by the Academies of R. Ishmael and R. Akiva

1. R. Ishmael and his academy laid down a principle of interpretation that "the Torah speaks in the language of ordinary people."[305] There are

---

fish in Moravia some 1700 years later; *see* Menahem Mendel Krochmal, *Resp. Ẓemaḥ Ẓedek* #28.

302. *See supra* pp. 316–317.

303. *See infra* pp. 1047–1049.

304. *See supra* p. 316.

305. *E.g.*, *Sifrei*, Numbers, Shelaḥ, sec. 112 (p. 121); TB Sanhedrin 64b; Keritot 11a. TJ Shabbat 19:2, 87b (19:2, 17a) has: "Repetitions of words [are not to be used as a basis for interpretation]; it is the style of the Torah to speak that way."

repetitions and redundancies in the narrative portions of Scripture for purposes of stress and emphasis, as in the words of Laban to Jacob: "Very well, you had to leave [lit. "go," which is said twice in the Hebrew—*halokh halakhta*], because you were longing [in the Hebrew, the word for "were longing" is also repeated—*nikhsof nikhsaftah*] for your father's house; but why did you steal my gods?"[306] This is the type of language people used in ordinary conversation.

R. Ishmael held that, by the same token, interpretation of the legal part of Scripture should not be based on repetitions or redundancies. For example, according to R. Ishmael, the repetition in the verse "she has not yet been redeemed"[307] (the Hebrew repeats the word "redeemed": *vehofdeh lo nifdatah*) does not call for an interpretation beyond the plain meaning, because "the Torah speaks in the language of ordinary people."

On the other hand, R. Akiva and his academy would find some interpretation for every redundancy, every repeated word, and even individual letters—"R. Akiva is the one who interprets the letter *vav*."[308]

2. According to R. Akiva and his academy, every Biblical use of the words *et* (the sign of the accusative case, placed before the direct object of a verb) or *gam* ("also," "moreover") indicates that the law is to be interpreted expansively, while the words *akh* ("however," "surely") or *rak* ("only," "but") indicate that the law is to be interpreted restrictively.[309] The extent to which R. Akiva carried his method of interpretation is shown by the following *baraita:*[310]

> It was taught: Simeon of Amsun and, according to some, Nehemiah of Amsun [this is Nahum of Gimzo, R. Akiva's teacher], interpreted every mention of the word *et* found in the Torah. When he reached the verse: "You shall revere the Lord your God" [in the Hebrew, the word *et* appears before "the Lord your God"] (Deuteronomy 6:13, 10:20) he withdrew [*i.e.*, he abandoned his approach and he halted his practice of expanding the law on the basis of the word *et*, for who besides God can be included in the commandment to revere Him?].
>
> His disciples said to him: "Master, what will happen to all of the words *et* that you interpreted?" He said to them: "Just as I was rewarded for inter-

306. Genesis 31:30. Another example is: "For in truth, I was kidnapped (*gunov gunavti*)," where "kidnapped" is repeated, *id.* 40:15.

307. Leviticus 19:20.

308. TB Yevamot 68b. *See also* Sanhedrin 51b, quoted *infra* in text accompanying n. 349; ET, VII, pp. 77–82, s.v. Dibberah Torah ki-leshon benei adam; *id.* at 158–160, s.v. Devarim ki-ketavam; ET, I, p. 316, s.v. Ein mikra yoẓe mi-dei peshuto.

309. Following R. Akiva's teacher, Nahum of Gimzo; *see supra* p. 316.

310. TB Bava Kamma 41b; Pesaḥim 22b.

preting them, so shall I be rewarded for withdrawing my interpretations."[311] Then R. Akiva came and interpreted (*limmed*):[312] "You shall revere *et* the Lord your God"—this means that you shall revere the Sages as well.

R. Akiva thus continued to interpret the word *et* even in this verse. Consistent with the principle "reverence for your teacher is like reverence of God,"[313] he interpreted the verse as comparing reverence for scholars to reverence for God. On the other hand, R. Ishmael and his academy did not interpret the words *et* and *gam* as being expansive, nor the words *akh* and *rak* as being restrictive.

3. Another important distinction between these two schools pertains to the group of canons of interpretation relating to generalization and specification. R. Ishmael interpreted these canons in the manner previously described.[314] However, R. Akiva, instead of "generalization and specification," adopted the approach of "inclusion and exclusion." R. Akiva's method broadens the scope of the legal conclusions to a much greater extent than R. Ishmael's method; this, too, is a continuation by each of the approach of his teacher.[315]

4. Another difference pertains to an important question of criminal law. There is a principle in Jewish law that "there is to be no punishment for any act not previously proscribed,"[316] *i.e.*, the Torah does not impose any punishment for a crime unless it has given a prior warning by declaring the act to be criminal. The law relating to forbidden sexual unions (*e.g.*, between son and mother, brother and sister, etc.) is an excellent example of the operation of this principle. Leviticus chapter 18 contains the admonitions against forbidden sexual unions, and Leviticus 20:10–21 prescribes the punishments for these transgressions.[317]

In light of this principle, R. Ishmael's view was that for each act not explicitly prohibited in the Torah but held to be prohibited as a consequence of one of the canons of Biblical interpretation (*e.g.*, inference *a fortiori*), the punishment for the act may not also be deduced through one of the canons

311. As much as if to say, "Until now I did well to interpret each *et*, but since I now realize that this *et* cannot be interpreted expansively, I abandon all the expansive interpretations of *et* that I have made up to now." *See* Rashi, Pesaḥim 22b, s.v. Et lo dareish.

312. The Hebrew *limmed* (lit. "he taught") means here "he expounded midrashically" or "interpreted." *See supra* n. 301 and pp. 276, 288.

313. M Avot 4:12; *see also* Rashi, Pesaḥim 22b, s.v. Lerabbot talmidei ḥakhamim.

314. *Supra* pp. 323–330.

315. *See supra* pp. 316–317 and sources cited there.

316. TB Yoma 81a; Zevaḥim 106b. *Cf.* the Latin maxim *nulla poena sine lege*.

317. *See Sifra*, Kedoshim, chs. 10–11 (pp. 92b–93a), for many examples; TB Makkot 5b: "We have learned of the punishment; from which verse [do we derive] the warning?" *See also* TB Yoma 81a.

because "liability to punishment cannot be based on an inference."[318] Or, as the Jerusalem Talmud puts it: "*Laws* may be deduced by means of an inference *a fortiori,* but *punishment* may not be deduced by means of such an inference."[319] On the other hand, R. Akiva took the contrary view that "punishments may be deduced by means of an inference,"[320] *i.e.,* punishment may be derived on the basis of an inference from one of the canons of interpretation when the punishment has not been explicitly prescribed in the Torah.

B. The Dispute Related Mainly to the Methods of Integrating the Law with Scripture, Not to the Substance of the Law

To understand the nature of these interpretive methods used by R. Akiva and his academy, which seem astonishing departures from the constraints of the meaning and substantive content of the Biblical text, we must refer again to the fundamental distinction between explicative exegesis and creative interpretation, on the one hand, and integrative interpretation, on the other.[321] As previously stated, from the beginnings of the *Halakhah,* integrative interpretation, which sought to connect existing law with the Scriptural text, functioned alongside creative interpretation, which created new law out of the Biblical verse. It is reasonable to assume that from the time of R. Neḥunya b. ha-Kanah and R. Nahum of Gimzo, and especially from the time of R. Ishmael and R. Akiva, the proportion of the corpus of Midrash that consisted of integrative interpretation became progressively greater.

The reason for this growing proportion of integrative interpretation was the massive development of the halakhic system. In addition to growing through interpretation, the *Halakhah* also continuously expanded through other legal sources, such as legislation, custom, actual incidents with legal implications, and legal reasoning. The Sages sought to connect these new laws (although not created by means of interpretation or exegesis) to Biblical verses, in order to make the laws easier to remember and to study, inasmuch as they were not written down, and in order to point up the interrelationship of the Oral Law and the Written Law.

As previously mentioned, this increase in the proportion of integrative interpretation had a decisive influence on the form and style of the exegesis. The interpreter who seeks to explain the Torah or to create new law out of the Torah must use an interpretive form constrained within the bounds of

318. TB Makkot 5b; *see also Tosefta* Shevu'ot 3:5.
319. TJ Yevamot 11:1, 62a (11:1, 11d); Avodah Zarah 5:12, 36b (5:12, 45b).
320. TB Sanhedrin 74a; Makkot 17b; Zevaḥim 106b.
321. *See supra* pp. 283–286.

the Biblical text and of logic, because the Biblical text is the source for the explanation or for the new law. On the other hand, the interpreter who seeks only to integrate an existing law with a Biblical verse enjoys a greater measure of freedom to depart from the plain meaning and the logical framework of the verse; it is sufficient if he supports the law by connecting it with the verse through an allusion, hint, or sign, in accordance with interpretive methodology accepted in the general culture of that time.[322]

The metaphorical and symbolic methods of interpretation developed by R. Nahum of Gimzo and by R. Akiva and his students were thus designed from the beginning to sustain and expand the methods of integrative interpretation connecting an already-existing law with Biblical texts. Indeed, in the majority of the disputes between R. Akiva and R. Ishmael, they disagreed not as to the substance of the law (which was known and accepted) but as to the manner and technique of connecting the law with Scripture. According to R. Akiva, one may find Scriptural support for existing law in any way possible; but according to R. Ishmael, in integrative as well as creative interpretation, the basis for connecting a law to a Biblical verse must be consistent with the logic and substantive content of the text.

The following is an example of a dispute between R. Ishmael and R. Akiva on the method of integrating a law with Scripture when the law itself was already in existence and well known:

The Mishnah states:[323] "If one throws a bill of divorcement to his wife while she is in her house or her courtyard, she is divorced." The Torah states: "He writes her a bill of divorcement and hands it to her" (lit. "gives it into her hand").[324] The law of the Mishnah, however, is that it is unnecessary actually to hand the document to the wife; a delivery is sufficient if the document is deposited on the wife's property, *i.e.*, her house or her courtyard.

How was this law deduced from the Scriptural verse? The reasoning was as follows:[325]

> "He writes . . . and hands it to her."[326] The requirement seems to be personal delivery. How do we know that it is also sufficient if it is deposited in her garden or courtyard? Scripture states: "he gives" and "he gives" [*i.e.*, the words "he gives" are stated twice in the same context, once in verse 1 and again in verse 3, and the repetition indicates that any type of delivery is per-

322. *See supra* p. 306 and n. 66, and the quotations there from I.M. Guttmann and S. Lieberman.

323. M Gittin 8:1.

324. Deuteronomy 24:1.

325. *Sifrei,* Deuteronomy, Ki Teẓe, sec. 269 (p. 290); TB Gittin 77a; TJ Gittin 8:1, 44a (8:1, 49b). Our quotation follows TJ. *See also infra* n. 327.

326. From Deuteronomy 24:1, quoted *supra* in text accompanying n. 324.

missible—not only putting it into the wife's hands but also depositing it in a place under her control].[327]

After giving this interpretation, the discussion in the Jerusalem Talmud continues:[328]

> Up to this point it is in harmony with R. Akiva. What about R. Ishmael? [*I.e.*, to this point the method of interpretation is R. Akiva's. How did R. Ishmael, who opposed this method and took the view that the Torah speaks in the language of ordinary people,[329] integrate this law with the Biblical verse?] R. Ishmael taught: The Torah states: "[Sihon]. . . , who had . . . taken all his land from his hand as far as the Arnon."[330] Did he [literally] take it from his hand? What, then, is the meaning of "his hand"? His control.

R. Ishmael explained the term "hand" in the verse "he . . . gives it into her hand" by analogy to a different passage in the Torah, about the war of Sihon against the king of Moab, where the term "hand" also appears. Just as in the account of the war of Sihon the meaning of "hand" is "control"—one does not capture land from anyone's physical hand but from his control—so in the case of a bill of divorcement the meaning of "he . . . gives it into her hand" is that he puts it under her control.

In this example, there was no dispute as to the correctness of the rule that actual delivery of a bill of divorcement into the wife's hand is unnecessary and that it is sufficient if the document is deposited on the wife's property. The difference of opinion related to the method of integrating this law with the Biblical text: R. Akiva did this by interpreting from a redundancy of language; R. Ishmael did it through a substantive interpretation of the term, by analogy to the meaning of this term in a different place in the Torah.

These differences of opinion between the two academies produced an additional effect: According to R. Akiva, we should take care to anchor every law in Scripture, even if this requires methods of interpretation going

327. In *Sifrei* and TB Gittin 77a, the text reads: "Scripture states: 'he gives'—in any fashion." Rashi (Gittin, *ad loc.*, s.v. Talmud lomar ve-natan mi-kol makom) explains: "Since it is not written, 'Into her hand shall he give it,' it implies [that] any sort of delivery [is sufficient]." The explanation in the body of our text follows the reading of TJ and the interpretations of *Korban ha-Edah* and *Penei Moshe* (s.vv. Talmud lomar ve-natan ve-natan), *ad loc. See also Torah Temimah* to Deuteronomy 24:1, subpar. 41.

328. TJ Gittin 8:1, 44a (8:1, 49b). *See* ed. Venice for a different reading.

329. *See supra* pp. 371–374.

330. Numbers 21:26: "Now Heshbon was the city of Sihon, king of the Amorites, who had fought against a former king of Moab and taken all his land from him [*mi-yado*, lit. "from his hand"] as far as the Arnon."

far beyond the meaning that the text will bear.[331] R. Ishmael, however, held that if a particular law cannot be integrated with Scripture in a logical manner, it is preferable for the law to stand independently on its own authority, even if it deviates from the plain meaning of the verse, inasmuch as *Halakhah* is fully authoritative whether it comes from tradition, legislation, or any other legal source.

The Sages emphasized this difference between the two schools of thought:

> R. Ishmael taught:[332] In three places the law overrides Scripture [*i.e.*, the law deviates from the plain meaning of the Torah], and in one place it overrides midrash [*i.e.*, it deviates from the conclusion that would follow from exegesis].
>
> The Torah refers to a "bill" [*sefer*, lit. "book" or "scroll"][333] of divorcement, but the accepted law is: anything which is detached. [A divorce is legally valid if written on any material—and not necessarily on the parchment of a book or scroll—as long as it is detached, in the sense of not being attached to the ground.][334]
>
> The Torah states: "He shall . . . cover it with earth."[335] The law is: with whatever produces vegetation.[336]
>
> The Torah states: "With an awl,"[337] but the law is: even with a wooden point, a thorn, or glass.
>
> In one place, the law is contrary to midrash. R. Ishmael taught: "On the seventh day he shall shave off all his hair[338] (a generalization)—of his head,

331. Except for the very few cases where it was simply impossible to integrate the law into Scripture. *See* Frankel, *Mishnah*, pp. 120–121.

332. TJ Kiddushin 1:2, 11b (1:2, 59d); TB Sotah 16a; *Midrash Tannaim*, Deuteronomy 24:1 (ed. Hoffmann, p. 154); *Mekhilta de-R. Ishmael*, Mishpatim, Tractate De-Nezikin, sec. 2 (p. 253). We have quoted the full text of TJ.

333. "He writes her a bill (*sefer*) of divorcement." Deuteronomy 24:1.

334. *See* Maimonides, *MT*, Gerushin, ch. 4.

335. Leviticus 17:10–14 prohibits the consumption of an animal's blood; only the flesh is permitted. Verse 13 establishes the obligation to cover the blood, and the Sages concluded that the blood of nondomesticated animals and fowl is required to be covered after slaughter. The verse reads: "And if any Israelite or any stranger who resides among them hunts down an animal or a bird that may be eaten, he shall pour out its blood and cover it with earth."

336. *E.g.*, even with linen waste, sawdust, or lime, etc. *See* Maimonides, *MT*, Sheḥitah 14:11.

337. The reference is to a Hebrew slave who says he loves his master and refuses to go free when his time comes. In that case, "you shall take an awl and put it through his ear . . . ." (Deuteronomy 15:17; similarly in Exodus 21:6: ". . . his master shall pierce his ear with an awl").

338. The reference is to the purification rites of a leper after he is cured (Leviticus 14:1–32). Verse 9 states: "On the seventh day he shall shave off all his hair—of his head, beard, and eyebrows. When he has shaved off all his hair, he shall wash his clothes and bathe his body in water; then he shall be clean."

beard, and eyebrows" (a specification). When the verse then states: "When he has shaved off all his hair," there is again a generalization. When a generalization is followed by a specification that is in turn followed by a generalization, one must be guided by what the specification implies.[339] Just as the specification involves places where hair is concentrated and clearly visible, the law should apply only to places where hair is concentrated and clearly visible,[340] yet the law is: he is to be shaved to look like a gourd.[341]

The *Halakhah* can therefore differ from and override both Scriptural language and inferences drawn from Scripture through one of the thirteen canons of Biblical interpretation—here, the canon of inference from a generalization followed by a specification that is in turn followed by a generalization. In all such instances, "R. Ishmael does not attempt to force the law into Scripture where the plain meaning of the verse is to the contrary. In such cases, he holds simply that it is 'the *Halakhah*,' and we accept it without proof from Scripture."[342]

Contrary to this approach of R. Ishmael and his school, the school of R. Akiva integrated all of the cited examples through Scriptural exegesis. With regard to the materials on which a bill of divorcement may be written:

A "bill" (*sefer*)—this would seem to require a scroll to be used. How do we know that even reeds, nutshells, olive tree leaves, and carob leaves can be used? Scripture states: "And he gives [it into her hand]"—this implies any kind of material.[343]

In connection with covering the blood, R. Akiva deduced the law from the same verse, Leviticus 17:13, by means of the exegetical rule of inclusion and exclusion.[344] With regard to the piercing of the slave's ear:

"And you shall take an awl"—how do we know that a thorn, a piece of glass, and the membrane of a stalk may also be used? Scripture states: "And you shall take." This includes anything that can be held in the hand.[345]

339. *See supra* pp. 326–327 for an explanation of this canon.

340. *I.e.*, in a visible place where there is a cluster of hairs.

341. *I.e.*, he is to shave all the hair on the entire body. *See* Maimonides, *MT*, Tum'at Ẓora'at 11:1.

342. Epstein, *Tannaim*, p. 536.

343. *Sifrei*, Deuteronomy, Ki Teẓe, sec. 269 (p. 289).

344. *Sifra*, Aḥarei Mot 11:10 (p. 84b).

345. *Sifrei*, Deuteronomy, Re'eh, sec. 122 (p. 180). The last sentence, "This includes anything that can be held in the hand," does not appear in *Sifrei*, but in TB Kiddushin 21b, after the quotation from *Sifrei*. According to TB Kiddushin, the deduction is not from the letter *vav* ("and") but from the entire word *ve-lakaḥta* ("and you shall take"), which is interpreted as encompassing anything that can be held in the hand. *See also* Epstein, *Tannaim*, pp. 535–536.

According to this approach, every law must be integrated with Scripture, even if the attempt is far-fetched and based only upon the vaguest hint that Scripture may be said to contain.

To summarize:

> The distinguishing feature of the interpretations of the School of R. Ishmael is their simplicity. They do not seek to circumvent the text in an effort to extract a law in any way possible, but they attempt to keep the exegesis close to the plain meaning of the text and do not base interpretation on any and all superfluities or redundancies.[346]

This applies to both creative and integrative interpretation. In contrast, R. Akiva and his academy used methods of interpretation that departed from the logic and plain meaning of the text, though this extreme approach was used mainly to integrate the law with Scripture:

> For R. Akiva, first and foremost, simply sought to connect accepted and well-known laws to Scripture and to strengthen and secure the links and interconnections between Scripture and the *Halakhah*.[347]

Although the midrashic approach based on redundancies, superfluous letters, and the like, was originally designed for integrative interpretation, and was chiefly used for that purpose, there were occasions when R. Akiva and his academy also used these methods of interpretation to create law from Scripture. These attempts provoked a sharp reaction from the Sages of R. Ishmael's school, as well as from other Sages.

The difference of opinion between R. Ishmael and R. Akiva on the law concerning a priest's married daughter who engages in harlotry is an instructive example.

Leviticus 21:9 states:

> And if the daughter of a priest defiles herself through harlotry, it is her father whom she defiles [lit. "profanes"]; she shall be put to the fire.

It was agreed that the verse does not refer to a priest's daughter who is neither married nor betrothed. R. Akiva's view is that the verse refers to a priest's daughter who is married, as well as to one who is betrothed.[348] According to R. Ishmael, on the other hand, the verse speaks only of a betrothed daughter; the punishment of a priest's married daughter is stran-

346. Epstein, *Tannaim*, pp. 535–536; and *see* pp. 537ff., pointing out that the disciples of R. Ishmael did not always follow the path of their teacher or the system of his academy.

347. Frankel, *Mishnah*, p. 120.

348. According to the original law, a period of time elapsed between betrothal, effected by giving the woman money (nowadays, a ring), and the nuptials, effected by entry under the *ḥuppah* (wedding canopy). *See infra* p. 974 n. 104.

gulation, which is the penalty for *any* married woman who has committed adultery. During the course of the discussion,[349] the following debate between R. Ishmael and R. Akiva is recorded:

> R. Akiva said to him: "Ishmael, my brother, I interpret the words '*and* if the daughter'" [*i.e.*, the letter *vav* ("and") contained in "*and* if the daughter" serves to include the married daughter of a priest]. R. Ishmael said to R. Akiva: "Should we put her to the fire because you interpret [the words] '*and* if the daughter'?"

Here, R. Akiva attempted to create new law through an interpretation based upon a superfluous letter, while R. Ishmael, together with most Sages,[350] strongly opposed reaching legal conclusions by way of this far-fetched interpretive method.

C. Criticism by the Sages of Symbolic Methods of Interpretation

We find additional references in halakhic literature to the strong opposition of many Sages to these far-fetched symbolic methods of interpretation.

The use of all methods of interpretation—even those based on logic and analogy—requires great caution not to exceed the bounds of plausibility. The Sages were sensitive to this need, as shown by the following interesting exchange:[351]

> R. Yose b. Tadai of Tiberias asked this question of Rabban Gamaliel: "My wife is permissible to me, yet I may not marry her daughter [the law is that if a man marries a woman who has a daughter, he may not marry his wife's daughter, as it is one of the forbidden sexual unions even though she is not his own daughter]. In the case of a woman married to another man, whom I may not marry, is it not an *a fortiori* inference (*kal va-ḥomer*) that I may not marry her daughter?"

R. Yose b. Tadai hypothesized an analogy that produced an absurd result, *i.e.*, to deduce by an inference *a fortiori*, from the case of his wife's daughter whom he may not marry, to the case of the daughter of another man's wife, whose marriage to him, according to his reasoning, should even more so be prohibited. The conclusion would then be that a man may not marry any woman who is the daughter of a married woman.

349. TB Sanhedrin 51b.

350. "In this method of exposition, most Sages did not agree with him and sometimes rejected his statements out of hand" (Frankel, *Mishnah*, p. 121).

351. Tractate Derekh Ereẓ Rabbah, ch. 1; *Yalkut Shim'oni*, Emor 631:75. *See also* Derekh Ereẓ Rabbah, ed. Higger, 3:6, p. 267.

The answer to R. Yose b. Tadai was as follows:

> He [Rabban Gamaliel] said to him: "First explain to me the law of the high priest, with regard to whom it is stated,[352] 'Only a virgin from his own kin shall he take to wife,'[353] and then I will explain the law relating to all Israelites, for you cannot draw a conclusion by means of *a fortiori* reasoning that negates a law stated in the Torah."[354] And Rabban Gamaliel placed him under a ban.

R. Yose b. Tadai's question was more ironic than serious. Furthermore, his *a fortiori* argument is fundamentally flawed in that it is based on erroneous logic. R. Yose assumed as a premise for his inference that he was permitted to marry his wife, whereas if the *a fortiori* inference were valid, he could never have married his wife in the first place, because she would not have been permitted to him, since she herself was the daughter of a married woman![355] Sensing R. Yose's ironic disdain of the entire midrashic approach, Rabban Gamaliel placed him under a ban. However, inherent in the discussion is an expression of skepticism that, in all likelihood, resulted from the use of excessive freedom in certain methods of midrashic interpretation.

The most significant and powerful shafts of criticism were aimed against the use of the far-fetched interpretive methods of R. Akiva and his academy, especially when these methods were employed to create law. At one point,[356] R. Ishmael told R. Eliezer, his teacher, who based an interpretation on the letter "*vav*" in the word *ve-ha-beged*—"and the garment" (Leviticus 13:47): "You seem to be telling the verse, 'Be silent until I make an interpretation!'" (*I.e.*, it is as if you tell the verse itself [namely, its plain meaning] to keep silent until you finish your interpretation.) R. Eliezer re-

352. Leviticus 21:14.

353. According to R. Yose's *kal va-ḥomer*, a high priest would never be able to marry. The *kal va-ḥomer* teaches that no man may marry a woman whose mother is married, which means that a man may marry only a woman whose mother is a widow or a divorcee, in which case the mother would also be eligible to be his wife. However, a high priest may not marry a widow or a divorcee, and therefore he could never marry at all, since there is no way for him to find a woman whose mother would be eligible to be his wife. *See Naḥalat Ya'akov* commentary to Tractate Derekh Ereẓ Rabbah, *ad loc.*

354. Since, according to the *kal va-ḥomer*, a high priest could never marry, the conclusion of the *kal va-ḥomer* negates a law of the Torah, because a high priest, like any other man, is obligated to marry. *Yalkut Shim'oni*, *supra* n. 351, adds: "'Only a virgin.' This teaches that he is commanded [to marry] a virgin," *i.e.*, the Torah does not merely grant him permission to marry a virgin, but requires him to do so as a specific religious duty attendant on his office. According to this view, the conclusion of the *kal va-ḥomer* is an even sharper negation of a law of the Torah. The fact that the *kal va-ḥomer* is invalid as applied to the high priest indicates that it is also invalid as applied to all Jews.

355. This would be true unless his wife was the daughter of a widow or a divorcee.

356. *Sifra*, Tazri'a 13:2 (p. 68a).

sponded: "Ishmael, you are a palm tree that grows on a mountain!" (*I.e.*, your fruits are few. Because you restrict the methods of interpretation you employ, your halakhic output is meager and insignificant.)[357]

On two other occasions,[358] R. Tarfon said to R. Akiva in response to his interpretive approach: "How long will you inflict us with your verbose exaggerations? Akiva, I cannot endure it!" Only after R. Akiva told R. Tarfon that his interpretation does not create law but merely integrates existing law with Scripture was R. Tarfon appeased. R. Tarfon then responded: "By Heaven, you have not been making things up. Blessed be Abraham, our father, whose descendant is Akiva. Tarfon had witnessed [the practice in question] but forgot; Akiva uses his own interpretation to arrive at the same legal conclusion. Therefore, whoever separates from you is as if he separates from his life."

Similarly, in another connection,[359] when R. Akiva based an interpretation on the word *be-shemen* ("with oil"), which appears twice in Leviticus 7:12, R. Eleazar b. Azariah said to R. Akiva: "Even if you keep saying all day long that the phrase 'with oil' excludes—or that it includes—I will pay no attention to you. The law is a tradition from Moses at Sinai"; *i.e.*, there is no possibility that the law was created by the Scriptural verse, or that the law can even be integrated with the verse; the source of the law is simply tradition—a law given to Moses at Sinai and transmitted from generation to generation.

The Sages' critical attitude toward the interpretive method of R. Akiva is reflected in the *aggadah*[360] previously discussed in connection with the term *halakhah le-Moshe mi-Sinai* (law given to Moses at Sinai).[361] In this *aggadah*, Moses requested God to permit him to sit in R. Akiva's academy and to hear how R. Akiva deduced myriads of laws on the basis of every jot and tittle of Scriptural text; and when Moses sat and heard, he "did not understand what was being said, and he felt faint." Moses was not comforted until he heard R. Akiva telling his students that the source of the laws that he "deduced" from the verse was not in the verse itself but in tradition, in *halakhah le-Moshe mi-Sinai*. In this *aggadah*, the Sages expressed their view that R. Akiva's symbolic interpretive methods should be accepted only to the extent that they succeed in finding support in the text for an already existing law, but not when they seek to create law.

357. *See* Rabad's commentary, *ad loc.*

358. *Sifra*, Va-Yikra, Dibbura De-Nedavah 4:5 (p. 6a), concerning sacrificial offerings; *Sifrei*, Numbers, Be-Ha'alotekha, sec. 75 (p. 70), concerning ineligibility for priestly functions.

359. *Sifra*, Ẓav, sec. 5, 11:6 (pp. 34b–35a).

360. TB Menaḥot 29b.

361. *See supra* pp. 204–207.

Notwithstanding this criticism of symbolic interpretive devices, the canons of Biblical interpretation and all the other accepted interpretive methods were used to explain Biblical law, create new laws and principles, and, by broadening or restricting the law as appropriate, resolve new problems produced by changes in circumstances and conditions. This great and crucial function of interpretation found its full expression in the statement of R. Yannai, the disciple of R. Judah Ha-Nasi and one of the leading early *amoraim* of the Land of Israel:

> If the Torah had been given cut-and-dried [*i.e.*, rigid and inflexible], one could not abide by it. Why is this so? "God spoke to Moses." Moses said to Him: "Master of the universe, tell me how the *Halakhah* is to be decided?" God said to him: "'Follow the majority' [Exodus 23:2]. If the majority is for acquittal, acquit him; if the majority is for guilt, find him guilty. This is so that the Torah can be interpreted in forty-nine ways to support the conclusion 'impure,' and forty-nine ways to support the conclusion 'pure.'"[362]

The giver of the Torah Himself, as it were, did not set down in the Torah final and unambiguous laws. His purpose was to make it possible for the halakhic authorities to search out the sense of the Torah, its hidden meaning. In that kind of searching out (midrash), some tend to leniency and others to severity, some would declare "pure" and others "impure." It is the interpretation accepted and confirmed by the majority of the halakhic authorities that is the resolution that the Torah intended. That interpretation is the *Halakhah*.

XI. EXEGETICAL INTERPRETATION OF THE TORAH IN THE AMORAIC PERIOD

A. Decline in the Use of Exegetical Interpretation of the Torah

In the amoraic period, Biblical interpretation was generally integrative, *i.e.*, confirming preexisting *Halakhah* with Scriptural support. However, the *amoraim* also considered themselves authorized to interpret the Torah to determine *Halakhah* by means of midrash, and "when they had determinative interpretations, they decided and established the law in accordance with those interpretations, . . . and there is no distinction between 'the

362. TJ Sanhedrin 4:2, 21a/b (11:2, 22a); *Midrash Tehillim* 12:4 (pp. 107–108). With regard to multiplicity of opinions in the *Halakhah* and decision according to the majority, *see further supra* pp. 261–263 and *infra* pp. 1061–1072.

leading early *tannaim'* and the later ones, and even between the *tannaim* and *amoraim*."[363]

However, in practice, Biblical exegesis no longer was a source of legal creativity.[364] The reason for this change is clear and well understood. At first, the Torah was the sole authoritative source for reaching legal conclusions in the halakhic system. However, from the time that mishnaic collections and halakhic *midrashim* were compiled, and especially from the time that the Mishnah of R. Judah Ha-Nasi was edited and acknowledged as authoritative at the end of the tannaitic and the beginning of the amoraic periods, the Mishnah became the book of laws that was interpreted and studied. It was the Mishnah that served as a foundation and starting point for the creation and continued development of the *Halakhah*.

Certainly, the Written Law remained even then the primary source of Jewish law; but it was in the nature of a basic and original source, the highest level in the hierarchy of values of the *Halakhah*, rather than a direct source for deriving legal rules and practical guidance in everyday life. Study, adjudication, and actual practice now found their source and direct sustenance in the Mishnah and in other tannaitic sources. For the same reason, not only were explicative exegesis and creative Biblical interpretation rare in the amoraic period, but even integrative interpretation progressively decreased. From that time, with the Mishnah being the authoritative and binding legal code, there no longer was any reason to integrate law with the Biblical text so as to give it Biblical sanction. The mere fact that a law was contained within the authoritative compilation of the Mishnah entitled it to full legal-halakhic recognition and authority.

B. Dispensing with the Need for Integrative Interpretation

Characteristic of this significant change in amoraic times are the surprised queries that one *amora* from time to time would ask another who sought to integrate a particular law with a Biblical verse when legal reasoning alone would have been a sufficient source from which the law could be derived.[365]

363. Albeck, *Mavo*, p. 54.

364. It should be borne in mind that the fact that an *amora* derived a specific law from a verse does not prove that the interpretation originated with him. It is entirely possible that the *midrash* was from tannaitic times and that it was merely transmitted by the *amora*. Occasionally, this can be proved by the existence of the same *midrash* in a tannaitic source. For such instances, *see* B. De Vries, *Toledot ha-Halakhah ha-Talmudit* [A History of Talmudic *Halakhah*], pp. 23–25. A similar phenomenon exists with respect to tannaitic *midrashim:* the material may considerably predate the *tanna* who transmitted it; *see supra* p. 314. The examples that De Vries cites (*op. cit.*, pp. 28–30) as creative *midrashim* of the amoraic period can all be explained as integrative *midrashim*, and thus they are no proof for the proposition that they were creating new law.

365. For legal reasoning as a legal source, *see infra* pp. 987ff.

Two examples follow.

1. Exodus 24:14 states that before Moses ascended to heaven to receive the tablets he instructed the elders: "Wait here for us until we return to you. You have Aaron and Hur with you; let anyone who has a legal matter approach them." Moses thus appointed Aaron and Hur as his surrogates and instructed the elders that all controversies should be brought before the two of them for resolution. This verse was interpreted by the *amora* R. Samuel b. Naḥmani in this manner: "How do we know that the burden of proof is on the claimant? Scripture states: 'Let anyone who has a legal matter approach (*yiggash*) them'—*i.e.*, let him bring (*yaggish*) proof to them."[366] R. Samuel b. Naḥmani interpreted the word *yiggash* (lit. "come near") as also meaning *yaggish* (in the causative, "cause to come near," "bring"), *i.e.*, the claimant must first bring proof of his contentions. This is clearly integrative interpretation, because the rule that the burden of proof is on the claimant had long been known and accepted;[367] R. Samuel b. Naḥmani sought only to integrate and support it with a Biblical verse.

In the course of the ensuing discussion, R. Ashi raised this objection: "Why do we need a verse? This rule is based on logic! Whoever has a pain goes to the doctor." R. Ashi, in other words, questioned the need for supporting this legal principle with a Biblical verse, because we can deduce it by simple logic: Just as it is the one who has a pain who goes to the doctor and describes his symptoms, and the doctor does not go searching for sick people, so, when someone has a claim against his neighbor, it is incumbent on him, the claimant, to first bring proof to substantiate his claim, and the defendant is not first required to show that he is not liable for that claim. According to R. Ashi, since the legal source of the principle that "the burden of proof is on the claimant" is legal reasoning, there is no need to integrate it with a Biblical verse.

2. In the Jewish law of pleadings, there is a principle to the effect that "the mouth that has prohibited is the mouth that has permitted."[368] This principle is illustrated in the following rule:[369]

> A woman who says, "I was married but now I am divorced," is believed, as the mouth that has prohibited is the mouth that has permitted; but if there

366. TB Bava Kamma 46b.

367. *See infra* pp. 992–993.

368. This principle constitutes the origin and basis of the rule of *migo* in Jewish legal procedure. That rule is to the effect that a claim, despite insufficiency of proof, is deemed valid because (*migo*) if the claimant desired to lie, he could have stated a more plausible case that would have been accepted as true. *See Tosafot,* Ketubbot 22a, s.v. Minayin she-ha-peh she-asar.

369. M Ketubbot 2:5.

> are witnesses that she was married, and she says, "I am divorced," she is not believed.

The rationale is that if a woman not known to be married says that she was married but has also been divorced, her statement that she was divorced is believed because it was only her own "mouth" (in saying she was married) that made her forbidden to any other man. Therefore, the same mouth that stated that she was married (a fact not known before she disclosed it) may release her from the obligations of the status of a wife by saying that she was divorced; and she need not bring any proof beyond her own word. However, if the fact that the woman was married is known not merely on the basis of her admission, but because witnesses so testified, her allegation alone is not sufficient to establish that she is divorced. In such a case, therefore, she may not remarry unless she produces evidence (such as a bill of divorcement or witnesses) to prove her allegation that she was previously divorced.

The Talmud comments on this *mishnah:*[370]

> Rav Assi asked: "How do we know that [the principle that] "the mouth that has prohibited is the mouth that has permitted" is from the Torah? Scripture states: 'I gave my daughter to this man to wife' [lit. 'I gave my daughter to man this to wife'—demonstrative or descriptive adjectives that precede nouns in English normally follow the noun in Hebrew].[371] 'To [a] man'—he prohibited her [to all;]. 'This'—he permitted her [to this man]."

R. Assi attempted to connect the law in the *mishnah* to a Scriptural verse through this interpretation: When the father says "I gave my daughter to [a] man," he is stating that she is married; and since, up to that point, he has not designated any particular man, the consequence of his general statement is that she becomes prohibited to everyone. However, when the father continues and says "this" (*i.e.*, this man), he designates and specifies the man whom his daughter has married, and thus permits her to that man.[372]

Here, too, the question is raised in the Talmudic discussion: "Why is a Scriptural verse necessary? It stands to reason! He prohibited her, and he permitted her!" In other words, what is the need for any reference to a Biblical verse? It is a principle based on logic and reasoning: he is the one who prohibited her, and therefore he can permit her.

370. TB Ketubbot 22a.

371. Deuteronomy 22:16, concerning a man who claims that the woman he married was not a virgin, states: "And the girl's father shall say to the elders, 'I gave my daughter to this man to wife, but he has taken an aversion to her.'"

372. *See* Rashi, Ketubbot 22a, s.v. Natati le-ish asrah; and *see infra* pp. 993–995.

We also find that occasionally when the *amoraim* sought a source for a particular rule of law that was known and accepted they would say: "If you wish, I will cite a Scriptural verse; if you wish, I will explain it on the basis of logic and reason (*sevarah*)."[373] *I.e.*, it is possible to base the source of that particular rule either on a Biblical verse or on logic, and the *amoraim* did not consider it mandatory to base the legal rule on the Biblical text.

There is no instance in the tannaitic period comparable to this phenomenon of dispensing with Scriptural support of a rule of law derivable by logical inference. The phenomenon is unique to the amoraic period, when resort to both creative and integrative interpretation progressively decreased.

C. General Guidelines for Use of Interpretive Methods

The *amoraim* made use of general guidelines, nonmidrashic in character, to give direction for the use of interpretive methods. This amoraic method of formulating general guidelines and principles manifests itself in many diverse areas of the halakhic system,[374] and sometimes the same general principle served in different areas of the *Halakhah*.[375]

An interesting example of such a general guideline is the principle that the *amoraim* based on the statement in Proverbs 3:17: "Her ways are pleasant ways and all her paths, peaceful." This verse, which describes the virtues of wisdom, and which in Jewish tradition was taken as particularly describing the virtues of the Torah and its students,[376] was accepted as a general guideline in the application of the methods of interpretation. The following are two examples:

1. Leviticus 23:40 states:

> On the first day [of the *Sukkot* festival] you shall take the product of *hadar* trees, branches of palm trees, boughs of leafy [lit. "thick"] trees, and willows of the brook; and you shall rejoice before the Lord your God seven days.

373. *E.g.*, TB Sanhedrin 30a; and *see further infra* pp. 1000–1004.

374. *See infra* pp. 622ff.

375. *E.g.*, the principle "Her ways are pleasant ways," immediately hereinafter discussed. Halakhic authorities in the post-Talmudic period used this principle as a methodological guideline for decision making. *See* M. Elon, "Ekronot Musariyyim ke-Normah Hilkhatit" [Moral Principles as Halakhic Norm], *De'ot*, XX (1962), pp. 62ff., at pp. 65–67. *See also id.*, *Samkhut ve-Oẓmah*, pp. 22, 26; *id.*, *Digest of the Responsa Literature of Spain and North Africa, Index of Sources*, I, Introduction, p. 25 (1981).

376. *See, e.g.*, TB Nedarim 62a; Gittin 59b; TJ Eruvin 3:2, 20b (3:3, 20d); 7:9, 49b (7:10, 24c).

The Talmudic discussion[377] centers on the identification of the tree meant by the Torah's reference to "boughs of leafy trees":

> The Rabbis taught: "Boughs of leafy trees" [refers to a tree] whose branches cover its bark. Which is it? It is the myrtle. Perhaps it is the olive tree? It must be leafy, and the olive tree is not. Perhaps it is the plane tree?[378] Its branches must cover its bark and the plane tree's do not.
>
> Perhaps it is the oleander?[379] Abbaye said: "'Her ways are pleasant ways,' and that is not true of the oleander" [which pricks the hand with thorns, as the edges of the leaves of that tree are as sharp as a needle; see Rashi, Sukkah 32b, s.v. Darkhei no'am].
>
> Rava said: "We deduce this [that is not the oleander] from 'Love truth and peace'"[380] [and using this tree does not partake of truth or of peace, as it is used to make a deadly poison. See Rashi, Sukkah 32b, s.v. Ha-emet ve-ha-shalom ehavu].

The plane tree and the olive tree were rejected because they are not consonant with the meaning of "boughs of leafy trees": the plane tree does not have "boughs of leafy trees," *i.e.*, its branches do not cover its bark, and the olive tree is not "leafy." This is customary midrashic interpretation to explain the content of a Biblical verse. The physical characteristics of the oleander do qualify as meeting the requirement of "boughs of leafy trees"; but the oleander could not have been the tree that the Torah intended, because it is thorny and pricks the hands. Thus, its use is not consonant with "pleasant ways," nor does it symbolize "truth and peace."[381]

The same considerations were applied to the identification of the tree that the Torah referred to in the phrase "branches of palm trees." Here, too, the Talmud[382] raises various possibilities of different types of trees:

> How do we know that "branches of palm trees" refers to the *lulav* (green sprouts of palm branches)? . . . Perhaps it is the spike? [Perhaps the reference is to a species of palm branches with prickly points?][383] Abbaye said: "It is written, 'Her ways are pleasant ways and all her paths, peaceful.'" [The spike is made of thorns, and many prickly points come out of it and scratch the hands. See Rashi, Sukkah 32a, s.v. Derakheha darkhei no'am.]

377. TB Sukkah 32b.

378. *See* Rashi, *ad loc.*, s.v. Dolba. *See also* J. Levy, *Wörterbuch*, s.v. Dolba.

379. A tree whose leaves are bitter and thorny and arranged as though woven, *see* Rashi, *ad loc.*, s.v. Hirduf. *See also* Levy, *Wörterbuch*, s.v. Hirduf.

380. Zechariah 8:19. The 1985 JPS *Tanakh* has "you must love honesty and integrity." This verse expressly relates to "occasions for joy and gladness"; the purpose of taking the boughs of leafy trees is also to rejoice before the Lord.

381. TB Pesaḥim 39a discusses whether one fulfills the obligation of eating bitter herbs on Passover by eating of the oleander tree.

382. TB Sukkah 32a.

383. *See* Rashi, Ketubbot 10a, s.v. Asvuhu kofri.

Here, too, the words "branches of palm trees" could possibly be intended to refer to the spike; however, as a consequence of the general guideline that one must interpret the Torah so that its ways are pleasant,[384] the branches of this tree are not included among the palm branches taken on the festival of *Sukkot*.[385]

2. We may conclude from a different example that if the use of the *kal va-ḥomer* canon (inference *a fortiori*) is contrary to the general interpretive guideline "Her ways are pleasant ways," the latter will govern and negate the conclusion based on the canon.

Deuteronomy 25:5 states:

> When brothers dwell together and one of them dies and leaves no son [lit. "and has no son"], the wife of the deceased shall not be married to a stranger outside the family. Her husband's brother shall unite with her and take her as his wife, performing the *levir's* duty.

What is the meaning of "and has no son"? It could mean that the husband left no child surviving him at his death, in which case his widow must either marry his brother or, if the brother does not wish to marry her, undergo *ḥaliẓah* (ceremony whereby the widow is released from the levirate tie) in order to be able to marry another man. If we interpret the verse this way, then if the decedent was survived by an only son who later died, the widow is exempt from the requirement of levirate marriage or *ḥaliẓah*.

However, during the course of the Talmudic discussion,[386] R. Judah of Deskarta argued that on the basis of an *a fortiori* inference the rule should be that even if the deceased was survived by a son, the wife is required to undergo either a levirate marriage or *ḥaliẓah* if the son subsequently dies. He based the argument on the law that an Israelite woman married to a priest may eat from the *terumah* (priestly tithe, which only priests and their families are permitted to eat) even after the death of her husband if she had a surviving son by the decedent, but she must cease eating from the *terumah* upon the death of this child. From this, he argued *a fortiori* to the case of levirate marriage: although the widow was not required to undergo a

384. Prickly palm branches were used to flog insolent persons; *see* TB Ketubbot 10a.

385. Even before Abbaye's interpretive rationale, it was known that the "boughs of leafy trees" were the myrtle and that "branches of palm trees" were the *lulav;* that was an ancient tradition. However, Abbaye established that it was inconceivable that the Torah intended these expressions to include the oleander and the spike, which are prickly, even though they fit the specifications of the verse, because such a result would be inconsistent with ways of pleasantness. Rava reached the same conclusion regarding the oleander on the basis of "love truth and peace."

386. TB Yevamot 87b.

levirate marriage when her husband died leaving a son surviving, she becomes obligated either to a levirate marriage or to *ḥaliẓah* when the son dies.[387]

In rejecting this argument, Rava stated: "Her ways are pleasant ways and all her paths, peaceful"; *i.e.*, according to the *a fortiori* argument, the situation could arise where the husband dies leaving a child, the widow remarries, and thereafter the child dies. In that case, if the argument were valid, the widow would have to undergo *ḥaliẓah* to remain with the man whom she has married, and the ceremony of *ḥaliẓah* may degrade her in the eyes of her current husband.[388] To prevent this result, we interpret the words "and has no son" as referring to the time of the former husband's death, and it makes no difference what happens afterward.

Rava's objection is not to the logical validity of the *a fortiori* argument. As a matter of logic, we would have to interpret the verse according to the conclusion that follows from that argument. But against the substantial force of the *a fortiori* canon, another countervailing principle of interpretation—"her ways are pleasant ways" (according to which the woman should not be demeaned before her current husband)—tips the scale in favor of the interpretation that "and has no son" refers only to the time of the former husband's death. Thus, if when the husband dies there is a surviving son, the widow is exempt, whether or not the son dies later.

The exposition by Solomon Luria (Maharshal) of the principle of "pleasant ways" in this connection is instructive: "The teachings of the Torah should produce pleasantness and equality of treatment; a matter should not be twisted so that one woman beams with joy and the second lives in sadness."[389] To put it another way, if we adopt the inference arising out of the *a fortiori* argument, the woman whose child dies before she remarries will not suffer from being required to obtain a release of levirate marriage through *ḥaliẓah* because, under the circumstances, *ḥaliẓah* has no adverse effect on her. However, the widow whose son by the decedent dies after her remarriage will be adversely affected by undergoing *ḥaliẓah* after her remarriage: she may be demeaned in the eyes of her current husband. This result violates the principle of "pleasant ways," which requires equal treatment for all and nondiscrimination in the application of legal rules.

387. For the explanation of why the relationship between levirate marriage and eligibility to eat *terumah* is such as to give rise to an *a fortiori* inference, *see* TB Yevamot 87b.

388. *See* Rashi, Yevamot 87b, s.v. Derakheha darkhei no'am.

389. *Ḥokhmat Shelomo*, Yevamot 87b. *See also* Maharsha, Yevamot (end), quoted *infra* pp. 530–531 n. 153.

XII. BIBLICAL EXEGESIS IN THE POST-TALMUDIC PERIOD

With the completion of the Talmud, there occurred a significant change in the extent to which Biblical exegesis was employed. The law that governed everyday life was the law contained in the elaborate and wide-ranging Talmudic literature. The solution to questions that arose was sought in the words of the *tannaim* and *amoraim* and not on the basis of Biblical exegesis. Talmudic literature, in the broad sense of the term, was accepted as a continuation of the Torah, and the law that was authoritative and binding was the law laid down in the Talmud. The connection with the Written Law was a spiritual connection. The Written Law conferred its authority on the entire system of Jewish law, but adjudication in everyday life was based upon Talmudic law as embodied in the halakhic *midrashim,* the Mishnah, the *Tosefta,* and the two Talmuds.

It should be pointed out, however, that the writings of the *geonim* and *rishonim* contain various interpretations of Biblical verses that are not contained in the halakhic *midrashim* now extant. Sometimes it appears that these interpretations were taken from collections of *midrashim* that the *rishonim* had but we do not.[390] Nevertheless, there were also occasions when the post-Talmudic halakhic authorities felt it necessary to use Biblical exegesis to support new law, arrived at through logical inference or created by legislation or custom, for which they sought to find support in the Torah itself. This post-Talmudic Biblical exegesis should be seen not as creative but as integrative interpretation. The *rishonim* themselves explicitly indicated that this was their approach:

> As to any matter that we know is valid but has not received Scriptural support, anyone may interpret the Biblical text and bring such support.[391]

We examine a few examples concerning which it is fair to assume—even if we cannot always prove—that these integrative interpretations were first made in the writings of the *rishonim.*

390. *See, e.g.,* Maimonides, *MT,* Avadim 2:12 (in regard to a Hebrew slave, who goes free after six years): "Even if he [the slave] fell sick and his master spent great sums of money on him, the slave owes the master nothing, as it is written, 'He shall be freed, without payment.'" The source of this midrashic law was unknown until the publication of *Mekhilta de-R. Simeon b. Yoḥai,* where it appears (Mishpatim 21:2, p. 161). *See further* M. Kasher, *Ha-Rambam ve-ha-Mekhilta de-R. Shim'on bar Yoḥai* [Maimonides and the *Mekhilta* of R. Simeon bar Yoḥai], pp. 108–109.

391. Aaron ha-Levi of Barcelona, quoted in *Nimmukei Yosef* to Alfasi, Bava Kamma, ch. "Ha-Ḥovel" (beginning). The statement is quoted there in explanation of TJ. *See Torah Temimah,* Introduction to Genesis, ch. 1, par. 9 (p. 15), and Radbaz's comment, quoted *infra* p. 332. For a detailed discussion of the subject, *see Yad Malakhi,* I, Kelalei ha-Dalet, #144.

A. Consecration of Something Not Yet in Existence

There is a principle in Jewish law that ownership of property not yet in existence cannot be transferred and that one cannot convey title to property not in one's possession; the act of acquisition cannot be legally effective when the object to be conveyed is not yet in existence or is not yet in the transferor's possession.[392] This principle applies not only to sales, but to all transactions, including gifts, consecrations to the Temple, and the like.

The law established in connection with consecration of property was:[393]

> One cannot consecrate anything that is not yet in existence. For example, [if one says,] "Whatever my nets in the sea will catch, [or] whatever fruit will be produced in my field is hereby consecrated," he has said nothing [*i.e.*, his statement has no legal effect].

The rule immediately following is:

> If one says to his neighbor, "This field that I have sold to you is hereby consecrated as of the time I buy it back from you," and he buys it back, it is not consecrated, because it was not in his possession when he purported to consecrate it.

The fish and the fruit were not yet in anyone's possession, so as to be able to be consecrated, and the field belonged to someone else and was not yet in the possession of the consecrator.

The inability to enter into transactions involving property not yet in existence or not within one's possession created serious obstacles to the development of commerce, since the subject of commercial transactions is often property that one will produce, obtain, or earn in the future. The halakhic authorities searched for legal methods to overcome this difficulty.

As to consecration and similar legal transactions, Maimonides found the solution by creating the possibility of an assumption of an obligation to consecrate that would apply even to something that does not yet exist.[394] He explained:[395]

> It seems to me[396] that even though one cannot consecrate property that does not yet exist, if one says "I take upon myself the obligation of consecrating

392. *See* Maimonides, *MT*, Mekhirah ch. 22.

393. *Id.*, *MT*, Arakhin va-Ḥaramin 6:26.

394. In the course of time, with respect to property not yet in existence, Jewish law developed the means of assuming an obligation not only for consecration to the Temple but in all types of transactions. *See infra* n. 400.

395. *MT*, Arakhin va-Ḥaramin 6:31–32.

396. This formulation indicates that the statement is original with Maimonides and does not appear in any earlier halakhic literary source; *see infra* p. 1205. This rule is also

> it," he is obligated to consecrate it when it comes into existence, because he must carry out his vow. If he does not consecrate it, he violates the commandments, "He shall not delay the performance of his vow," "He shall not break his pledge," and "He must carry out all that has crossed his lips" [Numbers 30:3], just as with all other vows.[397]
>
> For example, if one says "I undertake to consecrate all that my nets in the sea will catch," or "I undertake to give to the poor all the fruit that my field will produce," or "I undertake to consecrate or give for captives all that I will earn this year," or any other similar statement, he is required to give and to do whatever he has said when the specified objects come into his possession. These obligations are binding as vows and not as a matter of the law of consecrated property.

Maimonides thus distinguished between an act of consecration that immediately transfers ownership from the consecrator to the Temple—an act not possible with property not in existence or not in one's possession—and a present obligation to consecrate in the future when the property will be obtained or come into existence; this obligation is valid because it is in the nature of a vow. Consequently, when one obtains the property he must consecrate it, give it to the poor or for captives, or do whatever else his vow has obligated him to do.

Maimonides went on to supply a proof for his proposed rule:[398]

> I have proof for this from what Jacob our father said: "And of all that You give me, I will set aside a tithe for You" [Genesis 28:22], and it is also stated: "Where you made a vow to Me" [Genesis 31:13] . . . , and these are proper bases from which to derive an inference.

In other words, when Jacob promised to give a tenth of his property, he had no property and was referring to property that he would obtain in the future, yet the Torah itself tells us that the vow was effective and binding.[399]

This represented an innovative development by Maimonides in regard to an important rule of law. The innovation was in his use of the distinction between a conveyance of property for purposes of consecration, ransom of

---

mentioned in *MT,* Mekhirah 22:15 (*see infra* n. 400), but without the introductory "It seems to me."

397. These are the three prohibitions a person transgresses when he fails to fulfill a vow. *See* Maimonides, *MT,* Arakhin ve-Ḥaramin 1:1.

398. *Id.* 6:33.

399. Further on, Maimonides adduces an additional proof, based on the Talmud's discussion of the laws of the Nazirite. Rabad rejected this latter proof but accepted Maimonides' ruling on the basis of the proof from Jacob's vow. Rabad wrote: "The proof from Jacob is a proof; but that from the Nazirite is nothing."

captives, and the like, and an obligation to convey property for such a purpose in the future. First, he established the appropriateness of this distinction by the logical argument that the undertaking to convey for such a purpose has the quality of a vow, and then he buttressed his position by persuasively integrating it with the Scriptural text through Biblical exegesis.[400]

B. "Moving a Landmark" (*Hassagat Gevul*)

There is a doctrine in Jewish law prohibiting "moving a landmark" (*hassagat gevul*). This doctrine underwent many stages of expansion and development. The Torah, the original source of this phrase, used it to refer to the unlawful taking of a neighbor's land by physically moving the boundary markers into the neighbor's property so as to annex part of that property to the wrongdoer's own adjacent land. The Torah deals with this situation in two verses: (a) "You shall not move your neighbor's landmarks, set up by previous generations, in the property that will be allotted to you in the land that the Lord your God is giving you to possess";[401] and (b) "Cursed be he who moves his neighbor's landmark."[402]

Even in patriarchal times, it was customary to insist on precise landmarks, as is evidenced from the description of the field in Machpelah that Abraham bought from Ephron the Hittite.[403] The Hebrew prophets and wisdom literature condemn the movers of landmarks,[404] and the prohibition

400. Maimonides, *MT,* Mekhirah 22:15, refers to this law in the course of distinguishing it from other legal transactions that do not have the quality of vows:

> The law of consecration, the law of [charity for] the poor, and the law of vows are not like the law of acquisition by an ordinary person. For if a person says, "Whatever offspring my animal will have is consecrated to the maintenance fund of the Temple," or "will be forbidden to me," or "I will donate to charity," although the animal cannot thereby become consecrated because it does not yet exist, he is nevertheless obligated to perform his pledge, as it is written, ". . . he must carry out all that has crossed his lips" [Numbers 30:3].

See Rabad's comments, *ad loc.;* Sh. Ar. ḤM 212:7 and Rema's gloss thereto. In the course of time, Jewish law came to distinguish between, on the one hand, transferring or acquiring property rights, where the subject of the transaction must be something already in existence and in the possession of the transferor, and, on the other hand, the assumption of an obligation, which is binding, since the obligor undertakes it and he does exist. The binding effect of the obligation is not impaired by the fact that the obligation concerns something that does not yet exist or is not in the possession of the obligor. *See Resp. Rashba,* III, #65; Sh. Ar. ḤM 60:6 and *Sema, ad loc.,* subpar. 18. *See also supra* pp. 76–77 and *infra* pp. 587ff.

401. Deuteronomy 19:14.

402. *Id.* 27:17.

403. Genesis 23:17.

404. Hosea 5:10; Proverbs 22:28, 23:10; Job 24:2.

against moving one's neighbor's landmark is also discussed in Talmudic literature and in halakhic codes.[405]

As early as the time of the Talmud, but particularly in the post-Talmudic period, it became necessary to accord legal recognition and protection to rights not theretofore accorded specific protection by the law. The legal formulation and rationale of these rights were developed by broadening the doctrine of "moving a landmark" to include prohibiting the "moving" of various economic, commercial, and spiritual boundary lines.[406] One instance of how the doctrine was so broadened was the prohibition of "trespassing" against the trade or business of another.

In the Talmudic period, most Sages tended to support freedom of commercial and occupational competition.[407] The only condemnation of trespass against another's trade was moral and carried no legal sanction.[408] We do find that R. Huna laid down a legal rule that a resident of an alleyway who operates a handmill may restrain other residents of that alleyway from setting up a handmill nearby; the theory was that such conduct would constitute interference with his livelihood. This view, however, was not accepted as law; R. Huna b. Joshua ruled that an inhabitant of an alleyway may not restrain another inhabitant of the same alleyway from taking up the same occupation and may not even restrain a nonresident of the city from so doing if the nonresident pays taxes to the city in which he seeks to take up his trade.[409] Even this limited right to restrain competition by nonresidents was not yet fully defined and doctrinally elaborated; no legal sanctions, such as the payment of damages, were provided for.

With the limitations placed on the sources of livelihood for Jews in the Middle Ages, the question of limits on freedom of competition again became a matter of the most pressing concern. Among the occupations in which the government permitted the Jews to engage was the running of licensed concessions. A Jew who invested substantial labor and capital in the purchase of a concession in a particular area of commerce could lose his investment and his livelihood as a result of the competition of another Jew. From the tenth century C.E. on, there was much discussion in the responsa literature about the problem of the legal protection of concession rights, their scope, and the sanctions to be imposed for violating them.

405. Maimonides, *MT*, Genevah 7:11; Sh. Ar. ḤM 376:1.

406. Such as protection of copyrights, and protection of tenants' rights (even if noncontractual) where there is a scarcity of apartments. For further discussion, *see* M. Elon, EJ, VII, pp. 1460–1466, s.v. Hassagat gevul (reprinted in *Principles*, pp. 340–346).

407. M Bava Meẓ'ia 4:12; TB Bava Meẓi'a 60a/b; Bava Batra 21b.

408. TB Kiddushin 59a; Makkot 24a; Sanhedrin 81a.

409. TB Bava Batra 21b.

Some of the halakhic authorities expanded the right and some restricted it, but all acknowledged the basic right of exclusive concession to be a legally defined and recognized right.[410]

Understandably, the halakhic authorities sought a basis for recognizing the legal right of an individual to prevent a stranger from interfering with his concession, and for imposing sanctions against those who violated this right. This problem was dealt with in a case brought before Solomon Luria (Maharshal) in the seventeenth century in Poland.[411] The essential facts were these: A Jew acquired a right to operate a customs station. Another Jew gave the governor a greater sum of money to obtain the concession for himself. The governor transferred the concession to the second individual, thus causing substantial damage to the first concessionaire, who had invested much labor and money. The ousted concessionaire appealed to the Jewish court, and the judge turned to Maharshal for guidance as to whether the ousted concessionaire had any claim for damages. At the beginning of his responsum, Maharshal said:

> It is settled law that indirect causation of damage does not create liability.[412] If so, how can a judgment for damages be rendered if there is no legal basis? [*I.e.*, the second Jew who obtained the concession caused damages only indirectly and is therefore not liable to pay compensation under the settled law.] Therefore, I must explain why he [the second Jew] must cease his business and is liable even if the causation is only indirect.
>
> The reason is that he too is included in the "curse," as Roke'aḥ has written:[413] "Whoever interferes with the livelihood of his fellow is included in the category of 'Cursed be he who moves his neighbor's landmark.'" [It is true that] there were many who were surprised at this statement—is not the prohibition against moving a landmark applicable only to one who actually encroaches on another's property, and only in the Land of Israel? In any event, there is another even greater difficulty. . . . He [Roke'aḥ] should have said that the wrongdoer was guilty of violating "You shall not move your neighbor's landmarks."

Maharshal ruled that the second individual who ousted the first was liable, even though causation of the harm was only indirect. He relied on the ruling of Roke'aḥ that whoever interferes with the livelihood of his fellow is included in the category of "Cursed be he who moves his neighbor's landmark." However, Maharshal posed two problems in connection with

410. For details, *see* Elon, *supra* n. 406. The prohibition against "moving a landmark" applied not only to matters in which commerce was involved, but also to matters concerning the vocation of teachers, ritual slaughterers, rabbis, and the like. *See id.*

411. *Resp. Maharshal* #89.

412. As to this rule, *see supra* p. 219 n. 137.

413. For details on the author of *Sefer ha-Roke'aḥ*, *see infra* p. 1239.

this decision of Roke'aḥ: First, how can Roke'aḥ rely on the verse "Cursed be he who moves his neighbor's landmark," when according to Talmudic law the prohibition against moving a landmark applies only to real property and only in the Land of Israel,[414] whereas the question for decision by Roke'aḥ involved infringement of livelihood in Poland and Germany? Second, why, instead of relying on the verse containing the direct prohibition, "You shall not move your neighbor's landmarks," did Roke'aḥ rely on the verse containing the curse, "Cursed be he who moves his neighbor's landmark"? Maharshal responded to these two questions as follows:

> It seems to me that he received the tradition from his teachers that the verse "Cursed be he who moves his neighbor's landmark" is written to teach that the prohibition against "moving landmarks" also applies to trade and commerce. He [the second concessionaire] must return the customs station in its original condition without any additional payment or must pay compensation for the damage even though only indirectly caused.

Maharshal's explanation of the source of Roke'aḥ's view on the expansion of the prohibition against the moving of landmarks to include interference with another's livelihood is based on interpreting the two Biblical verses about moving landmarks: the first, "You shall not move your neighbor's landmarks," and the second, "Cursed be he who moves his neighbor's landmark." He argued that since the second verse, if it meant only what it seems to say, would be redundant, it should be interpreted as indicating the intent to broaden the prohibition to include trade and commerce and to impose liability for damages as a sanction for violating it.

Here again we have an example of exegesis of a Biblical verse by one of the foremost halakhic authorities of the sixteenth century, which, while it did not create law, did provide Scriptural support for the law and integrated the law with the Torah.

C. "Scheming Witnesses" (*Edim Zomemim*)

In the following example, we find a particular emphasis by a halakhic authority on the question of exegetical interpretation of the Torah after the completion of the Talmud. David b. Zimra (Radbaz), one of the leading halakhic authorities in the seventeenth century, was asked to clarify the law concerning witnesses found to have testified falsely that the defendant owed a sum of money; other witnesses appeared and testified concerning

414. According to the *Halakhah*, a person who steals another's land in the Land of Israel transgresses two prohibitions: "You shall not move your neighbor's landmarks" and "You shall not steal." Outside the Land of Israel, he transgresses only the latter. *See Sifrei*, Deuteronomy, Shofetim, sec. 188 (p. 227); Maimonides and Sh. Ar., both *supra* n. 405.

the first witnesses that "you were with us on the day your testimony stated the event occurred," and the first witnesses, therefore, could not have witnessed what they claimed to have seen. In such a case, the first witnesses, known as "scheming witnesses" (*edim zomemim*), are liable to pay the amount that they testified the defendant owed. The problem posed was whether the amount must be paid to the original defendant whom they sought to make liable for this amount or whether "the court may give it to whomever it wishes," on the theory that the liability of the scheming witnesses is in the nature of a penalty rather than compensatory damages.

In his responsum,[415] Radbaz wrote that the money should be paid to the individual against whom they falsely testified, and he supported this conclusion with, *inter alia,* the following rationale:

> If not for the fact that I hesitate to give a Biblical verse an interpretation not found in the Talmud, I would deduce this from a superfluous word. The verse states: "You shall do to him as he schemed to do to his fellow" [lit. "brother"].[416] "To his brother" is superfluous [it would have been enough to state: "You shall do to him as he had schemed to do"]. This is its meaning: "You shall do to him as he schemed to do," and this act shall be to his brother [*i.e.,* what he sought to accomplish with his false testimony, and what the court now does to the false witness, should be "to his brother"—the payment should be given to his brother, namely, the one against whom the witnesses gave false testimony]. There are similar interpretations in the Talmud, and you should use this rationale until you find a better one, as I, too, will do myself.

Radbaz approached the use of Biblical exegesis with diffidence, but in the end he saw in his exegesis an essential reason on which to base his conclusion that a scheming witness must make payment to the person he sought by his testimony to make liable.[417]

415. *Resp. Radbaz* #1049.

416. Deuteronomy 19:19.

417. This is certainly the law where the victim had already paid out the money as a result of the false testimony, since in monetary matters "You shall do to him as he schemed to do . . ." (*i.e.,* the sanction against scheming witnesses) applies even after the decision in the case has been carried out. *See Resp. Radbaz* #1049.

Radbaz reached his conclusion on the additional basis of an analogy drawn from the law of double payment for theft and an interpretation of the reasons underlying the Scriptural text:

> One should interpret the logic of Scripture: Since the victim of theft suffers anguish, it is only right that he should receive double payment; in this case, too, the one [*i.e.,* the victim of the scheming witnesses] who paid what he should not have had to pay has suffered anguish and is entitled to receive the double payment of the false witness because the same reason applies to both cases.

We have cited these illustrations to point out that Biblical exegesis did not completely cease even after the Talmud was completed. However, these illustrations, which can be supplemented by many others,[418] do not impair the correctness of the proposition that in halakhic literature after the completion of the Talmud, and especially after the middle of the geonic period,[419] neither creative nor integrative Biblical exegesis was employed to any significant extent. Interpretive activity and midrashic methods continued in full force, not in the area of Biblical exegesis but in the area of interpretation of the *Halakhah* (*midrash ha-halakhah*), of documents, and of legislation. These types of interpretation are reviewed in the chapters that follow.

This is true even when the decision in the case has not yet been carried out:

> He suffered anguish because they testified falsely against him to make him liable to pay money, and, had they not been discovered to be false, he would have paid. Therefore, the Torah awards him the payments, for all its ways are pleasant ways.

418. *See, e.g.,* the solution to the problem of authorizing entry into the house of a debtor to collect a debt. The problem resulted from Deuteronomy 24:10–11, which states:

> When you make a loan of any sort to your countryman, you must not enter his house to seize his pledge. You must remain outside, while the man to whom you made the loan brings the pledge out to you.

This prohibition was given a restrictive interpretation by Ramah and Rabbenu Tam. For details, *see* Elon, *Ḥerut,* pp. 56–64, quoting Ramah, who, "because it is work for the sake of Heaven," searched for a way to solve the problem although there was nothing in the Talmud or in the works of his teachers on which to base a solution. *See id.* at n. 25. *See also Tosafot,* Kiddushin 43b, s.v. Ve-hashta de-tikkun rabbanan shevu'at hesset; *Resp. Asheri* 84:2 (before the end). Further sources can be found in *Torah Temimah,* which occasionally quotes *midrashim* in the name of post-Talmudic scholars. Each source must, however, be scrutinized meticulously. *See also* Frankel, *Mishnah,* p. 17:

> The early generations [*i.e.,* the Talmudic Sages] built and completed the Torah by interpreting the verses of the Torah. This was not the method of the later authorities. After the Talmud was completed, they found the table set and the house built, and Scripture was no longer subject to further interpretation. If uncertainty arose about any law of the Torah, they did not resolve it by Biblical exegesis, but rather by turning to the Talmudic Sages for guidance.

In general, this statement is correct, but stated too categorically, since, as we have seen, there has occasionally been room for Biblical exegesis in the post-Talmudic era. *See also* M. Drori, "Shegagah ba-Mishpat ha-Ivri: Ta'ut ba-Din ve-Ta'ut ba-Uvdah" [Error in Jewish Law: Mistake of Law and Mistake of Fact], *Shenaton,* I (1974), pp. 72ff., at 85–86.

419. For Biblical exegesis in the geonic period, *see* Weiss, *Dor Dor ve-Doreshav,* IV, pp. 14ff. and p. 16 n. 6.

Chapter 10

INTERPRETATION OF THE *HALAKHAH*

I. The Nature of Halakhic Interpretation
II. Halakhic Interpretation in Ancient and Tannaitic Times
   A. Legislation Concerning *Agunot*—The Enactment Speaks of the Usual Situation
   B. Maintenance and Support of Daughters—Analogy from a Parallel Rule
   C. Indirect Evidence of Halakhic Interpretation
      1. Agency for the Purpose of Divorce
      2. Bailments
III. Halakhic Interpretation in the Amoraic Period
   A. Legal Capacity of Minors in the Law of Finders—Plain Meaning versus Nonliteral Interpretation
   B. Liability in Tort—Restricting the Rule to Limited Facts
IV. Halakhic Interpretation in the Post-Talmudic Period
   A. Guidelines for Judicial Decision Making—How Far Do Authoritative Materials Bind the Judge?
   B. Fraudulent Conveyances—Resourcefulness of the Halakhic Authorities in Combating Fraud
   C. Use of Traditional Canons in Interpreting Post-Talmudic Responsa

I. THE NATURE OF HALAKHIC INTERPRETATION

Up to this point, we have seen how the canons of interpretation and the other methods of exegesis of the Biblical text served as a source for the continued creation, development, and consolidation of the *Halakhah.* At a very early period, the Sages also began to apply the same midrashic methods, and with the very same objective, to the corpus of the *Halakhah* then existing.

> The *tannaim* dealt with these laws as they did with the Written Law; . . . they expounded them, and they derived new laws from them by means of rules of interpretation and logic.[1]

1. H. Albeck, *Mavo,* p. 63.

The reason is clear and quite understandable. From the moment that any halakhic collection, any enactment, or any other authoritative rule of Jewish law became an integral part of the *Halakhah*, it was itself automatically transformed into a subject of halakhic interpretation. It was only natural, and self-evident, that new legal rules being added to the corpus of the *Halakhah* themselves called for explication by means of all the available methods of interpretation. New laws had to be explained and interpreted logically, and new problems had to be solved by analogy and by the other midrashic methods.

In fact, the halakhic authorities used the term *midrash* to denote not only Biblical exegesis but also interpretation of *Halakhah:*

> In truth, the word *midrash* applies not only to Biblical exegesis but also to interpretation of enactments or ancient rules; for the meaning of *midrash* is "explanation" ["searching out," "clarification"], and this is also required for an old *takkanah* because when a long time has elapsed since its enactment it sometimes becomes necessary to investigate how it became enacted and also to analyze each and every word of it.[2]

For convenience in usage and definition, we shall call this interpretation "halakhic interpretation" (*midrash ha-Halakhah*), inasmuch as its function is to explain the *Halakhah*, in contrast to "Biblical exegesis" or "Biblical interpretation" (the type of interpretation discussed up to this point), which seeks to explain Biblical sections and verses.

Halakhic interpretation is the natural extension of Biblical interpretation. For a considerable time, halakhic interpretation functioned alongside Biblical interpretation; and, after Biblical interpretation ceased, halakhic interpretation continued to function in every period of Jewish law to the present day. In general, the halakhic authorities used the principles and rules of Biblical interpretation for halakhic interpretation as well,[3] although, with respect to one or another rule or principle of interpretation, they distinguished between Biblical and halakhic interpretation. This chapter briefly examines some of these aspects of halakhic interpretation in various periods of its history.

2. Frankel, *Mishnah*, pp. 96–97 n. 9.

3. Obviously, certain types of Biblical interpretation are inappropriate as methods of interpreting *Halakhah*, *e.g.*, the *gezerah shavah*, which is based on similar verbal expressions in connection with two quite different subjects, and was therefore qualified by the rule that no *gezerah shavah* may be used unless received by way of tradition from a teacher. *See supra* pp. 354–355.

II. HALAKHIC INTERPRETATION IN ANCIENT AND TANNAITIC TIMES

Examination of the teachings of the Sages sheds light on the various methods they used to interpret the legal rules with which they were dealing. These methods were sometimes explicitly stated and sometimes only implicit.

A. Legislation Concerning *Agunot*—The Enactment Speaks of the Usual Situation

One of the ancient enactments in the series of enactments adopted in order to enable the remarriage of *agunot* (*i.e.*, women "anchored" or "bound" by their marriage to husbands, as, for example, when the husband has disappeared) provided that a woman who accompanied her husband on a trip to a distant country and later returned alone, declaring "My husband has died," is to be believed in spite of the absence of witnesses to prove his death.[4] There was disagreement between the schools of Hillel and Shammai as to the scope and application of this enactment:[5]

> The School of Hillel said: "We have heard so [it is our understanding that a woman is believed when she declares "My husband has died"] only when she comes from the harvest in the same country and when the facts are similar to those in the actual case [as reported in the Talmud in which the Sages permitted the wife to remarry]."[6] The School of Shammai said to them: "The law applies whether she comes from the harvest, the olive grove, or the vintage, and whether or not she comes from outside the country; the Sages referred to the harvest only because it is the usual situation [*i.e.*, because it is common and frequent, and because those were the facts in that case]." The School of Hillel thereupon reconsidered and adopted the view of the School of Shammai.

The schools of Shammai and Hillel initially disputed whether the law under consideration should be interpreted expansively or restrictively, but they finally agreed that an expansive approach should be used, as the Sages often did when they interpreted a Biblical verse on the basis that "Scripture spoke of the usual situation."[7] For example:

4. M Yevamot 15:1. For a detailed discussion, *see infra* pp. 522–524.

5. M Yevamot 15:2.

6. *I.e.*, the woman's testimony is not accepted unless she and her husband had been harvesting in the heat of the day in a location near enough for her testimony to be verified, as in the precedent cited in TB Yevamot 116b, where the Sages permitted her to remarry.

7. *See Baraita of 32 Canons* (which appears in current editions of TB following Tractate Berakhot), where this is considered to be one of the canons of Biblical interpretation. *See*

> The same law applies to an ox and to all other domesticated animals that have fallen into a pit; [likewise] with respect to double payment [for their wrongful taking] and to their return if they are lost. The same also applies to a wild beast, a bird, etc. If so, why were only an ox and an ass specified? [In the Biblical discussion of these matters, the case is always put in terms of an ox or an ass, *e.g.*, Exodus 21:33; 22:3; 23:4.] Because Scripture spoke of the usual situation.[8]

B. Maintenance and Support of Daughters—Analogy from a Parallel Rule

In early *Halakhah* until the middle of the second century C.E., the duty of a father to support his children was only a religious and ethical, but not a legal, requirement.[9] The question arose as to whether the absence of a legal obligation existed only in respect to sons. Was there a legal obligation to support daughters, who, in contradistinction to sons, are entitled to support from the father's estate? Or were sons and daughters equally without legal entitlement to support during the lifetime of the father? With reference to this, the Mishnah says:[10]

> A father is not legally obligated to support his daughter. This is the midrashic reasoning that R. Eleazar b. Azariah presented to the Sages in the academy in Yavneh:[11] "The sons will inherit and the daughters will be supported." Just as sons do not inherit until after the death of their father, so daughters are not supported until after the death of their father.

R. Eleazar b. Azariah reached his conclusion that a father has no legal obligation to support his daughter during his lifetime by means of an analogical approach to the halakhic rule that "the sons will inherit and the daughters will be supported." Since the laws relating to sons and daughters were joined together in that single formulation, he reasoned that both are applicable under the same circumstances, namely, only after the death of the father. Just as the law entitling sons to inherit can, in the nature of things, apply only after the father's death, so the law relating to the support of daughters also applies only after the father's death.

What is the source of the formulation "the sons will inherit and the

---

examples given there and in *Mekhilta de-R. Ishmael,* Mishpatim, Tractate De-Kaspa, sec. 20 (p. 321).

8. M Bava Kamma 5:7.

9. *See supra* p. 116 for detailed discussion.

10. M Ketubbot 4:6.

11. The great house of learning in Yavneh, which was known as "the vineyard in Yavneh" (*kerem be-Yavneh*).

daughters will be supported," which R. Eleazar b. Azariah interpreted by analogy? This text is cited in the Mishnah as an ancient enactment relating to the laws of inheritance:[12] "When one dies leaving a large estate and surviving sons and daughters, the sons will inherit and the daughters will be supported." This is an instance where a *tanna* of the second generation deduced a legal rule by interpreting an early *halakhah,* the legal source of which was a *takkanah.*[13]

C. Indirect Evidence of Halakhic Interpretation

Sometimes, the evidence indicating the use of halakhic interpretation is not direct and explicit, but merely implies such use:

> The later *tannaim* drew conclusions from the statements of the early *tannaim* not only as to the same subject matter, but as to different issues as well. They inferred one matter from another; and if two subject areas had a common element, they applied to one area the reasons underlying a rule of law in the other, thus establishing a single rule for both areas. . . . They also carried over controversies of the early *tannaim* beyond their immediate subject matter, claiming that the rationale and reasoning in one matter required the *tannaim* to disagree on the same basis in other matters. They reported the earlier *tannaim* by name as being in disagreement on other matters, even though, in fact, these earlier *tannaim* explicitly disagreed only in one area and the statement that the controversy extended to other areas as well was based entirely on inference.[14]

The following are two illustrations of indirect evidence of halakhic interpretation.

1. AGENCY FOR THE PURPOSE OF DIVORCE

In connection with agency for divorce, the Mishnah says:[15]

> If one says [to his agent], "Give this *get* (bill of divorcement) to my wife in place X," and he gives it to her in a different place, it is invalid [because the husband took pains to stipulate that he should give her the divorce in the designated place]. [If, however, he says to the agent,] "She is in place X," and

12. M Bava Batra 9:1; Ketubbot 13:3 (where the text is in the present tense: "The sons inherit and the daughters are supported"). The Talmud calls this law a *takkanah* (enactment). *See* TB Bava Batra 131b, stating, in regard to R. Eleazar b. Azariah's interpretation, that "one *takkanah* can be deduced from another."

13. This example is dealt with more fully, *infra* pp. 427–428, in connection with the interpretation of documents, since the same language—"the sons will inherit and the daughters will be supported"—became part of the *ketubbah.*

14. H. Albeck, *Mavo,* p. 93.

15. M Gittin 6:3.

> the agent delivers it to her in a different place, it is valid [the husband's intent being only to inform the agent where she could be found].

This rule reflects the interpretive principle that one may deduce the intent of a juristic act from language used by the actor. Thus, it is concluded from one form of expression that the husband makes a point of requiring a particular place for the delivery of the *get* ("give . . . in place X") and therefore if the divorce is delivered in a different place it is invalid. A different form of expression ("she is in place X") does not lead to the conclusion that being in a particular place was a prerequisite for the divorce, and in that case the divorce is valid even if delivered elsewhere.

We find the same principle also applied to the subject of agency for marriage:[16]

> If one says [to his agent], "Go and betroth for me woman A in place X," and he goes and betroths her in a different place, she is not betrothed. [If, however, he says,] "She is in place X," and the agent betroths her in a different place, she is betrothed.

It seems likely that the interpretive principle was stated originally with respect to only one of the two situations, *i.e.*, either divorce or marriage, and that the later *tannaim* carried over the principle to the other situation.[17]

2. BAILMENTS

In connection with the laws of bailments, the Mishnah states:[18]

> If one deposits money [coins] with a money changer [an individual whose occupation is the examination and exchange of coins], and the coins are tied in a bundle, he [the money changer] may not use them; therefore, if they are lost, he does not bear the risk. If they are loose, he may use them; therefore, if they are lost, he bears the risk. [However, if one deposits them] with a householder [a private individual], whether they are tied in a bundle or loose, he [the householder] may not use them; therefore, if they are lost, he does not bear the risk. According to R. Meir, a shopkeeper is like a householder. R. Judah says: "A shopkeeper is like a money changer."

If the depositor gave money that was tied in a bundle, the law is that the bailee—whether a householder, money changer, or shopkeeper—may not use the money so entrusted to him. But if the money consists of loose coins, the right to use it depends on the type of bailee. If the bailee is one

16. M Kiddushin 2:4.

17. There is no evidence indicating whether the principle originated first in regard to agency for divorce or agency for marriage.

18. M Bava Meẓi'a 3:11.

who uses money in his business, the depositor is presumed to know that the bailee is likely to make use of it; and, therefore, the bailee may do so. (This is the rule, for example, in the case of a money changer, or, according to R. Judah, a shopkeeper.) If, however, the bailee is, for example, a private individual, such as a householder, he may not use the money even though left with him in the form of loose coins, because the money was given to him not to use but only for safekeeping. The law is the same with respect to a shopkeeper, according to R. Meir, since dealing in currency is not the shopkeeper's business.

We see from this distinction that one who may use the money is viewed as a paid bailee, since he receives a benefit from the deposit of the money with him—a "payment" for safeguarding it—and the burden of any loss falls on him if the money is stolen or lost ("he bears the risk"). However, one who may not use the money has the status of an unpaid bailee because he receives no benefit from the deposit of the money; and, therefore, he does not bear the burden of any loss resulting from theft or loss of the money ("he does not bear the risk").

The same principle applies in the law of *me'ilah* (lit. "sacrilege," *i.e.*, unlawful use of sacred property):[19]

> If one deposits coins [dedicated to sacred use] with a money changer, and the coins are tied in a bundle, he may not use them; therefore, if he uses them, he is guilty of sacrilege. If they are loose, he may use them; therefore, if he uses them, he is not guilty of sacrilege. [If one deposits them] with a householder, whether they are tied in a bundle or loose, he may not use them; therefore, if he uses them, he is guilty of sacrilege. According to R. Meir, a shopkeeper is like a householder. R. Judah says: "A shopkeeper is like a money changer."

In this *mishnah*, the same principle (with all of its consequences) that is applicable in the case of the bailee's responsibility for loss was applied to the issue of the guilt of the bailee for sacrilege. If the bailee may use the money and the depositor did not inform the bailee that the money was dedicated to sacred use, the bailee is not guilty of sacrilege if he uses it; "it is as if the depositor instructed him to use it, since it was not tied in a bundle, and he was carrying out his agency."[20] If, however, the bailee does

19. M Me'ilah 6:5. It is forbidden to use or derive benefit from a consecrated object. One who violates this prohibition through inadvertence is required to offer a sacrifice, called *asham me'ilot* (guilt offering for sacrilege), and pay to the Temple the value of the benefit derived, plus a fine.

20. Commentary of Obadiah Bertinoro to M Me'ilah 6:5. The depositor, however, has transgressed because he gave the bailee tacit permission to use the money by giving him the coins loose. *See* TB Bava Meẓi'a 43a.

not have permission to use it, then he is guilty of sacrilege if he does so; in that event, the use is on his own initiative, not within the scope of his authority as agent, and the prohibition of sacrilege therefore applies to him.

The consequence of whether the right to use the money did or did not exist was thus applied alike to the questions of liability for loss and of guilt of sacrilege. Here, too, it seems that, at first, the principle developed with respect to one of these issues, and the *tannaim* later applied the principle, by logical inference, to the other.[21]

III. HALAKHIC INTERPRETATION IN THE AMORAIC PERIOD

In the amoraic period, the momentum of halakhic interpretation vastly increased. By that time, the *amoraim* already had a series of redacted and authoritative collections of the *Halakhah,* especially the collection in the Mishnah of R. Judah Ha-Nasi. Just as the Sages of previous periods resorted primarily to Biblical exegesis to explain Scripture and to solve new problems, so the *amoraim* resorted mainly to interpretive methods to explicate the laws and to solve the new problems confronting them. As a matter of course, and for obvious reasons, the *amoraim* used the same canons and methods of interpretation to carry out their interpretive task as their predecessors had used for Biblical interpretation.

> Truly, if we examine the Talmud and its methods of interpreting the Mishnah, it will become clear to us that the Sages of the Gemara [that part of the Talmud that contains discussion of the Mishnah] adopted the canons and principles of Biblical interpretation as their own canons for the interpretation of the Mishnah.[22]

The *amoraim* adopted principles for the interpretation of the Mishnah similar in methodology to the tannaitic interpretations of Scripture, and they also added many of their own.[23] Moreover:

21. Here, too, there is no evidence indicating in which context the principle was first established.

22. Weiss, *Dor Dor ve-Doreshav,* III, pp. 10ff.; *see passim* for many examples of the use made by *amoraim* of the thirteen canons, and others as well, in interpreting the Mishnah and tannaitic *Halakhah. See also* H.L. Strack, *Introduction to the Talmud and Midrash,* p. 5 and nn. 33, 34, on the use of the term *talmud* in this connection.

23. *E.g.,* the rule that the letter *vav* is disjunctive as well as conjunctive (*see supra* p. 321) was also applied to tannaitic *dicta. See, e.g.,* M Yevamot 5:6: "If he submitted to *ḥaliẓah* from her and [*v*] then made a statement of betrothal to her, gave her a *get* (bill of divorcement), or [*v*] consummated marriage with her . . . ," where the first *vav* is interpreted as conjunctive, while the second is understood as meaning "or"; M Berakhot 6:8: "If a man

> It was the practice of the *amoraim* to subject the Mishnah and the *baraita* to minute analysis in the same way that the *tannaim* parsed Scripture, and their approach was that every redundancy in language was meant to convey something additional. Sometimes, they would pose questions that were not inherently difficult, but were raised only to give occasion for responses that would provide support for the statements of the *amoraim* and for new laws, by indicating that they rest on the teachings of the *tannaim*.[24]

Because of the greater quantity and detail of the halakhic discussion extant from the amoraic period as compared to the tannaitic, a study of the ways in which the *amoraim* used halakhic interpretation enables us to follow more closely how interpretive methods contributed to the development

---

ate figs or [*v*] grapes or [*v*] pomegranates, he should say the three benedictions after them," which means that if he ate any one of those kinds of fruit he must, in the opinion of the *tanna* quoted, recite grace after meals; M Avodah Zarah 4:10: "If a gentile fell into a wine vat and [*v*] came up again, or [*v*] if he measured it with a reed . . . ," where the second *vav* is to be understood as disjunctive. *See also* TB Bava Kamma 9a, where the *v* in R. Assi's statement "a quarter in land [*v*] a quarter in money" is to be understood as meaning "or," and Rashi, *ad loc.*, s.v. U-revi'a be-ma'ot.

Another rule relates to the explanation of a term repeated in a tannaitic source in the course of the same discussion: "Since [the *tanna*] had to use the term *nitkal* (collided with) in the last part of the *mishnah*, he also used it [rather than "broke"] in the first part" (TB Bava Kamma 27b–28a, *et al.*).

A new and important general principle created for interpreting tannaitic sources is: "Generalizations should not be applied literally" (lit. "one may not deduce [laws] from general statements") (TB Kiddushin 34a, *et al.*). *E.g.*, the word "all" in "the observance of all the positive commandments that are to be performed at specific times is incumbent on men but not on women" (M Kiddushin 1:7) is not to be taken literally, and at best means "most," since "the obligations to eat *mazzah* [unleavened bread] on the first night of Passover, to rejoice on the Pilgrimage Festivals, to participate in the *Hakhel* ceremony [Deuteronomy 31:10–13], to pray, to hear the *Megillah* [Scroll of Esther read on *Purim*], to kindle the *Hanukkah* and sabbath lights, and to consecrate the sabbath [with the *kiddush* ceremony] are positive commandments that are to be performed at specific times and yet each one is as incumbent upon women as upon men" (Maimonides, *Commentary on the Mishnah*, ed. Kafaḥ, p. 292). *See also* ET, I, pp. 112–113, s.v. O leḥallek; pp. 295–296, s.v. Ein lemedin min ha-kelalot.

Various other rules were formulated for the interpretation of the text of the Mishnah, such as "It is preferable to adopt a strained interpretation and explain a *mishnah* as being based upon two reasons and constituting the view of one *tanna*, rather than as being based upon one reason but constituting the view of two *tannaim*" (TB Kiddushin 63b, *et al.*; and *cf.* Rashi, Ketubbot 57a, s.v. Ha kamashma lan). Another example: "R. Joshua b. Levi said: 'Every place where R. Judah used the word *eimatai* (when) and *ba-meh* (in what) in a *mishnah*, he wished to explicate the view of the Sages [previously set forth].' R. Johanan said: '*Eimatai* is used when he wishes to explicate, but *ba-meh* is used when he wishes to disagree'" (TB Eruvin 82a, *et al.*). For many additional examples, *see* Israel Jacob Algazi, *Kehillat Ya'akov*, II, Ma'aneh Lashon, Leshon Ḥakhamim, Letters *alef* to *tav*.

24. H. Albeck, *Mishnah*, Zera'im, Berakhot, p. 336, and *see* the full discussion there. To the same effect is Weiss, *supra* n. 22.

of the *Halakhah* than how such methods contributed to Biblical exegesis in the tannaitic period.

Biblical interpretation is often stated very tersely and in quite general terms; the interpretation of a Biblical verse often consists of only a few words. In contrast, the materials for halakhic interpretation of the amoraic period include: (a) halakhic material of the tannaitic period, crystallized and clearly expounded in the Mishnah, the collections of *midrashim*, and various *baraitot*, all of which provide subjects for interpretation; and (b) detailed debates and discussions of the *amoraim* themselves in the two Talmuds, which include many details not only with regard to the *Halakhah* derived through interpretation, but also with regard to the interpretive process.

A comparison of the *Halakhah* in the tannaitic period with the *Halakhah* in the amoraic period provides us with many possibilities for examining the significant role played by amoraic interpretation (in the broad sense of this term, rather than merely in the limited sense of the thirteen canons) of tannaitic law in the continuing creativity and development of Jewish law. Several illustrative examples follow.

A. Legal Capacity of Minors in the Law of Finders— Plain Meaning versus Nonliteral Interpretation

The Mishnah states:[25]

> What is found by a minor son or daughter belongs to the father; what is found by an adult son or daughter belongs to the finder.

The literal meaning of this law seems clear: if the son is a minor, the object belongs to his father, and if the son is an adult, the object belongs to the son.

In the Talmudic discussion, however, there is a difference of opinion as to the meaning of this law:[26]

> Samuel said: "Why was it ruled that what a minor finds belongs to his father? Because at the time that he finds it he brings it quickly to his father and does not retain it in his possession."

Samuel's point was that the rationale for the legal principle that what a minor finds belongs to his father is that when the minor finds an object, he does not intend to keep it for himself but picks it up in order to bring to his father. An adult son, however, has the capacity and the intent to take

25. M Bava Meẓi'a 1:5.
26. TB Bava Meẓi'a 12a.

the found object for himself; therefore, it belongs to him. Samuel thus explained the law of the Mishnah according to the plain meaning of "minor" as referring to a person below the legal age of majority and an "adult" as one who has reached the age of majority. From this interpretation, two legal conclusions result:

1. A minor cannot obtain any rights for himself in an object that he finds, because he has no legal capacity, *i.e.*, no sufficient mental capacity to acquire an object for himself; his intent is to take the found object for the adult, his father.[27]
2. An adult under all circumstances always acquires for himself any object he finds, and what he finds does not belong to his father.

Later in the discussion, the view of R. Johanan, who disagreed with Samuel, is stated:

> He [Samuel] disagrees with R. Ḥiyya b. Abba; as R. Ḥiyya b. Abba said in the name of R. Johanan: "Adult" does not mean an actual adult and "minor" does not mean an actual minor. One who has reached the age of majority but is supported by his father is a "minor"; and one who has not attained his majority but is not supported by his father is an "adult."[28]

R. Ḥiyya b. Abba, in the name of R. Johanan, explained the terms "adult" and "minor" in the *mishnah* not on the basis of chronological age but rather as depending on the particular circumstances of each case. According to this view, a son who is of age but supported by his father is a "minor" with regard to a found object, and the object belongs to his father "on account of animosity";[29] *i.e.*, the Sages enacted that since the son is supported by his father, whatever the son acquires by finding should belong to his father, as otherwise there would be animosity between the father and the son and the father might withdraw his support. On the other hand, a son who is not supported by his father retains the object for himself even though he is a minor in terms of age.

Two conclusions contrary to those of Samuel can be drawn from R. Johanan's explanation of the *mishnah:*

1. A minor may retain a found object for himself if he is not supported by his father.[30]

27. *See Shittah Mekubbeẓet, ad loc.*, s.v. Ve-talmid ha-Rap: "Not only is this the case under Biblical law, but even under rabbinic law he does not have the legal capacity to acquire an object for himself."

28. TB Bava Meẓi'a 12b.

29. Rashi, *ad loc.*, s.v. A-de-rabbi Ḥiyya bar Abba.

30. He must, however, have reached at least the age at which he is able to comprehend his entitlement. Whether the rule is of Biblical or rabbinic origin is irrelevant.

2. Sometimes even an adult may not keep the object for himself, namely, when he is supported by his father.

Widely divergent legal conclusions thus resulted from different interpretations of the same *mishnah:* Samuel's, which accords with the plain meaning of the mishnaic text, and R. Johanan's, which uses midrashic methods to go beyond the plain meaning.

B. Liability in Tort—Restricting the Rule to Limited Facts

The Mishnah sets forth the following rule of tort law:[31]

> If someone leaves a jug in a public place and someone else comes along, stumbles over it, and breaks it, he [the one who breaks it] is not liable; if he [the one who breaks it] is injured by it, the owner of the jug is liable for the injury.

One who stumbles over the jug and breaks it is not liable for damages, because the jug was left unlawfully in the street, a public way. Moreover, if he was injured by the jug, its owner must compensate him for his injuries.

Two fundamental rules are stated in this *mishnah* with regard to one who leaves an object in the public domain:

1. One who stumbles over the object and breaks it is not liable.
2. If the object causes injury, the person who left the object in the public place is liable for the injury.

The second rule—that the owner of the object is liable for injury caused by him to others—is clear and reasonable, since the liability of one who leaves an object in a public place is similar to the liability of one who digs a pit in a public place. But what is the rationale of the law that a passerby who breaks the object is free from liability? Two different reasons were given in the Talmud: one is based on the plain meaning of the *mishnah* and accepts the legal principle that the *mishnah* intended to express, and the second is the result of an interpretation of the *mishnah* that is actually the opposite of the plain meaning of the text.

The first reason was given by some of the *amoraim* of the Land of Israel:[32]

> R. Abba said to R. Ashi: "This is what they say in the west [the Land of Israel] in the name of R. Ilaa:[33] 'People do not usually examine the road [while walking on it].'"

31. M Bava Kamma 3:1.

32. Quoted in TB Bava Kamma 27b.

33. This is the correct reading, *see Dikdukei Soferim, ad loc.* The printed version, however, has "Ulla."

According to this view, the reason for the nonliability of the passerby rests on the premise that he has no responsibility while he is walking along to be alert to objects that may be lying about on the road; the road is designated for human travel and "people do not usually examine the road [while walking on it]." Therefore, one who breaks the object while walking is not liable, because the owner had a duty to take care not to leave it in a public place.

The *amoraim* in Babylonia, as well as some of the *amoraim* in the Land of Israel, took a different view, based upon a diametrically opposite approach to an important issue of tort liability. This divergent view is mentioned at the outset of the Talmudic discussion of the subject:[34]

> Why is he free from liability [why should the passerby who broke the jug not be liable to pay for it]? He should have looked where he was going [and taken care not to break the jug].

The Talmud does not even raise the question of why the owner of the jug is liable for the injury caused to the passerby, because it is clear beyond any doubt that by putting the jug in a public place he creates a public obstruction, and he cannot be relieved of liability on the ground that the passerby should have exercised care not to stumble over the obstruction. However, by the same token, the fact that the owner of the object acted improperly should not free the passerby from liability for the damage that he caused, since the controlling principle is "one should be more careful not to cause damage than not to be damaged."[35] In other words, the duty to take care not to cause damage to another is stricter than the duty to take care not to be injured by someone else. And the question is, therefore, Why does the *mishnah* relieve the passerby from liability for breaking the jug?

In answer to this question, three *amoraim* restrict the scope of the legal rule relieving the passerby of liability, by interpreting the rule to apply only in certain specific factual circumstances. This is how the discussion continues:[36]

> It was said in the school of Rav in the name of Rav: "[The *mishnah* is referring to a case where] he filled the entire public area with jugs [and, therefore, the passerby who broke the jug is not liable as he had no alternative but to do so in order to proceed]."
>
> Samuel said: "The reference is to a dark place [the *mishnah* refers to a special situation—a dark place where a traveler could not see what is lying in the street]."

34. TB Bava Kamma 27b.
35. *Tosafot, ad loc.*, s.v. Amai patur iba'i leih le-iyyuni.
36. TB Bava Kamma 27b.

> R. Johanan said: "The reference is to a corner [the special circumstance is that the jug was placed in the intersection of two streets, and when the traveler turned the corner he did not see the jug and broke it]."

These three *amoraim* held that one who causes harm is generally liable even where the damage is to an object lying in a public area, notwithstanding the contributory negligence on the part of the owner of the object in placing it there. The plain meaning of the *mishnah* is in clear conflict with their view as to what the law should be. They attempted to reconcile this conflict by restrictive interpretation of the *mishnah;* they interpreted the *mishnah* as being confined to the special limited circumstances in which, even according to their view, the person who broke the jug is not liable.

In this illustration, too, different approaches to halakhic interpretation of the same *mishnah* yield two completely different and conflicting legal conclusions as to the extent of liability for causing damage.

On a different issue of tort law, we find the following rule:[37]

> The Rabbis taught: If one secretes thorns and broken glass in his neighbor's wall and the owner of the wall pulls it down, and the thorns and glass fall into a public place and cause injury, the one who secreted the thorns and glass is liable.

The person responsible for the injury here is the one who secretes the glass or thorns and not the person who tears down his own wall. The legal principle established here is that in such a case there is strict liability on the owner of the object that causes injury in the public place, but not on the one who was the immediate cause of the object's being there. R. Johanan explained (interpreted) this law as follows:

> This rule applies only to a wall in poor condition; but in the case of a sound wall, the one who secretes the dangerous object is not liable, and the owner of the wall is liable.

R. Johanan explained that the statement in the *baraita* that the one who secretes the glass is liable is applicable to a case where he does so in a wall that is in poor condition; he should realize that the wall would be torn down and the glass would fall into a public place. But if it is a sound wall, he need not foresee that the wall would be torn down, and he is therefore not liable. The owner of the wall, however, is liable because he should examine the wall before he tears it down, in order to ascertain whether glass or thorns are inside it.

37. TB Bava Kamma 30a.

This statement of R. Johanan changes the rule that is expressed by the plain meaning of the *baraita*. According to the *baraita*'s plain meaning, the owner of the object causing the injury is strictly liable. R. Johanan, however, held that, as a general rule, the owner of the wall is responsible, since he should examine it before tearing it down, and only if the wall is in poor condition, so that the owner of the object should foresee that the wall may soon be torn down, is he liable for any injury caused by the object.

Once again, we have here an example of the limitation of a legal principle, this time through a restrictive interpretation of the content of a *baraita*.[38]

IV. HALAKHIC INTERPRETATION IN THE POST-TALMUDIC PERIOD

In the same way that the *amoraim* interpreted the Mishnah and the other halakhic collections of the *tannaim*, the halakhic authorities in the post-Talmudic period interpreted the Talmudic *Halakhah;* and the authorities of every generation likewise interpreted the authoritative halakhic literature that had been added to Jewish law up to and including the generation immediately preceding their own. The halakhic authorities of every generation thoroughly examined and interpreted the text and the content of the writings of their predecessors. They expanded, developed, and created Jewish law, and they solved new problems that continually arose. The primary instrument by which they accomplished this was the employment of midrashic methods to interpret the Talmudic *Halakhah* and the authoritative halakhic literature then extant. Halakhic interpretation played a large and important role in the enormous development of the literary sources of the law—responsa, codificatory literature, commentaries, and novellae.[39]

The post-Talmudic authorities in their own halakhic interpretations used the methods and approaches to Biblical and halakhic interpretation that had been employed up to their time. Many and varied interpretive

38. *See further* Ravina's statement in the Talmudic discussion, and Maimonides, *MT*, Nizkei Mamon 12:9. For further development of this law, *see Resp. Asheri* 101:3 and the inconsistency between Sh. Ar. ḤM 410:29, which cites Ravina's law but ignores Asheri's conclusion, and Rema to ḤM 383:2, who cites Asheri's view. *Sema*, ḤM 410, subpar. 44, reconciles the inconsistency, and in so doing further develops the principle under discussion.

39. *See, e.g.*, Elon, *Ḥerut*, pp. 136–137 (proposal of Alexander Suslin ha-Kohen, author of *Sefer ha-Agudah*, for solving the problem of imprisonment for debt by means of interpretation of various laws dealt with in the Talmudic discussion); pp. 140–148 (view of Ribash); p. 192 (view of Yom Tov Lipmann Heller, author of *Tosafot Yom Tov*); pp. 240ff. (use of restrictive interpretation of a post-Talmudic law to solve the problem of delaying a debtor's burial); pp. 255ff.; and index, s.v. Interpretaẓyah.

approaches appear in the post-Talmudic halakhic material. Some coincide with the interpretive approach of the *amoraim* to the tannaitic *Halakhah*, while others differentiate between particular methods of interpretation in these two periods. A significant portion of these approaches represent new methods added over the course of time.[40] The halakhic authorities of every post-Talmudic period also used the thirteen canons of Biblical interpretation to interpret both the Talmudic *halakhah* and the halakhic statements of post-Talmudic scholars who preceded them. Many laws were deduced through *a fortiori* (*kal va-ḥomer*) reasoning[41] and by analogy; and, at times, the halakhic authorities explained why they used a particular canon in a

40. *See* ET, I, pp. 112–113, s.v. O leḥalek; pp. 295–296, s.v. Ein lemedin min ha-kelalot. For many further examples and a great deal of source material, *see* Algazi, *Kehillat Ya'akov, supra* n. 23 (end).

41. *E.g., Resp. Maharam of Rothenburg* (Prague, ed. Bloch) #85 reaches the conclusion that "the laborer has all of the privileges of the Hebrew slave by inference *a fortiori*. The Torah dealt generously with the Hebrew slave even though he was a transgressor. How much more so should a laborer, who is not a transgressor, be dealt with generously." The specific ruling was that a teacher who falls ill should not suffer any deduction from his pay for the time he is incapacitated, since a Hebrew slave incapacitated for three of the six years of his term of service is not required to make up the missing years of service.

As to the nature of the transgression by the Hebrew slave, *see Resp. Maharam of Rothenburg, supra* (also quoted in *Mordekhai*, Bava Meẓi'a #346), and particularly *Resp. Maharam of Rothenburg, supra*, #72. The transgression is the violation of a positive commandment of the Torah (Leviticus 25:55): "For it is to Me that the Israelites are servants: they are My servants, whom I freed from the land of Egypt, I the Lord your God." The Talmud interprets this verse: "'They are My servants'—not the servants of servants." TB Bava Kamma 116b, Bava Meẓi'a 10a, 77a. Thus, a Hebrew who sells himself into servitude violates the prohibition implicit in "they are My [*i.e.*, God's] servants" and not the servants of another master who himself is the servant of God. *See also Haggahot Mordekhai, ad loc.*

Maharam of Rothenburg, in the two responsa cited *supra*, understood this prohibition to be applicable only in the case of a Hebrew slave whose term of service is six years, but not in the case of a hired servant for a lesser period, such as one or two years, although TB Bava Meẓi'a 77a interprets the verse to mean that *any* laborer, even one who is employed for only one day, may quit before the day is out because he is not the "servant of servants."

Similarly, a *kal va-ḥomer* is utilized in *Resp. Naḥmanides* #3, quoted in S. Assaf, *Sifran Shel Rishonim*, pp. 58–59. The question submitted to Naḥmanides related to a monetary claim. The defendant first swore that he owed nothing, but afterward admitted owing half the amount claimed. The issue was whether the defendant had disqualified himself from taking a second oath—that he did not owe the other half of the claim—inasmuch as his admission showed that he had previously sworn falsely. Naḥmanides responded: "Imagine to yourself! If even a person who, in a locality where he is not known, says, 'I am not qualified [to be a witness],' cannot so disqualify himself [two competent witnesses being necessary for this], how much more so is this man—who volunteered an admission—not to be disqualified [from taking the second oath]. This is a *kal va-ḥomer* that cannot be refuted."

See also Resp. Rashba, II, #14: "Now I realize that the matter is a *kal va-ḥomer*"; *Resp. Maharshakh*, I, #44: "This matter can be deduced by a *kal va-ḥomer*." Such statements can be found in many responsa.

given context in halakhic interpretation. The following are brief illustrations.

A. Guidelines for Judicial Decision Making—How Far Do Authoritative Materials Bind the Judge?

In a long responsum on the law of adjoining landowners,[42] Abraham, son of Maimonides, made use of an analogy between two laws and between two points in the same law to answer the question referred to him, and he laid down the following guidelines for judicial decision making:[43]

> The principle of the matter is this: I say that a judge whose decisions follow only what is explicitly written is weak and indecisive. Such a practice contravenes the [Talmudic] *dictum*[44] that "a judge must be guided only by what his own eyes see." It [*i.e.*, to follow only what is explicitly written] is not correct. But the written laws are of prime importance, and the judge or decisionmaker must weigh them according to the circumstances of each case that comes before him, analogize his case to those that are similar, and derive branches from those roots.
>
> The many cases recorded in the Talmud, which represent only a fraction of the law, were not written without a purpose. That purpose is not that one should decide the law on a particular matter exactly as written there, but rather to enable the decisionmaker, familiar with them through repeated study, to acquire the power of balanced judgment and the proper approach to deciding cases. Even if the Talmud specifically stated that the law of adjoining landowners does not apply to one who has moved to another city, the judge must consider all aspects of the question and make his decision, particularly as the doctrine of adjoining landowners is based on the reasoning of the later authorities and is for the purpose of promoting the public welfare!

B. Fraudulent Conveyances—Resourcefulness of the Halakhic Authorities in Combating Fraud

In thirteenth century Spain, debtors increasingly failed to pay their debts and even secreted their assets by various sham arrangements in order to prevent their property from being reached to satisfy the debts.[45] The halakhic authorities searched for legal methods to negate the effect of these

42. On these laws, *see infra* pp. 625–626.
43. *Resp. Avraham b. ha-Rambam* #97 (pp. 147–148).
44. TB Bava Batra 131a.
45. *See* Elon, *Ḥerut*, pp. 118ff.

sham transfers. In one case brought before Asher b. Jehiel (Asheri),[46] "Reuben was obligated to Simeon on an oral loan, and he gave all his property to Levi in order to defeat Simeon's claim."[47] From a technical point of view, it was impossible to find a defect in Reuben's gift to Levi; but it was clear that the purpose of the transaction was to insulate the assets from Simeon, and in fact Reuben remained the real owner of the property. In time, he would by some means take the property back.

In a long responsum, Asheri ruled that the gift was invalid because, under the particular circumstances, the facts sufficiently demonstrated that Reuben's sole purpose was to secrete the assets from the creditor, and this chicanery invalidates the gift. In order to buttress this new legal principle, Asheri cited Talmudic discussions on different legal subjects in which the Sages took action against various types of defrauders.

One of his references was to the law with regard to an individual who purchased a small piece of land inside the seller's fields, following which he also purchased from the same seller the parcels of land adjoining the land he had previously acquired. It was ruled in the Talmud that if it could be concluded that the motive for the first sale was to make the purchaser an adjoining landowner in order to defeat the legal right of others owning property adjoining the seller's land, then the other landowners could oust the purchaser from the properties he subsequently purchased adjoining their own, because the entire transaction was fraudulent.[48] Asheri stated:[49]

> There is support for this in chapter *Ha-Mekabbel* [TB *Bava Meẓi'a* 108 a/b]: "It is fraud and we take it from him." The instant case is *a fortiori*. That case [in the Talmud] involved the law of the adjoining landowner, which is only a rabbinic enactment derived from the Biblical verse "You shall do what is right and good";[50] and the Sages were resourceful enough to block his fraud and prevent his scheme from succeeding. How much more so where one steals from his neighbor by deception, violates a Biblical law, and seeks to avoid paying his creditor, should we thwart his fraud and allow the creditor to collect his debt out of the gift!

46. *Resp. Asheri* 78:1.

47. Had the loan been evidenced by a written instrument, the gift to Levi would beyond question have been ineffective, since a loan by written instrument creates a lien on the debtor's property that would persist notwithstanding the transfer to Levi. *See infra* pp. 593–594.

48. TB Bava Meẓi'a 108a/b.

49. The same point is made in *Resp. Asheri* 78:3 in a more extensive form. The quotation at the beginning of this page is from 78:1, and that following the reference to this footnote is from 78:3. Asheri distributed 78:3 to all the scribes and witnesses, warning them not to participate in making documents intended to be used in fraudulent conveyances, since such documents are not valid. *See* Elon, *Ḥerut,* p. 125.

50. For a fuller discussion, *see infra* pp. 625–626.

Asheri cited additional examples where the Sages took action against defrauders, although none of them dealt with facts precisely in point. To explain the force of the argument from these examples, he added:[51]

> We see from all of these instances, that whenever anyone sought to fraudulently evade any prescription of the Sages and to scheme against his fellow, he was thwarted by the ingenuity of the Sages, who took action against him to frustrate his plan and nullify his evil design. And we shall draw inferences and reach conclusions by analogy from one case to another [*i.e.*, from the action taken by the Sages]. For the Sages of the Talmud were not able to specify everything that would happen in the future or all the new developments that would daily arise. Those who come after them follow in their footsteps and draw parallels from one case to another [when necessary to fashion new rules].

C. Use of Traditional Canons in Interpreting Post-Talmudic Responsa

In interpreting the *Halakhah,* the halakhic authorities used not only analogy and *a fortiori* reasoning, but also, as has been noted, the other canons as well. In the following example we find that a halakhic authority at the end of the fifteenth century interpreted the statements of a thirteenth-century authority by using the canon regarding inference from a generalization followed by a specification followed in turn by a generalization, and thereby solved the problem confronting him.

Judah Minz, one of the foremost authorities in Italy at the end of the fifteenth century, was asked[52] by the inhabitants of a certain community about a dispute concerning the financing of the completion of the synagogue, the construction of the ritual bath (*mikveh*) in the Jewish residential quarter, and the method of allocating food to the community's poor. The underlying question involved fundamental problems of Jewish public law in that period, namely: To what extent may a community's majority impose its decisions on the minority, and what is the criterion that should determine whether a member of the community must participate in financing construction of buildings designated for public use?[53] For example, is a member of the community required to participate in financing a public building for which he and the members of his household have no need?

Minz based his answer on a responsum given by Maharam of Roth-

51. *Resp. Asheri* 78:3, as to which *see also supra* p. 186 and *infra* pp. 1891–1894.

52. *Resp. Mahari Minz* #7.

53. For communal enactments and Jewish public law regarding this matter, *see infra* pp. 715–723.

enburg in a similar case, and he reached his decision by interpreting the responsum through use of the canon dealing with the inference to be drawn from a generalization followed by a specification followed in turn by a generalization.

After first establishing that Maharam of Rothenburg was accepted as a halakhic authority whose decisions are to be followed, Minz quoted Maharam's responsum as follows:

> To my friend and companion Abraham ha-Levi, concerning your question as to what should be done when there is dissension within your community and you are unable to come to a unanimous agreement on the choice of communal leaders. Everyone has a different viewpoint, and, as a result of the dispute, study is halted and the rule of law is impaired. There is no truth, justice, or peace in your city nor in the whole surrounding countryside. What is to be done?
>
> It seems to me that all taxpaying householders should be assembled and each one should take an oath[54] that he will present his point of view for the sake of Heaven and the welfare of the city and that he will follow the majority in regard to: choosing leaders; appointing officers; strengthening the charity fund; selecting tax collectors; building or renovating the synagogue; adding to or subtracting from, or buying, building, or renovating a wedding hall; and buying, building, or renovating a bakery. In the final analysis, all the needs of the community should be satisfied by them as they determine.
>
> If a minority were to refuse and fail to comply with the determination of the majority, or those whom the majority will appoint as their leaders, the majority has the power to use compulsion, according to both Jewish law and non-Jewish law, until the minority agrees to comply. If an appropriation of money is necessary, the minority must pay its share; whoever refuses to participate in the discussion in conformance with the oath shall have no voice in the matter, and the majority of those who took the oath will govern.
>
> In sum, the inhabitants of a city may compel one another to satisfy all important needs of the city, as stated in the *Tosefta Bava Meẓi'a:* "The townspeople may obligate each other to build a synagogue and to buy scrolls of the Torah, of the Prophets, and of the Hagiographa.[55] The inhabitants of an alleyway may obligate each other to build a sidepost and beam as a gateway to the alley."[56] Even though this is not such an important need, compulsion may be employed to satisfy it. How much more so for other needs that are more important! Let there be peace. Meir, son of Baruch of blessed memory.

54. The Hebrew reads *yekabbelu aleihem berakhah* (lit. "accept upon themselves a blessing")—a euphemism for taking an oath under penalty of execration for violation. "Blessing" (*berakhah*) is here used instead of "curse," as is sometimes done in English as well.

55. *Tosefta* Bava Meẓi'a 11:23; for further details, *see infra* pp. 679–680.

56. *Tosefta* Bava Meẓi'a 11:18.

Having quoted the responsum of Maharam of Rothenburg, Minz relied on it in deciding the case presented to him. He reached his decision in the following manner:

> Now, my dear friends, put your hearts to the road that leads to Beth-El [the house of God] and do not stray either to the right or left from what the illustrious scholar has shown us and what he taught and decided,[57] as his ways are pleasant ways and all his paths, peaceful.[58]
>
> This was his sequence: "*All* taxpaying householders should be assembled," etc., after which he made *specific* rulings—they should "follow the majority in regard to choosing leaders, etc.," following which he made a *general* ruling: "all the needs of the community should be satisfied by them as they determine."
>
> The generalization includes more than the specifications, and what it includes need not be of exactly the same character as the items referred to in the preceding specifications. It is a canon of Biblical interpretation that when a specification is followed by a generalization, the generalization includes more than the particulars specified. Afterward, at the end of his statement, he made an additional *generalization:*
>
> "In sum, the inhabitants of a city may compel one another to satisfy all important needs of the city. . . . The inhabitants of an alleyway may obligate each other to build a sidepost and beam. . . . Even though this is not such an important need, compulsion may be employed to satisfy it. How much more so for other needs that are greater!"
>
> We may conclude from all the foregoing that what is of public benefit or promotes the welfare of the community or of the majority of the community can be deduced from a similar instance, even if the similarity is not perfect. All or most of the instances listed in Maharam's responsum are not mentioned in the Mishnah, in any *baraita,* in the *Tosefta,* or in the Talmud; and even though they are not exactly the same, he arrived at them through reasoning based on the law that the townspeople may compel one another to purchase a synagogue and scrolls of the Torah, Prophets, and Hagiographa, and that the inhabitants of an alleyway may compel one another to build a sidepost and beam.
>
> He also stated that decisions of the majority must be followed, and that even if the opposing minority feel their arguments to be stronger, these arguments are of no force as against the majority and are to be disregarded, just as we would pay them no heed if they argued against hospitality to travelers, distribution of charity, or hiring a *minyan* [a quorum of ten for public prayer].
>
> The illustrious scholar made mention of an important point—that the majority may compel the minority to participate in the purchase, construction, or renovation of a wedding hall, even though this may mean overruling

57. *I.e.,* do not deviate in any respect from his ruling. *Cf. supra* pp. 243–244.
58. *Cf. supra* pp. 387–390 for the utilization of this verse in Biblical exegesis.

> many objections, such as: "I have no children yet," or "They are not yet adults," or "All my sons and daughters are already married," or "I may not have the wedding here," or "The expense is great." We reject arguments even as strong as these, and we build the wedding hall. Certainly, a ritual bath, which is not a matter of great expense, and for which the community has a much greater need than for a sidepost and beam or a wedding hall, is within the *a fortiori* inference that the illustrious scholar mentioned at the end of his opinion.
>
> The same applies to the complaints about the communal appointees. These complaints have no force, validity, or effect. Since the leaders are chosen by the majority, they have the same power as we have already declared the majority to possess. Moreover, since the building was certainly done publicly, and the majority did not object nor did anyone on behalf of the majority, they have therefore fulfilled their responsibilities, and there is no basis for any complaint against them.

The types of projects in which the majority may compel the minority to participate were deduced by Minz from the responsum of Maharam of Rothenburg through the application of the canon of inference from a generalization followed by a specification followed in turn by a generalization. In the course of his reasoning, he also used analogy to reach other conclusions, *e.g.*, that the degree to which an individual derives personal benefit from a particular communal undertaking has no legal relevance to the issue of the extent to which he may be compelled to participate in the project.

Not only did the halakhic authorities use the interpretive process in all eras to elucidate, develop, and expand Jewish law, but they carried on the process by applying the traditional canons and authoritative methods of interpretation.

Chapter 11
INTERPRETATION OF DOCUMENTS

I. *Doreshin Leshon Hedyot*
   A. *Doreshin Leshon Hedyot* as Meaning "Interpreting Ordinary Language"
      1. Interpretation of a *Ketubbah* by Hillel the Elder
      2. The Right to Collect the Amount of the *Ketubbah* on the Strength of the Testimony of the Wife Alone
      3. A Daughter's Legal Right to Support
      4. Interpretation of a Sharecropping Lease
   B. *Doreshin Leshon Hedyot* as Meaning "Ascertaining Lay Usage"
II. Principles of Documentary Interpretation
   A. Two Principles: (1) The Later Part of the Document Controls; and (2) Ambiguities Are Resolved Against the Holder of the Document (lit. "The Holder of the Document Has the Lower Hand")
   B. Interpretation According to the "Colloquial Usage of the People" (*Leshon Benei Adam*)

I. *DORESHIN LESHON HEDYOT*

A. *Doreshin Leshon Hedyot* as Meaning "Interpreting Ordinary Language"

Along with interpretation of *Halakhah,* there developed very early in Jewish law an additional category of interpretation that provided the basis for the interpretation of documents. This type of interpretation is known in the halakhic sources as *doreshin leshon hedyot.*

In the course of time, in Jewish law as in all other legal systems, various forms of legal documents were devised and used in everyday life, such as the *ketubbah,* deeds, bills of sale, promissory notes, wills, etc. These forms were sometimes developed by halakhic authorities and sometimes by custom and practice of the people; in either event, these instruments were incorporated into the general structure of Jewish law, and they broadened the scope and subject matter of the law.[1] Whether examining these docu-

1. *See infra* pp. 429–432 for a discussion of the fact that the terms of these instruments became part of the legal relationship between the parties to a transaction even when the parties had not expressly agreed to incorporate them.

ments for academic purposes or in order to reach decisions on practical questions, the halakhic authorities were, of course, required to understand the documents thoroughly and to explicate their contents. For this purpose, they employed the same methods they used for Biblical and halakhic interpretation; and, in the course of time, they developed additional, and sometimes different, methods.

The expression *doreshin leshon hedyot,* which appears in various Talmudic sources,[2] was explained as early as the geonic period as follows:[3]

> Judah al-Bargeloni[4] wrote: Rabbenu Hai is the author of a responsum saying, "The essential point is that Hillel the Elder and R. Yose and all those mentioned there, namely R. Meir, R. Judah, and their colleagues, would minutely examine and interpret *leshon ha-hedyotot, i.e.,* the ordinary language written in their legal documents, in the same way that they minutely examined and interpreted the words of the Torah, and would go beyond the simple meaning of the words to yield other meanings, such as the one discussed below, namely, the interpretation made by R. Eleazar b. Azariah of 'the sons will inherit and the daughters will be supported.'"[5]

As mentioned, the *ketubbah,* the text of which was composed by halakhic authorities, was among the documents to which this type of interpretation applied. The term "ordinary language" (*leshon hedyot*) is not therefore intended to exclude language composed by halakhic authorities, but rather to denote language other than "Scriptural language" or "Biblical language" or "the language of *Halakhah.*"[6] It means language that does not

2. *Tosefta* Ketubbot 4:9 *et seq.; Tosefta* Bava Batra 11:13; TJ Ketubbot 4:8, 29a (4:8, 28d); Yevamot 15:3, 78a (15:3, 14d); TB Bava Meẓi'a 104a.

3. Quoted by Naḥmanides in his novellae to Bava Meẓi'a 104a, s.v. Rabbi Meir hayah doresh leshon hedyot; also in *Shittah Mekubbeẓet,* Bava Meẓi'a 104a, s.v. Ve-zeh leshon ha-Ramban; also in the commentary of Zechariah Agamati on TB Bava Meẓi'a 104a, p. 143 (published with facsimile of ms. by Jacob Levin, London, 1961).

4. This is the *nasi* Judah b. Barzillai of Barcelona, an eleventh-century C.E. Spanish authority; for more about him *see infra* p. 1177–1178.

5. The interpretation made by R. Eleazar b. Azariah is discussed *supra* pp. 403–404 and *infra* pp. 427–428.

6. *Cf.* the terms *mamon hedyot* (ordinary money) as denoting unconsecrated secular property, and *mamon gavo'ah* (Temple, lit. "High" money) as denoting property belonging to the Temple, where *hedyot* is used antithetically to *gavo'ah* (= the [Most] High = God = the Temple). *See* the commentary of Zechariah Agamati, *supra* n. 3:

> And he [Hai Gaon], of blessed memory, also said: "The instruments are of *hedyot* nature, and we say of one who interprets their wording meticulously that he interprets *hedyot* language." Anything to be contrasted with *gavo'ah* is designated *hedyot,* as in M Kiddushin 1:6: "The Temple's (*gavo'ah*) right to property is acquired by payment of money [alone, no matter where the property is], but a lay (*hedyot*) person's right to property is acquired only through taking possession. Dedication to the Temple (*gavo'ah*) by oral declaration is the equivalent of delivery to a lay (*hedyot*) person." Doc-

derive its authority from being in the Torah or in the *Halakhah,* but nevertheless must be interpreted because it is contained in a document that has legal significance.

1. INTERPRETATION OF A *KETUBBAH* BY HILLEL THE ELDER

The following is a midrash of Hillel the Elder to the inhabitants of Alexandria, Egypt:[7]

> Hillel the Elder "interpreted ordinary language." It happened that when the men of Alexandria betrothed women, other men would appear [lit. "another man would come"] from the marketplace [or "street"] and snatch them [the women] away [to make them their own wives].[8] Such a case came before the Sages, and they were about to declare the children of the marriage to be *mamzerim.*[9] Hillel the Elder said to them: "Bring me your mothers' *ketubbah.*" They brought it to him and the text read: "When you enter my household,[10] you will be my wife according to the laws of Moses and Israel,"[11] and they did not declare the children to be *mamzerim.*[12]

Hillel the Elder sought to prevent children born of the marriages to the "second husbands" from being *mamzerim,* and he found the solution by interpreting the *ketubbah.* The language "When you enter my household,

---

uments relating to money, as distinguished from writings on matters of Torah, are also called *hedyot,* as in "One may not read *hedyot* documents on the sabbath."
See Tosefta Shabbat 13(14):1; TJ Shabbat 16:1, 79b (16:1, 15c); TB Shabbat 116b, where the term *hedyot* is contrasted with Holy Writ.

7. *Tosefta* Ketubbot 4:9; TJ Ketubbot 4:8, 29a (4:8, 28d–29a); Yevamot 15:3, 78a (15:3, 14d); TB Bava Meẓi'a 104a.

8. In other versions: "Another man would come and snatch her from the marketplace [or street]," but the version quoted in the text is the more reasonable. Under the influence of the Hellenic Egyptian law, the Jews of Alexandria looked upon betrothal as creating a monetary obligation between the parties, similar to *shiddukhin* in Jewish law—*i.e.,* an agreement to enter into a marriage—but not as creating for the parties the new personal status of a man and wife *vis-à-vis* the whole world, which traditional Jewish law accords to the couple upon betrothal (*erusin,* also called *kiddushin*). The *baraita* does not in fact deal with the case of kidnapping in the street, but with an outside party ("a man from the street") who "snatches her away" from her betrothed and marries her himself, since she was not regarded as a married woman. *See* A. Gulak, "Shetar Erusin u-Devarim ha-Niknim be-Amirah be-Dinei ha-Talmud" [The Document of Betrothal and Things that Can be Acquired by Oral Statements According to Talmudic Law], *Tarbiẓ,* III (1932), p. 361 n. 6, and pp. 365–366.

9. They reasoned that according to the *Halakhah,* she was already a married woman when the second man married her. For the definition of *mamzer, see supra* p. 353 n. 226.

10. Another reading: "the nuptial canopy (*ḥuppah*)."

11. In TB Bava Meẓi'a 104a, the words "according to the laws of Moses and Israel" are absent; in TJ Ketubbot and Yevamot, the reading is "according to the law of Moses and the Jews (*ke-dat Moshe vi-Yehuda'ei*)."

12. This concluding phrase is in TB Bava Meẓi'a 104a, but not in the other sources.

you will be my wife" can be interpreted according to its plain meaning, *i.e.*, as a statement of the fact that although after betrothal she is indeed (as the *Halakhah* provides) a married woman *vis-à-vis* the entire world, the actual married life of the couple would begin only after entry into the husband's household, symbolized by the *ḥuppah* (the nuptial canopy).[13] Hillel, however, interpreted the words to mean that the betrothal is conditional, *i.e.*, that it does not become effective until the bride joins the groom under the *ḥuppah*. Since she did not do so, but married someone else, it is clear that the betrothal was ineffective *ab initio;* consequently, her children by the second man are not *mamzerim*, because she was single and free to marry the man she did.[14]

Thus, through an interpretation of the *ketubbah*, Hillel the Elder solved a serious and frequently recurring problem that arose because the Jews of Alexandria were not completely meticulous in their observance of the halakhic laws of betrothal.[15]

13. In those days, there was an interval of some time between the betrothal (*kiddushin*) and the marriage proper (*nissu'in*), *i.e.*, between the presentation of the betrothal money (the ring) and joining under the nuptial canopy (*ḥuppah*). *See infra* p. 974 n. 104 and accompanying text.

14. *See* Hai Gaon, quoted by Judah al-Bargeloni, *supra* p. 423. Rashi states (Bava Meẓi'a 104a, s.v. Ketubbot iman) that it was customary to write out the *ketubbah* on the day of the betrothal. According to many halakhic authorities, the phrase *doreshin leshon hedyot* means that if the usual and customary practice is to include a certain term or condition in the document, that term or condition will be deemed to apply to the transaction even if not expressly incorporated in the particular document involved. *See* the discussion *infra* pp. 429–432.

Hillel therefore requested that the *ketubbot* of other Alexandrian couples be produced rather than the *ketubbah* in the case he was considering. *See* Naḥmanides to Bava Meẓi'a 104a, s.v. U-mah she-feresh, and *Shittah Mekubbeẓet, ad loc.*, s.v. Ve-zeh leshon ha-Rashba. *Resp. Rashba*, III, #17 states:

> In the case before Hillel, he did not require the production of the *ketubbot* of the mothers of those about to be declared *mamzerim*, but the *ketubbot* of other people of that locality, from which he ascertained that in most instances the *ketubbot* contained the same language [quoted in the *baraita*]. Thus, he was able to uphold all the documents (*ha-shetar*) [v.l.—all the others (*ha-she'ar*)] in which this provision did not expressly appear, on the ground that anyone writing out [a *ketubbah*] there did so on the understanding that the usual and customary provisions in other [*ketubbot*] would also be applicable to this *ketubbah*.

See also S. Lieberman, *Tosefta ki-Feshutah*, Ketubbot, pp. 245–247. *Resp. Rashba*, IV, #186, described the incident similarly:

> He examined the *ketubbot* of the people of that town and saw that they contained this provision. Therefore, although the *ketubbot* of the "snatched" brides did not contain the provision, Hillel nonetheless held their children not to be *mamzerim*, because anyone contracting a betrothal in that place who left that condition out of his *ketubbah* is presumed to have done so on the understanding that the usual and customary provisions in that locality would nevertheless apply.

15. *See supra* n. 8.

2. THE RIGHT TO COLLECT THE AMOUNT OF THE *KETUBBAH* ON THE STRENGTH OF THE TESTIMONY OF THE WIFE ALONE

In our discussion of the interpretation of *Halakhah,*[16] we cited the early *takkanah* with regard to the woman who took a trip abroad with her husband and returned alone, saying, "My husband has died." The enactment provided that she should be believed and she may remarry, despite the absence of testimony from two witnesses to prove her husband's death. After a halakhic disputation between the schools of Shammai and Hillel, this rule was accepted by both schools.[17]

The Mishnah (M Yevamot 15:3) records the following debate between the schools of Shammai and Hillel on the right of this woman to collect her *ketubbah:*

> The School of Shammai said: "She may remarry and collect her *ketubbah.*" [*I.e.,* just as her own testimony is sufficient to establish her eligibility to remarry, it is sufficient to give her the right to collect the amount of her *ketubbah* like any other widow.] The School of Hillel said: "She may remarry, but she may not collect her *ketubbah.*" [*I.e.,* although she may remarry, she is not entitled to collect the amount of her *ketubbah,* because the *ketubbah* is a monetary matter, and money cannot be recovered on the sole basis of her own testimony; confirmation is required by the testimony of two witnesses.]
>
> The School of Shammai said to them: "You have been permissive on the question of forbidden marriage, which is more serious than money; should you not also be permissive with regard to money, which is less serious?" [*I.e.,* if you were permissive in relying on the sole testimony of the woman to permit her to remarry, how can you not rely on her testimony to pay her *ketubbah,* which is a less serious matter?]
>
> The School of Hillel responded: "The law is that his brothers do not inherit on the basis of her testimony." [*I.e.,* in fact, for purposes of monetary law, her testimony is not credited, as evidenced by the fact that regardless of the sufficiency of her testimony to establish her eligibility to remarry, the property left by the husband is not divided among his brothers on the basis of her testimony, but witnesses must testify to his death before that may be done. Therefore, the woman also may not collect on her *ketubbah* without witnesses.]
>
> The School of Shammai replied: "We may deduce the rule from the *ketubbah* document [we can prove by interpreting the text of the *ketubbah*[18] that our view is correct]. He writes to her [in the *ketubbah*]: 'If you marry

16. *Supra* p. 402.

17. M Yevamot 15:1–2.

18. The Hebrew for "we can prove by interpreting" is *nilmod,* from the root *lamod,* which generally means "to learn." *See supra* pp. 276, 288 (the terms *limmud* [learning] and *talmud* [study], both from the same root *lamod,* also denote "interpretation.")

another, you may collect what is written to you' [*i.e.*, whenever the woman, for whatever reason, has the right to remarry, she may collect her *ketubbah*]."

The School of Hillel thereupon reconsidered and adopted the view of the School of Shammai.

It is stated in the Jerusalem Talmud[19] that after the School of Hillel acknowledged that the School of Shammai was correct, both schools "applied midrash to the *ketubbah*," *i.e.*, by interpreting the text of the *ketubbah*, they came to the conclusion that the woman in their case had the right to collect her *ketubbah*. They construed the text of the *ketubbah*—"if you marry another, you may collect what is written to you"—as being applicable to all circumstances in which a woman may lawfully remarry.[20]

Thus, through interpretation of the *ketubbah*, the legal rule was established that a woman who may remarry has the corresponding right to collect her *ketubbah*.

3. A DAUGHTER'S LEGAL RIGHT TO SUPPORT

An additional illustration of an interpretation of the *ketubbah* is the midrash by R. Eleazar b. Azariah before the Sages in the academy at Yavneh. He deduced there that a father's legal responsibility for support of his daughter exists only after his death, at which point it becomes a charge against his estate. R. Eleazar b. Azariah reached this conclusion from the halakhic text: "The sons will inherit and the daughters will be supported." He drew an analogy between support of the daughters and inheritance by the sons: just as the right to inherit arises only after the death of the father, so too does the obligation to support.[21] We have previously cited this *midrash* as an example of halakhic interpretation.[22] However, it is also an interpretation of the *ketubbah* because the same provisions are part of the conditions of the *ketubbah* regarding support of the offspring of the marriage. Indeed, this is precisely the point the Jerusalem Talmud made in this connection:[23] "R. Eleazar b. Azariah applied midrash to the *ketubbah*."

In the amoraic period, R. Huna deduced from this analogy an additional rule concerning support of a daughter, namely, that she has the right to collect on her claim for support from both the real and the personal property in her father's estate. This is contrary to the general rule that personal property in an estate is not liable for payment of the decedent's debts,

19. TJ Yevamot 15:3, 78a (15:3, 14d); Ketubbot 4:8, 29a (4:8, 29a).

20. On the need for interpretation of this provision of the *ketubbah*, *see Tosafot*, Yevamot 117a, s.v. Bet Hillel; *Tosafot*, Ketubbot 53a, s.v. She-ein ani kore bah . . . ; *id.* 81a, s.v. Man sham'et lei . . . .

21. M Ketubbot 4:6.

22. *Supra* pp. 403–404.

23. TJ Ketubbot 4:8, 29a (4:8, 28d); Yevamot 15:3, 78a (15:3, 14d).

and also contrary to the view of the *amora* Samuel that a daughter should not be treated differently from other creditors and should therefore not be entitled to look to the decedent's personal property for payment of her claim against the estate.

> R. Huna applied midrash to the *ketubbah:* R. Huna interpreted "the sons will inherit and the daughters will be supported" to mean that just as the sons inherit personal property, the daughters will also be supported out of personal property.[24]

4. INTERPRETATION OF A SHARECROPPING LEASE

An interpretation of a sharecropping lease provides another illustration of "interpreting ordinary language":[25]

> R. Meir made this interpretation:[26] If one leases a field from another [to work it and to give to the owner a percentage or a fixed measure of the produce], and after he [the tenant] acquires it, he neglects it [he lets it lie fallow and does not work it], we estimate how much it would have produced, and he gives that to him [*i.e.,* the tenant gives the landlord the percentage promised as if it had been produced], because his lease says [lit. "thus he writes for him"]: "If I neglect it and do not work it, I will pay out of the best."

This condition, on which both the lessee and the owner of the field agreed ("if I neglect it and do not work it, I will pay out of the best"), can be interpreted to mean that he is to pay out of the best of his own land for any damage caused to the land by not working it: "If he causes the land to deteriorate, he must pay compensation for the reduction in the value of the land."[27] R. Meir, however, interpreted the language of the lease to mean that the intent is to cover not merely damage caused to the land but rather all damage caused to the owner of the land, including his percentage of the produce that the land could have brought forth.[28]

24. TJ Ketubbot 4:8, 29b (4:8, 29a); Yevamot 15:3, 78b (15:3, 14d). *See also,* in the continuation of that discussion, the opinion of the *amora* Samuel, and the objections raised to the view of R. Huna; *see further infra* pp. 646–648.

25. *Tosefta* Ketubbot 4:10; TJ Yevamot 15:3, 78a (15:3, 14d); Ketubbot 4:8, 29a (4:8, 29a); TB Bava Meẓi'a 104a.

26. Heb., *darash R. Meir.* This is the version in the *Tosefta.* In TB Bava Meẓi'a the reading is: *R. Meir hayah doresh leshon hedyot,* "R. Meir used to interpret ordinary language." TJ Yevamot and Ketubbot, *supra* n. 25, have: *R. Meir avad ketubbah midrash,* "R. Meir applied midrash to the *ketubbah.*" The term *midrash ketubbah* (interpretation of the *ketubbah*) is a strange designation for interpretation of this sharecropping lease; *but see* Epstein, *Tannaim,* p. 502 and n. 10, where it is assumed that the term *ketubbah* refers not to a marriage *ketubbah* but to any document (*davar katuv,* lit. "anything written").

27. Naḥmanides to Bava Meẓi'a 104a, s.v. Rabbi Meir hayah doresh leshon hedyot. *See also* S. Lieberman, *Tosefta ki-Feshutah,* Ketubbot, p. 247.

28. Here, too, many authorities have commented that R. Meir intended that this be the rule even when the language he relied on for his interpretation does not appear in the

Talmudic sources contain additional illustrations of "interpreting ordinary language" in a *ketubbah,* in pledge agreements, and in other legal documents;[29] and this type of interpretation undoubtedly played a significant role in the development of the Jewish legal system.[30]

B. *Doreshin Leshon Hedyot* as Meaning "Ascertaining Lay Usage"

Many halakhic authorities saw in the doctrine of *doreshin leshon hedyot* a legal principle much broader and more far-reaching than a mere principle of interpretation. In their view, this principle serves to recognize the binding legal force of lay usage and practice even when the usage or practice has not been instituted by halakhic authorities:

> When halakhic authorities are said to be *doreshin leshon hedyot,* the meaning is that they are ascertaining usages and practices that laymen have engaged in on their own initiative, without legislation by the halakhic authorities, and even without formal communal agreement.[31]

Such a usage is legally binding even if the parties to a transaction do not incorporate it by specific reference in their legal document. Since laymen habitually engage in such legal transactions in accordance with the usage, the presumption is that the parties intend to conform their transaction to it, and the usage is therefore binding on them:

---

particular lease: "And even if it was not written, it is as though it had been written; for if the rule applies only when the provision is explicitly written into the lease, what did he [R. Meir] interpret? Obviously, he [the tenant] would have to honor his express undertaking since it was not an *asmakhta*" (*Tosafot,* Bava Meẓi'a 104a, s.v. Hayah doresh leshon hedyot). On this meaning of *asmakhta, see supra* p. 301 n. 51.

The phrase in the *baraita, "she-kakh kotev lo"* ("his lease says"), is thus not to be taken to mean "that the particular lease actually contained that provision, for if the actual presence of the provision in the lease had been a condition of R. Meir's interpretation, it [the *baraita*] should have stated *im katav lo* (if his lease said). . . . Indeed, whenever a Talmudic text states 'the document says' (*she-kakh kotev lo*), the meaning is that the provision customarily appears in such a document" (*Resp. Rashba,* III, #17). *See also* the discussion further in this chapter and *infra,* Appendix B, Example 2.

29. *See Tosefta,* TJ Yevamot and Ketubbot, and TB Bava Meẓi'a, *supra* n. 25.

30. The rule that R. Meir arrived at by his interpretation in the case of a field leased from its owner is to be found in M Bava Meẓi'a 9:3 without any mention that its source is in the interpretation of ordinary language. Hence, it is likely that there are other legal rules that owe their existence to this type of interpretation, but which are stated independently of their source. The difficulty of tracing a given legal rule to its legal source likewise exists regarding other legal sources.

31. *Resp. Rashba,* I, #662, which is parallel to *Resp. Rashba,* III, #433. The version in I is corrupt, so our text reflects both sources. The term "formal communal agreement" (*haskamah*) means a communal enactment; *see infra* p. 454 n. 28.

> Whatever laymen customarily write [in their documents] is considered to be incorporated in such a document even if one enters into a transaction without explicitly including it, because whoever enters into a transaction without explicitly providing for a particular contingency is regarded as having accepted all that is customary, and the usage is [binding on the parties] as if it were imposed by a court.[32]

Just as legislation, even if not explicitly mentioned by the parties, binds them when they enter into an agreement, lay usage also automatically becomes an integral part of the transaction.[33] The practice becomes binding simply by reason of its being customary usage. Not only is there no need for formal approval by the halakhic authorities, but there is no need even for approval by a communal enactment:[34]

> It should be noted that the provisions of the *ketubbah* and the gifts that one gives to his wife at the time of marriage depend on customary practice; even if it is not a practice agreed to by the townspeople [*i.e.*, by formal agreement or enactment] but a practice that laymen follow on their own, whoever does not expressly specify otherwise is deemed to act only in accordance with the lay practice, as was stated in chapter *Ha-Mekabbel* [*Bava Meẓi'a* 104b]: "R. Yose would *doresh leshon hedyot* ("ascertain lay usage").[35]

Elsewhere, Rashba explained:

> If the conditions of marriage in the agreement of betrothal and the *ketubbah* . . . and all other incidents of marriage are left unspecified, it is as if they were specified. There are some conditions that the halakhic authorities enacted for everyone when they saw that these were necessary, and these are the conditions of the *ketubbah* that are mentioned in the chapter. . . . Some were not enacted by the halakhic authorities, nor is there unanimous agreement as to them: they were practiced in some places by the people on their own and without formal enactment but simply *in pais*. Even as to these, if one does not expressly provide to the contrary, it is as if they were explicitly incorporated; and these are what the authorities are referring to when they speak of *derishat* (ascertaining) *hedyotot*.[36]

This additional meaning of *doreshin leshon hedyot* ("ascertaining lay usage") was accepted by most halakhic authorities along with the meaning

32. *Resp. Rashba*, III, #17. To the same effect are Hai Gaon as cited by Naḥmanides, Bava Meẓi'a 104a, s.v. U-mah she-feresh (end); *Tosafot*, Bava Meẓi'a 104a, s.v. Hayah doresh leshon hedyot; *Resp. Rashba*, I, #662, #778; II, #223; III, #210, #433; IV, #125; V, #167, *Resp. Ran* #54; *Resp. Ritba* #53.

33. *See also supra* nn. 14 and 28.

34. As to communal enactments, *see infra* pp. 678ff.

35. *Resp. Rashba Attributed to Naḥmanides* #14.

36. *Resp. Rashba*, IV, #186; *see also Resp. Rashba*, III, #433, quoted *supra* p. 429.

discussed in the first section of this chapter ("interpreting ordinary language").[37] This additional meaning does indeed have something in common with the first meaning, but it is also different in both its literal sense and basic thrust. This meaning puts major emphasis not on the word *doreshin*[38] but on the word *hedyot* ("ordinary"), by which it distinguishes spontaneous popular usage from practices stemming from the halakhic authorities, as well as from practices based on legislation by the general community. To a certain extent, this meaning involves some overlap with the general subject of custom in Jewish law, which is discussed later.[39] It bears noting here that the principle of *doreshin leshon hedyot,* in the alternative meaning discussed in this section, provided the halakhic authorities with the means to solve many legal problems in the laws of marriage, acquisition of property, and obligations.[40] The following is one illustration, which is also intrinsically interesting from a substantive point of view.

Rashba was asked the following question by the community of Saragossa in Spain:[41]

> Reuben brought gentile friends to Simeon's shop and they bought clothing from Simeon. Reuben then made a claim against Simeon for a commission, as the practice of shopkeepers has been to pay a commission to those who bring customers to their shops. Simeon responded that he was not obligated, in spite of the practice of the shopkeepers, inasmuch as he made no agreement with him [*i.e.,* Simeon argued that although this was the practice of the shopkeepers, he made no agreement to this effect with Reuben]. Who is correct?

Rashba responded to this interesting and not merely academic question as follows:

> Reuben, the claimant, is correct. Wherever there is such a practice by shopkeepers in regard to anyone who brings customers to a shop, silence about

37. *See Bet Yosef, Tur* ḤM 42:21, which leaves room for doubt whether Hai Gaon's explanation excludes the explanation here discussed. *Tosefta* Bava Batra 11:13 indicates that *doreshin leshon hedyot* originally had the meaning attributed to it by Hai Gaon (*i.e.,* interpreting ordinary language), since there it is impossible for it to mean anything else.

38. In this second meaning of *doreshin leshon hedyot,* the root *darosh* is not used in its special sense of "interpretation," but in a more general sense, denoting a thorough investigation into how things are generally done. *See* Rashi, Bava Meẓi'a 104a, s.v. Doresh leshon hedyot:

> It had become the practice of ordinary people to include in their documents certain provisions not instituted by halakhic authorities. He would ascertain the usage and rule accordingly.

39. *See infra* pp. 880ff.

40. *See* the sources cited *supra* n. 32.

41. *Resp. Rashba,* IV, #125.

> the practice is the same as agreement to it [*i.e.*, even if there was no mention of it in an express agreement by the parties, it is as if there was an agreement to incorporate the practice into the transaction], for it is on that basis that he participates in the business of the shopkeeper, brings him profits, and improves his business. Anything that the public practices without express agreement is the equivalent of an explicit agreement; such matters were referred to by the Sages as "*derishat leshon hedyot*," and they are listed in chapter *Ha-Mekabbel* [*Bava Meẓi'a* 104a].

Here, effect was given to a particular usage[42] that not only had no source in *Halakhah*, but was not even a matter of communal enactment. However, the general public acted in accordance with the practice. It was therefore necessary to ascertain (the second meaning of *doreshin*) this usage and to conclude that the shopkeeper agreed to pay the customary commission for procuring the customers.[43]

II. PRINCIPLES OF DOCUMENTARY INTERPRETATION

In addition to interpreting various terms and provisions of legal documents, Jewish law has dealt at some length with the general principles applicable to the interpretation of various kinds of legal documents. In contrast to "*doreshin leshon hedyot*" in the sense of interpreting non-Scriptural texts, where the object to a considerable extent has been to develop and create new legal rules, the object of the general principles of documentary interpretation discussed below has been to elucidate the contents of a particular

42. Later in the responsum, Rashba offered an additional reason for holding the shopkeeper, Simeon, liable: "Furthermore, how can this case of entering someone's shop and improving its trade, where the usual practice is to pay a commission for that service, be distinguished from the case of someone who enters his fellow's [unplanted] field without permission and improves it by planting?" There is, however, a basis for questioning the analogy: the person who enters someone else's field invests his own materials and work, whereas all Reuben did for Simeon was make the minimal effort involved in bringing the customers to Simeon's shop. Moreover, the case of the person who works someone else's land is subject to many rules that determine, *e.g.*, whether he is entitled to the profits or only to recovery of his out-of-pocket expenses. For these rules, *see* Sh. Ar. ḤM ch. 375. It may be assumed that the main reason for Rashba's decision was the first one, that of ascertaining lay usage.

43. The law was codified accordingly in *Tur* ḤM 42:21 and Sh. Ar. ḤM 42:15:

> Provisions customarily contained in documents are to be given effect even when the custom has not been established by halakhic authorities but reflects the lay practice of the local community. Furthermore, even if a particular document does not contain the customary provision, the document should be construed as if it did.

See also Shakh, ad loc., subpar. 36 (these rules apply only if it is certain that the parties knew of the customary practice; but if they did not, the custom does not become part of the transaction).

document, explain various terms contained in it, and resolve inconsistencies between the various parts of the document.

These laws of documentary interpretation are scattered throughout Talmudic literature;[44] we here examine only a few principles and set forth a few illustrations.

A. Two Principles: (1) The Later Part of the Document Controls; and (2) Ambiguities Are Resolved Against the Holder of the Document (lit. "The Holder of the Document Has the Lower Hand")

Two basic principles were laid down in the Mishnah for documentary interpretation when there is an inconsistency between different parts of a document.

The first is that if two clauses in the document are inconsistent, the later clause controls; it is presumed that the earlier statement was reconsidered and that the later clause states the final intention:

> If it [the instrument] states above [earlier], "a *maneh*" [a weight of gold or silver equivalent to 100 *zuzim*], and below, "200"—or above, "200," and below, "a *maneh*"—the later provision controls.[45]

The second principle is that if there is doubt as to the meaning of a document, the doubt will be resolved in favor of the alternative less burdensome to the obligor; ambiguities are resolved against the obligee or holder of the instrument.[46] Why is the holder of the instrument at this disadvantage? "Because he is the claimant, and a claimant cannot collect unless his claim is free from doubt. Therefore, the holder of any document that may reasonably be construed to have either of two meanings collects in accordance with the meaning that gives him the lesser recovery."[47]

44. Some of the laws are collected in M Bava Batra 10:1–2; *Tosefta* Bava Batra, ch. 11; TB Bava Batra 160a *et seq.*; TJ Bava Batra 10:1–3, 30b–31b (10:1–3, 17c); Maimonides, *MT*, Malveh ve-Loveh 27:14–17; *Tur* and Sh. Ar. ḤM chs. 42 and 61.

45. M Bava Batra 10:2; Maimonides, *MT*, Malveh ve-Loveh 27:14; Sh. Ar. ḤM 42:5. *See* Ri Migash to Bava Batra 160a, s.v. Katav mi-lema'alah; *Resp. Maharik* #10 (ed. Lemberg, 1798, p. 7a). Sometimes, if the meaning of the later provision is doubtful, the earlier language may be helpful in clarifying it. *See* M Bava Batra 10:2 and *MT*, Malveh ve-Loveh 27:14; Sh. Ar. ḤM 42:6; and *Resp. Maharik* #10.

46. TB Ketubbot 83b; Bava Batra 166a, 167a.

47. Maimonides, *MT*, Malveh ve-Loveh 27:16. *See also* Rashi, Ketubbot 83b, s.v. Yad ba'al ha-shetar al ha-taḥtonah. The reason for the rule is the ambiguity or uncertain meaning of the document. Consequently, if the holder of the document resorts to self-help and seizes the defendant's property to the extent necessary to satisfy his claim, the law will not require the holder to restore the property. *See* Maimonides, *supra*, and Sh. Ar. ḤM 42:8; *but see* Sh. Ar. ḤM 42:12; *Sema*, *ad loc.*, subpar. 32; *Shakh*, *ad loc.*, subpar. 27.

The Talmud contains many examples of this second principle. If a note states "the number of *zuzim* shall be," and the next word is erased, the holder of the note may claim only two *zuzim*, as the lowest plural number is two.[48] Also, "if it says: 'six hundred, and one *zuz*,' and it is not clear whether it means six hundred *zuz* plus one *zuz* or six hundred *istira*[49] plus one *zuz*, the Sages ruled that he collects six hundred *istira* plus one *zuz*, because ambiguities in the note are resolved against the holder."[50] However, ambiguities are resolved against the holder only if both of the possible meanings are reasonable. Thus, there is a reasonable basis for interpreting the note in the previous example as meaning either "six hundred *zuz* and one *zuz*" or "six hundred *istira* and one *zuz*," but the note cannot be construed as being for even less than six hundred *istira* and one *zuz*, *i.e.*, six hundred *perutot*[51] and one *zuz*, as this possibility is not reasonable. "Why do we not say that the meaning is six hundred *perutot* and one *zuz?* Because the number of *perutot* large enough to be the equivalent of *zuzim* is normally expressed and written by the scribe in terms of *zuzim*.[52] The same applies to all similar questions: at all times and in every place we follow the usual practice."[53]

The second principle, that ambiguities are resolved against the holder of the instrument, sometimes applies even when the difficulty is due to an inconsistency between earlier and later clauses of the instrument. This is so when the circumstances make it unreasonable to apply the principle that the later clause controls. For example, if the instrument states "a *maneh* that is 200," the holder of the instrument takes only 100 *zuzim* because it is clear that there is an error here and the later language does not reflect an intent to change the amount; and since it is uncertain whether 100 *zuzim* or 200 are intended, the ambiguity is resolved against the holder.[54] On the other hand,

> when an instrument states first "a *maneh*" and later "200," or first "200" and later "a *maneh*," the later clause controls. Why does not the lesser of the two

48. M Bava Batra 10:2; *Tur* ḤM 42:16.

49. The *istira* was a coin worth one-half of a *zuz; see* Rashbam, Bava Batra 167a, s.v. Yad ba'al ha-shetar al ha-taḥtonah, and *Tosafot,* Bava Batra 167a, s.v. U-mashvei leih zuzei.

50. Maimonides, *MT,* Malveh ve-Loveh 27:15, based on TB Bava Batra 166b–167a. For another example, *see Resp. Rashba Attributed to Naḥmanides* #108.

51. The *perutah* is the least valuable coin; a *zuz* contained 192 *perutot*.

52. If there are enough *perutot* to make up a *zuz*, then the scribe would include that number of *perutot* as *zuzim*, leaving only the remaining *perutot* to be expressed in terms of *perutot*. Therefore, if the number 600 had been intended to refer to *perutot*, he would have written "three *zuzim* and twenty-four *perutot*," or, in our case (where he wrote "600 and a *zuz*"), "four *zuzim* and twenty-four *perutot*."

53. Maimonides, *MT,* Malveh ve-Loveh 27:15, based on TB Bava Batra 166b–167a; Sh. Ar. ḤM 42:15. *See also Resp. Rashba*, II, #305, #269.

54. M Bava Batra 10:2.

> control? Because one is not dependent on the other. If it stated "a *maneh* that is 200" or "200 which are a *maneh*," he would take 100, but in the case of two clauses where the later is not dependent on the earlier, the later controls.[55]

In the course of time, various additional refinements were made to these two principles of interpretation of legal instruments. With reference to the principle that the later clause of the instrument controls, it was established that if there is even a remote possibility of harmonizing the conflict between the earlier and later clauses of the instrument, "we should give effect to each of them by employing any possible interpretation that renders them consistent . . . even if the reading is strained."[56] In such a case, rather than permitting the later clause to control on the presumption that the earlier clause has been retracted, we prefer to reconcile the two clauses "because people do not normally retract their statements immediately after having made them."[57]

Moreover, even if there is an inconsistency that cannot be reconciled, the earlier clause rather than the later sometimes controls. For example, if an instrument contains a detailed enumeration of the amounts from which the total sum is derived, and later only the total is stated, but the total is not the correct sum of the amounts enumerated, "we conclude that doubtless there was an arithmetical error and the detailed enumeration controls," even though it came earlier in the document than the total.[58]

A basic limitation on the principle that ambiguities in an instrument are resolved against the holder is that we apply this principle only when

> following the alternative less burdensome to the obligor does not render the instrument totally ineffective. However, if it is a question of giving effect to the instrument or invalidating it altogether, we do not rule that its holder is at a disadvantage but that he has the upper hand, as we should always attempt to uphold the validity of the instrument in any way possible, however strained. Whoever wishes to nullify or invalidate it, or to restrict its effect, has the burden of proof.[59]

This basic limitation was applied by Asheri in a responsum written about a century before the foregoing quotation from Ribash:[60]

55. Maimonides, *MT,* Malveh ve-Loveh 27:14.

56. *Resp. Ribash* #249, drawing this conclusion from TB Bava Batra 166b.

57. Sh. Ar. ḤM 42:5, and *Sema, ad loc.,* subpar. 10. To the same effect is *Resp. Rashba,* III, #386; *see infra* pp. 465–467.

58. Opinion of R. Isaiah, cited in *Tur* ḤM 42:8 and in Sh. Ar. ḤM 42:5.

59. *Resp. Ribash* #345.

60. *Resp. Asheri* 68:14.

> Your question concerns a note that states, "A has undertaken to give B fifteen *zehuvim* after Passover," but does not say "after the next Passover." You are in doubt as to whether he may collect immediately after the next succeeding Passover, or whether we should rule that the ambiguity should be construed against the holder and the reference may be to the last Passover of the fifth millenium plus ninety-nine years after the creation of the world.[61]
>
> Know that we apply the rule that ambiguities are resolved against the holder only where the instrument is not thereby completely nullified. . . . We say that its holder is at a disadvantage in order to weaken his position when the instrument is not precise and can be interpreted in two ways. [In such a case,] we interpret it to the disadvantage of its holder, since he is the claimant; but we do so only if he will not lose the benefit of the instrument altogether, as he would in this case if we interpret it to mean at the end of 6000 years. If so [*i.e.,* if that was the intent], why was the instrument written at all? Therefore, it seems abundantly clear that the reference is to Passover on a fixed date, and because of a mistake of the scribe the date was not written.
>
> We must now determine whether that date is Passover at the end of 6000 years or the next Passover. We have no way of choosing any other, for which one shall we choose? [*I.e.,* if not the next Passover, what is the basis for choosing any other Passover?] We cannot choose the last Passover, for if that was intended, why was the instrument written at all? Therefore, you must rule [that the instrument means] the next Passover. Thus, it seems that this note can be collected on the Passover next after [the instrument was executed].

This qualification that the rule resolving ambiguities against the holder does not apply where the effect of the rule would be to destroy the essential validity of the instrument was accepted as law.[62] Obviously, this exception does not apply where one of the parties to the instrument made a mistake of law, such as using a form of language to convey property that is not effective for that purpose or using the wrong language in a will. In such instances, the instrument is unquestionably ineffective.[63]

61. The intended year is 5999, as is clear from the continuation of the responsum. It would appear that Asheri picked that date on the basis of the Talmudic *dictum* that the world will exist for a total of 6000 years; *see* TB Avodah Zarah 9a.

62. *Tur* ḤM 42:14–15; Sh. Ar. ḤM 42:9; *see also Resp. Ribash* #480. Several principles derived from the responsum of Asheri quoted above have served as a basis for construing contracts in two decisions of the Supreme Court of Israel. Alperovitz v. Mizraḥi, 34(iv) *P.D.* 729, 735–737 (1980) (Elon, J.); Hiram v. Minister of Defense, 35(iv) *P.D.* 505, 509–510 (1980) (Hadassah Ben Itto, J.).

63. *See, e.g., Resp. Maharik* #94 (ed. Lemberg, p. 52c/d):

> It is quite plain that this [qualification of the rule construing ambiguities against the holder] applies only where the doubt concerns the intention of the borrower or donor, as when he obligates himself to pay "after Passover," in which case Rabbenu Asher [Asheri] ruled that repayment was due after the first Passover following the execution of the note, for that must have been the borrower's intention when he had the note

B. Interpretation According to the "Colloquial Usage of the People" (*Leshon Benei Adam*)

There is an important principle that terms used in an instrument should be interpreted according to their colloquial meaning and not in the sense in which they are used in Scripture or by the Sages. Therefore, when a testator makes a deathbed will (*ẓavva'at shekhiv me-ra*) bequeathing his property to his "sons," his grandsons are not included in the bequest; in the ordinary language of the people, it is not customary to refer to a grandson as a son, even though the Torah does sometimes use "son" to include grandson.[64]

The halakhic authorities drew a parallel between the interpretation of terms in documents and terms in a vow,[65] since in both instances the crucial factor is the meaning intended by the person whose document or vow is in question. An important principle in connection with vows is: "Follow the colloquial usage of the people,"[66] *i.e.*, follow the language of the ordinary people "of that place, that language, and that time."[67] Thus, the meaning of the terminology used by an individual taking a vow is the meaning that the vow has: (a) in the place where the vow was made, (b) in the language in which the vow was expressed, and (c) at the time when the vow was made (since the meaning of a particular expression can change over time even in the same place).[68] In these and in other respects, the halakhic au-

---

drawn; otherwise, what would have been the point of the document? Payment could be postponed until the Passover of the Great Jubilee! [Such an interpretation would contravene the principle that] a person does not intend his transactions to be exercises in futility. . . . But in a case such as ours, where the donor [mistakenly] thought the term "leave" was appropriate [this was a term used in the will, but it is legally ineffective], it is plain that we must rule that the holder of the document is at a disadvantage . . . even if it means that the document is totally ineffective. This is quite plain to anyone who understands [such matters].

Accord, Rema to Sh. Ar. ḤM 42:9.

64. TB Bava Batra 143b; *see also* Rashbam, *ad loc.*, s.v. Muttar bi-venei vanim, that with regard to the religious commandment to have children (to "be fertile and increase," Genesis 9:7), grandchildren are reckoned as children (based on TB Yevamot 62a/b); Maimonides, *MT,* Zekhiyyah u-Mattanah 11:1; Sh. Ar. ḤM 247:3; ET, III, pp. 346–347.

65. *E.g.*, TB Bava Batra 143b, where a *baraita* stating "If a man vows to derive no benefit from his children, he is permitted to derive benefit from his grandchildren" is cited as proof that the term "children" in a will does not include grandchildren. Similarly, TB Nedarim 63a/b, where the rule is that if a person vows not to taste wine "until the beginning of Adar" in an intercalated year when there are two months of Adar, he is presumed to have intended to refer to the first month of that name, just as when one writes in a document "until the beginning of Adar," we rule that he means Adar I.

66. TB Nedarim 51b.

67. Maimonides, *MT,* Nedarim 9:1, 13; Sh. Ar. YD 217:1.

68. For other examples of the interpretation of vows, *see* Maimonides, *MT,* Nedarim ch. 9; Sh. Ar. YD 217:1; and Talmudic sources cited in commentaries, *ad loc.*

thorities applied the method of interpreting vows to the interpretation of documents.

There are many discussions, especially in the responsa literature, in connection with this principle of interpreting documents according to the "colloquial usage of the people." The following is one example.

Rashba was asked:[69] "With reference to a month of 29 days, from which day does one count in the *ketubbah* and in other legal instruments: the first day or the second day?"[70] The meaning of the question is this: When an instrument says: "the first day of the month," and the "New Moon" (*Rosh Ḥodesh,* a semi-holiday celebrating the advent of each month) of that month consists of two days, of which the first day is legally the last day of the previous month, should we interpret the reference in the instrument to "the first day of the month" according to its halakhic meaning, in which case it would refer to the second day of the New Moon (technically, the first day of the month), or should we interpret it as the first day of the New Moon, which is technically the last day of the previous month?

Rashba responded that the second alternative is the proper construction because the colloquial usage of the people controls even when the technical halakhic meaning is to the contrary. His responsum states:

> In all instances in which we follow the colloquial usage of the people we count from the first day [of the New Moon], since the people refer to the New Moon as the first day [of the month]. The proof for this is the statement in Tractate *Nedarim:*[71] "If one says: 'I vow that I will not drink any wine in this month,' it is forbidden during the entire month, but the New Moon belongs to the future," *i.e.,* it is forbidden only in that month itself, but the next New Moon is considered as a part of the following month, and on the New Moon he is permitted [to drink wine].
>
> The Talmud posed the question: "'The New Moon belongs to the future'—is this not self-evident" inasmuch as he took a vow for only that very month and the next New Moon is part of the following month? The [Talmud's] response was: "The rule needed to be stated because when the [next] month is 29 days, it might be thought that the [first day of the] New Moon [of the next month] should be considered part of the previous month. The rule is therefore stated to make the law clear, since the people refer to it as the New Moon [*i.e.,* the beginning of the month]."

69. *Resp. Rashba,* VI, #151.

70. When the 30th day of the outgoing month is the first day of the New Moon (*Rosh Ḥodesh*) for the incoming month, but is legally regarded as the last day of the outgoing month, there are two New Moon days. Thus, the 30th day of Sivan would be the first day of the New Moon of Tammuz, whereas the first day of Tammuz would be the second day of the New Moon of Tammuz. When there are two New Moon days, the month that follows will generally have 29 rather than 30 days.

71. TB Nedarim 60a/b.

> In other words, if the *tanna* had not disclosed to us in the *mishnah* that the vow did not prevent drinking wine on the New Moon, we would be inclined to say that since the first day [of the next New Moon] is actually [*i.e.*, technically] part of the previous month, he should be prohibited on that day too. We are therefore told that the prohibition does not extend to that day, as in matters of vows we follow the colloquial usage of the people, and in regard to vows we start counting [the days of a month] from the first day of the New Moon.
>
> For these reasons, we also follow the colloquial usage of the people in the case of the *ketubbah* and all other legal instruments. . . . The principle that governs the interpretation of vows, namely, that words are to be interpreted in accordance with the colloquial usage of the people, also applies to the construction of legal instruments.[72]

This principle that documentary interpretation always follows the colloquial usage of the people gave rise to additional distinctions between the methods of documentary interpretation and the principles of Biblical and halakhic interpretation.

For example, in one community, the judges disagreed as to the interpretation of a document in which the husband wrote to his wife that he released her "from all claims and causes of action that he ever had against her." Some interpreted this language as a general release of all claims, while others took a more restrictive approach and interpreted the language as a release only of those claims related to the matters previously mentioned in that document. The latter view was based, *inter alia,* on the rule of interpretation that "generalizations should not be applied literally" (lit. "one may not deduce [laws] from general statements").[73]

This case was referred to Joseph Colon, who discussed it very thoroughly.[74] Colon construed the text of the instrument as a general release:

> I agree with the judge who interprets language as it is written. The language of an instrument is to be construed in accordance with its plain meaning, and here the ordinary meaning of the language clearly is that he absolves his wife, Rachel, from all claims and causes of action, since he set forth no exceptions. . . . Are we dealing with fools who would write "all claims" when they wish to refer only to a particular one?
>
> With regard to the view of the judge who rejected the ordinary meaning of the language referring to "all" claims and causes of action on the basis that generalizations should not be applied literally, that [principle] is not relevant here at all . . . , but is relevant only in regard to the statements of the *tannaim*

72. For additional examples, *see Resp. Rashba,* II, #233; IV, #161; *Resp. Rashba Attributed to Naḥmanides* #108, #268 *et al.*; *Resp. Ritba* #11 (=#203).

73. *See supra* p. 407 n. 23.

74. *Resp. Maharik* #10.

> because they would sometimes write cryptically and did not give a sufficient explanation.
>
> Moreover, we do not apply this rule even to statements of the *tannaim* except when absolutely necessary and there is no alternative. If, however, we are able to explain the statement in a different way, we do so. In the case at hand, we also should say that since the word "all" in the expression "all claims" may reasonably be taken literally, why should we strain ourselves to say that it does not mean precisely what it says?
>
> Moreover, it is a compelling presumption that no one voluntarily presents his adversary with a basis for a dispute or creates doubt for no good reason [*i.e.*, if the husband here had intended only a limited release, he would not have used the broad language that arguably gave the wife much more].

The halakhic authorities disagreed as to whether another rule of Biblical and halakhic interpretation should also be applied to documentary interpretation. The following question was referred to Rashba:[75]

> Reuben instructed his son Enoch and adjured him not to lend anyone more than a certain sum of money, except with the permission of Simeon and Levi ("*Shim'on ve-Levi*"). Simeon has now died. May Enoch lend the money with Levi's permission alone?

The nub of the question is this: Do the words "with the permission of Simeon and Levi" mean that he must have the permission of both, or can they be interpreted to mean that he need obtain only the permission of either one of them? In other words, is the letter *vav* conjunctive only, or also disjunctive?[76]

This was Rashba's response:

> This question is the subject of a dispute between R. Josiah and R. Jonathan[77] as to whether in all places where the verse reads, "A and [indicated in Hebrew by the letter *vav*] B," *e.g.*, "He has reviled his father and his mother (*ve-immo*)"[78] the meaning is [1] only A and B jointly or [2] A and B jointly, or either one separately. We have accepted the opinion of R. Jonathan, who held that the reference is both conjunctive and disjunctive except where Scripture explicitly specifies that it means *only* both jointly, as it did in connection with regard to *kilayim* [forbidden combinations], *e.g.*, "an ox and an ass *together*" [Deuteronomy 22:10, emphasis supplied].[79]

75. *Resp. Rashba*, V, #260.

76. This interpretive problem has been dealt with *supra* pp. 321–322 (in connection with Biblical interpretation) and p. 407 n. 23 (in connection with halakhic interpretation).

77. TB Shevu'ot 27a/b; *see supra* pp. 321–322.

78. Leviticus 20:9.

79. *See* the explanation *supra* p. 322 n. 131.

> Here, too, when he [the father] adjured him, the [son's] oath was that he would not lend without permission of either or both of them.

Rashba thus took the view that the problem of Biblical interpretation as to whether the letter *vav* is conjunctive only or also disjunctive is identical to the problem when that question arises in interpreting documents. He therefore concluded that since the law is in accord with R. Jonathan's view that the letter *vav* is disjunctive as well as conjunctive, the same result must follow in interpreting the document referred to him for construction. Therefore, he ruled that Enoch could make a loan on the basis of the permission of Levi alone.[80]

Other authorities disagreed, and held that this rule applies to the interpretation of the Torah but not to the colloquial usage of the people.

The following question was asked of Samuel de Medina:[81]

> Reuben sent a bill of divorcement to his wife and wrote in the document authorizing an agent to deliver the divorce: "If I do not come and appear before a distinguished court and [*v*] in the presence of my wife, the divorce will be effective; if I do come and appear before a distinguished court and [*v*] in the presence of my wife, the divorce will not be effective."
>
> A doubt has arisen whether [a] we should interpret the condition as referring to both acts together—before a court and in the presence of his wife; or [b] whether we should say that the *vav* stated prior to "in the presence of my wife" means "or," like the *vav* in "he has reviled his father and his mother [*ve-immo,* interpreted by R. Jonathan as meaning "or his mother"]," so that his appearance either before the court or in the presence of his wife will be sufficient to render the divorce ineffective.

The response of de Medina was that the *vav* cannot be read disjunctively and both conditions must be fulfilled. He stated, in relevant part:

> It seems to me that the law is that in order to nullify the divorce he must appear both before a court and in the presence of his wife. This is certainly true according to the view of R. Josiah . . . that the *vav* is conjunctive only . . . but [it is consistent] even with the opinion of R. Jonathan . . . since his interpretation of the *vav* as also being disjunctive applies only to Biblical language. . . . But in everyday matters the letter *vav* should certainly be given its primary and dominant meaning, namely, "and" and not "or." We have al-

80. Rashba made a similar ruling in another case of interpretation of documents in light of the conflicting opinions of R. Josiah and R. Jonathan; *see Resp. Rashba,* III, #206. *See also Resp. Rashba,* V, #266, on the Hebrew letter *kaf* when prefixed to a word in the sense of "as" or "like" for purposes of comparison, and *id.,* II, #237, on the use of the plural, where Rashba relies on Biblical language.

81. *Resp. Maharashdam,* EH, #48.

> ready seen in many places that there is a difference between Biblical language and colloquial language used by the people.

Later in his opinion, de Medina relied on other authorities who were also of the opinion that in interpreting colloquial usage, the *vav* is conjunctive and not disjunctive. In the course of discussion, he also cited the responsum of Rashba mentioned above, according to which the letter *vav* is also disjunctive even for documentary interpretation, but de Medina disagreed and expressed surprise at Rashba's view:

> The law is explicit that a basic principle applicable to vows and oaths is that one must follow colloquial usage.[82] Since this is so, the conclusion to be drawn from Rashba's responsum is that when people say "A and B," they really mean "A and/or B." This astonishes me. We have never found this to be so in our time.

According to de Medina, since all agree that the basic principle in documentary interpretation is that one follows the colloquial usage of the people,[83] *i.e.*, the ordinary meaning of the language at the time and place of the document, and since people in our time using the letter *vav* intend it only as conjunctive and not disjunctive, how then can the rule in Biblical exegesis properly apply when interpreting legal documents relating to everyday life?[84]

The foregoing discussion has not covered all the principles and rules of documentary interpretation; others could be added.[85] In halakhic literature, and especially in the responsa literature, there are many discussions of documentary interpretation that do not directly deal with the use of particular rules of interpretation, but rather with the explanation of various legal documents and with how to understand their content through an examination of their style, comparison of their various parts, investigation into the circumstances of their composition, explanation of their terms,

82. And as stated *supra,* this rule applies also to the interpretation of documents; *see* several responsa of Rashba himself, *supra* pp. 438–439.

83. *See supra* n. 82.

84. Maharashdam's surprise at Rashba was more than passing. He was unable to find any basis for Rashba's opinion, and remarked: "Therefore I need further information about the aforementioned responsum of Rashba concerning the case of Enoch." *See also Kehillat Ya'akov,* II, "Leshon Benei Adam," Letter *vav,* #57 (citing various opinions that distinguish between the use of the conjunctive *vav* in Hebrew and the conjunctive in other languages); ET, I, pp. 112–113, s.v. O le-ḥallek (at p. 113). *Cf.* sec. 7 of the Israeli Interpretation Law, 1981, regarding the interpretation of words such as the conjunction *o* ("or") when used in legislation.

85. *See* the abundant material in the various works on the principles of halakhic decision making (*see infra* pp. 1545–1548), particularly *Yad Malakhi; Kehillat Ya'akov,* II, "Leshon Benei Adam"; Shalom ha-Kohen Schwadron of Brezen, *Darkhei Shalom. See also Tur* and Sh. Ar. ḤM ch. 61, particularly Sh. Ar. ḤM 61:15–16.

etc.[86] Discussions of the latter type constitute the major portion of the vast halakhic material dealing with interpretation of various legal documents such as promissory notes, bills of sale, pledges, partnership agreements, leases, etc. All these have endowed Jewish law with a wealth and variety of material on the law of documentary interpretation.[87]

86. *See, e.g., Resp. Avraham b. ha-Rambam* #102–#104 (pp. 161–173); *Resp. Rashba,* II, #261; III, #203, #204, #208, #307; IV, #181, #213, #294; VI, #5, #151; *Resp. Ribash* #257.

87. Finding this material is now easier as a result of the compilation of the *Digest of the Responsa Literature of Spain and North Africa* published by the Institute for Research in Jewish Law of the Hebrew University of Jerusalem. *See infra* pp. 1525–1528. The entries under *Parshanut* ("Interpretation") in the *Legal Digest,* 1986, II, pp. 362–376, are detailed and comprehensive, and include cross-references to additional material relating to interpretation contained under other headings of the *Legal Digest. See id.,* I, Introduction, p. 27. The *Historical Digest* includes detailed material on all the forms of legal documents found in this responsa literature. This will facilitate reference to the appropriate responsa dealing with the interpretation of these documents. *See Historical Digest,* I, pp. 37–40, 103–106, 124–126, 259–272; *id.,* II, pp. 283–302.

The principles of interpretation discussed in this chapter have been considered in a number of decisions of the Supreme Court of Israel. *See, e.g.,* Board of Trustees of Bank Leumi of Israel, Ltd. v. Director of Estate Taxation, 32(iii) *P.D.* 202 (1978); Efrat v. Bureau of Customs, 35(iv) *P.D.* 729 (1981). *See also supra* n. 62.

Chapter 12
INTERPRETATION OF COMMUNAL ENACTMENTS

I. Authority to Interpret Communal Enactments
II. Interpretation in Accordance with the Language of the Enactment, Not the Subjective Intent of Those Who Enacted It
  A. Tax Law
  B. Family Law
  C. The Law of Landlord and Tenant
  D. Scope of Authority to Interpret as Limited by the Text of the Enactment
  E. "Scribal Errors" in the Text of the Enactment
III. Circumstances that Permit the Background and Objectives of the Enactment to Be Taken into Account
  A. Universally Agreed Intent
  B. Condemnation of Overnice Technicality in Interpreting Enactments
  C. Giving Weight to the Preamble and to the Promotion of Good Public Order
  D. Explanatory Remarks of the Enactors—Use and Limitations
IV. Inconsistency or Ambiguity in the Text
V. Methods of Interpreting Enactments

Another type of interpretation in Jewish law, related in point of theory to documentary interpretation, is the interpretation of communal enactments (*takkanot ha-kahal*).

The historical-legal phenomenon of legislation by the community or by its representatives and elected leaders is reviewed in detail later.[1] This phenomenon, which parallels legislation by the public or its representatives in other legal systems, already existed to a limited extent in the early stages of Jewish law, but started to become a major creative force from the tenth century C.E., as the Jewish communities in the various diasporas began to flourish. Communal enactments were the product of wide-ranging and fruitful legislative activity by Jewish communities over many centuries in numerous and broad areas of civil and criminal law; and, as is true of legislation in all legal systems, these enactments also gave rise to a large and

1. *See infra* pp. 678ff.

notable system of interpretive methods as a consequence of their application in actual life.[2]

I. AUTHORITY TO INTERPRET COMMUNAL ENACTMENTS

The interpretation of communal enactments was generally entrusted to the halakhic authorities to whom contending parties brought their controversies. The controversies were sometimes between individuals, sometimes between an individual and a community, and at times even between communities. A considerable portion of the responsa literature, involving public, civil, and criminal law, contains extensive discussions by the halakhic authorities on the interpretation of communal enactments pertaining to the subjects involved. The enactments themselves often expressly vested the halakhic authorities with the power to interpret them. Thus, for example, an enactment (*takkanah*) of the province of Moravia in the year 1650 provided:

> We have agreed to hold to an early *takkanah* and abide by the practice of our predecessors whereby if any enactment of the province is ambiguous, the rabbi of the province should take whatever action is needed to resolve all ambiguities. If there is any doubt as to the meaning of an enactment, the rabbi of the province should be requested to explain it, and his interpretation will govern.[3]

It is true that some enactments specifically provided that any doubt that might arise as to the meaning of any of their provisions should be resolved by the lay leaders of the community[4] of that time and, in that event, the power to interpret was vested in those leaders.[5] However, even where such a specific provision existed, it was quite possible that in the final analysis the matter was interpreted and decided by the halakhic authorities. An interesting illustration of this is the following case that was brought before Ritba in fourteenth-century Spain.[6]

2. The subject of the interpretation of communal enactments still awaits comprehensive research. The responsa literature is a rich source of relevant material. Our treatment covers only a few of the highlights of this vast subject.

3. I. Halpern, *Takkanot Medinat Mehrin* [The Enactments of the Community of Moravia], Enactment #292, pp. 97–98. *See also Pinkas Medinat Lita* [The Record Book of the Lithuanian Community], Enactment #753, p. 187, *and cf. id.*, Enactment #758, p. 188.

4. The communal leaders had different titles in different periods and places; among them: *mukademim, adelantados,* and *berurim. See supra* p. 27 n. 84.

5. *See, e.g., Resp. Rashba,* III, #409; V, #221, #289. *Cf. Pinkas Medinat Lita,* Enactment #758, p. 188.

6. *Resp. Ritba* #134.

> You have asked: The community enacted a *takkanah* concerning the payment of taxes, and among the provisions of that enactment it is stated: "Every Jewish man or woman who gives a daughter or sister in marriage to a man who does not pay taxes here . . . must pay a tax on the amount of money that is given with her."

It was thus provided in the enactment that the one who gives a dowry to a groom who lives in a different community must pay a certain proportion of the dowry (specified later in that enactment) as a tax imposed upon that property.[7]

The question referred to Ritba was this:

> Reuben, who has a daughter, gave his granddaughter in marriage to one who does not pay taxes to the community. The community now claims payment of the tax from Reuben . . . on the ground that the language of this provision obligates him to pay.
>
> Reuben answered that he is not obligated, as the language of the provision refers only to one who gives a daughter or sister in marriage, and he has given neither a daughter nor a sister in marriage; what he has given to his granddaughter is like giving to a stranger, as to which there is no obligation whatsoever to pay.
>
> The community replied that grandchildren are considered as children for all purposes, since the Sages declared that a person customarily calls his grandson "my son," and since she is his granddaughter, it is as if he gave his daughter in marriage.
>
> Reuben responded that nevertheless they are not children, and the Sages' own language proves this, as they said: "They are considered as children"—this being an expression of love for them. A person calls his grandson "my son" in his love and affection for him and not in any other sense; for, if one gives his property to his "sons," the grandsons do not share with them.[8]

The quoted language set forth the argument between the individual and the community with regard to the interpretation of the term "daughter" that appears in the enactment. At this point, an additional argument was mentioned:

> The community presented an additional argument: It is written in the *takkanah* that any doubt as to the meaning of the language should be decided

7. An enactment adopted in various communities provided that any person leaving the community within a stated period of time was required to pay the community's property tax. The object was to prevent leaving the locality from becoming a successful stratagem for tax evasion. For the same reason, a tax was imposed on anyone who transferred his assets from the jurisdiction of one community to another. *See* M. Elon, EJ, XV, pp. 837ff., at pp. 851–854, s.v. Taxation (reprinted in *Principles*, pp. 662ff., at p. 437).

8. TB Bava Batra 143b. *See also supra* p. 437.

according to the views of the *mukademim*,[9] and they have determined in this case that Reuben's granddaughter is the same as his daughter.

Reuben answered: The authority given them to decide according to their views was conferred on them only in case of doubt, and it is manifestly clear that a granddaughter is not a daughter. There is no ambiguity whatsoever that needs to be resolved by them.

The second argument thus related to the determination of the scope of the interpretive authority conferred on the communal leaders. According to the community's argument, since the enactment had an explicit provision conferring interpretive authority upon the communal leaders, their interpretation that a granddaughter is included in the term "daughter" was decisive; whereas, according to Reuben, this authority was conferred on them only if there was an ambiguity, but not when the meaning of the term was clear and unambiguous.

The response of Ritba was as follows:

My humble opinion is that Reuben's [first] argument is correct. The reason is that even though the Sages, of blessed memory, said on the basis of Scriptural texts that grandchildren are considered as children (as stated in Tractate *Yevamot* in chapter *Ha-Ba al Yevimto*),[10] this was stated only with reference to Biblical language. . . . But in the colloquial usage of the people in their everyday affairs, grandchildren are not called children, as indicated in chapter *Mi she-Met*,[11] where it is stated: "If one declares: 'Give my property to my sons' . . . Mar b. R. Ashi said: People do not call a grandson 'son.'"[12]

The legal conclusion is that people do not call grandchildren "children." As it is said: "Biblical language and the colloquial usage of the people are not the same."[13] It is clear from many places in the Talmud that in matters of acquisition of property, vows, and all other agreements (*haskamot*)[14] between individuals, or between individuals and groups, we follow the colloquial usage of the people, whether the result is lenient or severe.

This answered the first question: the language of the enactment was to be interpreted according to the colloquial usage of the people, pursuant

9. *I.e.*, the communal leaders; *see supra* n. 4.

10. TB Yevamot 62b.

11. TB Bava Batra 143b.

12. *See supra* p. 437 and accompanying notes.

13. The text in TB Avodah Zarah 58b and Ḥullin 137b is: "The language of the Torah is one thing, while the language of the Sages is another"; TB Nedarim 49a has: "R. Josiah's view is that one must follow Biblical language, while our *tanna*'s view is that, as far as vows are concerned, one must follow the colloquial usage of the people."

14. The term *haskamot* (agreements) as used by Spanish halakhic authorities also means "enactments" (*takkanot*).

to which grandchildren are not included in the term "children," and a granddaughter is not included in the term "daughter."

At this point, Ritba proceeded to respond to the second question, regarding the scope of the interpretive authority of the communal leaders:

> The reason Reuben is correct in his argument that there is no room for interpretation of this language by the communal leaders is that this language is not doubtful but clear. With regard to vows, which are a Biblical matter, we decide leniently and rule that if one takes a vow not to benefit from his children, he may benefit from his grandchildren;[15] but if the language [the meaning of "children" in the vow] were doubtful, the decision, as on any question of Biblical law, should have been in favor of the stricter alternative.[16] The conclusion is therefore as we have stated.

In other words, since it is clear that in the colloquial usage of the people grandchildren are not included in the term "children," the interpretation by the communal leaders—that the term "daughter" also includes a granddaughter—had no legal force. Their interpretive authority extended only to doubtful language, but not to language that is clear and unambiguous.[17]

The halakhic authorities were thus vested with the authority to interpret enactments, both directly and by way of defining the interpretive authority of others. In this extremely wide-ranging interpretive activity, these authorities established many principles for interpreting communal legislation. Indeed, as we saw from Ritba's discussion, the interpretation of enactments shared with the interpretation of private documents the basic principle that is the foundation for both types of interpretation, namely, that language should be construed in accordance with the colloquial usage of the people. However, since legislation enacted by the public had much greater and more general substantive significance and authority than documents drafted by individuals, the principles of interpretation devised for the interpretation of enactments were much more comprehensive and fundamental. The following sections take a closer look at some of these principles.

15. *See* TB Bava Batra 143b. *See also* n. 4 of J. Kafaḥ to *Resp. Ritba* #134. Kafaḥ was apparently unable to identify the source of the law in the Talmud. However, the source, which is TB Bava Batra 143b, is cited in Ritba's responsum itself.

16. *See supra* p. 212.

17. For a similar ruling, *see Resp. Rashba*, V, #221. Another detailed discussion of the enactment dealt with by Ritba is in *Resp. Rashba*, III, #406, which also includes a great deal of material on the interpretation of enactments.

II. INTERPRETATION IN ACCORDANCE WITH THE LANGUAGE OF THE ENACTMENT, NOT THE SUBJECTIVE INTENT OF THOSE WHO ENACTED IT

It is a fundamental principle that an enactment is not interpreted in accordance with the subjective intent of those who enacted it, but in accordance with the views and understanding of those authorized to interpret it.

A *takkanah* provided:[18]

> If anyone is in doubt as to the meaning of any of the provisions of the enactment, the authority to determine its meaning and application is vested in the communal leaders of the time.

Rashba was asked whether the enactment "should be interpreted according to the intent of those who enacted it or according to its sense." The response of Rashba was unequivocal:

> I have already said that it is entirely dependent on the interpretation given by the communal leaders of that time and neither on the intent of those who enacted the *takkanah* nor on the view of any halakhic authority or anyone other than the communal leaders of the time, since this was the original understanding and the entire community took an oath on this basis.

Similarly, particular terms in an enactment should not be interpreted in the light of the supposed motives of those who enacted it. In one community, an enactment was promulgated to remove the beams that protruded from the city wall. Some of the inhabitants of the community refused to remove the beams from their houses, arguing that these beams were smaller than the other beams and were therefore not included in the enactment. In his responsum,[19] Rashba first established that these beams were also included in the term "beams." It may be granted, Rashba continued, that, if we investigated the motive of those who enacted the *takkanah*, we would conclude that "the intent of the members of the earlier generation who enacted the *takkanah* was only to require whatever was necessary to protect the city and strengthen the walls, and thus they had in mind only large beams that could be taken hold of to climb the wall and the like." However, Rashba did not accept this approach:

> In any case, it seems to me that such matters are not to be the basis of fine distinctions, and we do not make the question turn on a matter of measurement. If we did that, the law would become relative and it would be necessary

18. *Resp. Rashba*, III, #409.
19. *Id.*, IV, #268.

> for you to provide a measure for the beams to enable us to tell you what your *takkanah* does or does not cover.

Therefore, Rashba concluded that only pieces of wood that were "the thinnest of the thin and are not called beams but simply sticks" were outside the scope of the enactment. The principle is:

> It all depends on the view of the court in each place in accordance with the terminology of ordinary usage; as in the case of all laws that concern civil disputes, vows, *ḥaramim* (bans and sanctifications), and oaths, the rule is to construe them according to the colloquial usage of the people.

This principle of statutory interpretation is regarded as of great importance in all legal systems. It is appropriate to examine a number of examples in Jewish law. We will look at three different legal subject areas: tax law, family law, and the law of landlord and tenant.

A. Tax Law

In his responsa, Rashba laid down the principle that it is improper to subject an individual to double taxation. Thus, if an individual lived in community A and owned property in community B, community A could not collect any tax from him on the property located in community B, because he was liable to pay a tax in community B on that property.[20] When a resident of one community owned property in a different community, this rule sometimes caused considerable loss to the community where he resided, as it could not collect any tax at all on this property. One community attempted to remedy this situation by means of the following enactment:

> Where individuals have immovable property outside the city . . . that property will be considered as being subject to tax like all property within the city; on the condition that there shall be credited [on account of the tax due] with respect to all of their taxable property, whether inside or outside the city, all expenses and taxes paid for the property outside the city, and the tax on the net balance shall be paid to the community.[21]

Thus, the enactment provided that a resident had to pay taxes to his community on property he owned elsewhere, but only after first being given a credit for taxes and expenses paid on that property to the commu-

20. For details, *see* M. Elon, EJ, XV, pp. 837ff., at p. 851, s.v. Taxation (reprinted in *Principles*, pp. 662ff., at p. 675); *infra* pp. 766–768.

21. *Resp. Rashba*, V, #282. The text of the enactment is quoted both in the question and in the response, with slight variations. The text as here quoted draws on both versions.

nity where it was located. In this way, the enactment sought to collect part of the tax from such property while at the same time protecting against double taxation. But "something unforeseen occurred"—the taxes and expenses for the property outside the community were extremely heavy, to the point that crediting those taxes and expenses would mean that the community in which Reuben lived would actually receive less taxes on Reuben's property than if the enactment had not been adopted.

The communal representatives argued that since the intent of the enactment was to produce a gain for the community and not a loss, the enactment was inapplicable to this situation; in opposition, it was argued that the language of the enactment should be followed and Reuben was entitled to the credit. The judge to whom this important dispute was brought referred it to Rashba and succinctly summarized the issue as follows: "Instruct me. Should we follow the language of the enactment or the intent of the community?"

Rashba concluded in his responsum that Reuben was correct:

> I do not see any sound principle on which the community's argument can be supported. I view the language of the *takkanah* and the condition that was enacted as clearly providing that they will allow a credit against the tax on all their property, whether in the city or outside the city, for all taxes and expenses paid out for property outside the city. This being so, they have explicitly taken this on themselves, even if this means that in effect they will have to pay the city's money for the expenses and taxes outside the city.
>
> This follows logically, inasmuch as they have become akin to partners in all their property; property outside the city has become the same as property in the city, and whatever is levied on both is paid out of the whole.
>
> Consider the case where the inhabitants of two principalities with two different rulers have become partners. Would not whatever is levied on each of them be paid out of the property of both as if they lived in one city?

After Rashba concluded that the language of the enactment made clear that the community sought to pool all the property of its residents in a single account and that, therefore, all expenses were to be charged against this combined account, he proceeded to consider the fundamental question, namely, whether the language or the subjective intent and motives of the enactors should control:

> If you wish to argue that in any event this was not the intent of the community, and in matters of vows, *ḥaramot* (bans and sanctifications), and oaths, the mouth must say what the heart wishes in order to be effective, that argument cannot prevail. That principle pertains only to the case where one intends to take a vow regarding a loaf of wheat bread and he utters the words

> "a loaf of barley bread." . . . [22] In that case, he has misspoken, and it is an inadvertent vow.
>
> However, in our case, both "mouth" and "heart" concurred; they did not err in their expression but in their intent. They did intend to give expression to what is stated and written; the statements are explicit and the condition is self-explanatory. It is as if they intended to say "a loaf of wheat bread" and they said "a loaf of wheat bread"; but they say that they erred, in that their intent was not that the tax and expenses would come to such a great sum as this. These, however, are unexpressed intentions, and an unexpressed intent is of no legal weight [lit. "words in the heart are not words"]!

It would be difficult to express more clearly than this the principle that enactments are to be interpreted according to the meaning of their language and not according to the subjective intent of the legislators when such intent is inconsistent with the meaning of the language used.

B. Family Law

One of the many types of enactments in the Jewish communities in Germany and Spain dealt with the question of the relative rights that the decedent's widow and his heirs had in his estate.[23] A question with regard to such an enactment was referred to Asheri:[24]

> As for your question concerning your *takkanah* providing that when a widow seeks a share of her husband's property, her husband's heirs have the advantage of an option: they may choose to give her half of the estate, if the estate is small; but if the estate is large, they may choose instead to give her the amount of her *ketubbah*. . . .

The enactment gave the heirs the option to give the widow the lesser of half of the estate or the amount of her *ketubbah*. If the estate was small and the value of the *ketubbah* was more than half the estate, the heirs would elect to give half of the estate; if the estate was large and the value of the *ketubbah* was less than half of the estate, the heirs would elect to give the widow the amount of the *ketubbah*.

The question that arose in connection with this enactment was as follows:

> Reuben divorced his wife just prior to his death; she claims her *ketubbah* and her marriage gifts, arguing that she is a divorcee and the *takkanah* speaks only

22. As when the intent of the one who made the vow was to refrain from eating wheat bread, but by mistake he misspoke and forswore "barley bread." TB Shevu'ot 26b.

23. *See infra* pp. 835–846.

24. *Resp. Asheri* 50:10. For another question relating to this enactment, *see id.* 55:7.

of a widow. The heirs argue that the divorce was given to her not for the purpose of allowing her to collect her *ketubbah,* but only to prevent the need for a levirate marriage;[25] therefore, [they contend], she has the status of a widow and they have the option of giving her half the estate. The heirs urge in support of their position that at the time that she requested a divorce, her husband Reuben said to her: "This is only because of my brother Simeon" [who, but for the divorce, would be obligated to enter into levirate marriage or participate in the ceremony of *ḥaliẓah*].

The woman was divorced just prior to the death of her husband; and under the circumstances there was no doubt—it was indeed undisputed—that she was divorced in order to obviate the need for levirate marriage. Therefore, the heirs argued that, in view of the background and intent of the enactment, it should apply to this case. The woman opposed this position on the ground that she had, in fact, been divorced, and the relative values of the estate and the *ketubbah* were such that it was more advantageous for her to receive the amount of the *ketubbah* rather than half the estate.

Asheri responded:

> The argument of the heirs is without merit. Since he gave her a divorce—for whatever reason—she is, in the final analysis, divorced; and she has a right to collect her *ketubbah,* inasmuch as he did not impose any condition in the bill of divorcement that would prevent her from collecting her *ketubbah.*

Since she had the status of a divorcee, the enactment did not apply to her, as it spoke of a "widow"; and the reasons for the divorce, as well as whether, in light of the background and the subjective intent behind the enactment, this woman was intended to be included in its scope, were irrelevant.

C. The Law of Landlord and Tenant

In many communities throughout the diaspora, Jews, whether voluntarily or by compulsion, generally lived in concentrated neighborhoods. This brought about a situation in which the demand for living quarters in those areas was greater than the supply, and, consequently, there were occasions when a Jew offered a landlord a higher rental than that paid by an existing Jewish tenant, in effect causing the existing tenant to be dispossessed of his home.

The communal leaders sought to prevent this socio-ethical dereliction;

25. A woman is obligated to enter into a levirate marriage or perform *ḥaliẓah* only if she was widowed, but not if she was divorced before her husband's death.

but they could not do so through an enactment that prohibited the landlord from renting the dwelling to another person in these circumstances, because the landlords were generally non-Jewish and, of course, were not bound by the enactments of the Jewish community. Therefore, the communal legislation was directed against the tenants; it was forbidden for a Jew to obtain living quarters by offering a higher rental and thereby cause the eviction of a fellow Jew from his dwelling.[26]

A question relating to such a *takkanah* was referred to Simeon b. Ẓemaḥ Duran (Rashbeẓ) in the fourteenth century in North Africa:[27]

> You have asked: The community has enacted [lit. "agreed"][28] that, under penalty of the ban,[29] none of its members may offer a higher rental than that paid by a tenant for a house or shop. The king has now given a place to live to an aide who came with him from Tunis,[30] and a dispute has arisen over this. Some take the view that this is not included in the enactment, as this is not a higher rental nor, in fact, any rental at all. Others argue that it is included in the enactment, as the intent of this enactment was that a member of the community should not be evicted from his home, and here one Jew has occasioned the eviction of another.

The question that arose is clear; and, as we shall presently see, the decision was not easy, because of the tension between indications of intent from the background circumstances of the enactment, on the one hand, and the language of the enactment, on the other. This was the response of Rashbeẓ:

> To respond: The lenient view is correct. The enactment does not say that a member of the community may not rent a dwelling that is already rented to another. It says only that he may not pay a rent higher than that paid by the tenant in occupancy. Here, he [the new tenant] did not pay a higher rent. Whoever seeks to make him liable must bring proof for his argument from the language of the enactment, and there is nothing in the enactment's language to indicate liability here.

26. These enactments, which are reminiscent of contemporary tenant protection laws, were common in all Jewish centers, with local variations. *See further infra* pp. 811–813.

27. *Resp. Tashbeẓ*, II, #61.

28. The Spanish and North African halakhic authorities frequently used the noun *haskamot* (agreements) for *takkanot*, and the verb *hiskimu* (they agreed) for *hitkinu* (they enacted).

29. The enactment was generally reinforced by the sanction of a ban.

30. The house was royal property rented to a Jew, who lived in it. Another Jew, who came from Tunis, then appeared and was given permission to live in the house; as a result, the first resident had to vacate the premises.

At this point, Rashbeẓ proceeded to discuss whether, under the circumstances, the broader intent of the enactment should nevertheless be regarded as being encompassed by its language:

> Concerning the arguments of the claimants, their position is that although the enactment provides only that one may not pay a higher rent, its purpose was to prevent any member of the community from ejecting another from his home in any manner whatever, even if no additional rent is paid, or if the landlord lets him have it rent-free. They contend that even though this purpose was not explicitly written into the enactment, the enactment should be deemed to have the same effect as if the purpose had been so written into it.
>
> This is their argument, but it has no validity. The law is that only when the intent of the author of a vow is entirely clear [*umdena de-mukhaḥ*—lit. "a surmise that is proven"] will that intent govern [*i.e.*, prevail over the language of the vow]; but when such intent is not so clear, we do not look to the intent of the author of the vow.

What Rashbeẓ was saying was that there are occasions when the background circumstances are so clear that they become a part of the enactment itself, *i.e.*, in such case the intent is "entirely clear" and not merely based on inference. Later in his responsum, Rashbeẓ provided an illustration of when it is possible to conclude that there is the "entirely clear" indication of intent.[31] However, he ruled that there was no such indication in this case:

> But in this enactment, where is the entirely clear indication that they intended the *takkanah* to apply to tenancies where the rent was not increased? If their enactment had followed upon an actual case in which an individual caused the eviction of another from his home without paying a higher rental, this would be an entirely clear indication, but here there is no evidence whatsoever to cause us to add to the enactment what is not mentioned in it.
>
> We do not change the meaning of language on the basis of a presumed intent; and, in addition, in this case, even if there were some slight indication

31. Such as the examples in TB Bava Kamma 80a, as set forth by Maimonides (*MT*, Nedarim 8:13):

> If a person swore an oath or took a vow that he would marry, or buy a house, or set out in a caravan, or embark on a sea voyage, he is not obligated to marry, buy, or set out at once, but [he may wait] until an opportune time. [In TB Bava Kamma and in *Resp. Tashbeẓ* the text reads: ". . . to buy a house or marry in the Land of Israel"; *Tosefta* Bava Kamma 8:14 has the same reading as Maimonides.]
>
> It once happened that a woman vowed that she would marry any man who proposed marriage, and many men who were not suitable for her did propose; but the Sages said, "She did not intend to accept the proposal of anyone but an appropriate suitor." This is the law in all similar cases.

On the question of when the matter is deemed to be covered by the language of the enactment, *see infra*.

> [tending to support the community's argument], the language of the enactment refers only to cases where a higher rental is paid, and we may not extend it to cases where there is no such increase.
>
> There is here no such indication whatsoever [of any broader intent than that expressed in the enactment]. To the contrary, there is an indication that they intended [to address] only a situation where a higher rental was offered. It was the practice of people to bid up rentals against one another, and the enactment was promulgated to protect the economic resources of the members of the Jewish community. There was no such practice on the part of the people, however, without payment of a higher rental; landlords do not ordinarily change tenants unless additional rental is involved.
>
> If a landlord of his own volition wishes Reuben as a tenant rather than Simeon, the community does not enact a *takkanah* concerning this; everyone has the right to rent his properties and lands to whomever he wishes, and it is not the practice of communities to enact *takkanot* concerning such instances. Certainly, with regard to the king's property, no one has ever considered trying to stop the king from doing with his property what he wishes.
>
> The conclusion to be drawn from all this is that the tenant has not violated the communal enactment.

Rashbeẓ' responsum evidences the great pains he took to decide the case. He reached his conclusion—that the enactment did not apply in the factual situation before him—on several grounds in addition to the basic point that the language of the enactment covered only offers of increased rental: (a) the objective of the enactment was to prevent increases in rental costs; (b) it was unlikely that those who adopted the enactment intended it to apply in a situation such as this, because it is unusual for a landlord to evict someone from a dwelling and rent it to another without receiving some additional rental; (c) it is not reasonable to assume that the community would limit an individual's freedom to use his property as he wishes when his use does not produce exorbitant profits; and (d) as mentioned at the end of the responsum, it should not be assumed that the community intended such a far-reaching enactment (*i.e.*, limiting use of property even where there is no exorbitant profit) to apply to tenancy of a dwelling belonging to the king.[32]

32. This last argument was made by way of additional support for the particular interpretation in this case and not because the law generally applicable to the king and his property is any different from that applicable to other property. Further on in the responsum, Rashbeẓ made another distinction—of both legal and historical interest—between the terms "a citizen of the town" and "a member of a community (*kehillah*)." He noted that "a person cannot belong to a community unless he is a citizen of the town, but he can be a citizen of the town and yet not be a member of a particular community, when the Jewish population is divided into two communities." At that time and in the succeeding period, it was not unusual for various Jewish communities—usually organized according to the place of origin

D. Scope of Authority to Interpret as Limited by the Text of the Enactment

The primary importance to be accorded to the text of the enactment is demonstrated by the following responsum concerning the scope of the authority vested in whoever is designated to decide questions that may arise in connection with the enactment.

The following question was asked of Rashba:[33]

> The townspeople wrote in their enactment: "All matters related to the enactment and all doubtful language in it shall be adjudicated according to [my] judgment. . . ." Do I have the right to decide at my discretion as I see fit to achieve the most beneficial results, or must I follow strictly the meaning of the text?

The question, in other words, was: Is the person designated in the enactment permitted to decide a matter according to his own view of what is necessary to achieve the most beneficial result, or is he confined by the meaning of the text of the enactment to the extent that it must control his decision even if it appears that a solution which departs from the language would be a better one?

Rashba responded:

> If they had written "all new matters and all doubtful language will be decided by [you]," you would be required to decide the new matter on the basis of your view of what is necessary for the achievement of the objective of the enactment and to interpret the doubtful language according to what you think it best should mean. You know that I have practiced this [*i.e.*, to give freedom of decision to the authorized decisionmaker] in our city in resolving ambiguities.
>
> However, they wrote, "All matters related to the enactment and all doubtful language in it shall be adjudicated according to [your] judgment." You may not decide at your discretion, but your opinion must seek to ascertain the meaning of the language, since they have only given you authority to determine what the text of the enactment means.
>
> Moreover, they did not state that it should be determined in the manner that you shall *declare*, but in the manner that you shall *adjudicate*.

Since the authority conferred in this case covered all matters relating to the *enactment*, and was to *adjudicate* the dispute, the person upon whom

---

of their members—to exist in the same town. For a detailed discussion of the existence of this situation in Salonika, *see infra* p. 865 and n. 301.

33. *Resp. Rashba*, IV, #308 and its parallel, V, #247. The version quoted here draws on both these sources.

the authority was conferred was constrained by the language and meaning of the enactment and was not entitled to decide on the basis of his view of what would achieve the most desirable result in regard to a matter within the scope of the enactment if such a decision would involve departing from the meaning of its text.

E. "Scribal Errors" in the Text of the Enactment

Of course, despite the importance of the text of the enactment in determining its meaning and construction, the language used will not inexorably dictate the outcome if it is reasonable to conclude that the language is the result of an error in recording. An interesting illustration of this is found in a responsum of Asheri:[34]

> May my master instruct me further. A community enacted a *takkanah* and agreed to exempt Reuben b. *Jacob* from the *takkanah*. The text of the *takkanah*, however, referred to Reuben b. *Isaac*. He now claims the right to exemption in accordance with the text of the communal document [*i.e.*, the enactment], on the ground that the text is to be followed in all cases of doubt.[35]
>
> Response. Concerning the error as between "Reuben b. Jacob" and "Reuben b. Isaac," if there is a doubt as to which of them was exempted, the text is to be followed. But if there is no doubt in the matter and all agree and declare that it was the intent to exempt Reuben b. Jacob, and the scribe erred, Reuben b. Jacob should not on that account suffer. That would not be a situation of doubt in which one follows the text. If the people disagree [as to which one was intended to be exempted], let them take a vote and follow the majority: if most of them say that they agreed to exempt Reuben b. Jacob and the scribe erred, they should follow the majority.

This, then, is in the nature of "scribal error," which may be discovered and corrected even if it requires the members of the community to be polled as to what they intended the enactment to say.

Since the nuances of the text of a *takkanah* were critical to its interpretation, the halakhic authorities made certain, before responding to a question calling for interpreting an enactment, that they had its full text in their

34. *Resp. Asheri* 6:8.

35. Apparently, the one who claimed the exemption was Reuben b. Isaac, who wanted to take advantage of the error. It is unlikely that the claimant was Reuben b. Jacob, claiming exemption on the basis of a "communal document"—not the enactment itself but rather a separate document given to him—which he relied on to show what the text of the enactment should have said. The ensuing discussion in Asheri's responsum is inconsistent with the interpretation that the claimant was Reuben b. Jacob.

possession,[36] and more than once they criticized a style that was obscure and unclear:

> I must first state that the language used in the communal enactment contained in the record book mentioned above upon which the entire controversy depends is cryptic and opaque.[37]

III. CIRCUMSTANCES THAT PERMIT THE BACKGROUND AND OBJECTIVES OF THE ENACTMENT TO BE TAKEN INTO ACCOUNT

A. Universally Agreed Intent

As we saw in the responsum of Rashbeẓ,[38] when the intent of those who adopted the enactment is "entirely clear," that intent can be considered even if not apparent from the language of the enactment. Precisely this notion is aptly expressed as a principle of interpretation of enactments in the writings of Rashba, who supported the principle by citing, *inter alia,* the same illustration used by Rashbeẓ.[39] After establishing the rule that an enactment should not be interpreted according to the subjective intent of those who enacted it, but according to the understanding of the language of the enactment by the one construing it,[40] he added the following:

> However, a universally agreed intent is like a stake that cannot be moved, in that everyone knows that the particular condition or provision unquestionably was promulgated on the basis of this intent, even where it is possible to interpret the language to the contrary.

An interesting illustration of this is found in the following responsum of Rashba:[41]

An enactment stated that the townspeople must be "in the synagogue" whenever a "ban" is proclaimed calling for the submission of truthful tax declarations, and that the tax officials must be "in the synagogue" when the townspeople submit their tax declarations as well as on other similar

36. *See, e.g., Resp. Rashba,* IV, #269; V, #280, #281. Responsum #280 is identical to *Resp. Ritba* #82; further study is therefore required to determine the actual authorship.

37. *Resp. Ritba* #120 (beginning, p. 138). *See further infra* pp. 1507–1508.

38. *Supra* pp. 454–456.

39. The case of the woman who, when vexed by her son, blurted a vow to marry any man who proposed marriage, which the Sages interpreted as including only proposals by suitors appropriate for her.

40. *Resp. Rashba,* III, #409, quoted *supra* p. 449.

41. *Resp. Rashba,* V, #222.

occasions. In the case under dispute, the officials were not *in* the synagogue but in the courtyard in front of the synagogue or in the upper chamber attached to the synagogue; and the other events referred to in the enactment also did not take place in the synagogue itself. The argument was made to Rashba that this was contrary to the requirement of the text of the *takkanah* and, hence, unlawful; that the term "synagogue" should be limited to where actual worship takes place, especially since the places where the events occurred have their own designations—"courtyard," "upper chamber," "enclosure" (*azarah*), "house of study." Rashba utterly rejected this argument, stating in part as follows:

> When one promulgates such an enactment, the context is controlling. There are times when even the enclosed yards and the upper chambers are included in "the synagogue," and sometimes they are not included in "the synagogue," which, in those instances, means only the place where the cantor prays. What is included depends on the specific matter under discussion.
>
> Thus, if the people vowed that all should go to the synagogue at the time of prayer, the intent is that they should enter the actual place where the cantor prays in order to join [in prayer], and the like.
>
> Similarly, an enactment that all should congregate in the synagogue at the time of the proclamation of a ban contemplates presence at those places in the synagogue where they will hear the cantor at the time of the ban.
>
> Also, the requirement that the communal leaders (*berurim*) should be present in the synagogue when the tax declarations are brought does not contemplate that they should be actually inside, for what need is there for them to be inside? On the contrary, the intent is only for them to be at the place where those who bring the declaration come.
>
> Likewise, by the requirement that the officials come there to consider matters of public welfare, it is intended only that they should be in any of the places there [about the synagogue] where they will be available to everyone, so that whoever has business with them can approach them.[42]

In this enactment, it is plausible to interpret the term "synagogue" narrowly as referring to the synagogue itself, because the places surrounding the synagogue have their own distinctive designations. However, Rashba rejected this approach, as there is a "universally agreed intent" that in certain circumstances the reference is to the synagogue itself, but in other circumstances the reference is to places in the synagogue area but not the synagogue itself.

42. An allusion to Exodus 24:14 (". . . You have Aaron and Hur with you; let anyone who has a legal matter approach them."). *See also* TB Bava Kamma 46b and *supra* p. 385.

B. Condemnation of Overnice Technicality in Interpreting Enactments

The halakhic authorities opposed using various overnice formalistic technicalities in the interpretation of enactments. One enactment,[43] which concerned the procedure for the payment of taxes, prescribed that if an individual's assets had increased during the year, he had to pay a specified amount of tax over and above what he paid the year before. The text of the enactment was as follows:

> Every Israelite who at the time of his accounting has had an increase in his principal, his funds, and all of his property, over their value at the time of his accounting in the previous year, shall calculate the increase, and pay the following tax thereon. . . .

Rashba was asked the following question:

> Reuben evaluated his property and found that he had more promissory notes than in the previous year. He also found that the notes he had the previous year had increased in value. He found that some of his other property had appreciated; but there was no increase in each one of the specific items, which the language of the foregoing provision requires, in that it states that he is not obligated unless he finds that all his property has increased in value. Who is correct?

Reuben's argument was that, according to the language of the enactment, additional tax had to be paid only if every item listed in the enactment had increased in value, but not when the increase involved only a portion of the property he had owned in the previous year.

Rashba rejected this extreme formalistic argument as follows:

> I find no validity or substance in Reuben's argument. The meaning is not that there must be an increase in every item specifically mentioned, but that there be an increase in one item or another in any portion of the property—whether all or only a part of it; it is normal to speak this way.
>
> Upon examining the matter, Reuben's argument is plainly invalid. The intent is clear that everyone should increase his tax payments every year according to the amount by which his worth increased over the previous year.[44]

43. *See Resp. Rashba*, III, #407.

44. *See also id.* #408 for another responsum on the subject of taxation in which Rashba also categorically rejected formalistic arguments of a different type.

C. Giving Weight to the Preamble and to the Promotion of Good Public Order

To understand the thrust of an enactment, the preamble was sometimes relied on, even though the preamble was not an integral part of the enactment.[45] Also, if the language of an enactment allowed for two interpretations, one of which benefited the public while the other had a harmful effect, it was determined that it should not be assumed that "the intent was to prohibit what is permissible, appropriate, and proper, for otherwise the enactments would not constitute measures for improvement but, to the contrary, would only cause the breakdown of restraints and make things worse rather than better."[46] Sometimes an enactment was even given a strained interpretation when necessary to obviate an alternative interpretation that would be detrimental, such as to prohibit public worship in a synagogue to be built in the future:

> Because to do this would prevent the public from carrying out a religious commandment . . . and certainly in the case of a noted and honorable community such as this, they are not to be suspected of promulgating something that I will not characterize as merely unhelpful but as perverse and disgraceful. One must give them the benefit of the doubt on this and say that they were inadvertent or erred in using that language, and it was not their intent . . . to include in their enactments the synagogues to be built in the future and to be dedicated to use by all, but their intent was only to cover the homes of individuals.[47]

D. Explanatory Remarks of the Enactors— Use and Limitations

There were times when it was permissible to resort to explanatory remarks by the enactors in order to determine the meaning of an enactment. In the case dealt with in the foregoing quotation from Ribash, the communal enactment stated:

> No Jew . . . shall pray with a quorum of ten except [here follows a list of the exceptions, namely, designated community synagogues and a specification of

45. *See, e.g., Resp. Rashba,* III, #427; V, #287; *Resp. Ribash* #331. *Cf.* in regard to reliance on legislative history (such as parliamentary debates, committee reports, and other such sources) in construing statutes, Salmond, p. 140; A.M. Applebaum, "Divrei ha-Keneset ke-Ra'ayah le-Ferush ha-Ḥok" [The Knesset Record as Evidence of Statutory Meaning], *Ha-Praklit,* XXI (1965), p. 411; Savitzky v. Minister of Finance, 19(ii) *P.D.* 369, 375–376, 378–379 (1965); Dan, Ltd. v. Attorney General, 20(iv) *P.D.* 253 (1966).

46. *Resp. Rashba,* V, #287.

47. *Resp. Ribash* #331.

> the occasions when it is permitted to pray in private homes, such as on the occasion of a wedding or in the house of a mourner].

On the basis of this language, some members of the community objected to public worship in a new synagogue that was built after the enactment; and, as we have seen, Ribash rejected this position by interpreting the enactment as being intended to prohibit public prayer only in private homes. The starting point of Ribash's reasoning was that it is impossible to conceive that a Jewish community would adopt an enactment against worship in a synagogue to be built in the future, because, among other things, such a *takkanah* would impede the performance of a religious commandment. However, since the plain meaning of the enactment would indicate that public worship is actually prohibited in synagogues to be built in the future, Ribash sought additional grounds to support his conclusion. He found that the preamble to the enactment referred to the fact that people were engaging in congregational worship in private homes and that, consequently, fewer people joined to worship in the synagogue. He concluded from this that the enactment was adopted to prevent public prayer in private homes. In addition, Ribash allowed those who drafted the enactment to clarify their intent:

> The most important reason of all in this connection is that most of the community say that their intent was directed only to the homes of individuals, and they may surely explain their intent. . . . In this case, where the people gave a reasonable explanation of the meaning of the enactment and the language of the enactment indicates that this was their intent, and the effect of their explanation is not to nullify the enactment altogether but to say "this is included in our enactment and this is not included," they may do so. Even if the minority does not agree with the majority in this explanation, the majority is to be followed, because the enactment applies only on the basis of the intent of the majority.

This was certainly a novel and far-reaching approach in the method of interpreting enactments, even if applied only to this particular enactment. Indeed, Ribash stated an important qualification that limits the circumstances in which it is possible to interpret an enactment on the basis of the explanation of its enactors:

> However, if we are to base this permissive conclusion solely on the explanation of the community—either all or most of them—as to what they intended, and we conclude that the language of the enactment, absent their explanation, denotes an all-inclusive prohibition [*i.e.*, but for the explanation of the enactors of the *takkanah*, its language would be interpreted as including both private homes and synagogues], their explanation would have to be that

> their intent was neither to enact an all-inclusive prohibition nor to use such all-inclusive language as was written; rather, their intent was to cover only private homes, but their language became confused.
>
> But if their intent was to use the all-inclusive language written into the enactment, then even if they did not actually intend to prohibit as broadly as their language stated, we follow the language and not the intent, as an unexpressed intent is of no legal weight.

Thus, according to Ribash, it is not sufficient that those who drafted the enactment should say that their intent was to a certain effect; they must also state that "it was their aim at the time of the enactment that this intent should be expressed by their language."[48] However, if they knew that the language was broader than their intent, their explanation will not have any weight because we follow the language and not the intent. In other words, the explanation is effective only if the explainers state that they erred in thinking that the language they used actually expressed their intention, *i.e.*, they state that in that sense "their language became confused."[49]

IV. INCONSISTENCY OR AMBIGUITY IN THE TEXT

Many responsa discuss the problem of the interpretation of an enactment when different parts of the text are inconsistent with each other. When this situation occurs in adversary litigation, the enactment should be interpreted in favor of the defendant:

> Wherever there is ground to interpret [the enactment] leniently for him [*i.e.*, in favor of the defendant], the law is that we do so . . . , and wherever there is ground to interpret it to preserve the *status quo*, we do so.[50]

The same rule applies to a claim between adverse parties, when the language of the enactment creating the claim is ambiguous and can bear either of two interpretations:

> Wherever there is doubt in a case before us as to the meaning of an enactment, we take a lenient approach and decide in favor of the defendant be-

48. *Id.*

49. A limitation such as this in regard to using the explanations offered by the framers of the enactment would prevent the use of such explanations in interpreting contemporary statutes. The argument that a mistake was responsible for use of language different from what the framers intended to use is acceptable only if the halakhic basis of an enactment is in the law of vows. In the case of contemporary legislation, however, statutory interpretation is limited much more closely by the statutory language actually used. For greater liberality in recourse to explanations offered by framers of an enactment, *see Resp. Ribash* #362.

50. *Resp. Rashba*, V, #281.

> cause: first, whatever is not part of the law cannot be made so until it is clearly included, and whenever this is not certain, the matter is to be governed by Talmudic law; and secondly, the burden of proof is on the claimant.[51]

Thus, where an enactment contains a provision contrary to the preexisting *Halakhah* (and communal enactments may properly include provisions that are inconsistent with the *Halakhah*),[52] and the precise meaning of the enactment is unclear, there is no alternative but to resolve the doubt in favor of the preexisting *Halakhah*. Moreover, even if the enactment contains no provision contrary to the preexisting *Halakhah*, but its meaning is unclear and one of the possible constructions favors the defendant, we may not find the defendant liable by a construction favorable to the plaintiff; the applicable principle in that case is that "the burden of proof is on the claimant."[53]

However, deciding in favor of the defendant cannot always adequately resolve the problem of conflicting provisions in an enactment. The following question presented to Rashba is an interesting case in point:[54]

> You have asked an additional question: The community enacted a *takkanah* with regard to administrators of the public funds, containing the following language: "The two administrators of the public funds shall not have the power to expend more than two *dinarim* or to make payment to anyone of more than two *dinarim* without the consent of a majority of their colleagues who are present in the town. No expenditure or payment of more than two *dinarim* and up to five *dinarim* may be made without the consent of all their colleagues who are present in the town."

In that community, there were five communal officials (*berurim*—including those who administered the public funds),[55] and Rashba was asked two questions with regard to the meaning of the language of the enactment: (1) Did the first part of the enactment validate an expenditure or payment where one of the three others joined with the two administrators, thus constituting a majority of the five, or did it require a majority of the other three to join with the two administrators of the fund, so that four of the five officials would be needed to authorize a valid expenditure or payment? (2)

51. *Id.*, III, #397.

52. *See id.*: "But all communities have laws and enactments on this matter that do not accord with Talmudic law, and they have the right to do so." For a detailed discussion of this point, *see infra* pp. 736–751.

53. *See further Resp. Rashba*, II, #339; III, #403, #431; *Resp. Asheri* 55:7; *Resp. Ritba* #157. Similarly in *Bet Yosef* to *Tur* ḤM 13:9, s.v. Katav ha-Rashba.

54. *Resp. Rashba*, III, #386.

55. *See id.*

In view of the clear contradiction between the first part of the enactment, which indicates that consent of the majority is sufficient for any expenditure or payment in excess of two *dinarim,* and the second part of the enactment, in which it is stated that any expenditure or payment of between two and five *dinarim* requires unanimous consent, could an expenditure of "up to five *dinarim* less an *agorah*" (a coin of very small value) be made with the consent of the majority, or was unanimous consent required?

Rashba responded to the first question by interpreting the language of the enactment as meaning that three were insufficient and that it was indeed necessary to have the consent of four:

> The two administrators cannot expend more than two *dinarim* without the concurrence of the majority of the remainder. The majority of the three remaining officials is two; and until those two join with the two administrators, the latter cannot expend more than two *dinarim,* as it is stated: "Without the consent of a majority of their colleagues." Thus, a majority of the *colleagues* of the two is necessary, and that majority consists of no less than two.

It was not possible to do the same with regard to the second question; here Rashba found no solution to the inconsistency:

> However, the text concerning whether a majority is sufficient or unanimous consent is required is extremely murky; and, according to the plain meaning of the language, it seems that one provision contradicts the other.
>
> The language of the *takkanah* you have enacted, that "the administrators . . . shall not have the power to expend more than two *dinarim* . . . without the consent of a majority of their colleagues," indicates that while the two have no authority to make an expenditure even of two *dinarim* plus one *perutah* without the joinder of a majority, nevertheless, if the majority [of their colleagues] consent, they may properly make any payment, without limitation as to amount.
>
> Later, however, a limitation is set forth to the effect that they do not have authority as to even one *perutah* more than two *dinarim* unless there is unanimous consent; the *takkanah* states: "No expenditure or payment of more than two *dinarim* and up to five *dinarim* may be made without the consent of all." It thus appears that according to this language, they do not have any authority to expend even a single *perutah* more than two *dinarim* without the concurrence of all the community leaders. It appears that the two provisions are contradictory.
>
> Furthermore, when there is unanimous consent, what is the point of the limitation to between two and five *dinarim?* If an expenditure or payment is by unanimous consent, what is the difference between five and a thousand?

After having thus analyzed the language of the enactment and expressed his amazement at how poorly it was drafted, Rashba continued as follows:

> It seems to me that if what you have sent me is an accurate text of the *takkanah,* it really was not drafted with care. Consequently, it is arguable that we should apply the rule that the later provision controls, in accordance with the law that when two provisions are inconsistent the later one controls, as is set forth in chapter *Get Pashut* in the Mishnah.[56]
>
> However, I maintain that whenever we can construe so as to give effect to both provisions, we should do so . . . even where this results in a construction favoring the holder of the document.[57]

Later in the responsum, Rashba did indeed attempt to reconcile the contradiction between the two parts of the enactment,[58] but he did not succeed. He concluded his responsum:

> It is quite possible that the language of the *takkanah* was the result of an error in recording it.

Rashba thus applied to interpretation of enactments the principles that the later provision controls and that contradictory provisions must be reconciled to the fullest possible extent, and he applied them in the same manner as in the case of interpretation of documents.[59] (We have already pointed out that the starting point for interpreting enactments is the interpretation of documents;[60] it follows, of course, that they both share common principles.) However, since Rashba failed to reconcile the inconsistency in the text of the enactment, and since the solution of accepting the meaning favorable to the defendant was inapplicable in this instance because there was no adversary litigation, there remained only the conclusion that the text was written with insufficient care and the source of the problem was an error in recording.[61]

56. M Bava Batra 10:2; *see supra* p. 433 concerning interpretation of documents.

57. *See supra* p. 435 for a similar rule regarding interpretation of documents.

58. In the course of his attempt to harmonize the text of the enactment, Rashba relied on a certain formulation commonly used by the halakhic authorities. Although the rule is that enactments must be interpreted according to the colloquial usage of the people, Rashba wrote that in this case "the framers of the enactment were halakhic authorities and therefore their language followed rabbinic [rather than colloquial] usage." However, his attempt failed because even this approach could not produce a consistent reading.

59. *See supra* nn. 56, 57.

60. *See supra* p. 444.

61. Apparently, in this instance Rashba did not ultimately apply the rule that the later provision controls, which he mentioned in the course of his responsum. The reason may be that the rule is based on the assumption that the writer of the document reconsidered the

Additional rules concerning the interpretation of unclear enactments are discussed in another responsum of Ribash,[62] which we now examine.

V. METHODS OF INTERPRETING ENACTMENTS

In addition to the general rules of interpretation of enactments, which we have discussed, there is a vast amount of material in the responsa literature dealing with various methodologies and particular rules used by the halakhic authorities in the interpretive process. We complete our examination of interpretation of enactments with some observations about these methods and rules.

We have already mentioned a number of times that the basic principle of interpretation of enactments is that they should be interpreted according to the colloquial usage of the people.[63] An interesting question in this connection was posed to Ribash by the leaders of the community of Teruel:[64]

> You, the communal leaders (may God protect you) have asked me to resolve your doubts with regard to the provisions of the *takkanah* and especially with regard to one section that contains the following language:
>
> "The aforementioned community has agreed that every *shetar* (legal instrument) that shall be formulated or written from this time forward in Teruel, or which any Jewish inhabitant of Teruel will present from this day forward, shall be put in writing by a scribe and shall be signed by him or his agent and by an additional witness.
>
> "Every *shetar* presented by any Jewish man or woman from this day forward that shall not be written by a scribe and signed by him and an additional witness shall from this day forward be null and void, reckoned as a broken potsherd that has no substance; and whoever presents such a *shetar* shall pay a fine of twenty *zehuvim*."
>
> You are now unsure whether . . . a *get* (bill of divorcement) is to be included in the category of *shetar* mentioned in this section; and, if it is held that a *get* is included in this *takkanah* so that the signature of the scribe is

---

earlier provision, *see supra* p. 433, but in the case under discussion, Rashba preferred the conclusion that there was no intent to retract, but rather a negligent error. *See also Resp. Rashba*, III, #387, for further discussion in the interpretation of another enactment of the same community dealing with commercial transactions.

62. *Resp. Ribash* #304.

63. *See supra* pp. 447–448 *et passim*.

64. *Resp. Ribash* #304. Teruel is a town in the region of Aragon in Spain that had a large Jewish community.

> required on the document, whether such a *get* is invalid on the very ground that the scribe signed along with one witness.[65]
>
> And if one takes the view that the signatures of the scribe and witness make the *get* invalid, what is the effect of the section of the *takkanah* that nullifies every *shetar* not having the signature of the scribe and witness?
>
> And if a *get* is included in the category of *shetar* mentioned in this section and [the conclusion is that] the signatures of the scribe and witness do not invalidate the *get*, what is the effect on the immemorial custom of your community under which a scribe did not sign a *get?*
>
> This is the essence of your question.

Ribash first dealt with the meaning of the terms *shetar* and *get* in the Talmud and came to the conclusion that in the language of the Sages, a *get* is included in the term *shetar; i.e.,* when the term *shetar* is used, a *get* is often meant to be included,[66] and the term *get* also often includes other types of legal instruments.[67] Ribash added that even in Biblical language there was a single term, *sefer* (lit. "scroll" or "book"), used to designate all types of documents, as in "*sefer keritut*" (bill of divorcement)[68] and "*sefer ha-miknah*" (deed of conveyance).[69] However, he reasoned, none of these established the meaning of the term *shetar* in the communal enactment:

> However, we do not interpret agreements, legal documents, and communal enactments in accordance with Biblical language or the language of the halakhic authorities, but in accordance with the colloquial usage of the people in the places where they reside. This is similar to the interpretation of vows, where the law is that one is guided by the colloquial usage of the people, even if their language is not the same as Biblical language . . . and the result is a more permissive interpretation.
>
> If the colloquial usage of the people is clear to us, we follow their language; and we draw no inferences from Biblical language or the language of the halakhic authorities, since Biblical language, the language of the halakhic

65. In both the Talmud and the codificatory literature, opinions are divided as to the validity of a *get* when the scribe who writes it also signs as a witness. Some authorities invalidate such a *get* on the theory that there may be cases where the husband does not intend that the scribe sign as witness. He might ask two men to have the document written by the scribe and signed by two designated witnesses other than the scribe; but those to whom the husband made the request, out of concern not to embarrass the scribe by implying that he is not an acceptable witness, may arrange to have the scribe sign as a witness. Such a *get* would be invalid because the scribe signed as a witness without authority from the husband. *See* TB Gittin 66b *et seq.*, 86b *et seq.*; Maimonides, *MT,* Gerushin 9:27; Sh. Ar. EH 130:18; and the subsequent discussion in Ribash's responsum.

66. *E.g.*, TB Gittin 10b; Kiddushin 5a/b.

67. *E.g.*, TB Gittin 10a, 36a, 86a; Bava Batra 160a, 173a.

68. Deuteronomy 24:1.

69. Jeremiah 32:12, 14.

> authorities, and the language of the people are each distinct from one another.
>
> In the colloquial usage of the people, the word *get* is used only to refer to bills of divorcement; no other type of legal instrument is ever called *get*, nor is a bill of divorcement referred to by the term *shetar*.
>
> This is true in most instances, and with only a few exceptions, even in the language of the halakhic authorities. Therefore, it seems that in this enactment the intent was to cover only legal instruments other than bills of divorcement.

It seems that Ribash was not satisfied to rest on this reason alone;[70] he advanced two additional grounds in support of his interpretation of the enactment.

The first ground is premised on the existence of a disagreement as to the validity of a *get* that a scribe both wrote and signed.[71] In view of this disagreement,

> How can they [the community in its enactment] agree that a *get* should be written in an invalid manner! Although many of the *geonim* . . . rule that the signature of the scribe along with one witness does not invalidate a *get*, yet how could those who enacted the *takkanah* venture into such a doubtful area and into the midst of a controversy on such a serious matter? The result would be that their *takkanah* [from the root meaning "to improve"] will only make things worse! For this reason, it is appropriate to say that the intent of those who enacted the *takkanah* was to include only legal instruments other than bills of divorcement.

The second ground was based on the practice of the community from the time that the enactment was adopted until the time that this question arose:

> In addition, custom provides proof in that the practice of the community even after that *takkanah* has been that the scribe does not sign bills of divorcement, and the communal leaders who enacted that *takkanah* did not rebuke them for this. This is equivalent to an explanation and interpretation that their

70. Perhaps the reason for Ribash's reservations was that, in the same collection of enactments in which the enactment under discussion appeared, other sections listed the *get* together with other legal instruments (*shetarot*). Ribash himself quoted another section of the same collection: "It shall not be permitted . . . to write any promissory note, or any instrument evidencing an obligation created by an act of acquisition (*kinyan*), or any instrument creating a lien (*shi'bud*), or any instrument of gift, or any instrument of pledge, or any bill of sale, or any receipt of deposit, or any *ketubbah*, or any *get*. . . ." Although Ribash also used this provision by way of comparison of the various sections and their sequence to prove that the term *shetar* in the section under discussion does not include a *get*, the contrary interpretation is also plausible.

71. *See supra* n. 65.

> intent in enacting the *takkanah* was not to include bills of divorcement in the term *shetar.* If that was not their interpretation, they should have protested against those who acted contrary to the *takkanah* or else they should have nullified it! However, the fact of the matter is that it never entered their mind to include bills of divorcement in their *takkanah.*

From these two additional grounds follow other important rules for interpreting an enactment of doubtful meaning: (a) if it is possible to interpret the enactment in a manner that avoids becoming involved in an issue embroiled in halakhic dispute, this interpretation is preferred; and (b) practice in actual daily life for a certain period after the enactment has been adopted may be helpful in construing the enactment.

In interpreting communal enactments, the halakhic authorities relied heavily on the overall examination of an entire collection of *takkanot,* and compared one section to another, either to distinguish between them or to apply the provisions of one to the other. They also used both the analogical canons and the canons of explicative interpretation,[72] and gave much consideration to the meaning of terms. These deliberations by the halakhic authorities added to the Jewish legal system many diverse methods of interpretation,[73] which constitute an inexhaustible source of doctrine for legislative interpretation.[74]

We shall end our study of interpretation of communal enactments with a brief and interesting responsum by Rashba:[75]

> Your question is: It is written in an enactment relating to the communal officials who are appointed from *Rosh Ha-Shanah* (the New Year) and thereafter: "Only those included in the tax register,[76] in the *albitka,*[77] in the sum of three *peshutim*[78] or more may be appointed"; and a doubt has arisen whether

72. *See, e.g., Resp. Rashba,* III, #396 for the interpretation of an enactment by the canon of "inference from a generalization followed by a specification" (*kelal u-ferat*).

73. In addition to the responsa already cited, the following are further examples: *Resp. Rashba,* I, #590; III, #330, #422–#425; V, #126, #221, #277, #279, #283, #284, #285, #288, #290; VI, #7; *Resp. Asheri* 55:9; *Resp. Ritba* #50; *Resp. Ribash* #249; *Resp. Tashbeẓ,* II, #5 (refers to I, #133); *Resp. Ḥavvot Ya'ir* #70 (an interpretation of the term *rashai*—permitted or entitled).

74. A great deal of the material in these responsa has now been classified by the Hebrew University's Institute of Research in Jewish Law in the course of the preparation of the digests of the responsa literature. These digests contain a substantial number of detailed entries relating to all aspects of interpretation dealt with in the responsa literature.

75. *Resp. Rashba,* IV, #312.

76. Hebrew *tevat ha-mas* (lit. "the tax coffer"); the term is particularly common in *Resp. Rashba.*

77. *Resp. Rashba,* IV, #313 states: "Now that the *albitka* has been done away with and no person knows anything about anyone else, it is impossible to know how much tax anyone pays."

78. This is the name of a coin.

the date of the above enactment or the time when the official is appointed is determinative.

The difference is important for one whose situation has changed between the two dates.

According to the enactment, only one who paid a designated amount of taxes could be appointed as a communal official. The question that arose was whether the decisive date when the condition of eligibility must be fulfilled was the time of the adoption of the enactment or the time of the appointment.

Rashba responded as follows:

My response: Whenever the term "was" or "is" is used in regard to various matters or in *takkanot,* the reference is to the time when that event takes place, not to a past time or to the present time.

In the case stated in the Mishnah[79]—"One who was thrown into a pit and called out that whoever heard his voice should write a bill of divorcement to his wife"[80]—the reference is not to someone who had been thrown into the pit at one time in the past but [to someone who was in the pit] at the time that he called out that whoever heard his voice should write a bill of divorcement.

We have also learned:[81] "If one puts out the [sabbath] candle because he fears the gentiles. . . ."[82] This does not refer to one who at the present time fears the gentiles but to one who was in fear at the time that he put out the candle!

In our case, the intent was to refer only to one who pays the required amount at the time that he is appointed.

The same applies to Scripture: "If he had a wife . . ."[83]—one who at that particular time had a wife.

This is clear; it does not need further explication.

Rashba used the question about that particular enactment as the occasion to lay down a rule of interpretation for a particular term ("was" or "is") whenever it appears in a particular context. He based his interpretation on Biblical language and the language of the Sages because here the

79. M Gittin 6:6; TB Gittin 66a.

80. The conclusion of the *mishnah* is: ". . . they shall write and give." Although the person did not actually say "give," it is assumed that the omission was due to the extraordinary circumstances.

81. M Shabbat 2:5; TB Shabbat 29b.

82. The passage in the *mishnah* concludes by stating that the person who extinguishes the candle in such cases does not violate the sabbath because he extinguishes it on account of the danger in keeping the lights burning.

83. Exodus 21:3: "If he came single, he shall leave single; if he had a wife, his wife shall leave with him."

term has had a consistent and uniform meaning. In this instance, the matter "is clear; it does not need further explication"—the consistency of meaning links all the three types of language on which the methodologies of interpretation and exposition in Jewish law are based: Biblical language, the language of the halakhic authorities, and the language of the people.

GLOSSARY

aggadah ("telling") the non-halakhic, non-normative portion of the *Torah she-be-al peh* consisting of historical, philosophical, allegorical, and ethical rabbinic teachings

aginut the state of being an *agunah*

agoria, *pl.* agoriot non-Jewish court

agunah ("anchored" or "bound") a woman unable to remarry because she is "bound," *e.g.*, to a husband who has disappeared and cannot be legally proved dead or who has abandoned her or who refuses to divorce her

aḥarei rabbim le-hattot "follow the majority" of a court or of legislative representatives

aḥaronim ("later ones") later halakhic authorities, generally referring to those from the sixteenth century onward. *See also rishonim*

am ha'areẓ ("people of the land") (1) national council; (2) hoi polloi; (3) ignorant, unlearned person; (4) a person not punctilious in observance, opposite of *ḥaver* and *ḥasid;* (5) the assembled public

amora, *pl.* amoraim (1) rabbis of the Talmudic period (220 C.E. to end of the fifth century C.E.); (2) *meturgeman,* which *see*

Anshei Keneset ha-Gedolah ("Men of the Great Assembly") Ezra, Nehemiah, and those who entered with them into the covenant to observe the laws of the Torah after the return of the Babylonian exiles. The Great Assembly was the supreme institution of the Jewish people during the time it was active, from the latter half of the fifth century B.C.E.

arba'ah shomerim ("four bailees") the four types of bailees in Jewish law—the unpaid bailee (*shomer ḥinam),* the borrower (*sho'el*), the paid bailee (*shomer sakhar*) and the hirer (*sokher*)

arev kabbelan one who has undertaken to be a surety by a declaration that entitles the creditor to look to him for payment without first pursuing a claim against the principal debtor

arka'ot (shel goyim) non-Jewish courts

arvit evening prayer

asharta judicial "certification" that a legal document has been properly authenticated

asmakhta ("something to lean on," "supportive device") (1) an action or transaction without an unqualified and deliberate intention to take the action or enter into the transaction; (2) a transaction involving a penalty or forfeiture; (3) exegesis identified by the Sages as integrative, not creative; (4) according to some, a strained and far-fetched (symbolic and figurative) exegesis that is necessarily only integrative

avak ribbit ("dust of interest") any form of benefit (other than actual stipulated interest) received by a lender that exceeds the value of the money or property lent; it is not expressly prohibited by the Torah, but is rabbinically proscribed because it partakes of the nature of interest

av bet din ("father of the court") (1) one of the two national leaders during the period of the Zugot; (2) presiding judge

avot nezikin ("fathers of damages") primary categories of causes of damage, namely, "ox" "pit," "grazing animal," and "fire." *See bor, mav'eh,* and *shor*

Bagaẓ acronym for *Bet Din Gavo'ah le-Ẓedek,* which *see*

bal tigra ("you shall not take away") the prohibition (Deut. 4:2, 13:1) against taking away from any commandments (*miẓvot*) set forth in the Torah; antonym of *bal tosif*

bal tosif ("you shall not add") the prohibition (Deut. 4:2, 13:1) against adding to the commandments (*miẓvot*) set forth in the Torah

baraita, ***pl.*** **baraitot** tannaitic *dictum* not included in the Mishnah (capitalized if referred to collectively)

be-di-avad ("after the fact," ***ex post*****)** usually employed in connection with the question whether an act in violation of a prohibition is not only a transgression but also without legal effect. *See also le-khateḥillah*

bein adam la-Makom ("between man and God") (1) involving human relationships with God; (2) pertaining to "religious" law as distinguished from civil law; (3) pertaining to matters of private conscience

bein adam le-ḥavero ("between a person and his fellow") (1) involving relationships between people; (2) pertaining to civil as distinguished from "religious" law

berurim ("selected ones," "arbiters") (1) members of the community council; (2) representatives for enacting legislation; (3) arbitrators selected by the parties; (4) lay judges; (5) communal leaders

bet din, ***pl.*** **battei din ("house of law")** (1) a court or panel of judges who adjudicate in accordance with the *Halakhah;* (2) a Jewish arbitral tribunal

Bet Din Gavo'ah le-Ẓedek "The High Court of Justice," the capacity in which the Supreme Court of Israel sits as a court of original jurisdiction to review administrative or governmental action claimed to be arbitrary or in excess of jurisdiction

bet din shel hedyotot ("a court of ordinary people") (1) a court lacking a rabbinic judge who is ordained; (2) a court composed entirely of laymen not knowledgeable in the law

Corpus Juris (Civile) ("Body of the [Civil] Law") (1) The Code of Justinian; (2) a comprehensive legal code that has achieved ultimate authoritative status

corpus juris the total body of law in a given legal system

darkhei shalom ("the ways of peace") the social and religious interest in peace and tranquillity

darshan (1) "exegete"; (2) preacher, homilist

dat (1) religious faith; (2) law, particularly law based on custom; (3) established practice

dayyan ("judge") a judge according to the *Halakhah;* a judge of a rabbinical court

de-oraita "Biblical"; the precise contours of this concept cannot be indicated in a glossary. *See* vol. 1, pp. 207ff.

de-rabbanan "rabbinic"; for the precise contours of this concept, *see* vol. 1, pp. 207ff.

derishah va-ḥakirah ("inquiry and examination") thorough interrogation of witnesses by the *dayyanim* of a *bet din*

din, ***pl.*** **dinim ("law")** (1) law generally; (2) "interpretation," particularly analogical or syllogistic interpretation or *a fortiori* reasoning; (3) sometimes, law included in the Order of *Nezikin;* (4) law based on a source other than custom or legislation

din Torah (1) Jewish law generally; (2) a case before a rabbinical court

dinei issur ve-hetter ("laws of prohibition and permissibility") laws governing religious and ritual matters, *i.e.,* matters involving relationships with God

dinei kenasot ("law of fines") (1) laws in civil cases pursuant to which the prescribed payment is not equivalent to actual loss suffered; (2) in modern usage, also a criminal fine or civil penalty

dinei malkot or **makkot ("laws of flogging")** laws relating to offenses punishable by flogging

dinei mamonot ("monetary laws") the body of Jewish law generally, but not completely, corresponding to civil law in contemporary legal systems

dinei nefashot ("law of souls") the body of Jewish law involving (a) capital crimes, (b) crimes punishable by corporal punishment, or (c) criminal law

din emet le-amito ("a judgment that is completely and truly correct") a judgment that combines principled decisionmaking with individualized fairness and equity based on thorough understanding of the particular circumstances as well as the law and the general background

divrei kabbalah ("matters of tradition") (1) the writings of the Prophets and the Hagiographa; (2) teaching transmitted orally by teacher to disciple, from one generation to the next; (3) Jewish mysticism (a much later meaning)

divrei soferim ("words of the Scribes") (1) equivalent to *de-rabbanan;* (2) matters essentially rooted in the written Torah but explained by the Oral Law; (3) enactments of the Scribes

divrei Torah ("words of the Torah") equivalent to *de-oraita* ("Biblical")

ed sheker "false witness"

edim zomemim ("scheming witnesses") witnesses who conspire to testify falsely

ein li ("I have nothing") an oath by a debtor attesting inability to pay the debt and undertaking to fulfill certain stringent requirements as to future earnings

erusin ("betrothal") (1) synonym for *kiddushin;* creates the personal status of husband and wife *vis-à-vis* the whole world, but marital rights between the couple do not arise until after *nissu'in, i.e.,* entry under the *ḥuppah* (marital canopy); (2) (in modern Hebrew) engagement

eruv ("merging") a method or device to (a) extend the boundaries within which one may walk or carry on the sabbath, or (b) permit food to be cooked on a festival for consumption on the sabbath immediately following

Even ha-Ezer one of the four principal divisions of the *Sefer ha-Turim* and the *Shulḥan Arukh,* dealing mainly with family law

exilarch the head of the internal Jewish government in the Babylonian diaspora

gabbai, *pl.* **gabba'im** (1) collector of dues, charitable contributions, or assessments; (2) director of a craft guild; (3) manager or director of a synagogue, with particular reference to the religious service

gaon, *pl.* **geonim** *see geonim*

garmi (geramei, gerama) (1) indirect causation; (2) harm other than by direct physical impact

GeFeT Hebrew acronym for "Gemara, Ferush, and Tosafot," *i.e.,* Talmud, Rashi, and Tosafot

Gemara ("completion" or "study" or "tradition") that part of the Talmud that contains discussion of the Mishnah

gematria a method of reaching or supporting conclusions on the basis of the numerical equivalents of letters of key words

gemirut da'at serious, deliberate, and final intent, without reservation, to enter into a legal transaction or perform a juristic act

geonic pertaining to the *geonim* or the gaonate

geonim heads of Talmudical academies (*yeshivot*), (the most famous being Sura and Pumbedita in Babylonia), from the end of the sixth or middle of the seventh century C.E. to the middle of the eleventh century C.E. in the west and the thirteenth century in the east

get bill of divorcement

get me'usseh ("a compelled divorce") a divorce that is invalid because given not voluntarily but rather as a result of improper compulsion

gezel mi-divreihem ("robbery by their words") theft under rabbinic law, *i.e.,* acts designated by the Rabbis as theft, although they do not constitute theft under Biblical law and were not prohibited by the Bible at all

gezerah ("decree") legislative enactment by the halakhic authorities; in the technical sense, as used by some authorities, limited to an enactment that extends or adds prohibitions beyond preexisting *Halakhah,* as distinguished from *takkanah,* an enactment prescribing performance of designated acts

gezerah shavah ("[comparison with] similar matter") inference from similarity of words or phrases. One of the thirteen canons of Biblical interpretation

guda ("wall") a ban

ha'anakah ("bonus," or "gratuity") a sum given to a Hebrew slave upon attaining freedom after six or more years of service; *see* Deuteronomy 15:11–18

haftarah, *pl.* **haftarot** prophetic reading that supplements the weekly Torah portions read during the synagogue service on sabbaths and other holy days

ḥakham, ***pl.*** **ḥakhamim ("sage")** (1) through the Talmudic period, rabbinic Sage; (2) in subsequent periods, halakhic authority, Talmudic scholar

halakhah le-ma'aseh a legal norm intended to be applied in practice, as distinguished from a theoretical or academic statement

Halakhah the generic term for the entire body of Jewish law, religious as well as civil

halakhah, ***pl.*** **halakhot ("the law")** (1) a binding decision or ruling on a contested legal issue; (2) a statement of a legal rule not expressly based on a Biblical verse, made in a prescriptive form; (3) in the plural, a collection of any particular category of rules

halakhah le-Moshe mi-Sinai ("law given to Moses at Sinai") (1) a law specifically given to Moses at Sinai, not indicated by or deducible from the Biblical text; (2) a law unanimously accepted by the Sages, having a tenuous connection with the Biblical text, given the designation to emphasize the law's authority; (3) a law so well settled that it is as authoritative as if it had explicitly been given to Moses at Sinai

halanat ha-din ("deferring judgment") deliberation in judgment

ḥaliẓah ("removal," "pulling off") release from levirate marriage by a rite whose central feature is removal of a sandal from a foot of the *levir. See* Deuteronomy 25:7–10. *See also levir*

ḥasid (1) pious; (2) equitable, more generous than the law requires; (3) punctilious in observance; synonym for *ḥaver*

haskamah, ***pl.*** **haskamot** (1) "agreement"; (2) (as the term was used by Spanish halakhic authorities) enactment

hassagat gevul (1) "removing a landmark" [*i.e.,* boundary marker]; (2) copyright infringement; (3) unfair competition; (4) unfair interference with contract or economic advantage

ḥaver (1) "friend," "comrade, "fellow"; (2) one punctilious in observance of the laws of ritual purity, (3) generally a halakhic scholar

ḥazakah (from ***ḥazak,*** **"strong")** (1) a mode of acquisition of property; (2) a legal presumption; (3) possession; (4) the rule that possession of real property for three years under claim of right is equivalent to a deed as proof of ownership; (5) an act of dominion such as putting up a fence or locking the premises

hedyot ("ordinary") (1) pertaining to mundane affairs, as distinguished from matters of Torah; (2) layman; (3) one untutored in the law

hefker bet din hefker ("ownerless [declared by] a ***bet din*** **is ownerless")** a halakhic court has the authority to expropriate property; the principle was later used as authority to legislate

hefker ẓibbur hefker ("ownerless" [declared by] the community is ownerless") the community has the authority to expropriate property and legislate

hekkesh ("analogy") analogical reasoning, a method of Biblical interpretation

hekkesh ha-katuv ("Scriptural analogy") analogy made by the Bible itself

henpek same as *asharta,* which *see*

ḥerem, ***pl.*** **ḥaramim ("ban")** (1) a ban as a sanction for transgression; (2) in its most severe form, total excommunication, an enforced exclusion from communal Jewish religious, social, and civic life; (3) oath; (4) sanctification

ḥerem ha-yishuv ("ban with respect to settlement") an enactment prohibiting settlement in a town without the consent of the townspeople, and providing penalties for violation

ḥezkat kashrut "presumption of propriety," *i.e.*, the presumption that persons behave correctly and that what should have been done has been properly done

ḥezkat shanim "possession for [a specified number of] years," which may serve as a substitute for proof of ownership

ḥiddushim, *sing.* **hiddush ("innovations")** novellae, *i.e.*, new legal interpretations and insights

hilkheta Aramaic for *halakhah*

hilkheta gemiri (1) "a determined [settled and accepted] rule"; (2) a rule handed down by tradition; (3) equivalent of *halakhah le-Moshe mi-Sinai*

hilkheta ke-vatra'ei "the law is in accordance with [the view of] the later authorities"

ḥiyyuv (1) contract; (2) obligation; (3) debt

ḥok (1) law; (2) statute; (3) regulation

hora'at sha'ah ("a directive for the hour") a temporary legislative measure permitting conduct forbidden by the Torah when such legislation is a necessary precaution to restore people to the observance of the faith; some legislation originally adopted or justified as a temporary measure has become an established part of Jewish law

Ḥoshen Mishpat one of the four principal divisions of the *Sefer ha-Turim* and the *Shulḥan Arukh*, dealing mainly with matters of *mishpat ivri*

ḥuppah the nuptial "canopy," under which bride and groom join in the concluding phase (*nissu'in*) of the marriage rite

innuy ha-din ("torture of the law") delay of justice, the law's delays

issur, also **issura ("prohibition")** and **issur ve-hetter ("prohibition and permission")** "religious" or ritual law; laws other than *dinei mamonot*

Jerusalem Talmud the Talmud of the *amoraim* of the Land of Israel

jus cogens ("compelling law") a mandatory legal norm not subject to variance or modification by agreement of the parties affected

jus dispositivum ("displaceable law") a legal rule that can be varied by agreement, as distinguished from *jus cogens*, which may not be varied by agreement

jus naturale ("natural law") law whose source is "in nature" and which is therefore common to all humanity; sometimes called "higher law," superior to law pronounced or enacted by human agency. *Cf.* Noahide laws

jus non scriptum ("unwritten law") in Roman law, law not reduced to writing, *e.g.*, custom. Not synonymous with the Jewish Oral Law

jus scriptum ("written law") in Roman law, law that has been reduced to writing. Not synonymous with the Jewish Written Law

kabbalah ("tradition") *See divrei kabbalah*

kabbalat kinyan assumption of an obligation made binding by exchange of a symbolic object (*sudar*) as "consideration" for the obligation

kallah (1) semiannual assembly of scholars and teachers at a *yeshivah*; (2) bride; (3) daughter-in-law

kal va-ḥomer ("easy and hard," "minor and major") inference *a fortiori* (one of the thirteen canons of Biblical interpretation)

karet, *pl.* **keritot** or **keretot ("extirpation"** or **"excision")** premature death by divine action as punishment for sin

kasher ("fit") (1) kosher; (2) competent (as applied to a witness)

kashrut ("fitness") dietary laws as to permissible and forbidden foods and food preparation. *See also ḥezkat kashrut*

kehillah the organized Jewish community, especially when possessed of juridical autonomy

kelalei ha-Talmud ("principles of the Talmud") methodology and rules of halakhic decision making

kerem be-Yavneh ("the vineyard in Yavneh") the academy of the Sages in Yavneh (also called Jabneh and Jamnia)

ketubbah, *pl.* **ketubbot ("writing")** marriage contract prescribing a wife's economic entitlements during the marriage and in the event of divorce or the husband's death, in addition to such other provisions as may be agreed by the parties

Ketuvim ("writings") the Hagiographa; *i.e.*, the third division of the Hebrew Bible, the other two being the Torah (Pentateuch) and the Prophets

kim li ("it is established for me") a plea that the defendant's position is supported by a halakhic authority, and that therefore the defendant is not liable. The plea lost its effectiveness with the acceptance of the *Shulḥan Arukh* as the authoritative code of Jewish law

king's law (*mishpat ha-melekh*) the legal authority of the Jewish king (later extended to other forms of Jewish governance), which includes the power to temper the *Halakhah* to meet social needs

kinyan ("acquisition") (1) a formal mode of acquiring or conveying property or creating an obligation; (2) ownership; (3) contract; (4) abbreviation of *kinyan sudar*

kinyan agav karka ("acquisition incident to land"); also **kinyan agav** a conveyance of land in which chattels are incidentally transferred without limitation as to quantity, kind, location, or value

kinyan ha-guf ownership or acquisition of property as distinguished from the right to income

kinyan ḥalifin ("acquisition by barter") exchange of one chattel for another, in which each party acquires the other's chattel

kinyan meshikhah ("acquisition by pulling") a mode of acquisition created by an enactment pursuant to which ownership is not acquired upon payment of the purchase money (which is sufficient under Biblical law to transfer ownership to the buyer) but is acquired only when actual possession is taken

kinyan perot (1) the right to income; (2) acquisition of the right to income

kinyan sudar ("acquisition by kerchief") symbolic barter. The transferee gives the transferor a symbolic object such as a *sudar* (kerchief) in exchange for the object that is the subject of the transaction. The *sudar* is returned to the transferee upon completion of the transaction. This mode of acquisition is also used to create a contractual obligation

kiyyum shetarot ("validation of legal instruments") judicial authentication and certification of legal instruments

Knesset the Israeli parliament

kohen "priest," a member of the tribe of Levi descended from the branch of the tribe authorized to perform the Temple service and other sacred duties

kol de-alim gaver ("whoever is the stronger [of claimants to property] prevails") whoever obtains possession by self-help when self-help is permissible may retain the property

kol di-mekaddesh ada'ata de-rabbanan mekaddesh ("all who marry do so subject to the conditions laid down by the Rabbis") a principle upon which the Rabbis were empowered to annul marriages

kum va-aseh ("arise and do") a category of legislation permitting the performance of an act prohibited by the Torah

lazeit yedei shamayim ("to fulfill a duty in the sight of Heaven") fulfilling a moral, but not legal, obligation

le-hatnot al mah she-katuv ba-Torah ("to contract out of a law contained in the Torah") by agreement between the parties, varying or rendering inapplicable a rule of the Torah

le-khatehillah ("in the beginning") *ex ante,* in the first instance. *See also be-di-avad*

le-ma'aseh ("for action") in actual practice, or for practical application as distinguished from *"le-halakhah"* ("for law," *i.e.,* as theoretical doctrine, not practical application)

le-migdar milta ("to safeguard the matter") the principle that authorizes the halakhic authorities, as a protective measure, to adopt enactments in the field of criminal law that prescribe action the Torah prohibits

lefi sha'ah ("temporarily") a principle authorizing legislation permitting conduct contrary to the Torah as a temporary measure under exigent circumstances

leshon benei adam ("colloquial usage of the people") (1) the principle that terms in a legal document should be construed according to their colloquial meaning, not in the sense used in Scripture or by the Sages; (2) according to R. Ishmael, the principle that the Torah speaks as people speak, and therefore there are redundancies in the Torah and not every word has midrashic significance

letakken olam ("to improve [or mend] the world") to promote the public welfare

levir brother-in-law of the widow of a man who has died leaving no children; he must marry the widow unless the rite of halizah is performed (Deut. 25:5–10). *See also halizah*

lifnim mi-shurat ha-din ("on the inside of the line of the law") acting more generously than the law requires

ma'amad sheloshtan ("a meeting of the three") a method of assignment of property rights or obligations: the creditor-assignor, in the presence of the debtor and the assignee, states that the ownership of the property or obligation is assigned to the assignee

ma'aseh, *pl.* **ma'asim** "act," "incident," "event," or "case" that is the source of a new halakhic norm or declarative of a preexisting norm

ma'aseh adif ("a *ma'aseh* takes precedence") a *ma'aseh* is entitled to particular deference

ma'aseh ha-ba ba-averah a transaction involving illegality

ma'aseh rav "a *ma'aseh* is [of] great [significance]"

ma'aseh yadeha "her [a wife's] handiwork," *i.e.*, the domestic services to which a husband is entitled from his wife in consideration of his obligation to support her

mah lo leshakker ("why should he lie") *see migo*

makkot mardut disciplinary flogging

malkot flogging; stripes

malshinut (1) "slander"; (2) informing, betrayal, *i.e.*, a slanderous accusation against a Jew of a kind that, if heard by a non-Jew, would likely cause harm to the person accused

mamon; also **mamona** "money" matters, *i.e.*, civil-law matters, as distinguished from religious-law matters

mamzer ("misbegotten") offspring of an incestuous or adulterous union that is subject to capital punishment by a court or extirpation (*karet*) by God; often mistranslated as "bastard," in the sense of one born out of wedlock

Mappah ("Tablecloth") the title of the commentary by Moses Isserles (Rema) on Joseph Caro's *Shulḥan Arukh* ("Set Table")

mattenat bari ("gift of a healthy person") a form of disposition of property essentially equivalent to a will, whereby the donor "gives" property to his beneficiaries but retains possession and control during his lifetime

mattenat shekhiv me-ra ("gift of one facing imminent death") gift in contemplation of death made by a *shekhiv me-ra*, or the last will and testament of a *shekhiv me-ra*, for which the usual formal requirements are relaxed

me-aḥar ("since") *see migo*

Megillah "scroll," usually referring to the Book of Esther

meḥusar amanah ("lacking in trustworthiness") a description applied by a court as a sanction to a person who reneges on a transaction as to which there is only an unenforceable oral agreement

me'ilah ("sacrilege") unlawful use of consecrated property

Mejelle the Ottoman code of civil law, based on Mohammedan principles and formally repealed in the State of Israel in 1984

melog, also **nikhsei melog ("plucked [usufruct] property")** property belonging to a wife, of which the income belongs to the husband and the principal remains the wife's; the husband is not responsible for loss or diminution in value of *melog* property as he is for *ẓon barzel* property

memrah, *pl.* **memrot ("statement")** a law originated by the *amoraim*

meshikhah ("pulling") *see kinyan meshikhah*

meturgeman (1) spokesman; (2) one who repeated aloud the words of a speaker to a large audience for whom it would be difficult to hear the speaker directly; (3) interpreter

me'un ("refusal") disaffirmance by a woman of a marriage entered into when she was a minor

meẓavveh meḥamat mitah "a testator on the brink of death," for whose will the usual formal requirements are relaxed

mezuzah (1) parchment scroll containing Deuteronomy 6:4–9 and 11:13–21, affixed to the right doorpost in a wooden, metal, or other case; (2) doorpost

mi-de-oraita *see de-oraita*

mi-de-rabbanan *see de-rabbanan*

middah, *pl.* **middot** (1) canon of interpretation; (2) desirable quality of character

middat ḥasidut ("the quality of piety or benevolence") pious or altruistic behavior

mi-divrei soferim ("from the words of the Scribes") *see divrei soferim*

midrash (1) interpretation of Scripture and *Halakhah*; (2) exegesis; (3) a particular midrashic text (when used in this sense in this work, *midrash* is italicized)

midrash ha-Halakhah interpretation of *Halakhah*

midrash mekayyem ("confirming exegesis") integrative exegesis, by which existing law is "integrated" or connected with a Biblical text

midrash yoẓer ("creative exegesis") exegesis that is the legal source of new law

migo ("since," "because" [Aramaic]) a procedural rule to the effect that a claim, despite insufficiency of proof, is deemed valid "since" (or "because") if the claimant had desired to lie, he could have stated a more plausible case that would have been accepted as true, and therefore the weaker claim actually made should also be accepted; also called *me-aḥar* and *mah lo leshakker*

mikveh ("collection of water") ritual bath

minhag (1) "custom" (in modern Hebrew, custom operating as an independent legal norm), *cf. nohag*; (2) legislative enactment (*takkanah*); (3) prescribed practice, *i.e.*, a legal rule for which the Torah itself is the source

minhag garu'a ("bad custom") custom deemed undesirable, which some halakhic authorities held for that reason legally ineffective

minhag ha-medinah ("custom of the region") local custom

minhag le-dorot ("a prescribed practice for the generations") a law for all time

minhag mevattel halakhah ("custom overrides the law") the principle that in monetary matters, custom controls even if contrary to the *Halakhah*

minḥah afternoon prayer

minyan ("number") a quorum of ten, the minimum number for public congregational prayer

mi she-para ("He Who punished . . .") an imprecation by the court addressed to a party who has violated a moral obligation for which there is no legal sanction

Mishnah the code of R. Judah Ha-Nasi, redacted about 200 C.E., which is the basis of the Gemara

mishnah, *pl.* **mishnayot** the smallest division of the Mishnah; the Mishnah is divided into Orders, tractates, chapters, and mishnayot (paragraphs)

mishnat ḥasidim ("standard of the pious") a higher ethical and personal standard than the law requires

Mishneh Torah Maimonides' Code, also called *Yad ha-Ḥazakah*

mishpat (1) adjudication, the act of judging; (2) decision; (3) justice; (4) a system of laws; (5) a legal right; (6) custom, usage, or practice

mishpat ivri ("Jewish law") that part of the *Halakhah* corresponding to what generally is included in the *corpus juris* of other contemporary legal systems, namely, laws that govern relationships in human society

mishpat ha-melekh *see* "king's law"

mishum eivah ("because of enmity") a principle of legislation to the effect that laws should be designed to prevent strife and enmity

miẓvah, *pl.* **miẓvot ("commandment")** (1) religious obligation; (2) good deed

miẓvah ha-teluyah ba-areẓ ("precept dependent upon the land") a precept directly relating to the Land of Israel, *e.g.*, the sabbatical year and the law of the firstfruits

mored a "rebellious" husband who refuses to cohabit with his wife

moredet a "rebellious" wife who refuses to cohabit with her husband

mu'ad ("forewarned") having given notice of propensity for causing harm. Opposite of *tam;* if the cause of harm is *mu'ad,* damages are higher than if the cause is *tam*

na'arah ("girl") a female minor, *i.e.*, a girl who is more than twelve years and one day old but has not reached the age of twelve years, six months, and one day

na'arut ("girlhood") the legal status of a *na'arah*

nasi, *pl.* **nesi'im ("patriarch")** president of the Sanhedrin

naval bi-reshut ha-Torah ("scoundrel within the bounds of the Torah") one who keeps within the letter but violates the spirit of the Torah

nekhasim benei ḥorin ("free [*i.e.*, unencumbered] property") property fully subject to execution of a judgment against the owner

nekhasim meshu'badim ("encumbered property"); nekhasim she-yesh lahem aḥarayut ("property bearing responsibility") real estate, which is responsible for and secures the owner's contractual obligations by virtue of an automatic lien created by entry into the contract

nekhasim she-ein lahem aḥarayut ("property bearing no responsibility") personal property, as to which no lien arises upon the creation of a contractual obligation

Nevi'im the Prophets, *i.e.*, the second division of the Hebrew Bible, the other two being the Torah and the Ketuvim (Hagiographa)

nezikin (1) damages; (2) torts; (3) injuries

niddui ("banning") semi-ostracism, a less severe ban than total excommunication

nikhsei melog *see melog*

niksei ẓon barzel *see ẓon barzel*

nissu'in ("marriage") joinder under the *ḥuppah* (wedding canopy). *See also erusin*

nohag (1) "usage," "conventional custom"; (2) in modern Hebrew, custom given operative effect not as an independent legal norm but because parties are presumed to have acted pursuant to it. *Cf. minhag*

nos'ei kelim ("armor bearers") commentaries and glosses to a legal code

novellae *see ḥiddushim*

ona'ah ("overreaching") taking unfair advantage, as by fraud or deception, in a legal transaction (Lev. 25:14)

ones, pronounced **o-nes ("force")** (1) coercion; (2) duress; (3) act of God (*vis major*); (4) rape

Oraḥ Ḥayyim ("The Way of Life") one of the four principal divisions of the *Sefer ha-Turim* and the *Shulḥan Arukh,* generally dealing with ritual and religious matters outside the scope of *mishpat ivri*

Oral Law (Torah she-be-al peh) all of Jewish law except the part explicitly written in Scripture

parshanut ("explanation") (1) commentary; (2) synonym for midrash

pasul unfit; opposite of *kasher*

pe'ah, *pl.* **pe'ot** "corner" of a field, where a portion of the crop must be left for the poor by the reapers

perat u-khelal ("specification and generalization," "particular and general") inference from a specification followed by a generalization. One of the thirteen canons of Biblical interpretation

peri eẓ hadar ("product of hadar trees") the *etrog* (citron)

perushim "commentaries"

pesak, *pl.* **pesakim** (1) legal ruling; (2) judgment in a litigated case

pesharah "compromise," "settlement"

peshat "plain meaning," as distinguished from midrash

pilpul a method of halakhic study characterized by subtle dialectics and finespun distinctions

piskei ba'alei battim ("judgments of householders") lay judgments

posek, *pl.* **posekim** (1) authoritative decisionmaker, decisor; (2) codifier

praesumptio juris a legal presumption whereby the law assumes the existence of a fact or condition unless the presumption is rebutted by proof to the contrary

prosbul a legal formula authorized by an enactment of Hillel whereby a debt would not be released by the sabbatical year, notwithstanding Deuteronomy 15:1–12, which prescribes such release

rabbinic period the period following the *geonim* to the present time. There are three subperiods: (a) the period of the *rishonim* (eleventh to sixteenth century C.E.), (b) the period of the *aḥaronim* (sixteenth century to the beginnings of the Jewish Emancipation in the late eighteenth century), and (c) the post-Emancipation period

regi'ah ("rest," "allocation of time [rega]" an agreement in restraint of trade allocating time for work and rest (*margo'a*)

resh galuta exilarch

rishonim (1) in prior historical periods, "earlier" halakhic authorities who lived longer ago than in the then recent past; (2) in contemporary usage, halakhic authorities from the eleventh to the sixteenth century. *See also aḥaronim*

rosh yeshivah head of a talmudical academy

Sanhedrin (1) the assembly of 71 ordained scholars constituting the supreme legislative and judicial authority of the Jews during the period of the Second Temple and some time thereafter; (2) the name of a tractate of the Talmud

savoraim ("reasoners") rabbinic Sages from the end of the fifth to the beginning of the sixth or middle of the seventh century C.E.

seder, *pl.,* **sedarim ("order")** (1) one of the six major divisions of the Mishnah; (2) the ritual meal on the first night of Passover

sefer halakhot a code that includes a discussion of the range of views of the various authorities

Sefer ha-Turim the code of Jewish law written by Jacob b. Asher

sefer keritut "bill of divorcement"; *see also get*

sefer pesakim a code written in prescriptive terms, without discussion of legal theory or conflicting opinions

semikhah ("laying on of hands") rabbinic ordination

sevarah "legal reasoning"

shali'aḥ "agent"

she'elot u-teshuvot ("questions and answers") responsa

Shekhinah Divine Presence, the "immanent" or "indwelling" aspect of God

shekhiv me-ra one who is dangerously ill and faces or otherwise reasonably apprehends imminent death

Shema three Biblical passages recited twice daily, beginning with "Hear (shema) O Israel" (Deut. 6:4), constituting the confession of the Jewish faith

shetar, *pl.* **shetarot** (1) legal document; (2) contract; (3) deed

shev ve-al ta'aseh ("sit and do not do") a category of legislation directing that an affirmative precept, obligatory according to Biblical law, not be performed

shevi'it ("seventh [year]") the sabbatical year

shevu'at ha-edut ("witness's oath") an oath by one formally called upon to bear witness, to the effect that the affiant has no knowledge of the matter about which he is called to testify

shevut ("[sabbath] rest") (1) work rabbinically forbidden on the sabbath; (2) the rabbinical prohibition of such work

shi'bud nekhasim ("encumbrance of property") (1) lien, security interest; (2) the general lien on the real estate of an obligor that arises automatically upon creation of the obligation

shi'buda de-oraita "Biblical lien"

shiddukhin an agreement to enter into marriage

shikkul ha-da'at (1) [judicial] "discretion"; (2) decision on a moot point of law; (3) the zone of permissible latitude of a *dayyan* to disagree with other authorities

shimmush (1) "service" to the Torah; (2) attendance upon a halakhic scholar; (3) apprenticeship to a halakhic authority

shi'ur (1) prescribed measure; (2) "lesson," talmudic lecture

sho'el ("borrower") a bailee in possession of property as a result of borrowing it from another

shofet (1) "judge"; (2) magistrate, ruler

shomer ḥinam "an unpaid bailee," *i.e.,* one who undertakes without compensation to preserve property of another

shomer sakhar a "paid bailee" who is compensated for his service in connection with the bailment

shufra de-shetara ("adornment of the *shetar*") clauses designed to enhance the effectiveness of a legal document, *e.g.,* waiver of certain defenses otherwise available

Shulḥan Arukh (the "Set Table") the code of Jewish law written by Joseph Caro in the sixteenth century; the most authoritative of the Jewish legal codes

sitomta ("seal") mark placed on a barrel or other large container identifying the owner; placing the mark was recognized as a mode of acquisition

sofer, *pl.* soferim ("counter," "scribe") (1) a halakhic authority of the period of Ezra the Scribe; (2) a scholar of the Talmudic period. *See divrei soferim*

sof hora'ah ("the end of instruction") the completion of the Talmud

sokher ("hirer") a bailee or lessee who pays for the right to possession of the bailed or leased property

sudar ("kerchief") the instrument used in the most widespread mode of acquisition in Jewish law. *See kinyan sudar*

sugyah, *pl.* sugyot (1) passage; (2) discussion; (3) issue; a Talmudic subject or area

sukkah "booth" or "tabernacle" erected for the festival of *Sukkot*

supercommentary a commentary on a commentary

takkanah, *pl.* takkanot ("improvement," "repair") legislative enactment by halakhic or communal authorities. *See also gezerah*

takkanah kevu'ah ("established enactment") legislation permanently in effect, as distinguished from a temporary measure. *See also hora'at sha'ah*

takkanat ha-kahal "communal enactment"

takkanat ha-shavim ("enactment for the encouragement of penitents") a category of enactments to encourage penitence and rehabilitation, *e.g.,* an enactment providing that a thief may be relieved of the obligation to return stolen property and may pay its value instead, when the property has been incorporated into a building and would be very expensive to retrieve

takkanat ha-shuk ("enactment for the market") an enactment to promote the security of transactions in the open market ("market overt") by protecting the purchaser from a thief at such a market against claims by the owner of the stolen property

takkanat medinah "a regional enactment," intended to be applicable to many Jewish communities (*kehillot*)

talmid ḥakham ("wise scholar") (1) halakhic scholar; (2) learned and pious person

Talmud the Mishnah and the discussion of the Mishnah by the *amoraim* of Babylonia (comprising the Babylonian Talmud) and the *amoraim* of the Land of Israel (comprising the Jerusalem Talmud)

talmud ("learning") (1) academic study; (2) midrash; (3) the colloquy between *tannaim* on a specific law

Talmud Bavli Babylonian Talmud

talmud lomar ("the text teaches") a statement introducing a conclusion derived by implication through exegesis

Talmud Yerushalmi Jerusalem Talmud

tam ("innocuous") not chargeable with notice of propensity to cause harm (opposite of *mu'ad*); if the cause of harm is *tam*, damages are less than if the cause is *mu'ad*

tanna, *pl.* tannaim rabbi of the Mishnaic period (first century to approximately 220 C.E.)

tanna kamma ("the first *tanna*") a *tanna* whose opinion is stated first, without attribution, in a *mishnah*

tenai, *pl.* tena'im (1) "condition"; (2) legislative enactment (*takkanah*); (3) in plural, (a) marriage contract, (b) formal betrothal contract

tenai bet din ("stipulation [or requirement] imposed by the court") a legislative enactment (*takkanah*); the term indicates that the legislation is based on prior private agreements that have become more or less standard

terumah ("contribution") (1) priestly tithe, which only priests and their families are permitted to eat; (2) in modern Hebrew, a donation

teshuvah (1) responsum; (2) "return," or repentance; (3) refutation

tikkun (ha-)olam ("improvement [or mending] of the world") promotion of the public welfare; the verb form, "to promote the public welfare," is *letakken olam*

tofes ("template") the main body of a legal document, containing basic and generally standard provisions relating to the type of transaction involved

tom lev ("purity of heart") (1) good faith; (2) wholeheartedness; (3) integrity; (4) sincerity

Torah ("teaching") (1) the five books of Moses (Pentateuch); (2) the entire Hebrew Bible; (3) doctrine; (4) custom; (5) the prescribed procedure; (6) divine revelation; (7) all Jewish study, the entire religious and ethical and cultural literature of Judaism

Torah min ha-shamayim ("Torah from Heaven") divine revelation, the article of Jewish faith that the Torah was given by God to the Jewish people

Torah she-be-al-peh ("Oral Law") (1) all Jewish law that is not set forth in Scripture; (2) the entire Teaching of Judaism, including aggadah

Torah she-bi-khetav "Written Law," *i.e.*, the law explicitly set forth in the text of the Torah

toref ("blank") the parts of a legal document relating to the individual aspects of the transaction, filled in as to the details of the particular transaction

Tosafot ("additions") critical and explanatory glosses on the Babylonian Talmud written by a school of scholars in France and Germany in the twelfth and thirteenth centuries

tosefet ketubbah ("addition to the *ketubbah*") an optional supplement to the mandatory minimum amount of the *ketubbah*

Tosefta ("additions") a collection of tannaitic statements supplementing the Mishnah

tovei ha-ir ("the good citizens of the town") lay judges or communal officials. Sometimes called "the seven *tovei ha-ir;*" they were the political and economic heads of the community

uvda Aramaic for *ma'aseh*—an act, incident, event, or case that gives rise to new law or is declarative of an existing norm

Va'ad Arba (ha-)Araẓot ("Council of the Four Lands") the central institution of Jewish self-government in Poland and Lithuania from the sixteenth to the eighteenth century

Written Law law explicitly set forth in Scripture

Yad ha-Ḥazakah the *Mishneh Torah,* Maimonides' Code

Yavneh (Jabneh, Jamnia) a town in Judea where R. Johanan b. Zakkai established an academy for teaching and studying the law after the destruction of the Temple in 70 C.E. *See kerem be-Yavneh*

yeshivah ("a place of sitting") academy for Talmudic study

yeẓe din ẓedek le-ẓidko ("let a righteous judgment justly issue") a judgment must do justice, let justice be done

Yom Tov ("good day") festival, holiday

Yoreh De'ah ("it will teach knowledge") one of the four principal divisions of *Sefer ha-Turim* and the *Shulḥan Arukh*

zaken mamre ("rebellious elder") a rabbi who adjudicates contrary to the ruling of the Sanhedrin

zav, *pl.* zavim ("bodily issue") *Zavim* is the title of a tractate of the Talmud in the Order of *Tohorot*

ẓavva'at shekhiv me-ra a deathbed will, or a will of one who apprehends imminent death. *See shekhiv me-ra*

ẓon barzel ("iron flock") assets of a wife over which a husband has almost complete dominion; he is responsible for any loss or diminution in value of these assets, as distinguished from *melog* property, since he has undertaken to preserve "like iron" the value of the *ẓon barzel* property at the time of the marriage

Zug, *pl.* Zugot ("pair") the *Zugot* consisted of the *nasi* and the *Av Bet Din,* who were the acknowledged leaders of the Jewish people from 160 B.C.E. to the beginning of the common era